LiViNG iN GOD'S

embrace

Michael Fonseca

LiViNG iN GOD'S

embrace

The Practice of Spiritual Intimacy

ave maria press   Notre Dame, Indiana

Imprimatur: The Most Reverend Patrick R. Cooney
                   Bishop of Gaylord
Given at Gaylord, MI on 15 November 1999

The *Imprimatur* is an official declaration that a book is free of doctrinal or moral error. No implication is contained therein that those who have granted the *Imprimatur* endorse its contents, opinions, or statements expressed.

International Standard Book Number: 0-87793-939-X

Cover and text design by Katherine Robinson Coleman

Printed and bound in the United States of America.

Library of Congress Cataloging-in-Publication Data
Fonseca, Michael.
        Living in God's embrace : the practice of spiritual intimacy /
        Michael Fonseca.
        p.   cm.
        Includes bibliographical references.
        ISBN 0-87793-939-X (pbk.)
        1. Spiritual life--Catholic Church. 2. Prayer--Catholic
Church. 3. Spiritual exercises. I. Title.
    BX2350.2 .F575 2000
    248.4'82--dc21   00-008399
                                              CIP

To Cherrie,
my spouse and soul friend,
whose life and example stir my soul
and nourish my well-being;
whose voice and inspiration
ring loud and clear
in many pages
of this book.

CONTENTS

Acknowledgments

This book was in the offing long before I put fingers to the keyboard. It is the fruit of much labor at the hands of some significant people in my life. God was an ever-present reality in the lives of my parents. Their example instilled in me a deep sense of God's presence from an early age. To them I am deeply grateful. I owe a debt of special gratitude to my Jesuit formators, mentors, and friends who formed and molded my spirituality through many years of spiritual formation when I was a member of the Society of Jesus. This book is a tribute of appreciation for their generous and devoted concern and love toward me.

I wish to acknowledge Cherrie, my wife, for her generous contribution through her unfailing support, solicitude, and honest feedback. She is my greatest fan who does not mince her words. My family members, especially Charles, my son, and Johanna, my sister-in-law, have been unfailing in their support and edifying through their example of coping with life's ups and downs. I am deeply grateful to Barb and Dennis Emery, Susie Erickson-Thompson, Carol and Matt Sobut, our dear friends who have been consistently supportive of my endeavors.

In a special way I wish to thank Randall Becker, a dear friend, for acting as my editor and literary critic. Without his help and time it would have been difficult to create this book. Fr. Don Bates, OSA, and Dr. Lawrence Dietrich have helped greatly with their valuable suggestions and feedback. Tricia Koles has helped to put together the manuscript, and I owe her many thanks.

I wish to acknowledge the profound influence that my colleagues at Saint Luke Institute, Silver Spring, Maryland, have had on my spirituality and world-view. Their dedication to their mission and support of my own efforts to integrate spirituality with psychology have made a lasting impression on me. Finally, I am especially grateful to the many directees, clients, and patients I have worked with over the years. Their graces, insights, and victories have become mine as well.

I wish to express my gratitude in a very special way to Ave Maria Press, especially in the persons of Bob Hamma, editorial director, and Julie Hahnenberg, managing editor. Their professionalism and gracious treatment have impressed and touched me greatly. Working with them has been a special privilege and joy.

My ultimate thanks go to God who began a good work in me a long time ago and gave me the tenacity and patience to bring it to completion.

Preface:
How to Use This Manual

In writing this book, I have tried to remain faithful to the wisdom and advice offered to me on numerous occasions by experienced spiritual and retreat directors over many years. Their offerings came in varied forms, but they always emphasized the basic truth of progress in the spiritual life: that the primary source of knowledge and wisdom is your relationship with God. Books and other sources of wisdom are helpful but will amount to little if a *personal experience of God* is missing. The *only* way to arrive at this wisdom from the Holy Spirit is to spend much time with God so that you can be molded and shaped by the divine Potter into a new creation. I consider my spiritual directors to be among the special graces given to me by a gracious God. Through implementation I have endeavored to make their unique discoveries my own.

Another great influence in writing this book has been my own experience as a spiritual and retreat director. Through this remarkable gift I have been privy to powerful conversion movements in many human hearts. In many instances God moved in some individual hearts in a way that left them and me both spellbound and tongue-tied. Their experiences of grace have become mine in an authentic way. Thanks to these two powerful sources of knowledge and wisdom, I have been able to put together the conferences and prayer exercises in this book.

THE BOOK'S FORMAT

I have used a retreat format in designing this book. Every chapter begins with a conference about a topic that will be the subject matter for prayer in that chapter. The ten prayer exercises that follow each chapter have been designed to help the seeker deepen his or her understanding of the topic, thereby allowing his or her own insights and graces to shape the experience. It might be helpful to read the whole book first, from beginning to end, as a way of getting the total picture, before you begin to use it as a manual of prayer and spiritual formation. The topics discussed in the six chapters follow the dynamics of a personal religious conversion movement as witnessed in an intensive process such as the Ignatian thirty-day retreat.

The first chapter acts as an introduction to the divine saga or adventure on which you will be embarking. The purpose is to give you a bird's-eye view of the journey. Various aspects of the context and process of prayer are discussed in this chapter. At first reading, you will recognize many of the points made from your own experience of prayer. Some suggestions will strike you as new and you might want to try them out and see if it makes sense to make them your own. In any case, it will be important for you to have ready access to the information to ensure adequate spiritual self-care as you move through the prayer exercises. It might prove useful to read and re-read this first chapter several times along the way until you are well acquainted with the various aspects of the journey.

The second and third chapters are grounded on the premise that repentance or conversion of heart can come only from God. A change of heart, mind, and soul is the result of God's unbounded love and compassion for us. Human effort alone can never bring about such a transformation. When human effort cooperates with God's action in the soul, however, graces and blessings flow abundantly. As a result, a true starting point in a healthy spiritual life is to begin by emphasizing God's love for us more than our love for God. Only after our hearts have been inundated with God's bountiful love and mercy will we reciprocate God's love for us through a life of generous and faithful service. The conferences in these two chapters highlight God's unswerving and unconditional love for us through numerous examples from scripture. The Old and New Testaments are replete with examples of ordinary men and woman who reached the heights of virtue and fidelity because their hearts had been deeply touched by God's graciousness.

Chapter Three makes two assertions: one, that God's love is mercy par excellence, and two, that we experience God's mercy especially in our brokenness. The most endearing and mysterious aspect of God's love is mercy, which is God's loving kindness shown to us especially when we have gone astray. There is only one way for such an assertion to be experienced deeply, and that is in the context of our sinfulness and messiness. Some of the most profound experiences of God have been made by seekers in the depths of their shame and guilt, when they brought everything to God and surrendered themselves because their lives had clearly become unmanageable. The exercises in the third chapter are designed with this backdrop in mind. The only reason for scrutinizing our past and befriending it is so that we might discover God's presence and providence in our history. It is always a source of relief and strength when, ever so slowly, we begin to discern the blessings that emerge from our misfortunes and mistakes.

Chapter Four makes the point that in order for prayer to be authentic we need to pray according to our God-given nature, which is that we have been created in God's image and likeness. We do well when we live according to this nature because then we are held in God's continual embrace. In such a context of intimacy, the seeker's prayer will be based on trust, openness, and love. Prayer becomes the context in which the seeker's relationship with God is explored, the problems and challenges of humanity are brought into God's presence, and where above all, we are led into the depths of God's own mystery.

The fifth chapter deals with the topic of discipleship or the translation of this very personal experience of intimacy with God into everyday life. While the life of a disciple is crisscrossed with activity and ministry in the service of the Lord, the key element of discipleship is contemplation or sitting at the feet of the Master, taking in his spirit and presence and becoming like him.

The last chapter is much like the first chapter in that it surveys the journey after the conversion experience. The emphasis is on managing yourself spiritually in the midst of everyday living and challenges. Is it possible to live an intense life of intimacy with God while being actively engaged and involved in the affairs of life? The advice on spiritual self-care seeks to address this question. From this renewed perspective, it will help greatly to read and re-read this chapter, as taking good spiritual care of oneself is a fine art that is learned slowly and painstakingly.

A word about the prayer exercises: there are ten exercises in each chapter. A productive way of using the manual is to use it over a period of six months, completing one chapter a month. This would mean doing the ten exercises over ten days and then making two repetition cycles. Repetitions serve a useful purpose as they help us go deeper into God's truth while tasting and relishing the mystery. Some of the exercises are quite exhaustive, and you might need the three attempts to do justice to them. The best way of benefiting from the prayer exercises is to read them in their entirety the evening before you pray on them. In this way you will be well acquainted with the contents of the exercise before you come to prayer. I have offered a scripture passage at the beginning of every prayer exercise. You may or may not find it helpful to actually use the quotation as material for your prayer. The hope is that the contents will help rather than distract you from your union with God. During your prayer period, the section marked "Session" is the one that really matters. The other sections are meant to act as catalysts to enhance your prayer experience. The best suggestion is to find out for yourself what is best for you. You might want to incorporate the quotation into your prayer or use it during the day as a reminder of your visit with God.

Some readers and practitioners of this manual will be individuals who function best when they have the support and encouragement of a group. If this is your case, you might want to start a peer group that would meet weekly or biweekly to share your experiences of the prayer sessions. You can meet over six months, taking one chapter a month. The group sessions would be the place to share your personal experiences of God as well as graces and insights received during the week(s), so that your group can benefit from the sharing and feedback. It is quite possible that this group experience will propel you into individual or group spiritual direction with an experienced director, if you are not yet in spiritual direction.

Finally, it is important to keep in mind that this book is a *manual* which means that it will work best for you when you *practice* the prayer exercises regularly and assiduously. Keeping a journal of your prayer experiences is a way of better understanding your journey with God. In the future, when you peruse your notes, you will discover that you are re-experiencing the consolations and graces you received the first time.

> The LORD bless you and keep you!

> The LORD let his face shine upon you, and be gracious to you!

> The LORD look upon you kindly and give you peace! (Nm 6:24-26)

My prayers and best wishes are with you.

CHAPTER ONE

Surveying the Journey

The saints and great spiritual teachers have written extensively about the proper context and process of prayer and have offered valuable tips and advice in their writings. This first chapter shares some of these valuable tips to help you prepare for and survey the territory you will cover in the course of your quest for God. We will first consider how best to create a proper context for your prayer, and second, look at the process you may go through as your journey with God unfolds.

YOUR PRAYER CONTEXT

Magnanimity

It is important to get your bearings about your relationship with God first and then to stick to them as a way of always keeping the right perspective on your life. When you decide to encounter God, it is no ordinary relationship about which you are talking. Given the nature of God, you will change and change profoundly in this encounter. If you begin with excuses, conditions, restrictions, and compromises, you will end up worshipping a false god, an idol that you have created in your own likeness and preference. If, however, you enter into this relationship with a deep respect and reverence for the transforming mystery of God, you will probably experience a profound conversion of heart, mind, and spirit, and come to a deeper appreciation of your true self as well. God does not ask us to be good and upright before we commit ourselves. If this were so, spirituality and a relationship with God would be relegated to the spiritually elite of this world. God asks that we come with hearts and minds that are open to the widest possible extent, that we allow ourselves to be overwhelmed by God's love and forgiveness. In the process, we will commit ourselves to loving and serving God and our neighbor with all our hearts and minds and souls. In the journey with God, it is essential that we have a large heart and a generous spirit. Then we will truly allow God to be God, and ourselves to be who we are—God's very own image and likeness.

Reverence

An essential ingredient or attitude that should be developed in our ongoing saga with God is a deep sense of reverence for God. True intimacy with God will always take into consideration the awesome mystery of God. It is important to keep in proper balance the immanence and transcendence of God in our prayer and everyday lives. Moses had a deep sense of unworthiness before the majesty and power of God. It rendered him speechless and awestruck at the burning bush and Mt. Sinai. At the burning bush we are told that Moses hid his face, because he was afraid to look at God (Ex 3:6). Isaiah, too, felt an acute sense of unworthiness and sinfulness before the holiness of God during his call to be a prophet. He exclaims, "Woe is me! I am lost, for I am a man of unclean lips . . . yet my eyes have seen the King, the LORD of hosts!" (Is 6:5). Jesus is both the Good Shepherd and the risen Lord. True reverence for who God is creates genuine intimacy that enlivens and transforms us. Familiarity, without reverence, breeds superficiality and self-centeredness.

Transition

It makes sense to create a sacred space when we come to prayer. We should set aside some time to transition into our prayer. Our relationship with God is unique among all our relationships, and it is important that we bring our whole person to the dialogue. St. Ignatius of Loyola recommends that we stand a step or two away from the place where we are going to pray and remind ourselves that we are in the presence of God, after which we make an act of reverence and humility. Then we beg God our Lord for the grace that all our intentions, actions, and operations may be directed purely to the praise and service of the Divine Majesty.[1] Transition brings closure to whatever it is we have been doing so we can go about the task of applying all our energies to communing with God.

Transitioning also helps us to collect our minds and bodies so that they are in the same place and pointed in God's direction. While St. Ignatius advises that this transition time last no longer than the space of an Our Father,[2] it is possible that you might need a longer period of time to become still and self-possessed. It is a good idea to take as much time as you need to become quiet, or else your prayer period could become more distracting and difficult than it need be. The psalmist has these wonderful words of advice:

> LORD, my heart is not proud;
>   nor are my eyes haughty.
> I do not busy myself with great matters,
>   with things too sublime for me.
> Rather, I have stilled my soul,
>   hushed it like a weaned child.
> Like a weaned child on its mother's lap,
>   so is my soul within me (Ps 131:1-2).

There are other effective ways of coming home to yourself so that you can be attentive to God's loving presence. Listening carefully to the sounds around you, without rejecting any sound either far or near, is a helpful way to arrive at a fair measure of quietness. Similarly, becoming aware of sensations in different parts of your body is another way of creating an effective transition into prayer; for example, focus on breathing—the sensation of inhaling in one nostril and exhaling in the other.

Developing Stillness

If you listen to novices talk about their prayer experience, you will often hear that the one difficulty they have is that their minds wander and they sense a restlessness in their bodies. In many instances, these difficulties become overwhelming and they are not able to genuinely immerse themselves into their prayer. Developing stillness in prayer is a priority, as it is an important step toward creating a listening heart. As previously mentioned, one way of creating stillness in prayer is by paying attention to a proper transition to prayer. Another help is to develop the habit, little by little, of remaining motionless for the whole period of prayer. Initially, you might be able to remain motionless for just a few minutes. If you persevere, before long you will be able to sit still for thirty minutes. You will realize that your body is no longer a hindrance to your communion with God; rather, your body has become an integral part of your prayer. You are praying with every fiber of your being. Your heart and mind and spirit now reflect your entire person.

Praying With Your Heart

The saints realized that prayer is a matter of the heart. While the mind is important in satisfying our curiosity about God and spiritual matters, repentance or a life pointed in the direction of God happens when the heart is moved. Knowledge of God makes sense when it leads to love of God. As St. John the Apostle points out in his first letter, the love of God consists first and foremost of God loving us (1 Jn 4:10). The saints insist that when we pray it benefits us to use methods that help quicken our hearts, or else no conversion will take place. The anonymous author of *The Cloud of Unknowing* states quite categorically that God can be reached only by love and not by intellectual knowledge. And in *The Spiritual Exercises*, St. Ignatius says, "It is not much knowledge that fills and satisfies the soul, but the intimate understanding and relish of the truth."[3] Prayer that focuses on letting God's word seep into our hearts the way a slow, steady drizzle sinks into the soil brings about the change of heart that brings salvation to self and others. But then, there are exceptions to every rule. There are some people who are very intellectually oriented. Their wills are moved to commitment and action through a thorough understanding and analysis of the reasons why they should do something, and they take the same approach to their discipleship.[4] It is important to respect one's approach to God and trust one's insights into oneself.

Integrating Your Body Into Your Prayer

As humans we have bodies that express who we are. If we pay close attention to our bodies, we will learn much about ourselves and about life in general. Many prayers have failed to germinate because the disciple sought to keep the body outside the realm of prayer. It is important that during your prayer you listen carefully to your body to see what God might be saying to you. Listen closely to both your feelings and bodily sensations during prayer and you will better understand the book of your life authored by the Holy Spirit.

Praying With Your Body

There will be times in prayer when the mind is wandering or is not interested in the matter at hand, and as a result the will or the heart becomes tired or spent. In such a situation it may be helpful to take an indirect approach to the dilemma. Do not address the problems of the mind by seeking answers from within the mind, but rather allow the body to bring about a creative solution. Pay attention to the body by focusing on breathing or bodily sensations, and remaining still during prayer. Sometimes it might even be necessary to experiment with different postures in order to help you come up with a creative solution that is in accord with God's will for you. As a result of engaging the body actively in your prayer, you will begin to notice that your mind is ceasing from its restlessness and is becoming more focused. Your heart has experienced an energizing transition to increased devotion and your awareness of God's presence has become a reality once again.

Posture in Prayer

All the great teachers of prayer and spirituality have emphasized the importance of posture in prayer. They realized from their own experience that the body is an integral part of our prayer. The right posture can create the delicate balance required between matter and spirit, and bring the disciple into the presence of God's mystery. Disciples have used various postures, such as kneeling, standing, sitting, prostrating, and lying on one's back. Some traditions have included slow and attentive walking. It is important to experiment with different postures in your prayer until you have come to a better understanding and a deeper appreciation of the connection between posture and the creation of a mood or attitude.

> *Kneeling* The kneeling posture denotes humility, submission, surrender, obeisance, and earnest supplication. There will be times in our prayer when kneeling would be an apt expression of humble adoration before God's mystery. At other

times we are faced with the unmanageability of our lives, and it seems most fitting to turn our lives over to the care of God on bended knees. When we kneel to seek the intervention of God's power in our lives or those of others, we make it very clear that God alone is the author of our lives and source of all grace. In a word, the kneeling posture can *intensify* our commitment to the relationship with God.

Sitting There are times when we are in a restful place in our relationship with God. Our hearts have been touched by God's unconditional acceptance of us, and sitting seems to be a conducive posture to savor and relish the experience. Similarly, when our hearts are burdened by difficult questions that will just not go away, sitting before and dialoguing with God seems to create the right ambiance. Sitting can also help create a spirit of docility, friendliness, and intimacy in prayer.

Standing When we stand we raise ourselves to our full height. In prayer, the standing posture can connote our full cooperation with God's higher purpose in whatever issue we are addressing in our lives. We also have fuller access to our energies and resources when we are in the standing posture. Offering praise and thanksgiving, with our arms outstretched, seems to come naturally in a standing posture.

Prostration Prostration is a demonstrative gesture. It has an expanse and sweep that makes it fitting for liturgical settings and celebrations. In any other setting it might be viewed as exaggerated. If you wish to experiment with the fruits of prostration in prayer, it may be most advantageous to do it in the privacy of your home or prayer room. Prostration is a powerful gesture to express our submission to and adoration of God. Prostration is a prayer of gesture, with or without the accompaniment of words. Some disciples might choose to do their prostrating in silence.

Lying on One's Back Lying on one's back as a posture in prayer can serve a useful, if limited, purpose. A useful purpose would be engaging in the prayer of remembrance, calling to mind God's many favors and blessings in life. This posture can also serve as a symbol of receptivity and contemplation as one beholds the azure sky dappled with cloud puffs, or the starry heavens away from the city lights. This posture is also good to perform the prayer of aspiration by closing your eyes, placing God's presence in your heart, and repeating the words of a short prayer formula over and over. This posture is not efficient when you are tired, unless you are using prayer as a help to sleep. Nor is this posture conducive to dealing with difficult and challenging issues in prayer.

The Amount of Time in Prayer

There is no hard and fast rule as to what the ideal amount of time is for prayer. Some advocate twenty minutes a session; others suggest thirty minutes. *The Spiritual Exercises* ask for five sessions a day, each lasting sixty minutes.[5] My own preference is to work toward an amount that ranges between thirty and sixty minutes, always trying to move closer toward the hour. Presuming that the seeker following this manual is a busy person and might not be able to realistically set aside more time, twenty to thirty minutes for the prayer exercises would be sufficient. However, a longer session is ideal because when prayer has become more sincere, and commitment more decisive, issues relating to one's sinful side and resistance to doing God's will start rearing their ugly heads, and it is imperative to stand one's ground and not flee. Staying the course of the stipulated time for prayer helps one overcome the resistance to God's inspirations and grace.

Spending Extra Time in Prayer

At times you will experience desolation in prayer, when nothing will seem to go well and God will seem distant and aloof. In these times the tendency will be to cut short the time for prayer, rationalizing that your time is being wasted in unproductive activity and might be used more constructively in something else. *The Spiritual Exercises* suggest that in order to fight against the desolation and conquer the temptation, it is better to remain in the prayer session a little longer than the stipulated time.[6] In this way, the seeker will get accustomed not only to resisting the temptation but even to overcoming it.

Contentment in Perseverance

There will be times in prayer when nothing seems to work well for you. The antidote mentioned above was that you extend your prayer time by a few minutes as a way of counteracting the impulse to give up. Your task is to do your prayer as well as you can. It is God's job to provide the results, or the apparent lack of them. If you have done your part, you have done well and that fact alone can and will give you peace and satisfaction.

The Importance of Repetition in Prayer

The Ignatian retreat recommends three repetitions a day.[7] The format goes as follows: The retreatant prays on a passage of scripture the first hour; in the second hour the retreatant does a repetition of the first hour; in the third hour the retreatant takes another scripture passage; in the fourth hour the retreatant does a repetition of the third hour; in the last hour the retreatant does a repetition of the repetitions. The understanding behind such a format seems to be that the truth of God's word is too profound to be grasped adequately in one sitting, hence the need for repetitions. Repetitions serve as a spiral process—they go deeper into the subject matter, to the point where the disciple's heart and will are moved and conversion ensues. A simple rule of thumb in prayer is that it is better to go deeper than wider. This same understanding lies behind the suggestion of doing two repetitions a month in every chapter of this book.

Preparation for Prayer

Some people find it helpful to plan for their day's visit with the Lord, especially if they like praying on scripture. If you are a morning person and visit with God upon rising or shortly thereafter, it might help to read a scripture passage before bedtime as a preparation for prayer the following day. When you are praying out of this book, before you retire for the night you can read and reflect briefly on the prayer exercise that you will be taking up the following day.

At Night

We all know how much our day is affected by how our night went. What goes on during your night sleep can and will affect, positively or negatively, your emotional and spiritual state of being. As a way of positively influencing the following day, think about the subject matter you will be taking up in prayer the following morning, and sleep with God's name in your heart and on your mind.

THE PROCESS OF YOUR PRAYER

In retreats and prayer workshops the following question arises periodically: "How do I know when I am experiencing God in my prayer or in my life?" Some of us have struggled for a long time with this question, not really knowing how to answer it satisfactorily because in our prayer we don't yet have a clear and definite sense that God is present to us. The saints, on the other hand, were quite sure they knew when they were experiencing God's presence or absence in their prayer, and some have written extensively on the subject. St. Ignatius of Loyola, for instance, came up with two sets of rules for the discernment of spirits.[8] In these rules he tries to provide a road map to others of what they can expect on their journey into the heart of God. The rules are based on his personal experiences with the presence and absence of God in his prayer and life. It would be worthwhile to review some of his experiences, which might already have become yours. The following review is based on my own interpretation of his rules, which I have come by as a result of my use of them as well as in the experience of offering spiritual direction.

Consolation

As a general rule, when we cooperate with God's action in our souls we will experience consolation. A consolation is any movement in the soul that propels us, strongly or gently, toward God and/or what is best for us. A consolation could come to us in the form of sentiments, desires, yearnings, feelings, insights, convictions, hopes, dreams, and so on. At the heart of consolation is a sense of peace and joy. Consolations can come to us on two levels. They can be described as *sensible* consolations and *spiritual* consolations. Sensible consolations will be experienced for the most part in and through our senses. Spiritual consolations, on the other hand, will often accompany sensible consolations. However, when they are experienced without the apparent accompaniment of sensible consolations, we detect them in the form of convictions, values, commitment, patience, perseverance, and so on. For example, we know that we have the conviction to remain in God's will, though there does not seem to be much enthusiasm to go with it. Given that consolations are movements that lead us toward God, it is fair to assume that the way to recognize God's presence in us is through the presence of consolations.

The Dynamics of Consolation

When we are visited by consolations, the spiritual life seems easy and attractive. Prayer comes readily to our lips because our hearts are being enkindled by God's presence. The relationship with God has a personal and intimate dimension to it. In fact, not surprisingly, many serious seekers will tell you that they are engaged in frequent conversation with God throughout the day. Making day to day decisions is an easier matter because our minds are producing good and noble thoughts. Our wills seem to be anchored in a stable commitment to God's will. Even when we are making difficult decisions that consume much time and energy, our state of consolation helps us to be patient and hopeful, because God is still a very real presence to us.

There are some lurking dangers inherent in the state of being in consolation. It is quite easy to get complacent and think that we are the architects of our consolations. While it is true that our cooperation with God's will helps us to be in a state of consolation, it is equally true that no amount of effort on our part can produce our consolations if God does not will them for us. In other words, consolations are God's gift which is to be received with gratitude and humility. It helps to remember that we are the caretakers and not the owners of our consolations. Treating our consolations with respect and using them to do God's will as generously as possible becomes a profound act of adoration of our Creator and Lord.

Being in consolation is a valuable time to get proper perspective on our lives and relationship with God. It is a spiritual state that helps to strengthen our good habits so that we are better prepared to face our dark side, especially when we are in a state of desolation. Being in consolation can help us to grow in humility and greater dependence on God's power and protection.

Desolation

Desolation is the exact opposite of consolation. A desolation is that kind of movement in our souls that thwarts our direction toward God and/or what is best for us. In time of desolation, our thinking goes awry. We are under the influence of evil. In many situations we will convince ourselves, through alibis and excuses, that harmful things are in fact good for us. We delude ourselves and become persons of the lie. Desolation could come to us as an insatiable desire for objects and behaviors that are harmful to our well-being, such as an inclination to act on our addictions, take the easy way out, be disinclined to spend time in prayer, postpone our duties and responsibilities, or nurse our grudges and resentments. We are on slippery ground in time of desolation. When God is absent from our hearts, the result is doubt, turmoil, anxiety, cynicism, bitterness, pessimism, and despair. We lose our peace and spiritual bearings. Desolation is a state we don't want to be in because it brings with it disintegration and alienation. Our normal spiritual state is that of consolation.

Dealing With Desolation

Desolation is a state of deceit. We are not living true to ourselves. It is important that we do our utmost as soon as possible to get out of desolation and into a state of consolation. St. Ignatius realized from his own experience of desolation that it was difficult for him to stick to decisions that had been made in a time of consolation. His tendency was to abandon or postpone these good decisions which formed the solid foundation of his state of consolation. If in time of desolation, however, he continued to do what he believed was right for him, his consolations, or a tangible sense of God's presence, would return to him. He also realized that his mind reveled in dissipation and pleasurable distractions when he was in a state of desolation. It was not a good time to make new decisions for himself. In other words, the appropriate time to make decisions for ourselves is when we are in consolation. In time of desolation, the rule is to stick to the decisions we made in time of consolation, and not make any new decisions until we return to consolation.

Desolation is a dangerous state of soul for the seeker. If we are not careful, harmful and unproductive behaviors once resorted to could resurface with a vengeance, or at least there will be a strong urge to return to them. Old feelings of guilt and shame about past sins and failures might come up, or great fear and anxiety about the future because of our failures in the past. The tendency will be to treat these experiences as shameful secrets, which are then kept hidden in our souls and allowed to poison our relationship with God and others. It is important that we counteract this tendency by creating for ourselves a network of supportive persons whom we trust and can talk to in such times. Such a network could include spiritual directors, confessors, spiritual companions, twelve-step sponsors, psychotherapists, and a support group.

Another interesting phenomenon of the spiritual life is the fact that all of us have our special vulnerabilities. When we are doing well and moving along in a state of consolation, our weaknesses hardly seem to plague us, or when they rear up we are able to squash them. They take on a hideous life of their own, however, when we are in desolation.

For example, if rejection is your Achilles' heel, in desolation you will tend to take everything personally and feel greatly marginalized as a result. If fear is your dominant demon, you could go into a paroxysm of suffocating anxiety and nauseating doubt. An important tool in the spiritual life is self-knowledge, which is acquired through relentless honesty with oneself and sincere feedback from others. The spiritual life requires us to know what our particular weaknesses are so that we learn to temper their insidious effects on us, especially in time of desolation. Such knowledge is best acquired through an honest examination of our behavior in a daily review, and honest dialogue with persons whom we trust.

Desolation is a time to be awake and alert, as a sentinel would be for the enemy. This is the time to examine more closely our behavior to see what the reason for desolation might be. It is also a time for extra prayer, especially the prayer of petition, asking God for help to do what is right in spite of our inclination to do the exact opposite. We may feel called to deny ourselves during this time as a way of purging our system of inordinate tendencies. Some might choose not to watch television, or might try to catch up with projects that have collected dust for a long time, such as cleaning out the garage or a desk. Many times it helps to engage in a work of charity that extends our generosity, like visiting a friend or family member in the hospital or helping somebody with a job. The whole idea is to treat desolation as an unwanted guest who will dominate our living and mental space if we don't get him out fast. Hopefully, along the way, we will have taught ourselves to use any means possible to return to the state of consolation.

In this connection I would like to mention fasting as an important tool for counteracting desolation as well as gaining valuable self-knowledge. Some have made fasting an important spiritual practice in the understanding that a tempered and appetite-regulated body gives rise to a transparent mind and a limpid spirit. I advocate the use of fasting with a note of caution. Unfortunately, some have used fasting as a way of punishing themselves for their sins, or "forcing" God to comply with their wishes. Such a rationale can damage one's discipleship and eventually lead to deeper desolation.

Desolation is a valuable stage, even though it is an unwelcome state, because it can provide us with many insights into ourselves and God. One reason for desolation could be the fact that we are not living according to the dictates of our conscience. Perhaps we are engaging in behaviors and thought processes that are unbecoming of God's will for us, from the blatant to the subtle. We could be flirting with doing something dishonest, or gossiping as a way of expressing our anger and resentment, or neglecting duties toward our children and clients, and so on. Desolation is a signal to us that we have wandered off the straight and narrow path toward enslavement of some kind.

At other times, however, we can experience desolation even though we are living in God's will. This is a circumstance that causes obvious bafflement. The question behind the puzzlement is: How could God send me desolation when I am doing my best to please and serve God? It is generally the novice disciple who experiences such bafflement, because, if he or she were to be honest, the quest is more for the consolations of God rather than the God of consolations. Gradually, the disciple comes to realize that God need never be beholden to desires and wishes that are self-serving. In his letter James says, "You ask but do not receive, because you ask wrongly, to spend it on your passions. Adulterers! Do you not know that to be a lover of the world means enmity with God?" (Jas 4:3-4).

Hopefully, we will see in time that purification of our expectations is essential if we are to make God the center of our lives rather than a satellite revolving around us. Desolation as an experience makes us realize that there is not much, or, more truthfully, nothing, that we can do without God's providence and help. In gradual stages, the disciple becomes humble and makes God the center and focus of his or her life. In the process, the ego is cut down to size, the disciple becomes obedient to God's will, and the journey into God's heart can really happen.

If we were to observe closely our experiences of desolation both when we cause it and when it comes to us as a measure of purification, we should notice a difference.

Generally, when desolation is the result of our own wrong-doing, we will experience an absence of both sensible and spiritual consolation. It will feel as if we are separated from God both on the level of feelings and sentiments, as well as on the level of our values and convictions. On the other hand, when desolation is present as a purification, what is absent is sensible consolation. Spiritual consolations will continue to be present and might actually increase in intensity. Our yearning for God and our commitment to doing God's will might even get stronger. Yet it is painful to remain in such a state. It is like traveling through the desert, knowing that you've got to go through this arid stretch before you can arrive at the oasis.

As you advance on the journey toward God, you will begin to recognize a two-fold sense within you. You are building up your confidence and familiarity with the process of prayer. God is becoming more recognizable to you. You have a much clearer sense of God's presence in you. While you still have occasional difficulty being consistent in your prayer practices, by and large being faithful and regular is no longer a concern for you. You are becoming, in other words, a seasoned traveler. Now you will find that the terrain is changing and you are being called upon to develop skills and insights you know you have and others you now need for the journey.

True and False Consolation

It might seem odd to think that in our relationship with God we can experience both true and false consolation. Then again, it would not be that odd if we reminded ourselves that we are easily prone to create illusion out of reality and live in falsehood and denial rather than face the truth. Many times we like to appear better than we are spiritually. Consequently, we might create a pseudo-state of consolation. Such a consolation does not last because it is founded on a lie. More tellingly, it has a deleterious effect on our relationship with God, as we resist salvation which can come only from an honest admission of our hypocrisy and sins.

Besides our own evil tendencies which can create false consolations in our prayer life, there are other circumstances

LIVING IN GOD'S EMBRACE

in our relationship with God that can confuse us. There are times when we will receive consolations from God without a previous cause. A good example of such a consolation is the encounter that Paul had with Jesus on his way to Damascus. He was not expecting such a radical change in his life. All of a sudden he is overwhelmed by the power and grace of Jesus. St. Ignatius believed that such a consolation need not be doubted because its source is clearly God.

Usually, consolations will have a previous cause. It will need to be looked at carefully to make sure that its source is indeed God. A simple example of a consolation having a previous cause is when you go on a weekend retreat and feel so inspired by the talks given that you decide on a daily prayer schedule that could affect your everyday duties. If the consolations are indeed genuine, they will produce lasting results in other areas of your life as well. As they unfold, the beginning, middle, and end of the process will be positive. On the other hand, if the source is anything other than God, there is a good likelihood that you will be led astray if you are not observant of the process as it unfolds in you. Such consolations will be experienced as authentic, at least initially, and they will produce all the results a consolation is supposed to produce, including peace, joy, fervor, enthusiasm to do God's will, and so on. However, such consolations are meant to lure and seduce with the purpose of throwing you into confusion and doubt. So the middle and end result of such a process will always lead to a state of desolation. In spite of your good-will and generosity, you will have been led astray because in some way you have not yet faced some of your demons. The ensuing desolation points to the work that needs to be done in your spiritual quest. The upshot of this is that it is important to closely monitor your consolations, from start to finish, as a way of making sure that they originate from and lead you toward God. In the beginning stages it is difficult to tell the difference between a true and false consolation. Through the middle and end stages, their paths will diverge rather dramatically, one leading you astray, the other to God. It is important that we look closely at the fallout of our decisions.

Examining Your Consciousness

In some spiritual traditions, there is a great emphasis on developing a keen awareness of everything that is going on within and around us. Different terms are used to describe this process. Terms like "awareness," "mindfulness," "discernment of spirits," and "at-oneness" emphasize the fact that our relationship with God is a creative, dynamic reality which has constant repercussions on our whole being. By closely observing what is going on in our breathing, bodily sensations, feelings, and thoughts, we will gain access to the diverse and subtle ways in which we enter into a communion relationship with God.

There are different ways to go about examining our consciousness during the day. It is important that you adopt a system that works for you. I wish to make a few suggestions and invite you to try them out so that you can come up with a way that works for you. Some disciples like the habit of taking a minute or two every waking hour to look at the process that has unfolded within them in the past hour in terms of consolation, desolation, insights, and the conscious presence of God. With this, one can choose two longer periods during the day, five to fifteen minutes in length, to do the same exercise, albeit in greater detail. We can also spend time in thanksgiving to God for the graces received during the day as well as in contrition and amendment for the wrong we have done. Examining our consciousness frequently during the day is a practice that grows on us in gradual stages. Initially we might have to put a lot of effort into developing this spiritual practice, but in time, doing so will become so second nature to us that we do it on a consistent basis throughout the day.

CHAPTER ONE HIGHLIGHTS

▲ A profound conversion of heart, mind, and spirit will occur if you enter into the relationship with a deep respect and reverence for the transforming mystery of God.

▲ Prayer is creating a sacred space where you can be overwhelmed with God's uncompromising love and acceptance.

▲ Prayer is a matter of the heart. Prayer that focuses on letting God's word seep into our hearts the way a slow, steady drizzle sinks into the soil brings about the change of heart that brings salvation to self and others.

▲ All the great teachers of prayer and spirituality have emphasized the importance of posture in prayer. The right posture can create the delicate balance required between matter and spirit and bring the disciple into the presence of God's mystery.

▲ A consolation is any movement in the soul that propels us, strongly or gently, toward God and/or what is best for us.

▲ Desolation is that kind of movement in our soul that thwarts our direction toward God and/or what is best for us.

▲ Desolation is a valuable stage—even though it is an unwelcome state—because it can provide us with many insights into ourselves and God.

▲ Examining our consciousness frequently during the day is a practice that grows on us in gradual stages. Initially we might have to put a lot of effort into developing this spiritual practice, but in time, doing so will become second nature to us, to the point where we are doing it on a consistent basis throughout the day.

Exercise One
PREPARATION FOR PRAYER (PART 1)

▲ Scripture

The LORD God formed man out of the clay of the
ground and blew into his nostrils the breath of
life, and so man became a living being. . . . The
LORD God then built up into a woman the rib that
he had taken from the man. . . . The man and his
wife were both naked, yet they felt no shame.
—Genesis 2:7, 22, 25

▲ Summary

The way we come home to God is by coming home to ourselves. Our bodies tell us a great deal about whether we are
at home with ourselves or not, and about the presence and
absence of God in our lives. Our bodies are a significant
arena of encounter with God. It is no wonder that we call
our bodies the temple of the Holy Spirit.

▲ Session

(20 minute duration)

Take up a comfortable sitting posture. Try keeping your
back as straight as possible without straining, and your
chin tilted forward slightly. Make the effort to be as still as
you can during the entire length of the exercise.

Listen to the sounds around you. Begin with the ones in the distance, away from your place of meditation. Then listen to the sounds in the room or chapel where you are sitting. Finally, listen to your own body sounds. *The cycle is outside sounds, inside sounds, body sounds.* Keep repeating this cycle until the time is up. At times you might want to be aware of all the sounds at one and the same time. Try to be as deliberate and conscious in your listening awareness as you can. If you get distracted, gently bring yourself back to the task at hand.

▲ Reflection

Many are pleasantly surprised that this exercise brings them peace and quiet. It gives them a sense of feeling grounded because it connects them with their surroundings.

This exercise dissolves the notion that sounds distract our concentration or focus. Rather, it illustrates the principle that focus or concentration is fostered when we are in harmony with ourselves and our surroundings. Distraction occurs when we are pulled apart in different directions.

Oftentimes, our likes and dislikes are based on our perceptions of reality and the labels and titles we place on it, rather than on reality itself. Similarly, our conclusions about God are often based upon our illusions about who God should be. This exercise is a small step toward understanding life and God as they are.

Exercise Two
PREPARATION FOR PRAYER (PART 2)

▲ Scripture

You formed my inmost being;
  you knit me in my mother's womb.
I praise you, so wonderfully you made me;
  wonderful are your works!
  —Psalm 139:13-14

▲ Summary

A central scriptural truth which undergirds our lives is that we have been created in God's image and likeness. Being intimate with God is at the heart of this birthright. The encounter with God has to take place within us, in the core of our being, *before* we can recognize God's whisperings all around us.

▲ Session

(20-30 minute duration)

Take up a comfortable sitting posture. Try keeping your back as straight as possible without straining, and your chin tilted forward slightly. If you are drowsy, although rested enough, it could be because your back is not erect. Make the effort to be as still as you can during the entire length of the exercise.

Focus on the area of your nostrils and upper lip, in particular on one nostril as you inhale, and on the other as you exhale, trying to become aware of sensations caused by your breathing in the area of your nostrils and upper lip. The idea is to become *aware* of your breathing and sensations, and *not* to alter your breathing. Try to be as deliberate and conscious in your awareness as you can. If you get distracted, gently but firmly bring yourself back to the task at hand.

▲ Reflection

Many are amazed at how still and silent they become through this exercise. Some, on the other hand, find this exercise to be quite difficult. To them the best advice is to be patient and persistent. Rome was not built in a day.

Your breathing will tell you much about yourself. Breathing from the diaphragm suggests harmony and rootedness. Breathing from the chest could imply anxiety and worry.

This exercise could be used as a preparation for prayer. It could be used as prayer itself, as breath signifies the gift of life. If you choose to use it as prayer, then as you inhale, become aware that you are breathing in God's life. As you exhale, you are sharing this gift of God's life with the universe.

Exercise Three

▲ Scripture

Do you not know that your body is a temple of the holy Spirit within you, whom you have from God, and that you are not your own? For you have been purchased at a price. Therefore glorify God in your body.
—1 Corinthians 6:19-20

▲ Summary

Besides being a temple of the Holy Spirit, our bodies are also broad canvases on which our life stories have been etched. Many colors in this kaleidoscope are bold and brassy. Many others are blurry and almost invisible. We need to have a true appreciation of all the colors if we are to be able to recognize ourselves as God's masterpieces.

▲ Session

(20-30 minute duration)

Take up a comfortable sitting posture. Try keeping your back as straight as possible, without straining, and your chin tilted forward slightly.

This exercise is about developing a keen awareness of your bodily sensations. Begin at the top of your head trying through your awareness to pick up sensations (like an itch, warmth, sweatiness, etc.) in each area. Then move your attention to your forehead, face, and the front of your neck, once again trying to become aware of any sensations in that area. The back of the head and neck is next. The right shoulder and arm, down to the fingertips, follow. Then it is the left shoulder and arm, down to the fingertips. The chest, stomach, and genitals are next, followed by the back, waist, and buttocks. Finally, it is the right leg, from the thigh to the toes, followed by the left leg, from the thigh to the toes. The next step is to move upward from the toes to the top of the head in reverse sequence. Continue this downward and upward movement until the time is up.

If at any point in the process you are having difficulty locating sensations, stay in that area for some time and it may happen that you will become aware of some. If, however, you are not able to pick up any sensations, proceed to the next section of your body.

▲ *Reflection*

This exercise is an excellent preparation for prayer. As your awareness of sensations sharpens and deepens, you will become aware of greater depths of stillness within you.

Sometimes the awareness will bring up memories and experiences which still need attention. It is God's way of asking you, through your body, to pay attention to your well-being by bringing closure to the issue.

Exercise Four
PREPARATION FOR PRAYER (PART 4)

▲ Scripture

> The LORD God formed man out of the clay of the ground and blew into his nostrils the breath of life, and so man became a living being.
> —Genesis 2:7

▲ Summary

Coming into God's presence always implies making a change of attitude and disposition because of the extraordinary Being we are about to encounter. We are coming into the presence of the Creator of the universe and Savior of the world, greater than the mightiest emperor, more compassionate than the most beneficent ruler. It is of primary importance that we ask the Holy Spirit to prepare us for our visits with God, every one of them portending a transformation of some kind.

▲ Session

(20-30 minute duration)

Take up a comfortable posture and allow for some time to settle down. After you are settled, focus on your breathing.

As you breathe in, imagine you are inhaling God's breath of life, and peace and joy are permeating your whole being, from the crown of your head to the tips of your toes. And as you exhale, imagine you are being exorcised of your demons of fear, anxiety, resentment, guilt, shame, and so on. It might help to imagine the inflow of peace and joy as a cool wind or a waft of flower-scented breeze, and the exit of your negativity as a motley crowd of unwelcome guests being pushed out the door. As you engage in this prayer of revitalization and house cleaning, you will become more centered and prepared to enter into your visit with God. It is important to end your prayer by surrendering yourself to the Holy Spirit and asking to always be docile and submissive to God's will for you.

▲ Reflection

As stated earlier, coming into God's presence always requires a change of attitude and disposition because of who God is. Every meeting with God is an encounter, as God's total Otherness calls for an adjustment in us. This prayer exercise is simple and easy to carry out. While it is prayer, it can also act as a wonderful preparation for a more intimate and profound meeting with God. It serves the same purpose as the penitential rite at the start of the eucharist: to cleanse and prepare ourselves for the unfolding mystery.

Exercise Five

▲ *Scripture*

By the LORD's word the heavens were made;
  by the breath of his mouth all their host.
The waters of the sea were gathered as in a bowl;
  in cellars the deep was confined.
                    —Psalm 33:6-7

▲ *Summary*

When we are distracted, it is a sign that we are being pulled in different directions. In this baffled state of mind, or non-awareness in many instances, we actually are trying to move in these various directions at the same time. The result of such an impossible maneuver is confusion, tension, frustration, and, at times, a sense of bursting at the seams. In extreme cases it might even feel like we are being stretched out on a rack. The antidote to distraction or being pulled apart is to create a sense of being pulled together, or harmony. The following exercise could help create harmony within you as you prepare for your visit with God.

▲ *Session*

(20-30 minute duration)

After you have taken up a comfortable sitting posture, imagine a favorite scene in nature that you love very much.

Your love for such a place probably comes from the fact that you have been nourished and rejuvenated every time you have visited this scene. It is possible that such a sacred space is one that you have visited just once or twice. Nevertheless, it is so indelibly etched in your mind and heart that its memory continues to permeate you with harmony and peace. For me, there are several such hallowed places, and I choose to go to them as on a pilgrimage. One such place is our garden where our family has engaged in a labor of love and creativity over the past few years. As I gaze lovingly on every tree, bush, and plant that we have planted and nurtured, they in turn share with me their gratitude, patience, resilience, and zest for life. In the exchange I am nurtured and made whole. It is important that you pay close attention to the details in the scene you choose, making personal connections with them. As a result the scene will come alive. It will cease to be merely a memory; it will become a living experience as well. You will be pulled together, ready to move in the direction of God in your visit. It is quite likely that as you contemplate the scene your heart will move toward God.

▲ Reflection

Creation is God's handiwork. If you look carefully at the wondrous artistry of the divine Sculptor and Artist, your eyes will sparkle with joy or be enraptured with amazement, and your heart will be moved into quiet adoration and praise. In the process you will experience harmony and communion with yourself, your surroundings, and with God.

Exercise Six

PREPARATION FOR PRAYER (PART 6)

▲ Scripture

"Blessed be the Lord God of Israel,
    for he has looked favorably on his people
    and redeemed them.
He has raised up a mighty savior for us
    in the house of his servant David,
as he spoke through the mouth of his holy prophets
from of old,
    that we would be saved from our enemies and
    from the hand of all who hate us.
Thus he has shown the mercy promised to our
ancestors,
    and has remembered his holy covenant. . . ."

▲ Summary

When remembering the various milestones in our journey with God, many of us are able to recall experiences that we would consider significant and special. Some of these experiences have been harbingers of a new direction or decision in our lives. Others have been instrumental in strengthening our resolve to persevere in a certain right course of action, or have provided us with a clarity of purpose that made our lives bearable and meaningful. Such experiences are not isolated incidents, as they contain God's mystery that is ever-present and life-giving. They become pools of living waters that we can bathe in whenever our spirits needs salving and repair.

▲ Session

(20-30 minute duration)

We are collected in ourselves when there is a sense of joy and harmony in our lives. The highlights in our relationship with God have been precisely such moments of joy and harmony. As a preparation for prayer or when we need to get perspective on our lives, it helps to return to these special moments we had with God. For some of us, such an experience might have been a pilgrimage we made which was a source of much grace and renewal. For others, it might be a special sense we received of God's presence in our lives that left a lasting impression upon us. During this session, take yourself back to such an experience and relive it as it occurred. You might notice that initially you will begin with the experience as it first took place. As you move along in prayer you might become aware that the experience is still very much alive in you, and is recreating itself into a new and special highlight in the present moment. You might want to do one of two things in the future. You might want to use this exercise as a preparation for prayer, in which case you would spend about five minutes or so in this exercise before you moved into your visit with God. Or, you might find enough nourishment in this exercise to consider it as your visit with God for the day. In the latter case, you might want to go the whole length of the time allotted.

▲ Reflection

Graces and visitations from God are alive in you in the present moment, even though they might have come to you a long time ago. This is true because they are both the sign and reality of the ever-living and present God in our midst. They become perennial sources of abundant healing and salvation. They are sacred icons that have breath and life. Our habitual contact with them regenerates God's life in us.

Exercise Seven
LONGING FOR GOD

▲ Scripture

LORD, hear my prayer;
  in your faithfulness listen to my pleading;
  answer me in your justice.
Do not enter into judgment with your servant;
  before you no living being can be just.
    —Psalm 143:1-2

▲ Summary

Saint Augustine noted that his heart was restless unless it rested in God. Restlessness can spring from a dissipated heart, as was Augustine's case before his conversion. In other circumstances, restlessness can be the painful consolation of a disciple's heart. The thirst for union with God can be so intense that the yearning feels like a painful void. Such a yearning for God is good as it keeps us focused in the right direction. Psalms 42 and 63 communicate such a longing for God in the disciple's heart.

▲ Session

(20-30 minute duration)

Spend a few minutes coming home to yourself by using an abbreviated form of any of the first six exercises. Then ask the Holy Spirit to cleanse your heart of all false longing and fill it with an intense yearning to behold the face of God. Repeat over and over some of the powerful phrases found in Psalms 42 and 63. Here is a sampling:

As the deer longs for streams of water,
  so my soul longs for you, O God (Ps 42:2).

My being thirsts for God, the living God.
　　When can I go and see the face of God? (Ps 42:3).

O God, you are my God—
　　for you I long!
For you my body yearns;
　　for you my soul thirsts,
Like a land parched, lifeless,
　　and without water (Ps 63:2).

Here is a sampling of adversity and affliction motivating the disciple's longing:

My tears have been my food day and night,
　　as they ask daily, "Where is your God?" (Ps 42:4).

Finally, the yearning leads to confidence and joy in the strength of God's presence:

Why are you downcast, my soul;
　　why do you groan within me?
Wait for God, whom I shall praise again,
　　my savior and my God (Ps 42:6).

When I think of you upon my bed,
　　through the night watches I will recall
That you indeed are my help,
　　and in the shadow of your wings I shout for joy.
My soul clings fast to you;
　　your right hand upholds me (Ps 63:7-9).

▲ Reflection

Words cannot communicate satisfactorily the vast depths of God's reality to us, but they can bring us to the cusp of God's mystery, beyond which it will be the Spirit's task to lead us. A slow, meditative repetition of hallowed phrases from the psalms, such as the ones in this exercise, could lead us to the sacred edge.

Exercise Eight
TRUE HAPPINESS

▲ *Scripture*

And Mary said:

"My soul proclaims the greatness of the Lord;
   my spirit rejoices in God my savior.
For he has looked upon his handmaid's lowliness;
   behold, from now on will all ages call me blessed."
       —Luke 1:46-48

▲ *Summary*

Relating with God is entering into a covenant relationship. Both parties pledge trust and loyalty to each other. On God's part the commitment is always total—there will never be any betrayal. On our part, the danger of reneging on our commitment always lurks in the background, as our shortcomings are part of our makeup. It is important to be aware of our ambivalence and ask God's help to stay on the path of covenant relationship.

▲ *Session*

(20-30 minute duration)

Take a few minutes to come home to yourself by using any one of the first six exercises. Then ask for the Spirit's knowledge to understand yourself and for the wisdom to stay on the tried and true path.

Psalm 1 describes the good and wicked person, both of whom are part of our makeup. The good person does not follow the counsel of the wicked, nor walks in the way of sinners, nor sits in the company of the insolent. The good person meditates on God's law day and night. He or she is like a tree planted near running water, that yields its fruit in due season and whose leaves never fade. Succinctly, a good person is a pillar of strength who habitually creates new life for those around. In what ways have you been a good person?

The wicked person is like chaff blown in the wind. In judgment the wicked shall not stand. Evil brings with it a state of desolation. Feelings like anger, resentment, jealousy, suspicion, fear, and anxiety dominate relationships with self, others, and God. In such a state, a downhill slide into a dark hole seems inevitable. Take a few minutes to remember your own states of desolation when you allowed evil influences to affect your happiness and make you like blown chaff, shifting and uprooted.

Finally, thank God for the times when you have been an instrument of peace and love; seek forgiveness for your failings, and courage and humility to depend on God in moments of weakness.

▲ *Reflection*

We are both good and evil. Experiencing our identity as God's likeness is possible only when we remain connected with God, especially in our moments of weakness. Then we will live out of our goodness and be able to keep our wickedness at bay.

Exercise Nine

GRATEFUL CONNECTIONS

▲ Scripture

It is good to give thanks to the LORD,
  to sing praise to your name, Most High,
To proclaim your love in the morning,
  your faithfulness in the night. . . .
          —Psalm 92:2-3

▲ Summary

It always helps to get the right perspective when a particular situation is causing us anxiety and confusion. The right perspective might not necessarily insulate us from the pain and discomfort, but it can make it bearable and give us a purpose that we did not have earlier. In a stressful situation, we can feel isolated and adrift, at times not wanting any connection with others, and at other times longing for meaningful contact. This prayer exercise is intended to generate within us the realization that even in our worst moments, when our vision is dimmed by disillusionment, we are still intimately connected with God and the world, and literally millions are concerned about our welfare.

▲ Session

(20-30 minute duration)

Take a few minutes to come home to yourself through awareness of sounds, your breathing, or bodily sensations.

Situate yourself in a place that is conducive for grateful remembering—a favorite place in your home, your garden, in the woods, or by the banks of a brook. Recall the numerous services you are inundated with every moment of your life. Recollect the bed you slept in and all the people involved in the making of every one of its components. Remember your home and all the people involved in producing its every fixture and component, and the workers who put it together. Continue doing this with your kitchen, bathrooms, furniture, light fixtures, heating and air conditioning, running hot and cold water, your garden, and on and on. Call to mind the countless individuals involved in supplying you with food and nourishment day after day, from the growers to the transport carriers, to the markets, the vendors, and so on. You can do the same with your automobile, the marvels of traffic and road engineering, the trust between motorists that gets you where you need to go, and so on. Your place of work, your friendships, and the list goes on and on. . . . And then there is God, your constant Provider of air, water, the earth, the seasons, the birds, animals, all of the above that you have already reflected on, and on and on. . . .

Finally, express your sentiments of gratitude, joy, and amazement to God, and possibly your feelings of guilt, shame, and embarrassment for taking your life for granted.

▲ Reflection

When we look at our lives from God's point of view, we know we are indeed princes and princesses, as God extends a solicitude and caring that is reserved for royalty. Such a perspective will give our lives a steady and firm foundation.

Exercise Ten
GETTING READY

▲ Scripture

> Trust in the Lord with all your heart,
>   on your own intelligence rely not;
> In all your ways be mindful of him,
>   and he will make straight your paths.
> —Proverbs 3:5-6

▲ Summary

When we plan a vacation, we usually take a long time to put it together. When we plan a career, we often invest years and considerable money into getting ourselves ready to carry out such a dream. The same approach applies to our relationship with God, but in a more profound way. It makes sense to see where you are in your relationship with God, what motivates you, and how far you are prepared to go in this adventure with the all Holy One. Knowing where you stand with God in the here and now can help you determine what still needs to be done and what steps you can take to do it.

▲ Session

(20-30 minute duration)

Take a few minutes to become quiet and dispose yourself for your visit with God by listening to the sounds around you, those in the distance and the ones near you. You can then reflect on the following questions and enter into a dialogue with God over your answers:

1. Who is God for me *today* and why do I *really* want to enter into a deeper relationship?

2. At what cost am I willing to pursue my relationship with God?

3. What is my resistance to giving an unqualified "yes" to God's invitation to intimacy?

4. How willing would I be to give up my resentments and grievances about the hand that I have been dealt to play in the game called "Life"?

5. What would be some of the prejudices and fears I would have to give up if I were to embrace Jesus' commandment to love everyone as myself, even my enemies?

6. If I allowed God to transform me, how would my life and circumstances change, and how would I look?

▲ *Reflection*

Some of us operate best when we have a glimpse of the whole picture because we know more clearly whether or not we want to commit ourselves to the task at hand. When it comes to the journey into the heart of God, we have the stories and experiences of the saints and mystics to give us *some* idea as to what the terrain will look like. Such information can encourage and support our resolve. But it cannot be a substitute for the real thing, which is making our *own* journey, blazing our *own* trail. The blueprint is locked up in God's mind, and we will know each step only when we are taking it. It takes faith to live this adventure. Faith is the disciple's eyes and heart knowing that the Master will always be journeying with him or her.

▲ Oftentimes our likes and dislikes are based on our perceptions of reality, the labels and titles we place on it, rather than on reality itself. Similarly, our conclusions about God are often based upon our illusions about who God should be.

▲ Your breathing will tell you much about yourself. Breathing from the diaphragm suggests harmony and rootedness. Breathing from the chest could imply anxiety and worry.

▲ Besides being a temple of the Holy Spirit, our bodies are also broad canvases on which our life stories have been etched. Many colors are bold and brassy; many others are blurry and almost invisible. We need to have a true appreciation of all our colors if we are to be able to recognize ourselves as God's masterpieces.

▲ Coming into God's presence always requires a change of attitude and disposition because of who God is. Every meeting is an *encounter*, as God's total Otherness calls for an adjustment in us.

▲ Creation is God's handiwork. If you look carefully at the wondrous artistry of the divine Sculptor and Artist, your eyes will sparkle with joy or be enraptured with amazement, and your heart will be moved into quiet adoration and praise.

▲ Graces and visitations from God are alive and *always* exist in the present moment, even though they might have first descended upon us a long time ago. They become perennial sources of divine healing and salvation. They are sacred icons that have breath and life. Our habitual contact with them regenerates God's life in us.

▲ Words cannot communicate satisfactorily the vast depths of God's reality to us. But they can bring us to the cusp of God's mystery, beyond which it will be the Spirit's task to lead us.

▲ We are both good and evil. Experiencing our identity as God's likeness is possible only when we remain connected with God, especially in our moments of weakness. Then we will live out of our goodness and be able to keep our wickedness at bay.

▲ When we look at our lives from God's point of view, we know we are indeed princes and princesses, as God extends a solicitude and caring that is reserved to royalty. Such a perspective will give our lives a steady and firm foundation. Even in our worst moments, when our vision is dimmed by disillusionment, we are still intimately connected with God.

▲ The blueprint of our spiritual journey is locked up in God's mind. We will know each step only when we are taking it. It takes faith to live this adventure. Faith is the disciple's eyes and heart knowing that the Master will always be a companion.

CHAPTER TWO

Nurtured
in
God's Embrace

The words of Jesus, "Many are called but few are chosen," could be appropriately applied to many seekers. In spiritual direction one can often detect this dilemma. On the one hand seekers yearn for a spiritual experience that will change them. They believe they are called to create something special out of their lives. They would like to leave the world a better place than when they first came into it. On the other hand, they are confused about the process. Their own efforts to seek and find God in their lives have left them with more questions than answers, more doubts than clarity of direction. They have been called, they think, but is there any assurance that they have been chosen? Is it possible, they wonder, to really enter into an intimate relationship with God, where communication will become communion?

Admittedly a personal and intimate relationship with God is a pure gift. Yet scripture tells us that there is nothing more precious that God would want to impart than sharing with us the divine life. Passages portraying God's special predilection for us literally jump out of the Old and New Testament pages. A few examples will make this assertion clear. In the Book of Genesis, the very first book of the Old Testament, through the creation story, the author is trying to make sense of this very special relationship that God has with creation and in particular with humans. The author seems overwhelmed trying to grasp the awesome mystery that a human person is. In a pithy statement, the depths of which will continue to be fathomed until the end of time, the author says:

> God created humankind in his image;
> in the image of God he created them;
> male and female he created them (Gn 1:27).

Indeed it is a mystery that even with such a noble identity many of us are stuck in the morass of low self-esteem and self-pity. By the same token, it is gratifying and encouraging when we meet a person who believes with all his or her heart and soul that he or she has been created in God's image and likeness, and, consequent with this identity, lives life in joy and hope. The psalmist is a good example of a person who is subdued into amazement and gratitude in trying to appreciate the core reality of our being in Psalm 8:

> What are humans that you are mindful of them,
>   mere mortals that you care for them?
> Yet you have made them little less than a god,
>   crowned them with glory and honor
>   (Ps 8:5-6).

Further, in Psalm 139 the psalmist continues to express great awe and gratitude at the way we have been created by God:

> You formed my inmost being;
>   you knit me in my mother's womb.
> I praise you, so wonderfully you made me;
>   wonderful are your works! (Ps 139:13-14).

Though we might be ordinary human beings on various levels of our lives, in our essence we belong to God's own house and lineage. Our destiny is a noble one because it has originated in the heart of God.

Many seekers fall by the wayside because the understanding of their personal reality is very one-sided. Some are so mired in their failures and deprivations of the past that they do not get beyond a jaundiced and pessimistic assessment of their lives. For them, life is both unfair and bad. Others have wasted years of their lives trapped in the vicious cycles of their addictions. Consequently, they do not think life is worth living. They have rarely, if ever, experienced the cornucopia of hope and consistency. Such people make a global assessment of their lives by taking a very one-sided view of their nature. "Nature" to them is the dark side of humanity, the flawed dimension of human life. Their spiritual lives, unfortunately, cannot be sustained by a paradigm that has excluded a true understanding of their nature, which is that they are indeed God's image and likeness, even though there is a dark side. And because they don't have the right perspective, they continue to engage in formulas and rituals that fail to breathe the Spirit of God into them. It is only on a true understanding of our nature that God's continued providence and grace can build.

GOD'S PLAN OF SALVATION

While it is true that life is in many ways unfair, we cannot get away from the even more compelling fact of God's intense yearning to be intimate with us. We are asked to take God seriously and live our lives as sons and daughters of the living God. St. Paul was tireless in proclaiming this plan of God's salvation to the early Christians because he was convinced that the heritage of being God's sons and daughters was indeed the bedrock of our meaning and joy in life. To the Ephesians he proclaims that "he chose us in Christ before the foundation of the world to be holy and blameless before him in love. He destined us for adoption as his children through Jesus Christ, according to the good pleasure of his will, to the praise of his glorious grace that he freely bestowed on us in the Beloved" (Eph 1:4-6). This message that we are precious to God, who wants a very special relationship with us as sons and daughters, is reiterated numerous times in scripture.

In Matthew, chapter 6, Jesus tells us to address God as "Father." The term "Abba" denotes a level of intimacy and trust that would transform a person if he or she experienced it. "Abba" is like a word that infants might use to address their parents when they are beginning to utter intelligible sounds. At one year of age, all an infant can do is rely totally on its parents. It has no other option. An infant grows up healthy and secure when this fundamental trust in its parents is honored. When this sacred trust is dishonored, society deals with the ravages of abuse and neglect. Interestingly enough, Jesus asks us as adults to address God as Abba. In other words, he wants us to put on the mind and heart of a tiny infant and have the unshakable conviction that God holds us in a warm embrace, is always by our side, and will never abandon us.

An apt image to convey this message is the picture of a mother nursing her baby, or playing with it, or just holding it in her arms with immense tenderness and protectiveness, to the point of being willing to sacrifice her own life for her infant. This invitation to be like an infant in our trust toward God comes to us from Jesus, even though he knows very well that many of us have had the experience or perception that life has given us a raw deal.

Several years ago I was directing an eight-day retreat for seminarians. Among the participants was a young man whose father had died before he was born. His mother had had a very difficult time raising her four children in the midst of poverty, deprivation, and discrimination. The young seminarian received a good Catholic high school education and went on to join his religious community. After some years in formation, he was disillusioned enough that he wanted to leave. The retreat was a last resort on his superior's part to help him make a proper decision. I was soon at my wits' end, not knowing how to deal with his profound sense of disillusionment and cynicism. In desperation I talked to him about the whole idea of addressing God as Abba, and the underlying assumptions that Jesus was making when he asked us to have the trust of an infant in its parent. He listened without comment and agreed, somewhat halfheartedly, to do as I suggested.

During his next prayer session he prayed in his room. He began his prayer as follows: "God, I have been told by my retreat director to address you as Abba. How can I ever address you as Father when you took away my own father before I was even born? I have never had the security of knowing a father as most children do. How can I address you as Father when you made life so difficult for my mother? . . ." And he proceeded to vent his resentments, dammed up within him for so many years. As he continued this angry dialogue with God, a clear image appeared before him. Across the room he saw God sitting in a high-backed chair, looking like a father figure, with a long flowing beard and deeply compassionate eyes, listening with rapt attention to his story of immense pain and abandonment.

In that instant, the young man became a toddler once again. He heard God address him by his name and ask him if he wanted to come to him. The seminarian answered in the affirmative but did not think he could toddle across the room. The Father extended his arm and very gently asked him to take his fingers and he would help him. When he came to God, he was asked if he wanted to come into God's lap. His answer was "Yes," and with that God swept him into his arms where he remained for the remainder of the retreat. Ever since then God has been Abba to him. The young man knew then what it meant to have a father, the best father he could possibly have. He continued his formation to be a priest, and his life has never been the same.

GOD'S WAYS ARE NOT OUR WAYS

While every seeker sincerely longs for this loving intimacy with God, many are hesitant to take this step. Jesus' message about Abba rings strangely in their ears, but they tell themselves, "It's too wonderful, so it can't be true." The truth is that every time we say the Lord's prayer, we dare to challenge our understanding of ourselves and the world. And while the stories of our broken and miserable lives are true, we are at the same time affirming a much greater and more important truth, which is that we are God's own sons and daughters.

The seeker who calls on God as Abba with trust and conviction soon realizes that being God's child is at the core of his or her reality. And such a truth sets us free. In other words, God's way of understanding us is very different from the way we understand ourselves. True spiritual and psychological health and freedom begin only when we put on the mind and heart of God, when we learn to look at and understand ourselves through God's eyes and thoughts. As Isaiah says:

> For my thoughts are not your thoughts,
> nor are your ways my ways, says the LORD.
> As high as the heavens are above the earth,
> so high are my ways above your ways
> and my thoughts above your thoughts
> (Is 55:8-9).

The parables illustrate the incomprehensible love that God has for us, his children. In Luke 15, Jesus tells us three parables, including the parable of the prodigal son. Were this just an ordinary story, the father would have sent his son packing when he returned after squandering away his inheritance. He would never have believed his story of feeling repentant over his sinful ways. In fact, the father would have been justified in thinking that the only change that occurred in his son was a change of diet. He would have felt rightly justified in letting his son sit on his blisters. In the same way, the elder son would have been rightfully rewarded and a celebration to honor him would have taken place.

However, Jesus is telling us a parable; his conclusion confounds our human way of thinking. The father's behavior is incomprehensible to the older boy, and to us. He just doesn't understand how his father can put the best clothes on his younger brother and celebrate his return. The father, in his own inimitable way, tries to communicate to both his sons another way of understanding human reality. The younger son and brother was dead, and now he has come alive. He had wandered away and now he has come home, no matter what his motivation might be.

The message seems to be that salvation and the process of becoming God-like can occur only when we have a genuine experience of being loved beyond measure, regardless of how wretched and perverse we might perceive ourselves to be. God never gives up on us, no matter how many times we might have given up on ourselves. And so it is always worth our while to pick up the pieces and return to God, who is always watchful for our arrival home.

Like the older son, many of us continue to be baffled by God's attitude and treatment of us. This other way of understanding reality just doesn't make sense. It takes simple, childlike faith to accept God's word, to believe that we are different from the way we perceive ourselves because God views us differently. We are precious in God's eyes because from all eternity we have been made in God's image and likeness, and no one can change that essential reality of our beings. It is not possible to become a true seeker if one has not experienced deeply God's all-encompassing love, where God is unwavering and faithful in good times and bad, in good conduct and bad, in holiness and sinfulness, in gloomy darkness and bright sunshine.

The right start is to understand clearly that the most important fact of discipleship is to be loved by rather than to love God. The two will go together, hand in hand, though too many discipleships have foundered because they believed that it was more important to love rather than to be loved by God. The emphasis on loving rather than being loved by God, or to put it more bluntly, the assumption that one can be the architect of one's own salvation in which God plays a secondary role, was condemned as a heresy by the church. The particular circumstances had to do with Pelagius, an English monk of the fifth century, who held that Jesus might be useful in our quest for salvation but was not necessary; that, in fact, we can save ourselves. Pelagius was condemned as a heretic because of his teaching that Jesus no longer had any real relevance.

In essence, a true disciple is someone who sits at the feet of the Master, constantly amazed and overwhelmed by the extraordinary love and acceptance of God for himself or herself. True holiness begins and ends in the heart of God. True religion is a matter of the heart. Understandably, one of Christianity's central tenets is that we cannot save ourselves. Salvation is God's business; allowing ourselves to be saved by falling into God's arms is ours.

THE FRUITS OF LOVE

Where there is love, joy and peace are present. This is a fact of our experience. In the presence of love we feel nourished and ennobled, and there arises in our hearts a desire to reciprocate the love we have received by doing something special for the giver. When a disciple has spent hours at the feet of the Lord tasting and relishing the loving kindness of the Master, gradually there arises in the heart a desire that grows ever stronger and deeper to respond in kind. Some disciples are so consumed by the gift of God's love that they feel called to give themselves entirely to God's service in whatever way God might call them.

The saints and mystics have talked about God's relationship with us in very endearing terms. Song of Songs contains the sublime portrayal and praise of the mutual love of the Lord and his people. The Lord is the Lover and his people are the beloved. Describing this relationship in terms of human love, the author follows Israel's tradition (found in Isaiah, Jeremiah, and Ezekiel) of characterizing the covenant between the Lord and Israel as a marriage.

On different occasions, I have had the wonderful privilege of hearing directees talk of their relationship with God in terms of an all-consuming relationship. They drew similarities between a passionate romance and their relationship with God. One of them talked about being wracked with an intense longing for God which would be slaked partially only in the presence of God. In every other activity during the day there was the sense that the Beloved was missing, creating in the person a ceaseless yearning for God.

Mary Magdalen was a person who related to the Lord with the same passion that a beloved has for her lover. After her conversion, Jesus was the light of her life. Wherever she went, she was consumed by the thought of him. She followed him wherever he went and was the first one to meet the risen Lord.

Abraham was utterly faithful to God's word to him. There was a vibrant and passionate relationship between God and Abraham. God made him a sweeping promise that he would be the father of a great nation, as many as the stars in the heavens. Abraham's faith was sorely tested. Even though Sarah was past her menopause, Abraham still believed that God would raise him a son. And his faith never wavered. When the apple of his eye was twelve years old, God again tested Abraham severely, to the point of asking him to sacrifice his son's life. But Abraham still believed in God's faithfulness to him. This relationship could not have endured all the hardships and vicissitudes that Abraham went through if there weren't a strong and enduring bond between God and him.

God desires to enter into a passionate relationship with us. The invitation asks us to accept the encounter, to enter into the fray and get swept away into God's embrace. It is quite possible that if we looked at the whole process as it might unfold with its various twists and turns, we would experience anxiety and worry about the outcome and the impact it might have on our lives. On the other hand, if we take it one day at a time, gradually the romance will unfold and, along with it, the maturity and depth of love we never imagined could be possible in our lives. Hopefully, the prayer exercises suggested in this chapter will help you grow and develop in your romance with God.

CHAPTER TWO HIGHLIGHTS

- ▲ Though we might be ordinary human beings on various levels of our lives, in our essence we belong to God's own house and lineage. Our destiny is a noble one because it has originated in the heart of God.

- ▲ Every time we say the Lord's prayer we dare to challenge our understanding of ourselves and the world. While the stories of our broken and miserable lives are true, we are at the same time affirming a much greater and more important truth: that we are God's own sons and daughters.

- ▲ True spiritual and psychological health and freedom begin only when we put on the mind and heart of God, when we learn to look at and understand ourselves through God's eyes and thoughts.

- ▲ The most important fact of discipleship is to be loved by rather than to love God, though the two will go hand in hand.

- ▲ One of Christianity's central tenets is that we cannot save ourselves. Salvation is God's business; allowing ourselves to be saved by falling into God's arms is ours.

- ▲ God clearly wants to enter into a passionate relationship with us. The invitation asks us to accept the encounter, to enter into the fray and get swept away into God's embrace.

Exercise Eleven
SELF-ACCEPTANCE

▲ Scripture

For God so loved the world that he gave his only Son, so that everyone who believes in him might not perish but might have eternal life. For God did not send his Son into the world to condemn the world, but that the world might be saved through him. Whoever believes in him will not be condemned. . . .
          —John 3:16-18

▲ Summary

Self-acceptance appears when self-hatred disappears. At times our self-hatred reigns and guilt lingers on because we are convinced that God can never forgive us. Jesus' understanding of God as Abba could help dismantle the caricature that we have formed of God. More important, our lives will change profoundly when we decide to accept Jesus' invitation to enter into a loving relationship with God as Abba.

▲ Session

(20-30 minute duration)

Spend a few minutes focusing on your breathing and the sensations in your nostrils and upper lip. After you have become quiet, you can move into the prayer session.

Jesus asks us as adults to address God as "Abba," or "Father," like a word used by a child to address its parent when it is first beginning to use intelligible sounds. At that tender age a child has no option except to depend *totally* on its parents. The child grows up healthy if that trust is honored. Whether our own trust in our fathers was honored or dishonored, Jesus asks us to become as a little child and, maybe for the first time in our lives, place our unconditional trust in God as Father.

Imagine a peaceful setting in nature, real or imagined, and you are once again a young child. You are seated in God's lap. Begin first by telling Abba about the obstacles and hurdles in the way of your being able to relate to him as Father. Imagine Abba's response to your objections, telling you how deeply and tenderly he has always loved you. Indeed, he cannot be Abba to you if you do not allow yourself to be loved and cared for by him. Next, say the "Our Father" with loving attention to the words and the presence of Abba holding you in his embrace. Repeat the prayer until the time is up.

▲ Reflection

Many of us have built our spiritual lives on emphasizing *our* love for God over God's love for us. This has led to numerous forms of Pelagianism, the belief that we can save ourselves without needing Jesus as our Savior. This prayer emphasizes spirituality as being the work of God in us. When our hearts have been deeply moved by God's all-embracing love for us, our lives will be marked by our own love for God and others, expressed through service and concern.

Exercise Twelve
THE EXCHANGE OF NAMES

▲ *Scripture*

Hark! my lover—here he comes
    springing across the mountains,
    leaping across the hills.
My lover is like a gazelle
    or a young stag.
Here he stands behind our wall,
    gazing through the windows,
    peering through the lattices.
My lover speaks; he says to me,
    "Arise, my beloved, my beautiful one,
    and come!"
        —Song of Songs 2:8-10

▲ *Summary*

A name is a very precious appellation because it communicates the identity of a person named in a very succinct and unique manner. God sometimes changed an individual's name as the first step toward forging a changed identity for and relationship with that person. In the Christian tradition the conversion of "Saul" to "Paul" is a classic example of this. This exercise is geared toward helping you gain a deeper appreciation of your own name given to you in baptism, as well as to realize that there are other precious names which characterize your identity and true self.

▲ Session

(15-20 minute duration)

Spend about five minutes coming home to yourself by doing any one of the first three exercises or a combination thereof.

Imagine yourself with Jesus in a peaceful and conducive setting, such as beside a fireplace in winter, or in a flower garden in summer, or in any other beautiful spot in nature. Begin your prayer by addressing Jesus by different names. Take your time and try to make sure your names reflect the deepest yearnings of your soul. If there are some names that resonate strongly, you can repeat them over and over in order to taste their inner depths.

It is then Jesus' turn to address you by names that best describe his relationship with you. You listen attentively as he showers you in his intimacy, commitment, and passion for you.

▲ Reflection

For some people it takes several sessions before their hearts are moved, either because they are not used to love being lavished upon them, or because they are burdened with guilt, fear, or resentment. It is important to repeat this exercise until the heart is moved, and it may take several sessions. The mystics insist that the only authentic way to God is through the heart. When the heart is moved, the mystery begins to make sense. This exercise can be a stepping stone toward appreciating the mystery that God is.

Exercise Thirteen
GOD'S PERSPECTIVE ON MY BIRTH

▲ *Scripture*

Blessed be the God and Father of our Lord Jesus
Christ, who has blessed us in Christ with every
spiritual blessing in the heavenly places, just as
he chose us in Christ before the foundation of the
world to be holy and blameless before him in
love. He destined us for adoption as his children
through Jesus Christ, according to the good pleasure of his will, to the praise of his glorious grace
that he freely bestowed on us in the Beloved.

—Ephesians 1:3-6

▲ *Summary*

Our birth is of God's making, no matter what the circumstances might have been or the spin others, or we ourselves, might have given to it. It therefore makes sense to
try to see our creation the way God does. Many have been
able to find precious graces and blessings in the midst of
their traumatized and painful histories. God is more present to us than we are aware, and sometimes such a realization may take a long time in coming to us.

▲ *Session*

(20-30 minute duration)

Spend about five minutes coming home to yourself using
any of the first six exercises or a combination thereof.

Imagine yourself at the site of the manger in Bethlehem. Create the scene in a way that is most conducive for you. Enter into the hearts and minds of Joseph, Mary, Jesus, and whoever else is present, and try to immerse yourself in their experience of Jesus' birth.

Next, create the scene of your own birth. Enter into the hearts and minds of your mother, father, yourself, and whoever else is present, and once again, try to immerse yourself in their experience of your birth.

Return to the scene of the manger. This time listen to the angels announcing peace and joy to the world through the birth of Jesus. Come back to the scene of your own birth, and listen to the message the angels are giving the world about the significance of *your* birth! What is the message? For how long have you known it? How have you lived it out so far?[1]

▲ Reflection

Those who have God's perspective on life are connected to a divine source of peace and joy which acts like a firm foundation in the vicissitudes of our lives. Such a source is both rare and possible at the same time. This prayer exercise can help you put on God's mind and heart so that you understand in greater depth the saying from Isaiah:

> For my thoughts are not your thoughts,
>   nor are your ways my ways, says the Lord (Is 55:8).

Exercise Fourteen

A VISIT FROM JESUS

▲ *Scripture*

> For by grace you have been saved through faith, and this is not your own doing; it is the gift of God—not the result of works, so that no one may boast. For we are what he has made us, created in Christ Jesus for good works, which God prepared beforehand to be our way of life.
>
> —Ephesians 2:8-10

▲ *Summary*

When good people endure self-loathing for long periods of time it means that their ability to assess themselves has gone awry. In such a situation, a gentle and loving assessment by an interested party can sometimes rectify the imbalance in this jaundiced view. The mystics recommend we try Jesus as our closest confidant.

▲ *Session*

(20-30 minute duration)

Imagine a beautiful setting in nature, real or imagined, where you own a custom-built home. With gratitude and joy you admire your home and its surroundings. You then go in and admire the various rooms, taking in every detail. As you are doing so, the phone rings and the caller is Jesus. He would like to visit with you in about fifteen minutes, as he is close by. What are your thoughts and sentiments as you prepare for the visit?

Fifteen minutes later you welcome Jesus into your home and the visit begins. You become aware of what's going on within you in Jesus' presence. At one point, Jesus draws close to you, looks you in the eye, and says, "You have your own version of your life story based on what others have said and your own self-appraisal. I want you now to listen to *my version* of your life story." You listen very attentively as Jesus tells you what he thinks of you. Then there is silence as you savor his assessment of you.

Next you muster up the courage to ask Jesus to tell you what it is that he wants from you. He smiles, thinks for a moment, and tells you what he wants from you. And you respond to his request.

Jesus then asks you to search your heart and make a request of him. You take your time and then tell him what it is that you desire from him.

Finally, it is time to part. The two of you spend some time in silence, savoring the intimacy and love between you. You bid farewell to each other, and Jesus departs. You spend some time pondering the mystery and gift of his presence in your home and heart.

▲ *Reflection*

Imagination is an effective way of entering into the mystery of God's love for us. In the course of prayer, mere imagination becomes imaginative faith when the seeker knows for a fact that God is indeed present. One can never stress too much the importance of knowing that one is loved unconditionally by God. Such a love is the bulwark of passionate commitment to God by otherwise frail and imperfect humans.

Exercise Fifteen
ENCIRCLED IN LOVE

▲ *Scripture*

Can a mother forget her infant,
   be without tenderness for the child of her womb?
Even should she forget,
   I will never forget you.
See, upon the palms of my hands I have written
your name.

—Isaiah 49:15-16

▲ *Summary*

Christian discipleship hinges on the reality that the disciple
is overwhelmingly and passionately loved by Jesus and has
firsthand experience of it. Jesus is the God who did not cling
to his divinity but emptied himself, even to the point of
becoming a slave in order to save humanity. This experience of wholehearted love transforms the disciple, eliciting
in him or her an equally passionate response of compassionate service and love.

▲ *Session*

(20-30 minute duration)

Take a few minutes to come home to yourself through
awareness of sounds, your breathing, or bodily sensations.

After you have become still, imagine a place that is very comfortable and conducive to intimacy. Invite your heavenly Father, Jesus, and the Holy Spirit as well as some of your favorite saints and other special persons who mean much to you to this place. It helps to keep the total number between seven and ten persons to ensure that the circle is intimate.

After the group has become comfortable with one another, you address them and tell them that you have brought them together for one specific purpose, namely, to share with you their memories, thoughts, and sentiments of appreciation of you. You listen in silence as they share with you their positive feedback, one by one. After each one there is silence to allow the impact to sink in. When they have finished, you respond to each one of them with your own thoughts and sentiments generated as a result of their positive regard for you. Make sure the three Persons of the Trinity offer you feedback as well.

▲ Reflection

The disciple's prayer is the context where one recognizes that God's palm is inscribed with his or her very own name. In this place of rest God avows everlasting love by stating that even if a mother were to forget the very child of her womb, God will never forget us. Prayer then is the swaddling cloth of comfort and well-being with which God covers us. As the disciple's heart is moved there is a true appreciation of one's wrongdoing and the need to make amends. The desire to be of service to others springs from the joy and exhilaration of being loved by God. This experience creates an intense desire to share one's blessings with others.

Exercise Sixteen

THE MYSTERY OF THE INCARNATION

▲ Scripture

And the Word became flesh and lived among us, and we have seen his glory, the glory as of a father's only son, full of grace and truth.

—John 1:14

▲ Summary

The Incarnation of Jesus is God's way of coming to our level, sharing in our lives and circumstances, so that we can understand our own nobility and heritage as sons and daughters of God. The planning for such a central event in our spiritual lives was done from all eternity. This prayer exercise helps us to appreciate God's perspective on the Incarnation.

▲ Session

(20-30 minute duration)

Spend about five minutes coming home to yourself through the awareness of sounds, your breathing, or bodily sensations.

Imagine the Holy Trinity having a conference where they are discussing the affairs of the world, and you are sitting in on their discussion. They are concerned that human beings are not participating in their own divine life in any great depth, and the ravages of sin are taking their toll. The

Trinity want to do something about that. They decide to send Jesus to us. He will become a human being like all of us, participate in our lives as one of us, and become our Redeemer by dying on the cross for us. Listen carefully to each Person of the Trinity, trying to fathom the depth of their love and concern for humanity. In particular, try to understand the magnitude of Jesus' mission. Do this by talking to each one of them as well as by listening to what they have to say to you.

▲ *Reflection*

God is unfathomable mystery. Yet we have been given clear hints and ways to experience God through revelation regarding Jesus Christ, and the universal plan of salvation. God's Word is inexhaustible in meaning and power. It takes many visits to the fountain of Life before one begins to appreciate dimly, yet significantly, the depths of God's love for each of us. St. Paul says, "At present we see indistinctly, as in a mirror, but then face to face. At present I know partially; then I shall know fully, as I am fully known" (1 Cor 13:12).

Exercise Seventeen
THE VIEWING

▲ *Scripture*

> When I see your heavens, the work of your fingers,
>   the moon and stars that you set in place—
> What are humans that you are mindful of them,
>   mere mortals that you care for them?
> Yet you have made them little less than a god,
>   crowned them with glory and honor.
> You have given them rule over the works of your hands,
>   put all things at their feet.
> > —Psalm 8:4-7

▲ *Summary*

While life brings pain and loss to us, such suffering can be meaningful if we have the right perspective and can accept life's terms realistically. On the other hand, when we refuse to accept the laws of human existence, we create suffering for ourselves that is not necessary. One of life's certainties is that we, and others we love, will die. Similarly, we will age, and no cosmetic camouflages can deny or keep at bay the aging process with all its ramifications. Acceptance will bring peace, though at times the process will be slow and painful. Kicking against the goad will bring misery and bitterness.

▲ *Session*

(20-30 minute duration)

Take up a comfortable sitting posture with your back erect and your chin tilted forward slightly. Spend about five minutes coming home to yourself through the awareness of sounds, your breathing, or bodily sensations.

Imagine that a famous sculptor has been commissioned to create two statues of you, one portraying you as you know yourself in your better and worse moments, and the other depicting you with your fulfilled dreams and wishes. You have had several visits with the sculptor in which you describe yourself as you are and would like to be.

A while later you receive the news that your statues have been completed, and you have been invited to a private viewing. You see yourself going to the viewing room and you get in touch with your feelings. As you approach the room, you notice that Jesus is waiting for you. He asks if he can view your statues with you. The two of you go into the room. First you unveil the statue of yourself as you are. Both Jesus and you take your time to observe the statue as well as your intimate reactions to it in silence. Next, you unveil the second statue of yourself as a person fulfilled. Again the two of you examine the statue and record your impressions and responses to it in silence. Then the two of you retire to a restful, comfortable place in the building and talk about your respective reactions and sentiments engendered by the viewing. In the dialogue, you learn more about yourself, and specifically, more about the way Jesus views you.

▲ *Reflection*

This exercise serves to give you better perspective on your life in order to help you embrace it with zest and optimism. Whatever the extent of your life's messiness might be, you have been created in God's likeness and are called to be whole and holy.

Exercise Eighteen
THE VISITATION

▲ *Scripture*

Simeon took Jesus into his arms and blessed God, saying:
"Now, Master, you may let your servant go
   in peace, according to your word,
for my eyes have seen your salvation,
   which you prepared in sight of all the peoples,
a light for revelation to the Gentiles,
   and glory for your people Israel."
     —Luke 2:29-32

▲ *Summary*

In one of his poems, Rabindranath Tagore asks, "Have you not heard his silent steps, he comes, comes, ever comes."[2] The disciple believes very strongly that God comes continually to us and there are many times when we do not recognize the divine visitations. There are several biblical figures who struggled for years as they waited for the Lord's coming into their lives. When it happened, their joy knew no bounds and their faith in God was even more strengthened.

▲ *Session*

(20-30 minute session)

Take a few minutes to come home to yourself through awareness of sounds, your breathing, or bodily sensations.

Recall the story of Joseph and his brothers. They sold him into slavery because they were jealous of him and resentful of their father, Jacob, for treating Joseph as his favorite son. Joseph went through many tribulations and eventually became a highly respected official in Egypt. The Lord came into his life in a very powerful way when he was reunited with his brothers and father under strange circumstances. (Read Genesis 37.)

The story of Elizabeth is a story in which a woman who was barren for years never gave up her yearning to bear a son. Against all odds and in spite of her husband's doubts, she bore a son who was God's special gift to her, and the Messiah's forerunner. (Read Luke 1:5-80.)

There is the tale of Simeon, a prophet who had become old and feeble as he waited for the coming of the Messiah. He was given the privilege of recognizing the Messiah in the baby who was being presented in the temple. (Read Luke 2:25-35.)

Spend time with each of these figures, appreciating their patience and faith as they waited for years for God to come to them. And in God's presence look at your own life and ask whether God has come to you and become Emmanuel.

▲ *Reflection*

Even when God seems to be stalling and withholding visitations, the saints and mystics always knew that God was still coming to them, albeit in subtle and imperceptible ways. If this were not the case, the wait would have been intolerable, if not impossible. In many of the psalms the author echoes the tension between yearning for God and knowing at the same time that God is there in some manner. Tagore put it well in his poem: "In sorrow after sorrow, it is his steps that press upon my heart, and it is the golden touch of his feet that makes my joy to shine."[3]

Exercise Nineteen
HUMAN HANDIWORK

▲ Scripture

Then God said, "Let us make humankind in our image, according to our likeness; and let them have dominion over the fish of the sea, and over the birds of the air, and over the cattle, and over all the wild animals of the earth, and over every creeping thing that creeps upon the earth."

So God created humankind in his image;
in the image of God he created them;
male and female he created them.
—Genesis 1:26-27

▲ Summary

We will never be able to plumb the depths of God's wondrous decision to make us in the divine likeness, because it boggles the mind to try to understand the meaning of what essentially is a mystery. However, even though we might never be able to fully fathom such a reality, pondering over and appreciating it will enrich our lives tremendously. One approach would be to reflect on the marvels of human creation which speak of God's wonderful intelligence and providence.

▲ Session

(20-30 duration)

Spend a few minutes coming home to yourself through the awareness of sounds, your breathing, or bodily sensations.

After you have become quiet and disposed for prayer, invite Jesus to sit beside you and together view various snapshots of human handiwork. You can imagine the two of you sitting by the window of a flying aircraft and being amazed by the sight below you: the grain fields, forests, villages and towns, streets and highways, lakes and rivers, automobiles and trucks moving along the roads, and so on. In all of this there is minute planning and hard work that have gone into the handiwork over many, many years.

Next, you can take a ride with Jesus on the expressway. Once again you can allow yourself to be impressed by the engineering and immense commitment on the part of thousands of human beings over the years to make it so convenient and safe for you to journey on these modern miracles. You can visit with Jesus the Taj Mahal in Agra, St. Peter's Basilica in Rome, the Eiffel Tower in Paris, the Sears Tower in Chicago, or any other masterpieces of human creation that have awed you. . . . Continue in this vein until you are satisfied and ready to spend some minutes in silent communion with Jesus, sharing the sentiments that have arisen in your heart, and listen to him respond to you.

▲ Reflection

For many of us it is characteristic to separate the sacred from the secular in our lives. We compartmentalize our lives, becoming aware of our relationship with God mostly when we are in church or saying our prayers. God seems to be absent when we are busy with the mundane and secular aspects of our lives. This exercise makes it clear that there is no separation between the sacred and the secular for the seeker. Our human handiwork is evocative of the throbbing presence of God in the wonderful workmanship we see all around us.

Exercise Twenty
MUNIFICENCE

▲ Scripture

I give thanks to my God always for you because of the grace of God that has been given you in Christ Jesus, for in every way you have been enriched in him, in speech and knowledge of every kind—just as the testimony of Christ has been strengthened among you—so that you are not lacking in any spiritual gift as you wait for the revealing of our Lord Jesus Christ.

—1 Corinthians 1:4-7

▲ Summary

God's bounty is all around us and within us. All that we have to do is be aware and be amazed. Gratitude and wonderment are healing salve to the soul. They give us the proper perspective we need when our worries and cares furrow us into enshrouding fear and debilitating anxiety. They tell us in no uncertain terms that there is a vast horizon beyond the hole we feel we are in, a silver lining to every one of our dark clouds, and, paradoxically, that resurrection sprouts from the seed of agony.

▲ Session

(30 minute duration)

Take a few minutes to come home to yourself through awareness of sounds, your breathing, or bodily sensations.

Choose a beautiful place in nature, real or imagined, which has an environment of great peace and serenity. The grandeur of the place puts you into a contemplative and receptive stance. Invite Jesus to enjoy this beautiful scene with you.

After you have contemplated the scene for some time, enter into a dialogue with Jesus by thanking him for all that you see around you in God's creation. You can then be grateful for all the material, human, and spiritual blessings you have received from God. You might want to tell Jesus how grateful you are for all the gifts and blessings you have received from family and friends. If you wish, you can thank Jesus for the many opportunities you have received to be a blessing and grace to others. It helps some people to make a list of their graces and blessings, both those received by them and those offered to others, before they do this prayer exercise. Try doing so if you think it is a good idea for you, and share it with Jesus. Then spend some time listening to Jesus respond to you.

▲ Reflection

While fear and anxiety contract the heart and furrow the brow, gratitude brings a sparkle to the eyes and raises one's vision to the eastern sky at dawn. Gratitude softens the spirit, making it malleable to receive God's consolations and blessings. No wonder the saints, beginning with St. Paul, exhort us to give thanks to God continually.

▲ Self-acceptance appears when self-hatred disappears. Sometimes, self-hatred reigns and guilt lingers on because we are convinced that God can never forgive us. Jesus' understanding of God as Abba could help dismantle the caricature that we have formed of God.

▲ The mystics insist that an authentic way to God is through the heart. When the heart is moved the mystery begins to make sense.

▲ Our birth is of God's making, no matter what the circumstances might have been or the spin others or we ourselves might have given to it. God is more present to us than we realize, and sometimes such a realization may take a long time in coming to us.

▲ When good people endure self-loathing for long periods of time, their ability to assess themselves has gone awry. A gentle and loving assessment by an interested party can sometimes rectify the imbalance in this jaundiced view. The mystics recommend we try Jesus as our closest confidant.

▲ Christian discipleship hinges on the reality that the disciple is overwhelmingly and passionately loved by Jesus and has made a firsthand experience of it.

▲ While life brings its fair share of pain and loss to us, such suffering is redemptive and meaningful if we have the right perspective and can accept life's terms realistically. Acceptance will bring peace, though at times the process will be slow and painful.

- Even when God seems to be stalling and withholding visitations, the saints always knew that God was still coming to them, albeit in subtle and imperceptible ways.

- There is no separation between the sacred and the secular for the seeker. Our human handiwork is evocative of the throbbing presence of God in the wonderful workmanship we see all around us.

- While fear and anxiety contract the heart and furrow the brow, gratitude softens the spirit and brings a sparkle to the eyes. No wonder the saints exhort us to give thanks to God continually.

CHAPTER THREE

Smitten
by
God's Mercy

In our human experience we tend to consider showing mercy toward our enemies as possibly the most difficult challenge we face in our lives. Jesus knew how difficult this was, yet he asked us to disregard the prevailing norm of treating our enemies as, well, enemies.

In Matthew's gospel, Jesus says, "You have heard that it was said, 'You shall love your neighbor and hate your enemy'" (5:43). Before Jesus' time there was a long-standing tradition of hating your enemies. It was not uncommon to exhort God in prayer to destroy the enemy. Psalm 35 says,

> Oppose, LORD, those who oppose me;
>   war upon those who make war upon me.
> Take up the shield and buckler;
>   rise up in my defense (35:1-2).

Jesus takes a deeply embedded tradition and stands it on its head. He says: "But I say to you, Love your enemies and pray for those who persecute you, so that you may be children of your Father in heaven; for he makes his sun rise on the evil and on the good, and sends rain on the righteous and on the unrighteous"(Mt 5:44-45). Jesus is clearly projecting an image of God that never existed in the consciousness of his hearers. In his mind there is no ambivalence about the fact that God's arms are outstretched to the same degree for saints and sinners alike. God's largesse is accessible by men and women of all stripes and colors, conduct and creed.

Luke addresses the same issue of love and mercy toward our enemies. He says, "Be merciful, just as your Father is merciful. Do not judge, and you will not be judged; do not condemn, and you will not be condemned. Forgive, and you will be forgiven" (Lk 6:36-37). In the face of this explicit teaching to love our enemies and do good to those who hate us, many of us are like the rich young man who was generous and interested in following Jesus, however, he was not willing to go all the way, to leave everything and follow Jesus (Mk 10:17-22).

Like the rich young man, we want Jesus, but on our own terms. While we may not have many material riches, there are always fears, resentments, and prejudices that we are not willing to give up. Gandhi was known to have said that giving up material possessions and living a simple life was rather easy for him. Giving up every form of deceit, prejudice, and hatred was an altogether different matter. Yet true salvation comes to us when we accept Jesus and his teachings for what they are, and allow them to govern our lives.

OUT ON A LIMB

One of the central aspects of Jesus' life and teaching was that he was merciful. He got himself into some very difficult situations because of his commitment to loving kindness. In the end it led to his passion and crucifixion. There was a power and magnetism that emanated from his merciful acts toward others. Many individuals experienced his unconditional acceptance and love, and their lives were transformed.

The Gospel of John tells a powerful story of an adulterous woman (8:1-11). Jesus was teaching in the temple precincts when a hostile crowd led a woman forward who had been caught in adultery. They made her stand there in front of everyone while they tested Jesus.

"Teacher," they said to him, "this woman has been caught in the act of adultery. In the law, Moses ordered such women to be stoned. What do you have to say about the case?" They were posing this question to trap Jesus so that they could have something with which to accuse him. Jesus bent down and started tracing on the ground with his finger.

When they persisted in their questioning, Jesus straightened up and said to them, "Let the one among you who has no sin be the first to cast a stone at her." A second time he bent down and wrote on the ground. Then the audience drifted away one by one, beginning with the elders. This left him alone with the woman, who continued to stand there before him. Jesus finally straightened up and said to her, "Woman, where did they all disappear to? Has no one condemned you?"

"No one, sir," she answered.

Jesus said, "Nor do I condemn you. You may go. But from now on, avoid this sin."

This incident is charged with powerful emotion, a veritable minefield that Jesus handled with courage, honesty, and warm compassion. He made it clear that to him compassion and forgiveness, when accepted with a repentant heart, bring about more righteous transformation than punitive justice. He was extremely discreet in the way he handled this situation. He did not get into a heated argument with the scribes and Pharisees and thereby lose the opportunity to minister to and save this condemned woman.

While the crowd was suspicious of Jesus, in some ways they were afraid of him and realized that he had a special charisma and power they seemed to lack. He could cure the sick, give sight to the blind and speech to the mute. And in some instances, to their consternation, he even forgave sin. It was this begrudging acknowledgment of his status as a teacher that possibly led them to face themselves and admit that they had no right to punish this woman when they themselves were in need of forgiveness.

In the final moments of face-to-face intimacy with Jesus, this woman was forever transformed. Jesus did not harangue or upbraid her. In his presence she experienced peace and mercy that changed her life. Jesus had loved her unconditionally and was willing to risk his life and reputation for her sake.

If we are to go by the popular tradition existing in the church, then this woman is identified as Mary Magdalen. Her encounter with Jesus resulted in her becoming an ardent seeker. Thereafter, she was with Jesus in the most difficult and challenging moments of his life. She was among the women who followed him to the Place of the Skull. She witnessed his crucifixion. She was the first one to whom Jesus appeared after his resurrection. Indeed, Mary became the witness to Jesus, par excellence.

LOVE'S RESPONSE TO FORGIVENESS

In the seventh chapter of Luke's gospel we read about a certain Pharisee, named Simon, who invites Jesus to dine with him. Jesus goes to the Pharisee's home and reclines to eat. A woman who is known in the town to be a sinner learns that Jesus is dining in the Pharisee's home. She goes there and brings in a vase of perfumed oil and stands behind him at his feet, weeping so that her tears fall upon his feet. Then she wipes them with her hair, kissing them and perfuming them with the oil. Simon sees this and says to himself, "If this man were a prophet, he would know who and what sort of woman this is that touches him—that she is a sinner." In the dialogue that follows between Jesus and Simon, Jesus extolls the woman's behavior and contrasts it sharply with Simon's own. Furthermore, Jesus forgives her sins and comments on the fact that she is able to love much because she is forgiven much.

This encounter between the woman and Jesus makes for an interesting study of the attitudes and dispositions of the different characters in this story. At first glance, Simon seemed to be well disposed toward Jesus. He was willing to run the risk of inviting Jesus to his home for a meal and be criticized for it by the orthodox segment of his community. But as a Pharisee he shared in the distrust and antagonism toward Jesus that many other Pharisees had. His true attitude toward Jesus became clear when Jesus was actually in his home. He seated Jesus for the meal without according him the most basic sign of hospitality, which is having Jesus' feet washed before he reclined to eat. Also, it is shocking that he allowed the woman who was branded as a sinner to enter his home. Were his motives insidious, since he knew that she wanted to meet Jesus, whose name would be tainted by his association with her?

Like most of us, Simon was probably a good person who was faced with the option of having to choose between teachings and rules that he had grown up with and the disturbing but magnetic teaching and presence of the man known as Jesus, who mingled with sinners and tax collectors and brought them the good news of God's salvation. For Simon, the good news according to Jesus was still too radical and scandalous and he could not yet recognize the woman's "sinful dimension" in himself.

If we are to remain faithful to the long-standing church tradition that the woman caught in adultery is this same penitent woman washing Jesus' feet, then her daring and audacity to come into the Pharisee's house uninvited has some understandable logic to it. She had been snatched from a humiliating and gruesome death by this man they called Jesus. Even more important, he gave her new life, filled with peace, hope, and joy. Her heart brimming with consolation, she was impelled to give herself completely to following this strange and dynamic Teacher who could forgive her sin and bring salvation to her soul. At the risk of being spurned and rejected by a hostile group of Pharisees assembled in Simon's house, she decided to meet with Jesus in this den of hostility as a way of expressing her gratitude, humility, and discipleship. She knew intuitively that Jesus had not been well received by Simon. He was insulted by his host who deliberately chose not to have his feet washed. Touchingly and unashamedly, she washed his feet with her tears and wiped them with her long tresses. Her tears expressed both her joy at being with Jesus as well as her sorrow for her life of sin, and above all, a clear commitment to following him in the face of open skepticism and ridicule. She was able to demonstrate such love because in her heart she had already known that she had been forgiven much by Jesus.

There is the moving story told by Anthony de Mello in his book *Taking Flight* of an old man who decides to go on an arduous pilgrimage to a holy place in the Himalayas. One evening as he eats his supper in a wayside inn, the innkeeper wonders aloud how he thought he could reach the holy place given the harsh terrain and climate and his own weak health. The old man replied in a serene voice that his body would somehow get there because his heart had already made the journey. Such is the substance of saints: when the heart has been moved, miracles occur. Mary Magdalen's heart had been moved by the love and compassion of Jesus. Consequently, her attitude and disposition were changed, and she demonstrated a courage and devotion that was breathtaking and admirable.

GOD IN OUR BROKENNESS

In chapter two of this book, there was a strong emphasis on God's earnest yearning for intimacy with us. God's love for us led to our creation in the divine image and likeness, and the suggestion was made that no matter how terrible and traumatic our respective histories might be, they can be healed and experienced as invitations to God's grace because of the all-important fact that we are indeed sons and daughters of God. However, I have observed again and again in spiritual direction that this unique heritage of being God's own offspring will not have any tangible impact on our behaviors and lives unless there is a relationship with God that is conscious, vibrant, and all encompassing.

Intimacy with anybody presupposes honesty and transparency. Intimacy with others is difficult and challenging because it presupposes a dual task: first, taking the risk of sharing personal secrets and shame, trusting that the other will receive your material with respect and compassion, and not knowing for sure whether this will in fact happen; and second, listening non-defensively to the feedback to your sharing, never really knowing whether it will build you up or devastate you. Implicit in the fear and challenge of intimacy is the reality that while we have been created in God's image and likeness, we are also sinners who are weak, flawed, and devious. Consequently, the only way to arrive at our true, God-given identity is through facing with honesty and courage our duplicity, deceit, and evil tendencies. The paradox of the spiritual life is that we discover God best in the heart of our addictions, failures, and messiness. The only way to the heart of God is through the humble admission of our sins and failings. The only meaningful way to experience God is as the Savior who loves us because of who God is rather than because of what we have done or not done. So it makes sense for the anonymous author of *The Cloud of Unknowing* to consider as a special grace the experience of seeing oneself as "a mass of sin"[1] before God.

In Psalm 139, the psalmist gives us a vivid rendering of the need to hold in delicate balance our wholeness/holiness on the one hand, and our sinfulness/wrongdoings on the other. God sees everything; no one can hide anything from the Creator. If, on the other hand, we take delight in being transparent before God, then there is a renewal of joy and gratitude in the midst of our fragility.

You formed my inmost being;
    you knit me in my mother's womb.
I praise you, so wonderfully you made me;
    wonderful are your works! (Ps 139:13-14).

Where can I hide from your spirit?
    From your presence, where can I flee?
If I ascend to the heavens, you are there;
    if I lie down in Sheol, you are there too
    (Ps 139:7-8).

If I say, "Surely darkness shall hide me,
    and night shall be my light"—
Darkness is not dark for you,
    and night shines as the day (Ps 139:11-12).

GOD IN OUR ADDICTIONS

Alcoholics Anonymous has developed a twelve-step spirituality that works for many who are unable to recover from their addiction. The first step is that "we admit we are powerless over alcohol—that our lives have become unmanageable." When an alcoholic truly accepts the truth of this statement, a profound change occurs. The alcoholic acknowledges utter powerlessness before the enslavement of alcohol as well as the serious damage the addiction has caused him or her and others. Indeed life has become unmanageable. Paradoxically, God's healing power and love can now enter into the picture. In the midst of the powerlessness, the alcoholic "comes to believe that a Power greater than ourselves can restore us to sanity," and "make a decision to turn our will and our lives over to the care of God as we understand Him."[2]

The rest of the steps are about facing one's shadow side and making "a searching and fearless moral inventory of ourselves" and admitting "to God, to ourselves, and to another human being the exact nature of our wrongs."[3] Those who seriously exercise themselves in the habit of admitting the exact nature of their wrongs will also humbly ask God to remove their defects of character and develop the practice and process of making amends to all whom they have hurt, directly or indirectly. As they face their shortcomings with candor and honesty, they will gradually find themselves looking directly into the eyes of God.

There is the right approach to addressing our faults and failings, and the wrong approach. The right approach creates honesty and integrity, which further generate a spiritual awakening that makes us want to live for and do God's will alone. The wrong approach leads to difficulty in accepting our character defects, resulting in denial, making excuses, lying, and a spirit of desolation. It is at best a half-hearted attempt at honesty, a charade of integrity, and a mockery of true spirituality. God is alive and well in the right approach, just as the seeker is. We are stymied and hobbled in the wrong one. God's salvation shines best in the humble acknowledgment of one's weaknesses.

CHAPTER THREE HIGHLIGHTS

- One of the central aspects of Jesus' life and teaching was that he was merciful. He got himself into some very difficult situations because of his commitment to loving kindness. In the end it led to his passion and crucifixion. Many individuals experienced his unconditional acceptance and love, and their lives were transformed.

- The paradox of the spiritual life is that we discover God best in the heart of our addictions, failures, and messiness. The only way to the heart of God is through the humble admission of our sins and failings.

- Implicit in the fear and challenge of intimacy is the reality that while we have been created in God's image and likeness, we are also sinners who are weak, flawed, and devious. Consequently, the only way to arrive at our true, God-given identity is through facing with honesty and courage our duplicity, deceit, and evil tendencies.

- Those who seriously exercise themselves in the habit of admitting the exact nature of their wrongs will also humbly ask God to remove their defects of character, and develop the practice and process of making amends to all whom they have hurt, directly or indirectly. As they face their shortcomings with candor and honesty, they will gradually find themselves looking directly into the eyes of God.

Exercise Twenty-One

THE WOMAN CAUGHT IN ADULTERY

▲ *Scripture*

> Then Jesus straightened up and said to her, "Woman, where are they? Has no one condemned you?" She replied, "No one, sir." Then Jesus said, "Neither do I condemn you. Go, and from now on do not sin any more."
> —John 8:10-11

▲ *Summary*

Some of Jesus' teachings and actions do not make sense to our human way of thinking. At times they create strong resistance within us because Jesus is calling us to a change of heart and direction. Whenever we embrace God's word with an open heart, mountains are moved and God's presence becomes more tangible.

▲ *Session*

(20-30 minute duration)

Take a few minutes to come home to yourself through the awareness of sounds, your breathing, or bodily sensations. After you have become quiet, recall the encounter from John's gospel of Jesus and the hostile crowd that has caught the woman in adultery. At first, imagine yourself to be one of the crowd, and go through your various mood changes, from the time you join the crowd to the time you decide you cannot cast a stone at the woman because you yourself have sinned. What is your sin? What role does Jesus play in making you confront your own hypocrisy and sinfulness?

Next identify yourself with the woman caught in adultery. Dialogue with her as a way of entering into her sentiments and dispositions. Ask yourself, what led her to commit adultery? What were her feelings as she was being led away for stoning? Then focus on Jesus as, with calm assurance, he deals with the crowd. His passion for truth and commitment to compassion mesmerize the crowd into silent admission of their own wrongdoing. Observe Jesus interacting on behalf of and with the woman as he leads her from hopelessness and despair to hope and trust; from shame and guilt to forgiveness and self-acceptance; from a terrible death by stoning to a life of peace and repentance. Express the sentiments aroused in your heart to God in prayer.

▲ Reflection

There are many things about Jesus and the spiritual life that we will never understand because they are so alien to our human way of thinking and relating with one another. Yet when we accept Jesus at his word and do as he tells us, we experience a transformation in our lives that astounds our sensibilities. Jesus' encounter with the adulteress is such a case. He chooses to make his point through a situation that would allow for no mercy or understanding. In the process, he confounds us all with his compelling honesty and persuasive compassion. A satisfactory understanding or explanation of life often comes to us after we have made our assent to God's will.

Exercise Twenty-Two
THE PENITENT WOMAN

▲ *Scripture*

Then turning toward the woman, he said to Simon, "Do you see this woman? I entered your house; you gave me no water for my feet, but she has bathed my feet with her tears and dried them with her hair. You gave me no kiss, but from the time I came in she has not stopped kissing my feet. You did not anoint my head with oil, but she has anointed my feet with ointment. Therefore, I tell you, her sins, which were many, have been forgiven; hence she has shown great love. But the one to whom little is forgiven, loves little."

—Luke 7:44-47

▲ *Summary*

The story of the penitent woman moves us deeply because it describes the honesty and courage of a person who loved much because she was forgiven much. The story gives us a deep insight into the power of Jesus' compassion and mercy, which brought out the best in the woman.

▲ *Session*

(20-30 minute duration)

Take up a comfortable sitting posture. Spend about five minutes coming home to yourself through the awareness of sounds, your breathing, or bodily sensations.

Imagine yourself in the home of Simon the Pharisee, observing closely and interactively the scene as it unfolds before you. There is Simon, who has invited Jesus, among other guests, to his home for a meal, but does not accord him the basic hospitality of having his feet washed. In keeping with his critical attitude he wonders whether Jesus could indeed be a true teacher since he allowed the woman, a known sinner, to touch him. There is the woman who hears that Jesus is at the house of Simon the Pharisee, where she would definitely be unwelcome. She decides to enter the lion's den and brave the mockery and hostility of the assembled guests. What then must have been her sense of Jesus to be willing to go through this humiliation? And there is the interaction between this woman and Jesus. She washes his feet with her tears, wipes them with her hair, and anoints them with expensive perfume. And Jesus is totally comfortable with her behavior in the midst of this critical group. He makes an eloquent defense of her actions and forgives her sins. She is able to love so much because she is first convinced of Jesus' compassion and acceptance of her. She leaves the house in peace, and salvation has come to her in the person of Jesus. Share your reflections and sentiments with Jesus.

▲ *Reflection*

The natural tendency of a person who has been deeply loved and accepted is to want to reciprocate with similar acts of kindness and compassion. The penitent woman displayed such courage and humility because she had received the grace of believing that Jesus would accept and forgive her completely, without any conditions. This conviction turned her life around, and even Jesus was amazed at her capacity for love.

Exercise Twenty-Three
SIN AND SALVATION

▲ Scripture

> But the tax collector stood off at a distance and would not even raise his eyes to heaven but beat his breast and prayed, "O God, be merciful to me a sinner." I tell you, the latter went home justified, not the former; for everyone who exalts himself will be humbled, and the one who humbles himself will be exalted.
>
> —Luke 18:13-14

▲ Summary

In his teaching, Jesus emphasized a strange paradox of the spiritual life: God's salvation and healing will come only to those who humbly and honestly admit their sins. Confession of sins highlights the reality that salvation can never be earned. Salvation comes only to the contrite of heart because there is an acknowledgment of one's powerlessness as well as a surrender to God's loving kindness and mercy.

▲ Session

(20-30 minute duration)

Take up a comfortable sitting posture. Take a few minutes to come home to yourself through awareness of sounds, your breathing, or bodily sensations.

In Luke 18, Jesus gives us the parable of the Pharisee and the tax collector, contrasting two opposing attitudes in a disciple's relationship with God. The Pharisee's attitude is one of self-righteousness. He is not like the rest of men, whom he sees as grasping, crooked, and adulterous, and definitely not like the tax collector, who is praying alongside him. He does not recognize any sin in himself, and has *earned* his merit or salvation with God.

The tax collector, on the other hand, does not even dare to raise his eyes to heaven. All he does is beat his breast and say, "O God, be merciful to me, a sinner." Jesus tells us that the tax collector went home from the temple justified, but the Pharisee did not.

Spend time with the Pharisee as a way of understanding the Pharisee in yourself. Spend much time with the tax collector, trying to understand the paradox he experienced in the temple, namely, that salvation came to him in the honest acknowledgment of his sins. Last, spend time with Jesus, who recognizes both the Pharisee and tax collector in you.

▲ Reflection

It is in God's nature to forgive our sins and bring healing to our spirits so that we can live as God's own sons and daughters. And because forgiveness and healing love can only be offered without coercion, we will experience this gift when we freely admit to sins and failings, and acknowledge our need for God. Many great sinners have been made into great saints by God's grace because they understood the paradox that in their brokenness are planted the seeds of God's holiness for them.

Exercise Twenty-Four
FEAR AND ANXIETY

▲ Scripture

God is love, and whoever remains in love remains in God and God in him. In this is love brought to perfection among us, that we have confidence on the day of judgment because as he is, so are we in this world. There is no fear in love, but perfect love drives out fear because fear has to do with punishment, and so one who fears is not yet perfect in love.

—1 John 4:16-18

▲ Summary

Love and joy, known as consolations, are the hallmarks of God's presence in our hearts. Fear and anxiety, on the other hand, stunt creativity, cripple the spirit, and draw us away from God and into ourselves. Where there is love, there is no fear. The presence of fear suggests the absence of God, unless one is willing to address it honestly.

▲ Session

(20-30 minute duration)

Take a few minutes to come home to yourself through the awareness of sounds, your breathing, or bodily sensations.

Ask help from the Holy Spirit to assist you in looking honestly at your fears, real and imagined. Then draw up lists of fears you have developed during the various stages of your life: childhood, adolescence, and adulthood. Also, make a separate list of fears that you have toward God. It is very possible that you will not be able to finish this exercise in one sitting.

After completing a list, choose some of the fears that are still bothering you, and bring them up in your prayer with Jesus. Try to make your dialogue with Jesus as honest and forthright as possible. Follow the same process for all your lists.

It might happen that for some of your fears you will need more than one session in prayer. Some of your fears may have grown lopsided, and it may take some time to cut them down to their realistic size, so that they become stepping stones toward greater trust and surrender to God. When faced head on, many of our fears will prove to be illusory.

▲ Reflection

Even if you had the body of a lion and a matching roar that went with it, you still wouldn't amount to much in the animal kingdom if you had the heart of a mouse. Similarly, an eagle would never be the king of birds if it convinced itself it was a chicken. We have been created in God's image and likeness. Our noble heritage is to live our lives in love and joy. However, many of us have convinced ourselves through our lists of many fears that we are made for an inferior destiny. When our fears are realistic, our ability to trust in God's providence remains intact. When they become exaggerated, they lessen our capacity to love, and increase our preoccupation with ourselves.

Exercise Twenty-Five
GUILT

▲ *Scripture*

Have mercy on me, God, in your goodness;
   in your abundant compassion blot out my offense.
Wash away all my guilt;
   from my sin cleanse me.
For I know my offense;
   my sin is always before me.
Against you alone have I sinned;
   I have done such evil in your sight.
            —Psalm 51:3-6

▲ *Summary*

We are all familiar with guilt. Guilt is like a weed that lies dormant and weak in a well tended lawn, but rears its ugly, nefarious head when neglect and drought are in season. Our guilt tells us that something has gone wrong in our moral universe, that some of our actions are not in accordance with the dictates of our conscience. Guilt is a strong and forceful demon which will only be exorcised by the power of honesty, humility, and courage.

▲ Session

(20-30 minute duration)

Take a few minutes to get in touch with yourself as a preparation for your meeting with God. You can do this by listening to the sounds around you, those in the distance and the ones near you.

Bring yourself into the presence of God in a place that is conducive for an intimate soul-washing visit with God. Imagine God looking at you with great tenderness and love, as a mother watches her newborn babe, or a father giving away his daughter on her wedding day.

After you have experienced God's benevolent gaze on you, call to mind your most shameful or guilt-ridden actions. It might help to make a list of these actions before you come to prayer. *Verbalize* them in God's presence. Share the feelings that accompany your narration, and ask God to make right what is wrong. Finally, ask God to let you know what you need to change in your life as a way of making amends.

▲ Reflection

Our guilt tells us that our compass needs fixing so that it can point us in the right direction. There are times when our guilt is exaggerated, being much greater than the wrong action warrants. This could be the result of our faulty perceptions, our unrealistic expectations of ourselves, and/or our unhealthy and self-defeating images of God. Whether our guilt is realistic or exaggerated, it is a force to reckon with and can be a useful tool on our spiritual journey.

Exercise Twenty-Six
RESENTMENTS

▲ *Scripture*

Jesus said to his disciples, "Occasions for stumbling are bound to come, but woe to anyone by whom they come! It would be better for you if a millstone were hung around your neck and you were thrown into the sea than for you to cause one of these little ones to stumble. Be on your guard! If another disciple sins, you must rebuke the offender, and if there is repentance, you must forgive. And if the same person sins against you seven times a day, and turns back to you seven times and says, 'I repent,' you must forgive."

—Luke 17:1-4

▲ *Summary*

We are relational beings. It is in our relationships with others that we know who we are and what motivates us. Those who experience the world as a friendly and inviting place will generally fare well in life. Those who view the world as hostile and inimical have a more difficult time establishing trust. This exercise seeks to address our hurts and distrust so that we can live in a conducive spiritual environment.

▲ *Session*

(20-30 minute duration)

Spend about five minutes coming home to yourself through the awareness of sounds, your breathing, or bodily sensations.

Our resentments are the single most destructive element in our relationships with others. They erect a barrier to freedom and intimacy with others, create a hovering cloud of pessimism around us and a slow internal paralysis of our creativity and joy. In this prayer we will attempt to look at our resentments honestly and transform them into stepping stones to healing and grace.

Imagine a scene in nature, real or imagined, that is conducive for a meeting with Jesus. Spend some time visiting with Jesus in this beautiful setting. Then bring into the scene, one by one, all those persons toward whom you bear resentments, beginning with your family of origin, and then moving on to others. In the presence of Jesus, tell each of them how you have been hurt by them. Listen to what each of them has to say to you. Extend your forgiveness to them if you are comfortable doing so at this time.

Next, bring into Jesus' presence all those persons whom you have hurt. Admit your insensitivity and failure to each of them in turn. Listen to what they have to say to you. It is quite possible that some among them might not be willing to forgive you yet.

Last, spend time with Jesus alone and tell him what this experience has meant to you. Listen attentively to the feedback he gives you about your interactions during the visit.

▲ Reflection

We function at our most creative when there is an abiding sense of peace and joy in our lives. As God's image and likeness, our nature is to love and be loved. Extending forgiveness to others and being forgiven is an essential part of being created in God's image and likeness. When we let go of our resentments, we receive the gift of peace.

Exercise Twenty-Seven
THE GOOD THIEF

▲ *Scripture*

He humbled himself,
becoming obedient to death, even death on a cross.
Because of this, God greatly exalted him
and bestowed on him the name
that is above every name,
that at the name of Jesus
every knee should bend,
of those in heaven and on earth and under the earth,
and every tongue confess that
Jesus Christ is Lord,
to the glory of God the Father.
—Philippians 2:8-11

▲ *Summary*

Two criminals were led along with Jesus to be crucified. When they came to Skull Place, they crucified him and the criminals, one on his right and the other on his left. One of the criminals hanging there reviled Jesus, saying, "Are you not the Messiah? Save yourself and us." The other, however, rebuking him, said in reply, "Have you no fear of God, for you are subject to the same condemnation? And indeed, we have been condemned justly, for the sentence we received corresponds to our crimes, but this man has done nothing criminal." Then he said, "Jesus, remember me when you come into your kingdom." He replied to him, "Amen, I say to you, today you will be with me in Paradise" (Lk 23:39-43).

▲ Session

(20-30 minute duration)

Spend about five minutes coming home to yourself through the awareness of sounds, your breathing, or bodily sensations.

With childlike faith implore the Holy Spirit to infuse your prayer with a deep understanding of your own sinfulness as well as the overwhelming power of God's love for you.

Re-create the scene of the Skull Place: Jesus hanging on the cross and the two criminals on either side of him. Crucifixion was given to the most hardened of criminals, so their crimes must have been grave. Jesus, however, is innocent and ironically the most despised of them all. Enter into conversation with the first criminal, who even in the throes of death is unrepentant and self-serving. He tries to manipulate Jesus into saving them all so that he can return to his old way of life. The other criminal has experienced a change of heart even within his desolation. He acknowledges his sins, accepts the consequences of his wrongdoing, and makes an act of faith in Jesus. Jesus responds favorably to him. Dialogue with this repentant criminal as you try to understand and savor the various steps in his conversion process. Finally, stay with Jesus and experience his power in the good thief's conversion, even as he is hanging on the cross. You can express the sentiments that arise in your heart during this visit to Skull Place.

▲ Reflection

Conversion of heart is God's gift that goes beyond our efforts. We have committed idolatry when we think that we are the creators of our own salvation, that repentance is a matter of white-knuckled willpower. The seeker who acknowledges sinfulness before God and humbly asks for God's salvation will receive it abundantly, as did the repentant criminal.

Exercise Twenty-Eight
ACKNOWLEDGING UNMANAGEABILITY

▲ Scripture

Out of the depths I call you, LORD;
  Lord, hear my cry!
May your ears be attentive
  to my cry for mercy.
If you, LORD, mark our sins,
  Lord, who can stand?
But with you is forgiveness
  and so you are revered.
  —Psalm 130:1-4

▲ Summary

Intimacy with God is not possible without a willingness to eschew deceit and lying from our conduct and lives. Serious seekers have a clear awareness that their sins and character defects can be addressed only by humbly acknowledging them, understanding and accepting their powerlessness before sin, and developing the conviction that God alone can restore them to their true nature as God's children. This prayer exercise seeks to help you get in touch with your powerlessness and unmanageability.

▲ Session

(20-30 minute duration)

Take a few minutes to come home to yourself through awareness of sounds, your breathing, or bodily sensations.

Situate yourself in a desert cave overlooking an arid plain and low lying hills in the distance. Jesus is seated next to you. It is twenty minutes before dawn and there is a stillness in the air that draws you to prayer and wholeness. This morning you have chosen to focus on the times when your life was unmanageable: you were embroiled in an addiction or attachment that brought you only illusory pleasure but shattered the transparency of your soul; you compromised your values and ideals and bore the onerous weight of desolation and alienation from yourself; you knew your prayer had become perfunctory and ritualistic and the pretense at holiness mocked you constantly; your spirit was embroiled in resentment and bitterness, and you chose to do battle rather than be at peace; you railed at the real and imagined weaknesses and faults of others, steadfastly pointing the finger at them and refusing to identify the same issues in your own life. . . . And as you continue with this search for your soul beyond the trappings of hypocrisy and deceit, you realize that there are more layers to unravel. Dawn is breaking as you finish your reflection and it is time for you to pour out your sentiments to Jesus in prayer. You acknowledge your need for him and humbly ask him to remove all your defects and shortcomings.

▲ Reflection

A humble confession of one's sins brings together humble honesty and the need for God on the seeker's part, and God's intense desire to save and love the sinner. Such a combination brings about the reign of God in the seeker's heart and life. The seeker becomes especially strong with God's grace in times of weakness and struggle. Such is the disposition of the poor in spirit.

Exercise Twenty-Nine
THE PRODIGAL SON

▲ *Scripture*

Fear not, you shall not be put to shame;
  you need not blush, for you shall not be disgraced.
The shame of your youth you shall forget,
  the reproach of your widowhood no longer
  remember.
For he who has become your husband is your Maker;
  his name is the LORD of hosts. . . .

  —Isaiah 54:4-5

▲ *Summary*

In the history of Christianity, there is perhaps no more powerful story about God's mercy and compassion than the parable of the prodigal son. It is a story that is both inspiring and challenging. Inspiring, because it reveals the Godlike nobility of the human heart when it works with God's grace. It is challenging because such unconditional acceptance and love of another is not possible until we have surrendered our wills and earnestly desire to live in God's will. In offering us this parable, Jesus is reminding us of our true identity and encouraging us to establish God's reign in our hearts as well as in the world.

▲ Session

(20-30 minute duration)

Take a few minutes to come home to yourself through the awareness of sounds, your breathing, or bodily sensations.

Read very slowly the parable of the prodigal son from the Gospel of Luke 15:11-32. Consider the following as you read it: The younger son committed the unpardonable sin of asking for his share of the inheritance while his father was alive and able-bodied. He had a change of diet rather than a change of heart when he decided to return to his father's home. His change of heart occurred in the experience of his father's joyous acceptance and unconditional love of him. The older son committed the unpardonable sin of questioning his father's decision in public.

After you have read the passage, spend time with each one of the characters. See in what way you can identify with each of them. Then talk with Jesus and try to find out what lesson and grace he has in store for you in this encounter with him.

▲ Reflection

This parable can act as a powerful means of entering into the heart of Jesus' teaching: Salvation comes only to the sinner who knows and accepts his or her sinfulness and is aware that only God can bring healing and salvation. Those who believe they are saved on their own merit are not able to hear and assimilate the good news. The challenge is to truly acknowledge our sinfulness and to stop pointing the finger at others and/or wallowing in self-pity and anger.

Exercise Thirty
THE CAPITAL SINS

Lo, the hand of the LORD is not too short to save,
nor his ear too dull to hear.
Rather, it is your crimes
that separate you from your God,
It is your sins that make him hide his face
so that he will not hear you.
—Isaiah 59:1-2

▲ *Summary*

Scrutinizing our evil ways as a means of understanding the ugliness and malice of sin has been a long-standing practice in Christian spirituality. The present-day adherents of this challenging tradition are the twelve-step programs and their members all over the world. They have realized that when they honestly acknowledge their defects before God and one another, God's power and compassion operate very tangibly in their lives. As a way of getting in touch with our own evil and acknowledging honestly our dark side, we will look at the seven capital sins as they operate in our lives.

▲ *Session*

(20-30 minute duration)

Take a few minutes to prepare yourself for your meeting with God by listening to the sounds around you. Then ask God for the gift of honest scrutiny of your life.

Imagine yourself in a comfortable setting with God alone. You are prepared to look honestly at the evil in you so that God's light might shine even more deeply in you.

Lust is substituting reality with falsehood; seeking ephemeral pleasure for lasting peace, substituting illusion for truth.

Anger (resentment) is the grudge you hold on to, pointing the finger at others rather than yourself, and insisting that you should have been dealt a different hand.

Greed is forgetting that you do indeed have enough. Greed is wanting to live on more than you actually need.

Pride is convincing yourself that you are bigger, greater, more powerful than you truly are. Pride was Lucifer's sin as he deluded himself that he was greater than God. Pride is attempting to build your home on somebody else's foundations.

Envy is wanting something that belongs to another; envy causes disquiet. Envy seeks happiness outside of oneself, and is a recipe for misery.

Gluttony is disrespect and misuse of creatures because one is seeking to fill a void and/or avoid pain. The antithesis to gluttony would seem to be contentment with who one is and what one has. Gluttony inevitably leads to alienation from self.

Sloth is living life as if God were not a force and presence in one's life. When sloth has come to stay, hopelessness and despair will soon follow.

▲ *Reflection*

The roots of our sin are deep. The nearer you come to God, the longer will the roots appear to be. The paradox is that greater exposure to the light will lead to their quicker demise. They never disappear altogether but keep diminishing in intensity if they remain exposed to God's mercy.

▲ The natural tendency of a person who has been deeply loved and accepted is to want to reciprocate with similar acts of kindness and compassion. The penitent woman displayed such courage and humility because she had received the grace of believing that Jesus would accept and forgive her completely, without any conditions.

▲ Many great sinners have been made into great saints by God's grace because they understood the paradox that in one's brokenness lie the seeds of God's holiness for them.

▲ When our fears are realistic, our ability to trust in God's providence remains intact. When our fears become exaggerated, they lessen our capacity to love and increase our preoccupation with ourselves.

▲ Our guilt tells us that something has gone wrong in our moral universe, that some of our actions are not in accordance with the dictates of our conscience. Guilt is a strong and forceful demon which will only be exorcised by the power of honesty, humility, and courage.

▲ We function at our most creative when there is an abiding sense of peace and joy in our lives. As God's image and likeness, our nature is to love and be loved. Extending forgiveness to others and being forgiven is an essential part of being created in God's image and likeness. When we let go of our resentments, we receive the gift of peace.

▲ The seeker who acknowledges sinfulness before God and humbly asks for God's salvation will receive it abundantly, as did the repentant criminal.

- A humble confession of one's sins brings together humble honesty and the need for God on the seeker's part, and God's intense desire to save and love the sinner. Such a combination brings about the reign of God in the seeker's heart and life.

- The roots of our sin are deep. The nearer you come to God, the longer will the roots appear to be. The paradox is that greater exposure to the light will lead to their quicker demise.

- Resentment is the grudge you hold on to, pointing the finger at others rather than yourself, and insisting that you should have been dealt a different hand.

- Gluttony is disrespect and misuse of creatures because one is seeking to fill a void and/or avoid pain. The antithesis to gluttony would seem to be contentment with who one is and what one has. Gluttony inevitably leads to alienation from self.

CHAPTER FOUR

*God's
Prayer
in Us*

The paradox of our human experience is that in order to get in touch with what is truly sublime in us we need to sink into our dregs. It is truly difficult to experience ourselves as God's image and likeness, as God's special predilection, if we have not been overwhelmed by our shadowy confusion and chaos. True salvation comes to the seeker who knows that his or her back is twisted out of shape and only the divine physician can straighten it out. With the confidence of a child who addresses his or her Father as "Abba," the seeker knows that all is and will be well because God never fails.

PRAYER OF THE BURDENED HEART

The prayer of the true seeker is the prayer of the *anawim*. The anawim were an oppressed and burdened lot of serfs and small landholders who were exploited by the rich and powerful landowners in the time of Jesus. They were never able to seek redress for their grievances because the legal profession was a corrupt group sympathetic to the landed gentry and priestly class. These oppressed people were described as the anawim, "people whose backs are bent double," because of the unjust burdens they had to carry. This image was then transferred to the religious consciousness of Israel to denote the right attitude and disposition a true seeker needed to possess in his or her relationship with God.

Like the anawim, true seekers realize they are powerless before their nefarious tendencies, and salvation is out of reach. They come before God in the clear realization that their backs are bent double with the weight of their sins and disorders. They know that trust and dependence on God will free them of their burdens. This is the case because trust in God is an honest acknowledgment of our evil and addictive tendencies as well as an assertion of confidence that God will always be faithful to us, no matter how difficult our situation might be.

Samuel's mother, Hannah, symbolizes eloquently the spirit of the anawim. In the first chapter of the first book of Samuel, we are told that Elkanah had two wives, Hannah and Peninnah. Peninnah had children, but Hannah was childless. Elkanah went regularly on pilgrimage with his family. When the day came for Elkanah to offer sacrifice, he would give a portion each to his wife Peninnah and to all her sons and daughters, but a double portion to Hannah because he loved her, though the Lord had made her barren. Peninnah turned her anger toward Hannah into a constant reproach that the Lord had left her barren. This went on year after year, each time they made their pilgrimage to the sanctuary of the Lord. After one such meal, Hannah presented herself to the Lord. Weeping copiously, she prayed in her bitterness: "O LORD of hosts, if you look with pity on the misery of your handmaid, if you remember me and do not forget me, if you give your handmaid a male child, I will give him to the LORD for as long as he lives; neither wine nor liquor shall he drink, and no razor shall ever touch his head" (1 Sm 1:11). Eli, the temple priest, rebuked Hannah because he thought she was drunk. But Hannah answered, "I am an unhappy woman. . . . I was only pouring out my troubles to the LORD. . . . My prayer has been prompted by my deep sorrow and misery" (1 Sm 1:15-16). We are told in the same chapter that Hannah bore a son whom she called Samuel, since she had asked the Lord for him. Once the child was weaned she took him to appear before the Lord and to remain there. The Lord favored Hannah so that she conceived and gave birth to three more sons and two daughters, while young Samuel grew up in the service of the Lord.

THE SAINT AND SINNER IN US

Jesus tells us the parable of the Pharisee and the tax collector in chapter eighteen of Luke's gospel. Jesus' intention was to address those who believed in their own self-righteousness while holding everyone else in contempt. In his prayer, the Pharisee kept his head unbowed. It was an act of self-glorification and a scathing criticism of the rest of men who were described as grasping, crooked, and adulterous. The Pharisee looked down with contempt on the tax collector praying in the same temple precincts. But the tax collector kept his head bowed to the ground. He dared not look up, as he knew full well that he was a sinner and unworthy in the sight of God. His prayer was heartfelt. He belongs to the anawim: "O God, be merciful to me, a sinner." Jesus tells us that the tax collector went home from the temple justified, but the Pharisee did not.

PELAGIANISM AND THE
TRUE PERSPECTIVE

As we explore the spirit of the anawim, we realize more clearly that there are two diametrically opposed aspects of our being that are in constant tension with each other. On the one hand, we are God's dwelling place, the temple of the Holy Spirit. We are indeed the apple of God's eye. We are also sinful and devious and capable of the most heinous crimes. It is important for the seeker never to lose sight of these two extremes and always to keep them in proper equilibrium. Many a discipleship has foundered because it has emphasized one extreme over the other.

Pelagius, an English monk of the fifth century, misunderstood that the central truth of discipleship is that our holiness and likeness to God is experienced *only* when we acknowledge our sinfulness and powerlessness and allow God to take over our affairs. Jesus can save only when the seeker humbly and honestly admits the need for salvation. We are all too aware in our own personal experience how often we like to appear better than we are and how easily we minimize our responsibility for failures and wrong doings—we are all Pelagian at times. Being Christian means waging an unceasing battle against the illusion that we are on a par with God, that being like God is the same as being God.

SELF INTEGRATION AND THE
TRUE PERSPECTIVE

There are other seekers who profess faith in Jesus as their Savior, yet their personal horizons are darkened by doubt, fear, resentment, and pessimism. They seem unable or unwilling to get beyond their own narrow and stifling confines to embrace a hope-filled discipleship of nourishing dependence on God. Some seekers are willing to pay the cost of discipleship and will undergo therapy or whatever else it takes to bring about a meaningful integration of their human history and God's plan for them. For some it might take a long time before their faith in God begins to glow with a quiet vibrancy. Then there are other seekers who are not willing to take the risk to find out if God can indeed bring healing and salvation to them. As stated earlier, our likeness to God is experienced only when we acknowledge our powerlessness and allow God's light to dispel the paralyzing darkness. True prayer becomes possible when we keep the right perspective on ourselves, holding our opposite extremes in equilibrium, and emphasizing God's loving us over our love for God, God's unfailing faithfulness over our fickle constancy and wavering commitment.

GOD'S UNFAILING LOVE AS OUR PRAYER CONTEXT

It would be interesting to hear what Jesus has to tell us about prayer, or more clearly, how we are to go about the business of relating to God. When one of his disciples asked Jesus to teach them how to pray, he taught them the "Our Father." The image of God as Abba expresses a context of great intimacy, love, and freedom that Jesus wants us to enter into when we dialogue with God. On different occasions and in very creative ways, Jesus tried to show us how very important it was to have the correct perspective when we connect with God.

In his own interactions, Jesus established for different individuals what God as Abba really meant. There is the touching story of Jesus washing the feet of his disciples at the Last Supper. The custom of having the feet of dinner guests washed was a sacred tradition in Jewish hospitality. However, the actual job of washing the feet was given only to non-Jewish slaves because it was considered so demeaning. Peter is shocked when Jesus begins to wash his disciples' feet and dry them with the towel he had around him. Peter's response was, "You shall never wash my feet" (Jn 13:8). Through his actions, Jesus was giving his disciples a very powerful message. He was telling them that they were so important that he was willing to go to any lengths to love and serve them, even to the extent of becoming a slave. It is no wonder then that Paul, in his letter to the Philippians says that though Jesus was in the form of God, he did not deem equality with God something to be grasped. Rather, he emptied himself and took the role of a slave. He humbled himself, obediently accepting even death, death on a cross! (Phil 2:6-8).

CONDITIONS FOR PRAYER RESULTING FROM GOD'S UNFAILING LOVE

Faith

When a seeker has experienced the magnanimity and selflessness of God's love in Jesus as many in the New Testament did, then there is an instant strengthening of faith in God, the sense that one is totally safe in God's arms, no matter what the situation might be. It is in this environment of trust and intimacy with God that Jesus asks us to have faith when we pray. On different occasions Jesus required the recipient of a miracle to have faith before he could do anything. In Luke, chapter seven, there is the moving story of the centurion who loved his servant who was sick to the point of death. He sent some Jewish elders to Jesus to seek a cure for him. When Jesus was only a short distance from his house, the centurion sent friends to tell him: "Lord, do not trouble yourself, for I am not worthy to have you enter under my roof. Therefore, I did not consider myself worthy to come to you; but say the word and let my servant be healed" (Lk 7:6-7).

Jesus showed amazement on hearing this, and turned to the crowd which was following him to say, "I tell you, not even in Israel have I found such faith" (Lk 7:9). When the group returned to the house, they found the servant in perfect health. The centurion was capable of such enormous faith in Jesus' power to heal because he was a generous man who loved greatly.

There is a simple reason why Jesus requires faith of the disciple: Faith is not faith if it does not lead to conversion of heart, where the seeker puts on the mind and heart of God. Every encounter with God is an invitation to leave behind the sins of the past and enter into the peace and joy of God's saving grace. Through the "Our Father," which is a prayer of petition, or intercession, Jesus impresses upon us the importance of bringing all our needs for salvation to his heavenly Father and they will be fulfilled. Some seekers are concerned that they might be indulging in selfishness when they pray for themselves. This concern is ill-founded in light of the fact that true faith leads to conversion, and asking God for help highlights the most important reality of our lives: that we are pure gift and totally dependent on God. Acknowledging our dependence on God through the prayer of petition is a profound act of adoration as well as thanksgiving.

Perseverance

Along with faith, Jesus asks us to persevere in our petition or intercession. Jesus exhorts us to, "Ask and it will be given to you; seek and you will find; knock and the door will be opened to you. For everyone who asks, receives; and the one who seeks, finds; and to the one who knocks, the door will be opened" (Mt 7:7-8). The literal translation from the Greek gives this passage a vitality and intensity that is amazing and baffling at the same time. Jesus is urging us to keep on asking, seeking, and knocking until we receive what we are looking for. Jesus seems to be contradicting himself by describing his heavenly Father as being only too eager to give us good things, and then asking us to insist and persevere till we receive what we want. As stated earlier, true faith leads to a change of heart. Oftentimes in our encounters with God we pay only lip service to God's prompting; we do not really mean what we say. A lack of perseverance could be an indication that a seeker does not want his or her prayer of petition to lead to repentance. Insisting on perseverance is God's way of telling us to clean up our act, to stop vacillating and make an unconditional commitment. No sooner do we pray with transparent hearts than God answers our prayers. If faith in God is supposed to lead to transformation of the disciple's heart, then perseverance in prayer is the disciple's way of confronting his or her fears and denials in the face of honest encounter with God.

Forgiveness

Along with perseverance, Jesus emphasizes forgiveness as an important condition for prayer. In the prayer Jesus taught us, we ask God to forgive us our trespasses as we forgive those who trespass against us. No matter how profound and limitless God's loving kindness might be toward us, we can receive mercy only in the measure we extend it to others. Our attitudes and behaviors toward others and ourselves need to be imbued with God's compassion and love, or else our prayer becomes hypocritical. In Mark 11:25 Jesus says: "When you stand to pray, forgive anyone against whom you have a grievance, so that your heavenly Father may in turn forgive you your transgressions." God is Love, and as noted earlier, we are the temples of God, and thus share in God's loving nature. Those who seriously seek God are open to the process of eradicating bitterness, anger, resentment, and hatred from their lives.

According to God's Will

In the last discourse found in John (chapters 14 through 17), Jesus makes it clear that he is the way, the truth, and the life, and that no one comes to the Father except through him. Further, Jesus states categorically: "If you remain in me and my words remain in you, ask for whatever you want and it will be done for you. By this is my Father glorified, that you bear much fruit and become my disciples" (Jn 15:7-8). These verses make it clear that the prayer of petition, whether it be for oneself or for others, will not be of a self-serving nature if the disciple is living according to God's will. Such a person's prayer is inspired by the Holy Spirit and such petitions will further advance God's reign in human hearts. When a seeker is striving to live in God's will, then a "no" from God is as good an answer as a "yes," because what is most important is that God's will be done, over and above the petition being answered or fulfilled.

The Power of Petition

There is a beautiful story from the Indian religious tradition which illustrates the power of the prayer of petition. There was a young couple who were childless. They petitioned earnestly with God to grant them children, and they kept getting a "No" for an answer. They even went on pilgrimage and offered alms to the poor as a way of convincing God of their plight and yearning. But nothing changed for them. One day a holy man was passing through their village on his way to a sacred place. He received hospitality from the couple. During the evening meal he inquired whether they had any children. With a downcast look the woman replied that they didn't have any, and proceeded to let the pilgrim know of their plight. He listened to them without comment. The following day he bade them farewell and proceeded on his journey. When he arrived at the holy place he entered into prayer. During his dialogue he insisted that God should grant the couple's wish to have children. God gave the pilgrim the same reply he gave the couple: "It is not in their destiny to have children." The holy man was unfazed. It was clear to him that he would persevere in his prayer until God had a change of mind. Five years later, the holy man went on the same pilgrimage. Once again he received hospitality from the young couple. This time as he entered their doorway he saw three kids playing on the dirt floor. He expressed his pleasure at the sight. The mother was all aglow and replied that their three children were the result of a holy man's prayers. Apparently, the couple had not recognized the pilgrim. The following day the pilgrim entered into prayer at the holy place. He thanked God for granting him this pilgrimage once again. In particular he thanked God for the special gift to the couple. Then with some bemusement he asked God why there was a change of mind. God answered: "It was not in their destiny to have children, but saints can change the destiny of humans."

The prayer of petition or intercession is quintessentially the prayer of one who is totally dependent on God for everything. Petition acknowledges this dependence and seeks its fulfillment in every aspect of life. Asking for ourselves so that we can do God's will with wholehearted devotion can only be called authentic and genuine. Every other form of prayer, whether it be thanksgiving, contemplation, or praise, hinges on the essence of the prayer of petition: the acknowledgment of our total dependence on our Creator and Savior.

CONCLUSION

The essence of our being is that we are dependent on God for everything. When we live our lives in this basic attitude of trust and dependence on God, we bear much fruit. Petition and intercession are the foundation of prayer because they express clearly this need for God. Other forms of prayer, like adoration, contrition, and thanksgiving, express the same reality of our dependence on God. Any time our prayer, whatever its form may be, captures the basic attitude of total dependence on God, it will bear much fruit and help bring about the establishment of God's reign in our hearts.

CHAPTER FOUR HIGHLIGHTS

▲ The paradox of our human experience is that in order to get in touch with what is truly sublime in us, we need to sink into our dregs. True salvation comes to the seeker who knows that his or her back is twisted out of shape and only the divine physician can straighten it out.

▲ The prayer of true seekers is the prayer of the surrendered heart. They know that trust and dependence on God will free them of their burdens.

▲ Being Christian means waging an unceasing battle against the illusion that we are God, that being like God is the same as being God.

▲ Faith is not faith if it does not lead to conversion of heart, where the seeker puts on the mind and heart of God. Every encounter with God is an invitation to leave behind the sins of the past and enter into the peace and joy of God's saving grace.

▲ No sooner do we pray with transparent hearts than God answers our prayers. If faith in God is supposed to lead to transformation of the disciple's heart, then perseverance in prayer is the disciple's way of confronting his or her fears and denial in the face of honest encounter with God.

▲ No matter how profound and limitless God's loving kindness might be toward us, we can receive mercy only in the measure we extend it to others.

▲ The prayer of petition or intercession is quintessentially the prayer of one who is totally dependent on God for everything. Petition acknowledges this dependence and seeks its fulfillment in every aspect of life.

▲ Other forms of prayer, like adoration, contrition, and thanksgiving, express the same reality of our dependence on God. Any time our prayer, whatever its form may be, captures the basic attitude of total dependence on God, it will bear much fruit and help bring about the establishment of God's reign in our hearts.

Exercise Thirty-One
BABYSITTING THE INFANT JESUS

▲ *Scripture*

Set me as a seal on your heart,
   as a seal on your arm;
For stern as death is love,
   relentless as the nether world is devotion;
   its flames are a blazing fire.
Deep waters cannot quench love,
   nor floods sweep it away.

—Song of Songs 8:6-7

▲ *Summary*

The heart is often moved by the simplest and most mundane activities when we have realized that all of life expresses God's presence, sometimes in gentle impulses, sometimes in visible throbs. There is always love and meaning present in everyday circumstances if one knows how to look. True prayer teaches one how to look and find God with spiritual eyes. Prayer often becomes profound when it is very simple and childlike.

▲ *Session*

(20-30 minute duration)

Spend about five minutes coming home to yourself through the awareness of sounds, your breathing, or bodily sensations.

St. Anthony of Padua was a learned man who was proclaimed a Doctor of the Church. He was born in Lisbon, Portugal, at the end of the twelfth century. One of his favorite ways of praying was to imagine himself before Mary, Joseph, and Jesus in the manger and ask if he could carry Jesus in his arms. He would see himself receiving permission to do so, and very tenderly and lovingly would hold Jesus in his arms and contemplate God's presence in this powerless little babe.

Make St. Anthony's prayer your own and imagine yourself carrying the infant Jesus in your own arms. While you do so, let the sentiments of your heart gush out in joyous exuberance or trickle forth in silent awe.

▲ Reflections

Love and joy expand when the heart is moved, and God becomes a more conscious presence in our lives. However difficult the circumstances of our lives might be, there is still the opportunity available for our hearts to be moved. It makes it easier and more possible to have God's perspective on life's vagaries when one drinks constantly from a perennial source of goodness and awe, such as the mystery of the infant Jesus being the Son of God. Faith transforms mystery into silent surrender.

Exercise Thirty-Two
JESUS, MY WILLING SERVANT

▲ Scripture

Yet it was our infirmities that he bore,
  our sufferings that he endured,
While we thought of him as stricken,
  as one smitten by God and afflicted.

—Isaiah 53:4

▲ Summary

God's transcendence conjures up visions of awesome splendor and remoteness, creating unease and fear in some of us. The Incarnation softens this picture because now God wears a human face, has a human form, and is in every way like us, save sin. Emmanuel, God dwelling among us, is God's way of entering into our lives while offering us the opportunity to participate in God's. This prayer exercise sets up our relationship with God through Jesus on a firm foundation of intimacy and bondedness.

▲ Session

(20-30 minute duration)

Spend about five minutes coming home to yourself through the awareness of sounds, your breathing, or bodily sensations.

The following prayer was composed by St. Teresa of Avila, and she recommended it highly to her sisters. Her suggestion was that, after you have come into God's presence, you imagine Jesus looking at you very lovingly and humbly. It may be helpful to carry on a conversation with Jesus as he looks at you in this very special way. Or you may be more comfortable allowing Jesus to look at you lovingly and humbly and absorbing his special attention in silence. Please choose what seems more conducive to you.

▲ Reflection

St. Teresa got to the essence of prayer in her understanding that God is reached through the heart. Conversion can occur when the heart is moved. This prayer highlights the basic attitudes of Jesus toward us. We are very special to Jesus, so that all he wants to do is love us passionately and totally, even to the point of becoming a servant for us. In New Testament times the feet of guests at a banquet were washed only by Gentile slaves because the task was considered too demeaning for a Jewish slave. Jesus chose to wash his disciples' feet to demonstrate the extent he was willing to go in his love for us. This prayer exercise is difficult for some people, especially those who suffer from low self-esteem, pervasive guilt, or shame. Hopefully, it will give you the experience and realization that Jesus loves you because he is good. You don't have to be good to be loved by God. The paradox is that we will refrain from doing evil when we feel deeply loved.

Exercise Thirty-Three
BENEDICT'S PRAYER

▲ Scripture

The shepherds said to one another, "Let us go now to Bethlehem and see this thing that has taken place, which the Lord has made known to us." So they went with haste and found Mary and Joseph, and the child lying in the manger. When they saw this, they made known what had been told them about this child; and all who heard it were amazed at what the shepherds told them. But Mary treasured all these words and pondered them in her heart.

—Luke 2:15-19

▲ Summary

The Benedictine method of prayer, also called *Lectio Divina*, has a central place in Catholic spirituality. It is a method of prayer that is very simple to use. Anybody can understand and use it without any difficulty. At the same time, it can stir the depths of one's soul in prayer because it is essentially the prayer of the heart.

▲ Session

(20-30 minute duration)

Take a few minutes to become still by listening to the sounds around you. After you have become quiet, ask the Holy Spirit to help you with your prayer.

The Benedictine method of prayer has four simple steps to it: *lectio*, or reading; *repetitio*, or repetition; *oratio*, or prayer; and *contemplatio*, or contemplation. Begin by taking a passage from scripture and reading it very slowly. It helps to choose the passage or passages before you come to prayer. When you approach a phrase that appeals to you, repeat the phrase over and over until its meaning begins to sink into your spirit, generating different movements or sentiments within you. Repeating means repeating, *not* reflecting, though some reflection will take place in the act of repetition. The third step is prayer, or raising to God the sentiments created in your heart. In time you will learn your best way of praying with the contents of your heart. The fourth step, contemplation, is taken only when it happens to you. It happens when your prayer moves from words and conversation to silent communion with God. It is as if a new way of connecting with God has opened up within you. When the fourth step happens, you will know it. Meanwhile, don't worry about it.

Follow the same procedure for the rest of the scripture passage. Any non-scriptural passage or vocal prayer that is special to you could serve as subject matter for this method of prayer. It is important to go through the steps slowly and deliberately, focusing your attention on the task at hand. It is beneficial that you try to go through the whole passage during your time of prayer, unless it is very long, or you are being moved deeply and strongly. When God brings you to contemplation, the steps will have served their purpose until you are ready to return to them.

▲ Reflection

The Benedictine method of prayer has been used by countless holy men and women through the centuries. It has the uncanny knack of unlocking the precious treasures of God's heart and bringing us to the cusp of contemplation. It unlocks the treasures of our own hearts as well, bringing about a deeper integration between our hearts and minds.

Exercise Thirty-Four
THE ECHO

▲ *Scripture*

Do not store up for yourselves treasure on earth, where moth and decay destroy, and thieves break in and steal. But store up treasures in heaven, where neither moth nor decay destroy, nor thieves break in and steal. For where your treasure is, there also will your heart be.
—Matthew 6:19-21

▲ *Summary*

An echo in a canyon is more impressive and resonant than a sound against a low lying ridge. The greater hollow creates a more inviting space for lingering reverberation. The echo is a very real way of communicating with the vast chasm in front of us, of touching and embracing it through the sound waves created by our voice. The enduring echo is a good image of God's pervasive action in our lives. In a very real way, and with the help of our imagination, we can visualize God's voice reverberating in the depths of our being, touching us and sanctifying us with the divine presence.

▲ *Session*

(20-30 minute duration)

Take a few minutes to prepare yourself for this holy meeting through the awareness of your bodily sensations.

Begin your prayer by asking God to remove fear, doubt, anxiety, and guilt from your heart, thus creating a bigger and more inviting space for a bigger and better sound. Next, imagine yourself as a vast, empty canyon, and invite God to fill and sanctify it with the divine presence. You can sing in a slow, resonant voice the following phrases, creating your own music, and imagining them entering every tiny space in your being and birthing God's love and presence in you. It is helpful to make appropriate pauses after every recitation, to allow the echo-prayer to envelop you in its warm embrace. The prayer is:

Kyrie eleison, Christe eleison (Lord have mercy, Christ have mercy).

My God and my All.

The Lord is my Salvation.

Behold the Lamb of God who takes away the sin of the world.

The Lord is my Shepherd, there is nothing I shall want.

Jesus, Son of David, have mercy on me, a sinner.

As you proceed in your prayer, you might want to create your own phrases. End your prayer with a "Glory Be."

▲ Reflection

Mahatma Gandhi believed that there was more power in the name of God than in the atom bomb. When he recited the holy name of God he believed with all his heart that God's power would be unleashed in his life and actions. Echoing God's names in ourselves is a way of recognizing and appreciating the power of God's image in us.

Exercise Thirty-Five
SANCTIFYING THE UNCONSCIOUS

▲ *Scripture*

Bartimaeus, a blind man, the son of Timaeus, sat by the roadside begging. On hearing that it was Jesus of Nazareth, he began to cry out and say, "Jesus, son of David, have pity on me." And many rebuked him, telling him to be silent. But he kept calling out all the more, "Son of David, have pity on me." Jesus stopped and said, "Call him." So they called the blind man, saying to him, "Take courage; get up, he is calling you." He threw aside his cloak, sprang up, and came to Jesus. Jesus said to him in reply, "What do you want me to do for you?" The blind man replied to him, "Master, I want to see." Jesus told him, "Go your way; your faith has saved you." Immediately he received his sight and followed him on the way.

—Mark 10:46-52

▲ *Summary*

Call it by whatever name, but there is a dark, sinister side to us. Admitting our powerlessness over our evil ways can set the stage for a genuine dependence on God's power and salvation in our lives. Our character defects are not erased with one great stroke. They are deeply ingrained habits of disordered behavior which can be tempered and brought within control only through the practice and development of good habits. One such habit is the practice of the presence of God through the recitation of a prayer formula.

▲ Session

(20-30 minute duration)

Spend about five minutes coming home to yourself through the awareness of sounds, your breathing, or bodily sensations.

Imagine yourself in a very dark, cold, and dingy room. The darkness is all enveloping—a total lack of light and warmth. This image is a fairly accurate picture of your sinister side. You are now going to invite God's light into this benighted place by reciting the prayer formula, "Lord Jesus, have mercy on me, a sinner," paying loving attention to the words and the presence of Jesus in your darkened heart. Every time you recite the prayer, it is as if you are lighting a tiny candle to illumine the darkness. Gradually, the darkness fades as the light brightens and spreads in every direction. Make sure you keep appropriate pauses in your recitation, depending on how your heart is moved, as a way of tasting and relishing the profound truth of God's mystery contained in the words of the prayer formula.

▲ Reflection

The darkness in us is a fact of our lives. Equally true is the fact that we can decide whether we will live in this darkness or allow the light of God's love and presence to enter in. This prayer exercise, known as the Jesus Prayer, emphasizes the need to always live in the light of God's presence as a way of neutralizing the darkness in us. Salvation can come only from God. But even God needs our humble and honest cooperation.

Exercise Thirty-Six
THE DISCIPLE'S PRAYER

▲ *Scripture*

"And I tell you, ask and you will receive; seek and you will find; knock and the door will be opened to you. For everyone who asks, receives; and the one who seeks, finds; and to the one who knocks, the door will be opened.

—Luke 11:9-10

▲ *Summary*

True discipleship is born in the understanding that one is powerless in the face of character defects, addictions, and sin. Salvation and healing can come only from the genuine realization that God's power and presence in one's life is the key. The disciple's prayer is an appreciation of God's constant presence, and a childlike trust that God will be there in every peaceful and painful moment.

▲ *Session*

(20-30 minute duration)

Do an awareness exercise in preparation for prayer. After you have a sense that you are quiet and settled, ask God to give you a forgiving and trusting heart so that you can make known your petitions with childlike simplicity.

Think of those persons you wish to pray for, and in your mind gather them into a circle. Jesus is present in your midst. Try to create an ambiance that is conducive to intimacy and community. Take each one of these individuals that you wish to pray for and first thank God for all the graces and blessings they have received and given to others in their lives. Then intercede with Jesus on their behalf. As you do so, imagine all the others extending their hands toward the individual being prayed for and interceding with you. Jesus listens attentively to your prayer. Keep doing this for everyone present. Then imagine the whole group thanking God and interceding for you in the same way. Finally, it is Jesus' turn to respond, and he speaks directly to your hearts about the sentiments aroused in him while you and the group offered thanksgiving and petition.

▲ Reflection

When disciples gather to pray, Jesus is present in their midst and the Holy Spirit prays on their behalf. Such prayer is childlike in its trust that God will move mountains. Such total confidence in the power and love of God creates in the disciple an equally strong desire to do everything to cooperate with God's will. No wonder, then, such prayer is heard.

Exercise Thirty-Seven
THE PEDAGOGUE

▲ Scripture

And it happened that, while he was with them at table, he took bread, said the blessing, broke it, and gave it to them. With that their eyes were opened and they recognized him, but he vanished from their sight. Then they said to each other, "Were not our hearts burning within us while he spoke to us on the way and opened the scriptures to us?"

—Luke 24:30-32

▲ Summary

In ancient Greece the *paidagogos* was a family servant who from a child's early years acted as his mentor. The *paidagogos* helped the child learn through the companionship itself. Clement of Alexandria described Christian life in terms of the Word acting as our Pedagogue, or Mentor. A continuing dialogue takes place between Christ and the Christian person in varying circumstances and stages of development.

▲ Session

(20-30 minute duration)

Spend about five minutes coming home to yourself by doing any one of the first three exercises or a combination thereof.

This prayer is a companion prayer, and so it extends to the whole day, embracing every situation, opportunity, and moment. Jesus, the companion-guide, is wayfaring with us constantly. He is more enduring than our own shadow, and more present than our very breath. Here are some hints to help you develop a loving and permeating relationship with Jesus as a way of putting on his mind and heart:

♦ Situate Jesus in your heart, and during the day be aware of his loving presence by reciting a prayer formula over and over. Let the prayer formula be short so that it is easy to create a rhythm with it. You can recite it to the accompaniment of your breathing if you are seated, or your walking when you are up and about.

♦ When driving or walking, some people find it preferable to have Jesus in the passenger seat or alongside them. Some are more comfortable carrying on a non-stop dialogue with Jesus throughout the day, about themselves, their work, relationships, family, life, and Jesus himself. And gradually, they learn to listen to him as well.

♦ Whatever the nature of your companion-prayer, you might find it beneficial to infuse a generous dose of thanksgiving and intercession into it.

▲ Reflection

In its etymology a companion is someone with whom you share bread. In Jesus' time, sharing a meal was an honor because the guest was being invited to partake of the life of the host, symbolized by the meal. Through the companion-prayer, the disciple gradually begins to share in the very life of Christ. It is no coincidence that Jesus is called the Bread of Life. The disciple's life becomes eucharist.

Exercise Thirty-Eight

THE ODE TO JOY

▲ Scripture

> You visit the earth and water it,
>   make it abundantly fertile.
> God's stream is filled with water;
>   with it you supply the world with grain.
> Thus do you prepare the earth:
>   you drench plowed furrows,
>   and level their ridges.
> With showers you keep the ground soft,
>   blessing its young sprouts.
> You adorn the year with your bounty;
>   your paths drip with fruitful rain.
> The untilled meadows also drip;
>   the hills are robed with joy.
> The pastures are clothed with flocks,
>   the valleys blanketed with grain;
>   they cheer and sing for joy.
>   —Psalm 65:10-14

▲ Summary

If there is one characteristic to describe a vital spiritual life, it is joy. Joy is the exhilaration one experiences at the energy of spring, when the song and laughter of the birds commences before the break of dawn and ends temporarily when darkness curtains off the day. Joy is amazement at the exuberance of nature, as every bush and tree bursts forth with new growth. Joy is the stillness of our beings, in whose presence others are able to see a clearer image of themselves. Joy is the assurance that God lives in us and our life is a miracle.

▲ Session

(20-30 minute duration)

Take a few minutes to come home to yourself through awareness of sounds, your breathing, or bodily sensations.

As a way of exercising yourself in the art and practice of being joyous, retire into a special place in nature, real or imagined, and compress into this one sitting an entire cycle of the seasons, beginning with your favorite one, and going through all four. Be attentive to the rise and fall of the sounds of birds and bees, insects, animals, and the wind. Observe the splash of colors in the sky, the shades of greens and browns, yellows, reds, and oranges in the vegetation, and the rich tones of the earth. Listen to the silence hanging breathless on a cold winter's night, and the blaze of stars in a jet black yonder. Feel the cool wind caress your face as you sit in the summer shade of a maple tree. Recall the changes over the years in the bushes and trees you planted in your garden. Become aware of God sitting by your side and taking in the beauty and grandeur along with you. Enter into silent communion with the Creator as words fail you to describe what is essentially indescribable.

▲ Reflection

St. Ignatius of Loyola would go into rapture during many of his nightly visitations with the starry heavens. The grandeur awed him into awareness of the stupendous majesty and splendor of the Divine Presence. It was a sacred ritual that brought much profit to his soul. St. Francis of Assisi had the same reverence and passion for nature, calling the animals and birds and plants his brothers and sisters. Creation is indeed the Face of God, on whose surface the divine compassion and providence are etched for all to see and experience.

Exercise Thirty-Nine
THE LADDER PRAYER

▲ *Scripture*

"But when you pray, go to your inner room, close
the door, and pray to your Father in secret. And
your Father who sees in secret will repay you. In
praying, do not babble like the pagans, who think
that they will be heard because of their many
words. Do not be like them."
—Matthew 6:6-8

▲ *Summary*

Saint John Climacus was a desert father who wrote *The
Ladder of Divine Ascent.* To him is attributed a very simple
method of prayer which could act as a ladder leading the
disciple into the heart of God. The name "Climacus"
suggests "the ladder" in Latin. This simple prayer form
emphasizes the encounter with God happening in the heart
of the disciple. When the heart is moved, change occurs. In
order for the heart to be moved, the truth of God's mystery
contained in the words of a prayer needs to be plumbed.
John Climacus' method is the kind of prayer that can help
you plumb the depths of God's truth.

▲ Session

(20-30 minute duration)

Do some awareness exercise in preparation for prayer. Then ask God to give you a childlike disposition of trust and candor as you raise your heart to God through the ladder prayer.

John Climacus left very simple directions for this prayer. Take the prayers that you are accustomed to saying on a regular basis and try to recite them with *perfect attention* to the words and the presence of God. If at any point in the recitation of the prayer you are distracted, go back to the point of distraction and continue again to try to recite the prayer with perfect attention. There will be times when you will not be able to remember where and when you got distracted. In that case it is best to continue trying to pray the rest of the prayer with perfect attention. In the course of twenty to thirty minutes you will be able to recite several of your favorite prayers. At times you might want to read your prayers with perfect attention from a prayer manual.

▲ Reflection

A good time to engage in this form of prayer is when your disposition toward God is one of receptivity. There is both a willingness and an ability to listen to God. The mind has slowed down. There is less need to talk and use many words, and a greater affinity for listening to God. There will be other times in your life when you are harried and pulled forth in various directions all at once. This prayer is a good way of becoming centered and pointed in one direction—toward God.

Exercise Forty
TRUSTING GOD

> Where can I hide from your spirit?
>> From your presence, where can I flee?
> If I ascend to the heavens, you are there;
>> if I lie down in Sheol, you are there too.
> If I fly with the wings of dawn
>> and alight beyond the sea,
> Even there your hand will guide me,
>> your right hand hold me fast.
>> —Psalm 139:7-10

▲ *Summary*

In the presence of fear and anger, trust has about the same chances of survival as a grain of wheat in parched soil. In the face of the belief that God is infinite and perfect, it defies good logic to recognize that we could still have smoldering resentments toward our Creator, but we do. This exercise recognizes the ambiguous and contradictory sentiments we often have toward God. Acknowledging their presence in us will oftentimes be the start of a deeper trust and intimacy with God.

▲ *Session*

(20-30 minute duration)

Take up a comfortable sitting posture with your back erect and your chin tilted forward slightly. Spend about five minutes coming home to yourself through the awareness of sounds, your breathing, or bodily sensations.

In order to truly come into the divine presence, you must be willing to allow God to know your innermost sentiments in the relationship. Begin with the negative emotions, which need to be cleared up before the positive emotions can flow. Go over the various stages of your life, beginning with your birth, and recall the anger and resentment you have harbored toward God regarding the various circumstances of your life. Then get in touch with the different fears you developed over the years toward God, like the fear of retribution in this life, fear of eternal damnation in the next, and so on. You might also want to share any lingering doubts you may have about God's love for you.

After you are satisfied that you've addressed the negative emotions, you can focus on your positive sentiments. You might want to focus on the different ways God has loved and blessed you over the years, directly and through others.

End the exercise pondering some of God's expressions of love for you:

♦ For God so loved the world that he gave his only Son, so that everyone who believes in him might not perish but might have eternal life. For God did not send his Son into the world to condemn the world, but that the world might be saved through him (Jn 3:16-17).

♦ In this is love: not that we have loved God, but that he loved us and sent his Son as expiation for our sins (1 Jn 4:10).

▲ Reflection

When talking about God we are really talking about our *images* of God, which reflect the truth of God's mystery in some way, but also detract from the true nature of God. It is important that we work through the dross in our images so that we can know the true God more intimately. This prayer exercise is a step in that direction.

- There is always love and meaning present in the every-day circumstances of life if we know how to look. True prayer teaches one how to look and find God. Prayer often becomes profound when it is simple and childlike.

- It is easier to have God's perspective on life's vagaries when one drinks constantly from a perennial source of goodness and awe, such as the mystery of the infant Jesus being the Son of God. Faith transforms mystery into silent surrender.

- Emmanuel, God dwelling among us, is God's way of entering into our lives while offering us the opportunity to participate in God's.

- The Benedictine method of prayer has been used by countless holy men and women through the centuries. It has the uncanny knack of unlocking the precious treasures of God's heart and bringing us to the cusp of contemplation. It unlocks the treasures of our own hearts as well, bringing about a deeper integration between our hearts and minds.

- Mahatma Gandhi believed that there was more power in the name of God than in the atom bomb. When he recited the holy name of God he believed with all his heart that God's power would be unleashed in his life and actions. Echoing God's names in ourselves is a way of recognizing and appreciating the power of God's image in us.

- The darkness in us never disappears. It is a fact of our lives. Equally true is the fact that we can decide whether we live in this darkness or allow the light of God's love and presence to enter in. The Jesus Prayer tradition emphasizes the need to always live in the light of God's presence and love as a way of neutralizing the darkness in us.

▲ True discipleship is born in the understanding that one is powerless in the face of character defects, addictions, and sin. The disciple's prayer is an appreciation of God's constant presence, and a childlike trust that God will be there in every peaceful and painful moment.

▲ If there is one characteristic to describe a vital spiritual life, it is joy. Joy is the stillness of our beings in whose presence others are able to see a clearer image of themselves. Joy is the certainty that God lives in us and our life is a miracle.

▲ When talking about God we are really talking about our images of God, which reflect the truth of God's mystery in some way, but also detract from the true nature of God. It is important that we work through the dross in our images so that we can know the true God more intimately.

CHAPTER FIVE

In the
Master's Footsteps

CALLED BY NAME

The distinguishing mark of Christian discipleship is that the seeker is called by Jesus Christ to be a disciple, or follower. This call presupposes a personal relationship with Jesus, so that the person desires to walk in the Master's footsteps and continue with the mission of establishing God's reign in human hearts. A two-fold dynamic is at work in this interactive process. There is a clear sense on the seeker's part that Jesus is invested in the disciple's life; Jesus loves him or her passionately, and invites this person to a covenant relationship in which fidelity and intimacy will always be a cherished standard, at least on God's part. The seeker is awed by this commitment and passion, and in turn gives himself or herself to the Master in humble and ardent following.

The Old and New Testaments are replete with calls to various men and women. There is a definite commitment on God's part toward the individual. God is doing the choosing, and to make clear that the persons were being set aside for God's service, their names would sometimes be changed by God. God changed Abram's name after the covenant was established with him. Henceforth he would be called Abraham because he was to become the father of a host of nations. When Jesus commissioned Simon to be his apostle, he changed his name to Peter, which means the rock. Saul's name was changed to Paul.

In addition to the name change, disciples would also experience their world being turned inside out. Often they would be asked to leave their homeland and go live and work in a foreign country, as was the case with Abraham, Paul, and Barnabas. At times the individuals would be asked to give up their chosen profession and work for God in unfamiliar territory. Peter and his brother Andrew were fishermen; fishing was the family profession, but Jesus asked them to give up their trade and become fishers of men and women. Levi was a tax collector, but Jesus called him away from his profession and changed his name to Matthew to signify the deeper change toward becoming a herald of the good news.

IDENTIFICATION WITH THE MASTER

A salient feature of discipleship is that the disciples become identified with the Teacher. They share in the mission; they pledge their lives to a person and vision whose outcome is not clear. All they know is that they have enough faith and trust in their leader and are prepared to pledge their lives to him. Jesus' disciples were chosen from various walks of life. They traveled with him wherever he went. Soon they were identified as his disciples. They belonged to his inner circle. They began to witness miracles and heard sermons from Jesus that were lofty and radical. Some among the disciples began dreaming of setting up an earthly kingdom here on earth, with Jesus as their king. They had succumbed to the temptation every disciple is faced with, namely, to prefer one's own ambitions and dreams to those of the Teacher; to make self, rather than the Master, the focus of one's life. Before long their vision of what the mission should be began clashing with the mission that Jesus had received from his Father—that the kingdom he was establishing was the reign of God in people's hearts through repentance and total dependence on God. Jesus was not talking of an earthly kingdom where power and possession are its dominant passions. Soon the two visions were on a collision course.

Not only would Jesus not be an earthly king, even worse he would be crucified as a common criminal. What greater despair and disillusionment could the disciples be subjected to than having their dreams shattered so terribly? What greater test to their discipleship than to have their Master's reputation and vision sullied and shattered beyond repair?

Their faith in Jesus was sorely tested, and there were enough signs to suggest that his band of disciples had reneged on their commitment to him. Judas went so far as to betray his Master and commit suicide. Peter, the chosen leader among them, denied his Master three times. They slept during Jesus' agony in the garden rather than watch and pray with him. Only John was present at the crucifixion along with Mary. They were totally devastated after Jesus' death on the cross. Their morale had been splintered.

They were completely discouraged, and a pall of hopelessness loomed over them. Their own dreams of glory and honor turned out to be illusions. It was almost impossible for them to hold on to Jesus' vision for the world after his crucifixion and death.

Their experience of drinking from the dregs of darkness and despair helped them greatly to understand the true nature of discipleship. If there was one lesson they learned from the events of Jesus' passion and death, it was that they were powerless. Only a total trust and dependence on their Master and his mission could redeem their discipleship and make it authentic. This truth they realized through the resurrection event.

TRANSFORMATION

The resurrection event clarified and strengthened their understanding of discipleship as no other event in the life and teaching of Jesus did. The teachings impressed and challenged the apostles as they knew they were in the presence of God's messenger. The miracles were signs confirming the fact that Jesus was sent by God, and also attested to the fact that Jesus was indeed God because he could both forgive sins and heal physical and spiritual illness. All these events pointed to the resurrection, to the claim that Jesus was indeed God. But the apostles were able to make the connections only after the resurrection event.

Before that they had to die to their own dreams and expectations of what the good news was all about. No wonder they sank into disillusionment and despair during and after the crucifixion. But their eyes and hearts were opened by the resurrection event, which brought about a profound transformation in them. Thomas had sulked and buried himself in his despair and impenetrable doubt, yet Jesus' love and concern held sway over his stubbornness. He was asked to put his hand in Jesus' wounded side and his fingers in the nail imprints, and the encounter set aside any lingering hesitation he might have. Peter had denied his Master three times, but the risen Lord asked him to feed his lambs and his sheep. The disciples on their way to Emmaus encountered the risen Lord. As their hopelessness

LIVING IN GOD'S EMBRACE

melted away, the passion in their hearts was rekindled. They returned to the other disciples full of enthusiasm and the good news that Jesus is risen from the dead. For whatever reason, Judas was not willing to bring his shame and deception to Jesus and allow himself to be accepted and transformed by Jesus' loving forgiveness.

The resurrection event reaches its climax in the feast of Pentecost when the Holy Spirit descends upon the disciples with power and mighty works. The disciples are transformed from hiding cowards to profiles of courage and freedom. No longer afraid, Peter proclaims the good news in the open and works miracles and wonders in Jesus' name. He is willing to go to prison and endure suffering and persecution for the sake of his Master.

God's power surges though the workings of the Holy Spirit as seen in the wondrous deeds performed by the disciples after the resurrection. There is a captivating joy and dynamism present now in the Christian fellowship. They have truly become identified with Jesus' mission, which has also become theirs. The change in the disciples shows truly what the call is about. As Dietrich Bonhoeffer put it, "When Christ calls a man, he bids him come and die."[1]

God's power is clearly visible in the life and works of the disciples when they stay true to the teachings of Jesus. Their discipleship brings about the establishment of God's reign in human hearts when they are single-minded in their focus on God's mission for them, and conform their own desires to God's will for them. Many others have followed in their wake through the centuries and have manifested the same power and deeds of God through fidelity to their calling. Now it is our turn to be transformed into disciples of Jesus.

THE ESSENCE OF DISCIPLESHIP

The Beatitudes capture both the spirit of Jesus and the essence of discipleship. One of my scripture professors was fond of saying that there was only one beatitude that really mattered, the first one: "Blessed are the poor in spirit, for theirs is the kingdom of God." The other seven beatitudes were contained in the first and would be fulfilled if we were truly imbued with the first one. He then proceeded to break up the first beatitude into three components: blest are they; poor in spirit; the kingdom of God is theirs. Next, he asked us to identify the component which resonated the most with us. Interestingly enough, the majority of the class selected the phrase, "poor in spirit." He smiled mischievously knowing that he had suckered us into revealing our brand of discipleship. In our minds it was clear that discipleship was difficult and demanding. It was up to *us* and within *our* power to sacrifice and lay down our lives for the flock. That was the basic reason why most of us chose the phrase "poor in spirit." Unless *we* made ourselves poor in spirit we could not enter the kingdom of heaven. After generating plenty of interest and curiosity, he proceeded to give us a translation of the beatitude from the Greek. It went something like this: "Oh, the great joy of those whose backs are bent double, for God reigns in their hearts." In other words, if God is to reign in our hearts and bring us great joy and peace, our backs must be bent double.

As stated in chapter four, the anawim were the people whose backs were bent double because of the injustices and discrimination suffered by them. They felt powerless and in need of help. This image was transferred into the religious consciousness of Israel to signify the right attitude and disposition to have before God. God comes to the rescue of those who in their powerlessness seek refuge in the Almighty One. The disciples realized that they could not depend on themselves because of their sinfulness, and so they placed all their confidence in God, and endeavored to live their lives in total trust every step of the way.

A disciple is a seeker who tries to be in constant touch with God during all of his or her waking hours. Only then does being created in God's image and likeness become a living reality and not just wishful thinking. Discipleship becomes walking in the footsteps of the Master. When true discipleship becomes a reality, wanting to fulfill all of the beatitudes becomes a way of life.

CHAPTER FIVE HIGHLIGHTS

- ▲ The distinguishing mark of Christian discipleship is that the seeker is *called* by Jesus Christ to be a disciple, or follower. There is a clear sense on the seeker's part that Jesus is invested in the disciple's life. The seeker is awed by this commitment and passion, and in turn gives himself or herself to the Master in humble and ardent following.

- ▲ If there was one lesson the disciples learned from the events of Jesus' passion and death, it was that they were powerless. Only a total trust and dependence on their Master and his mission could redeem their discipleship and make it authentic. They realized this truth through the resurrection event.

- ▲ God's power is clearly visible in the life and works of the disciples when they stay true to the teachings and spirit of Jesus. Their discipleship brings about the establishment of God's reign in human hearts when they are single-minded in their focus on God's mission for them and conform their own desires to God's will for them.

- ▲ A disciple is a seeker who tries to be in constant touch with God during all of his or her waking hours. Only then does being created in God's image and likeness become a living reality and not just wishful thinking. Discipleship becomes walking in the footsteps of the Master.

Exercise Forty-One
DISCIPLESHIP

▲ Scripture

Philip found Nathanael and told him, "We have found the one about whom Moses wrote in the law, and also the prophets, Jesus son of Joseph, from Nazareth." But Nathanael said to him, "Can anything good come from Nazareth?" Philip said to him, "Come and see." Jesus saw Nathanael coming toward him and said of him, "Here is a true Israelite. There is no duplicity in him."

—John 1:45-47

▲ Summary

Discipleship is walking in the Master's footsteps. The disciple's feet will never quite fill out the imprints of the Master's steps, but in walking and being with the Master, a slow and profound transformation takes place. The Master's voice is heard and his presence felt in and through the disciple. Much of ministry becomes the communication of the good news that the disciple has received and personalized.

▲ Session

(20-30 minute duration)

Take a few minutes to come home to yourself through awareness of sounds, your breathing, or bodily sensations.

Imagine yourself in a setting that is familiar to you where you meet Jesus in person. He looks into your eyes with a gaze that penetrates your being and dissolves camouflage and deceit. He asks you the question, "What do I need to do for you so that you can follow me with love and eagerness, beyond all fear and anxiety?" You ponder this question for a while and listen to your heart for the answer you will give. First, you come up with a list of obstacles in the path of your discipleship, such as your fear of change, your gnawing doubt in your ability to commit, your burdened sense of guilt, your many-layered shame, and so on. Scrutinize, confront, cut down to size each of these obstacles so that they stand naked in their truth, without any exaggeration. Then discuss each of them with Jesus as you rest in the comfort of his presence.

Now it is Jesus' turn to speak. He calls you by name, asking you to come and follow him, while assuring you that he will be with you always. In response to Jesus, offer yourself and ask him to receive you as a gift.

▲ Reflection

Discipleship, or the continual process of looking into the eyes of God, is God's gift to us. It becomes a gift difficult to receive when we have convinced ourselves that conversion of heart is our doing and we are not up to it. However, when we understand that it is God who brings about the change in us and our job is to ask for this gift with childlike faith, we will receive it.

Exercise Forty-Two
PETER THE PILGRIM

▲ *Scripture*

Now when Jesus came into the district of Caesarea Philippi, he asked his disciples, "Who do people say that the Son of Man is?" And they said, "Some say John the Baptist, but others Elijah, and still others Jeremiah or one of the prophets." He said to them, "But who do you say that I am?" Simon Peter answered, "You are the Messiah, the Son of the living God." And Jesus answered him, "Blessed are you, Simon son of Jonah! For flesh and blood has not reveled this to you, but my Father in heaven. And I tell you, you are Peter, and on this rock I will build my church, and the gates of Hades will not prevail against it. I will give you the keys of the kingdom of heaven. . . ."

—Matthew 16:13-19

▲ *Summary*

Peter was a diamond in the rough. If he were looking for an important leadership position in the church of today, he wouldn't have passed muster in the eyes of many evaluators. The discerning eye would have noted that there was too much work on himself that needed to be done. The man was much too impetuous and histrionic. Yet Jesus chose Peter to be his apostle and the head of his church. What then did Jesus see?

▲ *Session*

(20-30 minute duration)

Take a few minutes to come home to yourself through awareness of sounds, your breathing, or bodily sensations.

Imagine you are having a heart-to-heart conversation with Peter. He is now an old man with gray-white hair and you are talking to him about his discipleship and yours. He brings his past to life before you. He talks about his life as a fisherman and his family. He was truly comfortable with fish and boats. All of a sudden he was yanked out of his security and asked to follow this strange teacher called Jesus.

He gives you his first impressions of Jesus. He talks about his reactions to Jesus' teachings and miracles, and how his dream of an earthly messiah was shattered. He describes the transfiguration experience, the last supper, his denial of Jesus and his shame and guilt over it, his appointment as head of the church, the Ascension, the descent of the Holy Spirit and the impact it had on his own life, and his preaching and suffering in the service of his Master.

As you listen, you know you are in the presence of God's mystery as this very ordinary man, with all his defects and failings, was transformed by the power and love of Jesus and became his trusted disciple and spokesperson. You spend time with Peter and Jesus and ask them to help you understand and appreciate your own discipleship.

▲ *Reflection*

If discipleship is about being called by the Master, then its power and mystery originate in the caller and not the one being called. God often seems to call a person who in the eyes of the world is a misfit for the job. St. Paul's words, "When I am weak, then I am strong," (2 Cor 12:10) echo this paradox. The power of God comes forth in the weakness of the disciple because he or she depends more completely on God's power.

Exercise Forty-Three
MARY'S FIAT

▲ Scripture

Standing by the cross of Jesus were his mother and his mother's sister, Mary the wife of Clopas, and Mary of Magdala. When Jesus saw his mother and the disciple there whom he loved, he said to his mother, "Woman, behold, your son." Then he said to the disciple, "Behold, your mother."

—John 19:25-27

▲ Summary

When contemplating Mary's life, we are often swayed by the privileges she received from God, like being chosen to be the virgin mother of Jesus. Such an emphasis on her privileged status has tended to remove her from our company, setting her apart as a person who was very different from us. The truth of the matter is that Mary's life was anything but privileged. She faced innumerable questions and doubts about her role as the mother of Jesus. In saying "Yes" to God's plan of salvation, she faced the horrors of hell, more than any mother could ever envisage for her child.

▲ Session

(20-30 minute duration)

Take up a comfortable sitting posture. Try keeping your back straight without straining, and your chin tilted forward slightly. Spend about five minutes coming home to yourself through the awareness of sounds, your breathing, or bodily sensations.

Imagine yourself with Mary in the three following vignettes:

1. In the context of the annunciation, Mary knows clearly that Jesus belongs to God and the world. This message is impressed upon her heart during the presentation of Jesus in the Temple. Simeon's words, "You yourself a sword will pierce," left her with no doubt as to where Jesus' priorities would be. (See Lk 1:46-55 and 2:34-35.)

2. Imagine Mary on the fringes of the crowd gathered before Pilate as he sat in judgment over Jesus. She hears those heart-rending words from the mob: "Crucify him, crucify him; give us Barabbas instead." (See Mt 27:20-23; Mk 15:6-15; Lk 23:18-25; Jn 19:6.) Try to stay with her experience.

3. Imagine yourself with Mary at the foot of the cross, witnessing and participating in Jesus' last moments (See Jn 19:25-27). Try to enter into her sentiments and feelings at the time.

▲ *Reflection*

In everyone's cross there lie the seeds of resurrection. Some never get to appreciate the power of the resurrection because they are too busy grumbling about life's twists and turns. Those who understand that God exhibits many facets, all of which reflect God's loving nature, and are therefore willing to accept life's terms, know great peace. As Rabindranath Tagore says, "In sorrow after sorrow it is his steps that press upon my heart; and it is the golden touch of his feet that makes my joy to shine."[2]

Exercise Forty-Four
THE DOUBTING THOMAS

▲ *Scripture*

But Thomas, one of the twelve, was not with them when Jesus came. So the other disciples told him, "We have seen the Lord." But he said to them, "Unless I see the mark of the nails in his hands, and put my finger in the mark of the nails and my hand in his side, I will not believe."

A week later his disciples were again in the house, and Thomas was with them. Although the doors were shut, Jesus came and stood among them and said, "Peace be with you." Then he said to Thomas, "Put your finger here and see my hands. Reach out your hand and put it in my side. Do not doubt but believe." Thomas answered him, "My Lord and my God!" Jesus said to him, "Have you believed because you have seen me? Blessed are those who have not seen and yet have come to believe."

—John 20:24-29

▲ *Summary*

Doubt and confusion are always present in faith. The believer knows there will be light at the end of the tunnel even though there is darkness and sagging hope all around. In times of crisis the questioning mind seems stronger than the trusting will. Thomas trusted until he was thrown into chaos and despair. His world shattered with his Master's crucifixion. It took his Master's resurrection to restore him to a renewed commitment of faith and trust in Jesus.

▲ Session

(20-30 minute duration)

Spend about five minutes coming home to yourself through the awareness of sounds, your breathing, or bodily sensations. Implore the Holy Spirit to deepen your faith in the power of the risen Jesus.

Next, imagine Thomas and yourself several years after the resurrection. Thomas has had much time to reflect on his following of Jesus. You seek to get a deeper look into the inner recesses of his discipleship so that you are strengthened in your own.

Thomas tells you about his youthful dreams for Israel and himself. He wanted Jesus to be an earthly messiah who would rid Israel of its foreign yoke and establish God's reign. For a while everything seemed to go according to plan. Then came the rapid unraveling of this heady vision as he saw his Master arrested, tortured, and sentenced to a criminal's crucifixion. From the heights of optimism and glory, he plunged into the abyss of disillusionment and despair. From a world of connections and community, he moved into the wilderness of isolation. The ardent follower had become a pathetic mockery of discipleship. But Jesus still had other plans for him.

Thomas tells you of his encounter with the risen Christ, how amazing light and unspeakable joy permeated his intense darkness and despair as he placed his hand and fingers in Jesus' wounds, and how his faith and trust have been unwavering since then. With Thomas you ponder over your own discipleship and what it needs to bring back its sparkle.

▲ Reflection

Discipleship is God's gift to us. It can only be fully appreciated when we place our trust in God's continual help along the way. Our faith might bend; hopefully it will not break.

Exercise Forty-Five
THE PARALYZED MAN

▲ *Scripture*

Not finding a way to bring him in because of the crowd, they went up on the roof and lowered him on the stretcher through the tiles into the middle in front of Jesus. When he saw their faith, he said, "As for you, your sins are forgiven." Then the scribes and Pharisees began to ask themselves, "Who is this who speaks blasphemies? Who but God alone can forgive sins?" . . . "But that you may know that the Son of Man has authority on earth to forgive sins"—he said to the man who was paralyzed, "I say to you, rise, pick up your stretcher, and go home." He stood up immediately before them, picked up what he had been lying on, and went home, glorifying God.
> —Luke 5:19-21; 24-25

▲ *Summary*

Jesus' miracles were signs that God's reign was in our midst. Jesus forgave sins, indicating thereby that he was God, and he worked miracles to show that he had the power to do so. True discipleship hinges on the firm conviction that Jesus is *my* Savior. He has the power both to forgive my sins and work miracles in my life if I come to him with the disposition of the paralyzed man.

▲ *Session*

(20-30 minute duration)

Take a few minutes to come home to yourself through awareness of your breathing. You can beseech the Holy Spirit to give you the heart of a true disciple in this visit.

Jesus was surrounded by Pharisees and teachers of the law who had come from every village of Galilee and from Judea and Jerusalem to listen to him. There was a large crowd as well in attendance. Obviously this was a significant gathering. Some men came to the gathering carrying a paralytic on his mat. They were unable to get near Jesus because of the crowd. They do the bold and unthinkable. They go up on the roof and let him down with his mat through the tiles, into the presence of Jesus.

Impressed by their faith, Jesus first forgives the man his sins. The Pharisees and scribes begin to discuss whether Jesus is God or blasphemer. Jesus then heals the paralyzed man, making him whole. He makes it clear to the Pharisees and scribes that he could heal because he had the power to forgive. The man stands erect and goes home praising God. The crowd is seized with astonishment and gives praise to God.

Visit with the paralyzed man and his friends as they tell you of his predicament and what prompted them to come to Jesus. Rejoice with him in his deep sense of awe and gratitude at God's graciousness toward him. Visit with the Pharisees and scribes and listen sympathetically as they struggle with their resistance to accept the New Way. Visit with the crowd and enter into their sentiments as well. Last, spend time with Jesus, being amazed and awed by his compassion to forgive and his power to heal. Then ask him for the forgiveness and miracle you need in your own life.

▲ Reflection

Miracles happen only when we acknowledge our powerlessness over our sins. God can come to us only when we are humble and honest. When we are persons of deceit and sin, we tie God's hands and block grace from flowing into us.

Exercise Forty-Six
SAUL'S CONVERSION

▲ *Scripture*

For you heard of my former way of life in Judaism, how I persecuted the church of God beyond measure and tried to destroy it, and progressed in Judaism beyond many of my contemporaries among my race, since I was even more a zealot for my ancestral traditions. But God, who from my mother's womb had set me apart and called me through his grace, was pleased to reveal his Son to me, so that I might proclaim him to the Gentiles.

—Galatians 1:13-16

▲ *Summary*

Paul fitted to a T the profile of a religious fanatic, willing to go to great extremes for his beliefs. But God's grace was greater than his fanaticism. He became a changed man, an ardent apostle who suffered much persecution from the very same people he once served.

▲ *Session*

(20-30 minute session)

Spend about five minutes coming home to yourself by doing any one of the first three exercises. Ask the Holy Spirit to help you appreciate God's power as exhibited in Paul's conversion so as to inspire your own spiritual journey.

The rest of Paul's conversion story goes as follows:

> Now as he was going along and approaching Damascus, suddenly a light from heaven flashed around him. He fell to the ground and heard a voice saying to him, "Saul, Saul, why do you persecute me?" He asked, "Who are you, Lord?" The reply came, "I am Jesus, whom you are persecuting. But get up and enter the city, and you will be told what you are to do." The men who were traveling with him stood speechless because they heard the voice but saw no one. Saul got up from the ground, and though his eyes were open, he could see nothing; so they led him by the hand and brought him into Damascus. For three days he was without sight, and neither ate nor drank (Acts 9:3-9).

Spend time with Paul and ask him to reflect on his conversion experience. Try to get a sense of what he needed to convert from and what his experience of Jesus was like. Then enter into a dialogue with Jesus about this transforming experience and ask the same questions of yourself: What is it you need to convert from and what has your experience of Jesus been like so far?

▲ Reflection

Conversion of heart is a mystery that is baffling, especially when it is dramatic and sudden as in the case of Saul. Here was a man who was a true Pharisee. He believed that he was righteous in the eyes of God. In the name of God he expressed his rage, cruelty, and vengeance. At the same time he had the generosity required of a true seeker, and he was able to respond to Jesus' invitation to follow him.

Exercise Forty-Seven
APPEARANCES ARE DECEPTIVE

▲ *Scripture*

As Jesus passed on from there, he saw a man named Matthew sitting at the customs post. He said to him, "Follow me." And he got up and followed him. While he was at table in his house, many tax collectors and sinners came and sat with Jesus and his disciples. The Pharisees saw this and said to his disciples, "Why does your teacher eat with tax collectors and sinners?" He heard this and said, "Those who are well do not need a physician, but the sick do. Go and learn the meaning of the words, 'I desire mercy, not sacrifice.' I did not come to call the righteous but sinners."

—Matthew 9:9-13

▲ *Summary*

The tax collectors were despised by the Jewish community because they raised taxes from their own people for the Roman rulers. Many of them extorted more than the required amount, which they kept for themselves. Some, however, were honest tax collectors, such as Zacchaeus. Others, who were dishonest, came into contact with Jesus and changed their ways once and for all. Matthew seemed to be such a person.

▲ *Session*

(20-30 minute duration)

Spend about five minutes coming home to yourself through the awareness of your bodily sensations. Ask the Holy Spirit for the right perspective on yourself and others so that your actions may be guided by the truth of who people are rather than by labels.

In the ninth chapter of Matthew's gospel we are told the story of Matthew's call, which has been cited above. During your prayer arrange for visits with Jesus, Matthew, some of the tax collectors known as sinners, and the Pharisees who complained against Jesus. Talk to Matthew and the other tax collectors about the change of heart they experienced in Jesus' presence. Talk to the Pharisees about their spirituality and see in what way you can identify with them. Finally, talk to Jesus about his understanding of salvation, ministry, and mission. You might want to close by sharing your own sentiments with Jesus.

▲ *Reflection*

The secret to changing a sinner's heart is love. A sinner becomes capable of living and acting like a saint when his or her heart has been moved powerfully by God's love and compassion. The history of the church is replete with examples of great sinners becoming great saints after God touched their hearts. Hopefully your prayer will access God's immense love for you and change you radically.

Exercise Forty-Eight
THE RICH YOUNG MAN

▲ Scripture

> Jesus said to him, "If you wish to be perfect, go, sell what you have and give to the poor, and you will have treasure in heaven. Then come, follow me." When the young man heard this statement, he went away sad, for he had many possessions.
> —Matthew 19:21-22

▲ Summary

There is the amazing story of the rich young man who wanted to know what he must do to possess everlasting life. He had kept all the commandments; he wanted to do more. Although he was generous, he was not yet willing to be radical enough to give up his possessions and be Jesus' disciple.

▲ Session

(20-30 minute duration)

Take a few minutes to focus on your breathing as a way of becoming still and preparing yourself for your visit with Jesus. Focus on one nostril as you breathe in, and the other as you breathe out, trying to become aware of sensations in the area of your nostrils and upper lip. After you have composed yourself, you can enter into your prayer.

The young man was truly generous and faithful in keeping God's commandments, but he was not satisfied with his service because he wanted to do more for God. Jesus invites him to divest himself of his possessions and become his disciple. He turns down Jesus' offer with sadness because he does not want to part with his many possessions. The disciples are dismayed at Jesus' reflection that it is easier for a camel to pass through a needle's eye than for a rich man to enter the kingdom of God. Jesus' response to them is that for humans it is impossible but for God all things are possible.

Spend time with the young man thinking about his generosity, which is willing to go far but not the whole distance. Then get in touch with your own ambivalence to go all the way as God wants, in different areas of your life. Spend time with the disciples and get in touch with their helplessness regarding Jesus' teaching on detachment.

Finally, ask Jesus to help you understand his message that the possession of God is better and greater than any other possession, and that the possession of God is possible only when one is willing to give up everything for it, a grace which can be received only from God but one that is there for the asking.

▲ Reflection

Alcoholics Anonymous has a simple creed: fake it till you make it. If you engage in behaviors that are right for you and persevere in them, the conviction will follow. Asking occasionally to put on the mind of Jesus is a simple matter in prayer. Doing it on a consistent basis is more difficult because you will *have* to address your ambivalence.

Exercise Forty-Nine
THE REUNION

▲ *Scripture*

Faith is the realization of what is hoped for and evidence of things not seen. Because of it the ancients were well attested. . . . By faith Abraham obeyed when he was called to go out to a place that he was to receive as an inheritance; he went out, not knowing where he was to go. By faith he sojourned in the promised land as in a foreign country, dwelling in tents with Isaac and Jacob, heirs of the same promise; for he was looking forward to the city with foundations, whose architect and maker is God. By faith he received power to generate, even though he was past the normal age—and Sarah herself was sterile—for he thought that the one who had made the promise was trustworthy. So it was that there came forth from one man, himself as good as dead, descendants as numerous as the stars in the sky and as countless as the sands on the seashore.

—Hebrews 11:1-2; 8-12

▲ *Summary*

Jubilee celebrations and family reunions are important because they give us a good sense of our roots. We realize that we are not isolated beings. We are linked to a past that helps us clarify who we are in the present and want to be in the future. Stories of our forebears help us appreciate our true heritage. It is equally important that we learn to appreciate our Christian roots, which go back some twenty centuries to a man called Jesus who was the Son of God.

▲

▲ *Session*

(20-30 minute duration)

Take a few minutes to come home to yourself by listening to the sounds around you, those in the distance and the ones nearest to you, including your own body sounds. After you have become quiet, you can imagine the following scenario taking place:

It is twenty years after Jesus' resurrection. You have arranged for a special reunion. You have picked out a villa in the mountains or by the sea, and have spent much time planning this event. You have invited Jesus and some of the people who became his disciples during his lifetime, like Jesus' mother, Mary Magdalen, Peter, the centurion's servant, the man born blind, Veronica, Paul, and so on. You have been able to collapse the centuries and include some modern-day disciples as well. You assemble them in a cozy setting, and invite each of them to share with Jesus and the group how their lives have changed as a result of their encounter with the Master. You take your turn as well to tell about your discipleship. At the end, Jesus responds to all of you, and to you in particular, sharing his sentiments that came up during the sharing.

▲ *Reflection*

Nothing is more contagious in the spiritual life than listening to a truly inspiring story. Listening to our forebears in the faith share with us the story of their conversion through Jesus can be a source of inspiration and enthusiasm for our own discipleship. Hopefully, at some point in our prayer, we will know that we are actually in contact with our Christian ancestors, and not merely remembering or imagining their presence.

Exercise Fifty
THE LOST SHEEP

▲ Scripture

Let the scoundrel forsake his way,
  and the wicked man his thoughts;
Let him turn to the LORD for mercy;
  to our God, who is generous in forgiving.
For my thoughts are not your thoughts,
  nor are your ways my ways, says the LORD.
As high as the heavens are above the earth,
  so high are my ways above your ways
  and my thoughts above your thoughts.

—Isaiah 55:7-9

▲ Summary

Jesus did some of his most effective teaching through the use of parables. Many of Jesus' parables have unexpected endings. The conclusions do not make logical sense to us. The parables often make a clear statement that God does not think as we do. God's perspective is very different from ours. God draws conclusions that are baffling to us. On the other hand, conversion of heart and salvation come to the seeker who understands and embraces God's point of view.

▲ Session

(20-30 minute duration)

Spend about five minutes coming home to yourself through the awareness of sounds, your breathing, or bodily sensations. With childlike faith implore the Holy Spirit to infuse your prayer with a deep understanding and appreciation of God's perspective toward the sinner.

The parable of the lost sheep is found in Luke, chapter fifteen. It is the story of a shepherd who has a hundred sheep. He loses one of them and leaves the ninety-nine behind to go after the one lost sheep. Had this parable been an ordinary story with a logical ending, the shepherd would have ensured the safety of his ninety-nine sheep to make sure he did not lose another one. Only then would he have either gone after the lost sheep or written it off as a business loss.

You can consider the following questions in a dialogue with Jesus: What message is Jesus giving you through this parable? Are you convinced that Jesus would go to any lengths to love and save you? Are you willing to make Jesus your most prized treasure, more precious than family, wealth, and even life itself?

▲ Reflection

Often we judge God's involvement with us on human terms, namely, that acceptance and love come only with perfection and merit. Through his parables Jesus seems to be telling us that doing good and making sacrifices in the service of others are most effective when they come from a heart that feels deeply loved and forgiven.

- Discipleship is walking in the Master's footsteps. The disciple's feet will never quite fill out the imprints of the Master's steps, but in walking and being with the Master, a slow and profound transformation takes place. The Master's voice is heard and his presence felt in and through the disciple.

- If discipleship is about being called by the Master, then its power and mystery originate in the caller and not the one being called. God has often called a person who to others might be considered a misfit for the job.

- In everyone's cross there lie the seeds of resurrection. Those who understand that God wears many faces, all of which reflect God's heart, and are therefore willing to accept life's terms, know great peace.

- In times of crisis, faith in the power and presence of God feels like an empty boast, and the questioning mind seems stronger than the trusting will. Thomas' world shattered with his Master's crucifixion. It took the Master's resurrection and faith in him to restore Thomas to a renewed commitment and trust in Jesus.

- God can come to us only when we are humble and honest. When we are persons of deceit and sin, we tie God's hands and block grace from flowing into us.

- The secret to changing a sinner's heart is love. A sinner becomes capable of living and acting like a saint when his or her heart has been moved powerfully by God's love and compassion. The history of the church is replete with examples of great sinners becoming great saints after God touched their hearts.

- Asking occasionally to put on the mind of Jesus is a simple matter in prayer. Doing it on a consistent basis is more difficult because you will have to address your ambivalence.

- When we hear stories of our ancestors, we learn to appreciate the stuff of which we are made. It is equally important that we learn to appreciate our Christian roots, which go back more than twenty centuries to a man called Jesus who was the Son of God.

- Many of Jesus' parables have unexpected endings. The conclusions do not make logical sense to us. God seems to draw conclusions that are baffling to us. Conversion of heart comes to the seeker who understands and embraces God's point of view.

CHAPTER SIX

*From Tabor
to Jerusalem*

LIVING OUT THE EXPERIENCE

When you have been through an intense spiritual experience, as during a thirty-day retreat or a spiritual renewal program, you will notice that the period after the experience is crucial to the survival and growth of your intimacy with God. There are a host of folk and spiritual songs which attest to the "mountaintop" experience with God, and the "valley" experience which naturally follows for many seekers. The mountaintop experience itself is so profound that it cannot possibly be nurtured in the seeker's old ways of doing things. The old habits and way of thinking become challenged by this new illumination.

The seeker will have no other choice except to create enhanced and more effective ways of living out this greater intimacy with God, or the gift will have no appreciative value. During the renewal process the seeker learned new and more effective ways of translating this powerful experience of God into everyday life, however, the new habits were in their nascent stage and the renewal program provided an ideal context in which to try them out. The situation back home, in everyday living circumstances, will be different and more challenging to the spiritual life. Fundamental changes in one's lifestyle will be prompted. There won't be the same kind of support and encouragement as experienced on the mountaintop. There will be a much greater need to create a suitable network of support, both internal and external, to help the deepening relationship with God to flourish.

After working your way through this manual, it is my hope that you have encountered a significant experience of God. Now, you will need to nurture and protect your experience to enable continued growth, and for that to happen there is a need to emphasize a viable support network in your life.

RECAPPING THE EXPERIENCE

Before we look at some of the fundamental changes in lifestyle that you will need to make to support and strengthen your intimacy with God, it will help to recapitulate the essence of the disciple's relationship with

God. There are two products from living in the reality that God is at the center of our lives. The first grace is a deep joy and gratitude that wells up within the depths of our being. Whatever our weaknesses might be, they cannot overshadow the fact that we have been created in God's image and likeness and are loved totally and unconditionally by God, "Abba." Knowing we are sons and daughters of the living God creates a sense of nobility and blessedness. Being convinced that God resides in us and loves us unconditionally creates a sense of the sacred and holy in us. We therefore make a concerted effort to think and act as befits those created in God's image and likeness.

The second result is the sharp contrast we experience between our spiritual and selfish selves. As a consequence of the meaningful intimacy that is developing with God, we become even more aware of our own propensity to avoid the truth. So we ask for God's guidance and presence in every activity we are engaged in during the day. As we continue in this manner, God's presence becomes all-encompassing in our lives. The bedrock of Christian spirituality is to know that we are "a lump of sin," in the words of the anonymous author of *The Cloud of Unknowing*, even though we have been created in the image and likeness of God. This pervasive sense of sinfulness is never totally eliminated as long as we are wayfarers on this earth.

True seekers understand that there is *one way* to control and diminish this shadowy and insidious power within them. They realize that freedom from this attraction to evil does not lie within themselves, but in God. Alcoholics Anonymous appreciates the powerlessness of the human being before the seductive and manipulative power of addiction and evil, and realizes that the *only way* out is to acknowledge our powerlessness and ask God to take over our lives. By a strange paradox, these seekers are happy to be weak because in their weakness they experience God's power. In the same light, all seekers can be relieved to know that we have "sinned and fallen short of the glory of God," (Rom 3:27) because only then can we experience the saving love and compassion of Jesus. Honesty and humility become the fundamental virtues of the human journey.

What are some of the attributes and habits you need to develop if you are to preserve and deepen this special relationship you now have with God? A daily period of prayer, an inventory of your conduct, a grateful attitude, befriending your past in God's embrace, leaving the future alone, practicing the presence of God, and inspirational spiritual reading would be some of the good habits to develop as a major part of your internal support system.

Daily Prayer

Ideally, if you were living in a state of consolation because of the special relationship you have with God, it would seem redundant to ask whether you prayed on a daily basis. Visiting with God on a daily basis would seem to be the most natural thing to do. However, intimacy with God, while precious, is a very challenging experience. If you are serious about surrendering completely to God, you will be left with no other option than to be changed radically.

It is difficult to embrace such a challenge all at once. Invariably, the time will come when you will find excuses for skipping your daily meeting with God. At first these excuses will seem like legitimate reasons to you. If you pray in the morning, you might find it convenient to forego your session because you went to bed late. If you pray at night before going to bed, you will somehow find a reason to go to bed early that evening because you have to get up early the following morning.

I have met several individuals who have developed a fidelity to their daily prayer session over the course of many years. It is remarkable to see how their relationship with God has deepened as a result of this daily contact with God. It is important, therefore, that you make a serious commitment to your daily prayer session because the fruits of such a commitment will be immense. It helps greatly to ask God on a daily basis to give you the gift of prayer, the desire to spend time with God alone, even when things are not going well for you.

Doing a Daily Inventory

The rationale for doing a daily moral inventory of our lives is the reality that only God is the architect of our salvation. The gift of salvation can be given only to those who acknowledge their need for it. In other words, salvation comes to those with a meek and humble heart. Looking honestly at the way we give in to deceit and dishonesty in our everyday actions and thoughts is equivalent to acknowledging our sinfulness, which we then bring to God and ask for mercy and guidance to live in God's truth. Doing a daily inventory sharpens the awareness of our character defects and heightens the need to depend on God's power and help. In the Christian tradition, the moral inventory is done during the examination of conscience. Some opt to do it twice daily, others prefer only at the end of the day. Whatever your preference may be, it is important that you create a sacred space within and around you so that your mind and heart are receptive to the prompting of the Holy Spirit leading you to the truth. Along with asking God for forgiveness and guidance, you could also take this opportunity to thank God for the continual guidance and love you receive at every step of the way.

Developing a Grateful Attitude

Gratitude is the result of being loved and appreciated. There is heartfelt gratitude when there is enormous love and compassion shown toward us. Seekers who have made a profound experience of God's love and who live from that embrace tend to develop some wonderful qualities. They become sensitive to God's blessings and graces to them and to those around them. The world of God's largesse and bounty becomes known to them. They develop a true appreciation of the goodness and love around them. An offshoot of this attitude of thanksgiving is that people are attracted to them because they emanate an inner joy and peace.

It is easier to be grateful when things are going well for us, when we are in the state of consolation. It is much more difficult to be thankful when we are lost and confused and there are more questions than answers. But even in these difficult situations, the reality of God loving us totally and passionately and continuing to be present to us in every moment of our lives does not change. So it makes sense to be grateful to God even when things are not going well for us. In fact, it presents an opportunity for experienced seekers to thank God even for situations that they do not particularly like. They know that all is well even when their world is a mess.

Befriending Your Past in God's Embrace

It is very important to engage in therapeutic prayer on a regular basis. You will not come home to the true God if you do not come home to your true self. Coming home to your true self is an arduous task. It takes humility and honesty to discard the illusions you have created about yourself and arrive at the reality of your life as it is.

While such an endeavor is going to be painful, it will result in freedom and joy because the truth does set us free. In coming home to your true self you will discard your false images of God and enter into an authentic and transparent relationship with your Creator and Lord. It is important, therefore, to pray about your past in the spirit of Psalm 139, to take the different events of your life, positive and negative, look at them honestly in God's presence, and see how God was indeed present in them even though you might have had no consciousness of God when they actually occurred. Hopefully, at some stage in your life you will come to see that while your history was flawed in many ways and your setbacks made you suffer greatly on many an occasion, in the final analysis, you did indeed get a good package deal from the Lord. The circumstances of your life were indeed the wrappings enclosing the gift that is and was the Lord from the very moment of your conception.

Leaving the Future Alone

Leaving the future alone is easier said than done, except for someone who has discovered that the present moment is indeed all there is and that it is full of the presence and promise of the risen Christ. For seekers who are in love with the Lord, the present is full of joy and expectation. They arrive at the conclusion that the future will take care of itself if the present moment is attended to with eagerness and devotion. When their anxieties and worries overshadow their peace and joy in the present moment, they engage in therapeutic prayer and consciously surrender themselves into God's loving embrace. At times, therapeutic prayer is not enough, and they will need to go and speak to someone who acts as their pastor, mentor, or director. Ultimately, life is a gift when we can stay in the present moment. We tend to live in the future mainly when things are not going well for us. The future is not ours to see, but if God is in our present moment, God will definitely be there in our future as well.

Practicing God's Presence

It could be helpful for you to make a first-hand experience of the various Christian traditions that emphasize the practice of the presence of God. The most ancient tradition is that of the Jesus Prayer, which was developed by the desert fathers and mothers in the Middle Ages. The tradition emphasizes three simple steps. The first step is to recite the prayer formula, "Lord Jesus Christ, have mercy on me, a sinner," over and over. The second step is to place the presence of God in your heart. The third step is to recite the prayer formula over and over, paying loving attention to the words and the presence of God in you. In the course of your prayer, especially when you are quiet and still, you might notice that the pace of the recitation will slow down because your spirit needs more time to taste and relish the words of the formula. The idea is to set the rhythm of your recitation to the responses of your heart to the prayer. Generally the rhythm slows down as the feelings and sentiments increase.

Another well known tradition is attributed to St. Ignatius of Loyola. It was his custom to practice the presence of God during the day by focusing constantly on God's magnanimity and goodness toward him and the world through the prayer of gratitude. He would devise various ways of remembering God's goodness during the day. He found the practice so helpful that he recommended it very strongly at the end of the thirty-day retreat as a practice to be continued during one's everyday life.

Brother Lawrence is also a well known practitioner of the constant presence of God. He did it by engaging in constant conversation with God throughout the day. He would bring everything to prayer and found it to be the bedrock of his spiritual life.

All three traditions talk about the salutary effects this practice brings to the seeker, leading to a profound conversion of heart and ardent discipleship.

Inspirational Reading

We are social beings. We enrich our lives greatly through the inspiration and example of those around us. Reading inspirational books that warm our spirits and fire our idealism is a good way of benefiting from the lives and good example of enlightened human beings. Through books we can come into contact with the enlightened experience of others with whom we would never otherwise come into contact. It goes without saying that the regular reading of the Bible would help to move your spirit into God's heart.

EXTERNAL SUPPORTS

Several external supports come to mind when thinking of a healthy support network: the celebration of the sacraments, spiritual direction (including retreats and soul-companioning), and doing some ministry.

Sacramental Life

The celebration of the eucharist becomes an important focal point for the seeker. Participation in the eucharist is a manifold blessing. It gives the disciple the opportunity to participate in Christ's own passion, death, and resurrection in preparation for living out his or her own paschal mystery. Many disciples find the celebration so meaningful that they decide to participate in the eucharist more than once a week.

Another great advantage of participation in the liturgy is the gradual initiation into the life of the church as a worshipping community through the cycle of feasts and seasons of the liturgical calendar.

The sacrament of reconciliation is another great blessing of the sacramental life. It makes sense to go on a regular basis and have a regular confessor who comes to know you and can give you proper guidance.

Spiritual Direction

It is both a great opportunity and privilege to be in spiritual direction with a director who is close to God and has great wisdom and insight as a result of this experience, as well as proper training. The spiritual journey is complex and has twists and turns that will sometimes baffle us. There is also the added challenge of integrating our history with God's call to discipleship. A good spiritual director will help point us constantly in God's direction, always keeping the relationship with God in the forefront of our lives.

For those who are in a twelve-step fellowship, the importance of the sponsor cannot be emphasized enough. Once again the sponsor is an individual who has and continues to walk the same journey as the one being sponsored. Furthermore, the sponsor has had and continues to have the same difficulties and challenges that the one being sponsored faces. In such relationships where God is the focus, Jesus is very much present. Such a relationship becomes a sacrament offering us the gift of God's presence. Soul-companioning, or having a friend with whom you can share the intimate moments of your walk with God, will generate many sacred moments as well.

Doing Some Ministry

Ultimately, true love is expressed in deeds. You will know that your experience of God's love for you is authentic when you begin to express your love and concern for others through acts of kindness, thoughtfulness, and cheerful service. For some of us, there will be no need to look for situations in which to express our love for God—the circumstances of our lives provide plenty of opportunities to be Christ's presence to others. What will change, however, is our attitude in our daily activities. We will try to communicate a new spirit of peace and joy that we have found in God. For others, there might be a clear preference to identify a ministry and spend a few hours every week in service. Hopefully, the time will come when your ministry will become a prayer experience where God's presence and help will become more discernible. To take it a step further, the time might arrive when your whole day will seem like a continual ministry where God is coming to you and you are instrumental in bringing God to others.

CHAPTER SIX HIGHLIGHTS

▲ Being convinced that God resides in us and loves us unconditionally creates a sense of the sacred and holy in us. We therefore make a concerted effort to think and act as befits those created in God's image and likeness.

▲ If you are serious about surrendering completely to God, you will be left with no other option than to be changed radically. It is important, therefore, that you make a serious commitment to your daily prayer session, because the fruits of such a commitment will be immense.

▲ Doing a daily inventory sharpens the awareness of our character defects and heightens the need to depend on God's power and help.

▲ Gratitude is the result of being loved and appreciated. Seekers who have made a profound experience of God's love and live from that embrace tend to develop a true appreciation of the goodness and love around them. An offshoot of this attitude is that people are attracted to them because they emanate an inner joy and peace.

▲ You will not come home to the true God if you do not come home to your true self. It takes humility and honesty to discard the illusions and mirages you have created about yourself and arrive at the reality of your life as it is.

▲ In coming home to your true self you will discard your false images of God and enter into an authentic and transparent relationship with your Creator and Lord.

▲ Life is a gift when we can stay in the present moment. We tend to live in the future mainly when things are not going well for us. The future is not ours to see, but if God is in our present moment, God will definitely be in our future as well.

▲ The spiritual journey is complex and has twists and turns that will sometimes baffle us. There is also the added challenge of integrating our history with God's call to discipleship. A good spiritual director will help point us constantly in God's direction, always keeping the relationship with God in the forefront.

Exercise Fifty-One
HOMAGE TO OUR ANCESTORS

▲ Scripture

On the evening of that first day of the week, when the doors were locked, where the disciples were, for fear of the Jews, Jesus came and stood in their midst and said to them, "Peace be with you." When he had said this, he showed them his hands and his side. The disciples rejoiced when they saw the Lord. Jesus said to them again, "Peace be with you. As the Father has sent me, so I send you." And when he had said this, he breathed on them and said to them, "Receive the holy Spirit."

—John 20:19-22

▲ Summary

Various religious traditions pay special attention to ancestor homage. The tradition seems to emphasize the fact that death is not the end of our relationship with our forebears; rather, death signals the advent of a special communication with them, on the level of the spirit. The Christian tradition emphasizes the communion of saints. Our spiritual roots go back centuries to the time of Christ and the founding of his church. It is important that we stay in close touch with our Christian roots through our communion with the saints.

▲ Session

(20-30 minute duration)

Spend about five minutes coming home to yourself through the awareness of sounds, your breathing, or bodily sensations. With childlike faith implore the Holy Spirit to give you a deeper appreciation of the communion of saints in your life.

In your mind, assemble a small group of individuals from the past around Jesus. You can include some biblical figures if you so desire. (My own favorites are Mary's husband, Joseph, the faithful one; Nathaniel, the man without guile; and Paul, who felt passionately about the community of the faithful being the body of Christ.) Choose some deceased members of your own immediate and extended family, persons who influenced you spiritually. You might want to choose a teacher, priest, or religious sister or brother who influenced you. After you have brought them together, interact with each one, thanking each of them for the blessings they have bestowed upon you through their example. Listen to them respond to you by sharing with you the highlights of their relationship with Jesus. Finally, listen to Jesus tell you about the importance of staying intimately connected with his Body, the communion of saints here on earth as well as in heaven. He then bestows his blessing on the group.

▲ Reflection

The "I" can only be known if there is a "you." The self can only be known in the context of a relationship with another. In our human existence we need to have a healthy experience of community, or else our identity is shrouded in confusion and isolation. The same is true for our spiritual selves. We function best when we have a good sense of our spiritual roots—the history, traditions, and sacred practices of the religious community with which we are affiliated. Our ecclesial community is both the living faithful and the saints who have gone before us to live with God.

Exercise Fifty-Two
MOVING INTO TRUST

▲ *Scripture*

Lo, I am about to create new heavens
  and a new earth;
The things of the past shall not be remembered
  or come to mind.
Instead, there shall always be rejoicing and
happiness
  in what I create;
For I create Jerusalem to be a joy
  and its people to be a delight;
I will rejoice in Jerusalem
  and exult in my people.
                    —Isaiah 65:17-19

▲ *Summary*

Trust is the bedrock of one's identity. When trust is absent, fear, anxiety, and a pervasive restlessness will dominate. But even in the most extreme case of mistrust, there is hope. Erik Erikson believes, "there is little that cannot be remedied later; there is much that can be prevented from happening at all."[1] Salvation is the establishment of trust in God which can then extend to oneself and to others.

▲ *Session*

(20-30 minute duration)

Take a few minutes to come home to yourself through the awareness of sounds or bodily sensations. After you have become quiet, come into God's presence and ask yourself the following questions:

▲ Is the story of my life satisfactory?

▲ Do I have any regrets?

▲ If I were given the opportunity to change my self-image, how would I do it?

▲ Where have I usually gone for answers to my questions?

Check to see if God's opinion of you agrees with yours. Here is a sample of the way God thinks of you:

> God created humankind in his image,
>   in the image of God he created them;
>   male and female he created them (Gn 1:27).

> When I see your heavens, the work of your fingers,
>   the moon and stars that you set in place—
> What are humans that you are mindful of them . . . ?
> Yet you have made them little less than a god,
>   crowned them with glory and honor (Ps 8:4-6).

> You formed my inmost being;
>   you knit me in my mother's womb.
> I praise you, so wonderfully you made me;
>   wonderful are your works!
> My very self you knew . . . (Ps 139:13-14).

> But Zion said, "The LORD has forsaken me;
>   my Lord has forgotten me."
> Can a mother forget her infant,
>   be without tenderness for the child of her womb?
> Even should she forget,
>   I will never forget you.
> See, upon the palms of my hands I have written your name (Is 49:14-16).

If your thinking agrees with God's, you can spend time in gratitude and praise. If it does not, then you have the opportunity to challenge your conclusions about yourself.

▲ Reflection

Moving from mistrust to trust is giving up the familiar and choosing to listen to the quiet voice within us that calls us to greater freedom and life. We are so wedded to our viewpoint that we tend to ignore God's view of us. Pondering over the above scripture passages is important until gradually they subdue our doubts and suspicions.

Exercise Fifty-Three
REDEMPTIVE SUFFERING

▲ *Scripture*

Then Jesus said to all, "If anyone wishes to come after me, he must deny himself and take up his cross daily and follow me. For whoever wishes to save his life will lose it, but whoever loses his life for my sake will save it. What profit is there for one to gain the whole world yet lose or forfeit himself?

—Luke 9:23-25

▲ *Summary*

It is an inevitable fact that life brings much suffering with it. Unfortunately some or much of this suffering is of our own doing. When we approach suffering with honesty and forgiveness toward others and ourselves, our suffering becomes redemptive. We learn from it, grow through it, and the paschal mystery becomes reality for us. On the other hand, when we approach suffering with sustained anger, lingering resentment, bitterness, and self-pity, the result is misery and unhappiness.

▲ *Session*

(20-30 minute duration)

Take a few minutes to come home to yourself through awareness of sounds, your breathing, or bodily sensations.

In one of his poems from his collection called *Gitanjali*, Rabindranath Tagore writes, "Have you not heard his silent steps, He comes, comes, ever comes. In sorrow after sorrow, it is his steps that press upon my heart, and it is the golden touch of his feet that makes my joy to shine."[2] The saints and mystics arrived at a place in their journey with God where they understood from their own experience that suffering can be redemptive, that the seeds of resurrection are contained in the pain and agony of their lives.

Let us look at the dilemmas some of the biblical characters faced in their journey into the heart of God. Joseph faced the dilemma of keeping or putting away his wife because she was inexplicably with child. He accepted God's word that the child was of the Holy Spirit. He continued to be Mary's husband, was put to the test in the future, and remained steadfast. Hosea embraced his wife in spite of her infidelity, as a sign of God's own passion and love for Israel. A painful cross in his personal life became a powerful symbol of God's fidelity to him and his people.

Choose two incidents of suffering in your life, one that caused you misery and bitterness and another that you approached with honesty and forgiveness and experienced salvation as a consequence, and discuss them with Jesus.

▲ *Reflection*

Suffering is part of our human condition. Many of our psychological and spiritual problems arise because we choose to avoid facing our responsibilities by creating pleasurable illusions that in the end leave us feeling depressed and dismayed. At other times we make ourselves miserable by demanding an eye for an eye or a tooth for a tooth. Jesus' way alone brings salvation: "Love your enemies and do good to those who hate you" (Mt 5:44).

Exercise Fifty-Four
MY HOME, GOD'S SANCTUARY

▲ Scripture

The house of the wicked will be destroyed,
  but the tent of the upright will flourish.

In the house of the just there are ample resources,
  but the earnings of the wicked are in turmoil.
    —Proverbs 14:11; 15:6

▲ Summary

Emmanuel is one of Jesus' names. It means "God-with-us." We refer to ourselves as temples of the Holy Spirit. In our religious language and everyday consciousness, we stress the link between the human and the spiritual, the mundane and the supernatural, the secular and the sacred. Our homes are dear to us—we want them to be safe and secure places where we are nourished and renewed. Has your home become God's dwelling place for you?

▲ Session

(20-30 minute duration)

Take a few minutes to come home to yourself by using any one of the first six exercises. Then ask God for the grace to appreciate deeply the constant and lively presence of God in your home.

Jesus has responded to your invitation to visit you. The purpose is to help you discover his love and presence in your home. You are elated as you welcome him. You begin by seating him on your favorite couch in your favorite room. Very gently and lovingly you remove his sandals and wash his dust-covered feet. Your gesture moves him deeply. You then offer him food and beverage as you converse with each other.

The theme is one of gratitude at how, day after day and year after year, you have been nurtured and strengthened by God's bounty in your home. You thank Jesus that your dining table has often been his sacrament of loving providence and care for you and the many family members and guests who have been nurtured by your hospitality. You express your sorrow for the many times when you have been unaware of his presence as he sat at the same table with you.

Next, you visit every room in your home and relive your moments of comfort, joy, peace, and security, and in all those circumstances you remember that God was present and providing for you. For example, the beautiful designs in the hardwood floors are the oak trees' expressions of praise to their Creator as they grew straight and tall for numerous decades. Jesus reminds you of all the other labors of love that were instrumental in putting together this cozy sanctuary you call home. You spend time expressing your sentiments of gratitude, joy, and amazement to Jesus, as you wander in and out of the rooms.

▲ Reflection

Many of our most precious memories embrace our family members and traditions in the context of our home. If our home is our sanctuary in which we nurture our intimacies and joys, then such a place is where God is. It behooves us to place this presence in our consciousness.

Exercise Fifty-Five
YIELDING: SURRENDER AND BOUNTY

▲ *Scripture*

Though he was harshly treated, he submitted
and opened not his mouth;
Like a lamb led to the slaughter
or a sheep before the shearers,
he was silent and opened not his mouth.
Oppressed and condemned, he was taken away,
and who would have thought any more of his
destiny?
—Isaiah 53:7-8

▲ *Summary*

Yield is an interesting word that can be a treasure-trove of rich spiritual meaning. In its verb form it means to give in, give way to, or surrender. In its noun form it signifies an amount produced, or a harvest. The spiritual life emphasizes the strange connection between surrender and the production of much fruit. The two meanings seem to be mutually exclusive. Paradoxically, though, they complement each other. The good news is that when we yield to God, we produce a hundredfold. Surrender to God is the equivalent of true spiritual freedom and joy.

▲ *Session*

(20-30 minute duration)

Take up a comfortable sitting posture with your back erect and your chin tilted forward slightly. Spend a few minutes coming home to yourself through the awareness of sounds, your breathing, or bodily sensations.

Ponder the following statements of Jesus that emphasize surrender and yielding:

"Love your enemies, and pray for those who persecute you" (Mt 5:44).

"Remove the wooden beam from your eye first; then you will see clearly to remove the splinter from your brother's eye" (Mt 7:5).

"Be merciful, just as your Father is merciful. Stop judging and you will not be judged" (Lk 6:36-37).

Ponder the following truths about nature that emphasize yielding and bounty:

- ▲ the spectacular display of colors before the deciduous trees shed their leaves and then wait in patience for the next resurgence of abundance in spring;

- ▲ the grain field that yields to the furrowing plow so that its seeds can germinate and grow and multiply a hundredfold;

- ▲ the forest fire that scourges the land, yet provides for abundant new growth.

Ponder your own yielding to doing and receiving concrete acts of kindness, compassion, and understanding, especially with persons you consider to be difficult.

Spend some time with Jesus, sharing the sentiments and thoughts that have arisen from your reflections.

▲ Reflection

The spiritual life is full of paradoxes, one of which is that God's salvation is not possible without an honest admission of sin and guilt. True spiritual freedom can come only to the disciple who stretches out his or her hands to God in supplication. Ministry is the giving from one's abundance—the abundance which was received from God in the first place. When we allow ourselves to be weak and transparent before God, we become strong with God's power and presence.

Exercise Fifty-Six
LIVING WITH WISDOM

▲ Scripture

> For the first step toward discipline is a very earnest
> desire for her;
>> then, care for discipline is love of her;
>> love means the keeping of her laws;
> To observe her laws is the basis for incorruptibility;
>> and incorruptibility makes one close to God;
>> thus the desire for Wisdom leads up to a kingdom.
>> —Wisdom 6:17-20

▲ Summary

The Book of Proverbs is a superb collection of spiritual wisdom, providing not only much food for thought and nourishment for the soul but offering answers to many of our personal questions as we try to find our way in this labyrinth called life. It helps to familiarize ourselves with the proverbs, even commit many of them to memory, so that they come to mind when we most need them—in our daily pursuit of God's will for us.

▲ Session

(20-30 minute duration)

Spend a few minutes focusing on your breathing as a way of becoming quiet and receptive to your forthcoming visit with God. As you begin, you may want to take a few deep, cleansing breaths.

Consider the following proverbs about right behavior and then talk to God about your sentiments and conclusions:

There are six things the LORD hates,
  yes, seven are an abomination to him;
Haughty eyes, a lying tongue,
  and hands that shed innocent blood;
A heart that plots wicked schemes,
  feet that run swiftly to evil,
The false witness who utters lies,
  and he who sows discord among brothers
  (Prv 6:16-19).

A path to life is his who heeds admonition,
  but he who disregards reproof goes astray
  (Prv 10:17).

For lack of guidance a people falls;
  security lies in many counselors (Prv 11:14).

A soothing tongue is a tree of life,
  but a perverse one crushes the spirit (Prv 15:4).

Better a dry crust with peace
  than a house full of feasting with strife (Prv 17:1).

Fine words are out of place in a fool;
  how much more, lying words in a noble! (Prv 17:7).

When a man walks in integrity and justice,
  happy are his children after him! (Prv 20:7).

He who conceals his sins prospers not,
  but he who confesses and forsakes them obtains
  mercy (Prv 28:13).

▲ Reflection

Our behaviors are a reliable window into our souls. They mirror back to the world and to us, if we are willing to look, our true attitudes and convictions. The Book of Proverbs provides a salutary dose of reality and truth. If we take the proverbs seriously by putting them in practice, the gift of wisdom will be ours.

Exercise Fifty-Seven
HUMILITY—THE WAY OF TRUTH

▲ Scripture

> My son, conduct your affairs with humility,
>   and you will be loved more than a giver of gifts.
> Humble yourself the more, the greater you are,
>   and you will find favor with God.
> For great is the power of God;
>   by the humble he is glorified.
> What is too sublime for you, seek not,
>   into things beyond your strength search not.
> What is committed to you, attend to;
>   for what is hidden is not your concern.
>   —Sirach 3:17-21

▲ Summary

Humility could be viewed as the bedrock of true spirituality. It acts as the solid base on which an authentic spiritual way can be built. Humility is closely connected to truth. The humble human is transparent and so experiences new life. Many disciples have adopted humility as a way of thinking, living, and doing. St. Francis of Assisi is a good example. In this exercise you are invited to adopt humility as your way of life.

▲ Session

(20-30 minute duration)

Spend a few minutes coming home to yourself through the awareness of sounds.

Follow the Benedictine method of prayer: *reading* each phrase, *repeating* it several times until your heart is moved, and *praying* your sentiments to God.

"My soul proclaims the greatness of the Lord;
   my spirit rejoices in God my savior.
For he has looked upon his handmaid's lowliness"
(Lk 1:46-47).

"But the tax collector stood off at a distance and would not even raise his eyes to heaven but beat his breast and prayed, 'O God, be merciful to me a sinner.' I tell you, the latter went home justified, not the former; for everyone who exalts himself will be humbled, and the one who humbles himself will be exalted" (Lk 18:13-14).

Who, though he was in the form of God,
. . . he emptied himself,
taking the form of a slave,
coming in human likeness . . .
he humbled himself,
becoming obedient to death, even death on a cross
(Phil 2:6-8).

"You call me 'teacher' and 'master,' and rightly so, for indeed I am. If I, therefore, the master and teacher, have washed your feet, you ought to wash one another's feet" (Jn 13:13-14).

Draw near to God, and he will draw near to you. . . . Humble yourselves before the Lord and he will exalt you (Jas 4:8, 10).

▲ Reflection

The word "humility" is derived from the Latin *humus*, which means "soil" or "the earth." The ground is a symbol of stability and strength. Our homes can be strong and sturdy because they have firm foundations in the ground. The earth is also a symbol of giving and nurture. All living plants, animals, and humans derive their sustenance from the earth. Humility has the same effect on the person who chooses to be humble. Such a disciple becomes a symbol of stability, trustworthiness, and support in the community.

Exercise Fifty-Eight
THE MORTAL PRESENCE

▲ Scripture

It was now about noon and darkness came over the whole land until three in the afternoon because of an eclipse of the sun. Then the veil of the temple was torn down the middle. Jesus cried out in a loud voice, "Father, into your hands I commend my spirit"; and when he had said this he breathed his last. The centurion who witnessed what had happened glorified God and said, "This man was innocent beyond doubt." When all the people who had gathered for this spectacle saw what had happened, they returned home beating their breasts; but all his acquaintances stood at a distance, including the women who had followed him from Galilee and saw these events.

—Luke 23:44-49

▲ Summary

Death is a fact of our lives. We do not know when or how we shall breathe our last. We do know, however, that we will die. While death is inevitable, the thought of it causes fear and anxiety in many of us, so we conjure up ingenious ways of discounting and denying this reality. Denying or ignoring death does not make it go away. Rather, such behavior only increases its fearful presence and hold on us. The only healthy way to deal with the reality of death is to reflect upon it and understand its great significance as a spiritual tool. In many religious traditions, meditating on the reality of death has been an important prayer exercise. We shall try to do the same in this exercise.

▲ Session

(20-30 minute duration)

Take a few minutes to prepare yourself for prayer. What better way to do this than by focusing on your breathing, which signifies the gift of life. Try to be deliberate as you pay attention to your breathing in and out. After you have become calm and centered, imagine yourself in the presence of Jesus. Imagine you have only one hour left to live, and through the following questions you review your life in dialogue with Jesus:

- ▲ What is the present state of your relationship with Jesus? Talk to him about it.

- ▲ For what blessings and graces are you most grateful? Choose a few specific ones.

- ▲ What has been your contribution to the world? Try to name it.

- ▲ Do you have any regrets about the way you lived?

- ▲ Is there still some unfinished business left? Be specific in naming it.

- ▲ When you meet Jesus face to face shortly, what will the two of you say to each other? Let Jesus respond after you.

▲ Reflection

Death holds no fear or worry for those who are accustomed to living their lives in the present moment, applying all their attention and energies to whatever task is before them. They are motivated by love and truthfulness. Joy has become their distinguishing mark. For them death becomes the passageway through which they will meet the same God they have known very intimately on this side of the divide. The difference in death is that they will behold God face to face and know themselves with utmost clarity as God's very own image and likeness.

Exercise Fifty-Nine
THERAPEUTIC PRAYER

▲ Scripture

>I wait with longing for the Lord,
>   my soul waits for his word.
>My soul looks for the Lord
>   more than sentinels for daybreak.
>More than sentinels for daybreak,
>   let Israel look for the Lord,
>For with the Lord is kindness,
>   with him is full redemption,
>And God will redeem Israel
>   from all their sins.
>
>   —Psalm 130:5-8

▲ Summary

We are familiar with Psalm 139, where the psalmist captures the reality of the all-knowing and ever-present God in our lives. It is one thing to acknowledge *intellectually* that God is aware of every facet of our being and behavior. Such an acknowledgment will not necessarily bring about a real submission to God's authority over our lives. It is another matter, however, to allow ourselves to be constantly guided by the reality of God's omnipresence in every circumstance of our lives. In such a relationship, a growing transparency between God and us develops. We bring everything to God without censor or censure, similar to the process in psychotherapy or spiritual direction or twelve-step sponsorship. The fruits of such a relationship with God are trust, intimacy, serenity, and spiritual growth.

▲ Session

(20-30 minute duration)

Take up a comfortable sitting posture with your back erect and your chin tilted forward slightly. Spend a few minutes coming home to yourself through the awareness of sounds, your breathing, or bodily sensations.

The ideal way of praying therapeutically would be to ask how God is present in the daily events of your life *as* they occur, especially the ones that are difficult and stressful. Hopefully the day will come when you are in frequent dialogue with God about your interior movements. Meanwhile, setting time aside, as during this prayer session, to do therapeutic prayer is a good way of training yourself to become a pray-er all through the day.

For this session, imagine you are visiting with Jesus in a comfortable setting. Begin by telling Jesus what your feelings are in the present moment. Some of these feelings will be related to events of the past or to a forthcoming agenda. It is important as well to get to the assumptions underlying your feelings.

Your preference might be to revisit some painful or joyful event of the past to see how God was present. There might be areas of anger and resentment into which you have not yet allowed God. Similarly, there might be joyful experiences whose depths you have not yet plumbed. Therapeutic prayer is the context in which everything from your past and present is content for honest dialogue with God.

▲ Reflection

Various images can be used to express the kind of intimacy that is required in therapeutic prayer. The image of God as your soul-friend is an apt one, as through honest dialogue you have become comfortable with God dwelling in your innermost recesses.

Exercise Sixty
TAKING STOCK

▲ *Scripture*

As long as I kept silent, my bones wasted away;
   I groaned all the day.
For day and night your hand was heavy upon me;
   my strength withered as in dry summer heat.
Then I declared my sin to you;
   my guilt I did not hide.
I said, "I confess my faults to the Lord,"
   and you took away the guilt of my sin.
Thus should all your faithful pray
   in time of distress.
Though flood waters threaten,
   they will never reach them.

—Psalm 32:3-6

▲ *Summary*

Taking stock, or getting proper perspective on one's life, is an important spiritual tool. We might not know how our lives will unfold in the future, but we can always know where we stand if we learn to ask ourselves the right questions and try to answer them as truthfully as possible. Knowing where one stands is equivalent to being grounded in oneself. When we are rooted in ourselves, the uncertainties and problems of life assume realistic proportions.

▲ *Session*

(20-30 minute duration)

Take a few minutes to come home to yourself through awareness of sounds, your breathing, or bodily sensations.

After you have become still, try to come up with answers to

the following questions in order to help you better understand and appreciate the present context of your life. It helps to create a comfortable setting where God and you can visit with each other over these questions. Let the answers come to you from your heart, rather than trying to generate them with your mind.

- ▲ What is the one gift/grace/blessing that you are most grateful for *now*?
- ▲ What is your deepest wish for yourself and why has it not yet been fulfilled?
- ▲ What is your greatest regret and how have you tempered it?
- ▲ What is the most loving way in which *you* have experienced God?
- ▲ What is the most loving way in which *God* has experienced you?
- ▲ What is your greatest fear and how do you trust in its presence?
- ▲ If you were allowed only one task or action to perform for the rest of your life, what would it be?

▲ *Reflection*

As a serious seeker you will take stock of your discipleship frequently. Twelve-step programs strongly recommend doing a moral inventory alone and with someone else, and doing so on a regular basis. Examinations of consciousness and retreats are times when we square up with ourselves. Taking stock oftentimes has more to do with God's activity in us rather than how we are doing.

▲ We function best when we have a good sense of our spiritual roots—the history, traditions, and sacred practices of the religious community with which we are affiliated. Our ecclesial community is both the living faithful and the saints who have gone before us to live with God.

▲ Moving from mistrust to trust is giving up the familiar and known, and choosing to listen to the quiet voice within us that calls us to greater freedom and life. We are so wedded to our viewpoint that we tend to ignore God's view of us.

▲ Life brings much suffering with it. Unfortunately, some or much of this suffering is of our doing. When we approach suffering with honesty and forgiveness toward others and ourselves, our suffering becomes redemptive.

▲ Many of our most precious memories embrace our family members and traditions in the context of our home. If our home is our sanctuary in which we nurture our intimacies and joys, then such a place is where God is. It behooves us to make conscious this presence.

▲ The spiritual life emphasizes the strange connection between surrender and the production of much fruit. The good news is that when we yield to God, we produce a hundredfold. Surrender to God is the equivalent of true spiritual freedom and joy.

▲ "He who conceals his sins prospers not,
    but he who confesses and forsakes them obtains
    mercy" (Prv 28:13).

▲ Denying or ignoring death does not make it go away. Rather, such behavior only increases its fearful presence and hold on us. The only healthy way to deal with the reality of death is to reflect upon it and understand its great significance as a spiritual tool.

▲ It is one thing to acknowledge intellectually that God is aware of every facet of our being and behavior, it is another matter to allow ourselves to be constantly guided by the reality of God's omnipresence in every circumstance of our lives. In such a relationship a growing transparency between God and us develops. The fruits of such a relationship with God are trust, intimacy, serenity, and spiritual growth.

▲ We might not know how our lives will unfold in the future, but we can always know where we stand if we learn to ask ourselves the right questions and try to answer them as truthfully as possible. Knowing where one stands is equivalent to being grounded in oneself. When we are rooted in ourselves, the uncertainties and problems of life assume realistic proportions.

Notes

▲ Chapter One

1. *The Spiritual Exercises*: 46
2. *The Spiritual Exercises*: 75
3. *The Spiritual Exercises*: 2
4. "The Spiritual Direction of 'Thinking' Types," Carolyn Osiek, R.S.C.J., *Review for Religious*, Volume 44, 1985, pp. 209-219.
5. *The Spiritual Exercises*: 12
6. *The Spiritual Exercises*: 13
7. *The Spiritual Exercises*: 118; 120; 121
8. *The Spiritual Exercises*: 313-327; 328-336

▲ Chapter Two

1. The inspiration for this exercise came from the prayer exercise called "The Advent" from *Wellsprings: A Book of Spiritual Exercises*, by Anthony de Mello.
2. Rabindranath Tagore, "Song Offerings, Number 45," *Gitanjali*. Boston: Branden Publishing Company, 1996.
   3. Ibid.

▲ Chapter Three

1. *Cloud of Unknowing and Book of Privy Counseling*, William Johnston, ed. Image Books, 1996.
2. Adapted from *How It Works*, third edition, chapter 5, page 59, steps one and three, Alcoholics Anonymous.
3. Adapted from *How It Works*, third edition, chapter 5, page 59, step five, Alcoholics Anonymous.

▲ Chapter Five

1. Dietrich Bonhoeffer, *The Cost of Discipleship*, Chapter 4, "Discipleship and the Cross," page 99, revised edition, Macmillan Publishing Company, Inc.

2. Rabindranath Tagore, "Song Offerings, Number 45," *Gitanjali*. Boston: Branden Publishing Company, 1996.

▲ Chapter Six

1. Marie Lawrence, OSF, "Psycholosocial Development of Malcolm X Through Erikson's Eight Stages," thesis submitted to St. Louis University, December 1974.
2. Rabindranath Tagore, "Song Offerings, Number 45," *Gitanjali*. Boston: Branden Publishing Company, 1996.

◀ 32ND ANNUAL EDITION ▶

CHILDREN'S WRITER'S & ILLUSTRATOR'S MARKET

2020

Amy Jones, Editor

WD
WRITER'S DIGEST
BOOKS

Children's Writer's & Illustrator's Market 2020. Copyright © 2019 Penguin Random House LLC. Published by Writer's Digest Books, an imprint of Penguin Random House LLC. Printed and bound in the United States of America. All rights reserved. No part of this book may be reproduced in any form or by any electronic or mechanical means including information storage and retrieval systems without permission in writing from the publisher, except by a reviewer, who may quote brief passages in a review.

ISSN: 0897-9790
ISBN-13: 978-1-4403-0123-0
ISBN-10: 1-4403-0123-9

Edited by: Amy Jones
Designed by: Wendy Dunning

CONTENTS

BUSINESS & PROMOTION

MARKETS

RESOURCES

INDEXES

FROM
THE EDITOR

//

Welcome to the 32nd Annual Edition of the *Children's Writer's and Illustrator's Market*!
In this edition, my goal was not just to balance the articles and listings, but within
the articles, to include useful information for writers of the wide age spectrum that
encompasses children's writing. So you'll find articles that speak to everything from
picture books to YA novels.

In the section of craft articles you'll find brilliant excerpts from Ann Whitford Paul's
book, *Writing Picture Books Revised and Expanded Edition*, plus articles about creating
compelling characters. You'll also find interviews with bestselling authors including
Jacqueline Woodson, Cassandra Clare, N.K. Jemisin, and more. Learn more about
promoting your work, whether self-published or traditionally published, and much more
in the collection of business and promotion articles.

As usual, the listings in this edition run the gamut from book publishers in the
United States and abroad; magazines; agents and art reps; clubs and organizations;
conferences and workshops; and contests, awards, and grants.

With the help of these resources, I hope 2020 will be your most satisfying and
productive year yet.

Amy Jones
Managing Content Director
Children's Writer's & Illustrator's Market
http://twitter.com/AmyMJones_5

HOW TO USE
CHILDREN'S WRITER'S & ILLUSTRATOR'S MARKET

//

As a writer, illustrator, or photographer first picking up *Children's Writer's & Illustrator's Market*, you may not know quite how to start using the book. Your impulse may be to flip through the book and quickly make a mailing list, then submit to everyone in hopes that someone will take interest in your work. Well, there's more to it. Finding the right market takes research. The more you know about a market that interests you, the better chance you have of getting work accepted. We've made your job a little easier by putting a wealth of information at your fingertips. Besides providing listings, this directory has a number of tools to help you determine which markets are the best ones for your work. By using these tools, as well as researching on your own, you raise your odds of being published.

USING THE INDEXES

This book lists hundreds of potential buyers of material. To learn which companies want the type of material you're interested in submitting, start with the indexes.

Subject Index

But let's narrow the search further. Take your list of young adult magazines, turn to the **Subject Index**, and find the **Fashion** subheading. Then highlight the names that appear on both lists (**Young Adult** and **Fashion**). Now you have a smaller list of all the magazines that would be interested in your teen fashion article. Read through those listings and decide which seem (or look) best for your work.

Illustrators and photographers can use the **Subject Index** as well. If you specialize in painting animals, for instance, consider sending samples to book and magazine publishers listed under **Animals** and, perhaps, **Nature/Environment**. Because illustrators can simply send general examples of their style to art directors to keep on file, the indexes may be more helpful to artists sending manuscript/illustration packages who need to search for a specific subject. Always read the listings for the potential markets to see the type of work art directors prefer and what type of samples they'll keep on file, and obtain art or photo guidelines if they're available online.

Age-Level Index

Age groups are broken down into these categories in the Age-Level Index:

- **PICTURE BOOKS OR PICTURE-ORIENTED MATERIAL** are written and illustrated for preschoolers to eight-year-olds.
- **YOUNG READERS** are for five- to eight-year-olds.
- **MIDDLE READERS** are for nine- to eleven-year-olds.
- **YOUNG ADULT** is for ages twelve and up.

Age breakdowns may vary slightly from publisher to publisher, but using them as general guidelines will help you target appropriate markets. For example, if you've written an article about trends in teen fashion, check the **Magazines Age-Level Index** under the **Young Adult** subheading.

USING THE LISTINGS

Some listings begin with symbols. Many listings indicate whether submission guidelines are indeed available. If a publisher you're interested in offers guidelines, get them and read them. The same is true with catalogs. Sending for and reading catalogs or browsing them online gives you a better idea of whether your work would fit in with the books a publisher produces. (You should also look at a few of the books in the catalog at a library or bookstore to get a feel for the publisher's material.)

A Note for Artists & Photographers

Along with information for writers, listings provide information for illustrators and photographers. Illustrators will find numerous markets that maintain files of samples for possible future assignments. If you're both a writer and an illustrator, look for markets that accept manuscript/illustration packages and read the information offered under the **Illustration** subhead within the listings.

If you're a photographer, read the information under the **Photography** subhead within listings to see what format buyers prefer. For example, some want the highest resolution .jpg available of an image. Note the type of photos a buyer wants to purchase and the procedures for submitting. It's not uncommon for a market to want a résumé and promotional literature, as well as sample URLs linking to previous work. Listings also note whether model releases and/or captions are required.

QUICK TIPS FOR WRITERS & ILLUSTRATORS

If you're new to the world of children's publishing, reviewing this edition of *Children's Writer's & Illustrator's Market* may have been one of the first steps in your journey to publication. What follows is a list of suggestions and resources that can help make that journey a smooth and swift one:

1. MAKE THE MOST OF *CHILDREN'S WRITER'S & ILLUSTRATOR'S MARKET*. Be sure to take advantage of the articles and interviews in the book. The insights of the authors, illustrators, editors, and agents we've interviewed will inform and inspire you.

2. JOIN THE SOCIETY OF CHILDREN'S BOOK WRITERS AND ILLUSTRATORS. SCBWI, more than 22,000 members strong, is an organization for both beginners and professionals interested in writing and illustrating for children, with more than seventy active regional chapters worldwide. It offers members a slew of information and support through publications, a website, and a host of Regional Advisors overseeing chapters in almost every state in the U.S. and a growing number of locations around the globe. SCBWI puts on a number of conferences, workshops, and events on the regional and national levels (many listed in the **Conferences & Workshops** section of this book). For more information, visit www.scbwi.org.

3. READ NEWSLETTERS. Newsletters, such as *Children's Book Insider*, *Children's Writer*, and the *SCBWI Bulletin*, offer updates and new information about publishers on a timely basis and are relatively inexpensive. Many local chapters of SCBWI offer regional newsletters as well.

4. READ TRADE AND REVIEW PUBLICATIONS. Magazines such as *Publishers Weekly* (which offers two special issues each year devoted to children's publishing and is available on newsstands as well as through a digital subscription) offer news, articles, reviews of newly published titles, and ads featuring upcoming and current releases. Referring to them will help you get a feel for what's happening in children's publishing.

5. READ GUIDELINES. Most publishers and magazines offer writers' and artists' guidelines that provide detailed information on needs and submission requirements, and some magazines offer theme lists for upcoming issues. Many publishers and magazines state the availability of guidelines within their listings. You'll often find submission information on publishers' and magazines' websites.

6. LOOK AT PUBLISHERS' CATALOGS. Perusing publishers' catalogs can give you a feel for their line of books and help you decide where your work might fit in. If catalogs are available, visit publishers' websites, which often contain their full catalogs. You can also ask librarians to look at catalogs they have on hand. You can even search Amazon.com by publisher and year. (Click on "book search" then "publisher, date" and plug in, for example, "Lee & Low" under *publisher* and "2019" under *year*. You'll get a list of Lee & Low titles published in 2019, which you can peruse.)

7. VISIT BOOKSTORES. It's not only informative to spend time in bookstores—it's fun, too! Frequently visit the children's section of your local bookstore (whether a chain or an independent) to see the latest from a variety of publishers and the most current issues of children's magazines. Look for books in the genre you're writing or with illustrations similar in style to yours, and spend some time studying them. It's also wise to get to know your local booksellers; they can tell you what's new in the store and provide insight into what kids and adults are buying.

8. READ, READ, READ! While you're at that bookstore, pick up a few things, or keep a list of the books that interest you and check them out of your library. Read and study the latest releases, the award-winners and the classics. You'll learn from other writers, get ideas, and get a feel for what's being published. Think about what works and doesn't work in a story. Pay attention to how plots are constructed and how characters are developed, or the rhythm and pacing of picture book text. It's certainly enjoyable research!

9. TAKE ADVANTAGE OF INTERNET RESOURCES. There are innumerable sources of information available online about writing for children (and anything else you could possibly think of). It's also a great resource for getting (and staying) in touch with other writers and illustrators through listservs, blogs, social networking sites, and e-mail, and it can serve as a vehicle for self-promotion.

10. CONSIDER ATTENDING A CONFERENCE. If time and finances allow, attending a writers conference is a great way to meet peers and network with professionals in the field of children's publishing. As mentioned earlier, SCBWI offers conferences in various locations year round. (See scbwi.org and click on "Events" for a full conference calendar.) General writers' conferences often offer specialized sessions just for those interested in children's writing. Many conferences offer optional manuscript and portfolio critiques as well, giving you feedback from seasoned professionals. See the **Conferences** section of this book for information on conferences.

11. NETWORK, NETWORK, NETWORK! Don't work in a vacuum. You can meet other writers and illustrators through a number of the things listed earlier—SCBWI, conferences, online. Attend local meetings for writers and illustrators whenever you can. Befriend other writers in your area (SCBWI offers members a roster broken down by state)—share guidelines, share subscriptions, be conference buddies and roommates, join a critique group or writing group, exchange information, and offer support. Get online—subscribe to listservs, post on message boards and blogs, visit social networking sites and chatrooms. Exchange addresses, phone numbers, and e-mail addresses with writers or illustrators you meet at events. And at conferences, don't be afraid to talk to people, ask strangers to join you for lunch, approach speakers and introduce yourself, or chat in elevators and hallways.

12. PERFECT YOUR CRAFT AND DON'T SUBMIT UNTIL YOUR WORK IS AT ITS BEST. It's often been said that a writer should try to write every day. Great manuscripts don't happen overnight; there's time, research, and revision involved. As you visit bookstores and study what others have written and illustrated, really step back and look at your own work and ask yourself, *How does my work measure up? Is it ready for editors or art directors to see?* If it's not, keep working. Join a critique group or get a professional manuscript or portfolio critique.

13. BE PATIENT, LEARN FROM REJECTION, AND DON'T GIVE UP! Thousands of manuscripts land on editors' desks; thousands of illustration samples line art directors' file drawers. There are so many factors that come into play when evaluating submissions. Keep in mind that you might not hear back from publishers promptly. Persistence and patience are important qualities in writers and illustrators working toward publication. Keep at it—it will come. It can take a while, but when you get that first book contract or first assignment, you'll know it was worth the wait.

BEFORE YOUR
FIRST SALE

If you're just beginning to pursue your career as a children's book writer or illustrator, it's important to learn the proper procedures, formats, and protocol for the publishing industry. This article outlines the basics you need to know before you submit your work to a market.

FINDING THE BEST MARKETS FOR YOUR WORK

Researching markets thoroughly is a basic element of submitting your work successfully. Editors and art directors hate to receive inappropriate submissions; handling them wastes a lot of their time, not to mention your time and money, and they are the main reason some publishers have chosen not to accept material over the transom. By randomly sending out material without knowing a company's needs, you're sure to meet with rejection.

If you're interested in submitting to a particular magazine, see if it's available in your local library or bookstore, or read past articles online. For a book publisher, obtain a book catalog and check a library or bookstore for titles produced by that publisher. Most publishers and magazines have websites that include catalogs or sample articles (websites are given within the listings). Studying such materials carefully will better acquaint you with a publisher's or magazine's writing, illustration, and photography styles and formats.

Many of the book publishers and magazines listed in this book offer some sort of writers', artists', or photographers' guidelines on their websites. It's important to read and study guidelines before submitting work. You'll get a better understanding of what a particular publisher wants. You may even decide, after reading the submission guidelines, that your work isn't right for a company you considered.

SUBMITTING YOUR WORK

Throughout the listings, you'll read requests for particular elements to include when contacting markets. Here are explanations of some of these important submission components.

Queries, Cover Letters, & Proposals

A query is a no-more-than-one-page, well-written letter meant to arouse an editor's interest in your work. Query letters briefly outline the work you're proposing and include facts, anecdotes, interviews, or other pertinent information that give the editor a feel for the manuscript's premise—enticing her to want to know more. End your letter with a straightforward request to submit the work, and include information on its approximate length, date it could be completed, and whether accompanying photos or artwork are available.

In a query letter, think about presenting your book as a publisher's catalog would present it. Read through a good catalog and examine how the publishers give enticing summaries of their books in a spare amount of words. It's also important that query letters give editors a taste of your writing style. For good advice and samples of queries, cover letters, and other correspondence, consult *Guide to Literary Agents 2020*, as well as *Formatting & Submitting Your Manuscript, 3rd Ed.* and *The Writer's Digest Guide to Query Letters* (all published by Writer's Digest Books).

- **QUERY LETTERS FOR NONFICTION.** Queries are usually required when submitting nonfiction material to a publisher. The goal of a nonfiction query is to convince the editor your idea is perfect for her readership and that you're qualified to do the job. Note any previous writing experience and include published samples to prove your credentials, especially samples related to the subject matter you're querying about.
- **QUERY LETTERS FOR FICTION.** For a fiction query, explain the story's plot, main characters, conflict, and resolution. Just as in nonfiction queries, make the editor eager to see more.
- **COVER LETTERS FOR WRITERS.** Some editors prefer to review complete manuscripts, especially for picture books or fiction. In such cases, the cover letter (which should be no longer than one page) serves as your introduction, establishes your credentials as a writer, and gives the editor an overview of the manuscript. If the editor asked for the manuscript because of a query, note this in your cover letter.
- **COVER LETTERS FOR ILLUSTRATORS AND PHOTOGRAPHERS.** For an illustrator or photographer, the cover letter serves as an introduction to the art director and establishes professional credentials when submitting samples. Explain what services you can provide as well as what type of follow-up contact you plan to make, if any. Be sure to include the URL of your online portfolio if you have one.

- **RÉSUMÉS.** Often writers, illustrators, and photographers submit résumés with cover letters and samples. They can be created in a variety of formats, from a single page listing information to color brochures featuring your work. Keep your résumé brief, and focus on your achievements, including your clients and the work you've done for them, as well as your educational background and any awards you've received. Do not use the same résumé you'd use for a typical job application.
- **BOOK PROPOSALS.** Throughout the listings in the **Book Publishers** section, listings refer to submitting a synopsis, outline, and sample chapters. Depending on an editor's preference, some or all of these components, along with a cover letter, make up a book proposal.

A *synopsis* summarizes the book, covering the basic plot (including the ending). It should be easy to read and flow well. The gold standard for synopsis length is one page, single-spaced.

An *outline* covers your book chapter by chapter and provides highlights of each. If you're developing an outline for fiction, include major characters, plots, and subplots, and book length. Requesting an outline is uncommon, and the word is somewhat interchangeable with *synopsis*.

Sample chapters give a more comprehensive idea of your writing skill. Some editors may request the first two or three chapters to determine if they're interested in seeing the whole book. Some may request a set number of pages.

Manuscript Formats

When submitting a complete manuscript, follow some basic guidelines. In the upper-left corner of your title page, type your legal name (not pseudonym), address, and phone number. In the upper-right corner, type the approximate word count. All material in the upper corners should be single-spaced. Then type the title (centered) almost halfway down that page, the word "by" two lines under that, and your name or pseudonym two lines under "by."

The first page should also include the title (centered) one-third of the way down. Two lines under that, type "by" and your name or pseudonym. To begin the body of your manuscript, drop down two double spaces and indent five spaces for each new paragraph. There should be one-inch margins around all sides of a full page. (Manuscripts with wide margins are more readable and easier to edit.)

Set your computer to double-space the manuscript body. From page two to the end of the manuscript, include your last name followed by a comma and the title (or key words of the title) in the upper-left corner. The page number should go in the top right corner. Drop down two double spaces to begin the body of each page. If you're submitting a novel, type each chapter title one-third of the way down the page. For more information on manuscript formats, read *Formatting & Submitting Your Manuscript, 3rd Ed.* (Writer's Digest Books).

Picture Book Formats

The majority of editors prefer to see complete manuscripts for picture books. When typing the text of a picture book, don't indicate page breaks and don't type each page of text on a new sheet of paper. And unless you are an illustrator, don't worry about supplying art. Editors will find their own illustrators for picture books. Most of the time, a writer and an illustrator who work on the same book never meet or interact. The editor acts as a go-between who works with the writer and illustrator throughout the publishing process. *How to Write and Sell Children's Picture Books* by Jean E. Karl (Writer's Digest Books) offers advice on preparing text and marketing your work.

If you're an illustrator who has written your own book, consider creating a dummy or storyboard containing both art and text, and then submit it along with your complete manuscript and sample pieces of final art (hi-res PDFs or JPGs—never originals). Publishers interested in picture books specify in their listings what should be submitted. For tips on creating a dummy, refer to *How to Write and Illustrate Children's Books and Get Them Published*, edited by Treld Pelkey Bicknell and Felicity Trotman (North Light Books), or *How to Write, Illustrate, and Design Children's Books* by Frieda Gates (Lloyd-Simone Publishing Company).

Writers may also want to learn the art of dummy-making to help them through the writing process with things like pacing, rhythm, and length. For a great explanation and helpful hints, see the article "Cut and Paste" by Ann Whitford Paul in the Craft & Technique section (excerpted from *Writing Picture Books Revised and Expanded*, Writer's Digest Books 2018).

Mailing Submissions

Your main concern when packaging material is to be sure it arrives undamaged. If your manuscript is fewer than six pages, simply fold it in thirds and send it in a #10 (business-size) envelope. For a SASE, either fold another #10 envelope in thirds or insert a #9 (reply) envelope, which fits in a #10 neatly without folding.

Another option is folding your manuscript in half in a 6" × 9" (15cm × 23cm) envelope, with a #9 or #10 SASE enclosed. For larger manuscripts, use a 9" × 12" (23cm × 30cm) envelope both for mailing the submission and as a SASE (which can be folded in half). Book manuscripts require sturdy packaging for mailing. Include a self-addressed mailing label and return postage. If asked to send artwork and photographs, remember they require a bit more care in packaging to guarantee they arrive in good condition. Sandwich illustrations and photos between heavy cardboard that is slightly larger than the work. The cardboard can be secured by rubber bands or with tape. If you tape the cardboard together, check that the artwork doesn't stick to the tape. Be sure your name and address appear on the back of each piece of art or each photo in case the material becomes separated. For the packaging, use either a manila envelope, a foam-padded envelope, or a mailer lined with plastic air bubbles. Bind nonjoined edges with reinforced mailing tape and affix a typed mailing label or clearly write your address.

Mailing materials first class ensures quick delivery. Also, first-class mail is forwarded for one year if the addressee has moved, and it can be returned if undeliverable. If you're concerned about your original material reaching its destination, consider other mailing options such as UPS. No matter which way you send material, never send it in a way that requires a signature for receipt. Agents and editors are too busy to sign for packages.

Remember, companies outside your own country can't use your country's postage when returning a manuscript to you. When mailing a submission to another country, include a self-addressed envelope and International Reply Coupons, or IRCs. (You'll see this term in many listings in the Canadian & International Book Publishers section.) Your postmaster can tell you, based on a package's weight, the correct number of IRCs to include to ensure its return. If it's not necessary for an editor to return your work (such as with photocopies), don't include return postage.

Unless requested, it's never a good idea to use a company's fax number to send manuscript submissions. This can disrupt a company's internal business. Study the listings for specifics and visit publisher and market websites for more information.

E-mailing Submissions

Most correspondence with editors today is handled over e-mail. This type of communication is usually preferred by publishing professionals because it is easier to deal with as well as free. When sending an e-mailed submission, make sure to follow submission guidelines. Double-check the recipient's e-mail address. Make sure your subject line has the proper wording, if specific wording is requested. Keep your introduction letter short and sweet. Also, editors and agents usually do not like opening unsolicited attachments, which makes for an awkward situation for illustrators who want to attach .jpgs. One easy way around this is to post some sample illustrations on your website. That way, you can simply paste URL hyperlinks to your work. Editors can click through to look over your illustration samples, and there is no way your submission will be deleted because of attachments. That said, if editors are asking for illustration samples, they are most likely used to receiving unsolicited attachments.

Keeping Submission Records

It's important to keep track of the material you submit. When recording each submission, include the date it was sent, the business and contact name, and any enclosures (such as samples of writing, artwork or photography). You can create a record-keeping system of your own or look for record-keeping software in your area computer store.

Keep copies of articles or manuscripts you send together with related correspondence to make follow-up easier. When you sell rights to a manuscript, artwork, or photos, you can "close" your file on a particular submission by noting the date the material was accepted, what rights were purchased, the publication date, and payment.

Often writers, illustrators, and photographers fail to follow up on overdue responses. If you don't hear from a publisher within their stated response time, wait another month or so and follow up with an e-mail asking about the status of your submission. Include the title or description, date sent, and a SASE (if applicable) for response. Ask the contact person when she anticipates making a decision. You may refresh the memory of a buyer who temporarily forgot about your submission. At the very least, you will receive a definite "no" and free yourself to send the material to another publisher.

Simultaneous submissions

Writers and illustrators are encouraged to simultaneously submit—sending the same material to several markets at the same time. Almost all markets are open to this type of communication; those that do not take simultaneous submissions will directly say so in their submission guidelines.

It's especially important to keep track of simultaneous submissions, so if you get an offer on a manuscript sent to more than one publisher, you can instruct other publishers to withdraw your work from consideration. (Or, you can always use the initial offer as a way to ignite interest from other agents and editors. It's very possible to procure multiple offers on your book using this technique.)

AGENTS AND ART REPS

Most children's writers, illustrators, and photographers, especially those just beginning, are confused about whether to enlist the services of an agent or representative. The decision is strictly one that each writer, illustrator, or photographer must make for herself. Some are confident with their own negotiation skills and believe acquiring an agent or rep is not in their best interest. Others feel uncomfortable in the business arena or are not willing to sacrifice valuable creative time for marketing.

About half of children's publishers accept unagented work, so it's possible to break into children's publishing without an agent. Writers targeting magazine markets don't need the services of an agent. In fact, it's practically impossible to find an agent interested in marketing articles and short stories—there simply isn't enough financial incentive.

One benefit of having an agent, though, is it may speed up the process of getting your work reviewed, especially by publishers who don't accept unagented submissions. If an agent has a good reputation and submits your manuscript to an editor, that manuscript will likely bypass the first-read stage (which is generally done by editorial assistants and junior editors) and end up on the editor's desk sooner.

When agreeing to have a reputable agent represent you, remember that she should be familiar with the needs of the current market and evaluate your manuscript/artwork/photos accordingly. She should also determine the quality of your piece and whether it is salable. When your manuscript sells, your agent should negotiate a favorable contract and clear up any questions you have about payments.

Keep in mind that no matter how reputable the agent or rep is, she has limitations. Representation does not guarantee sale of your work. It just means an agent or rep sees potential in your writing, art, or photos. Though an agent or rep may offer criticism or advice on how to improve your work, she cannot make you a better writer, artist, or photographer.

Literary agents typically charge a fifteen percent commission from the sale of writing; art and photo representatives usually charge a twenty five or thirty percent commission. Such fees are taken from advances and royalty earnings. If your agent sells foreign rights or film rights to your work, she will deduct a higher percentage because she will most likely be dealing with an overseas agent with whom she must split the fee.

Be advised that not every agent is open to representing a writer, artist, or photographer who lacks an established track record. Just as when approaching a publisher, the manuscript, artwork, or photos, and query or cover letter you submit to a potential agent must be attractive and professional looking. Your first impression must be as an organized, articulate person. For listings of agents and reps, turn to the **Literary Agents & Art Reps** section.

UNLEASH YOUR STORYTELLING SUPERPOWER

....

Gabriela Pereira

Some say that at the heart of every story is a compelling character. I agree, but with one crucial caveat: Characters aren't just a necessary ingredient for your story—they *are* your story. Without them you have nothing more than a sequence of plot points. Characters humanize your story and give readers someone to root for. It's one thing to watch a newsreel or read a news report of a dramatic event, but when you experience that story through a character, it suddenly becomes more personal and powerful.

Compare, for example, Stephen Crane's newspaper account "The Sinking of the *Commodore*" (*The New York Press*, 1897) with his short story "The Open Boat," published in *Scribner's* magazine the following year. The former gives a sequence of events summing up what happened and when, who died, and how. The short story puts us in the boat, standing shoulder to shoulder with the desperate men as they bail the rising water and eventually abandon ship. Both accounts are from the same author, who was aboard the ship as it went down, but the short story is far more engaging. In it we see the events unfold as those sailors would have experienced them. When we craft stories around a character, we're not just telling it to our readers. We're showing them what it feels like to be there.

CHARACTER TYPES AND DESIRES

Every writer is drawn to a character archetype that she is particularly adept at bringing to life on the page. When it comes to the protagonist (or main character of your story), there are four such types. But before we dive into the particulars of each one, it's important to understand where these archetypes come from.

The protagonist is the focal point for your story. Who this character is and what she wants will drive the plot from beginning to end. The archetypes for this main character come from the intersection between her personality type and what she wants.

What Is Your Protagonist's Type?

Every character in literature falls into one of two types. No matter how nuanced or multifaceted your protagonist may be, at her most basic she is either an *everyman* or a *larger-than-life hero*.

The everyman protagonist—or what I like to call the ordinary Joe (or Jane)—is a regular guy going about his regular life, until something happens that turns his world upside down. The ordinary Joe is an unlikely hero caught in extraordinary circumstances. Though he is out of his league, he eventually rises beyond his ordinariness and does something astonishing. While at first glance the everyman might not be anything special, with the right motivation he can become a hero.

At the other end of the scale we have the larger-than-life hero. This character is so powerful and amazing, she seems almost perfect. We already know all the incredible things this character can do, so instead the key with bringing this character to life is to show a hint of vulnerability, a chink in the armor. After all, even Superman has his kryptonite.

Keep in mind these two personality types are not separate categories so much as they are opposite ends of the same spectrum. Most characters fall somewhere in the middle of two extremes, and as the story progresses they shift toward the opposite pole. I call this concept the "Opposite is Possible" theory. As writers it is our job to show that our main characters can become the opposite of how they appear at the beginning of the story. This is not about making your protagonist behave in ways that seem outlandish or *out of character*. Rather, the goal is to show the potential for change and plant the right hints, so when your everyman or larger-than-life hero does begin to shift, it doesn't force the reader out of the story. Remember that in every story, your protagonist must change in some way. Regardless of whether this change is extreme or subtle, you need to craft that main character with that possibility for change already baked into the narrative.

What Does Your Character Want?

"Make your character want something!" If you have taken a writing class or read any books about the craft, you have likely heard this advice. But it's not enough to make your protagonist want just anything. It has to be something so important to your character that the pursuit of that desire will keep your story moving. Making your character want a glass of water is not that compelling if he can simply get up and walk to the kitchen. But if your character is stranded on a raft in the middle of the ocean, then a glass of water takes on a whole new level of significance.

Just as there are two types of protagonists, there are also only two fundamental things your character can want. On one hand, your character might want to change something, whether in himself or the world around him. Or his most fervent desire might be the preservation of the status quo. Of course, no story is ever quite that simple, and often your character will want many different, sometimes contradictory things. When you consider all these desires, however, you will usually find that your character leans toward one type over the other. As with the character types, what your character wants exists on a spectrum rather than as two binary extremes.

At this point we have established that the protagonist's personality and desire fall on two distinct spectrums, but what does any of this have to do with us as writers? That's where the concept of the storytelling superpower comes in.

UNDERSTANDING YOUR STORYTELLING SUPERPOWER

When you intersect the protagonist's personality type with what she wants, you get one of four archetypes: the underdog, the disruptor, the survivor, and the protector. The storytelling superpower matrix shows how we get each of these archetypes from looking at character type and desire. The underdog is an everyman character who wants to change something in himself or the world around him. The disruptor also wants to effect change,

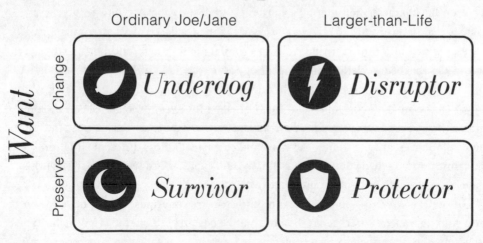

but in this case the character is in the larger-than-life category. The survivor and protector, on the other hand, both want to preserve something in their lives or their world, with the survivor as the everyman type and the protector as a larger-than-life hero.

As writers, we each tend to gravitate toward one of these archetypes over the other three. Look at stories you've written or ones you love to read. Chances are, one of these archetypes keeps coming up again and again. Think also about how you view yourself, and it's likely that the archetype you most like to write (or read about) is the one you identify with the most. This is not to say that you never identify with the other types, but it's likely that one of these resonates with you more than the others. I call this preferred archetype your *storytelling superpower*.

Identifying your storytelling superpower isn't meant to set limitations or compartmentalize your creativity. Rather, when you understand your natural tendencies and preferences, it allows you to play to your strengths and stretch yourself beyond your comfort zone. After all, if one archetype tugs at your heartstrings more than the others, you'll likely pour more passion and creative energy into crafting that character, which in turn will make your writing shine.

The Three Layers of Character Development

As you'll soon discover, each archetype has positive qualities as well as weaknesses. Understanding these pros and cons will help you ratchet up the stakes and increase the conflict in your story. You will also learn to identify aspects of your character that can be off-putting to your readers, making them want to stop reading altogether. Training yourself to identify these red flags will help you craft characters and stories your readers can't help but love.

To understand each storytelling superpower archetype, you need to consider three layers of that character: her internal state, her external situation, and how readers will relate to her. In business, a *SWOT analysis* assesses an idea based on its strengths, weaknesses, opportunities, and threats. We'll do a similar analysis here, adding an extra layer to consider the reader relationship. (See the opposite page.)

Strengths and weaknesses are positive or negative traits within your character. Who is your character at his core, and what does he believe in? Every protagonist carries some internal baggage, and these qualities will affect how he reacts to various events. These internal qualities are also somewhat fixed and consistent across different situations, which means that when your character finally *does* experience a transformation at this internal layer, it will feel significant to the reader.

The external layer—opportunities and threats—are situations that happen around or to your character. What scenarios bring out the best in your character? Which situations cause her to misbehave? And, even more interesting, what environments can you

Character Analysis

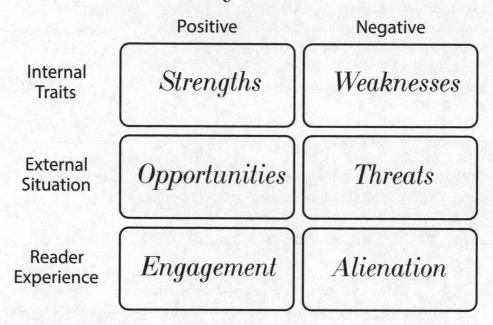

	Positive	Negative
Internal Traits	*Strengths*	*Weaknesses*
External Situation	*Opportunities*	*Threats*
Reader Experience	*Engagement*	*Alienation*

create to generate more conflict and tension for your protagonist? Conflict is what makes your story interesting, and while in some rare circumstances the character's internal state might be enough to create that tension, often the juiciest conflict arises from a mismatch between your protagonist's internal qualities and the environment where she finds herself.

Finally, you must also consider the relationship your character has with your reader. Which of your character's internal qualities will your readers find engaging, and which will alienate them? Does the character make choices or react to external situations in ways that resonate with readers, or are his behaviors repellent? There are also certain signature stories (e.g., rags to riches, fish out of water, etc.) that tend to work better with some archetypes than the others. Knowing what these signature stories are will help you determine if you are crafting the best narrative for your character.

MEET THE ARCHETYPES

The Underdog
The quintessential underdog is a relatable character with a deep desire to change something in herself or in the world around her. From Katniss Everdeen in Suzanne

Collins's *The Hunger Games* to Marty McFly in the Back to the Future film series, underdogs are regular people caught in extraordinary circumstances but who manage to rise to the occasion and do something heroic. Underdogs have a lot of pluck and determination, and they're not afraid to do whatever it takes to reach their goals. However, these characters may sometimes feel like they have something to prove, so they pick battles they cannot win. And while their "bring it on" attitude might be inspiring and may get them through challenging circumstances, underdogs don't cope well with situations that demand retreat.

In terms of reader engagement, this archetype is one of the most compelling because people love rooting for underdogs. When readers see an underdog come out on top, it makes them think, *If he can do it, maybe I can, too.* But if taken too far, the underdog can seem self-righteous, like they have a chip on their shoulder. And when underdogs stubbornly make bad choices or pick the wrong battles again and again, readers may stop feeling sympathy for the character.

Signature underdog stories include rags-to-riches narratives, epic David-and-Goliath-style battles, and classic comebacks in which a character who used to be on top needs to earn back his former glory. Because the underdog is so relatable and these stories often have such high stakes, underdogs are compelling characters that readers find irresistible.

This is one of the most prevalent archetypes in short fiction, in part because the scope of the short story favors everyman characters over their larger-than-life counterparts. Also, it's easier to convey a character's transformation within a condensed word count if the protagonist is already seeking out change in the first place, as is the case with underdogs. To see the underdog in action, look at Mrs. Mallard in Kate Chopin's "The Story of an Hour," the nameless narrator in "The Yellow Wallpaper" by Charlotte Perkins Gilman, or Pinky in Claire Davis's story "Labors of the Heart."

The Disruptor

Disruptors are larger-than-life characters who rebel against the status quo. They will do whatever it takes to change their societies, overcome all odds, and defeat tyranny. From Elizabeth Bennet in *Pride and Prejudice* by Jane Austen, to the title character in F. Scott Fitzgerald's *The Great Gatsby*, to Tris Prior in Veronica Roth's Divergent series, disruptors take on many different forms. They are charismatic leaders who know how to persuade and inspire the people around them, though they sometimes focus so much on their mission that they wind up hurting the people around them. And, like underdogs, disruptors may concentrate so much on instigating change that despite their larger-than-life qualities they might pick fights they cannot win.

This archetype is especially powerful if you want to infuse your writing with a broader message. Because disruptors possess a strong vision, they can serve as a vessel to communicate your own opinions or ideals from behind the scenes. The danger is that if you make the allegory or satire too heavy-handed, you may end up sounding preachy and alienating your readers. Also, with all that passion and charisma comes narcissism and a lack of empathy. Disruptors don't always play well with others, and there is a fine line between being a rebel and a bully. To make your disruptor a sympathetic or even likable character, you need to make her motivations clear to your readers and have her show at least some vulnerability.

This may be the reason why disruptors are far less common in short stories than in book-length literature. It takes time to tease out a character's motivations and show her weaknesses. Short fiction may not give you the necessary space to give your disruptor the depth she needs to engage your readers. This is where supporting characters can be useful in making a disruptor protagonist seem less bad by comparison. For instance, in Flannery O'Connor's "A Good Man Is Hard to Find," the grandmother is clearly unlikable—at the beginning of the story, it is hard for readers to sympathize with her. But when The Misfit holds the family captive and begins killing people, suddenly the grandmother doesn't seem quite as terrible, and we almost feel sorry for her. Similarly, Neddy Merrill in "The Swimmer" by John Cheever is a vapid, entitled snob, but as we see his life slowly deteriorate, we can't help but feel compassion for him.

The Survivor

Until now, we have looked at characters who want to change something either in themselves or in the world around them. Now we shift gears to archetypes driven by a desire for preservation. True to his name, a survivor character will do whatever it takes to preserve his life as he knows it. This may be a literal battle for survival or simply a desire not to shake up the status quo, but to the character it feels like a life-and-death struggle. Whether he is stranded on a desert island, kidnapped by an evil genius, or fighting to beat a terminal illness, readers will admire a survivor for his pluck, determination, and sheer creative willpower.

Like underdogs, survivors are of the everyman type, so readers see a part of themselves reflected in these characters and feel inspired when they persist against all odds. There is also something inherently hopeful in this archetype. Despite the doom and gloom that often follows these characters, they hold fast and persist even if all seems lost. Taken to the extreme, survivors can become self-reliant to a fault, often isolating themselves and failing to ask for help even when they desperately need it.

As writers, we also need to be careful not to let the character's struggle derail the story and make the issue or problem the story's only raison d'être. It's one thing to craft your narrative around a character who overcomes a trauma, but there has to be more to the story than the trauma alone. A beautiful example is the short story "Everyday Use," in which author Alice Walker explores issues of race, culture, and what it means to honor your heritage. While these themes are very present throughout, this is not a "racial heritage story" but is instead a story in which the theme comes to light in how differently the two main characters interpret and understand their racial heritage, and the conflict that subsequently arises between them.

The Protector

Protectors are larger-than-life heroes. Whether or not they wear capes, boots, and spandex, when the world is in danger, they are compelled to protect it and those they love. As with survivors, protectors are driven by a desire to preserve rather than to shake things up. Whether it's Iron Man, James Bond, or the nerdy and militant Dwight Schrute from the television series *The Office*, protectors show almost superhuman fortitude in their quest to defend what they believe in, prevent disasters, and stand up to the forces of evil.

Protectors are the most popular and prevalent character archetype, in part because heroic characters are powerful and inspiring. With all this power, however, often comes arrogance, and protectors can become obsessed with status and might even misuse their power. Also, these characters do not like to follow rules or be subordinate to someone else, and they detest change, especially if it undermines their authority. As with all larger-than-life characters, the way to make protectors engaging and relatable to readers is to show a hint of vulnerability and imperfection.

Protectors often are more likable than their disruptor counterparts. After all, it's easier for readers to root for a hero who is trying to *save* the world than for one who wants to *take over* the world or *change* it in his favor. However, the horror genre often features a counterexample in which the larger-than-life protector character is extremely unlikable. This can be seen in early classics from Nathaniel Hawthorne and Edgar Allan Poe. Unsympathetic protectors in these works are compelling because readers want to see them suffer. In Hawthorne's "Young Goodman Brown" and "The Birthmark," and in many of Poe's short stories, the appeal of the story isn't that the character succeeds but that he fails. And the best way to make a reader root against a character is to make that character unlikable.

YOUR CHARACTER'S TRANSFORMATION

It's important to remember that these four archetypes are not fixed categories. Remember that change is inherent in any work of fiction; if your character doesn't change in some way, then it's a static dossier, not a story. Keep in mind that this change does not have to be extreme. You do not need to push your character from one pole to its opposite. Instead, it can be a subtle shift.

Remember, too, that the character's desire needs to drive this transformation. In Flannery O'Connor's "A Good Man Is Hard to Find," we see the grandmother change from a narcissistic and manipulative matriarch into a desperate woman begging for her life. The story is so heart wrenching because she starts out trying to control and dominate everyone in her family but ends up losing all control—including over her own life. As you craft your characters, consider not only what they want and how they will transform throughout the story, but also how that desire will affect and support that change.

Your story's resolution hinges on how you resolve your protagonist's quest for what they desire. Does your character get what she wants? If so, does she still want it? The ending will depend on how you answer these two questions, but keep in mind that your character's personality, what she wants, and how she transforms in pursuit of it, are all inextricably linked. The key is to weave these threads together without tying up your story in a neat bow. Often what distinguishes a great story from a mediocre one is the artistry of the ending, which both resolves the character's quest for the thing she wants and also transforms her. When the ending feels unexpected *and* inevitable—surprising but also deeply satisfying to the reader—you know a story is truly exceptional.

GABRIELA PEREIRA is a writer, speaker, and self-proclaimed word nerd who wants to challenge the status quo of higher education. She is the instigator of DIYMFA.com, host of the podcast DIY MFA Radio, and has an MFA in creative writing from The New School. Her book *DIY MFA: Write with Focus, Read with Purpose, Build Your Community* is out now from Writer's Digest Books. To find out your storytelling superpower and learn how to unleash its full potential, take the quiz at DIYMFA.com/STSP.

TELLING YOUR STORY

by Ann Whitford Paul

"... the work of art as completely realized is the result of a long and complex process of exploration. ..." —JOYCE CARY

Remember when you were young, how you loved dressing up like Little Red Riding Hood or Superman? Remember how you changed clothes to play? Maybe you put on a firefighter helmet. Maybe you wore a crown. What does playing dress-up have to do with writing picture books? A lot!

In much the same way you changed outfits, you can change your story by telling it in different ways. Most picture-book stories are told by an *outside* narrator who speaks of the characters using third-person pronouns such as *he, she, it,* and *they*. In a completely unscientific study of twenty-five books I've typed up since the first edition of my book, *Writing Picture Books*, the majority—seventeen—were written in third person. Five stories were told by a character who was a *participant* in the story—a first-person narrator. That adds up to twenty-three.

And the odd-duck stories? *Smile Pout-Pout Fish* by Deborah Diesen is told in the apostrophe form, where the narrator talks to something that can't talk back. *Suppose You Meet a Dinosaur: A First Book of Manners* by Judy Sierra is told in the second person, where the writer addresses the reader and listener. Test picture books on your shelves or in the library to see for yourself. You, too, will find most books are told by an outside narrator—in the third person.

Novelist Willa Cather said, " … there are only two or three human stories, and they go on repeating themselves as fiercely as if they had never happened before. …" If we accept her statement, then the only way to differentiate our writing from other stories on the same topic is to write them uniquely. Today more than ever, you *must* make your story so original it will leap into an editor's hands and shout, "Publish *me!*"

To do that, explore different ways of telling your story. You may discard each experiment and go back to your original, but, trust me; no journey is wasted in pursuit of a story.

Let's play around with a familiar story by Aesop from 600 B.C.

THE ANT AND THE DOVE

An Ant went to the bank of a river to quench its thirst and being carried away by the rush of the stream, was on the point of drowning. A Dove sitting on a tree overhanging the water plucked a leaf and let it fall into the stream close to her. The Ant climbed onto it and floated in safety to the bank. Shortly afterwards a birdcatcher came and stood under the tree and laid his lime-twigs for the Dove, which sat in the branches. The Ant, perceiving his design, stung him in the foot. In pain the birdcatcher threw down the twigs, and the noise made the Dove take wing.
ONE GOOD TURN DESERVES ANOTHER.

Narrative voice—third-person-limited point of view

This story above is told in the popular, traditional form of an outside observer who relates what happens but doesn't participate in the action. Notice the narrator doesn't go into Dove's head. He starts his story with Ant and stays with her. As you've seen from my informal study, most picture books are told in this manner—by a single outside observer who goes only into the head of the main character.

Jacob's New Dress by Sarah and Ian Hoffman tells the moving story of a boy named Jacob who wants to wear a dress to his preschool. His mother is supportive, his father is slow to accept it, and one boy at school declares that boys don't wear dresses.

Jacob, though, knows what he wants and has the guts to do what feels right for him. The narrator doesn't allow us into any head but Jacob's. We know the other characters' feelings only by what Jacob hears them say. Read this book, not only for voice but for the way Jacob is an active character insisting on what he wants and solving his problems without much adult interference.

Change the point-of-view character

What happens if I tell this story with Dove as the main character?

One early morning Dove was munching seeds while sitting on the branch of a tree that overhung a river. "Help! Help!" he heard a thin voice squealing. Ant, struggling against the current, was thrashing about.

Dove couldn't let her drown. Thinking quickly, he tossed down a leaf. "Climb aboard," he sang. Ant did as directed and rode safely to shore.

That very afternoon, Dove was enjoying his nap when he was jarred awake by a loud scream and the sight of a birdcatcher hobbling off. Ant, the very same one he had rescued earlier, explained, "The birdcatcher was preparing a trap for you. I bit his foot, and off he ran." Dove was so grateful he sang to Ant.

"I'm not your mother;
I'm not your brother,
but I believe one good turn
deserves another."

This example is still told from only one point of view—Dove's. Switching main characters allowed me to expand on his role and put it in a song (a cheesy one), highlighting his singing ability.

Third-person-omniscient (or multiple) point of view

Let's see how this story might read if the narrator jumps between the heads of each character.

Ant went to the bank of a river to quench her thirst but lost her footing and tumbled into the water. The rush of the stream was carrying her away. She was sure she was a goner.

Luckily Dove was sitting on a tree branch overhanging the water and understood she was in danger. He didn't want Ant to drown, so he plucked a leaf and dropped it close to her. Ant couldn't believe her good fortune. She climbed onto it and floated safely to the bank.

Shortly afterwards a birdcatcher came and stood under Dove's tree. The birdcatcher, dreaming of dove supper, laid his lime-twig trap. But he didn't see Ant.

A good thing too, for Ant, grateful to Dove for saving her life, wanted to return the favor. Hidden by the grass, she crept, crept, crept closer . . . closer and BIT that birdcatcher.

"Yeow!" he howled. Dove awakened with a jerk just in time to see the birdcatcher hobble away.

In this telling, I'm initially in Ant's head, but then I move to Dove's. I even spend time in the birdcatcher's head.

While older readers can easily move from one character's viewpoint to another's, picture-book listeners, who are new to books, story, and plot, may have more trouble. It's best to make the action easy for them to follow. Staying in one character's head allows the listener to know whom to focus on and identify with.

However, *Extra Yarn* by Mac Barnett is an example of a successful book told in third-person-omniscient point of view. The story starts out with Annabelle, the main character, knitting sweaters from a box of never-ending yarn. She knits sweaters for everyone and then for animals. At that point, the author peers into the minds of the townspeople, who are sure she'll run out of yarn. But she doesn't.

Annabelle knits sweaters for houses, churches, barns, and birdhouses. The author also enters the mind of a jealous archduke who tries to buy her box of yarn. When she turns him down, he hires thieves to steal it. You'll have to read the book to find out what happens next. Being a knitter myself, this book appealed to me, but non-knitters will enjoy it, too. It has the feel of an old tale, and the illustrations won Jon Klassen a Caldecott Honor.

First-person, or the lyrical voice

In this point of view, the narrator is one of the story's participants. *I* and *we* are the key words that let you know you're in a first-person story. What happens when our story is told by Ant?

> Danger was the farthest thing from my mind. I was at the bank of a river and thirsty, so I leaned down for a drink. *Splash!* Into the water I fell, and the rushing current carried me away from shore. "Help! Help!" I cried, but we ants are small in body and in voice. No one could hear me. I was a goner for sure.
>
> Lucky for me, Dove was sitting on a branch overhanging the water and tossed me a leaf. I grabbed it, climbed aboard, and floated to shore. Was I grateful?
>
> You bet, and soon I had a chance to show it. A birdcatcher came to Dove's tree and started making a trap for him out of lime-twigs. Time for action!
>
> I stung him badly on the foot. "OWWWWWWWWWWW!" he howled. The noise warned Dove, who took flight and was saved. Just goes to show that one good turn deserves another.

With this first-person perspective, listeners experience the action and emotion along with Ant. They get into her head and feel her gratitude for her narrow escape. The story's tone changes.

If I'm having trouble getting into my character's head, I write a version in this voice to get to know her better. Perhaps I'll like it and leave it in the lyrical voice, but I may rewrite it again in third person. Either way, my experimentation wasn't wasted because I gained a deeper understanding of my character's feelings.

However, first person has drawbacks. Telling your story this way doesn't allow you an opportunity to write about offstage actions. The main character—the *I*-writer—must be on every page. Also, telling it in this manner lets the reader know that the narrator survives. We might not know in what state, but we're certain he lived to tell the tale.

Check out *Ralph Tells a Story* by Abby Hanlon. Ralph's teacher tells him that stories are everywhere. His classmates always find them, and although Ralph tries and tries, he fails to come up with a story. Since the book is narrated by Ralph, we feel his pain and suffer with him. More importantly, we rejoice in his success when he finally does tell a story.

Now I'm going to tell the story again in first person, but with the birdcatcher as the narrator. Here's the opening:

> I woke this morning with a longing for dove stew. Delicious, delightful, delectable dove stew. I'm not one for inaction. Not me. I gathered string and lime-twigs and set off to make my dream a reality.

You can see how if you wrote this to the end, it wouldn't be the story we started with. That change is what we're after, something to liven up a tired and much-told tale. First-person voices may take several different forms, including letters and journal/diary entries.

One long letter

> Dear Mother,
>
> So much has happened since I left your nest, I had to write. Thank you for teaching me to not ignore those in need. Yesterday, I was sitting on a branch in the loveliest of trees, minding my business, enjoying the breeze. The peace was broken by squeals from the stream below. A poor ant was struggling to swim to shore, but the current was too strong. I couldn't swoop down and pluck her from the water. My beak might have broken her in two, so I came up with an alternate plan. I plucked a leaf from the tree and tossed it down. The ant had just enough energy to pull herself aboard and float to safety.
>
> That might have been the end of the story, but after she'd dried off, caught her breath, and calmed down, along came a birdcatcher. I remember your lesson about flying away from those nasty people, and I would have, but I was dozing and didn't realize he was setting a trap for me. Luckily that birdcatcher was wearing sandals. Even luckier for me that ant was nearby and knew exactly what was up! She bit that birdcatcher's foot! I'd be surprised if you couldn't hear his scream from where you live. You can bet it startled me. Off I flew, and off the birdcatcher hopped, clutching his foot, moaning in pain.
>
> I'm so thankful you taught me that we eat seeds, not insects. If that ant hadn't been around to save me, I shudder to think what would have happened. For one thing, you certainly wouldn't be reading this letter.
>
> Your Loving Son,
> Featherly

My favorite example of a published book told in a single letter is *Nettie's Trip South* by Ann Turner. In this compelling story, Nettie writes to her friend Addie about her experiences visiting the South just before the Civil War. Among other incidents, she describes attending a slave auction and the horror of watching two young children being separated. She returns home forever changed. Although this book was published in 1987, it remains in print. I urge you to read this beautiful and poignant story.

A more contemporary book that takes the form of one letter is *Love, Mouserella* by David Ezra Stein, where a little mouse writes her grandmother a letter about all she's done since her grandmother returned to her home in the country.

Journal or diary

Monday

Dear Diary,

What an exciting day! If it hadn't been for me, there would have been one less ant in this world. I was minding my own business on a low tree branch overhanging a river when I heard the tiniest of screams from an ant splashing in the water, struggling to reach shore. It was easy to see if no one helped her, she would drown. But no one rushed to the rescue. Where were her mom and dad? Her cries grew more frantic, so I tugged a fat maple leaf off of the tree and tossed it down. That ant had just enough strength to pull herself up onto the leaf and float to shore. She was one grateful ant and thanked me profusely.

Friday

Dear Diary,

Remember that ant I wrote about? Now I'm the one who's grateful and thanking her profusely. Here's why:

I was dozing on my tree branch when a horrific howling awakened me just in time to see that birdcatcher, the bane of my existence, clutching his foot and hopping away. I had no idea what to make of this crazy behavior until the ant I'd dropped the leaf to scampered up the tree trunk and explained how she'd stopped that mean man from laying a trap for me: She bit his foot! Good thing the birdcatcher was wearing sandals and good thing the ant knew this was my tree. I'd saved her, so she saved me.

Diary of a Spider by Doreen Cronin is written in diary form and is a great follow-up to her earlier success, *Diary of a Worm*. Now let's be a bit more daring with the story.

Second person

The word *you* is a clue here. Using *you*, the author invites the reader into the story. This is how Aesop's fable might read if written in second person:

If you saw your neighbor's dog tangled up in its leash, what would you do?

I hope you'd rush to its rescue.

Why?

Because someday maybe that dog could help you. And that day might come as soon as the very next day.

You'll hear that dog bark, bark, barking and after you get over your annoyance at the noise, you'll go outside and see smoke coming out of your trash can. You'll grab a hose and spray out the fire. And you'll know it really is true that one good turn deserves another.

Notice here, I took the story in a completely different direction, getting rid of the dove and the ant and inserting a dog. That's the fun of experimenting. Your story can fly off to places you'd never imagined even though the new version was always where it was supposed to be.

Suppose You Meet a Dinosaur makes use of this point of view, but you don't need to look further than the If You Give a … series written by Laura Numeroff: *If You Give a Mouse a Brownie, If You Give a Cat a Cupcake, If You Give a Dog a Donut, If You Give a Moose a Muffin*, and on and on. In each of these, the author talks to the reader. Check out at least one of them to see how involving this form of inviting the listener to participate in the action can be.

In all the retellings, notice I didn't switch the voice midstory. This would confuse our young audience. They wouldn't know who the main character was or with whom to identify. Once you start a picture book in one point of view, stick to it.

A FEW FINAL WORDS

Isn't it interesting to see how changing the point of view can affect a story so markedly? I hope you'll experiment with this in your story and in any future stories you write.

ANN WHITFORD PAUL has published more than twenty picture books (including board books, early-readers, a poetry collection, plus a variety of fiction and non-fiction, rhymed and prose picture book, including the popular series that began with *If Animals Kissed Goodnight*). Many of her poems have appeared in anthologies and her essays have been published by several newspapers. She lives with her husband in Los Angeles and hopes you'll visit her website www. annwhitfordpaul.com. This essay is excerpted from *Writing Picture Books Revised and Expanded Edition* (Writer's Digest, 2018).

THROUGH THE LOOKING GLASS

As publishing endeavors to address diversity and inclusion in fiction, an inevitable question arises: Can authors write characters whose experiences are outside of their own?

by Diana M. Pho

Questions of representation in literature are a tale as old as time, coupled with that other great conundrum: How can we write about experiences outside of our own? The best fiction has the ability to transport readers into another's shoes and make readers consider a new perspective. And while the question of writing the Other is evergreen, the assessment of how to do so successfully is an ever-evolving story.

When I think about why writing across difference is so important, I remember my childhood and how books changed my perception of the world and of myself. Two specific books were a huge influence—Laurence Yep's 1982 novel *Dragon of the Lost Sea* and George Selden's 1960 book *The Cricket in Times Square*—but between them, their treatment of Chinese characters and culture couldn't be more different. Yep spent much time doing research into Chinese myths and legends before even taking up the project, and I was completely swept away by the adventures of the dragon princess Shimmer and the human orphan Thorn on their quest to restore the Inland Sea. *The Cricket in Times Square*, on the other hand, featured racist stereotypes: Sai Fong, who teaches the newspaper boy Mario about the importance of crickets in Chinese culture, speaks with a broad transliterated accent and works out of a derelict laundromat. Mario and his family benefit from talented Chester the cricket, while Sai Fong remains a mystical minor character.

While both books were praised during their time, *The Cricket in Times Square* sent a certain message about Asian characters: We all talked in broken English, held ignoble jobs and acted only in service to the white characters. Yep's story, however, showed how characters who looked like me could be heroes, and demonstrated that not all fantasies must take place in medieval Europe.

A few lessons for today's authors can be drawn here. One is that writers are capable of composing stories that uplift the marginalized (or, alternatively, ones that push them down). The second is that while Selden might not have realized how racist his portrayal was, and certainly the mostly white literary community of the time didn't either, it doesn't excuse the fact that the book has biased content. And a third lesson is the understanding that writing effective diverse stories is a skill that *can* be learned. Later on in high school, I picked up Robert Olen Butler's 1992 short story collection, "A Good Scent From a Strange Mountain." I was astounded by the way Butler captured life in the Vietnamese immigrant community, which resonated with my own family experiences. Writing the Other *is* possible. It's simply a matter of doing so respectfully, and responsibly.

WRITING IS HARD, BUT WRITING #OWNVOICES IS HARDER

In conversations about the challenge of getting published and the current movements around diversity and inclusion, one misconception I've heard from many aspiring authors is that marginalized writers are getting an "advantage." Historically, culturally dominant voices have had a leg up in publishing (typified by straight, white, able-bodied men). In recognition of that imbalance, it's true that publishers are working hard to right the ship by supporting more books by diverse writers. This is not to hit any sort of "quota," but to bring enriching stories and voices to the marketplace that have long been missing. For example, Angie Thomas's 2017 novel, *The Hate U Give*, has a powerful take on police brutality, made more so from being written by a black woman affected by this violence. The hashtag #ownvoices has been used online to elevate stories about underrepresented communities as told by writers in those communities.

Despite recent efforts, statistics still show that #ownvoices stories are being left behind in the industry. It's a misunderstanding to think that marginalized authors have a sudden advantage because "diversity is trendy." To take some recent numbers from children's literature: According to the Cooperative Children's Book Center annual survey, multicultural content increased from 28 percent in 2017 to 31 percent in 2018, but the number of black, Native and Latinx *writers* only increased from 6 percent to 7 percent. This means that publishers are choosing to publish more white authors who write multicultural content than writers of color. More evidence can be found in the genres I edit, science fiction and fantasy. *Fireside Magazine* has done extensive work in recording the lack of black writers published in short fiction in their 2016 #BlackSpecFic report, which has been corroborated by *FIYAH* magazine's Presence of Blackness (POB) Score Report of 2018. Such cases illustrate how power dynamics impact who gets published, how they get published and who gets ignored.

On top of institutional challenges, underrepresented writers face cultural challenges as well. Because of the historic lack of marginalized stories in pop culture, minority writers must deal with the added pressure that their individual story comes to inherently represent the whole of their community. Even the blockbuster success *Crazy Rich Asians* was hit with backlash that it did not represent the entire Asian diaspora. Policing identities has also become an issue: That is, whether a marginalized person can prove they have the "credentials" to write about their own experiences. This has been especially harmful to queer writers who've felt forced to out themselves in order to write about the LGBTQ community.

As long as the majority of industry decision-makers remain white, straight, able-bodied and affluent, anyone who falls outside of those categories will have additional obstacles to overcome in order to be published.

INVADER, TOURIST, OR GUEST: A WRITER'S GUIDE TO CULTURAL DIFFERENCE

Bearing all that in mind, what kind of responsibility does a writer then shoulder when writing characters whose experience extends outside of their own identity? One ethical approach has been described in Nisi Shawl's essay "Appropriate Cultural Appropriation." (Shawl also co-wrote *Writing the Other*, the classic volume on this subject, with co-author Cynthia Ward.) Shawl asks creators what mindset they have when looking to add other cultures or experiences in their work: Are they an "invader," a "tourist" or a "guest"?

An "invader," as the term implies, is the most harmful approach, in which writers act without any regard for the feelings of the community or the responsibilities in representing them. "Invaders arrive without warning, take whatever they want for use in whatever way they see fit," Shawl explains. "Theirs is a position of entitlement without allegiance."

Examples of an invader mindset include:

- cursory research focusing on what seems "exotic" to your world-building
- projection of stereotypes, desires or fantasies about a different gender when writing characters instead of making them dynamic people
- assuming that not including queer people or people of color in a story is being "historically accurate."

Writers who act as "tourists" are a step-up. Tourists acknowledge they are outsiders deeply interested and invested in learning more about the Other. As this term also implies, however, tourists can act positively or negatively—think immersive traveler Anthony Bourdain in "Parts Unknown" versus an undergraduate on spring break in Cancun. A respectful tourist mindset embodies these qualities:

- an honest curiosity and willingness to learn, and ability to ask questions from experts when help is needed
- awareness that a writer should respect cultural boundaries and not impose their own biases
- ability to compensate the community for their experiences, whether through financial means or meaningful, equal knowledge-sharing
- realization that a story offers a visit to a new experience, but also making conscious efforts to boost the originators.

A negative example of a tourist mindset would be "going native": the assumption that one can instantly gain expertise through limited time or experience, and showing such superficial knowledge off in a self-important way.

According to Shawl, acting as a "guest"—being someone with insider knowledge, familiar connections and trust—is a level of authenticity and craft a writer can strive for, but is a status that must be given to them by the community they wish to represent. No one can assume to be a guest, but must instead be welcomed as one.

FURTHER READING

- *Fireside Magazine*. "#BlackSpecFic special report." medium.com/fireside-fiction-company/blackspecfic-571c00033717
- *FIYAH Magazine*. "POB Score: A FIYAH Project." fiyahlitmag.com/blackspecfic/the-pob-score-project
- Lee and Low Books. "The Diversity Gap in Children's Book Publishing." blog.leeandlow.com/2018/05/10/the-diversity-gap-in-childrens-book-publishing-2018
- Nisi Shawl. "Appropriate Cultural Appropriation." writingtheother.com/appropriate-cultural-appropriation
- Nisi Shawl and Cynthia Ward. *Writing the Other: A Practical Approach*. Aqueduct Press: 2005.aqueductpress.com/books/978-1-933500-00-3.php
- Daniel José Older. "12 Fundamentals Of Writing 'The Other' (And The Self)." buzzfeed.com/danieljoseolder/fundamentals-of-writing-the-other
- Uma Krishnaswami. "Interview Wednesday: Stacy Whitman of Tu Books." umakrishnaswami.blogspot.com/2011/07/interview-wednesday-stacy-whitman-of-tu.html

THE NEXT STEPS IN WRITING DIVERSITY

After examining the different approaches as described by Shawl, here are some follow-up actions I'd recommend based on my own editorial experience:

1) Know yourself—and your limitations.

Being able to effectively write from the experience of others requires not just strong ability, but also a level of awareness about yourself and your role as a storyteller. As Daniel José Older acknowledges in his essay "12 Fundamentals of Writing 'The Other' (And the Self)," it's a writer's job to enter into someone else's head. But can writers take ownership of the stories and experiences of another in the process? Would doing so help enrich the reading experience, or would it be considered a type of theft? Older suggests that writers ask themselves: *Why do you feel it falls to you to write someone else's story? Why do you have the right to take on another's voice? And should you do this?*

Especially considering the statistics mentioned earlier, it's important to consider what socio-political advantages you may possess, and how your story might overshadow or limit opportunities for a marginalized community.

2) Do your research—then do research on your research.

Research is key, but *how* you research even more so. Look at your sources and consider whether they hold any possible bias. For example, the popular 19th century photographer Edward Curtis tended to romanticize and mislabel his Native American subjects, thus turning their experience into art that didn't accurately or respectfully depict the community he was portraying. Make sure to use museums, libraries, documentaries, academic sources, community cultural centers and trusted experts to inform your portrayal.

3) Get some sensitivity readers.

Sensitivity readers (also known as cultural consultants) act like a critique group, except their specialty is evaluating authenticity and flagging any possible incorrect or damaging elements. Always use more than one such reader, as one person should not be treated as if their advice represents an entire people. Change readers with each major revision to maintain a fresh perspective. Be prepared to get some great insights, but also be ready to act accordingly if a sensitivity reader says a story aspect is offensive or inappropriate and must be scrapped. Sensitivity readers should not be treated like stamps of approval, but as advisors whose opinion must be taken seriously. Also, be sure to fairly compensate sensitivity readers—their work is equivalent to a developmental edit and should be treated as such.

4) Realize your story is still your responsibility, not anyone else's.

When your work is published, its criticism will span broadly: Some story aspects may be praised for their authenticity, while others may be seen as inaccurate. Inevitably, you will make mistakes. *That's okay.* No piece of art can be perfect. It's also not the critic's fault for pointing out flaws. While there are many ways to handle reviews, criticism regarding cultural appropriation, racism, sexism or another form of oppression should not be ignored or cast aside, no matter how much work you've done to avoid harm. You, and only you, are responsible for addressing these criticisms. At the very least, sincerely apologize and make amends to do better, as evidenced with concrete actions.

Reflecting on what you've now learned, does writing across difference sound complicated? Well, it should be! Understanding that alone is the tip of the iceberg. That said, with time, craft and true ethical dedication to your work, it *is* possible to portray diversity effectively. In doing so, you'll also master a good chunk of what it means to be a quality writer. It is an act of courage to put your book out into the world, no matter your background. It is also an act of deep understanding and respect to write the Other well. Poet Nikki Giovanni may have summed up the matter best: "Writers don't write from experience. Writers write from empathy."

DIANA M. PHO is a Hugo Award-nominated editor at Tor Books and Tor.com Publishing. She is also a published academic, playwright, and activist. This essay was previously published in the February 2019 issue of *Writer's Digest*.

SINISTER, YET SYMPATHETIC

The key to a great story is a villain that readers can relate to. These tips from several international bestselling authors show how to enchant readers with the sinister.

....

by Sam Boush

Imagine Little Red Riding Hood: ruddy cheeks, basket full of goodies, off to Grandma's house with not a care in the world. She's taking in the sights, smelling flowers, throwing that towel over her meat pies to keep them warm and fresh. The very picture of innocence: unaware that these woods hold danger.

Then, BAM! You know what happens next.

Except this time, it doesn't.

No wolf emerges from the forest, salivating over the savory treats. No heroic woodcutter, no gobbled granny. No threat. No danger. No salvation.

Where's the story in that? Without tension or drama, there's no story at all. And none of it can happen without the most important character: the villain.

Without an antagonist, *Little Red Riding Hood* is a nature walk, *Jaws* is a day at the beach, and *First Blood* is just Rambo sleeping rough. Without a villain, Harry Potter's parents are never murdered, Gotham City's worst crime is jaywalking, and Luke and Leia grow up in a stable, non-planet-destroying household.

Bad guys, please save us from these boring outcomes!

You already know that a story needs a villain. Where we all struggle, however, is making our antagonist convincing, memorable, and frightening all at the same time. It's one of the most fundamental problems every storyteller faces: how to bring an antagonist to life, making them believable in the eyes of readers and letting them reveal their sinister true selves.

Seven international bestselling fiction writers have offered their advice on how to create a compelling villain. They've shared their best practices to help you build the best villain possible—a character every bit as important as your protagonist.

MAKE YOUR VILLAIN RELATABLE

People don't do things just because they're bad. Sure, there are rotten people out there, but most of us behave out of a place of self-rationalization. Villains are the same.

"Villains are tricky," says Robert Dugoni, *Wall Street Journal* bestselling author of the Tracy Crosswhite series. "If you make them too over the top, they're not believable, and if they're not believable they're not frightening. I think most villains are born of circumstance, not genetics. So for an author, I think the question to ask is, 'How far would you go in the same circumstance?' Because what is truly frightening is when the villain is relatable."

Antagonists, like protagonists, think what they're doing is right. Your villain doesn't think they're bad. From their perspective, they're doing what they think is—if not exactly good—at least justifiable. And the more they're driven by a justified purpose, the more relatable they'll be.

None of us would go as far as the murderers that Dugoni's protagonist, homicide detective Tracy Crosswhite, encounters. Though we're not killers ourselves, we can certainly understand the blur in the line between good and evil, which these villains choose to step over. Maybe we've even stepped over lesser lines at one time or another. But what makes a villain relatable is, despite their worst actions, understanding how that journey to the gray area happens.

Maybe it's an obsession with the dark side that goes too far. A white lie that snowballs. A slope that gets a little too slippery, a little too fast. Whatever brings your villain to cross the line, it's more memorable and enthralling if the reader can relate to their decisions, even while disagreeing with them.

KNOW YOUR VILLAIN'S MOTIVATION

In the Harry Potter series, Severus Snape's heart was broken by Lily. In Shakespeare's *Othello*, Iago was unfairly passed over for promotion. In the Lord of the Rings series, Sméagol found one of those rings of power, beginning his transformation into Gollum.

And in the Song of Ice and Fire series, Cersei Lannister was pawned off as a child bride to a king.

What do all these characters have in common? They broke bad as an outcome of circumstance, not because they were just built that way. Like the rest of us, villains are made by their experiences.

Readers want the same from your antagonist. They want to know what brought them to this place of wickedness and what motivates them to go beyond the norms of behavior, toward evil deeds. Readers want to know what continues to drive the villain, despite pressures to give up, admit mistakes and pay for their crimes.

"The most convincing villains are the ones who appear to be completely normal on the surface," says Karin Slaughter, whose books (including the Grant County series) have sold more than 35 million copies worldwide. "They seem just like you or me or your best friend from college or favorite cousin. But once you start to pay attention to their actions, you see that they are very self-oriented and incredibly motivated by something, whatever their own brand of something is, to satisfy themselves at any expense."

So, what motivates your antagonist?

There are many possible reasons for doing evil. Your villain might be activated by greed, raising one favored group over another or revenge. Almost anything will do, as long as it fits with the character and explains why they behave the way they do.

By explaining your villain's motivation, you allow your reader to understand them, even empathize with them.

MAKE YOUR VILLAIN A WORTHY RIVAL

The nature of the protagonist and antagonist are of two opposing forces. The protagonist works to push forward a goal. The antagonist works against that same goal. At the heart of it, this is what makes a story.

But it's not much of a story when the villain doesn't stack up. To be a counterbalance, the villain needs to be a power in her own right. Formidable. Frightening. Moreover, to create real tension, the antagonist should be of an even greater power than the protagonist, so that the reader genuinely worries that the hero won't prevail.

"The villain has to be very skilled at what they do," says Andy Weir, *The New York Times* bestselling author of *The Martian*. "They have to be a good threat or rival to the protagonist."

Granted, Weir recognizes that his antagonists aren't often people and good stories sometimes have nature as the villain. This works just as well. What's a more terrifying villain than a cold red planet 34 million miles from home?

In fact, using place as a villain is common. In *Jurassic Park*, the park is the principle menace, not the bumbling computer programmer, Dennis Nedry. The same applies in many stories. Alice's wonderland is the real villain in *Through the Looking Glass*, just as is Wonka's factory in *Charlie and the Chocolate Factory*.

ALLOW YOUR VILLAIN SOME HUMANITY

Your villain isn't all evil. No one is. In fact, a good villain has hopes and dreams, a past, longings and desires. They're just like the rest of us: human, imperfect.

"Give him a deeply complex, yet relatable reason for doing the evil that he does," says David Baldacci, international bestselling author of *Wish You Well* and *The Christmas Train*. "Allow him a smidgen of redeemable backstory to keep the reader honest and engaged."

Even if you choose to make your villains something other than human, you can still give them personality. Weir's protagonist in *The Martian* has a love/hate relationship with Mars, so not surprisingly, Weir recommends showing the humanity of villains. "The villain is best if they are also likeable," he says. According to Weir, you've succeeded in creating a great villain "if the audience actually roots for them to succeed in the short term. Though, of course, the audience should be rooting against them in the climax."

When your reader really gets to know a villain and sees they aren't all bad, that's when the fun begins. As much as readers love to hate a bad guy, the thing that really gets them hooked is when they also start to see themselves in the villain.

AVOID CLICHÉD VILLAIN DIALOGUE

"Bwa-ha-ha," the villain said, dry-washing her hands in her underground lair. "I'll get you, protagonist, if it's the last thing I do! Say goodbye to your trusty sidekick!"

That may have been painful to read (it was painful to write), but I hope it serves as an example of—and fair warning against—clichéd villain dialogue. We've all seen these kinds of lines in books, movies and TV. It's lazy. It's forgettable. And most of all—the cardinal sin—it's boring.

So how do you write better dialogue for your villain?

Lois Lowry, author of the Newbery Medal-winning books *Number the Stars* and *The Giver,* has written some of the most compelling villains for young readers, including Nazis and politicians. She suggests looking to contemporary examples of humans you might find maleficent and listening to what they say. She also notes that "verbs are always good for villains: *leered*, *hissed*, *muttered*, *lied*."

Caroline Kepnes, author of *You* (which also became a hit Netflix series), recommends getting inside your villain's head. "Explore the difference between the said and the unsaid," she says. "Write the inner monologue that's happening as the scene plays out. Highlighting the mental gymnastics that happen behind the scenes, in the mind, will help ground your characters. You might cut all of it, but you'll learn so much about your characters by analyzing the dimensions of motive and the hidden wounds within each line of dialogue."

When it comes to writing dialogue between your protagonist and antagonist, it comes back to motivation. Kepnes, whose most famous villain is an unrelenting stalker, has some great advice here, too. "The more you know your villain, the more you will create opponents who are specifically threatening," she says. "At the end of the day, we all have certain personality types that bring out the best in us, the worst. I always want to relate to the universal tension, the idea that we all, at times, feel as if people were sent to unnerve us."

DISPLAY YOUR VILLAIN'S BEST SIDE

While a villain's evil deeds are their most notable, it's often their unique (and sometimes even positive) qualities that set them apart. After all, who would Hannibal Lecter be if all he did was dine on human flesh, without the charm and charisma that made him memorable? Or Sherlock Holmes's archenemy, Professor Moriarty, without his cunning? Or Dolores Umbridge without her perfectionism?

"I think creating a compelling villain is no different from creating a compelling protagonist," says Emily St. John Mandel, author of the National Book Award-finalist novel *Station Eleven*. "I'm not sure anyone is completely evil or completely good; so I think a compelling hero or heroine needs to have flaws, and I think a compelling villain needs to have virtues. Your villain will be no less frightening for taking an interest in animal rescue or donating to humanitarian causes or being an excellent parent, but he or she will be a more interesting person for the reader to think about."

Characters often resonate when negative characteristics are offset with positive. Michael Corleone from *The Godfather* wouldn't be the classic bad guy he is in later books if not for his love of family and willingness to sacrifice for them. Similarly, the pirate Long John Silver is dastardly across the board in *Treasure Island*, except in his protective nature toward the young protagonist, Jim. For both Corleone and Silver, we can't bring ourselves to hate them, even though we know they're awful people.

In the end, this insight into character is what makes a universal story. Maybe the hero prevails. Maybe the antagonist comes away victorious. Maybe no one wins, and the conflict lives on. But through the journey, the reader is able to connect with all the characters, believe them, understand them and relate to them.

Even the villain.

SAM BOUSH is the author of *All Systems Down* (Lakewater Press, 2018). His second book, *All Threats Within*, will be published in September 2019. This article was previously published in the July/August 2019 issue of *Writer's Digest*.

CUT AND PASTE

Making a Mock-Up Book

....

by Ann Whitford Paul

"Putting together the … book dummy is a necessary process—it is the foundation for your book and lies at the heart of good bookmaking."
—Uri Shulevitz

You've written your story. You've revised the opening until it's tight and engaging. You've experimented with different ways to tell your story and chosen the best one. Your characters are strong, unique, and believable; your plot is a page-turner, and the ending resolves the main conflict. You've tied things together so that your audience will be satisfied and will want to read or hear the book again. Your manuscript, whether written in poetry or prose, is poetic. You've worked to use the right words, and you've cut out unnecessary ones. You should be finished, but. …

You're not done yet! You need to make a dummy. A dummy is a layout of your text onto thirty-two pages. It's helpful in determining if the structure of your story fits the picture-book format.

"But I'm not an illustrator," you plead. "I write the words. Illustrators may find making a dummy a positive exercise, but it's a waste of time for me."

Trust me on the helpfulness of dummies. For years I tried to get away with not doing them. Making check marks or stars on the hard copy of my manuscript was surely enough to show me where the page turns came and if I had enough illustration possibilities. *Wrong!* I am one of the converted—a born-again dummy maker. I never send out a manuscript without first doing a dummy—a visual and tactile way of evaluating my story.

Most of us who write for children are kids at heart. Creating a dummy takes you away from your computer and gives your back and neck a break. Cutting and pasting allows you to use different hand and arm muscles, so it can be a nice change of pace.

We think of a dummy as the last stage of the revision process, but it may expose less obvious problems and lead to more revisions and more dummies. None of my dummies are for my editor to see. Some writers sketch out a simple, rough dummy early in the writing process, sometimes even before a word is written. They do this storyboard on a single sheet of paper, dividing it into separate pages and spreads as I have done below:

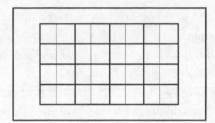

A spread is two facing pages that end up with an illustration that fills and spans both of those pages. You can purchase these forms in most art stores. The writer then uses single words or brief phrases to indicate action, page turns, etc. This initial dummy/storyboard does not include the story text. Its purpose is to give a general overview of the story's spacing.

The dummy we're going to make next is closer to a finished book with numbered pages you can turn. Print a hard copy of your story, and then grab some blank paper, lift-off tape, and scissors.

THE DUMMY FORM

Staple sixteen pieces of 8½" × 11" (22cm × 28cm) paper together along the left side. Picture-book manuscripts rarely have enough text to fill full pieces of paper, so save a tree and use only eight sheets of 8½" × 11" (22cm × 28cm) paper. Cut them in half, either vertically (portrait) or horizontally (landscape). You will then have pieces measuring either 5½" × 8½" (14cm × 22cm) or 11" × 4¼" (28cm × 11cm). Depending on what side you staple it, your dummy may be long or tall. Choose what shape you want your dummy to be, depending on the amount of text and the line lengths. If your text lines are short, you can have a taller dummy. If they are long, you should make a longer dummy.

If you have a particularly brief text, use just four pages of paper; cut them into quarters, and staple them together.

Number your pages from one to thirty-two. The first is page one. Turn the page, and put a two on the back of page one. Number three will go on the right-hand page. Continue in this manner until you reach the back page, which should be thirty-two.

CUTTING AND PASTING

Now you're ready to cut and paste sections of your manuscript onto the pages. To do that, you need to consider how many pages will be taken up by front matter. This can include four different items.

1. **HALF-TITLE PAGE:** This usually appears on page one and traditionally is the title with only a small illustration.
2. **FULL-TITLE PAGE:** This usually appears on pages two and three and includes the title and the writer's, illustrator's, and publisher's names.
3. **COPYRIGHT INFORMATION:** This usually appears on page four.
4. **DEDICATIONS:** They usually appear on page five, directly preceding your story's opening page.

Notice, the repetition of the phrase *usually appears*. These days publishers display a wide range of creativity in laying out front matter. You should browse through picture books to see the variety of ways front-matter information may be presented, but for right now you can familiarize yourself with the approaches listed below.

- Page one of *Me and Momma and Big John* by Mara Rockliff has a half title on page one, and the story opens with a double-spread on pages two and three. The copyright and dedications appear at the end of the book.
- *School's First Day of School* by Adam Rex is a forty-page picture book. Because the endpapers are part of those forty pages, the front matter begins on page four with the dedication and copyright info, and then the half title is on page five. The story begins on pages six and seven.
- *Old Robert and the Sea-Silly Cats* by Barbara Joosse is another forty-page book and begins completely differently. The first sentence is on page one. Pages two and three are a full-title page, and the dedication and copyright info appear on page forty.
- *Bike On, Bear!* by Cynthea Liu has a half title with no illustration on page one. Page two is dedication and copyright info, and page three is another half title, this time with an illustration. The story begins on page four.

- *Mousequerade Ball: A Counting Tale* by Lori Mortensen has a half title on page one, copyright info on page two, and dedications on page three. The story begins on page four.
- *Dot.* by Randi Zuckerberg begins with a half title on page one, copyright info on page two, and dedications on page three, but page four is blank—no picture, no text. The story begins on page five.

When you cut and paste your manuscript, plan where that information will go. Usually I start pasting my story on page six. If I find I need more story pages, I tighten my front matter. Don't use ordinary tape. You need a lift-off tape—Scotch brand calls it "removable tape"—so you can shift text from one page to another without creating tears. I'm a creature of habit and prefer tape, but non-permanent glue sticks and sprays work as well.

BREAKING UP THE TEXT

Always cut whenever one of the following story elements changes.

1. **LOCATION:** Your character leaves the house, enters a store, or goes to a friend's house. The different setting calls for a different picture, which means it's time to move on to the next page.
2. **CHARACTERS:** A new character is introduced, or a character disappears. Mother comes home from work, the tooth fairy sneaks into the bedroom, or the cat hides, but the result is the same: The picture must change.
3. **ACTIONS:** Two characters are fighting. Someone breaks up the fight, and then the characters start working together. Each of these would signal the need for a different illustration.

Note that on odd pages it is not enough to have simple changes in the story. There should be developments dramatic enough to compel your reader to turn the page. Try to leave your character in peril on the odd-numbered pages.

Using your lift-off tape, paste your text onto the pages of your dummy. An important benefit of making a dummy is that it shows whether you have those necessary page turns we discussed in the previous chapter. You'll need to do some experimentation and realigning to decide where your text works best.

Once your dummy is as complete as you can make it, read it aloud with pen or pencil in hand. The act of reading and turning the pages, as your reader will, allows you to see the story in a new way. Then make the necessary changes to your dummy.

I'm always surprised to find changes need to be made because I wait to dummy my manuscript until I think my story is ready to send off. Invariably, though, I discover places for revision I hadn't noticed before. Pay special attention to the following questions when evaluating your dummied manuscript.

Can Your Story Fit into Thirty-Two Pages?

Perhaps your story is quite short and would work better as a board book. But maybe your story needs forty pages. Beware if you are a first-time writer with a manuscript that needs more than the traditional thirty-two pages. Publishing a new writer's book is an expensive gamble for the publishing house. Any additional pages might cause an editor to think twice about buying your story.

Does Your Story Have Enough Illustrations?

The minimum number of pictures is thirteen double-spreads and one single-spread. Thoughts cannot be easily illustrated. The days of characters with thought bubbles over their heads have passed. Nevertheless, dialogue is often printed comic-book style in those kinds of bubbles. Some dialogue can be illustrated. "I'm leaving right now" indicates action and could be illustrated with Rabbit leaving her den. "I'm not sure what to do" would be more difficult. Negative statements, such as "He didn't jump" or "She didn't read her book," would require great creativity on the illustrator's part. Look at *My Favorite Pets: by Gus W. for Ms. Smolinski's Class* to see how Harry Bliss deals with the negative statements Jeanne Birdsall wrote.

Does Your Text Suggest a Variety of Illustrations?

Does your story take place entirely in one room? While Margaret Wise Brown got away with that in *Goodnight Moon,* give your illustrator a break and vary the illustration possibilities. Give your listener a break, too, so she won't be looking at the same pictures over and over again.

Does the Reader Know Your Book's Premise Within the First Three Pages?

After the front matter, no more than three pages should be required to give your reader a good idea of your story's subject matter. Really, though, allowing three pages is being generous. All that opening material should be on the first page.

Does Your Story Have Page Turns?

Not every page needs a cliff-hanger, but something should be left unanswered or unfinished so the reader wants to proceed.

Is the Action Spread Over Thirty-Two Pages?

Or is it clumped together at the beginning or the end? Are big chunks of text on some pages and little slivers on others? Ask yourself whether all that text is important and if some can be deleted.

Are There Spots with Unnecessary Words?

Scrutinize any clumps of dialogue and description. Can they be condensed? Can they be eliminated? Seeing one's text on the page reveals new possibilities for edits.

Does Your Climax Happen in the Story's Final Pages?

Ideally, your climax will occur near page thirty or thirty-one. If it happens on pages sixteen and seventeen, you have a problem and need to cut much of what comes afterwards. On the other hand, you might consider adding more action to your story's middle section.

Do You Tie Up Loose Ends Nicely?

You have until the last page to accomplish this. We discussed this in detail in chapter twelve, which focused on endings. With your dummy, you'll see how well you've handled this element of your story.

Is Your Storytelling Concise, Poetic, and Dramatic?

To answer this question, read your dummy one last time for an overview of how your plot and language work together.

COLOR-TESTING THE DUMMY

After you've made your dummy, get out your highlighters. Use the green highlighter for the *wow* moment, that initial intriguing development that compels the reader to proceed. Turning the pages can sometimes show you the *wow* moment isn't that much of a *wow*.

Next use a blue highlighter to show where the problem of the story is revealed. If this wasn't within the first three pages of text, text juggling and cutting are in order. Using that same blue highlighter, mark the place where the problem is solved. If it comes before pages twenty-eight and twenty-nine, revise to bring it closer to the end of your text. Circle dramatic moments in red. Are there enough? Where did they occur? If they're all close together or too far apart, can they be moved, expanded, or shortened? Then with an ordinary pen or pencil, go through your dummy story again and star places where some question or drama creates a page turn. Remember: These should come on every odd-numbered page. And last of all, the dummy will show if there's a satisfying wrap-up moment on page thirty-two. If you have that, draw yourself a smiley face.

Here's a sample page of one of my dummies, with corrections and changes for you to see.

Pretty sloppy, isn't it?

A FEW FINAL WORDS

Your dummy doesn't have to be neat and pretty. It's only for you. Don't send it to an editor, but don't trash it. Save each dummy. Later, you can compare it to the published book. The layout may be the same or wildly different. That doesn't matter. Just make sure your story fits the picture-book format. Don't be a dummy—make a dummy!

ANN WHITFORD PAUL has published more than twenty picture books (including board books, early-readers, a poetry collection, plus a variety of fiction and non-fiction, rhymed and prose picture book, including the popular series that began with *If Animals Kissed Goodnight*). Many of her poems have appeared in anthologies and her essays have been published by several newspapers. She lives with her husband in Los Angeles and hopes you'll visit her website www. annwhitfordpaul.com. This essay is excerpted from *Writing Picture Books Revised and Expanded Edition* (Writer's Digest, 2018).

JACQUELINE WOODSON

The bestselling National Ambassador for Young People's Literature talks character building, confronting controversial subjects, and the real-world importance of books for kids and teens.

....

by Jera Brown

///

Jacqueline Woodson writes about issues that make her feel powerless.

Most recently, that means police brutality as well as mass deportation and its impact on American families. The author of more than 30 books for children, middle-grade, and adult readers, Woodson writes to better understand difficult subjects, but also with the high-minded goal of provoking tangible change—something she has believed literature capable of since she herself was a young reader.

To Woodson, the power of literature comes from creating what Dr. Rudine Sims Bishop—pioneering Ohio State University emeritus professor of children's literature—refers to as "mirrors" and "windows." Says Woodson: Readers "need mirrors to see reflections of themselves in literature, which is reaffirming, but they also need a window to see how the 'Other' lives."

Woodson has used her own background as a black queer woman and her ability to write rich, diverse char-acters to expand the "mirrors and windows" available for children and adults, with an extensive body of work comprising poetry, memoir, fiction, picture books, and cultural criticism.

Among her many accolades, 2014's *Brown Girl Dreaming*, a memoir in verse (using poetic forms instead of traditional paragraphs), was named a Newbery Honor Book and earned Woodson her second Coretta Scott King Award, along with a National Book Award for Young People's Literature. She's the author of four additional Newbery Honor Books: *The Evolution of Calpurnia Tate*, *After Tupac and D Foster*, *Feathers* and *Show Way*. The memoir *Another Brooklyn*, released in 2016, scored Woodson her fourth National Book Award nomination.

In 2018, Woodson began a two-year term for the Library of Congress as National Ambassador for Young People's Literature—an honor previously held by such accomplished authors as Katherine Paterson, Kate DiCamillo, and, most recently, Gene Luen Yang. Established in 2008, the role is designed to raise awareness about the impact of literature on lifelong literacy, starting with the development of young readers.

This August (2018), Woodson is releasing two more books: *Harbor Me* is a middle-grade novel about a group of fifth- and sixth-graders whose families struggle with poverty, deportation and incarceration. *The Day You Begin* is a picture book illustrated by Mexican artist Rafael López that narrates the first-person account of Woodson's great-grandfather—the only black boy in his classroom.

Woodson took a brief respite from her busy schedule to talk with WD about her body of work and the importance of books for kids and teens.

You've said when you feel powerless toward something, you write about it. What exactly do you mean by that?

My writing is always [prompted by] this whole series of questions that I'm asking myself: *Why does this happen? Why does that person behave that way? What is the impact of that behavior? How is that person going to change? What's going to be the catalyst to their change?*

This new book, *Harbor Me*, is about kids dealing with a number of things, including police brutality and someone's father getting deported. And for me, the question is: *What happens when this happens? How do we keep moving forward and what are the tools we have?* [In] figuring that out in the narrative, I'm also figuring it out in my real life, and that's what makes it healing and bearable.

Harbor Me has many protagonists. How do you effectively portray such a diverse set of characters?

Oh my goodness, they surprise me sometimes. The main part of the process was [just] writing. There were holes in their lives, and there were holes in their characters, and the rewriting and the filling in—I think of it the way artists might think of their art process. You're adding layers and layers and layers until your character makes sense, and then you're adding more layers until your character has their metamorphosis. So with each of these characters, it's that same question that is part of the hero's journey, which is: *What is their original world? What is it saying?*

The first character we meet is Esteban. His ordinary world was the world with his mother, father, and sister—and then one day his father doesn't come home. Then he's no longer in that ordinary world because his father has been taken by Immigration and Customs Enforcement. What's going to happen to him? Who are going to be his allies? I just start kind of flushing it out with those questions and see where they take me.

As a YA writer, you often write about "controversial" topics, such as addiction and interracial relationships. Early in your career, you learned from none other than Judy Blume that your books were being banned or challenged by parents in some school systems as a consequence. Is that still the case? How did that make you feel?

I'm sure my books are being challenged all over the place, but it's not like I would know that, right? It's not like someone's calling me up and saying, "Yo, we challenged your book in Waco, Texas." I know that it's a place I never get invited to do a school visit. I've never been invited to Brigham Young University, which has this huge children's literature component. I'm sure that's about race or sexuality or gender—who knows? You don't know how and when you're being challenged until someone like Judy Blume says, "Oh yeah, you're being challenged."

I get asked a lot about my literature in terms of the controversy of it, which, it's not controversial to me. I'm writing about everyday life and real issues and real people— I mean real characters who are trying to find their footing. And I think the thing that is called "controversial" is the thing that makes other people uncomfortable. I'm not uncomfortable writing about this stuff. I write because I think it's so necessary. I would be uncomfortable *not* writing about it.

Do you think writers with marginalized identities or marginalized stories need a unique sense of bravery and boldness in order to make it [in publishing]?

I think every writer needs some bravery and some boldness, and a little bit of a unicorn in them to make it. Eighty percent of writing is about persevering, and when your book bombs, not saying, "I quit," but saying, "Okay, that book bombed, but I have plenty of other stories locked and loaded for my career." You can't go into this fearfully and you can't go into this with a chip on your shoulder saying, "I have a right to have my book make *The New York Times* bestseller list in its first week of publishing." It's not going to happen for 99 percent of writers. You have to go in with integrity, and with faith, and you have to go into this willing to work really hard to get your book out there.

And it's a balance! I mean, I look on Twitter and I see people [where] every single post is about their new book. I'm like, *Stop it already; you're going to drown your book*! Because writing isn't just about writing, it's about the social context in which you're writing. It's about paying attention to the world, and if you publish a book and it's just about your book, you're already failing the rest of the world.

What advice do you have for YA writers tackling topics that might make others uncomfortable?

I think the most dangerous thing a writer can do is think about how a reader is going to react to their writing, because you never know. You don't know the reader, and if you're going to self-censor, if you're so busy thinking about the audience, who are you writing for? The first person you should be writing for is yourself. If you start out thinking, "What does the reader need?" you're going to fail. You're going to be wrong.

That's often the advice I hear for adult writers, but assumed it'd be different for those writing for kids.

Well, the thing about writing for young people is … you have to know your audience. And I think that's something that might be a little bit different.

If you don't know that when you're writing a middle-grade novel, your protagonists can't be 17 going on 40, then you don't know this genre. You have to know if you're writing about kids in fifth grade, your protagonist needs to be 10 or 11. But does that mean knowing your reader *specifically*? Not so much.

Do you read differently when you're writing middle-grade versus YA or adult novels?

Yes and no. When I'm writing for adults and picture books, I read a lot more poetry. When I'm writing for young adults, that's when I catch up on all my friends' books, and then when I'm writing for middle-grades, I'm usually not reading at all. I want to get into [my own] world, and when reading other people's middle-grade books, it's going to take me into *their* world. Or [if] I'm reading adult stuff, it's going to make my [middle-grade] characters sound too old.

Do you have any advice for writers interested in publishing both YA and adult books?

I think people should just write what they want to write. A lot of times [we] think that we have [to have] the golden elixir that's going to be the answer. The only answer I can give is to *write the dang book*. Write two books at once if that's what's coming to you; write four books. But this is a process, and I'm sure writers have heard this a lot of times, and I think sometimes it's hard to hear, but it is a process. And I've seen so many people who want to know about publishing before they even put pen to paper.

I used to send out short stories and poetry back in the '90s, and we had to send it out by regular mail. But the minute the rejection came back, I always had the next envelope waiting. *Paris Review* rejected it? Let me try *The New Yorker*. Because I just wanted to keep it off my desk, and while it was out there, I wasn't sitting there not writing. I was working on the next thing.

As National Ambassador of Young People's Literature, one of your goals is to spend time with kids in underserved communities. What communities are you focusing on?

I'm hoping to visit a lot of young people in juvenile detention centers and underserved schools. Next week I'm going to Alabama, and I've done some Skyping with women in prison. ... I've been to one school that was primarily autistic kids. I was just in Philadelphia and went to a number of Title I schools and community centers, including one that was [for] adults and children. I've been home like three days, so I feel like I should be able to list more places. It's been such a blur: a lot of young people. I mean, it's been fabulous, and it's [also] been some work.

What do those interactions look like, and what have you learned from these visits?

I just love [the kids] so much! They're still very passionate about reading. Part of my [National Ambassador] platform is [the idea that] Reading = Hope × Change. The gist of it was to get people in rooms together to talk. And I've re-learned how interested young people are in engaging and being heard. That gets reconfirmed every time I step into a room with them. A lot of times people think young people are just so into their devices and kind of checked out. One place I went to had a large population of Muslim kids, and so a lot of girls wore hijabs. Just listening to them talk about their spiritual lives and their academic lives was amazing, and [they asked] me about my own spiritual life as a writer and what that means.

What role do you believe literature should play in the lives of young readers?

I think the role that it plays in the lives of young readers, and the role that it can play in the lives of *all* readers, is to create conversation: to be able to engage across lines of socioeconomics, race, gender, and sexuality, and to be the jumping-off point for that conversation. A lot of times people are scared to have very hard conversations, or what they *perceive* to be very hard conversations, and what literature can do is introduce those conversations through characters and make it a safer entry into talking about stuff. When people feel passionate about good books, they want to share them. They want to engage in discussions around them. It also changes people. It stops the routines.

You have two kids. How has your writing changed since becoming a parent? For instance, do you find yourself writing with them in mind, or do you see characters differently?

My kids make me laugh, so I think my writing has gotten funnier at points. I took myself very seriously B.C. (Before Children), and now I definitely feel like having a 16-year-old daughter … a lot of *Another Brooklyn* was inspired by me watching her negotiate the world. I remember my own self at 16, but my kids definitely gave me feedback whether I asked for it or not. And they make me laugh in a way that shows me that young people are finding their way and laughter comes to them. It's not all just brooding.

Is there any parting wisdom you'd like to give aspiring writers?

I know every writer says this, but you can't be a writer if you don't read. It's really important to read the same book again and again and study how other writers do stuff. And of course, read in your genre. You don't know how many people who aspire to write for young people have come to me and said, "Well, I can't be bothered with reading those books."

JERA BROWN is a freelance writer and columnist for *Rebellious Magazine*. Selections from her memoir have been published in *The Rumpus* and *Big Muddy*. This interview was previously published in the September 2018 issue of *Writer's Digest*.

CASSANDRA CLARE

The YA sensation unveils the practical magic behind her bestselling Shadowhunter series and demystifies the secrets of writing for different age groups and fostering representation in fiction.

....

by Jess Zafarris

///

Cassandra Clare wrote her first published novel in a closet. That is, in one of those "cozy" New York City spaces, wherein the bed doubles as an office chair and the desk looks suspiciously like a windowsill. At the time, she worked the night shift as a copy editor for the *National Enquirer*, spending daylight hours in her cramped apartment, cranking out chapters, researching agents, writing queries, reworking her manuscript and, eventually, signing a contract for publication of the soon-to-be *New York Times* bestselling YA novel *City of Bones*.

That book would prove to be the first of several bestsellers in a multi-series collection of 12 novels (and counting)—plus several short story anthologies—known as the Shadowhunter Chronicles: tales from an urban fantasy world brimming with angels, demons, warlocks, vampires, and faeries, plus the enemies and allies thereof. Of those, perhaps the best-known series within the broader universe is The Mortal Instruments sextet. Clare's follow up, the Infernal Devices prequel trilogy, harks back to the Victorian Era, and the December 2018 release of *Queen of Air and Darkness* completes The Dark Artifices, a sequel trilogy to Mortal Instruments. Fans of Clare can expect to further explore the Shadowhunter universe in a new trilogy, The Eldest Curses, the first of which will be released in Spring 2019.

Despite her early successes, it wasn't until the stellar release of her *third* book that the YA superstar was finally able to ditch her tabloid gig and embrace novel-writing full time. Today, the 45-year-old's books have sold over 50 million copies worldwide in more than 35 languages and have been adapted into film, television, and two manga series.

Clare, whose real name is Judith Lewis, pens her books like clockwork: She's published at least one Shadowhunter book per year since 2007, with additional short stories and collaborative works interspersed among them. Often, she says, the processes overlap such that she's plotting out one book while copy editing its predecessor.

Many of her co-authored works, like The Bane Chronicles novellas with Sarah Rees Brennan and Maureen Johnson, belong to the Shadowhunter universe, while the five-book middle-grade Magisterium series with Holly Black, author of The Spiderwick Chronicles, ventures into an entirely new world.

In conversation with WD, Clare shares her thoughts on plotting a multi-part series, venturing out into middle-grade, collaborating with other writers, and more.

Your world is so intricate. Tell me about your plotting process. How do you lay out your narratives?

I'm an outliner. I know there are people who are plotters and people who are more pantsers, but I am definitely a plotter. I need to know what is going to happen in a story. So I generally start with what I call a "macro-plot," in which I sort of take the story from Point A, where it begins, to the end, and try to lay out the significant moments. And I think pacing is a good way of looking at it, because I'm looking at the moments where the story turns.

For me, there are basically five points where the story turns: You've got the beginning of the story. Then you've got the inciting incident, something that changes things for the character so that the story [takes off]. And that'll be a realization or an event: a birth, a death, something that causes you to answer the question of, *Why now?—Why are you telling this story now, from this point?* And then you have your midpoint, where the story often reverses itself or changes and you learn new information. You usually have the low point of the story where things seem lost for your characters. And then you have your denouement.

I try to plot those out, and that forms a spine on which everything else is built. Then I'll do what I call a "micro-plot," in which I actually plot out each chapter and what is happening in terms of the characters and the arcs and the events that are occurring in order to create a full story.

Obviously those things will change. They're not going to stay completely the same as I move through the story; some things will work, some things won't work. But for me, it helps to have that as a guide. And I think that does help me keep these books, which are quite sprawling and involve a lot of characters, as tightly plotted as possible.

Most of your books take place in the same universe, but you didn't write the series in chronological order. How do you ensure consistency and continuity when you're writing these novels that jump around in time?

I know. I keep thinking, *Why did I do that?* But that's me. I try to be disciplined in my outlining and whatnot, but sometimes it's a case of "follow your bliss"—I do the stories that I'm the most excited about at the time. And it just happened that, when I was finishing up Mortal Instruments, the thing I was most excited about was doing a historical. I had this idea and I loved it, and I wanted to do it. So I jumped back in time and did The Infernal Devices, which is set in 1878. Then I jumped *forward* in time and did The Dark Artifices. And now I'm jumping back to 1903 and doing [a new series called] The Last Hours.

It's imperative for me that I have a bible. I think they often call it that in TV writing as well, where everything is noted down. You know, the genealogy of all the families, what things and how they work, the rules of magic. The location of all the major known places in the books. I refer back to that. If somebody ever stole it, I would be so doomed.

The dialogue in your books feels so natural. Do you have any advice for crafting strong conversations?

Listen to the way people actually talk. To an extent, all written dialogue is stylized where we take out the *ums* and the *ifs* and the *sort ofs* and the minimizing language. And remember that there is a rhythm. That the back-and-forth of talking is rhythmic: Somebody gives information, somebody else reacts. You have to get that pattern down. I love writing dialogue. It's one of my favorite things.

When I was writing Infernal Devices, one thing that was helpful to me was sitting down and listening to audiobooks and plays written in the Victorian Era, so I could get the cadence of Victorian dialogue and the way that they talked. I did it as a sort of immersion thing. For about six months, I only read books, watched movies, and listened to plays that were written in the specific time period my characters were operating in, so that I was sort of walking around thinking in that kind of language.

You have a very dedicated fan base. Have you used their feedback to shape what you've written?

Definitely—when they give me feedback on certain characters or things that they love. I'm very interactive with my fans, and they're very interactive with me. For instance, they absolutely love the character Magnus Bane in The Mortal Instruments series.

He's an immortal warlock, and I thought, *There's no reason he couldn't be in The Infernal Devices*, so I put him in. People love him so much and it was great to see him at a different stage of his life. It was in large part fan feedback that caused me to include him as a significant character in that other series.

That character—Magnus—is gay, correct? And beyond him, diversity is core to your books. Why is having a diverse cast of characters important to you, and how do you avoid falling victim to stereotypes when you're writing these characters?

[Magnus's boyfriend] Alec is based on a friend of mine I knew when I was younger who committed suicide because he was gay and his family did not accept that. Alec was a way of giving him—though he wasn't around—a story that he would have loved. He, like me, was a big fan of science fiction and fantasy, a big fan of stories and adventurers and kickass fighters. To see a character who was like him, who was this badass demon fighter and got to have all these adventures, would have meant the world to him. What I thought when I created Alec was, *This will hopefully be something that can mean a lot to people who want to see themselves reflected.* There's not enough representation across all the boards.

And in the same vein, I've tried to create many other characters that people can see themselves in. There are autistic Shadowhunter characters. There are trans characters. There are characters with different body types. There are characters of different ability, and all these characters of different races and ethnicities. Being a Shadowhunter—being this cool sort of hero—isn't restricted to any one kind of person.

In terms of avoiding stereotypes, it's something that you have to keep an eye out for. When I create characters that are not like me, I always use sensitivity readers. When I was writing, for instance, the trans character Diana, who is in The Dark Artifices, I met with many trans women who live in my area and talked to them extensively about how to build her character, how to know exactly what to avoid. That was my first question. I sat down [and asked], "What do you not want to see in this character? What do you not want me to express?" And then when the book was done, I had trans readers give me their feedback and changed it accordingly.

Mortal Instruments is often referred to as a YA "urban fantasy" series, but you've said in the past that it has also been categorized as YA romance. How do you feel about those genre designations?

They're marketing designations. When I first sold my book, it was sold as urban fantasy. And that's what we looked at it as. And then *Twilight* came out and suddenly all of these publishers were pushing books toward being marketed as romance. There is romance in The Mortal Instruments, absolutely. I love romance and I love writing it, so that's not a problem. There were definitely books that I saw out there that were not romance that were sort of shoehorned into this category. Then we got *The Hunger Games*, and everything was marketed as a dystopia.

One thing about having a career that's now spanned about a decade is that no longer happens to me. In the early days of my books, my publisher did a lot of designing kind of romantic-looking marketing for them—part of that paranormal romance marketing boom. I'm glad that has faded away. Now the books are marketed as their own thing.

One of the things I love about YA, actually, is that it's not broken down into those categories [as much as adult fiction]. It's all together in the bookstore. So you write a mystery and then a romance and then a science-fiction book, they're all going to be shelved together. But if you're an adult author, all of those books would be shelved separately in the bookstore. YA encourages intersectional fiction. It doesn't matter if your book is difficult to shelve. If you've written a science-fiction romance, you don't have to worry about where it's going to end up.

How does your process change when you're writing with co-authors?

I've written with a bunch of co-authors who are friends of mine—Robin Wasserman, Sarah Rees Brennan, Maureen Thompson—on the anthology series we've done, which are short stories set in my [Shadowhunter] world. I was influenced to do this by classic urban fantasy, books like the Thieves' World [anthologies] I grew up reading where groups of writers would get together and write different stories all set in the same world. This was something that I grew up thinking of as completely normal, and then I realized it wasn't something that people were still doing. I was like, "Let's bring it back."

That was interesting because these are all people who are very familiar with my world and my characters. We have workshops on my books together. They definitely know what they're doing. So we would sit there and kind of back-and-forth these ideas. It was almost like working in a writer's room on a television show, where you all know the characters and you all know the world and you're sort of tossing ideas back and forth—that could happen or this other thing could happen.

And then when I wrote with Holly Black, and we created Magisterium, which is a five-book series for middle-grade, it was totally different. We had to build the world from the ground up, *together*. It wasn't my world; it was *our* world. We were both equally responsible for building all the pieces of the magic system. And I didn't have any veto power. With the anthologies, I'm kind of like the showrunner because it's my world. But with this, Holly and I had equal say. It's a different balance. They're both fun in different ways.

Did you find writing for middle-grade more difficult?

I was worried that I wouldn't have a middle-grade voice. That was how the whole discussion with Holly started—I was reading Percy Jackson in an airport. I said [to Holly], "I have this idea that I think would be a great middle-grade book but I don't know if I have a middle-grade voice." She wrote The Spiderwick Chronicles, which are classics, and she sort of sat up and said, "I have a middle-grade voice."

We decided then [that] we could write this together. When we sat down to write the beginning—because we were going to use it to sell the publishers—she plopped it down in front of me and said, "Let's see your middle-grade voice." I was like, "You know, this is like teaching someone to swim by throwing them into the pool." But I started writing and she was like, "This is great. This is exactly what middle-grade is like." I was like, "Oh, thank god."

I think I got there not because I have an inherent ability to do this, but because I'd read a ton of middle-grade before I had sat down to start. If you want to write in a genre you're not used to, the best thing you can do is sit down and spend a couple of weeks reading in that genre.

JESS ZAFARRIS was the content director for Writer's Digest. She is now the executive director of marketing and communications at Gotham Ghostwriters. This article was previously published in the February 2019 issue of *Writer's Digest*.

N.K. JEMISIN

The master fantasy world-builder reveals her secrets to success on Patreon and speculates on how the imagination might test-drive our future.

....

by Jera Brown

N.K. Jemisin wants to be a "storyteller of a writer." It's an ambition she claims not to have mastered, but many who have lost themselves in Jemisin's tales of captive gods and stone eaters are sure to disagree.

Through her three epic fantasy series (the Inheritance trilogy, the Dreamblood duology and the Broken Earth trilogy) as well as dozens of short stories and a novella, Jemisin has become known as a master world creator, each world brought to life through their detailed histories and unique mythology. And even though Jemisin's stories are set in universes where magic is commonplace, Jemisin's writing feels pressingly relevant to our own world. Her stories are based on flawed power structures and deeply held prejudices with devastating consequences. There's also hope—a constant theme through Jemisin's latest book, *How Long 'til Black Future Month.* The short story collection, published in November 2018, imagines futures for people of color like herself.

Storytelling is not just about the tales themselves, but also the connection between the storyteller and their audience. Outside of her work, Jemisin cultivates a bond with her readers through means such as her writing groups and outspoken activism in the fantasy and science fiction communities. This bond has paid off. In 2016, Jemisin quit her day job to focus on writing full-time with the generous support of her fans through the Patreon platform.

Among Jemisin's accolades, her debut novel, *The Hundred Thousand Kingdoms,* was short-listed for the James Tiptree Jr. Award, earned the Sense of Gender Award from the Japanese Association for Gender, Fantasy, and Science Fiction, and a Locus Award for Best

First Novel. In 2018, when *The Stone Sky* (the final book in Jemisin's Broken Earth trilogy) won the Best Novel Hugo award, Jemisin became the first author to win three Hugo Best Novel awards in a row. The novel also earned a Nebula Award for Best Novel and a Locus award for Best Fantasy Novel.

Jemisin spoke to *Writer's Digest* about her relationship to her readers and how she creates other worlds.

You were able to move into writing full time thanks to the support of your fans via Patreon. Can you tell us about making that decision?

It was not my decision 100 percent. I liked my day job [as a career counselor and academic advisor], and I really didn't want to give the job up. But at the time, my mother was ill and deteriorating. And my writing career had become more than full time. *The Fifth Season* came out and sold like gangbusters, which is great. But it meant that I immediately started getting a deluge of interview requests, and when you have a nine-to-five job, you can only do interviews between 5:30 and seven, and you've got to eat somewhere in there, and write on top of that.

Some things had started to give, and the things that had started to give were my health and my sanity. It was to the point where the only reason I hadn't quit already was because I was afraid of the finances of the writer's life, because I had done that before. Back at the beginning of my career, I had taken about a year-and-a-half off after I got the contract for the Inheritance trilogy. I discovered that I did not function well not having structure, not having people to interact with other than family, not having a purpose or sense of fulfillment. Because the thing about my day job was helping real people in real time and working with marginalized kids.

So given the stress that I was under, either I was going to break or I had to do something. That was when I decided to try Patreon.

What was that experience like?

Honestly, I didn't think it was going to work. There were some popular authors and artists who were making a great deal of money through Patreon, but I was just a midlist author. At the time, the Dreamblood series was the only thing that I had the royalty statement for, and I knew the sales of the last book of the series were not fantastic. So I was like, *If I do this, am I going to end up on the street?* That was the fear. I launched it on a Friday afternoon around 5:00 thinking nobody's going to pay any attention and by the end of the weekend, it was fully funded, and I was quitting my job.

Terror was the feeling that I had beforehand going into it and shock afterward. I still am making more than my initial goal of $3,000 a month, which was just enough to cover my rent and health insurance (at least before Trump, that was enough to cover my health insurance).

What advice do you have for other writers considering pursuing fan-based funding?

First and foremost, you do have to be a known person. I've seen friends who were writers that didn't have any books out attempting it, and it doesn't usually go well. The sense that I get from the people who contribute to my Patreon is that they do so out of a sense of personal relationship. They've read my books, and they feel like they know me on some level. And, to a degree, they do, because I put a lot of myself into my books.

They want to contribute to the writer that they've seen already and make sure that that writer produces more work. It's not just an altruistic thing on their part; it's a desire for more of the same.

So if you are a writer who's got some stuff out there and feel like you've built even a small audience, then it can be useful for you. You're not necessarily going to get rent and insurance money, but you are very likely going to get enough to cover a few utility bills. Even just $200 a month can make difference because everybody's living paycheck to paycheck. People should just manage their expectations going into it.

Make sure your story doesn't get too detailed. When you're explaining to people what you need, you don't want them to start, like, trying to work out your budget for you. I've seen mostly women feeling uncomfortable asking about money and so they literally delineate every single line of what they would spend XYZ on, and because they are working in a patriarchal environment, men jump in and start nitpicking how they're spending the money. When you go and look at men's Patreon [profiles], they're not offering you their life story. They're literally saying, "I need X for Y," and that's all you need to say.

What do your supporters expect in return?

You owe your readers whatever you've promised them. Once a month, I post an original vignette or a short story based on the world of the books that I've written so far. But you do have to deliver on that.

Now the readers can be reasonable about it; when I tell my readers I am deep in deadline hell and can't produce the thing that I told them I was going to try and produce for a while, for example.

The people I've seen have trouble with it are the ones that are not able to deliver on anything, and people will vote with their dollars for that.

In the introduction to your newest book, *How Long 'til Black Future Month*, you explained that you write "proof of concept" stories to "test drive potential novel worlds." Once the concept seems viable, where do you go from there?

If you read "Stone Hunger," [from *How Long 'til Black Future Month*] and then read the Broken Earth series, you would see where I did not like the way that "Stone Hunger" depicted the magical form orogeny. In that short story, it was very "sense specific." The character thought of everything in terms of the taste of food, and that wasn't going to work, because I wanted it to be effectively a science that had gone wrong.

Once I finish the proof-of-concept story and have sent it to people and have seen how they react to it, then I decide from there what I need to change or refine in order to make the world building work for a novel. What that usually means is that I simply start writing. I start doing test chapters to see what voices work best. I tried many voices with the Broken Earth until the second person thing just kind of clicked and seemed like the right voice, and that's a purely instinctual thing.

And, as I went forward, I realized that the concept of the magic from the short story wasn't going to work, but the rest of the world was fine.

You took a year off of novel writing to focus on short stories. The process improved your longer fiction by teaching you about the "quick hook and the deep character" and by giving you "space to experiment with unusual plots and story forms." How did you learn to trust whether your experimental forms were working?

Nearly all of the short stories [in *How Long 'til Black Future Month*] were run through one writing group or another. I didn't do a lot of experimental stuff to begin with, because I didn't know what the hell I was doing, and because I didn't even really know how to read experimental stuff at first. That was partly what that year was about. One of the magazines that I read during that year was *Strange Horizons*, for example, which does a lot of wide-ranging styles, everything from the very didactic to slipstream or interstitial, and a lot of new weird stuff. So that helped me learn how to read it, and then I finally felt more willing to try and write it.

In your blog and when you speak publicly, you frequently mention your readers.

Well, we're storytellers. Storytellers work with an audience. That's normal, isn't it?

I'd hope so. I do think that many writers seem to go off into their own world and are less interested in that dialogue and more interested in just presenting something.

Well, that's their personal choice, and not everybody feels comfortable with it. I get it. To me though, I've always wanted to be a storyteller. When I was a teenager, I used to babysit kids, and I would tell them stories to entertain them. I've traveled to lots of different places in the world. I've seen storytellers, and I've always admired the hell out of them. It's a different art form from writing. It is an art form that I have nowhere near mastered, but I try to be a storyteller of a writer and to me that's what it's supposed to be. But everyone's mileage varies, I guess.

In your acceptance speech for your latest Hugo Award, you explain, "As this genre finally, however grudgingly, acknowledges that the dreams of the marginalized matter, and that all of us have a future, so will the world." Do you believe that speculative fiction has the power to change society?

I didn't used to think so, and then I started to realize, first off that I was underestimating it, and then second of all that other people had already done that calculation and were using it for evil. It sounds kind of corny, but I started to realize it when right-wingers tried to take over fandom. When you started trying to take over every bit of media, and you suddenly see Nazis in video games and comic books trying their damnedest to squish out people who are different from young, straight, white boys, and harassing and trying to dox them, there's a reason for that.

I don't necessarily think it's a one-for-one relationship. I don't think that I'll write a book and it'll change the world. But I do tend to think that the things we are capable of imagining and believing are our future are influenced by all of the media that we consume.

Growing up, I had a really hard time imagining a future for myself and for other black people because when you looked at science fiction, you did not see black people in the future. There had been some kind of unspoken apocalypse that wiped us all out, and Asians, and everybody else too. Certainly that's not what the creators of those works intended to convey, but that was what their work did convey by their exclusion.

People often point out—and I don't know how true this is—but one of the reasons that America became comfortable enough with the idea of a black man and the presidency to elect Obama was because, in TV and film, presidents had been black for quite some time. So we pursue in reality the things that we're capable of imagining and those of us who are in industries or fields that play with imagination have a responsibility to depict futures that are for everyone. And I think that if we can manage to start doing that, then it makes it easier for people in the present day who are trying to influence policy to say, "Look, this is just like in *Star Trek*, we can do blah, blah, blah."

Is there anything else you'd like to convey to other writers?

The industry is changing in some good ways. It's still got a lot of the old blind spots, and it's still struggling to fully embrace futures and mythologies other than what it's familiar with, and that's not entirely surprising. Business has always been reactive rather than proactive. Artists may sometimes have to go outside of traditional channels in order to get our vision realized, but I do like the fact that more people now have the ability to get their work out there.

People encouraged you to self-publish after the *Killing Moon*—your first novel that landed you an agent—didn't find a publisher, but you wanted the book to be in libraries ... Is the only channel other than traditional press self-publishing?

There's small press publishing, but small press publishing also doesn't get you in the library. But you decide on the publishing method that satisfies what it is that you want. A lot of people simply want to make the maximum amount of money possible. For them, self-publishing is perfect because they can control how much they spend on production and marketing. And there's no nobody else kind of like taking chunks out of that profit. They're willing to pay in time for that flexibility. I am not willing to pay in time. Time is my most precious resource, not money.

JERA BROWN is a freelance writer and columnist for *Rebellious Magazine*. Selections from her memoir-in-progress have been published in *The Rumpus* and *Big Muddy*. This interview appeared in the May/June 2019 issue of *Writer's Digest*.

LEIGH BARDUGO

Unstoppable

....

by Baihley Gentry

Leigh Bardugo has always written the stories she wanted to write.

When querying her debut, *Shadow and Bone*—in which she introduced readers to a Czarist Russia-inspired world where individuals called Grisha have the mystical ability to manipulate matter—Bardugo was faced with a publishing-industry reality. Although young adult novels were popular at the time, and her premise was unique and compelling, no literary agents seemed interested in epic or high fantasy books for young readers.

She forged ahead anyway.

"I knew very little about the market. I learned that many [agents] would not even entertain the idea of that kind of book," she says. "It's wise to know what's out there, [but don't] let that hinder you. If you have an idea, pursue it. [Think] about things that make your story a story that only you could tell—those are the things that will stand out."

The strength of that story did eventually resonate with a rep, and the series was sold in a three-book deal in 2010. Within a week of its release in 2012, *Shadow and Bone* sky-rocketed to the top of *The New York Times* bestseller list—as did her six books after that: 2013's *Siege and Storm* and 2014's *Ruin and Rising*, which rounded out the Grisha trilogy; 2015's *Six of Crows* and 2016's *Crooked Kingdom*, a "heist-con" duology Bardugo likens to "*Ocean's 11* meets *Game of Thrones*"; and her two latest stand-alones in 2017: *The Language of Thorns*, her first short story collection, and *Wonder Woman: Warbringer*, about the superhero's teen years.

In sum, her books have sold more than 1 million copies combined internationally, and have earned such accolades as RT Reviewers Choice Awards in 2012 and 2015, and multiple starred reviews from *Publishers Weekly*, *Kirkus Reviews* and *School Library Journal*. Bardugo regularly writes short stories for Tor.com, and she has appeared in various anthologies, including *Last Night a Superhero Saved My Life* with notable names like Jodi Picoult and Neil Gaiman, and *Slasher Girls & Monster Boys* alongside Jonathan Maberry and Kendare Blake.

Despite the impressive trajectory of her career, the path from aspiring author to bestseller was a circuitous one.

Born in Jerusalem and raised in Southern California, Bardugo's lifelong aspiration to be a writer led her to earn a degree in journalism from Yale. While struggling for years to finish a first draft of a novel ("I didn't know yet that I was an outliner, and how badly I needed structure in order to work"), she took jobs in copywriting, advertising, and as a Hollywood makeup and special effects artist.

It wasn't until she brushed off "some pretty wonky ideas" espoused by media, TV, and film about what it meant to produce creative work that Bardugo was able to embrace a "terrible, messy, ugly first draft." That experience taught her some thing valuable: "Let go of the idea that somehow you can outsmart a first draft," she says. "Because I have never met anybody who can."

The YA fantasy maestro took a break from promoting *The Language of Thorns* and *Wonder Woman: Warbringer* to talk world-building, personal perseverance and more.

The runaway success of a debut can put a lot of pressure on subsequent follow-ups. How did you manage to cope with that so gracefully?

When a book lists, there's the illusion of runaway success. My [first book] listed, but it's not as if you hit *The New York Times* bestseller list and all of a sudden they give you the keys to a magical clubhouse and you've suddenly arrived. That's one book, and a book does not make a career. Certainly, I had a wonderful push from my publisher and got very lucky. I'm very aware of what it means to have a publisher back you. But your job as a writer, no matter what else is happening, is to continue to produce work—whether you're succeeding or failing. [You have to put] aside ideas about sales or success or ambition, and just work.

You know, I think I have a journey that looks smooth from the outside. And I'm always a little hesitant to talk about it because I don't want people to get a false impression about what it takes to get published. But [up until the point of publishing *Shadow and Bone*], I did face plenty of rejection, and even after I signed with [my agent], every single one of those rejections stung. Because the marvel of the information age is that you're still getting email rejections months and months after you sent them. [Laughs]. And so, until *Shadow and Bone* came out, I would read those rejections—because, of course, I had to read every single one of them—and I would think, *Well, maybe they're right and everybody else is wrong.* Part of the journey is that horrific balance of, you know, delusions of grandeur and abject humility that I think writers walk the line of all the time.

You've talked about losing faith in your ability to become a professional writer. What would you tell others who are struggling with that same feeling?

I want to be really clear about something: I think we kind of fetishize the creative life. We have the vision of what it means to be an author, where you sit in your garret or looking out at your view and you give everything to your art and you commit fully to it. But the reality is that most of us have bills to pay. We have loans to pay off. We have educations to pay for. Some of us have children to take care of or other relatives or dependents or responsibilities.

And the idea that somehow you're not a real writer if you are pursuing taking care of yourself and your life, as you pursue your art, is an incredibly damaging one. Very few people have the wherewithal or the safety net to be able to pursue writing full time from moment one. And I want people to understand that you can absolutely work a job, sometimes two jobs, and have those responsibilities—and still write. I didn't fail to become a writer, and therefore had to take a job. I had to take a job to keep a roof over my head because I had student loans to pay off. And that's the way it works.

For writers trying to balance life and art, how would you encourage them to stay motivated in pursuing their passion?

Set realistic goals. Sometimes that means doing something like NaNoWriMo, or it means saying, "I'm just going to write 500 words a day, but I'm going to write 500 words a day." Or "I'm going to do writing sprints for 30 minutes before work." Or in the 45 minutes when my kid is napping, or whatever it is. Carve out a time, find a process that works for you and don't compare yourself to anybody else.

[And] get offline. Stop reading about what other authors are doing. Stop reading reviews. Let yourself be immersed in the story that you're writing.

Remember: There is no expiration date on your talent. I did not publish my first book until I was 35 years old. If you have a story to tell, it doesn't matter when you tell it. Just get it onto the page and let go of any of the ideas that somehow it's less worthwhile because it took you a little longer to get there than it took others.

Man, you're inspiring me!

[Laughs.] Oh, good. Do it. Do it.

You've said before that there is no right way to write a book. You've been publishing at least one book per year since 2012, which is an impressive output. Describe your process.

I'm an outliner. I write through a three-act structure. I build all of my books in pretty much the exact same way: I have the idea, I write it out onto a single page so that I essentially have a book that is one-page long, and then I begin to fill in all of the things that I know. I build this kind of ramshackle zero-draft, that operates as an extended outline, and that is what becomes the musculature of the book. Now, when I get into the work of actually writing the scenes and revising the book into something that it can be, that process changes a little depending on the project.

....

A big part of writing is the discomfort of the work not being what you want it to be and the feelings of doubt or failure that come with not being able to make the idea instantly into what you want it to be.

....

Everybody processes differently, but [the exact method] is something you can keep coming back to when you feel psychologically embattled. A big part of writing is the discomfort of the work not being what you want it to be and the feelings of doubt or failure that come with not being able to make the idea instantly into what you want it to be.

Your books have very elaborate, well-rounded worlds. I haven't read a book in a long time where I felt so there. When world-building, where do you typically begin?

I start with my characters and with the story, the plot. When a reader enters the first chapter of your book, they're trying to get their bearings. It's our job as authors to give them the signals they need in order to be able to navigate that world. The great challenge of world-building is not building the world. You could build a world with maps and languages and all these things [and still be missing something]. It's releasing that information to the reader. The world-building that really falls into place first is what I always describe as the sense of power—helping readers understand how power flows in the book. That could mean governmental power, personal power, magical power, whatever. But [determining how power flows] is going to determine how your characters behave on the page, and what they're able or not able to do.

You had help creating the Grisha Trilogy's Ravkan language from David Peterson, who assisted with developing the Dothraki language in HBO's *Game of Thrones*. What was that like?

David and I met at Worldcon several years ago. I went to a presentation of his on Dothraki. He has been kind enough to be a resource for me as we've worked through the [Grisha] books, although we do occasionally butt heads because he wants me to be much more ambitious in my language in the book, and he's very probably right.

You write a lot of diverse characters without falling victim to stereotypes. Do you think attitudes about diversity in publishing have shifted, or does the industry still have a ways to go?

I think both of those things are true. I think that there's a new dedication to making sure that not only is representation better, but that marginalized authors and voices that maybe didn't have voices before are increasingly given platforms in publishing. And that is not only as writers, but as editors and in everything from publicity to sales. That said, I don't think there's any question that there's a long way to go because that is a long process and because until the fundamental power structures change, until the gatekeepers are different, I don't think we're going to see the kind of change that we really need to see—in the way not only that stories are told, but in the way they reach readers.

I'm sure many authors ask you what's trending in YA. What do you think is the ideal balance of writing what you're passionate about and understanding what's drawing readers in the industry?

You have to know the market. So you have to know what's selling, what isn't selling anymore, what people are fatigued by. But that doesn't mean you can say, "Oh, well, I [can't write that ever]." There was a period of time where people would say, "Oh, no more vampire books," or "no more dystopians," or no more this or that. But that is really false because what that actually meant was no more of that particular kind of story. We need a different take on vampires or we need to see a dystopian that is simply described as science fiction. YA shifts and moves faster than most other categories because so much work is being generated and consumed so quickly. And to be frank, I think if I brought *Shadow and Bone* out now, it would not have the same reception it had in 2012. Be aware of the market, but really, being aware of the market is just one part of being a storyteller and thinking about craft.

What's next for you?

Well, *King of Scars* is the first book in my upcoming duology that continues the story of the Grishaverse, and will pick up the story of Nikolai Lantsov, the young king of Ravka. And I'm [also working on] *Ninth House,* my first novel for adults. It is the start of a series set at Yale, a dark fantasy that focuses on the secret societies among East Coast elites. I've got a couple of other things cooking, but nothing I can discuss just yet.

I heard you have a band, which is probably the coolest side hustle ever. What type of music do you play?

Our lead guitarist would probably punch me for this, but I've always described it as "geek rock." It's sort of like if you put the Pixies and the New Pornographers and a little bit of They Might Be Giants in a blender. I mostly sing. Unfortunately, all of our lives got taken over by adulthood: Our guitarist had a baby. Our bassist had a baby. Our drummer bought a house. I landed my dream job. But we do occasionally meet up for band brunch and one of these days we'll have a reunion show.

I think that when you're writing, being creative in other ways is really useful and therapeutic. And whether that's creating visual art or making music—or hell, even baking—as long as you're doing something that's keeping you engaged and keeping you from chewing over reviews on Goodreads, I think you're better off.

BAIHLEY GENTRY is the former associate editor of *Writer's Digest*, in which this interview originally appeared in March/April 2018.

MELISSA DE LA CRUZ

by Cris Freese

When you think of young adult fiction, it's hard to think of someone more prolific than Melissa de la Cruz. Her more-than forty-five books have appeared atop a slew of bestseller's lists—*The New York Times*, *Publishers Weekly*, *IndieBound*, *USA Today*, *Wall Street Journal*, and *The Los Angeles Times*. Her books have been published in over twenty countries.

Much of the reason for her success—and her love of fiction for young adults—is because she never wants to grow up.

That translates to optimism and idealism, which has certainly translated into her fiction. It shines brightly in her novel, *Something in Between*, where Jasmine de los Santos has her dreams of attending college on scholarship ripped away, as she discovers her family is in the United States illegally. The resulting fight to protect herself and her family is beautiful—and needed in today's world.

And, of course, refusing to grow up helped with The Descendants series, as de la Cruz wrote the prequels to the hit Disney television movie.

De la Cruz is also known for her Blue Bloods series—with more than three million copies in print—and The Witches of West End series, which was also turned into a two-season drama series on Lifetime.

When you look at the list of novels, you realize its de la Cruz's work ethic that's truly prolific. And as the co-director of Yallfest and co-founder of Yallwest, she's constantly giving back to young adult readers and writers—interacting with more than 30,000 people every year.

A former fashion and beauty editor, de la Cruz has written for *The New York Times*, *Marie Claire*, *Harper's Bazaar*, *Glamour*, *Cosmopolitan*, *Allure*, *The San Francisco Chronicle*, *McSweeney's*, *Teen Vogue*, *CosmoGirl!*, and *Seventeen*.

De la Cruz grew up in Manila and moved to San Francisco with her family. She now lives in West Hollywood with her husband and daughter.

She took some time out of her busy schedule to answer a few questions for *Children's Writer's & Illustrator's Market*.

How did you get started writing? Who or what inspired you?

I've always wanted to be a writer. Ever since I can remember. But I was eleven years old when I read about the Sweet Valley High ghostwriters in the newspaper—Francine Pascal created the series, but the books were written by young 22-year-old women. Up until then, I thought all authors were 90 years old or dead. It was the first time I thought, hey, if they can do this, I can do this too.

How did your immigration experience influence *Something in Between*? I read that it took 20 years for you to get your green card!

Yes, when my family was approved for a green card, my sister and I were over the age of 21, and so we were in limbo. They have changed the law now so that adult unmarried children now get green cards with their parents, but back then, there was no such law that covered people with our status. So, I got my green card when I married my husband, when I was 31.

My experience made me empathize a lot with Jasmine's plight. I totally remember what it was like to feel American in your heart and mind, but not actually be American on paper. The heart of the story has my heart in it.

> I totally remember what it was like to feel American in your heart and mind, but not actually be American on paper.

Was it your intention to maintain a sense of ever-optimism throughout *Something in Between*? Jasmine strikes me as someone who never gives up, and always sees the best in the world and people.

Yes, I'm a pretty optimistic person and I gave that to Jasmine. I think immigrants have an innate optimism—only people who have a lot of hope and faith and grit leave everything they ever know and move to a foreign country. Sometimes, when I think about how my parents did this, it takes my breath away. And their kids want so much to make it all "worth it." That kind of sacrifice is a huge responsibility.

What drove you to branch out into something very different with this novel? Did you feel like readers needed this story in today's climate?

>*Seventeen* magazine and Harlequin asked me to write a story about immigration, and I felt I could not say "no," since I knew this experience intimately.

How much of you is in Jasmine?

>I'm actually more like Royce, who wants to be a writer, who was spoiled and privileged. I modeled Jasmine after friends I knew from honors summer camps—[those] girls who were perfect: cheerleaders and class presidents and plucky, poor immigrant kids.

What was the most difficult part about writing *Something in Between*, a story that so obviously hits close to home?

>The emotional arc of the story was really difficult, and the helplessness and despair were really hard to feel again.

You're prolific, in terms of the number of novels you've published. How are you able to keep spinning new ideas and pumping out more stories?

>Ideas are the easiest part, writers have so many ideas and interests. I think, as creative people, we are open to the world and when we discover something that fascinates us, we want to delve into it more. I don't have hobbies; I just like working and reading and being with my family. I'm not distracted by entertainment—I watch very little television, and I read a ton of books.

Is it more difficult to work with and develop your own idea, or to build off of and adapt an existing idea, like with Descendants?

>It's so much easier to be in a world you've created. I enjoy working in other people's universes, but I prefer to work on my own.

How did your relationship with Disney come about?

>We did 15 books together before *Blue Bloods*. They asked me to lend my talents to the Descendants world, and I loved the idea. I'm a huge Disney kid; I know those characters and movies like my own and it was an honor to add to the story.

Talk about your writing process. Are you a plotter? How do you keep track of multiple characters when you have multiple points of view, such as *The Isle of the Lost*?

>I'm a huge outliner and plotter. I've always written in multiple POV—it's my preferred way to write, ever since *Au Pairs*.

Which character do you like most in The Isle of the Lost? Who do you relate to?

I love Carlos. He's my favorite, as he's the most like me—the brainy kid in the back, a little anxious, a little nerdy.

Who was the most fun to write? How were you able to dive into well-known Disney villains and develop them into realistic characters?

I looooved writing Mal and Maleficent. Always so fun to be evil! But they are real people to me. I can always find the humanity in a character.

Where did the idea of starting with The Mayflower in Blue Bloods come from? How did that develop?

It came from reading an article about the descendants of the Mayflower, they were all these famous Americans—from George Bush to Oprah to Alec Baldwin—and I thought, *What if the reason all these people are power and famous is because they're vampires?* Then *Blue Bloods* was born.

How were you able to set apart this series from other popular vampire novels?

I wanted to write my own mythology, and I was also inspired by *Paradise Lost*. Both the Mayflower and *Paradise Lost* angle—that my vampires were angels—were in my original outline.

What drives you to write for children and teens? Why those categories?

I guess, like Peter Pan, I refuse to grow up. I think my worldview is very much a kid's, I'm very optimistic, idealistic, and I still find new things in the world to be fascinated by—adulthood is very jaded. I'm pretty much the opposite of that.

Any parting advice for aspiring authors?

Keep trying. Don't give up!

....

CRIS FREESE is a former editor of *Children's Writer's & Illustrator's Market*, a freelance writer, and literary intern with Corvisiero Literary. Follow him on Twitter @crisfreese.

....

MARIEKE NIJKAMP

by Cris Freese

Marieke Nijkamp is not your typical *New York Times* bestselling author. She was born and raised in the Netherlands and edited the anthology *Unbroken: 13 Stories Starring Disabled Teens*. She's also the author of *This Is Where It Ends* and *Before I Let Go*.

Recently, she took time out to discuss her writing process, projects, and more for readers of *Children's Writer's & Illustrator's Market*.

Your first two novels have featured some really strong female characters. How were you able to create characters who have stood out?

I set out to create interesting, well rounded characters. It's actually one of my favorite parts of the creative process. I love discovering characters' hopes and dreams, loves and fears, nightmares and secret desires. I want all my characters to be as complex as possible. Obviously gender plays a part in that, because our gender identity informs who we are to ourselves and in the eyes of the world. Female characters are going to have different experiences than AND be read and perceived differently from male characters. And so too nonbinary characters.

One of the most impressive things about your writing is how you capture emotion. What inspired Kyra and Corey in *Before I Let Go*?

I wanted to tell a story about friendship and grief and what it means to be different in a place where difference isn't accepted. I wanted to write a book about responsibility and guilt and the stories we tell ourselves and the stories we tell about ourselves. I wanted to set a mystery in the deepest, cruelest Alaskan winter. *Before I Let Go* allowed me to do all of those things at once.

Have you been to Alaska before? What went to the choice of that setting?

No, alas! I would love to visit Alaska someday, and I tried to plan a research trip while writing the book, but it didn't work due to a number of reasons. Thankfully, I had a few very gracious Alaskan readers who offered advice as I worked on the book.

As for the choice of setting: I always wanted to set a story in Alaska. I love winter, and I've always found there's something magical about snow covered days. That tied into this particularly story quite well.

In many ways, I felt like Corey possessed some of the "outsider" qualities (at least upon returning to Lost Creek) that Tyler had in *This Is Where It Ends*. (Really, I think Kyra had them too!) Was that intentional? Can you talk about your choices in creating characters rejected by society (in some ways)?

I love writing about outsiders. As a disabled, nonbinary, queer creator I feel quite drawn to characters that don't fit in well with the societal "norm" (whatever that even means). More than that too, it's the world I know best. For the longest time, I wasn't able to rhyme the world I saw in books with the world I saw around me, because one did not reflect the other. Thankfully, that's changing and I love being able to add to that. We "outsiders" deserve to have heroes.

Having said that, I don't actually feel Tyler fits that pattern. He is one of the most mainstream characters I've written: he's a white, cishet boy who is angry at the world around him. He's easily in a position of most of acceptance. Certainly he deals with trauma and hardships, and he deserved to get help for that, but so do many of the other characters in *TIWIE*. None of them resorted to picking up a gun and killing people.

You walked a line between with the supernatural in *Before I Let Go*. What made you make that choice when it came to Kyra's art?

Story ideas can come from the wildest places. A lot of what happens in Lost came from an article I once read, which essentially linked medieval mysticism to mental illness. And I was very curious what would happen if I took that idea as a basis for exploring mental illness (and ableism) in a modern context. So naturally it involved some mysticism too. Or a belief system, in any case. And that required certain unexplainable things.

Was it difficult to create that question of whether what was happening in Lost Creek was supernatural or not? What made you choose to have the town so accepting of Kyra?

I wanted to explore the idea of acceptance a bit in this book. Personally, I don't think the town was accepting of Kyra. Is it acceptance when it's conditional on usefulness? Is it acceptance when it chooses to ignore humanity? Kyra wanted to be loved for all she was, with all she was. As someone whose passion was stories and storytelling, who loved fiercely, who lived with bipolar disorder. Not in spite of. Unconditionally. And she deserved nothing less.

Both of these novels really deal with loss as a teenager, and comprehending and dealing with it. When approaching heavy topics, do you have a hard time writing?

Of course approaching heavy topics isn't always easy, and I definitely need to occasionally step away and go for a walk, but it helps that I try to write the books I would love to read. I write stories I'm passionate about, and that keeps me going.

What was your writing process like for both of these novels?

I'm a plotter at heart, so for both (and honestly, all my stories) I had very extensive notes and a very extensive outline before I even put pen to paper. I love knowing what the shape of the story is before I create it, what the ending is I'm working toward. I greatly admire people who can write a story by the seat of their pants, but I'm not one of them.

And just for the record, that's okay! We all have our own process. I love discovering other people's processes, but I've learned I shouldn't try to emulate them, because I can work best when I'm working my way.

How did you originally get your agent, Jennifer Udden?

A Twitter pitch contest! I was hanging out on the #PitMad hashtag to answer questions and help people with pitches, which is something I was lucky enough to do quite a lot back then. I was querying *This Is Where It Ends* at the time, so I figured I'd throw in my own pitch too. Jen requested I query her when she saw it, and the rest, as they say, is history.

Did you have any reservations about querying *This is Where It Ends*? Particularly with the number of school shootings in the United States?

I had reservations about writing *TIWIE*, exactly because it's such a sensitive subject. I wanted to make sure I could write the story respectfully, truthfully, and without doing harm. I strongly believe it's my responsibility as a writer to always consider whether I'm the right person to write a story, because some stories quite simply do not belong to me. Once I found a way to do right by *TIWIE*, I pursued that.

By the time I started querying, I knew I wanted to work with an agent who understood that responsibility, and I'm very glad I found her.

Forget the subject matter of *This Is Where It Ends* for a second—how difficult was it to write a story that occurs over the course of just fifty-four minutes? How did you plot that story out?

It was really tricky and I loved doing it. I had a spreadsheet that tracked all of the main characters and some of the ensemble on a minute-by-minute basis and having that structure was beautiful.

Was the story complicated by writing from four different POVs? How were you able to not only create four completely different characters, but four completely different voices? Sometimes, characters can begin to sound the same, but not in this case.

> I wrote the story four times, from four different POVs. Only when I had all the ingredients did I shuffle and start blending it together. So that helped me a lot in keeping the voices separate.

Was it difficult to write a character like Tyler? What went into his development?

> Oh, absolutely. Not in the least because I didn't want to create a situation wherein my one interpretation could be seen as the quintessential profile of a school shooter. That wouldn't be responsible. So I stuck to the research there is, spent a lot of time frustrated with the Dickey Amendment, and started with the common characteristics—most of the shooters are white boys, most of them are angry, and in the vast majority of cases, mass shootings aren't a result of mental illness.
>
> From there, I recreated Tyler in a similar way as we would try to recreate our understanding of shooters in a real life situation: through other people's stories, by trying to sort out all the puzzle pieces, and interpretation.

What is the best advice you've received as a writer? What advice would you give to writers just starting out?

> Write your truth. Be brave. Never stop learning.

What one or two things do you wish you'd known when you started writing?

> Some no's are not-yets. Some stories are not-yets too. Both of that is perfectly fine.

CRIS FREESE is a former editor of *Children's Writer's & Illustrator's Market*, a freelance writer, and literary intern with Corvisiero Literary. Follow him on Twitter @crisfreese.

BLOGGING BASICS

by Robert Lee Brewer

In these days of publishing and media change, writers have to build platforms and learn how to connect to audiences if they want to improve their chances of publication and overall success. There are many methods of audience connection available to writers, but one of the most important is through blogging.

Since I've spent several years successfully blogging—both personally and professionally—I figure I've got a few nuggets of wisdom to pass on to writers who are curious about blogging or who already are.

Here's my quick list of tips:

1. **START BLOGGING TODAY.** If you don't have a blog, use Blogger, WordPress, or some other blogging software to start your blog today. It's free, and you can start off with your very personal "Here I am, world" post.
2. **START SMALL.** Blogs are essentially simple, but they can get complicated (for people who like complications). However, I advise bloggers start small and evolve over time.
3. **USE YOUR NAME IN YOUR URL.** This will make it easier for search engines to find you when your audience eventually starts seeking you out by name. For instance, my url is http://robertleebrewer.blogspot.com. If you try Googling "Robert Lee Brewer," you'll notice that My Name Is Not Bob is one of the top five search results (behind my other blog: Poetic Asides).
4. **UNLESS YOU HAVE A REASON, USE YOUR NAME AS THE TITLE OF YOUR BLOG.** Again, this helps with search engine results. My Poetic Asides blog includes my name in the title, and it ranks higher than My Name Is Not Bob. However, I felt the play on my name was worth the trade off.
5. **FIGURE OUT YOUR BLOGGING GOALS.** You should return to this step every couple months, because it's natural for your blogging goals to evolve over time. Initially,

your blogging goals may be to make a post a week about what you have written, submitted, etc. Over time, you may incorporate guests posts, contests, tips, etc.

6. **BE YOURSELF.** I'm a big supporter of the idea that your image should match your identity. It gets too confusing trying to maintain a million personas. Know who you are and be that on your blog, whether that means you're sincere, funny, sarcastic, etc.

7. **POST AT LEAST ONCE A WEEK.** This is for starters. Eventually, you may find it better to post once a day or multiple times per day. But remember: Start small and evolve over time.

8. **POST RELEVANT CONTENT.** This means that you post things that your readers might actually care to know.

9. **USEFUL AND HELPFUL POSTS WILL ATTRACT MORE VISITORS.** Talking about yourself is all fine and great. I do it myself. But if you share truly helpful advice, your readers will share it with others, and visitors will find you on search engines.

10. **TITLE YOUR POSTS IN A WAY THAT GETS YOU FOUND IN SEARCH ENGINES.** The more specific you can get the better. For instance, the title "Blogging Tips" will most likely get lost in search results. However, the title "Blogging Tips for Writers" specifies which audience I'm targeting and increases the chances of being found on the first page of search results.

11. **LINK TO POSTS IN OTHER MEDIA.** If you have an e-mail newsletter, link to your blog posts in your newsletter. If you have social media accounts, link to your blog posts there. If you have a helpful post, link to it in relevant forums and on message boards.

12. **WRITE WELL, BUT BE CONCISE.** At the end of the day, you're writing blog posts, not literary manifestos. Don't spend a week writing each post. Try to keep it to an hour or two tops and then post. Make sure your spelling and grammar are good, but don't stress yourself out too much.

13. **FIND LIKE-MINDED BLOGGERS.** Comment on their blogs regularly and link to them from yours. Eventually, they may do the same. Keep in mind that blogging is a form of social media, so the more you communicate with your peers the more you'll get out of the process.

14. **RESPOND TO COMMENTS ON YOUR BLOG.** Even if it's just a simple "Thanks," respond to your readers if they comment on your blog. After all, you want your readers to be engaged with your blog, and you want them to know that you care they took time to comment.

15. **EXPERIMENT.** Start small, but don't get complacent. Every so often, try something new. For instance, the biggest draw to my Poetic Asides blog are the poetry prompts and challenges I issue to poets. Initially, that was an experiment—one that worked very well. I've tried other experiments that haven't panned out, and that's fine. It's all part of a process.

SEO TIPS FOR WRITERS

Most writers may already know what SEO is. If not, SEO stands for *search engine optimization*. Basically, a site or blog that practices good SEO habits should improve its rankings in search engines, such as Google and Bing. Most huge corporations have realized the importance of SEO and spend enormous sums of time, energy, and money on perfecting their SEO practices. However, writers can improve their SEO without going to those same extremes.

In this section, I will use the terms of *site pages* and *blog posts* interchangeably. In both cases, you should be practicing the same SEO strategies (when it makes sense).

Here are my top tips on ways to improve your SEO starting today:

1. **USE APPROPRIATE KEYWORDS.** Make sure that your page displays your main keyword(s) in the page title, content, URL, title tags, page header, image names and tags (if you're including images). All of this is easy to do, but if you feel overwhelmed, just remember to use your keyword(s) in your page title and content (especially in the first and last 50 words of your page).

2. **USE KEYWORDS NATURALLY.** Don't kill your content and make yourself look like a spammer to search engines by overloading your page with your keyword(s). You don't get SEO points for quantity but for quality. Plus, one of the main ways to improve your page rankings is when you ...

3. **DELIVER QUALITY CONTENT.** The best way to improve your SEO is by providing content that readers want to share with others by linking to your pages. Some of the top results in search engines can be years old, because the content is so good that people keep coming back. So, incorporate your keywords in a smart way, but make sure it works organically with your content.

4. **UPDATE CONTENT REGULARLY.** If your site looks dead to visitors, then it'll appear that way to search engines too. So update your content regularly. This should be very easy for writers who have blogs. For writers who have sites, incorporate your blog into your site. This will make it easier for visitors to find your blog to discover more about you on your site (through your site navigation tools).

5. **LINK BACK TO YOUR OWN CONTENT.** If I have a post on Blogging Tips for Writers, for instance, I'll link back to it if I have a Platform Building post, because the two complement each other. This also helps clicks on my blog, which helps SEO. The one caveat is that you don't go crazy with your linking and that you make sure your links are relevant. Otherwise, you'll kill your traffic, which is not good for your page rankings.

6. **LINK TO OTHERS YOU CONSIDER HELPFUL.** Back in 2000, I remember being ordered by my boss at the time (who didn't last too much longer afterward) to ignore any competitive or complementary websites—no matter how helpful their content—because they were our competitors. You can try basing your online strat-

egy on these principles, but I'm nearly 100 percent confident you'll fail. It's helpful for other sites and your own to link to other great resources. I shine a light on others to help them out (if I find their content truly helpful) in the hopes that they'll do the same if ever they find my content truly helpful for their audience.

7. **GET SPECIFIC WITH YOUR HEADLINES.** If you interview someone on your blog, don't title your post with an interesting quotation. While that strategy may help get readers in the print world, it doesn't help with SEO at all. Instead, title your post as "Interview With (insert name here)." If you have a way to identify the person further, include that in the title too. For instance, when I interview poets on my Poetic Asides blog, I'll title those posts like this: Interview With Poet Erika Meitner. Erika's name is a keyword, but so are the terms *poet* and *interview*.

8. **USE IMAGES.** Many expert sources state that the use of images can improve SEO, because it shows search engines that the person creating the page is spending a little extra time and effort on the page than a common spammer. However, I'd caution anyone using images to make sure those images are somehow complementary to the content. Don't just throw up a lot of images that have no relevance to anything. At the same time ...

9. **OPTIMIZE IMAGES THROUGH STRATEGIC LABELING.** Writers can do this by making sure the image file is labeled using your keyword(s) for the post. Using the Erika Meitner example above (which does include images), I would label the file "Erika Meitner headshot.jpg"—or whatever the image file type happens to be. Writers can also improve image SEO through the use of captions and ALT tagging. Of course, at the same time, writers should always ask themselves if it's worth going through all that trouble for each image or not. Each writer has to answer that question for him (or her) self.

10. **USE YOUR SOCIAL MEDIA PLATFORM TO SPREAD THE WORD.** Whenever you do something new on your site or blog, you should share that information on your other social media sites, such as Twitter, Facebook, LinkedIn, online forums, etc. This lets your social media connections know that something new is on your site/blog. If it's relevant and/or valuable, they'll let others know. And that's a great way to build your SEO.

Programmers and marketers could get even more involved in the dynamics of SEO optimization, but I think these tips will help most writers out immediately and effectively while still allowing plenty of time and energy for the actual work of writing.

BLOG DESIGN TIPS FOR WRITERS

Design is an important element to any blog's success. But how can you improve your blog's design if you're not a designer? I'm just an editor with an English Lit degree and no formal training in design. However, I've worked in media for more than a decade now and can share some very fundamental and easy tricks to improve the design of your blog.

Here are my seven blog design tips for writers:

1. **USE LISTS.** Whether they're numbered or bullet points, use lists when possible. Lists break up the text and make it easy for readers to follow what you're blogging.
2. **BOLD MAIN POINTS IN LISTS.** Again, this helps break up the text while also highlighting the important points of your post.
3. **USE HEADINGS.** If your posts are longer than 300 words and you don't use lists, then please break up the text by using basic headings.
4. **USE A READABLE FONT.** Avoid using fonts that are too large or too small. Avoid using cursive or weird fonts. Times New Roman or Arial works, but if you want to get "creative," use something similar to those.
5. **LEFT ALIGN.** English-speaking readers are trained to read left to right. If you want to make your blog easier to read, avoid centering or right aligning your text (unless you're purposefully calling out the text).
6. **USE SMALL PARAGRAPHS.** A good rule of thumb is to try and avoid paragraphs that drone on longer than five sentences. I usually try to keep paragraphs to around three sentences myself.
7. **ADD RELEVANT IMAGES.** Personally, I shy away from using too many images. My reason is that I only like to use them if they're relevant. However, images are very powerful on blogs, so please use them—just make sure they're relevant to your blog post.

If you're already doing everything on my list, keep it up! If you're not, then you might want to re-think your design strategy on your blog. Simply adding a header here and a list there can easily improve the design of a blog post.

GUEST POSTING TIPS FOR WRITERS

Recently, I've broken into guest posting as both a guest poster and as a host of guest posts (over at my Poetic Asides blog). So far, I'm pretty pleased with both sides of the guest posting process. As a writer, it gives me access to an engaged audience I may not usually reach. As a blogger, it provides me with fresh and valuable content I don't have to create. Guest blogging is a rare win-win scenario.

That said, writers could benefit from a few tips on the process of guest posting:

1. **PITCH GUEST POSTS LIKE ONE WOULD PITCH ARTICLES TO A MAGAZINE.** Include what your hook is for the post, what you plan to cover, and a little about who you are. Remember: Your post should somehow benefit the audience of the blog you'd like to guest post.

2. **OFFER PROMOTIONAL COPY OF YOUR BOOK (OR OTHER GIVEAWAYS) AS PART OF YOUR GUEST POST.** Having a random giveaway for people who comment on a blog post can help spur conversation and interest in your guest post, which is a great way to get the most mileage out of your guest appearance.

3. **CATER POSTS TO AUDIENCE.** As the editor of *Writer's Market* and *Poet's Market,* I have great range in the topics I can cover. However, if I'm writing a guest post for a fiction blog, I'll write about things of interest to a novelist—not a poet.

4. **MAKE IT PERSONAL, BUT PROVIDE NUGGET.** Guest posts are a great opportunity for you to really show your stuff to a new audience. You could write a very helpful and impersonal post, but that won't connect with readers the same way as if you write a very helpful and personal post that makes them want to learn more about you (and your blog, your book, your Twitter account, etc.). Speaking of which …

5. **SHARE LINKS TO YOUR WEBSITE, BLOG, SOCIAL NETWORKS, ETC.** After all, you need to make it easy for readers who enjoyed your guest post to learn more about you and your projects. Start the conversation in your guest post and keep it going on your own sites, profiles, etc. And related to that …

6. **PROMOTE YOUR GUEST POST THROUGH YOUR NORMAL CHANNELS ONCE THE POST GOES LIVE.** Your normal audience will want to know where you've been and what you've been doing. Plus, guest posts lend a little extra "street cred" to your projects. But don't stop there …

7. **CHECK FOR COMMENTS ON YOUR GUEST POST AND RESPOND IN A TIMELY MANNER.** Sometimes the comments are the most interesting part of a guest post (no offense). This is where readers can ask more in-depth or related questions, and it's also where you can show your expertise on the subject by being as helpful as possible. And guiding all seven of these tips is this one:

8. **PUT SOME EFFORT INTO YOUR GUEST POST.** Part of the benefit to guest posting is the opportunity to connect with a new audience. Make sure you bring your A-game, because you need to make a good impression if you want this exposure to actually help grow your audience. Don't stress yourself out, but put a little thought into what you submit.

ONE ADDITIONAL TIP: Have fun with it. Passion is what really drives the popularity of blogs. Share your passion and enthusiasm, and readers are sure to be impressed.

ROBERT LEE BREWER is a senior editor with the Writer's Digest Writing Community and author of *Solving the World's Problems* (Press 53). Follow him on Twitter @robertleebrewer.

THE AGENT QUERY TRACKER

Submit smarter and follow up faster with these simple spreadsheets to revolutionize your record-keeping.

Tyler Moss

Everyone knows the real magic of writing comes from time spent in the chair, those sessions in which your fingertips flitting across the keyboard can barely keep pace with the electric current sparking through your brain.

Those in-between periods, full of administrative tasks—the querying, the tracking of payments, the day-to-day doldrums that occupy the interstitial moments of a writer's life—become an afterthought. But when such responsibilities are given short shrift, the inevitable result is disorganization—which at best can impede creativity and at worst can have dire consequences. Missed payments, embarrassing gaffes (querying the same agent twice, or realizing you have no record of where your previous agent submitted your last novel), and incomplete records come tax time are entirely avoidable headaches.

Still, organized record-keeping takes work. Which is why we decided to do it for you.

This does not have to mean you're about to start spending more time on these tasks—in fact, quite the opposite. Once you invest in a standard process up front, each future action will require little more than filling out a few cells in a spreadsheet. (Learn to love them as I have for their clean, quadrilateral beauty.)

You can use the simple guides on the following pages to customize forms of your own, whether you're querying an agent, tracking the places your agent is submitting, or working on your freelancing career between projects.

AGENT QUERY TRACKER

AGENT	Example: Booker M. Sellington		
AGENCY	The Booker M. Sellington Agency		
E-MAIL	BMS@bmsagency.com		
DATE QUERIED	8/1/16		
MATERIALS SENT	Query, Synopsis, first 10 pages		
DATE FOLLOWED UP	9/1/16		
RESPONSE	Request for additional materials		
ADDITIONAL MATE-RIALS REQUESTED	Full manuscript		
DATE FOLLOWED UP	10/15/16		
RESPONSE	Offer of representation		
NOTES	Specializes in thrillers		

Few writers hit the jackpot and manage to land a literary agent on their first query. As this process can take weeks or months, and as agency guidelines vary widely, it can be helpful to keep a detailed record of whom you have contacted, what agency they work for, what materials you've sent in, and the specifics of their responses. Customize your own tracker starting from these column headings:

- **AGENT, AGENCY, & E-MAIL:** Where you are sending your query
- **POLICY AGAINST QUERYING MULTIPLE AGENTS AT AGENCY:** [Optional Field] Some agencies have a no-from-one-agent-means-no-from-the-whole-agency policy; noting this saves you time and embarrassment, particularly at larger firms where multiple reps might seem like a potential fit
- **DATE QUERIED & MATERIALS SENT:** When and what you submitted, always following guidelines (query letter, first ten pages, synopsis, proposal, etc.)
- **"NO RESPONSE MEANS NO" POLICY:** [Optional Field] Agents who specify in their guidelines that no response equates to a rejection, meaning you shouldn't follow up
- **DATE FOLLOWED UP:** In the event of no response and excluding those with the policy noted above
- **RESPONSE:** A rejection, a request to see more, or any constructive feedback
- **ADDITIONAL MATERIALS REQUESTED & DATE SENT:** Typically a full or partial manuscript is requested if your query garners interest

- **DATE FOLLOWED UP:** For a full or partial, follow up after at least four weeks if there's no response (unless you have an offer for representation elsewhere, in which case you'll follow up immediately to request a decision or withdraw your manuscript from consideration)
- **RESPONSE:** The agent's final feedback or response
- **NOTES:** Any helpful info on your interaction with the agent or agency, or feedback that could be addressed before additional querying (e.g., "The protagonist often behaves erratically and inconsistently," or "The manuscript could use a proofread")

If you opt to forgo seeking representation and instead are submitting directly to publishers that accept unagented submissions, then I suggest you make a separate spreadsheet to track that information, swapping the headings **AGENT** and **AGENCY** for **ACQUIRING EDITOR** and **IMPRINT/PUBLISHER**, respectively.

ORGANIZE YOUR QUERIES

Both versions of the tracker are available for download at writersdigest.com/GLA-18.

AGENT SUBMISSIONS TO PUBLISHER TRACKER

IMPRINT/PUBLISHER	Example: Pendant Publishing		
ACQUIRING EDITOR	Elaine Benes		
DATE SENT	8/1/16		
DATE FOLLOWED UP	9/1/16		
RESPONSE	Pass		
EDITOR'S COMMENTS	Says a "book about nothing" is not right for their Spring 2018 lineup		
ADDITIONAL NOTES	Suggests changes to plot in which the judge sentences protagonist to be the antagonist's butler		

After signing with an agent, it's critical to stay in close communication as she sends your manuscript to publishers. Such records allow you to stay involved in the direction of your career, gather essential data about the imprints your agent believes you'd be best suited for, and pinpoint commonalities or contradictions in feedback. And if you must someday sever ties with your agent, you'll have what you need to help your new representation pick up right where your old representation left off. Keep record of the following details.

- **IMPRINT/PUBLISHER, ACQUIRING EDITOR, & DATE SENT:** The details of exactly where and when your agent submitted your manuscript
- **DATE FOLLOWED UP:** Date on which your agent followed up with the acquiring editor if you did not receive an initial response
- **RESPONSE:** Accepted, rejected, revise-and-resubmit request
- **EDITOR'S COMMENTS:** A one-line description highlighting any relevant feedback received
- **ADDITIONAL NOTES:** Miscellaneous information about the publisher, editor or the overall interaction between agent and publishing house

---

PRO TIP: SAVE SPREADSHEETS TO GOOGLE DRIVE

Recently I read a news story in which a writer in New Orleans ran into his burning home to save the manuscripts of two completed novels stored on his computer—the only place he had them saved. Luckily, he weathered the blaze and escaped with laptop in hand. Though we can admire his dedication to his work, there are any number of digital-age options that could've prevented this horrible scenario—among them, Google Drive.

The system is ideal for uploading a fresh document of your manuscript every time you make changes, storing files online in addition to on your computer (Google Drive has an online storage function similar to services such as Dropbox and Microsoft OneDrive).

Google Drive allows you to create documents, spreadsheets, slide shows, and more, all of which can be accessed from anywhere—laptop, tablet, smartphone—by logging into a free Google account. Such items are easily shared with your co-author, agent, or publicist for more efficient record keeping or file sharing. It's also a great place to create and modify the trackers from this article.

Simply log in to your account at google.com/drive (or create one for free), hit the New button in the top left corner of the interface and click on Google Sheets. This will open a new window with a clean spreadsheet, where you can then begin entering the appropriate column headings. Title the spreadsheet by clicking "Untitled spreadsheet" at the top of the page. Once complete, you'll be able to open up your Freelance Payment Tracker or Agent Query Tracker on any device with an Internet connection—far from flames or flood.

FREELANCE PITCH TRACKER

SUBJECT	**Example:** Essay about meeting Stephen King in the waiting room at the dentist		
PUBLICATION	*Writer's Digest*		
EDITOR	Tyler Moss		
E-MAIL	wdsubmissions@ fwmedia.com		
PITCH SUBMITTED	8/1/16		
FOLLOW UP	8/15/16		
RESULT	Accepted		
DEADLINE	10/15/16		
NOTES	$0.50 cents/word for 600 words		

For freelance writers, ideas are currency—but they don't exist in a vacuum. Once you've brainstormed a solid premise and started to pitch potential markets, the resulting interactions can quickly clutter your in-box. Avoid losing track by recording your pitches in a spreadsheet with the following column headings:

- **SUBJECT:** One-line description of your story idea
- **PUBLICATION:** Name of magazine, website, or newspaper you pitched to
- **EDITOR & E-MAIL:** Where you sent your pitch
- **PITCH SUBMITTED:** When the query was sent
- **FOLLOW UP:** The date on which you plan to follow up if you haven't received a response (typically two weeks later, unless the submission guidelines specify otherwise)
- **RESULT:** Accepted, rejected, asked to rework
- **DEADLINE:** If accepted, date story is due
- **NOTES:** Additional info, based on your interactions with the editor (e.g., "Publication pays too little," or "Editor rejected pitch, but encouraged pitching again soon")

In addition to keeping track of irons currently in the fire, this spreadsheet is invaluable for later looking up contact info of editors you haven't e-mailed in a while.

If you want to track submissions to literary journals, simply switch out the column headings **SUBJECT** and **PUBLICATION** with **STORY TITLE** and **JOURNAL**, respectively, ax the **FOLLOW UP** column (journals tend to operate on slower, more sporadic schedules, sometimes without full-time staff), and replace the **DEADLINE** column with **READING FEE** (so you can evaluate and track any submission expenses where applicable).

ORGANIZE YOUR FREELANCE LIFE

Find both the freelance pitch and journal versions of this pitch tracker available for download at writersdigest.com/GLA-18.

FREELANCE PAYMENT TRACKER

ARTICLE HEADLINE	Example: Tongue Tied		
PUBLICATION/URL	*Ball & String Magazine*		
PAYMENT	$500		
DATE PUBLISHED	July 2016		
TOTAL WORDS	1,000		
$/WORD	$0.40 cents/word		
INVOICE #	#2014-1		
INVOICE SUBMITTED	8/12/16		
PAID	8/30/16		

When you've been commissioned to write a piece, it's vital to document the status of your payment. Not only will it keep you from missing a check, but it's incredibly useful for noting what a publication has paid you in the past and comparing the rates of different publications for which you freelance—which can help you prioritize your time by targeting the most lucrative outlets. It's also a lifesaver come April 15.

As depicted in the example spreadsheet above, you can use the following column headings to trace the path of your payments:

- **HEADLINE:** Title of the finished, published piece
- **PUBLICATION/URL:** Outlet that published the article and, if applicable, the URL where the article can be found online
- **PAYMENT:** Total payment received for work
- **DATE PUBLISHED:** Date article went live online, or issue month if for a print magazine or journal
- **TOTAL WORDS & $/WORD:** Length of the piece and amount you were paid per word, found by dividing the total payment by the total number of words (a common standardization for freelance payment rates)
- **INVOICE # & SUBMITTED:** Unique number of the invoice you submitted for this particular article (if applicable), and date on which it was submitted

- **PAID:** Date on which you received the payment, most commonly via check or direct deposit

Of course, you can also use this same basic format to develop a spreadsheet that covers advances, royalties, speaking honoraria, etc. Use the basic format outlined here to construct your own customized version.

TYLER MOSS is the former editor-in-chief of *Writer's Digest*. He is currently the content director at Wanderu. Follow him on Twitter @tjmoss11.

GETTING AN AGENT 101

....

by Jennifer D. Foster

Considered the "gatekeepers" to (large) publishing houses, literary agents are often your best bet to getting your foot in the door and making a name for yourself in the book (and even the motion picture, but that's another story!) world. But do you really need an agent? And exactly how do you find one? What are the tell-tale signs of a reputable (and not-so-reputable) literary agent? And how do you make the author-agent relationship work? Key insights, helpful tips, and sound advice from authors, editors, publishing consultants, editorial directors, literary agents, writing instructors, and heads of professional writing organizations give you the inside track.

WHAT LITERARY AGENTS DO

While the Writers' Union of Canada website states that "about 70 percent of the books published in Canada do not have an agent-assisted contract," it's a radically different story in the United States. In her book *Publishing 101: A First-Time Author's Guide to Getting Published, Marketing and Promoting Your Book, and Building a Successful Career* (Jane Friedman, 2015), Jane Friedman reveals that "in today's market, probably about 80 percent of books that the New York publishers acquire are sold to them by agents." But before taking the often-challenging plunge of getting a literary agent, do your homework to determine it you actually need one to get your manuscript published. And in order to figure that out, it's necessary to understand what, exactly, literary agents are and what they do. Jennifer Croll, editorial director of Greystone Books in Vancouver, explains it this way: "Agents act as both scouts and filters—they sort through what's out there and actively search to find the authors and proposals that are most likely to be published." Linden MacIntyre, award-winning journalist, internationally bestselling and Scotiabank

Giller Prize–winning author, and former host of *The Fifth Estate*, concurs. "Agents know the world of publishing, who matters, and established agents are known and recognized by editors and publishers. A recommendation from a credible agent will usually assure that someone of influence in publishing will read the manuscript."

Trevor Cole, Toronto, Ontario–based, award-winning author of *The Whisky King*, *Hope Makes Love,* and *Practical Jean*, further clarifies. An agent is beneficial "if you are committed to producing well-crafted book-length prose on a consistent professional basis." And, he says, "if the agent is part of a large house, they will have international contacts and sub-agents who can give your book its best chance at international distribution." Quite simply, "if an agent loves a book you've written, they will go to bat for it hard," he says, adding, "and once an editor agrees to buy the book, the agent's job is to get the best possible financial deal for you." Geoffrey Taylor, director of the International Festival of Authors in Toronto, Ontario, says that "an agent is the conduit for an author's work. This could mean anything from national to world rights. It could include all print forms, electronic, and video/film platforms." He says that agents have a lot of "experience with contracts and can usually negotiate better terms and a higher cash advance against future sales." Terence Green explains further. "A book contract can easily be twenty pages or more. An agent familiar with the publishing business understands which clauses are negotiable, and to what degree, and can customize the boilerplate contracts often tendered as a matter of rote to ones that are more palatable and fair-minded to all parties." Martha Kanya-Forstner, editor-in-chief of Doubleday Canada, and McClelland & Stewart, and vice-president of Penguin Random House Canada, reveals that "it is exceptionally difficult for authors to negotiate the value of their own work, [and it is] much better to have an agent secure the best deal possible and ensure that all terms of that deal are then met."

Martha Webb, proprietor and literary agent with CookeMcDermid in Toronto, Ontario, sees the agent's role as that of career guide and activist. "We are an author's advocate throughout the life of their work, and the liaison between the author and publisher. Our goal is to find the best possible publishing arrangements for the author's work …to support and advocate for their interests throughout the process and to advise them throughout their writing career." Carolyn Forde, literary agent and international rights director for Westwood Creative Artists in Toronto, Ontario, sums up the advocate role this way: "The agent supports and advises their clients. We do many, many contracts a year, and most authors won't do more than one a year (and even that would be considered a lot), so we do know what's industry standard, what's author friendly and what isn't."

In an online interview with Authornomics, agent Katherine Sands, with the Sarah Jane Freymann Literary Agency in New York, takes it even further, explaining that "literary agent now means content manager … the work is hands-on with a role in developing and marketing an author's name and material for print, digital, and other media—

not just centered around a book deal." She believes "the digital age is revolutionizing everything and reinvented agents are now far more involved in creating opportunities for writing clients' content in emerging markets: for books, to be used online, with partners, in podcasts, in products, and in digital media to accrue sales. The new agent focus is on how writers can market and maximize their works across a wide slate." Lori Hahnel, Calgary-based author of *After You've Gone, Love Minus Zero,* and *Nothing Sacred* and creative writing teacher at Mount Royal University and the Alexandra Writers' Centre Society, notes another role of the agent—that of editor. "Today more than ever, agents are taking on an editorial role. As publishers employ fewer and fewer editors, they need the manuscripts they get from agents to be in nearly publishable form when they're submitted."

Agents also handle other types of administrative and editorial-type tasks, such as checking royalty statements and hunting down overdue royalty checks; submitting books to reviewers and literary contests; and submitting future manuscripts to editors/publishers.

DETERMINING NEED

"Academic writing, and those working in less commercially successful genres likely don't need an agent," says Webb. Friedman, in her blog post "How to Find a Literary Agent for Your Book," adds that "if you're writing for a niche market (e.g., vintage automobiles) or wrote an academic or literary work, then you might not need an agent." Why? "Agents are motivated to take on clients based on the size of the advance they think they can get. If your project doesn't command a decent advance, then you may not be worth an agent's time, and you'll have to sell the project on your own." Kelsey Attard, managing editor of Freehand Books in Calgary, Alberta, says that "it depends on your goals … and also it depends on your genre. There are virtually no agents who represent poets, for example." Anita Purcell, executive director of the Canadian Authors Association, expounds further. "If you write poetry, short stories, or novellas, agents are not likely to take you on, and you have a better chance pitching directly to smaller presses that specialize in your particular genre." And, she adds, "authors who have been offered a contract with a publisher may want to get an agent to represent their interests before actually signing the contract. It is far easier to land an agent when you've got a firm offer from a publisher in hand."

Croll notes that those who want to work with an independent (indie) publisher can most likely get by without an agent. But, literary representation is essential for any writer wanting to make money by accessing most major publishing houses and editors, especially since the merging of many publishing companies has resulted in huge conglomerates with multiple imprints. "Editors often review agented submission first—and give them more consideration—because those submissions have already gone through a sort of vetting process," says Croll. And, shares Attard, "those biggest publishers typically don't accept unsolicited submissions from unagented authors." In the same online interview with Authornomics, Sands paints this picture: "Try this test at home: call a leading publisher tomorrow and try to get anyone to discuss your work. An agent has the green-light to do this, but a civilian is unlikely to penetrate the publisher's robotic turnaround, shielding editors from unrepresented writers." And, she poses, "betcha you can't find out which newly-hired editor would really love your literotic chiller about a sexy ichthyologist who must solve eco-system crime in Namibia."

Dawn Green, British Columbia–based author of *In the Swish* and *How Samantha Became a Revolutionary*, has this perspective. "I think any author who wants to just be an author, just be writing novels full time, requires an agent who will allow them time to focus on their craft." Stephanie Sinclair, senior literary agent with Transatlantic Agency in Toronto, Ontario, shares Dawn Green's sentiment: "The contracts are often very tricky, and without an agent, the process can end up taking up so much time, the author has no time/energy left to write! My job is to help my authors, so they can just focus on the writing." Like Sands, Dawn Green also holds that "an agent needs to help a writer market and brand themselves. It's that classic difference between art and business." And, she adds, "today, it seems that more time needs to be put into the social media and networking side of things, and that is not easy for most introverted writers to do."

Taylor Brown, Wilmington, North Carolina–based bestselling author of the novels *Fallen Land, The River of Kings,* and *Gods of Howl Mountain*, views the author-agent relationship from this lens. "Once your work has been published in book form, your agent's help only becomes that much more important. I think of an agent as a 'corner man' or woman of sorts." As well, he says, "they can do everything from giving feedback on manuscripts to helping interpret communications from your publisher to acting as a sounding board for important career changes. I could hardly imagine this career without an agent."

BEFORE THE QUERY

Most (good) literary agents receive hundreds of submissions a week from prospective clients, so time is precious, and second chances are rare. Part of doing your homework in finding an agent, before even entering the literary agent querying process, is ensuring your manuscript is the absolute best it can be. You want to be ready to hit "Send" as soon as an agent requests pages. In a guest blog post about finding a literary agent for The Writers' Workshop, novelist Harry Bingham says that means having a rock-solid product. "Write a good book. A stunning one. A dazzling one. One that echoes in the consciousness. One that makes a professional reader (i.e. agent/editor) sit up late with tears in their eyes." Sands agrees. In her book *Making the Perfect Pitch: How to Catch a Literary Agent's Eye* (The Writer Books, 2004), she says, "Literary agents must be enchanted, seduced, and won over to take you on as a client."

But how do you ensure this? Have your manuscript professionally evaluated; give it to trusted beta readers for invaluable constructive feedback. "They will find idiosyncrasies in your manuscript that will surprise you and also offer suggestions. Then after you make the edits, send the manuscript to a copy editor. Agents can spot professionalism a mile away," says Lynne Wiese Sneyd, owner of LWS Literary Services in Tucson, Arizona, and literary consultant for the Tucson Festival of Books. Hiring a professional editor will ensure the manuscript is error-free and at-the-ready for agent consideration. Brown shares Wiese Sneyd's philosophy. "A professional editor who has a record of helping shepherd books to publication is simply invaluable. You cannot depend on the agent seeing the potential in your work. They are not looking for potential. They are looking for a book they can sell right now."

THE QUERY: SOME DOS AND DON'TS

Also, make sure your pitch to an agent is bang-on in every aspect. If you can't write an enticing query letter, you may not convince a literary agent that you can write a compelling book. Jan Kardys, a literary agent at Black Hawk Literary Agency LLC in Redding, Connecticut, and chairman of the Unicorn Writers' Conference, offers these tips for honing your query and book summary: "It is helpful for writers to study book publishers' websites and study catalog copy. Once you study author's bio(s) and read the descriptions of their books, you get great ideas." Sinclair explains the pitch process this way: "Know who you are submitting to. When people send letters referencing some of my other clients and my taste, I know they have done their homework, which makes me immediately pay close attention." According to Sands, "it's the pitch and nothing but the pitch that gets a writer selected from the leaning tower of queries in a literary agent's office … The writing you do about your writing is as important as the writing itself." It is "part 'hello,' part cover letter, part interview for the coveted job of book author," she says. Agents, she stresses, "are looking first for a reason to keep reading, then for a reason to represent you … you want your pitch to give crystal clear answers—fast."

Some of those answers, says Croll, include being able to clearly describe the market for your book—who is going to buy it. "Selling your manuscript to a publisher is how an agent makes a living—that is their source of income. They are motivated to take on authors who will create work they can actually sell." And remember that your query letter is a form of communication, "so try to come across as a real person and not a pitching robot following a formula," advises Webb. Purcell couldn't agree more. "Always personalize your letter: make sure you use the agent's name and spell it correctly. If possible, find something you share in common, whether it's having the same birthplace, a mutual love of horror, or having met at a writers' conference." Like Webb, Purcell says "the query letter should not read like a form letter that is sent to every agent and publisher."

Hahnel, like Wiese Sneyd, suggests soliciting feedback from respected beta readers. The input will help "polish your query and your sample chapters until they shine." Purcell suggests taking it a step further. Writers "should ask experienced authors to review their query letter before submitting it." Why go to all this effort? "The bar is very, very high now, and so anything you can do to put your best foot forward is in your best interest," stresses Forde.

Hahnel also recommends having "a synopsis ready. Not all agents ask for them, but some will." As for a query letter, she says "don't clutter it with unnecessary information, such as courses you've taken or retreats you've gone on." Be polite and professional, says Hahnel, and ensure a confident and positive tone. "Don't say negative things like, 'I'm not sure if you'll like this.' or 'You probably won't want to read all of this.'" Attard recommends this: "Be brief, engaging, and also (at least for literary writing) let your manuscript be the star." Forde offers similar sound advice for a query. "Keep it short and concise—tell me about the book and about you. Don't try to be cute or memorable. Don't compare your book to the best book in the genre. If you say it's the next Harry Potter, what I hear is that you have unrealistic expectations." Purcell has this sage query-writing advice. "Agents often say that what catches their interest most is when writers manage to avoid some of the pitfalls of new writers, such as telling the agent that they're good writers (show, don't tell), or that all their family and friends loved the manuscript (of course they did, they love you), or that they've been wanting to be published authors since they were six years old (few writers haven't)." She says what also catches agents' interest is "when writers seem to have a strong understanding of their genre, as well as the distinction between commercial, upmarket, and literary writing."

A FEW WISE WORDS ON PLATFORM

Purcell says that it's all about branding right now "And writers should look at their social media platforms and their website, if they have one, with a critical eye that asks: 'What is my current brand and how appealing is that brand to a potential agent or publisher? Are there any posts or images that might turn an agent or publisher off?'" And, she adds, "if they're unpublished, writers need to think about what makes them stand out as good candidates for representation by the agent. Have they won any writing competitions? Are they authorities on the subject matter?"

WHERE TO FIND AGENTS

Once your manuscript is ultra-polished and ready for publication, and you've decided to take the leap and find an agent, one way is to conduct online research. "I think a writer should be a good sleuth," says Dawn Green. "And most agents/agencies are clear on their websites about what they are looking for." She also suggests researching to see if agents have given (online) interviews and made additional comments about what they're looking for in a manuscript.

Publishers Marketplace is a helpful online research tool. For a $25 monthly membership, writers/authors can get snapshots of top literary agencies, seeing which books agents have sold and editors' buying patterns. A membership also offers industry news updates and deal reports. The "Dealmaker" lists a contact database and a rights and proposals board posting—all helpful for determining which agent to pitch and also for knowing how to entice each one. "It's one of the most extensive databases of agents," says Wiese Sneyd. "It's an amazing resource."

Word of mouth is also helpful. Ask authors (especially in your genre) you know and trust, and whose work you respect who their agent is and request a candid assessment of their professional and personal style. "Referrals from existing clients are also an excellent way to get an agent's attention, so if you are able to ask an established writer, do so," recommends Forde. With Brown, he's the one making the connection for the writer. "In several cases, I have come across an unrepresented writer whose work I admire and recommended them to my agent."

Another method is to read the acknowledgment section of books with a similar audience or vibe to yours, as well as those of your favorite authors, who often list their agent with a huge "thank you." In a *Forbes'* blog post by contributor Nick Morgan, he succinctly explains the process: "Find books that are similar to what you hope yours will be, and that you like, and read the acknowledgments. Every writer thanks her agent fulsomely in the acknowledgments, or she'll never publish again."

Writers' conferences are also another viable route to find agents who are actively seeking new titles/authors. These agents are often speakers/panelists there, offering writers the chance to meet with them one-on-one to pitch their manuscript. "Face-to-face meetings with agents can help you get a foot in the door—as long as you keep it professional and respectful," notes Purcell. Hahnel knows "two people who were able to sign with agents at 'speed-dating' sessions at conferences," but, she stresses, "I understand it's not a super-common occurrence." Taylor says to attend myriad industry events, including in-store appearances, book launches and festivals. "Talk to people. Often those in attendance are part of the book industry. Always tell people you are an author. You never know who you may be talking to."

QueryTracker.net has helped more than 2,400 authors find a literary agent. Among its many online freebies are a detailed database of more than 1,500 agent profiles, including author comments from their experience with said agent; an agent query-tracking feature; and data that lists agent reply rates, typical response times, etc. Writersdigest.com also offers a handy online feature called "New Agency Alerts" that profiles "new literary agents actively seeking writers, books, and queries now. These agents are building their client lists." Agentquery.com, which says it's "the internet's largest free database of literary agents," lets you search for agents (around one thousand of them) by category, offers an online social networking community (great for the query process) and provides agent and agency updates. Attard maintains that authors and writers should check out the deal listings on *Publishers Weekly*, and *Quill & Quire*, investigating the agents listed in those deal announcements. And annual print directories, such as the *Literary Market Place: The Directory of the American Book Publishing Industry* (which offers listings to "reach the people who publish, package, review, represent, edit, translate, typeset, illustrate, design, print, bind, promote, publicize, ship, and distribute"), are often available in your local library's reference section, says Purcell.

Brown suggests submitting to literary magazines and contests. "These publications still attract the attention of agents," he assures. He also recommends using social media. Brown "drew the attention of a couple of agents after becoming active on Twitter." Why? "I believe some of the younger literary agents monitor social media for young writers who are making waves with their essays or stories." Attard is in agreement. "Some agents are active on social media, so follow a few and get a sense of what they like and don't like, and what you should avoid doing! It can be really valuable to get a sense of how they work."

And while a seasoned, big-name agent may be able to get you an impressive advance on your book and secure an ironclad contract, don't be afraid to go with a newer literary agent, someone who's "hungry" and will most likely have more time and offer a high level of personal attention to champion not only your book, but also your literary career. Attard suggests that "if an agent is new without many prior sales, consider their history in the industry. Do they have the connections necessary to be successful?" And, cautions Webb, "a junior agent—and everyone needs to start somewhere—should be a junior agent within a reputable agency, who has the support of more senior agents behind her." In the same vein is the size of the literary agency. "This doesn't necessarily correlate with the quality of the agent or the size of the deal you can expect," verifies Friedman in her blog post "How to Find a Literary Agent for Your Book."

THE "GOOD" AGENT

What are the signs of a good literary agent? According to the website of the Canadian Authors Association, "reputable agents will be up to date on current publishing trends … and serve as experts in market sales, so they will help ensure your book gets a good cover design, and more attention from the publisher's publicity department." Purcell affirms that agents "represent you [the author], not the publisher, and will negotiate for more money, subsidiary rights, and protection clauses. Good agents are also in it for the long haul: they are as interested in building the author's career as they are in selling the first book."

MacIntyre shares the same mindset. He says that many writers aren't interested in the "bureaucracy and the fine points of the book business," so a good agent, "in addition to possessing literary instincts and professional connections, has a mercenary skill set. An agent should be a partner and a friend, but strong enough to speak truth to vanity. An agent will offer an essential service but is not a servant." He also says good agents attend myriad international book fairs; have strong professional relationships with influential editors; "play bad-cop where money matters matter; play mom/dad when the creative muse becomes petulant and sulky; pick up the tab (now and then); offer tactful commentary and advice (but not instruction) on creative issues; and know the difference between momentary insecurity and reality-based despair." MacIntyre also believes good agents have "the sensibilities and judgment of an editor; the skills of an accountant; the temerity of a union boss; a sense of humor, irony; good taste in food, drink and literature; and patience."

Kanya-Forstner stresses that "the best agents search widely and actively for new, diverse and challenging voices; for writers who bring something essential to the conversations in which they participate." She says that "the best agents are the most discerning, taking on only those clients whose work they know they can champion with the utmost integrity and confidence. The work they then submit comes with the weight of their endorsement and credibility." To Kanya-Forstner, "the best agents make it their business to be familiar with the sensibilities and interests of individual editors and with the publishing identity and strengths of individual imprints. The best agents pride themselves on being successful matchmakers."

Kardys says a "talented agent" will suggest to a writer several tactics, such as building a platform before the book deal—social media, contact lists, and doing events or writing articles/stories; provide ideas on how to market the book; and edit the writer's book summary." For her, "ideally, the best literary agents have a background as a former book editor, subsidiary rights experience at a book publisher, or the agent has started their publishing career by working for another literary agency before leaving to start their own agency."

Cole sees a good agent as "someone who seems to 'get' your work, who understands what you're writing now, and what you want to write in the future." And, adds Kanya-Forstner, since "publishing is a constantly changing business, the best agents stay on top of market trends, shifts in buying habits and retail practices." Terence Green describes the good agent in these terms: "A good agent knows editors and what they are looking for. They can provide shortcuts to editors. Many editors won't even look at unsolicited manuscripts, trusting the judgment of respected agents." So, the good agent, he says, is "in essence, the editor's first reader, winnowing the field appropriately for the editor." Friedman believes a good agent is not only an author's business manager, but also an author's "mentor and cheerleader." She shares these wise sentiments in her blog post: Literary agents are "also there to hold your hand when things go wrong with the editor or publisher. They prop you up when you're down, they celebrate your successes publicly, they look for opportunities you might not see, and they attend to your financial best interests as well as your big-picture career growth." Purcell stresses that "because the bulk of their work involves sales and negotiation, [editors] should be confident and assertive in their dealings, but always professional and respectful in their treatment of people, including you." She also believes agents should be "strategic thinkers" with strong social media skills. And "being well-organized is also a useful quality in a literary agent, since they need to juggle a variety of authors, editors, and projects."

THE "BAD" AGENT

While the list of qualities and skills of a good agent is long, the list for a "bad" one is comparable. Since there is no worldwide professional organization responsible for vetting agents and maintaining agent standards, virtually anyone can hang out their "Agent" shingle. Beware of sweet-talking scammers, secretive behavior, those who don't treat you as a business partner, those who don't communicate respectfully and clearly, and those who don't reply in a timely manner. They aren't legit agents. Never, ever give a literary agent money upfront—not as a retainer, not for administrative expenses, and not for a reading fee/feedback. An agent only gets paid—somewhere between 10 and 15 percent of an author's earnings—when an author gets paid and the publisher's advance is received. And 20 to 25 percent is standard for foreign sales (when translation rights are licensed to foreign book publishers), since the commission is often split between foreign and domestic agents. Cole says that "if you send a manuscript to an agent and she doesn't respond after a few months, that's an agent I wouldn't bother approaching further." And, he stresses, "if you're working with an agent, and she can't give you a list of the publishers she's sent your manuscript to, that's an agent who probably isn't working hard for you." Similarly, Taylor says that "if your agent is not directing you towards a deal, perhaps it is not the best fit."

Kardys feels the following are red flags: "A writer should not work with an agent who has no experience in the book field or hasn't offered suggested changes in the manuscript." However, she says, "if the book requires major work, an agent shouldn't sign up a writer as a client." And "if the agent doesn't know the basic points of a contract, the payment structures for an advance and the latest changes in the book marketplace, you should be cautious," she warns. Friedman, in her blog post, stresses that "if an agent passes you a publisher's boilerplate contact to sign with no changes, you may be in big trouble." Hahnel says to avoid agents with "non-existent client lists or sales history." And, she alerts, "beware of agents who only work with a few publishers."

According to a Science Fiction & Fantasy Writers of America blog post by A.C. Crispin, "real agents don't advertise. They don't have to. If you see an agency name in a sponsored Google ad or in the back of a writer's magazine, odds are they're a scam." And, says

Crispin in that same post, "any agent that claims their client list is 'confidential' should be regarded with wariness, and their credentials should be investigated with extra care." Also, avoid agents who don't help with improving your query and/or proposal package. In her blog post, Friedman says only a few authors can put together a "crackerjack proposal." She stresses that "an agent should be ensuring the pitch or proposal is primed for success, and this almost always requires at least one round of feedback and revision."

Membership in the newly founded Professional Association of Canadian Literary Agents (PACLA), which only permits established literary agents to join and has a strict Code of Practice, or in the Association of Authors' Representatives, Inc. (AAR), for which its some 400 member must meet the highest standards and subscribe to its bylaws and Canon of Ethics, is a positive sign, but not necessarily a guarantee. Friedman states that "people in the industry should recognize the name of your agent." She also warns that if no online mention or reference to your agent can be found and if the agent isn't a member of the AAR, "that's a red flag. Check his track record carefully. See who he's sold to and how recently." And, forewarns Purcell, "generally speaking, if an agent is pursuing you rather than the other way around, think twice—most agents already have a stable of promising authors and rarely need to be the wooer." These are all reasons why, says, Terence Green, "one must do one's 'due diligence' in the matter, just as one would before venturing into any business investment."

HOW TO KEEP THE GOOD ONES

If you do secure a literary agent, be mindful that, like in any good relationship, the author-agent "marriage" can only thrive on mutual trust and respect, shared enthusiasm and open communication. Says Purcell: "I think it's important to have a connection with your literary agent. If there isn't a genuine and mutual feeling of respect and liking for one another, the relationship may sour over time." Sinclair thinks "it's important that you can enjoy a meal together. It's an intimate relationship in a way, so you want to be sure you like each other!" Cole advises to "be reliable, meet your deadlines and appreciate [your agent's] hard work." And Webb says to "be open to feedback and trust that your agent wants to make a success of your book and your career." But, don't expect to sit back and let your agent do all of the legwork. "Be proactive about your career, boosting your platform whenever you can, and be someone who editors want to work with," she advises. Wiese Sneyd concurs. "Learn the business ahead of time. Respect an agent's time. Avoid excessive emails. Don't expect an agent to teach you the ins and outs of publishing. You'll have questions, of course, but enter the relationship as a savvy author."

Kardys advises to "always put in writing the obligations and duties of the writer and the agent" and to "encourage open communication and timelines." She also stresses to "listen carefully when your agent tells you to build your social media platform and make a list of email contacts, as later you will not have time to do this intense work when your book is published." Brown's suggestions are also a list of dos. Only a small percentage of writers get to have an agent represent their work, he says, and "there will be ups and downs and stressors of all kinds." But, he notes, "it's important to keep in mind that many writers only dream of having such problems! So try to enjoy the whole experience, even the worries and frustrations. They are all part of the story."

MAKING THE FINAL DECISION

Kanya-Forstner advises that "agents are only as good as the authors they represent, or for new agents, as good as the writers whose work they champion on social platforms and in public discourse about books." Refer to an agent's client list, which rights they've sold, when and in which countries, view their photograph, their (literary) likes and dislikes (Goodreads is a good resource to check), their Twitter feed, their website or their company's website, and weigh it all with any kind of gut feeling you may have to help you make your final choice. It all boils down to feelings and sensibilities—a kind of personal chemistry. MacIntyre concurs: "Basically, it will come down to a gut-level response, based on impressions and the compatibility of personalities." Author Chuck Sambuchino takes a similar stance. In his online WritersDigest.com article entitled "11 Steps to Finding the Agent Who'll Love your Book," he says that, after making your list of agents to contact, "rank agents in the likelihood of a love match."

THE SUBMISSION PROCESS IN A NUTSHELL

After doing your research into finding suitable agents, it's absolutely essential to find out what each agent wants in a submission. "Be professional, read about the formatting details the agency wants and let your story do the selling," says Dawn Green. Purcell shares in her tips, adding, "it's important to find out what their preferences are and to follow their guidelines faithfully. If they want the manuscript double-spaced in the courier font with one-inch margins, that's what you should give them. You're sending them a message if you don't." Sambuchino concurs in his online piece. "Getting through the front door is often about playing by the rules. Don't send anything less—or more—than each agent has asked for." If the agent specifies that they don't want attachments, "that means they want the query letter and up to ten pages of the manuscript imbedded in the body of the email, even if that looks ugly," says Purcell. Also, says Sambuchino, be sure you're submitting to four to eight agents only at a time, giving each agent their own separate email or mailed package. "Keep things professional. No gimmicks." And don't argue if/when you get a "no thank you" reply. "An agent is not attacking you. They know the business, they know what sells, and they are honestly trying to help your words get noticed," says Dawn Green, adding not to take agent criticism personally. Taylor suggests that if you receive a "no," be sure to "follow up with a thank you and ask if they might suggest who might be interested.

Sometimes advice comes your way, or even your work gets a second look. Often publishing is luck and timing."

BEYOND THE QUERY

Be sure to keep track of your submissions and their results. Sambuchino says that "if you aren't getting any page requests, your query needs work. If you're getting partial requests but then nothing, your first draft pages aren't snagging the reader. If you're getting full requests but no nibbles, it's time to take a look at the full manuscript again." Use each rejection and any feedback you may get from an agent to fine-tune your next set of submissions. "This is not an easy business, and rejection is the norm, not the exception. I like to think of rejections as marks of honor," says Brown. "It's not how many times you get knocked down; it's how many times you get back up. Each rejection is one step closer to publication. Keep the faith. Keep going. It's worth it." And be prepared to wait for as long as it takes to find your perfect match. "My experience," clarifies Terence Green, "has always been that this is not a business for the impatient."

Perhaps the best advice to keep in mind during this journey comes from Cole: "Too many beginning writers with a half-finished manuscript think the first thing they need to do is get an agent, as if that will solve everything and ensure a flourishing writing career. It doesn't work that way," he warns. "The first thing you need to do is master your craft and produce a damn good book. An agent can't make you a good writer. An agent can't make you a success. That's up to you."

JENNIFER D. FOSTER is a Toronto, Canada-based freelance writer and editor, and her company is Planet Word. Her clients are from the book and custom publishing, magazine, and marketing and communications fields and include House of Anansi Press, Art Gallery of Ontario, TC Media Inc., *Quill & Quire*, PwC Management Services, *The Globe and Mail*, and *Canadian Children's Book News*. When Jennifer's not busy spilling ink for her first novel, she enjoys mentoring novice editors and writers, theater, traveling, gardening, camping, women's roller derby, urban hiking, baking, and yoga. Jennifer is administrative director of Rowers Reading Series and vice-president of Canadian Authors Association, Toronto branch. Find her online at lifeonplanetword.wordpress.com.

30-DAY PLATFORM CHALLENGE

Build Your Writing Platform in a Month

....

by Robert Lee Brewer

///

Whether writers are looking to find success through traditional publication or the self-publishing route, they'll find a strong writer platform will help them in their efforts. A platform is not marketing; it's the actual and quantifiable reach writers have to their target audience.

Here is a 30-day platform challenge I've developed to help writers get started in their own platform-building activities without getting overwhelmed. By accomplishing one task for one day, writers can feel a sense of accomplishment and still handle their normal daily activities. By the end of the month, writers should have a handle on what they need to do to keep growing their platform into the future.

DAY 1: DEFINE YOURSELF

For Day 1, define yourself. Don't worry about where you'd like to be in the future. Instead, take a look at who you are today, what you've already accomplished, what you're currently doing, etc.

EXAMPLE DEFINE YOURSELF WORKSHEET

Here is a chart I'm using (with my own answers). Your worksheet can ask even more questions. The more specific you can be the better for this exercise.

NAME (AS USED IN BYLINE): Robert Lee Brewer

POSITION(S): Senior Content Editor - Writer's Digest Writing Community; Author; Free-lance Writer; Blogger; Event Speaker; Den Leader - Cub Scouts; Curator of Insta-poetry Series

SKILL(S): Editing, creative writing (poetry and fiction), technical writing, copywriting, database management, SEO, blogging, newsletter writing, problem solving, idea generation, public speaking, willingness to try new things, community building.

SOCIAL MEDIA PLATFORMS: Facebook, LinkedIn, Google+, Twitter, Tumblr, Blogger.

URLs: www.writersmarket.com; www.writersdigest.com/editor-blogs/poetic-asides; http://robertleebrewer.blogspot.com/; www.robertleebrewer.com

ACCOMPLISHMENTS: Named 2010 Poet Laureate of Blogosphere; spoken at several events, including Writer's Digest Conference, AWP, Austin International Poetry Festival, Houston Poetry Fest, and more; author of Solving the World's Problems (Press 53); published and sold out of two limited edition poetry chapbooks, *Enter* and *Escape*; edited several editions of *Writer's Market* and *Poet's Market*; former GMVC conference champion in the 800-meter run and MVP of WCHS cross country and track teams; undergraduate award-winner in several writing disciplines at University of Cincinnati, including Journalism, Fiction, and Technical Writing; BA in English Literature from University of Cincinnati with certificates in writing for Creative Writing-Fiction and Professional and Technical Writing.

INTERESTS: Writing (all genres), family (being a good husband and father), faith, fitness (especially running and disc golf), fantasy football, reading.

IN ONE SENTENCE, WHO AM I? Robert Lee Brewer is a married Methodist father of five children (four sons and one daughter) who works as an editor but plays as a writer, specializing in poetry and blogging.

As long as you're being specific and honest, there are no wrong answers when it comes to defining yourself. However, you may realize that you have more to offer than you think. Or you may see an opportunity that you didn't realize even existed.

DAY 2: SET YOUR GOALS

For today's platform-building task, set your goals. Include short-term goals and long-term goals. In fact, make a list of goals you can accomplish by the end of this year; then, make a list of goals you'd like to accomplish before you die.

EXAMPLE GOALS

Here are some of examples from my short-term and long-term goal lists:

SHORT-TERM GOALS:

- Promote new book, *Solving the World's Problems*.
- In April, complete April PAD Challenge on Poetic Asides blog.
- Get *Writer's Market 2016* to printer ahead of schedule.
- Get *Poet's Market 2016* to printer ahead of schedule.
- Lead workshop at Poetry Hickory event in April.
- Etc.

LONG-TERM GOALS:

- Publish book on platform development for small businesses.
- Raise 5 happy and healthy children into 5 happy, healthy, caring, and self-sufficient adults.
- Continue to learn how to be a better husband and human being.
- Become a bestselling novelist.
- Win Poet Laureate of the Universe honors.
- Etc.

Some writers may ask what defining yourself and creating goals has to do with platform development. I maintain that these are two of the most basic and important steps in the platform-building process, because they define who you are and where you want to be.

A successful platform strategy should communicate who you are and help you get where you'd like to be (or provide you with a completely new opportunity). If you can't communicate who you are to strangers, then they won't realize how you might be able to help them or why you're important to them. If you don't have any goals, then you don't have any direction or purpose for your platform.

By defining who you are and what you want to accomplish, you're taking a huge step in establishing a successful writing and publishing career.

DAY 3: JOIN FACEBOOK

For today's task, create a profile on Facebook. Simple as that. If you don't have one, it's as easy as going to www.facebook.com and signing up. It takes maybe 5 or 10 minutes. If that.

10 FACEBOOK TIPS FOR WRITERS

Many readers probably already have a Facebook profile, and that's fine. If you have already created a profile (or are doing so today), here are some tips for handling your profile:

- Complete your profile. The most checked page on most profiles is the About page. The more you share the better.
- Make everything public. Like it or not, writers are public figures. If you try to hide, it will limit the potential platform.
- Think about your audience in everything you do. When your social media profiles are public, anyone can view what you post. Keep this in mind at all times.
- Include a profile pic of yourself. Avoid setting your avatar as anything but a head-shot of yourself. Many people don't like befriending a family pet or cartoon image.
- Update your status regularly. If you can update your status once per day, that's perfect. At the very least, update your status weekly. If your profile is a ghost town, people will treat it like one.
- Communicate with friends on Facebook. Facebook is a social networking site, but networking happens when you communicate. So communicate.
- Be selective about friends. Find people who share your interests. Accept friends who share your interests. Other folks may be fake or inappropriate connections trying to build their "friend" totals.
- Be selective about adding apps. If you're not sure, it's probably best to avoid. Many users have wasted days, weeks, and even months playing silly games on Facebook.
- Join relevant groups. The emphasis should be placed on relevancy. For instance, I'm a poet, so I join poetry groups.
- Follow relevant fan pages. As with groups, the emphasis is placed on relevancy. In my case, I'm a fan of several poetry publications.

In addition to the tips above, be sure to always use your name as it appears in your byline. If you're not consistent in how you list your name in your byline, it's time to pick a name and stick with it. For instance, my byline name is Robert Lee Brewer—not Robbie Brewer, Bob Brewer, or even just Robert Brewer.

There are times when I absolutely can't throw the "Lee" in there, but the rest of the time it is Robert Lee Brewer. And the reasoning behind this is that it makes it easier for people who know me elsewhere to find and follow me on Facebook (or whichever social media site). Name recognition is super important when you're building your writer platform.

DAY 4: JOIN TWITTER

For today's task, create a Twitter account. That's right. Go to www.twitter.com and sign up—if you're not already. This task will definitely take less than 5 minutes.

As with Facebook, I would not be surprised to learn that most readers already have a Twitter account. Here are three important things to keep in mind:

- **MAKE YOUR PROFILE BIO RELEVANT.** You might want to use a version of the sentence you wrote for Day 1's task. Look at my profile (twitter.com/robertleebrewer) if you need an example.
- **USE AN IMAGE OF YOURSELF.** One thing about social media (and online networking) is that people love to connect with other people. So use an image of yourself—not of your pet, a cute comic strip, a new age image, flowers, robots, etc.
- **MAKE YOUR TWITTER HANDLE YOUR BYLINE—IF POSSIBLE.** For instance, I am known as @RobertLeeBrewer on Twitter, because I use Robert Lee Brewer as my byline on articles, in interviews, at speaking events, on books, etc. Be as consistent with your byline as humanly possible.

Once you're in Twitter, try finding some worthwhile tweeps to follow. Also, be sure to make a tweet or two. As with Facebook, people will only interact with your profile if it looks like you're actually there and using your account.

SOME BASIC TWITTER TERMINOLOGY

Twitter has a language all its own. Here are some of the basics:

- **TWEET.** This is what folks call the 140-character messages that can be sent on the site. Anyone who follows you can access your tweets.
- **RT.** RT stands for re-tweet. This is what happens when someone shares your tweet, usually character for character. It's usually good form to show attribution for the author of the original tweet.
- **DM.** DM stands for direct message. This is a good way to communicate with someone on Twitter privately. I've actually had a few opportunities come my way through DMs on Twitter.
- **#.** The #-sign stands for hashtag. Hashtags are used to organize group conversations. For instance, Writer's Digest uses the #wdc to coordinate messages for their Writer's Digest Conferences. Anyone can start a hashtag, and they're sometimes used to add humor or emphasis to a tweet.
- **FF.** FF stands for follow Friday—a day typically set asides to highlight follow-worthy tweeps (or folks who use Twitter). There's also a WW that stands for writer Wednesday.

DAY 5: START A BLOG

For today's task, create a blog. You can use Blogger (www.blogger.com), WordPress (www.wordpress.com), or Tumblr (www.tumblr.com). In fact, you can use another blogging platform if you wish. To complete today's challenge, do the following:

- **CREATE A BLOG.** That is, sign up (if you don't already have a blog), pick a design (these can usually be altered later if needed), and complete your profile.
- **WRITE A POST FOR TODAY.** If you're not sure what to cover, you can just introduce yourself and share a brief explanation of how your blog got started. Don't make it too complicated.

If you already have a blog, excellent! You don't need to create a new one, but you might want to check out some ways to optimize what you have.

OPTIMIZE YOUR BLOG

Here are some tips for making your blog rock:
- **USE IMAGES IN YOUR POSTS.** Images are eye candy for readers, help with search engine optimization, and can even improve clicks when shared on social media sites, such as Facebook and Twitter.
- **USE HEADERS IN POSTS.** Creating and bolding little headlines in your posts will go a long way toward making your posts easier to read and scan. Plus, they'll just look more professional.
- **WRITE SHORT.** Short sentences (fewer than 10 words). Short paragraphs (fewer than five sentences). Concision is precision in online composition.
- **ALLOW COMMENTS.** Most bloggers receive very few (or absolutely zero) comments in the beginning, but it pays to allow comments, because this gives your audience a way to interact with you. For my personal blog, I allow anyone to comment on new posts, but those that are more than a week old require my approval.

DAY 6: READ AND COMMENT ON A POST

For today's task, read at least one blog post and comment on it (linking back to your blog). And the comment should not be something along the lines of, "Hey, cool post. Come check out my blog." Instead, you need to find a blog post that really speaks to you and then make a thoughtful comment.

Here are a few possible ways to respond.

- **SHARE YOUR OWN EXPERIENCE.** If you've experienced something similar to what's covered in the post, share your own story. You don't have to write a book or anything, but maybe a paragraph or two.
- **ADD ANOTHER PERSPECTIVE.** Maybe the post was great, but there's another angle that should be considered. Don't be afraid to point that angle out.
- **ASK A QUESTION.** A great post usually will prompt new thoughts and ideas—and questions. Ask them.

As far as linking back to your blog, you could include your blog's URL in the comment, but also, most blogs have a field in their comments that allow you to share your URL. Usually, your name will link to that URL, which should either be your blog or your author website (if it offers regularly updated content).

It might seem like a lot of work to check out other blogs and comment on them, but this is an incredible way to make real connections with super users. These connections can lead to guest post and interview opportunities. In fact, they could even lead to speaking opportunities too.

DAY 7: ADD SHARE BUTTONS TO YOUR BLOG

For today's challenge, add share buttons to your blog and/or website.

The easiest way to do this is to go to www.addthis.com and click on the Get AddThis button. It's big, bright, and orange. You can't miss it.

Basically, the site will give you button options, and you select the one you like best. The AddThis site will then provide you with HTML code that you can place into your site and/or blog posts. Plus, it provides analytics for bloggers who like to see how much the buttons are boosting traffic.

If you want customized buttons, you could enlist the help of a programmer friend or try playing with the code yourself. I recently learned that some really cool buttons on one friend's blog were created by her husband (yes, she married a programmer, though I don't think she had her blog in mind when she did so).

Plus, most blogging platforms are constantly adding new tools. By the time you read this article, there are sure to be plenty of fun new buttons, apps, and widgets available.

Here's the thing about social sharing buttons: They make it very easy for people visiting your site to share your content with their social networks via Facebook, Twitter, LinkedIn, Instagram, Pinterest, and other sites. The more your content is shared the wider your writer platform.

DAY 8: JOIN LINKEDIN

For today's challenge, create a LinkedIn profile. Go to www.linkedin.com and set it up in a matter of minutes. After creating profiles for Facebook and Twitter, this task should be easy.

LINKEDIN TIPS FOR WRITERS

In many ways, LinkedIn looks the same as the other social networks, but it does have its own quirks. Here are a few tips for writers:

- **USE YOUR OWN HEAD SHOT.** You've heard this advice before. People want to connect with people, not family pets and/or inanimate objects.
- **COMPLETE YOUR PROFILE.** The more complete your profile the better. It makes you look more human.
- **GIVE THOUGHTFUL RECOMMENDATIONS TO RECEIVE THEM.** Find people likely to give you recommendations and recommend them first. This will prompt them to return the favor.
- **SEARCH FOR CONNECTIONS YOU ALREADY HAVE.** This is applicable to all social networks. Find people you know to help you connect with those you don't.
- **MAKE MEANINGFUL CONNECTIONS WITH OTHERS.** Remember: It's not about how many connections you make; it's about how many meaningful connections you make.
- **MAKE YOUR PROFILE EASY TO FIND.** You can do this by using your byline name. (For instance, I use linkedin.com/in/robertleebrewer.)
- **TAILOR YOUR PROFILE TO YOUR VISITOR.** Don't fill out your profile thinking only about yourself; instead, think about what your target audience might want to learn about you.

LinkedIn is often considered a more "professional" site than the other social networks like Facebook, Instagram, and Twitter. For one thing, users are prompted to share their work experience and request recommendations from past employers and current co-workers.

However, this site still offers plenty of social networking opportunities for people who can hook up with the right people and groups.

DAY 9: RESPOND TO AT LEAST THREE TWEETS

For today's task, respond to at least three tweets from other tweeps on Twitter.

Since Day 4's assignment was to sign up for Twitter, you should have a Twitter account—and you're hopefully following some other Twitter users. Just respond to at least three tweets today.

As far as your responses, it's not rocket science. You can respond with a "great article" or "cool quote." A great way to spread the wealth on Twitter is to RT (retweet) the original tweet with a little note. This accomplishes two things:

- One, it lets the tweep know that you appreciated their tweet (and helps build a bond with that person); and
- Two, it brings attention to that person for their cool tweet.

Plus, it helps show that you know how to pick great resources on Twitter, which automatically improves your credibility as a resource on Twitter.

DAY 10: DO A GOOGLE SEARCH ON YOURSELF

For today's task, do a search on your name.

First, see what results appear when you search your name on Google (google.com). Then, try searching on Bing (bing.com). Finally, give Yahoo (yahoo.com) a try.

By searching your name, you'll receive insights into what others will find (and are already finding) when they do a search specifically for you. Of course, you'll want to make sure your blog and/or website is number one in the search results. If it isn't, we'll be covering SEO (or search engine optimization) topics later in this challenge.

OTHER SEARCH ENGINES

For those who want extra credit, here are some other search engines to try searching (for yourself):

- DuckDuckGo.com
- Ask.com
- Dogpile.com
- Yippy.com
- YouTube.com

(Note: It's worth checking out which images are related to your name as well. You may be surprised to find which images are connected to you.)

DAY 11: FIND A HELPFUL ARTICLE AND LINK TO IT

For today's task, find a helpful article (or blog post) and share it with your social network—and by social network, I mean that you should share it on Facebook, Twitter, and LinkedIn at a minimum. If you participate on message boards or on other social networks, share in those places as well.

Before linking to an article on fantasy baseball or celebrity news, however, make sure your article (or blog post) aligns with your author platform goals. You should have an idea of who you are and who you want to be as a writer, and your helpful article (or blog post) should line up with those values.

Of course, you may not want to share articles for writers if your platform is based on parenting tips or vampires or whatever. In such cases, you'll want to check out other resources online. Don't be afraid to use a search engine.

For Twitter, you may wish to use a URL shortener to help you keep under the 140-character limit. Here are five popular URL shorteners:

- bit.ly. This is my favorite.
- goo.gl. Google's URL shortener.
- owl.ly. Hootsuite's URL shortener.
- deck.ly. TweetDeck's URL shortener.
- su.pr. StumbleUpon's URL shortener.

By the way, here's an extra Twitter tip. Leave enough room in your tweets to allow space for people to attribute your Twitter handle if they decide to RT you. For instance, I always leave at least 20 characters to allow people space to tweet "RT @robertleebrewer" when retweeting me.

DAY 12: WRITE A BLOG POST AND INCLUDE CALL TO ACTION

For today's task, write a new blog post for your blog. In the blog post, include a call to action at the end of the post.

What's a call to action?

I include calls to action at the end of all my posts. Sometimes, they are links to products and services offered by my employer (F+W Media) or some other entity. Often, I include links to other posts and ways to follow me on other sites. Even the share buttons are a call to action of sorts.

Why include a call to action?

A call to action is good for giving readers direction and a way to engage more with you. Links to previous posts provide readers with more helpful or interesting information. Links to your social media profiles give readers a way to connect with you on those sites. These calls to action are beneficial to you and your readers when they are relevant.

What if I'm just getting started?

Even if you are completely new to everything, you should have an earlier blog post from last week, a Twitter account, a Facebook account, and a LinkedIn account. Link to these at the end of your blog post today. It's a proper starting place.

And that's all you need to do today. Write a new blog post with a call to action at the end. (By the way, if you're at a loss and need something to blog about, you can always comment on that article you shared yesterday.)

DAY 13: LINK TO POST ON SOCIAL MEDIA PROFILES

For today's challenge, link your blog post from yesterday to your social networks.

At a minimum, these social networks should include Facebook, Twitter, and LinkedIn. However, if you frequent message boards related to your blog post or other social networks (like Instagram, Pinterest, etc.), then link your blog post there as well.

I understand many of you may have already completed today's challenge. If so, hooray! It's important to link your blog to your social media accounts and vice versa. When they work together, they grow together.

Is it appropriate to link to my blog post multiple times?

All writers develop their own strategies for linking to their articles and blog posts, but here's my rule. I will usually link to each blog post on every one of my social networks at least once. Since I have a regular profile and a fan page on Facebook, I link to each of those profiles once—and I only link to posts once on LinkedIn. But Twitter is a special case.

The way Twitter works, tweets usually only have a few minutes of visibility for tweeps with an active stream. Even tweeps with at least 100 follows may only have a 30-minute to hour window of opportunity to see your tweet. So for really popular and timely blog posts, I will tweet them more often than once on Twitter.

That said, I'm always aware of how I'm linking and don't want to become that annoying spammer that I typically avoid following in my own social networking efforts.

LINKING TIPS

Some tips on linking to your post:
- Use a URL shortener. These are discussed above.

- Apply title + link formula. For instance, I might Tweet this post as: Platform Challenge: Day 13: (link). It's simple and to the point. Plus, it's really effective if you have a great blog post title.
- Frame the link with context. Using this post as an example, I might Tweet: Take advantage of social media by linking to your blog posts: (link). Pretty simple, and it's an easy way to link to the same post without making your Twitter feed look loaded with the same content.
- Quote from post + link formula. Another tactic is to take a funny or thought-provoking quote from the post and combine that with a link. Example Tweet: "I will usually link to each blog post on every one of my social networks at least once." (link). Again, easy stuff.

DAY 14: JOIN INSTAGRAM

For today's task, create an Instagram (instagram.com) profile.

Many of you may already have Instagram profiles, but this social networking site and app is a little different than Facebook and Twitter. While all three offer opportunities for sharing video and photos, Instagram really emphasizes visual elements.

That might not seem like a good fit for writers, who are often more about text than visual cues. But there are opportunities for writers on this platform. And it's one more venue where the people (or your potential audience) are.

Here are a few getting started tips for Instagram:

- Complete your profile completely. Use your name, concisely describe who you are and what you're about, and make your profile public.
- Use an image of yourself. Not a cartoon. Not an animal. Not a piece of art. Remember that people like to connect with other people.
- Post new content regularly. Let people know you are using your account. A new post every day or three is a good way to achieve this.
- Use unique and relevant hashtags. These provide a way for people with similar interests who aren't already connected to you to find you.

DAY 15: MAKE THREE NEW CONNECTIONS

For today's task, make an attempt to connect with at least three new people on one of your social networks.

Doesn't matter if it's Facebook, Twitter, LinkedIn, or Instagram. The important thing is that you find three new people who appear to share your interests and that you try to friend, follow, or connect to them.

As a person who has limited wiggle room for approving new friends on Facebook, I'd like to share what approach tends to work the best with me for approving new friend requests. Basically, send your request and include a brief message introducing yourself and why you want to connect with me.

That's right. The best way to win me over is to basically introduce yourself. Something along the lines of, "Hello. My name is Robert Lee Brewer, and I write poetry. I read a poem of yours in *XYZ Literary Journal* that I totally loved and have sent you a friend request. I hope you'll accept it." Easy as that.

Notice that I did not mention anything about checking out my blog or reading my poems. How would you like it if someone introduced themselves and then told you to buy their stuff? It sounds a bit telemarketer-ish to me.

While it's important to cultivate the relationships you already have, avoid getting stuck in a rut when it comes to making connections. Always be on the lookout for new connections who can offer new opportunities and spark new ideas. Your writing and your career will benefit.

DAY 16: ADD E-MAIL FEED TO BLOG

For today's challenge, add an e-mail feed to your blog.

There are many ways to increase traffic to your blog, but one that has paid huge dividends for me is adding Feedblitz to my blog. As the subscribers to my e-mail feed have increased, my blog traffic has increased as well. In fact, after great content, I'd say that adding share buttons (mentioned above) and an e-mail feed are the top two ways to build traffic.

Though I have an account on Tumblr, I'm just not sure if it offers some kind of e-mail/RSS feed service.

The reason I think e-mail feeds are so useful is that they pop into my inbox whenever a new post is up, which means I can check it very easily on my phone when I'm waiting somewhere. In fact, this is how I keep up with several of my favorite blogs. It's just one more way to make your blog content accessible to readers in a variety of formats.

If I remember, this task didn't take me long to add, but I've been grateful for finally getting around to adding it ever since.

DAY 17: TAKE PART IN A TWITTER CONVERSATION

For today's task, take part in a Twitter conversation.

Depending upon the time of month or day of week, there are bound to be any number of conversations happening around a hashtag (mentioned above). For instance, various conferences and expos have hashtag conversations that build around their panels and presentations.

Poets will often meet using the #poetparty hashtag. Other writers use #amwriting to communicate about their writing goals. Click on the hashtag to see what others are saying, and then, jump in to join the conversation and make new connection on Twitter.

DAY 18: THINK ABOUT SEO

For today's task, I want you to slow down and think a little about SEO (which is tech-speak for search engine optimization, which is itself an intelligent way of saying "what gets your website to display at or near the top of a search on Google, Bing, Yahoo, etc.").

So this task is actually multi-pronged:

- Make a list of keywords that you want your website or blog to be known for. For instance, I want my blog to be known for terms like "Robert Lee Brewer," "Writing Tips," "Parenting Tips," "Platform Tips," "Living Tips," etc. Think big here and don't limit yourself to what you think you can actually achieve in the short term.
- Compare your website or blog's current content to your keywords. Are you lining up your actual content with how you want your audience to view you and your online presence? If not, it's time to think about how you can start offering content that lines up with your goals. If so, then move on to the next step, which is ...
- Evaluate your current approach to making your content super SEO-friendly. If you need some guidance, check out my SEO Tips for Writers below. There are very simple things you can do with your titles, subheads, and images to really improve SEO. Heck, I get a certain bit of traffic every single day just from my own SEO approach to content— sometimes on surprising posts.
- Research keywords for your next post. When deciding on a title for your post and subheads within the content, try researching keywords. You can do this using Google's free keyword tool (googlekeywordtool.com). When possible, you want to use keywords that are searched a lot but that have low competition. These are the low-hanging fruit that can help you build strong SEO for your website or blog.

A note on SEO: It's easy to fall in love with finding keywords and changing your content to be keyword-loaded and blah-blah-blah. But resist making your website or blog a place that is keyword-loaded and blah-blah-blah. Because readers don't stick around for too much keyword-loaded blah-blah-blah. It's kind of blah. And bleck. Instead, use SEO and keyword research as a way to optimize great content and to take advantage of opportunities as they arise.

SEO TIPS FOR WRITERS

Here are a few SEO tips for writers:

- Use keywords naturally. That is, make sure your keywords match the content of the post. If they don't match up, people will abandon your page fast, which will hurt your search rankings.
- Use keywords appropriately. Include your keywords in the blog post title, opening paragraph, file name for images, headers, etc. Anywhere early and relevant should include your keyword to help place emphasis on that search term, especially if it's relevant to the content.
- Deliver quality content. Of course, search rankings are helped when people click on your content and spend time reading your content. So provide quality content, and people will visit your site frequently and help search engines list you higher in their rankings.
- Update content regularly. Sites that are updated more with relevant content rank higher in search engines. Simple as that.
- Link often to relevant content. Link to your own posts; link to content on other sites. Just make sure the links are relevant and of high interest to your audience.
- Use images. Images help from a design perspective, but they also help with SEO, especially when you use your main keywords in the image file name.
- Link to your content on social media sites. These outside links will help increase your ranking on search engines.
- Guest post on other sites/blogs. Guest posts on other blogs are a great way to provide traffic from other relevant sites that increase the search engine rankings on your site.

DAY 19: WRITE A BLOG POST

For today's task, write a new blog post.

Include a call to action (for instance, encourage readers to sign up for your e-mail feed and to share the post with others using your share buttons) and link to it on your social networks. Also, don't forget to incorporate SEO.

One of the top rules of finding success with online tools is applying consistency. While it's definitely a great thing if you share a blog post more than once a week, I think it's imperative that you post at least once a week.

The main reason? It builds trust with your readers that you'll have something to share regularly and gives them a reason to visit regularly.

So today's task is not about making things complicated; it's just about keeping it real.

DAY 20: CREATE EDITORIAL CALENDAR

For today's task, I want you to create an editorial calendar for your blog (or website). Before you start to panic, read on.

First, here's how I define an editorial calendar: A list of content with dates attached to when the content goes live. For instance, I created an editorial calendar specifically for my Platform Challenge and "Platform Challenge: Day 20" was scheduled to go live on day 20.

It's really simple. In fact, I keep track of my editorial calendar with a paper notebook, which gives me plenty of space for crossing things out, jotting down ideas, and attaching Post-It notes.

EDITORIAL CALENDAR IDEAS

Here are tips for different blogging frequencies:

- Post once per week. If you post once a week, pick a day of the week for that post to happen each week. Then, write down the date for each post. Beside each date, write down ideas for that post ahead of time. There will be times when the ideas are humming and you get ahead on your schedule, but there may also be times when the ideas are slow. So don't wait, write down ideas as they come.
- Post more than once per week. Try identifying which days you'll usually post (for some, that may be daily). Then, for each of those days, think of a theme for that day. For instance, my 2012 schedule offered Life Changing Moments on Wednesdays and Poetic Saturdays on Saturdays.

You can always change plans and move posts to different days, but the editorial calendar is an effective way to set very clear goals with deadlines for accomplishing them. Having that kind of structure will improve your content—even if your blog is personal, fictional, poetic, etc. Believe me, I used to be a skeptic before diving in, and the results on my personal blog speak for themselves.

One more benefit of editorial calendars

There are times when I feel less than inspired. There are times when life throws me several elbows as if trying to prevent me from blogging. That's when I am the most thankful for maintaining an editorial calendar, because I don't have to think of a new idea on the spot; it's already there in my editorial calendar.

Plus, as I said earlier, you can always change plans. I can alter the plan to accommodate changes in my schedule. So I don't want to hear that an editorial calendar limits spontaneity or inspiration; if anything, having an editorial calendar enhances it.

One last thing on today's assignment

Don't stress yourself out that you have to create a complete editorial calendar for the year or even the month. I just want you to take some time out today to think about it, sketch some ideas, and get the ball rolling. I'm 100 percent confident that you'll be glad you did.

DAY 21: SIGN UP FOR SOCIAL MEDIA TOOL

For today's task, try joining one of the social media management tools, such as Tweet-deck, Hootsuite, or Seesmic.

Social media management tools are popular among social media users for one reason: They help save time and effort in managing multiple social media platforms. For instance, they make following specific threads in Twitter a snap.

I know many social media super users who swear by these tools, but I actually have tried them and decided to put in the extra effort to log in to my separate social media accounts manually each day.

Here's my reasoning: I like to feel connected to my profile and understand how it looks and feels on a day-to-day basis. Often, the design and feel of social media sites will change without notice, and I like to know what it feels like at ground zero.

DAY 22: PITCH GUEST BLOG POST

For today's task, pitch a guest blog post to another blogger.

Writing guest posts is an incredible way to improve your exposure and expertise on a subject, while also making a deeper connection with the blogger who is hosting your guest post. It's a win for everyone involved.

In a recent interview with super blogger Jeff Goins, he revealed that most of his blog traffic came as a result of his guest posting on other blogs. Some of these blogs were directly related to his content, but he said many were in completely different fields.

GUEST POST PITCHING TIPS

After you know where you want to guest blog, here are some tips for pitching your guest blog post:

- Let the blogger know you're familiar with the blog. You should do this in one sentence (two sentences max) and be specific. For instance, a MNINB reader could say, "I've been reading your Not Bob blog for months, but I really love this Platform Challenge." Simple as that. It lets me know you're not a spammer, but it doesn't take me a long time to figure out what you're trying to say.

- Propose an idea or two. Each idea should have its own paragraph. This makes it easy for the blogger to know where one idea ends and the next one begins. In a pitch, you don't have to lay out all the details, but you do want to be specific. Try to limit the pitch to 2-4 sentences.
- Share a little about yourself. Emphasis on "a little." If you have previous publications or accomplishments that line up with the blog, share those. If you have expertise that lines up with the post you're pitching, share those. Plus, include any details about your online platform that might show you can help bring traffic to the post. But include all this information in 1-4 sentences.
- Include your information. When you close the pitch, include your name, e-mail, blog (or website) URL, and other contact information you feel comfortable sharing. There's nothing more awkward for me than to have a great pitch that doesn't include the person's name. Or a way to learn more about the person.

What do I do after the pitch is accepted?

First off, congratulations! This is a great opportunity to show off your writing skills. Here's how to take advantage of your guest post assignment:

- **WRITE AN EXCEPTIONAL POST.** Don't hold back your best stuff for your blog. Write a post that will make people want to find more of your writing.
- **TURN IN YOUR POST ON DEADLINE.** If there's a deadline, hit it. If there's not a deadline, try to turn around the well-written post in a timely manner.
- **PROMOTE THE GUEST POST.** Once your guest post has gone live, promote it like crazy by linking to your post on your blog, social networks, message boards, and wherever else makes sense for you. By sending your own connections to this guest post, you're establishing your own expertise—not only through your post but also your connections.

DAY 23: CREATE A TIME MANAGEMENT PLAN

For today's task, create a time management plan.

You may be wondering why I didn't start out the challenge with a time management plan, and here's the reason: I don't think some people would've had any idea how long it takes them to write a blog post, share a link on Twitter and Facebook, respond to social media messages, etc. Now, many of you probably have a basic idea—even if you're still getting the hang of your new-fangled social media tools.

Soooo ... the next step is to create a time management plan that enables you to be "active" socially and connect with other writers and potential readers while also spending a majority of your time writing and publishing.

As with any plan, you can make this as simple or complicated as you wish. For instance, my plan is to do 15 minutes or less of social media after completing each decent-sized task on my daily task list. I use social media time as a break, which I consider more productive than watching TV or playing Angry Birds.

I put my writing first and carve out time in the mornings and evenings to work on poetry and fiction. Plus, I consider my blogging efforts part of my writing too. So there you go.

My plan is simple and flexible, but if you want to get hardcore, break down your time into 15-minute increments. Then, test out your time management plan to see if it works for you. If not, then make minor changes to the plan until it has you feeling somewhat comfortable with the ratio of time you spend writing and time you spend building your platform.

Remember: A platform is a life-long investment in your career. It's not a sprint, so you have to pace yourself. Also, it's not something that happens overnight, so you can't wait until you need a platform to start building one. Begin today and build over time—so that it's there when you need it.

DAY 24: TAKE PART IN A FACEBOOK CONVERSATION

For today's task, take part in a conversation on Facebook.

You should've already participated in a Twitter conversation, so this should be somewhat similar—except you don't have to play with hashtags and 140-character restrictions. In fact, you just need to find a group conversation or status update that speaks to you and chime in with your thoughts.

Don't try to sell or push anything when you join a conversation. If you say interesting things, people will check out your profile, which if filled out will lead them to more information about you (including your website, blog, any books, etc.).

Goal one of social media is making connections. If you have everything else optimized, sales and opportunities will take care of themselves.

DAY 25: CONTACT AN EXPERT FOR AN INTERVIEW POST

For today's task, find an expert in your field and ask if that expert would like to be interviewed.

If you can secure the interview, this will make for a great blog post. Or it may help you secure a freelance assignment with a publication in your field. Or both, and possibly more.

How to Ask for an Interview

Believe it or not, asking for an interview with an expert is easy. I do it all the time, and these are the steps I take.

- **FIND AN EXPERT ON A TOPIC.** This is sometimes the hardest part: figuring out who I want to interview. But I never kill myself trying to think of the perfect person, and here's why: I can always ask for more interviews. Sometimes, it's just more productive to get the ball rolling than come up with excuses to not get started.
- **LOCATE AN E-MAIL FOR THE EXPERT.** This can often be difficult, but a lot of experts have websites that share either e-mail addresses or have online contact forms. Many experts can also be reached via social media sites, such as Facebook, Twitter, LinkedIn, Instagram, etc. Or they can be contacted through company websites. And so on.
- **SEND AN E-MAIL ASKING FOR AN E-MAIL INTERVIEW.** Of course, you can do this via an online contact form too. If the expert says no, that's fine. Respond with a "Thank you for considering and maybe we can make it work sometime in the future." If the expert says yes, then it's time to send along the questions.

How to Handle an E-mail Interview

Once you've secured your expert, it's time to compose and send the questions. Here are some of my tips.

- **ALWAYS START OFF BY ASKING QUESTIONS ABOUT THE EXPERT.** This might seem obvious to some, but you'd be surprised how many people start off asking "big questions" right out of the gate. Always start off by giving the expert a chance to talk about what he or she is doing, has recently done, etc.
- **LIMIT QUESTIONS TO 10 OR FEWER.** The reason for this is that you don't want to overwhelm your expert. In fact, I usually ask around eight questions in my e-mail interviews. If I need to, I'll send along some follow-up questions, though I try to limit those as well. I want the expert to have an enjoyable experience, not a horrible experience. After all, I want the expert to be a connection going forward.
- **TRY NOT TO GET TOO PERSONAL.** If experts want to get personal in their answers, that's great. But try to avoid getting too personal in the questions you ask, because you may offend your expert or make them feel uncomfortable. Remember: You're interviewing the expert, not leading an interrogation.
- **REQUEST ADDITIONAL INFORMATION.** By additional information, I mean that you should request a headshot and a preferred bio—along with any links. To make the interview worth the expert's time, you should afford them an opportunity to promote themselves and their projects in their bios.

Once the Interview Goes Live ...

Link to it on your social networks and let your expert know it is up (and include the specific link to the interview). If you're not already searching for your next expert to interview, be sure to get on it.

DAY 26: WRITE A BLOG POST AND LINK TO SOCIAL PROFILES

For today's task, write a new blog post.

In your blog post, include a call to action and link it on your social networks. Also, don't forget SEO.

Remember: One of the top rules of finding success with online tools is applying consistency. While it's definitely a great thing if you share a blog post more than once a week, I think it's imperative that you post at least once a week.

The main reason? It builds trust with your readers that you'll have something to share regularly and gives them a reason to visit regularly.

If this sounds repetitive, good; it means my message on consistency is starting to take root.

DAY 27: JOIN ANOTHER SOCIAL MEDIA SITE

For today's task, join one new social media site. I will leave it up to you to decide which new social media site it will be.

Maybe you'll join Pinterest. Maybe you'll choose Goodreads. Heck, you might go with RedRoom or some social media site that's not even on my radar at the time of this article. Everything is constantly evolving, which is why it's good to always try new things.

To everyone who doesn't want another site to join ...

I understand your frustration and exhaustion. During a normal month, I'd never suggest someone sign up for so many social media sites in such a short period of time, but this isn't a normal month. We're in the midst of a challenge!

And no, I don't expect you to spend a lot of time on every social media site you join. That's not always the point when you first sign up. No, you sign up to poke around and see if the site interests you at all. See if you have any natural connections. Try mingling a little bit.

If the site doesn't appeal to you, feel free to let it be for a while. Let me share a story with you.

How I Came to Rock Facebook and Twitter

My Facebook and Twitter accounts both boast more than 5,000 followers (or friends/sub-scribers) today. But both accounts were originally created and abandoned, because they just weren't right for me at the time that I signed up.

For Facebook, I just didn't understand why I would abandon a perfectly good MySpace account to play around on a site that didn't feature the same level of music and personal blogging that MySpace did. But then, MySpace turned into Spam-opolis, and the rest is history.

For Twitter, I just didn't get the whole tweet concept, because Facebook already had status updates. Why tweet when I could update my status on Facebook?

But I've gained a lot professionally and personally from Facebook and Twitter—even though they weren't the right sites for me initially. It's not like Facebook is going to be around forever.

The Importance of Experimentation

Or as I prefer to think of it: The importance of play. You should constantly try new things, whether in your writing, your social media networks, or the places you eat food. Not only does it make life more exciting and provide you with new experiences and perspective, but it also helps make you a more well-rounded human being.

So don't complain about joining a new social media site. Instead, embrace the excuse to try something new, especially when there are only three more tasks left this month (and I promise no more new sites after today).

DAY 28: READ POST AND COMMENT ON IT

For today's task, read and comment on a blog post, making sure that your comment links back to your blog or website.

If you remember, this was the same task required way back on Day 6. How far we've come, though it's still a good idea to stay connected and engaged with other bloggers. I know I find that sometimes I start to insulate myself in my own little blogging communi-ties and worlds—when it's good to get out and read what others are doing. In fact, that's what helped inspire my Monday Advice for Writers posts—it gives me motivation to read what others are writing (on writing, of course).

DAY 29: MAKE A TASK LIST

For today's task, make a task list of things you are going to do on each day next month. That's right, I want you to break down 31 days with 31 tasks for each day—similar to what we've done this month.

You see, I don't want you to quit challenging yourself once this challenge is over. Of course, you get to decide what the tasks will be. So if you aren't into new social media sites, don't put them on your list. Instead, focus on blog posts, commenting on other sites, linking to articles, contacting experts, or whatever it is that you are going to do next month to keep momentum building toward an incredible author platform.

Somewhere near the end of the month, you should have a day set aside with one task: Make a task list of things to do on each day of the next month. And so on and so forth. Keep it going, keep it rolling, and your efforts will continue to gain momentum and speed. I promise.

DAY 30: ENGAGE THE WORLD

For today's task, engage the world.

By this, I mean that you should comment on status updates, ask questions, share answers, start debates, continue debates, and listen—that's right, don't be that person who dominates a conversation and makes it completely one-sided.

Engage the world by entering the conversation. Engage the world by having the courage to take risks and share things of consequence. Engage the world by having the courage to make mistakes and fail and learn from those mistakes and failures.

The only people who never fail are those who never try, and those people never succeed at anything except avoiding failure and success. Don't be that person. Engage the world and let the world engage you.

ROBERT LEE BREWER is a senior editor with the Writer's Digest Writing Community and author of *Solving the World's Problems* (Press 53). Follow him on Twitter @robertleebrewer.

DIVERSE BOOKS MATTER

The push to publish a broader range of voices is no fad—it's an industry course correction long overdue. Here, a literary agent unpacks the movement taking books by storm.

by Ammi-Joan Paquette

One of the most common questions I'm asked as a literary agent at writers' conferences these days—and one that I'm always happy to hear—is some variation on: "How do you feel about the increased focus on diversity in publishing? What changes are you seeing in this area?"

Why am I happy to hear it? Because it's a question that didn't really come up five years ago, or at least not to this extent. It *should* be coming up, and the fact that it does so with increasing frequency is in itself a sign of the industry's change and forward progress.

But first, a caveat: This won't be an article detailing the history, statistics, or specific trajectory of diversity in publishing. I'm neither a scholar nor an analyst, and while I do love a good spreadsheet, I am not qualified to deliver any type of comprehensive treatise. What I hope to do here is share my broader perspective as an active member of the publishing community—both as a consumer of books and someone who helps funnel them along toward your bookshelves. Thus here's a primer, if you will, for those who may be less familiar with the subject and could use an overview on diversity in publishing today.

WHAT READERS WANT

To begin, someone who may not be up on the movement might be wondering: *What's this all about?* Well, historically, published books have largely focused their lens on white, straight, able-bodied characters. *What's wrong with that*, you ask? It's not what's there that's the problem; it's what's *not* there. Seeing ourselves reflected in the books—and media—we consume can be a way of legitimizing our own journey, struggles and questions. Seeing the reflection of someone else's journey, a journey that may be entirely unlike our own, provides an essential portal into the experiences of others, fostering empathy, understanding and growth. Simply put, readers want, *need*, to see themselves in the books they read. In recent years, that need has begun to be addressed with a growing range of books reflecting a broader, truer lens. A more diverse selection of books means more mirrors to reflect our experiences, and more windows to offer glimpses into lives unlike our own. Win-win, right?

"As someone obsessed with and who writes small-town America, if you don't see diversity in your town, you're not looking hard enough."
—Julie Murphy, author of *Dumplin'*

WHAT AGENTS & EDITORS WANT

Certainly I cannot speak for all of the publishing community, but from what I've seen as a literary agent working largely in publishing for young readers, I can safely say: There is a great and a growing hunger for diverse books—in terms of culture, race, sexuality, gender, ability, class, and beyond. When I meet with editors and talk about what they're looking to acquire, almost invariably the conversation will come around to: "I want to see more diverse books, and books by diverse authors."

"We talk about representation every single day. When I started in publishing two decades ago at a different company, we weren't allowed to use the word 'gay' in describing a character unless it was specifically tagged a 'gay book' and was geared toward that community only. Now it feels like there is a real push toward diversity, a focus on and celebration of that." — John Morgan, executive editor at Imprint, a part of Macmillan Children's Publishing Group

This appetite is also seen in the formation of social media campaigns to enhance visibility for underrepresented voices, such as the popular #DVpit event on Twitter (created by literary agent Beth Phelan), where authors can pitch their diverse projects in real-time. Interested agents and editors can—and do—request these manuscripts, and the event already has an impressive rate of authors signing with agents and getting book deals. And initiatives like We Need Diverse Books have provided resources and a rallying point for writers of marginalized communities and beyond.

Bear in mind: This is a process. The skewed balance of worldview in literature didn't happen overnight, and the shift to a more accurate and complete representation will not happen overnight either. But readers are hungry for it. Agents are hungry for it. Editors are hungry for it. What comes next?

WHAT WRITERS CAN DO

Some people have called diversity in publishing a "trend." Let me be clear, it's nothing of the sort. It is, and will continue to be, a gradual shifting—*a correction in the market*, so to speak—an increased awareness for those writing and publishing from a place of privilege that there are important stories out there that were formerly overlooked. It's an initiative that I believe will only grow more as marginalized authors continue to gain confidence and experience and wherewithal to make their stories known, and as publishers continue not only to diversify their acquisitions, but also their staff at every step of the publishing process.

"'Diversity' should just be called 'reality.' Your books, your TV shows, your movies, your articles, your curricula, need to reflect *reality*."
—Tananarive Due, author of *The Living Blood*

One contentious issue right now is the debate over whether authors can—or should—write from a perspective that is outside their own race or culture. Those arguing against point to the glut of inauthentic voices crowding the shelves and taking space and attention from those writing from their "own voice" viewpoints. On the other side, some argue that authors writing only their own distinct gender, race, culture and specific background would make for dull books indeed.

On one thing all sides agree, however: Any author writing outside their culture should do so thoughtfully, respectfully, and deliberately. If you're considering doing so, ask: *Why am I the one telling this particular story? What is my touch-point or connection that makes me an authentic narrator for this character?* Next, be willing to put in the work. Research is good, but that alone isn't enough. Talk, interview, experience. Bring in readers of the race or culture in question to critique your work—and then *listen* to what they're saying, and make the necessary changes.

WHAT THE FUTURE HOLDS

One has only to look at *The New York Times* bestsellers list or the National Book Awards list to see how whole-heartedly readers and critics alike are taking to this shift toward greater and more accurate representation. In the last year, books by authors of color have repeatedly sold in high-stakes auctions, with foreign and film deals flocking in their wake. This is especially the case in YA and children's publishing, but adult fiction is catching on as well. It turns out that people like to see themselves in the books—and media—they consume. It makes logical, and financial, sense.

What does this all mean for you? If you're a marginalized writer: There's never been a better time to tell your story. If you're writing from a place of privilege: Be willing to educate yourself, and in the works you do create, strive for honesty, authenticity, inclusivity.

Publishing is experiencing a period of growth. Things are changing, yet more change is still needed. Diversity is not a fad, trend or marketing gimmick. It is a lifestyle; a requirement. The new normal.

AMMI-JOAN PAQUETTE is a senior literary agent with Erin Murphy Literary Agency and the author of many books for young readers. This article previously appeared in the March/April 2018 issue of *Writer's Digest*.

OPERATION AMAZON

Indie authors and bestsellers alike must harness the force of Amazon to maximize sales. Here are 4 covert success strategies for authors taking on the world's largest bookseller.

....

by Rob Eagar

Amazon sells more books than anyone else. Therefore, if you want to sell more books, you must learn how to sell more books through Amazon.

Amazon is more than a website. It's the most powerful book-selling machine ever invented. The good news is that Amazon's power isn't reserved just for elite bestsellers. Their system was designed to help any author capture more sales.

Jeff Bezos founded the company in 1994 under the original name, Cadabra, until a lawyer confused it with "cadaver." Another name, Relentless, was also floated by Bezos, but people thought it sounded too sinister. (Fun fact: Type "Relentless.com" into your internet browser and see where it goes.) The name "Amazon" was eventually chosen because it starts with the letter "A" and is the name of the world's largest river. Who would have thought the name would come to mean so much more?

Today, Amazon completely dominates the publishing industry. Take a moment to consider these mind-blowing statistics:

- Amazon sells close to 50 percent of all print books in America.
- Amazon sells over 70 percent of all e-books in America.
- Amazon is the largest sales account for almost every publisher in America.
- Amazon paid 1,000 indie authors over $100,000 each in book royalties in 2017.
- Amazon's market share continues to increase both in America and abroad.

Note: The term "indie author" in the list above refers to an independent author who self-publishes using Amazon's KDP service. These authors manage the writing, formatting, and marketing functions for their books, but receive a royalty rate of 35–70 percent.

Just as nothing can stop the Amazon River from flooding its banks in South America, nothing seems to stop Amazon from expanding its efforts to sell more books. All the while, their only legitimate competition, Barnes & Noble, continues to struggle with sluggish sales while looking for someone to purchase the company. If these facts don't get your attention, allow me to make things very clear:

Amazon sells more books than anyone else. Therefore, if you want to sell more books, you must learn how to sell more books through Amazon.

It doesn't matter if you're self-published or traditionally-published. It doesn't matter if you write fiction or nonfiction. It doesn't matter if you're a first-time author or an experienced bestseller. Today, success for every author hinges on selling more books on Amazon.

Authors may not be able to control Amazon's dominance over the publishing industry. But, it's possible to use Amazon's power to your advantage if you know these four secrets:

SECRET 1: USE AMAZON'S "HIDDEN DOOR" TO IMPROVE YOUR BOOK'S MARKETING COPY.

Language is the power of the book sale. If your book's marketing description is bland on Amazon's website, your sales will be stunted. But if your marketing copy sizzles, your sales can skyrocket. Therefore, it's imperative to make your book appear as enticing as possible to shoppers on Amazon. But, many authors mistakenly believe their Amazon copy can't be changed.

For example, if you're a traditionally published author, maybe you're disappointed with boring or outdated marketing text that a publisher put on your book's Amazon page. If you self-published, maybe you used a third-party company to get your book listed on Amazon. So, you feel blocked from making important changes to your book's marketing copy.

Here's a little secret: Amazon offers a hidden "back door" that lets you update your book's marketing text whenever you desire. Did your book recently receive an amazing endorsement, win an industry award or hit a bestseller list? Did you create a sizzling new marketing hook that you'd love for readers to see? You can update your book's Amazon description with this information whenever you desire.

The solution to updating your text on Amazon is simple. You can access any book you've written by using the Author Central account that Amazon provides for free. Go to authorcentral.amazon.com/ to create an account.

Once your account is active, you receive full control to adjust your marketing text, editorial reviews and author bio at any time. You're also able to separately manage each edition of your book, including the paperback, hardcover, and e-book formats.

Use this powerful secret to improve the way your books are displayed to shoppers on Amazon.

SECRET 2: GROW YOUR AUTHOR EMAIL LIST USING AMAZON'S HUGE AUDIENCE.

Amazon attracts more book readers than any other sellers on the planet. Did you know those readers can be converted into followers on your author email list? There are multiple ways to do it for free.

First, add a page to the front and back of your book manuscript promoting an exclusive incentive for readers to join your author email list. Then, provide a website link to a landing page on your website for people to claim your offer. This simple trick by itself can add a lot of new subscribers each month.

Second, you can self-publish a permanently free e-book on Amazon using their Kindle Direct Publishing (KDP) service. The content could be a novella, short story or concise nonfiction teaching guide. Within the free e-book, add a page at the front and back promoting an exclusive incentive to join your email list. I call this tactic a "bait book," because the free item serves as appealing bait to attract new readers.

Technically, Amazon doesn't allow authors to sell permanently free books on their site. But, they have a permanent price-matching policy against all other retailers. So, you can sell an e-book at other retailers for free, such as Barnes & Noble, and ask Amazon to match the price of zero.

Once you set up a "bait book," it will remain a constant tool on Amazon's website to help build your email list while writing your next book. You can even purchase Amazon ads to drive additional traffic to your e-book and generate more email signups. The best part is that everything can be created for free.

SECRET 3: AMAZON WILL REVEAL HOW TO TARGET NEW POTENTIAL READERS.

Wouldn't it be great if Amazon told you who bought and read your book? Obviously, they don't share their customer data with anyone. But, they do offer a secret way to identify your target audience.

Go to your book detail page on Amazon and look at the section that says, "Customers who bought this item also bought …" This data reveals similar titles and authors to you and your book. Why is this data helpful? It explains where to find potential readers who would like your book.

For instance, if you see "Author X" frequently displayed in your "Customers Also Bought" list, then you know that fans of Author X may also be fans of your book. Here's the logic behind this approach. Amazon's system verified that people who bought a copy of your book also bought a book by Author X. So, if some fans of Author X liked your book, then there might be more fans of Author X who would like your book as well.

How do you put this data to good use? Buy inexpensive online advertising for your book that targets fans of Author X. Amazon, Facebook, and BookBub allow authors to buy advertising that targets fans of other authors. In other words, you can make an educated guess using Amazon's purchase history that fans of Author X will also like your book.

In a short amount of time and on a small budget, you can test your hypothesis to see if it's true. Sometimes, this approach will work, and you'll immediately generate new book sales from your advertising campaigns. Other times, the results may not pan out. But, it's better than shooting in the dark. Using the Also Boughts technique is like letting Amazon shine a light on new marketing opportunities.

SECRET 4: THE AMAZON "SALES RANKING" CAN IDENTIFY PIVOTAL MARKETING EFFORTS.

Amazon is famous among authors for creating the "Best Sellers Rank," which is a number assigned to each book on their website that represents recent sales on an hourly basis. (You can find the ranking for your book under the "Product details" section mid-way down the Amazon product page.) Some authors, including me, have been known to obsess over their book's ranking by continually checking the number several times a day.

In reality, the Best Sellers Rank is an unreliable number that doesn't account for accurate book sales. However, the Amazon ranking does have a secret ability to reveal when specific marketing activities are working well.

Since Amazon provides one of the few pieces of real-time sales data, authors can observe their book's Best Sellers Rank to notice any aberrations. If you see your book's ranking dramatically improve within a 24-hour period, you can deduce that a specific marketing activity had a positive impact.

For example, I recently worked on a major book launch for an author client. As I monitored the Best Sellers Rank for my client's book during the launch week, I noticed one day that the number quickly shot up from #2,500 to #141. This dramatic change signaled that a lot of new sales had recently occurred.

When I noticed this change, I contacted the author and asked, "What marketing activities did you conduct in the past 24 hours?" He replied that a national radio station in New York City had interviewed him the previous morning. Then, he added, "I think they also posted my interview on their YouTube channel."

I quickly searched YouTube, found my client's interview and noticed that the video had already been viewed over 100,000 times. Bingo! That interview was the catalyst driving an immediate surge of book sales. Based on this discovery, I urged my client to drive more attention to that persuasive video interview. Since then, that video has been viewed over 293,000 times and still helps drive book sales today.

But, here's the key point. We might not have identified that powerful marketing video if we hadn't noticed the dramatic change in the Best Sellers Rank for my client's book. The sudden spike gave us a clue to find the video and use it to propel more book sales.

Likewise, you can benefit by monitoring (not obsessing over) your book's Best Seller Rank and watching for sudden spikes. If you see a dramatic improvement, then quickly analyze what activities you conducted in the past 24-48 hours. The analysis can help define which marketing activities best motivate readers to take action and buy your book. Those are the activities you want to duplicate and repeat on a frequent basis.

Success comes much easier when you know which marketing activities cause readers to purchase. Use your book's Amazon Best Sellers Rank to help identify the tactics that work best. Armed with that knowledge, you can transform a mediocre book launch into a bestselling campaign.

Amazon has always been a secretive organization. For example, they never reveal how many books or Kindle devices they actually sell. But, they are several marketing secrets any author can utilize on Amazon to boost book sales. Use the "hidden door" within your Author Central account to improve your book's marketing copy. Grow your author email list by promoting free incentives to Amazon customers. Use the Also Boughts information to help target potential new readers. Then, monitor your book's Best Sellers Rank to identify marketing tactics that produce real-time results.

It's no secret that Amazon dominates the publishing industry. But, the secret to selling more books on Amazon doesn't need to remain a mystery.

ROB EAGAR (RobEagar.com) is a marketing consultant who has coached more than 600 authors and helped books hit the *New York Times* bestseller list in three different categories. This article was previously published in the May/June 2019 issue of *Writer's Digest*.

FUNDING YOUR WRITING WITH PATREON

by Lucy A. Snyder

Many writers dream of quitting their day jobs and becoming full-time freelancers. And while that *is* achievable, it's a difficult prospect for poets, playwrights, and midlist-fiction writers. Writing organizations such as the Science Fiction & Fantasy Writers of America consider a minimum professional rate for fiction to be six cents a word. Many novels only receive advances of $5,000–$10,000. Think about your basic living costs. A book that took years to write may only cover rent for a few months. Making up the difference as a freelancer is challenging, to say the least!

The good news: Crowdfunding can fill that uncomfortable financial gap. Kickstarter and Indiegogo are great for funding specific projects such as novels, plays, anthologies, and poetry collections. But if you're seeking ongoing, monthly support for your creative endeavors, take a closer look at Patreon (patreon.com).

THE BIG IDEA

Launched in 2013, Patreon is conceptually the modern version of the old system whereby artists and writers sought out wealthy patrons for support—but the key difference is that popular Patreon creators are supported by dozens or hundreds of people rather than a single rich benefactor. In practice, Patreon gives creators tools for publishing a wide variety of subscription content. Editors use it to publish monthly online magazines, and fiction writers use it to serialize their novels-in-progress. Artists post sketches-in-progress or commissions for individual patrons. Others post videos or audio tracks of music or narration. Educators can use the built-in integration with Discord (a voice/text-chat system) to host discussions or workshops.

And while you post as much content as your imagination can summon, the site handles all the billing. Creators can charge by the post or by the month. Opting for monthly charges lets you set up tiered rewards as you would with Kickstarter. Rewards can be anything you can legally fulfill: For instance, for $2 a month, my supporters get a weekly poem; for $3 a month they receive weekly writing prompts plus my poetry. For $30 a month, they receive all my writing plus detailed feedback on 2,000 words of their own work. Patreon takes 5 percent of processed payments, plus additional processing fees to move funds to PayPal or Stripe. Some creators resent the fees, but most see them as a fair trade for a suite of extremely versatile tools.

GETTING STARTED WITH PATREON

1. Research Patreons like yours at graphtreon.com, and emulate successes.
2. Craft a compelling personal narrative about why you're seeking patrons.
3. Offer a variety of appealing patron rewards. Avoid rewards that require shipping.
4. Focus on rewards that you are *certain* you can consistently provide.
5. Plan to spend time promoting your campaign on social media every month.
6. Recruit friends and colleagues to help with promotion. Word of mouth is critical.
7. Make a content creation/posting calendar and stick to it.
8. Poll your patrons periodically to gauge their satisfaction.
9. Reassess your promotional tactics and ability to meet reward goals after a couple of months; change your strategies as needed.

THE BENEFITS

Income is the first thing people wonder about when they start exploring Patreon. Graphtreon is an extremely useful tool for tracking and analyzing various campaigns. Go to graphtreon.com/patreon-creators/writing to view the writers who have the most total patrons or who earn the most money per month. The site collects a great deal of insightful data, and before you set up your own Patreon you should take a look at the top creators' pages to figure out what you can learn from their successes.

Authors Seanan McGuire and N.K. Jemisin bring in thousands of dollars per month through their Patreons. McGuire rewards her patrons with stories, writing tutorials, and more. Jemisin is able to write fiction full time because of her campaign. Her rewards range from cute cat videos to ARCs of her forthcoming books.

True, most don't earn as much as McGuire or Jemisin—each had an established readership *before* they launched their campaigns—but their success shows what's possible.

My Patreon covers a significant chunk of my mortgage each month. I treat it like a serious part-time job, and the work I've put into it has definitely paid off.

Authors who take a casual approach typically earn $50–$150 per month. That's enough to cover a utility bill, which can make a huge difference for some households. And if your Patreon isn't performing well? Seek feedback and try new tactics; you're free to change your campaign whenever and however you like.

Some writers use the money they bring in to fund others' Patreons. This is a way to create goodwill and to network with other writers. If your campaign's earnings are too small to matter to you personally, use them to boost others and get access to great content in the process. Community and connections matter, and Patreon gives you the tools to build both.

But Patreon isn't just about the money. It's also a vehicle for creative inspiration. I love writing poetry, but it doesn't pay very well. Over time I'd abandoned it for fiction; I wanted to change that. So, I set my poem-a-week reward level. The result? I've been writing a whole lot of new poetry, and my subscribers enjoy it. Use Patreon to set (and meet!) new goals for yourself.

THE LONG HAUL

Unlike other crowdfunding, Patreon campaigns don't have a pre-set ending. You'll post your promised content monthly, weekly, maybe even daily. Compared to the sprint of Kickstarter, the marathon of Patreon can be exhausting. You risk turning something fun into a chore.

You have to keep promoting if you want to build followers. Even if you're posting solid content, count on losing a patron (or several) every month as people's finances and interests change. Many of us find self-promotion to be tedious and somewhat shameful, and having to constantly go out with your hat in your hand can be demoralizing. Focus on providing a good value to your subscribers and emphasize that in your promotional efforts.

Avoiding burnout is crucial for ensuring that you can maintain a solid campaign. By all means, set some reward levels that will challenge you creatively, but for the rest? Play to your strengths and interests. For instance, if you have several finished novels that you've trunked, dust those off, revise them and serialize them. Sit down and figure out what you can comfortably accomplish in a month, and then focus on doing what you do best. Chances are, if it's something you love, your patrons will love it, too.

LUCY A. SNYDER (lucysnyder.com) is the Bram Stoker Award-winning author of a dozen books and more than 100 short stories. This essay was originally published in the October 2018 issue of *Writer's Digest*.

THE ATTENTION DEFICIT

The lure of Facebook and Twitter can prove disastrous for a writer's productivity. Next time the social media sirens call, use these pointers to last yourself to the mast of your manuscript.

by Julie Duffy

What if I said I could show you how to complete a brilliant novel in just three months—but that you might not be able to handle my solution?

Would you read on?

Of course you would. Because that opening line was engineered to manipulate your cognitive processes. I promised your brain an escape from pain, a little hit of pleasure, and also a bit of uncertainty. (*Will you like my solution? Will you hate it?*)

Now, what if I told you that I know why you lose so much writing time thanks to the lure of social media? And that I have the solution. And that you might not like it …

STEALING YOUR ATTENTION

This scenario may sound familiar: You're determined to write 1,000 words on your work-in-progress on a given day, but then you encounter a tricky spot. Sitting back from the keys for a second, you reach for your phone. You see some notifications on Facebook, mentions on Twitter, comments on Instagram. You decide to check them out … and suddenly 45 minutes of your allotted writing hour have disappeared! You didn't *want* to waste that time on social media, but somehow you were pulled in.

It's no accident. Apps like Facebook, Twitter and Instagram ping us constantly, hooking us on the little doses of dopamine our brains release whenever we see that someone has "Liked" our latest post. Every time you refresh your feed, the app is counting on your brain getting excited by something psychologists (and gambling addiction specialists) call "variable response." (*Will you like what you see, or will it enrage you? Is this email going to be the one in which the agent you queried offers to represent you, or rejects you?*) It's the same neurological process that keeps Aunt June feeding quarters into a casino slot machine. *Maybe this time it'll finally land on the jackpot …*

Tobias S. Buckell, author of the novel *Arctic Rising*, describes Twitter as "like heroin [with its] constant little hits of interestingness."

Shouldn't we be able to resist?

YOUR MOST VALUABLE ASSET

As it turns out, ignoring that vibration in your pocket is not a simple matter of willpower. In the flooded digital market-place, the most valuable commodity is your attention, and you'd better believe that tech companies are heavily invested in research and development to make themselves irresistible. As consumer psychology and behavioral design consultant Nir Eyal chronicles in his 2014 book, *Hooked: How to Build Habit-Forming Products*, "Instead of relying on expensive marketing, habit-forming companies link their services to the users' daily routines and emotions." Several recent news stories have even featured early employees of Facebook and other tech companies apologizing for knowingly hijacking our brains. In fact, there's a whole department at Stanford dedicated to a new field they call "Captology" (Computers as Persuasive Technology).

Your brain and your habits are being rewritten, without you even noticing.

WHY YOU'RE HOOKED

You probably reach for your phone whenever you're bored, dissatisfied, or uncomfortable (while waiting in line, around company you dislike, stuck on a plot problem). Do it often enough and you create what psychologists call a "behavior triggered by situational cues"— otherwise known as a *habit*. And because it's a habit, you are likely to repeat it any time you're in a similar situation.

In the example above, your actions are trigged by an internal cue: your emotions. The notifications that apps send replicate this artificially, acting as an external trigger. In turn, that chime then foments a strong urge to open the app and find out what people are saying.

That's not just vanity; it's chemical. The brain releases dopamine—a chemical neurotransmitter that makes us feel good—in anticipation of that reward. The uncertainty of not knowing exactly what's behind the notification on your screen makes the effect even stronger—conditioning you to click, every time.

TIME TO CUT THE CORD?

So, how do we go about increasing our productivity and actually dedicating distraction-free time to our writing? Is the only answer to go cold turkey, deleting all our social media accounts?

For most, that's simply not an option.

Kate McKean, vice president and literary agent at Howard Morhaim Literary Agency, cautions, "More and more of a book's marketing hinges on the community a writer may build online."

New York Times bestselling author Sarah Dessen actually finds social media to be a boon: "When you write for a living, like I do, and you have the long gaps between when you're publishing things, it is a nice way to be able to interact with people between books."

Not to mention that writing is a solitary business. "Twitter, in particular, is my water cooler," Dessen adds. "It's a way that I've been able to bond with a lot of other writers who are also sitting at home, obsessing in various places. It links us all together."

And don't forget all the great writing and research resources that are online.

So, what's a writer to do?

SIT DOWN & WRITE

The good news is that if we know we're being manipulated, we can use that knowledge to change our behavior. Better yet, we can trick our brains into supporting our own goals, instead of someone else's.

The key, then, is to trigger our brains to focus on what we *want* to focus on—made possible through an acronym I call SIT: Separation, Integration, and Triggers.

SEPARATION. A study published in the *Journal of the Association for Consumer Research* in April 2017 found that it's distracting to have your phone in the same room as you—even switched off. This "automatic attention" is the same cognitive process that lets you hear your name across a crowded room, even though you weren't consciously eavesdropping. Your subconscious reserves attention for things you've trained it to believe are important. By immediately following up on your phone's every chirp, you've given it permission to cut through your creative concentration.

Thus consider separating yourself from the most distracting aspects of your technology. That might mean disconnecting from social media that doesn't serve you.

Elizabeth Bear, the Hugo and Sturgeon award-winning author of *The Stone in the Skull*, says, "I've pretty much managed to quit Facebook … I can't follow the conversations unless I make it a full-time job." Instead, she focuses on communicating with her readers via her email list.

Some less drastic actions you can take: Disconnect Wi-Fi while you're working, or turn off push notifications for the apps that most steal your attention. If you *must* be available, settings like Do Not Disturb mode will block calls and mute audible notifications from everyone and everything except contacts you designate. Consider putting your gadgets in Airplane Mode, or leaving them in another room.

INTEGRATION. Not all technological manipulation is evil. Now that you know technology can rewrite your brain, you can use those same tools to help you achieve your goals—instead of distracting you.

Bear uses the app Cold Turkey (getcoldturkey.com) "to keep [herself] from falling down research rabbit holes." This program allows her to block certain websites on the fly or at scheduled times. Similar apps include Freedom (freedom.to) and Self-Control (selfcontrolapp.com).

Buckell uses Tweetbot (tapbots.com/tweetbot) to help him "keyword-block" his social media drug of choice, Twitter. This limits his feed to a slim stream of topics that *support* his creativity, rather than contribute to the noise.

I use an app called Forest (forestapp.cc) that helps me focus for short bursts of time by providing a positive outcome if I leave my phone alone (a virtual tree grows) and a negative one if I navigate away before the allotted time is up (the tree dies). It may sound silly, but it really does make me pause before clicking over to social media.

TRIGGERS. Instead of being prompted by negative emotions or external notifications, you can design triggers you control.

Dr. BJ Fogg of Stanford University pioneered a technique he calls "Tiny Habits" to reinforce new habits. Pick the smallest possible new goal, and tie it to something you already do. For example, you could decide that every time you sit at your desk, you'll immediately open your work-in-progress and read the last paragraph you wrote. Once that becomes a habit, you can add to it with additional micro-goals like, "Write 300 new words."

You can also establish other triggers that tell your brain it's time to write: Buy a scented candle that you light before opening your laptop; put on the same concerto every time you work on your novel; meditate for five minutes prior to sitting down.

Dessen allows herself 15 minutes at the start of the writing day to check Twitter, "but then I have to just go and write." Whether she knows it or not, she has created a trigger that her brain recognizes as the start of her workday.

Another psychological trick is Mental Contrasting with Implementation Intentions, more colloquially known as WOOP. To WOOP, take the old idea of visualizing an objective you want and go a step further, by turning that desire into actionable steps.

Here's how: State a wish (W); visualize the best outcome (O); pin down your objections or obstacles (O); and make a plan (P) to counteract your objection ("If [obstacle] happens I will [more positive response]"). For example, "If I get distracted by social media while writing, I will blow out—then relight—my scented candle, and start writing again immediately."

WOOP-ing creates clarity around the steps necessary to reach a goal, making your brain anticipate its reward and allowing you to focus on working toward it.

In short—you've been manipulated. But now that you know how that omnipresent device is sapping your precious productivity, you can turn the tables and employ tactics to redirect your focus back to the work that matters.

Won't it feel good to once again have your brain working for you?

....

JULIE DUFFY is the founder of StoryADay May (storyaday.org), a 31-day creativity challenge and online community focused on short stories. This article was previously published in the May/June 2018 issue of *Writer's Digest*.

....

THE 5 REJECTIONS YOU MEET IN YOUR INBOX

Rejections are a reality of the writing trade, but even a pass can provide valuable insight to carry forward your career.

by Jeff Somers

When I was a kid, I was a huge baseball fan. I lived and breathed the game: I played Little League,[1] collected baseball cards, watched or listened to games every day, and played in fantasy leagues. It was the statistical aspect of the game that fascinated me—especially the realization that baseball was a game where the best hitters in the world made an out *70 percent* of the time[2]. I mean, that's a lot of failure for people making millions of dollars playing a game. Looking back, my decision to pursue writing professionally was probably influenced by this fascination. What other profession is so rife with rejection and failure?[3]

My relationship with rejection goes back to my childhood as well. When I was 16, I made an unforced error and sent a lightweight, silly short story to a magazine that took

---

1 I was impressively terrible at it, too, as a pudgy, bespectacled child with the hand-eye coordination of a tree stump. I'm pretty sure I established the little-known 10th position known as Left Out.
2 Unless you're Ty Cobb, in which case you only made an out 60 percent of the time. His secret power was sociopathy.
3 Fun fact: I have literally sold 3 percent of everything I've ever submitted.

itself and its politics really, *really* seriously. To say their rejection note was mean would be an understatement; I think I got my first gray hair after reading it.[4]

I learned two important lessons that day (three, if you count the unrelated but *absolutely vital* lesson that there is, in fact, such a thing as "too much cologne"): One, research your markets. And two, the dark rule of professional writing is that if you submit your writing, you will get rejection letters.

NO PAIN, NO GAIN

If you have any desire to be a professional writer, you're going to have to get used to rejection. Even established, well-published writers (my ears are burning) get rejections. The trick to dealing with rejection letters is to remind yourself that editors turn down stories and pitches for a long list of reasons—just because your story didn't make a particular cut doesn't mean that it's terrible and should be ritualistically burned in the basement.[5] Rejections come for a variety of reasons, some of which have nothing to do with the quality of your work at all. Your work could be rejected because:

- You misunderstood the market's focus and your story is wrong for their editorial vision (see previous page and weep for 16-year-old Jeff[6]).
- There were other stories that just hit the (mysterious, unknowable, totally subjective) mark.
- The editor has a specific pet peeve about grammar or style that you violated.[7]

Is it possible the reason is because your story stinks? Sure![8] But it doesn't matter. Rejection is just the cost of doing business when you're a writer. As a man who collects a lot of rejections every year, I can't help but be amused by writers who fear rejection or allow themselves to be cowed by the thought of having a story or novel rejected. Over the years, I've figured out that every rejection you'll ever get in your lifetime will fall into one of five fundamental categories—and there are concrete lessons you can take away from each.

While every editor you might submit a story, novel, poem, or article to is a unique being, they will reject your story with a note that falls into one of the following categories. While rejection stings, you can at least gain some insight into either your own work or the value of that market simply by analyzing which category it comes from.

---

4 To give you an idea how much rejection I've experienced since, I now resemble Anderson Cooper.
5 Just be prepared, because sometimes the combination of fire, ritual, and really, really bad writing opens a portal you do not want open in your basement. At the very least, don't burn your manuscripts when you're expecting guests later.
6 Also weep for him because of the mullet.
7 For example, some snobs really go after you if misspell words or paste in whole paragraphs from Wikipedia or end every sentence with a semicolon for no discernible reason other than you were extremely hungover when writing the story. Like I said: snobs.
8 <bursts into tears>

1. To Whom It May Concern: The Impersonal Form Letter

WHAT IT IS: You know it; it begins "Dear author" and it is exactly the same text that every other rejected author received. Sometimes it contains an apology concerning the lack of personalization. More often it is robotic, brief, and very clearly a template. In the bad old days, these were frequently poor photocopies—the text off-center, the paper darkened by the dead dreams of a million authors who came before you.

THE LESSON: You're in the Game.
No, seriously—your takeaway from an impersonal form letter rejection is that you are a professional writer. You wrote something, submitted it to a market, and took your rejection like a grown-up. Congratulations! You just fulfilled the only three prerequisites to be able to tell people you're a professional writer. More important, you've taken the one step that is absolutely crucial to publishing your work—you got it out there. You publish exactly zero of the stories you don't start or finish, yes—but more important you publish exactly zero of the stories you don't *submit*. Bonus: The editor wasn't moved to send you a personal note of disdain or a dead rodent, so your work couldn't have been *that* bad.[9]

2. The Sympathetic Feedback Dump

WHAT IT IS: It's a rejection, but they really, *really* want you to know why, so it is also feedback. Sometimes it's just a few brief notes regarding the decision to reject you, sometimes it's three pages of really dense thoughts on a story you wrote in the backseat of a car while road tripping to a Foo Fighters concert. Feedback isn't always *pleasant*, of course, but it's always *welcomed*, so these sorts of rejections should be treasured.

THE LESSON: You moved someone.
Some of these feedback-dump rejections are the result of editorial policy—everyone gets a glimpse of the editors' thoughts. Some are sporadic and imply that you really got to the reader—either way, your lesson is that although they ultimately turned you down, they were *thinking about what you wrote*. Making someone think and react to your words is amazing no matter what the outcome, and you should feel pretty good that you inspired someone to write about your work, even if their response contains the phrase *for the love of all that is holy, stop writing*.[10]

3. The Insult: Do You Even Write?

WHAT IT IS: The dark inverse of The Sympathetic Feedback Dump, this rejection is a mean-spirited rundown of all your flaws as a writer, a professional, and possibly a citizen

---

9 Plus, form letters and emails allow you to pretend you got yours by mistake.
10 Maybe especially if it contains that phrase.

of the world and/or universe (depending on genre). This rejection will explain in terrifying detail the low opinion this editor has of your work.[11]

THE LESSON: The market's not worth it.

You just learned something about this market—that it's not worth your time. There's a right way and a wrong way to offer criticism, and sending you a note that is not only a rejection of something you worked hard at but also a callous teardown tells you that you don't want to be a part of this market. Look, it's part of our job to synthesize criticism into better work, but an insulting rejection just means the person running that market has no idea how to do it right—and is a good predictor of how they treat the authors they *do* buy content from. That being said, while it's probably a bad market, it might be *useful* feedback. Most insulting rejections are just mean, but any time you receive less-than-stellar feedback on your work is an opportunity to take a step back and ask yourself if it's justified.

4. The Ramble

WHAT IT IS: You're not sure. You've read it three times and you're still not certain whether you sold the story, got rejected, or have just been invited to join some sort of literary cult promising you eternal life just as soon as the asteroid hits New York.[12] In fact, The Ramble is usually so bad it gets the details wrong—you're addressed by someone else's name, the story's title is mixed-up and re-arranged and at least half of it seems to be someone's letter to their grandmother. Their *deceased* grandmother.

THE LESSON: You dodged a bullet.

Even if you *did* sell the story to these clowns, your chances of ever actually seeing it in print—much less getting *paid* for it—are slim to none.[13] Cross them off your list of potential markets and get on with your life, because if your job boils down to writing something compelling that people will want to read, their job is to communicate clearly with you.

5. The Sales Pitch

WHAT IT IS: "Thanks for showing us your work, we really enjoyed reading it. It's not right for us, but … maybe if you buy a subscription, you'll have better luck next time." Essentially, after destroying your self-confidence with a rejection, they hit you up for some cash.

---

11 The only thing worse is the insulting acceptance, wherein the editor says congrats, they're buying your work, and then spends three pages telling you how awful it is.
12 Note to all crazy people out there: I wish to join this exact cult. Hit me up.
13 Chances a Rambler wants to pay you in their own cryptocurrency: 97 percent.

THE LESSON: This market doesn't value writers.

Look, there's nothing wrong with a magazine or web site pitching subscriptions, and if you are determined to sell a story to a certain market you could make worse decisions than reading some sample issues. But a rejection note that urges you to buy a sub is emotionally manipulative, and implies that they're more concerned with extracting money *from* writers than paying them to supply excellent, incredible writing.

Rejection is tough, but every rejection is an opportunity to learn—either about your own writing or about the market. The key to surviving the submissions process is to understand that rejection comes to us all. It's up to you what you take away from it.

JEFF SOMERS (jeffreysomers.com) is the author of *We Are Not Good People* and eight other novels. His Writer's Digest book, *Writing Without Rules,* was published in 2018. This article was previously published in the March/April 2019 issue of *Writer's Digest*.

BOOK PUBLISHERS

There's no magic formula for getting published. It's a matter of getting the right manuscript on the right editor's desk at the right time. Before you submit it's important to learn publishers' needs, see what kind of books they're producing, and decide which publishers your work is best suited for. *Children's Writer's & Illustrator's Market* is but one tool in this process. (Those just starting out, turn to the article "Quick Tips for Writers & Illustrators" in this book.)

To help you narrow down the list of possible publishers for your work, we've included several indexes at the back of this book. The **Subject Index** lists book and magazine publishers according to their fiction and nonfiction needs or interests. The **Age-Level Index** indicates which age groups publishers cater to.

If you write contemporary fiction for young adults, for example, and you're trying to place a book manuscript, go first to the Subject Index. Locate the fiction categories under Book Publishers and copy the list under Contemporary. Then go to the Age-Level Index and highlight the publishers on the Contemporary list that are included under the Young Adults heading. Read the listings for the highlighted publishers to see if your work matches their needs.

Remember, *Children's Writer's & Illustrator's Market* should not be your only source for researching publishers. Here are a few other sources of information:

- The Society of Children's Book Writers and Illustrators (SCBWI) offers members an annual market survey of children's book publishers for the cost of postage or free online at www.scbwi.org. (SCBWI membership information can also be found at www.scbwi.org.)
- The Children's Book Council website (www.cbcbooks.org) gives information on member publishers.
- If a publisher interests you, send a SASE for submission guidelines or check publishers' websites for guidelines *before* submitting. To quickly find guidelines online, visit The Colossal Directory of Children's Publishers at www.signaleader.com.
- Check publishers' websites. Many include their complete catalogs, which you can browse. Web addresses are included in many publishers' listings.

- Spend time at your local bookstore to see who's publishing what. While you're there, browse through *Publishers Weekly* and *The Horn Book*.

SUBSIDY & SELF-PUBLISHING

Some determined writers who receive rejections from royalty publishers may look to subsidy and co-op publishers as an option for getting their work into print. These publishers ask writers to pay all or part of the costs of producing a book. We strongly advise writers and illustrators to work only with publishers who pay them. For this reason, we've adopted a policy not to include any subsidy or co-op publishers in *Children's Writer's & Illustrator's Market* (or any other Writer's Digest Books market book).

If you're interested in publishing your book just to share it with friends and relatives, self-publishing is a viable option, but it involves time, energy, and money. You oversee all book production details. Check with a local printer for advice and information on cost or check online for print-on-demand publishing options (which are often more affordable).

Whatever path you choose, keep in mind that the market is flooded with submissions, so it's important for you to hone your craft and submit the best work possible. Competition from thousands of other writers and illustrators makes it more important than ever to research publishers before submitting—read their guidelines, look at their catalogs, check out a few of their titles, and visit their websites.

ABBEVILLE FAMILY

Abbeville Press, 116 W. 23rd St., New York NY 10011. (646)375-2136. **Fax:** (646)375-2359. **E-mail:** abbeville@abbeville.com. **Website:** www.abbeville.com. Our list is full for the next several seasons. *Not accepting unsolicited book proposals at this time.* **Publishes 8 titles/year. 10% of books from first-time authors.**

FICTION Picture books: animal, anthology, concept, contemporary, fantasy, folktales, health, hi-lo, history, humor, multicultural, nature/environment, poetry, science fiction, special needs, sports, suspense. Average word length 300-1,000 words.

HOW TO CONTACT Please refer to website for submission policy.

ILLUSTRATION Works with approx 2-4 illustrators/year. Uses color artwork only.

PHOTOGRAPHY Buys stock and assigns work.

ABDO PUBLISHING CO.

8000 W. 78th St., Suite 310, Edina MN 55439. (800)800-1312. **Fax:** (952)831-1632. **E-mail:** nonfiction@abdopublishing.com. **Website:** www.abdopublishing.com. ABDO publishes nonfiction children's books (pre-kindergarten to 8th grade) for school and public libraries—mainly history, sports, biography, geography, science, and social studies. "Please specify each submission as either nonfiction, fiction, or illustration. Publishes hardcover originals. **Publishes 300 titles/year.**

TERMS Guidelines online.

ABRAMS

115 W. 18th St., 6th Floor, New York NY 10011. (212)206-7715. **Fax:** (212)519-1210. **E-mail:** abrams@abramsbooks.com. **Website:** www.abramsbooks.com. **Contact:** Managing Editor. Publishes hardcover and a few paperback originals. **Publishes 250 titles/year.**

🚫 Does not accept unsolicited materials.

FICTION Publishes hardcover and "a few" paperback originals. Averages 150 total titles/year.

TIPS "We are one of the few publishers who publish almost exclusively illustrated books. We consider ourselves the leading publishers of art books and high-quality artwork in the U.S. Once the author has signed a contract to write a book for our firm the author must finish the manuscript to agreed-upon high standards within the schedule agreed upon in the contract."

ABRAMS BOOKS FOR YOUNG READERS

195 Broadway, 9th floor, New York NY 10007. **Website:** www.abramsyoungreaders.com.

🚫 Abrams no longer accepts unsolicited mss or queries.

ILLUSTRATION Illustrations only: Do not submit original material; copies only. Contact: Chad Beckerman, art director.

ALADDIN

Simon & Schuster, 1230 Avenue of the Americas, 4th Floor, New York NY 10020. (212)698-7000. **Website:** www.simonandschuster.com. Aladdin also publishes Aladdin M!X, for those readers too old for kids' books, but not quite ready for adult or young adult novels. **Contact:** Acquisitions Editor. Aladdin publishes picture books, beginning readers, chapter books, middle grade and tween fiction and nonfiction, and graphic novels and nonfiction in hardcover and paperback, with an emphasis on commercial, kid-friendly titles. Publishes hardcover/paperback originals and imprints of Simon & Schuster Children's Publishing Children's Division.

HOW TO CONTACT Simon & Schuster does not review, retain or return unsolicited materials or artwork. "We suggest prospective authors and illustrators submit their mss through a professional literary agent."

ALGONQUIN YOUNG READERS

P.O. Box 2225, Chapel Hill NC 27515. **Website:** algonquinyoungreaders.com. Algonquin Young Readers is a new imprint that features books for readers 7-17. "From short illustrated novels for the youngest independent readers to timely and topical crossover young adult fiction, what ties our books together are unforgettable characters, absorbing stories, and superior writing.

FICTION Algonquin Young Readers publishes ficiton and a limited number of narrative nonfiction titles for middle grade and young adult readers. "We don't publish poetry, picture books, or genre fiction."

HOW TO CONTACT Query with 15-20 sample pages and SASE.

ILLUSTRATION "At this time, we do not accept unsolicited submissions for illustration."

TERMS Guidelines online.

AMBERJACK PUBLISHING

P.O. Box 4668 #89611, New York NY 10163. (888)959-3352. **Website:** www.amberjackpublishing.com. Amberjack Publishing offers authors the freedom to write without burdening them with having to promote the work themselves. They retain all rights. "You will have no rights left to exploit, so you cannot resell, republish or use your story again."

FICTION Amberjack Publishing is always on the lookout for the next great story. "We are interested in fiction, children's books, graphic novels, science fiction, fantasy, humor, and everything in between."

HOW TO CONTACT Submit via online query form with book proposal and first 10 pages of ms.

Ⓐ AMULET BOOKS

Imprint of Abrams, 115 W. 18th St., 6th Floor, New York NY 10001. **Website:** www.amuletbooks.com. *Does not accept unsolicited mss or queries.* **10% of books from first-time authors.**

FICTION Middle readers: adventure, contemporary, fantasy, history, science fiction, sports. Young adults/teens: adventure, contemporary, fantasy, history, science fiction, sports, suspense.

ILLUSTRATION Works with 10-12 illustrators/year. Uses both color and b&w. Query with samples. Contact: Chad Beckerman, art director. Samples filed.

PHOTOGRAPHY Buys stock images and assigns work.

ARBORDALE PUBLISHING

612 Johnnie Dodds, Suite A2, Mt. Pleasant SC 29464. (843)971-6722. **Fax:** (843)216-3804. **E-mail:** submissions@arbordalepublishing.com. **Website:** www.arbordalepublishing.com. **Contact:** Acquisitions Editor. "The picture books we publish are usually, but not always, fictional stories with nonfiction woven into the story that relate to science or math. All books should subtly convey an educational theme through a warm story that is fun to read and that will grab a child's attention. Each book has a 4-page *'For Creative Minds'* section to reinforce the educational component. This section will have a craft and/or game as well as 'fun facts' to be shared by the parent, teacher, or other adult. Authors do not need to supply this information with their submission, but if their ms is accepted, they may be asked to provide additional information for this section. Mss should be less than 1,000 words and meet all of the following 4 criteria: fun to read—mostly fiction with nonfiction facts woven into the story; national or regional in scope; must tie into early elementary school curriculum; must be marketable through a niche market such as a zoo, aquarium, or museum gift shop." Publishes hardcover, trade paperback, and electronic originals. **Publishes 12 titles/year. 50% of books from first-time authors. 99% from unagented writers.**

FICTION Picture books: animal, folktales, nature/environment, science- or math-related. No more than 1,000 words. Holiday-specific, cats or dogs

NONFICTION Prefer fiction, but will consider nonfiction as well.

HOW TO CONTACT All mss should be submitted via e-mail to Acquisitions Editor. Mss should be less than 1,000 words. All mss should be submitted via e-mail. Mss should be less than 1,000 words. 1,000 mss received/year. Accepts electronic submissions only. Snail mail submissions are discarded without being opened.

Acknowledges receipt of ms submission within 1 month. Publishes book 18 months after acceptance. May hold onto mss of interest for 1 year until acceptance.

ILLUSTRATION Works with 20 illustrators/year. Prefers to work with illustrators from the US and Canada. Uses color artwork only. Submit Web link or 2-3 electronic images. Contact: Acquisitions Editor

TERMS Pays 6-8% royalty on wholesale price. Pays small advance. Book catalog and guidelines online.

TIPS "Please make sure that you have looked at our website to read our complete submission guidelines and to see if we are looking for a particular subject. Manuscripts must meet all four of our stated criteria. We look for fairly realistic, bright and colorful art-no cartoons. We want the children excited about the books. We envision the books being used at home and in the classroom."

Ⓐ ATHENEUM BOOKS FOR YOUNG READERS

Simon & Schuster, 1230 Avenue of the Americas, New York NY 10020. **Website:** kids.simonandschuster.com. Publishes hardcover originals.

FICTION All in juvenile versions. "We have few specific needs except for books that are fresh, interesting and well written. Fad topics are dangerous, as are works you haven't polished to the best of your ability. We also don't need safety pamphlets, ABC books, coloring books and board books. In writing picture book texts, avoid the coy and 'cutesy,' such as stories about characters with alliterative names." Agented submissions only. No paperback romance-type fiction.

NONFICTION Publishes hardcover originals, picture books for young kids, nonfiction for ages 8-12 and novels for middle-grade and young adults. 100% require freelance illustration. Agented submissions only.

TERMS Guidelines for #10 SASE.

TIPS "Study our titles."

BAILIWICK PRESS

309 East Mulberry St., Fort Collins CO 80524. (970)672-4878. **Fax:** (970)672-4731. **E-mail:** info@ bailiwickpress.com. **Website:** www.bailiwickpress. com. "We're a micro-press that produces books and other products that inspire and tell great stories. Our motto is 'books with something to say.' We are now considering submissions, agented and unagented, for children's and young adult fiction. We're looking for smart, funny, and layered writing that kids will clamor for. Authors who already have a following have a leg up. We are only looking for humorous children's fiction. Please do not submit work for adults. Illustrated fiction is desired but not required. (Illustrators are also invited to send samples.) Make us laugh out loud, ooh and aah, and cry, 'Eureka!'"

HOW TO CONTACT "Please read the Aldo Zelnick series to determine if we might be on the same page, then fill out our submission form. Please do not send submissions via snail mail or phone calls. You must complete the online submission form to be considered. If, after completing and submitting the form, you also need to send us an e-mail attachment (such as sample illustrations or excerpts of graphics), you may e-mail them to aldozelnick@gmail.com." Responds in 6 months.

ILLUSTRATION Illustrated fiction desired but not required. Send samples.

Ⓐ BALZER & BRAY

HarperCollins Children's Books, 10 E. 53rd St., New York NY 10022. **Website:** www.harpercollinschildrens.com. "We publish bold, creative, groundbreaking picture books and novels that appeal directly to kids in a fresh way." **Publishes 10 titles/year.**

FICTION Picture Books, Young Readers: adventure, animal, anthology, concept, contemporary, fantasy,

history, humor, multicultural, nature/environment, poetry, science fiction, special needs, sports, suspense. Middle readers, young adults/teens: adventure, animal, anthology, contemporary, fantasy, history, humor, multicultural, nature/environment, poetry, science fiction, special needs, sports, suspense.

NONFICTION "We will publish very few nonfiction titles, maybe 1-2 per year."

HOW TO CONTACT Contact editor. Agented submissions only. Agented submissions only. Publishes book 18 months after acceptance.

ILLUSTRATION Works with 10 illustrators/year. Uses both color and b&w. Illustrations only: send tearsheets to be kept on file. Responds only if interested. Samples are not returned.

PHOTOGRAPHY Works on assignment only.

TERMS Offers advances. Pays illustrators by the project.

Ⓐ BANTAM BOOKS

Imprint of Penguin Random House LLC, 1745 Broadway, New York NY 10019. (212)782-9000. **Website:** www.penguinrandomhouse.com. *Not seeking mss at this time.*

BAREFOOT BOOKS

2067 Massachusetts Ave., 5th Floor, Cambridge MA 02140. (617)576-0660. **Fax:** (617)576-0049. **E-mail:** help@barefootbooks.com. **Website:** www.barefootbooks.com. **Contact:** Acquisitions Editor. "We are a small, independent publishing company that publishes high-quality picture books for children of all ages and specializes in the work of artists and writers from many cultures. We focus on themes that support independence of spirit, encourage openness to others, and foster a life-long love of learning. Prefers full manuscript." Publishes hardcover and trade paperback originals. **Publishes 30 titles/year. 35% of books from first-time authors. 60% from unagented writers.**

FICTION "Barefoot Books only publishes children's picture books and anthologies of folktales. We do not publish novels."

HOW TO CONTACT Barefoot Books is not currently accepting ms queries or submissions. 2,000 queries received/year. 3,000 mss received/year.

ILLUSTRATION Works with 20 illustrators/year. Uses color artwork only. Reviews ms/illustration packages from artists. Send query and art samples or dummy for picture books. Query with samples or send promo sheet and tearsheets. Responds only if interested. Samples returned with SASE. Pays authors royalty of 5% based on retail price. Offers advances. Sends galleys to authors. Originals returned to artist at job's completion.

TERMS Pays advance. Book catalog for 9x12 SAE stamped with $1.80 postage.

⊙ BARRONS EDUCATIONAL SERIES

250 Wireless Blvd., Hauppauge NY 11788. **Fax:** (631)434-3723. **Website:** www.barronseduc.com. **Contact:** Wayne R. Barr, manuscript acquisitions.

FICTION Picture books: animal, concept, multicultural, nature/environment. Young readers: adventure, multicultural, nature/environment, fantasy, suspense/mystery. Middle readers: adventure, fantasy, multicultural, nature/environment, problem novels, suspense/mystery. Young adults: problem novels. "Stories with an educational element are appealing."

NONFICTION Picture books: concept, reference. Young readers: biography, how-to, reference, self-help, social issues. Middle readers: hi-lo, how-to, reference, self-help, social issues. Young adults: reference, self-help, social issues, sports.

HOW TO CONTACT Query via e-mail with no attached files. Full guidelines are listed on the website. Submit outline/synopsis and sample chapters. "Nonfiction submissions must be accompanied by SASE for response." Due to the large volume of unsolicited submissions received, a complete evaluation of a proposal may take 4-6 weeks. Please do not call about the status of individual submissions. Publishes book 1 year after acceptance.

ILLUSTRATION Works with 20 illustrators/year. Reviews ms/illustration packages from artists. Query first; 3 chapters of ms with 1 piece of final art, remainder roughs. Illustrations only: Submit tearsheets or slides plus résumé. Responds in 2 months.

TERMS Pays authors royalty of 10-12% based on net price or buys ms outright for $2,000 minimum. Pays illustrators by the project based on retail price. Catalog available for 9x12 SASE. Guidelines available on website.

TIPS Writers: "We publish pre-school storybooks, concept books and middle grade and YA chapter books. No romance novels. Those with an educational element." Illustrators: "We are happy to receive a sample illustration to keep on file for future consid-

eration. Periodic notes reminding us of your work are acceptable." Children's book themes "are becoming much more contemporary and relevant to a child's day-to-day activities, fewer talking animals. We are interested in fiction (ages 7-11 and ages 12-16) dealing with modern problems."

BEHRMAN HOUSE INC.

11 Edison Place, Springfield NJ 07081. (973)379-7200. **Fax:** (973)379-7280. **E-mail:** customersupport@behrmanhouse.com. **Website:** www.behrmanhouse.com. **Contact:** Editorial Committee. Publishes books on all aspects of Judaism: history, cultural, textbooks, holidays. "Behrman House publishes quality books of Jewish content—history, Bible, philosophy, holidays, ethics—for children and adults." **12% of books from first-time authors.**

NONFICTION All levels: Judaism, Jewish educational textbooks. Average word length: young reader—1,200; middle reader—2,000; young adult—4,000.

HOW TO CONTACT Submit outline/synopsis and sample chapters. Responds in 1 month to queries; 2 months to mss. Publishes book 18 months after acceptance.

ILLUSTRATION Works with 6 children's illustrators/year. Reviews ms/illustration packages from artists. "Query first." Illustrations only: Query with samples; send unsolicited art samples by mail. Responds to queries in 1 month; mss in 2 months.

PHOTOGRAPHY Purchases photos from freelancers. Buys stock and assigns work. Uses photos of families involved in Jewish activities. Uses color and b&w prints. Photographers should query with samples. Send unsolicited photos by mail. Submit portfolio for review.

TERMS Pays authors royalty of 3-10% based on retail price or buys ms outright for $1,000-5,000. Offers advance. Pays illustrators by the project (range: $500-5,000). Book catalog free on request. Guidelines online.

BELLEBOOKS

P.O. Box 300921, Memphis TN 38130. (901)344-9024. **Fax:** (901)344-9068. **E-mail:** bellebooks@bellebooks.com. **Website:** www.bellebooks.com. BelleBooks began by publishing Southern fiction. It has become a "second home" for many established authors, who also continue to publish with major publishing houses. **Publishes 30-40 titles/year.**

FICTION "Yes, we'd love to find the next Harry Potter, but our primary focus for the moment is publishing for the teen market."

HOW TO CONTACT Query e-mail with brief synopsis and credentials/credits with full ms attached (RTF format preferred).

TERMS Guidelines online.

TIPS "Our list aims for the teen reader and the crossover market. If you're a 'Southern Louise Rennison,' that would catch our attention. Humor is always a plus. We'd love to see books featuring teen boys as protagonists. We're happy to see dark edgy books on serious subjects."

BERKLEY

An imprint of Penguin Random House LLC, 1745 Broadway, New York NY 10019. **Website:** penguinrandomhouse.com. The Berkley Publishing Group publishes a variety of general nonfiction and fiction including the traditional categories of romance, mystery and science fiction. Publishes paperback and mass market originals and reprints. **Publishes 700 titles/year.**

"Due to the high volume of manuscripts received, most Penguin Group (USA) Inc. imprints do not normally accept unsolicited mss. The preferred and standard method for having mss considered for publication by a major publisher is to submit them through an established literary agent."

FICTION No occult fiction.

NONFICTION No memoirs or personal stories.

HOW TO CONTACT Prefers agented submissions. Prefers agented submissions.

BESS PRESS

3565 Harding Ave., Honolulu HI 96816. (808)734-7159. **Fax:** (808)732-3627. **Website:** www.besspress.com. Bess Press is a family-owned independent book publishing company based in Honolulu. For over 30 years, Bess Press has been producing both educational and popular general interest titles about Hawai'i and the Pacific.

NONFICTION "We are constantly seeking to work with authors, artists, photographers, and organizations that are developing works concentrating on Hawai'i and the Pacific. Our goal is to regularly provide customers with new, creative, informative, educational, and entertaining publications that are directly connected to or flowing from Hawai'i and other islands in the Pacific region." Not interested in material that is unassociated with Hawai'i or the greater Pacific in theme. Please do not submit works if it does not fall into this regional category.

HOW TO CONTACT Submit your name, contact information, working title, genre, target audience, short (4-6 sentences) description of your work, identifies target audience(s), explains how your work differs from other books already publishing on the same subject, includes discussion of any additional material with samples. All submissions via e-mail. Responds in 4 months.

TERMS Catalog online. Guidelines online.

TIPS "As a regional publisher, we are looking for material specific to the region (Hawaii and Micronesia), preferably from writers and illustrators living within (or very familiar with) the region.", "As a regional publisher, we are looking for material specific to the region (Hawaii and Micronesia), preferably from writers and illustrators living within (or very familiar with) the region."

BETHANY HOUSE PUBLISHERS

Division of Baker Publishing Group, 6030 E. Fulton Rd., Ada MI 49301. (616)676-9185. **Fax:** (616)676-9573. **Website:** bakerpublishinggroup.com/bethanyhouse. Bethany House Publishers specializes in books that communicate Biblical truth and assist people in both spiritual and practical areas of life. Considers unsolicited work only through a professional literary agent or through manuscript submission services, Authonomy or Christian Manuscript Submissions. Guidelines online. *All unsolicited mss returned unopened.* Publishes hardcover and trade paperback originals, mass market paperback reprints. **Publishes 90-100 titles/year. 2% of books from first-time authors. 50% from unagented writers.**

HOW TO CONTACT Responds in 3 months to queries. Publishes a book 1 year after acceptance.

TERMS Pays royalty on net price. Pays advance. Book catalog for 9 x 12 envelope and 5 first-class stamps.

TIPS "Bethany House Publishers' publishing program relates Biblical truth to all areas of life—whether in the framework of a well-told story, of a challenging book for spiritual growth, or of a Bible reference work. We are seeking high-quality fiction and nonfiction that will inspire and challenge our audience."

Ⓐ BEYOND WORDS PUBLISHING, INC.

20827 NW Cornell Rd., Suite 500, Hillsboro OR 97124. (503)531-8700. **Fax:** (503)531-8773. **E-mail:** info@beyondword.com. **Website:** www.beyondword.com. **Contact:** Submissions Department (for agents only). "At this time, we are not accepting any unsolicited queries or proposals, and recommend that all authors work with a literary agent in submitting their work." Publishes hardcover and trade paperback originals and paperback reprints. **Publishes 10-15 titles/year.**

NONFICTION For adult nonfiction, wants whole body health, the evolving human, and transformation. For children and YA, wants health, titles that inspire kids' power to incite change, and titles that allow young readers to explore and/or question traditional wisdom and spiritual practices. Does not want children's picture books, adult fiction, cookbooks, textbooks, reference books, photography books, or illustrated coffee table books.

HOW TO CONTACT Agent should submit query letter with proposal, including author bio, 5 sample chapters, complete synopsis of book, market analysis, SASE. Agent should submit query letter with proposal, including author bio, 5 sample chapters, complete synopsis of book, market analysis, SASE.

BLACK ROSE WRITING

P.O. Box 1540, Castroville TX 78009. **E-mail:** creator@blackrosewriting.com. **Website:** www.blackrosewriting.com/home. Author provides illustrations, fully-illustrated or samples. **Contact:** Reagan Rothe. Black Rose Writing is an independent publishing house that strongly believes in developing a personal relationship with their authors. The Texas-based publishing company doesn't see authors as clients or just another number on a page, but rather as individual people.. people who deserve an honest review of their material and to be paid traditional royalties without ever paying any fees to be published. Black Rose Writing, established in 2006, features books from an array of fiction, nonfiction, and children's book genres, all having one thing in common, an individual's originality and hardship. It can take endless hours to finish a deserving manuscript, and Black Rose Writing applauds each and every author, giving them a chance at their dream. Because Black Rose Writing takes full advantage of modern printing technology, the company has an infinite print run via print-on-demand services. Black Rose Writing's success with their authors is due mainly to their many lines of promotion, (examples: showcasing book titles at festivals, scheduling book events, flexible marketing programs, and sending out press releases and review copies, etc.) and they provide a broad distribution (Ingram, Baker & Taylor, Amazon, Barnes & Noble, and more..) that larger book publishers also reach. We are proud members of IBPA (Independent Book Publishers Association), a recognized ITW (International Thriller Writers) publisher, members of Publishers Marketplace, and currently serving on the Ingram Publisher Advisory Board. Publishes fiction, nonfiction, and illustrated children's books. **Publishes 150+ titles/year. 75% of books from first-time authors. 80% from unagented writers.**

HOW TO CONTACT "Our preferred submission method is via Authors.me, please click 'Submit Here' on our website." "Our preferred submission method is via Authors.me, please click 'Submit Here' on our website." 3,500 submissions received/year. Responds in 3-6 weeks on queries; 3-6 months on mss. Publishes ms 4-6 months after acceptance.

ILLUSTRATION Must be provided by author.

TERMS Royalties start at 20%, e-book royalties 25% Catalog online. Guidelines online.

Ⓐ BLOOMSBURY CHILDREN'S BOOKS

Imprint of Bloomsbury USA, 1385 Broadway, 5th Floor, New York NY 10018. **Website:** www.bloomsbury.com/us/childrens. No phone calls or e-mails. *Agented submissions only.* **Publishes 60 titles/year. 25% of books from first-time authors.**

HOW TO CONTACT *Agented submissions only.* Responds in 6 months.

TERMS Pays royalty. Pays advance. Book catalog online. Guidelines online.

BOOKFISH BOOKS

E-mail: bookfishbooks@gmail.com. **Website:** bookfishbooks.com. **Contact:** Tammy Mckee, acquisitions editor. BookFish Books is looking for novel lengthed young adult, new adult, and middle grade works in all subgenres. Both published and unpublished, agented or unagented authors are welcome to submit. "Sorry, but we do not publish novellas, picture books, early reader/chapter books or adult novels." Responds to every query.

HOW TO CONTACT Query via e-mail with a brief synopsis and first 3 chapters of ms.

TERMS Guidelines online.

TIPS "We only accept complete manuscripts. Please do not query us with partial manuscripts or proposals."

BOYDS MILLS PRESS

Highlights for Children, Inc., 815 Church St., Honesdale PA 18431. (570)253-1164. **Website:** www.boydsmillspress.com. Boyds Mills Press publishes picture books, nonfiction, activity books, and paperback reprints. Their titles have been named notable books by the International Reading Association, the American Library Association, and the National Council of Teachers of English. They've earned numerous awards, including the National Jewish Book Award, the Christopher Medal, the NCTE Orbis Pictus Honor, and the Golden Kite Honor. Boyds Mills Press welcomes unsolicited submissions from published and unpublished writers and artists. Submit a ms with a cover letter of relevant information, including experience with writing and publishing. Label the package "Manuscript Submission" and include an SASE. For art samples, label the package "Art Sample Submission." All submissions will be evaluated for all imprints.

FICTION Interested in picture books and middle grade fiction. Do not send a query first. Send the entire ms of picture book or the first 3 chapters and a plot summary for middle grade fiction (will request the balance of ms if interested).

NONFICTION Include a detailed bibliography with submission. Highly recommends including an expert's review of your ms and a detailed explanation of the books in the marketplace that are similar to the one you propose. References to the need for this book (by the National Academy of Sciences or by similar subject-specific organizations) will strengthen your proposal. If you intend for the book to be illustrated with photos or other graphic elements (charts, graphs, etc.), it is your responsibility to find or create those elements and to include with the submission a permissions budget, if applicable. Finally, keep in mind that good children's nonfiction has a narrative quality—a story line—that encyclopedias do not; please consider whether both the subject and the language will appeal to children.

HOW TO CONTACT Responds to mss within 3 months.

ILLUSTRATION Illustrators submitting a picture book should include the ms, a dummy, and a sample reproduction of the final artwork that reflects the style and technique you intend to use. Do not send original artwork.

TERMS Catalog online. Guidelines online.

CALKINS CREEK

Boyds Mills Press, 815 Church St., Honesdale PA 18431. **Website:** www.boydsmillspress.com. "We aim to publish books that are a well-written blend of creative writing and extensive research, which emphasize important events, people, and places in U.S. history."

HOW TO CONTACT Submit outline/synopsis and 3 sample chapters. Submit outline/synopsis and 3 sample chapters.

ILLUSTRATION Accepts material from international illustrators. Works with 25 (for all Boyds Mills Press imprints) illustrators/year. Uses both color and b&w. Reviews ms/illustration packages. For ms/illustration packages: Submit ms with 2 pieces of final art. Submit ms/illustration packages to address above, label package "Manuscript Submission." Reviews work for future assignments. If interested in illustrating future titles, query with samples. Submit samples to address above. Label package "Art Sample Submission."

PHOTOGRAPHY Buys stock images and assigns work. Submit photos to: address above, label package "Art Sample Submission." Uses color or b&w 8×10 prints. For first contact, send promo piece (color or b&w).

TERMS Pays authors royalty or work purchased outright. Guidelines online.

TIPS "Read through our recently published titles and review our catalog. When selecting titles to publish, our emphasis will be on important events, people, and places in U.S. history. Writers are encouraged to submit a detailed bibliography, including secondary and primary sources, and expert reviews with their submissions."

ⓐ CANDLEWICK PRESS

99 Dover St., Somerville MA 02144. (617) 661-3330. **Fax:** (617) 661-0565. **E-mail:** bigbear@candlewick.com. **Website:** www.candlewick.com. "Candlewick Press publishes high-quality, illustrated children's books for ages infant through young adult. We are a truly child-centered publisher." Publishes hardcover and trade paperback originals, and reprints. **Publishes 200 titles/year. 5% of books from first-time authors.**

○ *Candlewick Press is not accepting queries or unsolicited mss at this time.*

FICTION Picture books: animal, concept, contemporary, fantasy, history, humor, multicultural, nature/environment, poetry. Middle readers, young adults: contemporary, fantasy, history, humor, multicultural, poetry, science fiction, sports, suspense/mystery.

NONFICTION Picture books: concept, biography, geography, nature/environment. Young readers: biography, geography, nature/environment.

HOW TO CONTACT "We currently do not accept unsolicited editorial queries or submissions. If you are an author or illustrator and would like us to consider your work, please read our submissions policy (online) to learn more."

ILLUSTRATION "Candlewick prefers to see a range of styles from artists along with samples showing strong characters (human or animals) in various settings with various emotions."

TERMS Pays authors royalty of 2½-10% based on retail price. Offers advance.

TIPS *"We no longer accept unsolicited mss. See our website for further information about us."*

CAPSTONE PRESS

Capstone Young Readers, 1710 Roe Crest Dr., North Mankato MN 56003. **E-mail:** author.sub@capstonepub.com; il.sub@capstonepub.com. **Website:** www.capstonepub.com. The Capstone Press imprint publishes nonfiction with accessible text on topics kids love to capture interest and build confidence and skill in beginning, struggling, and reluctant readers, grades pre-K-9.

FICTION Send fiction submissions via e-mail (author.sub@capstonepub.com). Include the following, in the body of the e-mail: sample chapters, resume, and a list of previous publishing credits.

NONFICTION Send nonfiction submissions via postal mail. Include the following: resume, cover letter, and up to 3 writing samples.

HOW TO CONTACT Responds only if submissions fit needs. Mss and writing samples will not be returned. "If you receive no reply within 6 months, you should assume the editors are not interested."

ILLUSTRATION Send fiction illustration submissions via e-mail (il.sub@capstonepub.com). Include the following, in the body of the e-mail: sample artwork, resume, and a list of previous publishing cred-

its. For nonfiction illustrations, send via e-mail (nf.il.sub@capstonepub.com) sample artwork (2-4 pieces) and a list of previous publishing credits.

TERMS Catalog available upon request. Guidelines online.

CAROLRHODA BOOKS, INC.

1251 Washington Ave. N., Minneapolis MN 55401. **Website:** www.lernerbooks.com. "We will continue to seek targeted solicitations at specific reading levels and in specific subject areas. The company will list these targeted solicitations on our website and in national newsletters, such as the SCBWI Bulletin." Interested in "boundary-pushing" teen fiction. *Lerner Publishing Group no longer accepts submissions to any of their imprints except for Kar-Ben Publishing.*

ⓐ CARTWHEEL BOOKS

Imprint of Scholastic Trade Division, 557 Broadway, New York NY 10012. (212)343-6100. **Website:** www.scholastic.com. Cartwheel Books publishes innovative books for children, up to age 8. "We are looking for 'novelties' that are books first, play objects second. Even without its gimmick, a Cartwheel Book should stand alone as a valid piece of children's literature." Publishes novelty books, easy readers, board books, hardcover and trade paperback originals.

FICTION Again, the subject should have mass market appeal for very young children. Humor can be helpful, but not necessary. Mistakes writers make are a reading level that is too difficult, a topic of no interest or too narrow, or mss that are too long.

NONFICTION Cartwheel Books publishes for the very young, therefore nonfiction should be written in a manner that is accessible to preschoolers through 2nd grade. Often writers choose topics that are too narrow or "special" and do not appeal to the mass market. Also, the text and vocabulary are frequently too difficult for our young audience.

HOW TO CONTACT *Accepts mss from agents only. Accepts mss from agents only.*

TERMS Guidelines available free.

CEDAR FORT, INC.

2373 W. 700 S, Springville UT 84663. (801)489-4084. **Website:** www.cedarfort.com. "Each year we publish well over 100 books, and many of those are by first-time authors. At the same time, we love to see books from established authors. As one of the largest book publishers in Utah, we have the capability and enthusiasm to make your book a success, whether you are a new author or a returning one. We want to publish uplifting and edifying books that help people think about what is important in life, books people enjoy reading to relax and feel better about themselves, and books to help improve lives. Although we do put out several children's books each year, we are extremely selective. Our children's books must have strong religious or moral values, and must contain outstanding writing and an excellent storyline." Publishes hardcover, trade paperback originals and reprints, mass market paperback and electronic reprints. **Publishes 150 titles/year. 60% of books from first-time authors. 95% from unagented writers.**

HOW TO CONTACT Submit completed ms. Query with SASE; submit proposal package, including outline, 2 sample chapters; or submit completed ms. Receives 200 queries/year; 600 mss/year. Responds in 1 month on queries; 2 months on proposals; 4 months on mss. Publishes book 10-14 months after acceptance.

TERMS Pays 10-12% royalty on wholesale price. Pays $2,000-50,000 advance. Catalog and guidelines online.

TIPS "Our audience is rural, conservative, mainstream. The first page of your ms is very important because we start reading every submission, but good writing and plot keep us reading."

CHARLESBRIDGE PUBLISHING

85 Main St., Watertown MA 02472. (617)926-0329. **Fax:** (617)926-5720. **E-mail:** tradeeditorial@charlesbridge.com. **Website:** www.charlesbridge.com. "Charlesbridge publishes high-quality books for children, with a goal of creating lifelong readers and lifelong learners. Our books encourage reading and discovery in the classroom, library, and home. We believe that books for children should offer accurate information, promote a positive worldview, and embrace a child's innate sense of wonder and fun. To this end, we continually strive to seek new voices, new visions, and new directions in children's literature. We are now accepting young adult novels for consideration." Publishes hardcover and trade paperback nonfiction and fiction, children's books for the trade and library markets. **Publishes 50 titles/year. 10-20% of books from first-time authors. 40% from unagented writers.**

FICTION Strong stories with enduring themes. Charlesbridge publishes both picture books and transitional bridge books (books ranging from early readers to middle-grade chapter books). Our fiction titles include lively, plot-driven stories with strong, engaging characters. No alphabet books, board books, coloring books, activity books, or books with audiotapes or CD-ROMs.

NONFICTION Strong interest in nature, environment, social studies, and other topics for trade and library markets.

HOW TO CONTACT Please submit only 1 ms at a time. For picture books and shorter bridge books, please send a complete ms. For fiction books longer than 30 ms pages, please send a detailed plot synopsis, a chapter outline, and 3 chapters of text. If sending a young adult novel, mark the front of the envelope with "YA novel enclosed." Please note, for YA, e-mail submissions are preferred to the following address; yasubs@charlesbridge.com. Only responds if interested. Full guidelines on site. https://charlesbridge.com/pages/submissions Follow guidelines online. https://charlesbridge.com/pages/submissions 4,000 submissions/year. Responds in 3 months. Publishes 2-4 years after acceptance.

TERMS Pays royalty. Pays advance. Guidelines online. https://charlesbridge.com/pages/submissions

TIPS "To become acquainted with our publishing program, we encourage you to review our books and visit our website where you will find our catalog."

CHICAGO REVIEW PRESS

814 N. Franklin St., Chicago IL 60610. (312)337-0747. **Fax:** (312)337-5110. **E-mail:** csherry@chicagoreviewpress.com; jpohlen@chicagoreviewpress.com; lreardon@chicagoreviewpress.com; ytaylor@chicagoreviewpress.com. **Website:** www.chicagoreviewpress.com. **Contact:** Cynthia Sherry, publisher; Yuval Taylor, senior editor; Jerome Pohlen, senior editor; Lisa Reardon, senior editor. "Chicago Review Press publishes high-quality, nonfiction, educational activity books that extend the learning process through hands-on projects and accurate and interesting text. We look for activity books that are as much fun as they are constructive and informative."

FICTION Guidelines now available on website.

NONFICTION Young readers, middle readers and young adults: activity books, arts/crafts, multicultural, history, nature/environment, science. "We're interested in hands-on, educational books; anything else probably will be rejected." Average length: young readers and young adults—144-160 pages.

HOW TO CONTACT Enclose cover letter and a brief synopsis of book in 1-2 paragraphs, table of contents and first 3 sample chapters; prefers not to receive e-mail queries. For children's activity books include a few sample activities with a list of the others. Full guidelines available on site. Responds in 2 months. Publishes a book 1-2 years after acceptance.

ILLUSTRATION Works with 6 illustrators/year. Uses primarily b&w artwork. Reviews ms/illustration packages from artists. Submit 1-2 chapters of ms with corresponding pieces of final art. Illustrations only: Query with samples, résumé. Responds only if interested. Samples returned with SASE.

PHOTOGRAPHY Buys photos from freelancers ("but not often"). Buys stock and assigns work. Wants "instructive photos. We consult our files when we know what we're looking for on a book-by-book basis." Uses b&w prints.

TERMS Pays authors royalty of 7.5-12.5% based on retail price. Offers advances of $3,000-6,000. Pays illustrators and photographers by the project (range varies considerably). Book catalog available for $3. Ms guidelines available for $3.

TIPS "We're looking for original activity books for small children and the adults caring for them—new themes and enticing projects to occupy kids' imaginations and promote their sense of personal creativity. We like activity books that are as much fun as they are constructive. Please write for guidelines so you'll know what we're looking for."

CHILDREN'S BRAINS ARE YUMMY (CBAY) BOOKS

Children's Brains are Yummy Productions, LLC, P.O. Box 670296, Dallas TX 75367. **E-mail:** submissions@cbaybooks.com. **Website:** www.cbaybooks. blog. **Contact:** Madeline Smoot, publisher. "CBAY Books currently focuses on quality fantasy and science fiction books for the middle grade and teen markets. We are not currently accepting unsolicited submissions. We do not publish picture books." **Publishes 3-6 titles/year. 30% of books from first-time authors. 80% from unagented writers.**

HOW TO CONTACT Responds in 2 months. Publishes ms 24 months after acceptance.

ILLUSTRATION Accepts international material. Works with 0-1 illustrators/year. Uses color artwork only. Reviews artwork. Send resume and tear sheets. Send samples to Madeline Smoot. Responds to queries only if interested.

PHOTOGRAPHY Buys stock images.

TERMS Pays authors royalty 10-15% based on wholesale price. Offers advances against royalties. Average amount $500. Pays advance. "We are distributed by IPG. Our books can be found in their catalog at www. ipgbooks.com." Brochure and guidelines online.

CHRONICLE BOOKS

680 Second St., San Francisco CA 94107. **E-mail:** submissions@chroniclebooks.com. **Website:** www. chroniclebooks.com. "We publish an exciting range of books, stationery, kits, calendars, and novelty formats. Our list includes children's books and interactive formats; young adult books; cookbooks; fine art, design, and photography; pop culture; craft, fashion, beauty, and home decor; relationships, mind-body-spirit; innovative formats such as interactive journals, kits, decks, and stationery; and much, much more." **Publishes 90 titles/year.**

FICTION Only interested in fiction for children and young adults. No adult fiction.

NONFICTION "We're always looking for the new and unusual. We do accept unsolicited manuscripts and we review all proposals. However, given the volume of proposals we receive, we are not able to personally respond to unsolicited proposals unless we are interested in pursuing the project."

HOW TO CONTACT Submit complete ms (picture books); submit outline/synopsis and 3 sample chapters (for older readers). Will not respond to submissions unless interested. Will not consider submissions by fax, e-mail or disk. Do not include SASE; do not send original materials. No submissions will be returned. Submit via mail or e-mail (prefers e-mail for adult submissions; only by mail for children's submissions). Submit proposal (guidelines online) and allow 3 months for editors to review and for children's submissions, allow 6 months. If submitting by mail, do not include SASE since our staff will not return materials. Responds to queries in 1 month. Publishes a book 1-3 years after acceptance.

ILLUSTRATION Works with 40-50 illustrators/year. Wants "unusual art, graphically strong, something that will stand out on the shelves. Fine art, not mass market." Reviews ms/illustration packages from artists. "Indicate if project *must* be considered jointly, or if editor may consider text and art separately." Illustrations only: Submit samples of artist's work (not necessarily from book, but in the envisioned style). Slides, tearsheets and color photocopies OK. (No original art.) Dummies helpful. Résumé helpful. Samples suited to our needs are filed for future reference. Samples not suited to our needs will be recycled. Queries and project proposals responded to in same time frame as author query/proposals."

PHOTOGRAPHY Purchases photos from freelancers. Works on assignment only.

TERMS Generally pays authors in royalties based on retail price, "though we do occasionally work on a flat fee basis." Advance varies. Illustrators paid royalty based on retail price or flat fee. Book catalog for 9x12 SAE and 8 first-class stamps. Ms guidelines for #10 SASE.

CHRONICLE BOOKS FOR CHILDREN

680 Second St., San Francisco CA 94107. (415)537-4200. **Fax:** (415)537-4460. **Website:** www.chroniclekids.com. "Chronicle Books for Children publishes an eclectic mixture of traditional and innovative children's books. Our aim is to publish books that inspire young readers to learn and grow creatively while helping them discover the joy of reading. We're looking for quirky, bold artwork and subject matter." Publishes hardcover and trade paperback originals. **Publishes 100-110 titles/year. 6% of books from first-time authors. 25% from unagented writers.**

FICTION Does not accept proposals by fax, via e-mail, or on disk. When submitting artwork, either as a part of a project or as samples for review, do not send original art.

HOW TO CONTACT Query with synopsis. 30,000 queries received/year. Responds in 2-4 weeks to queries; 6 months to mss. Publishes a book 18-24 months after acceptance.

TERMS Pays variable advance. Book catalog for 9x12 envelope and 3 first-class stamps. Guidelines online.

TIPS "We are interested in projects that have a unique bent to them—be it in subject matter, writing style, or illustrative technique. As a small list, we are looking for books that will lend our list a distinctive flavor. Primarily we are interested in fiction and nonfiction picture books for children ages up to 8 years, and nonfiction books for children ages up to 12 years. We publish board, pop-up, and other novelty formats as well as picture books. We are also interested in early chapter books, middle grade fiction, and young adult projects."

CLARION BOOKS

Houghton Mifflin Co., 215 Park Ave. S., New York NY 10003. **Website:** www.hmhco.com. "Clarion Books publishes picture books, nonfiction, and fiction for infants through grade 12. Avoid telling your stories in verse unless you are a professional poet. *We are no longer responding to your unsolicited submission unless we are interested in publishing it. Please do not include a SASE. Submissions will be recycled, and you will not hear from us regarding the status of your submission unless we are interested. We regret that we cannot respond personally to each submission, but we do consider each and every submission we receive."* Publishes hardcover originals for children. **Publishes 50 titles/year.**

FICTION "Clarion is highly selective in the areas of historical fiction, fantasy, and science fiction. A novel must be superlatively written in order to find a place on the list. Mss that arrive without an SASE of adequate size will *not* be responded to or returned. Accepts fiction translations."

NONFICTION No unsolicited mss.

HOW TO CONTACT Submit complete ms. No queries, please. Send to only *one* Clarion editor. Query with SASE. Submit proposal package, sample chapters, SASE. Responds in 2 months to queries. Publishes a book 2 years after acceptance.

ILLUSTRATION Pays illustrators royalty; flat fee for jacket illustration.

TERMS Pays 5-10% royalty on retail price. Pays minimum of $4,000 advance. Guidelines online.

TIPS "Looks for freshness, enthusiasm—in short, life."

CRAIGMORE CREATIONS

PMB 114, 4110 SE Hawthorne Blvd., Portland OR 97124. (503)477-9562. **E-mail:** info@craigmorecreations.com. **Website:** www.craigmorecreations.com.

NONFICTION "We publish books that make time travel seem possible: nonfiction that explores pre-history and Earth sciences for children."

HOW TO CONTACT Submit proposal package. See website for detailed submission guidelines. Submit proposal package. See website for detailed submission guidelines.

CREATIVE COMPANY, THE

P.O. Box 227, Mankato MN 56002. (800)445-6209. **Fax:** (507)388-2746. **Website:** www.thecreativecompany.us. "We are currently not accepting fiction submissions." **Publishes 140 titles/year.**

NONFICTION Picture books, young readers, young adults: animal, arts/crafts, biography, careers, geography, health, history, hobbies, multicultural, music/dance, nature/environment, religion, science, social issues, special needs, sports. Average word length: young readers—500; young adults—6,000.

HOW TO CONTACT Submit outline/synopsis and 2 sample chapters, along with division of titles within the series. Responds in 3-6 months. Publishes a book 2 years after acceptance.

PHOTOGRAPHY Buys stock. Contact: Photo Editor. Model/property releases not required; captions required. Uses b&w prints. Submit cover letter, promo piece. Ms and photographer guidelines available for SAE.

TERMS Guidelines available for SAE.

TIPS "We are accepting nonfiction, series submissions only. Fiction submissions will not be reviewed or returned. Nonfiction submissions should be presented in series (4, 6, or 8) rather than single."

CRESTON BOOKS

P.O. Box 9369, Berkeley CA 94709. **E-mail:** submissions@crestonbooks.co. **Website:** crestonbooks.co. Creston Books is author-illustrator driven, with talented, award-winning creators given more editorial freedom and control than in a typical New York house. **50%% of books from first-time authors. 50%% from unagented writers.**

HOW TO CONTACT Please paste text of picture books or first chapters of novels in the body of e-mail. Words of Advice for submitting authors listed on the site.

TERMS Pays advance. Catalog online. Guidelines online.

CURIOSITY QUILLS

Whampa, LLC, P.O. Box 2160, Reston VA 20195. (800)998-2509. **Fax:** (800)998-2509. **E-mail:** editor@curiosityquills.com. **Website:** curiosityquills.com. **Contact:** Alisa Gus. Curiosity Quills is a publisher of hard-hitting dark sci-fi, speculative fiction, and paranormal works aimed at adults, young adults, and new adults. Firm publishes sci-fi, speculative fiction, steampunk, paranormal and urban fantasy, and corresponding romance titles under its new Rebel Romance imprint. **Publishes 75 titles/year. 60% of books from first-time authors. 65% from unagented writers.**

FICTION Looking for "thought-provoking, mind-twisting rollercoasters—challenge our mind, turn our world upside down, and make us question. Those are the makings of a true literary marauder."

NONFICTION Writer's guides, on a strictly limited basis.

HOW TO CONTACT Submit ms using online submission form or e-mail to acquisitions@curiosityquills.com. 1,000 submissions/year. Responds in 1-6 weeks. Publishes ms 9-12 months after acceptance.

TERMS Pays variable royalty. Does not pay advance. Catalog available. Guidelines online.

DARBY CREEK PUBLISHING

Lerner Publishing Group, 1251 Washington Ave. N., Minneapolis MN 55401. (612)332-3344. **Fax:** (612)332-7615. **Website:** www.lernerbooks.com. "Darby Creek publishes series fiction titles for emerging, striving and reluctant readers ages 7 to 18 (grades 2-12). From beginning chapter books to intermediate fiction and page-turning YA titles, Darby Creek books engage readers with strong characters and formats they'll want to pursue." Darby Creek does not publish picture books. Publishes children's chapter books, middle readers, young adult. Mostly series. **Publishes 25 titles/year.**

"We are currently not accepting any submissions. If that changes, we will provide all children's writing publications with our new info."

FICTION Middle readers, young adult. Recently published: *The Surviving Southside* series, by various authors; *The Agent Amelia* series, by Michael Broad; *The Mallory McDonald* series, by Laurie B. Friedman; and *The Alien Agent* series, by Pam Service.

NONFICTION Middle readers: biography, history, science, sports. Recently published *Albino Animals*, by Kelly Milner Halls, illustrated by Rick Spears; *Miracle: The True Story of the Wreck of the Sea Venture*, by Gail Karwoski.

ILLUSTRATION Illustrations only: Send photocopies and résumé with publishing history. "Indicate which samples we may keep on file and include SASE and appropriate packing materials for any samples you wish to have returned."

TERMS Offers advance-against-royalty contracts.

ⒶDELACORTE PRESS

An imprint of Random House Children's Books, a division of Penguin Random House LLC, New York, 1745 Broadway, New York NY 10019. (212)782-9000. **Website:** randomhousekids.com; randomhouse-teens.com. Publishes middle grade and young adult fiction in hard cover, trade paperback, mass market and digest formats.

◯ All query letters and manuscript submissions must be submitted through an agent or at the request of an editor.

DIAL BOOKS FOR YOUNG READERS

Imprint of Penguin Random House LLC, 1745 Broadway, New York NY 10019. (212)782-9000. **Website:** www.penguinrandomhouse.com. "Dial Books for Young Readers publishes quality picture books for ages 18 months-6 years; lively, believable novels for middle readers and young adults; and occasional nonfiction for middle readers and young adults." Publishes hardcover originals. **Publishes 50 titles/year. 20% of books from first-time authors.**

FICTION Especially looking for lively and well-written novels for middle grade and young adult children involving a convincing plot and believable characters. The subject matter or theme should not already be overworked in previously published books. The approach must not be demeaning to any minority group, nor should the roles of female characters (or others) be stereotyped, though we don't think books should be didactic, or in any way message-y. No topics inappropriate for the juvenile, young adult, and middle grade audiences. No plays.

HOW TO CONTACT Accepts unsolicited queries and up to 10 pages for longer works and unsolicited mss for picture books. Will only respond if interested. Only responds if interested. "We accept entire picture book manuscripts and a maximum of 10 pages for longer works (novels, easy-to-reads). When submitting a portion of a longer work, please provide an accompanying cover letter that briefly describes your manuscript's plot, genre (i.e. easy-to-read, middle grade or YA novel), the intended age group, and your publishing credits, if any." 5,000 queries received/year. Responds in 4-6 months to queries.

ILLUSTRATION Send nonreturnable samples, no originals, to Lily Malcolm. Show children and animals.

TERMS Pays royalty. Pays varies advance. Book catalog and guidelines online.

TIPS "Our readers are anywhere from preschool age to teenage. Picture books must have strong plots, lots of action, unusual premises, or universal themes treated with freshness and originality. Humor works well in these books. A very well-thought-out and intelligently presented book has the best chance of being taken on. Genre isn't as much of a factor as presentation."

Ⓐ⬟ DK PUBLISHING

Penguin Random House, 1450 Broadway, Suite 801, New York NY 10018. **Website:** www.dk.com. "DK publishes photographically illustrated nonfiction for children of all ages." *DK Publishing does not accept unagented mss or proposals.*

DUTTON CHILDREN'S BOOKS

Penguin Random House, 1745 Broadway, New York NY 10019. **Website:** www.penguinrandomhouse.com. Dutton Children's Books publishes high-quality fiction and nonfiction for readers ranging from preschoolers to young adults on a variety of subjects. Currently emphasizing middle grade and young adult novels that offer a fresh perspective. De-emphasizing photographic nonfiction and picture books that teach a lesson. Publishes hardcover originals as well as novelty formats. **Publishes 100 titles/year. 15% of books from first-time authors.**

◯ "Cultivating the creative talents of authors and illustrators and publishing books with purpose and heart continue to be the mission and joy at Dutton."

FICTION Dutton Children's Books has a diverse, general interest list that includes picture books; easy-to-read books; and fiction for all ages, from first chapter books to young adult readers.

HOW TO CONTACT Query. Responds only in interested. Query. Responds only if interested. Query. Only responds if interested.

TERMS Pays royalty on retail price. Offers advance. Pays royalty on retail price. Pays advance.

Ⓞ EDUPRESS, INC.

Teacher Created Resources, 12621 Western Ave., Garden Grove CA 92841. (800)662-4321. **Fax:** (800)525-1254. **Website:** www.edupress.com. **Contact:** Editor-in-Chief. Edupress, Inc., publishes supplemental curriculum resources for PK-6th grade. Currently emphasizing Common Core reading and math games and materials.

"Our mission is to create products that make kids want to go to school."

HOW TO CONTACT Submit complete ms via mail or e-mail with "Manuscript Submission" as the subject line. Responds in 2-4 months. Publishes ms 1-2 years after acceptance.

ILLUSTRATION Query with samples. Contact: Cathy Baker, product development manager. Responds only if interested. Samples returned with SASE.

PHOTOGRAPHY Buys stock.

TERMS Work purchased outright from authors. Catalog online.

TIPS "We are looking for unique, research-based, quality supplemental materials for Pre-K through 6th grade. We publish mainly reading and math materials in many different formats, including games. Our materials are intended for classroom and home schooling use. We do not publish picture books."

WILLIAM B. EERDMANS PUBLISHING CO.

2140 Oak Industrial Dr. NE, Grand Rapids MI 49505. (616)459-4591. **Fax:** (616)459-6540. **E-mail:** info@eerdmans.com. **Website:** www.eerdmans.com. "The majority of our adult publications are religious and most of these are academic or semi-academic in character (as opposed to inspirational or celebrity books), though we also publish general trade books on the Christian life. Our nonreligious titles, most of them in regional history or on social issues, aim, similarly, at an educated audience." Publishes hardcover and paperback originals and reprints.

NONFICTION "We prefer that writers take the time to notice if we have published anything at all in the same category as their manuscript before sending it to us."

HOW TO CONTACT Query with SASE. Query with TOC, 2-3 sample chapters, and SASE for return of ms. Responds in 4 weeks.

TERMS Book catalog and ms guidelines free.

ELLYSIAN PRESS

E-mail: publisher@ellysianpress.com. **Website:** www.ellysianpress.com. **Contact:** Maer Wilson. "Ellysian Press is a speculative fiction house. We seek to create a sense of home for our authors, a place where they can find fulfillment as artists. Just as exceptional mortals once sought a place in the Elysian Fields, now exceptional authors can find a place here at Ellysian Press.

We are accepting submissions in the following genres only: Fantasy, Science Fiction, Paranormal, Paranormal Romance, Horror, along with Young/New Adult in these genres. Please submit polished manuscripts. It's best to have work read by critique groups or beta readers prior to submission. PLEASE NOTE: We do not publish children's books, picture books, or Middle Grade books. We do not publish books outside the genres listed above." Publishes fantasy, science fiction, paranormal, paranormal romance, horror, and young/new adult in these genres. **25% of books from first-time authors. 90% from unagented writers.**

HOW TO CONTACT "We accept online submissions only. Please submit a query letter, a synopsis and the first ten pages of your manuscript in the body of your e-mail. The subject line should be as follows: QUERY – Your Last Name, TITLE, Genre." If we choose to request more, we will request the full manuscript in standard format. This means your manuscript should be formatted as per the guidelines on our website. Please do not submit queries for any genres not listed above. Please do not submit children's books, picture books or Middle Grade books. You may email queries to submissions(at)ellysianpress(dot)com. Responds in 1 week for queries; 4-6 weeks for partials and fulls. Publishes ms 12+ months after acceptance.

TERMS Pays quarterly. Does not pay advance. Catalog online. Guidelines online.

ELM BOOKS

1175 Hwy. 130, Laramie WY 82070. (610)529-0460. **E-mail:** leila.elmbooks@gmail.com. **Website:** www.elm-books.com. **Contact:** Leila Monaghan, publisher. "Follow us on Facebook to learn about our latest calls for science fiction, mystery and romance stories. We also welcome submissions of middle grade fiction featuring diverse children. No picture book submissions."

FICTION "Follow us on Facebook to learn about our latest calls for science fiction, mystery and romance stories. We also welcome submissions of middle grade fiction featuring diverse children. No picture book submissions."

HOW TO CONTACT Send inquiries for middle grade fiction featuring diverse children via e-mail to Leila.elmbooks@gmail.com. No mail inquiries.

TERMS Pays royalties.

ENTANGLED TEEN

Website: www.entangledteen.com. "Entangled Teen and Entangled digiTeen, our young adult imprints publish the swoonworthy young adult romances readers crave. Whether they're dark and angsty or fun and sassy, contemporary, fantastical, or futuristic. We are seeking fresh voices with interesting twists on popular genres."

FICTION "We are seeking novels in the subgenres of romantic fiction for contemporary, upper young adult with crossover appeal."

HOW TO CONTACT E-mail using site. "All submissions must have strong romantic elements. YA novels should be 50K to 100K in length. Revised backlist titles will be considered on a case by case basis." Agented and unagented considered.

TERMS Pays royalty.

FACTS ON FILE, INC.

Infobase Learning, 132 W. 31st St., 16th Floor, New York NY 10001. (800)322-8755. **Fax:** (800)678-3633. **E-mail:** llikoff@infobaselearning.com; custserv@ infobaselearning.com. **Website:** www.infobase-learning.com. **Contact:** Laurie Likoff. Facts On File produces high-quality reference materials in print and digital format on a broad range of subjects for the school and public library market and the general nonfiction trade. Publishes hardcover originals and reprints and e-books as well as reference databases. **Publishes 150-200 titles/year. 10%% of books from first-time authors. 45%% from unagented writers.**

NONFICTION "We publish serious, informational e-books for a targeted audience. All our books must have strong library interest, but we also distribute books effectively to the trade. Our library books fit the junior and senior high school curriculum." No computer books, technical books, cookbooks, biographies (except YA), pop psychology, humor, fiction or poetry.

HOW TO CONTACT Query or submit outline and sample chapter with SASE. No submissions returned without SASE. Responds in 2 months to queries. Responds in 6 months to 1 year.

ILLUSTRATION Commissions line art only.

TERMS Pays 10% royalty on retail price. Pays $3-5,000 advance. Reference catalog available free. Guidelines online.

TIPS "Our audience is school and public libraries for our more reference-oriented books and libraries, schools and bookstores for our less reference-oriented informational titles."

FAMILIUS

1254 Commerce Way, Sanger CA 93657. (559)876-2170. **Fax:** (559)876-2180. **E-mail:** bookideas@familius. com. **Website:** familius.com. **Contact:** Acquisitions. Familius is a value's driven trade publishing house, publishing in children's, parenting, relationships, cooking, health and wellness, and education. The company's mission is to help families be happy. Publishes hardcover, trade paperback, and electronic originals and reprints. **Publishes 60 titles/year. 30% of books from first-time authors. 70% from unagented writers.**

FICTION All picture books must align with Familius values statement listed on the website footer.

NONFICTION All mss must align with Familius mission statement to help families succeed.

HOW TO CONTACT Submit a proposal package, including a synopsis, 3 sample chapters, and your author platform. Submit a proposal package, including an outline, 1 sample chapter, competition evaluation, and your author platform. 200 queries; 100 mss received/year. Responds in 1 month to queries and proposals; 2 months to mss. Publishes book 12 months after acceptance.

TERMS Authors are paid 10-30% royalty on wholesale price. Advances periodically paid to participating illustrators. Catalog online and print. Guidelines online.

FARRAR, STRAUS & GIROUX FOR YOUNG READERS

Macmillan Children's Publishing Group, 175 Fifth Ave., New York NY 10010. (212)741-6900. **Fax:** (212)633-2427. **Website:** www.fsgkidsbooks.com.

FICTION All levels: all categories. "Original and well-written material for all ages."

NONFICTION All levels: all categories. "We publish only literary nonfiction."

HOW TO CONTACT Submit cover letter, first 50 pages by mail only. Submit cover letter, first 50 pages by mail only.

ILLUSTRATION Works with 30-60 illustrators/year. Reviews ms/illustration packages from artists. Submit ms with 1 example of final art, remainder roughs. Do not send originals. Illustrations only: Query with tearsheets. Responds if interested in 3 months. Samples returned with SASE; samples sometimes filed.

TERMS Book catalog available by request. Ms guidelines online.

TIPS "Study our catalog before submitting. We will see illustrators' portfolios by appointment. Don't ask for criticism and/or advice—due to the volume of submissions we receive, it's just not possible. Never send originals. Always enclose SASE."

Ⓐ FEIWEL AND FRIENDS

Macmillan Children's Publishing Group, 175 Fifth Ave., New York NY 10010. (646)307-5151. **Website:** us.macmillan.com. Feiwel and Friends is a publisher of innovative children's fiction and nonfiction literature, including hardcover, paperback series, and individual titles. The list is eclectic and combines quality and commercial appeal for readers ages 0-16. The imprint is dedicated to "book by book" publishing, bringing the work of distinctive and oustanding authors, illustrators, and ideas to the marketplace. This market does not accept unsolicited mss due to the volume of submissions; they also do not accept unsolicited queries for interior art. The best way to submit a ms is through an agent.

TERMS Catalog online.

Ⓐ FIRST SECOND

Macmillan Children's Publishing Group, 175 5th Ave., New York NY 10010. **E-mail:** mail@firstsecondbooks. com. **Website:** www.firstsecondbooks.com. First Second is a publisher of graphic novels and an imprint of Macmillan Children's Publishing Group. First Second does not accept unsolicited submissions.

HOW TO CONTACT Responds in about 6 weeks.

TERMS Catalog online.

FORWARD MOVEMENT

412 Sycamore St., Cincinnati OH 45202. (513)721-6659; (800)543-1813. **Fax:** (513)721-0729. **E-mail:** editorialstaff@forwardmovement.org. **Website:** www.forwardmovement.org. "Forward Movement was established to help reinvigorate the life of the church. Many titles focus on the life of prayer, where our relationship with God is centered, death, marriage, baptism, recovery, joy, the Episcopal Church and more. Currently emphasizing prayer/spirituality." **Publishes 30 titles/year.**

NONFICTION "We are an agency of the Episcopal Church. There is a special need for tracts of under 8 pages. (A page usually runs about 200 words.) On rare occasions, we publish a full-length book."

HOW TO CONTACT Query with SASE or by e-mail with complete ms attached. Responds in 1 month.

TERMS Book catalog free. Guidelines online.

TIPS "Audience is primarily Episcopalians and other Christians."

FREE SPIRIT PUBLISHING, INC.

6325 Sandburg Rd., Suite 100, Minneapolis MN 55427-3674. (612)338-2068. **Fax:** (612)337-5050. **E-mail:** acquisitions@freespirit.com. **Website:** www.free-spirit.com. "Free Spirit is the leading publisher of learning tools that support young people's social-emotional health and educational needs. We help children and teens think for themselves, overcome challenges, and make a diffcrence in the world." Free Spirit does not accept general fiction, poetry or storybook submissions. Publishes trade paperback originals and reprints. **Publishes 25-30 titles/year.**

FICTION "Please review catalog and author guidelines (both available online) for details before submitting proposal. If you'd like material returned, enclose a SASE with sufficient postage."

NONFICTION "Many of our authors are educators, mental health professionals, and youth workers involved in helping kids and teens." No general fiction or picture storybooks, poetry, single biographies or autobiographies, books with mythical or animal characters, or books with religious or New Age content. We are not looking for academic or religious materials, or books that analyze problems with the nation's school systems.

HOW TO CONTACT Query with cover letter stating qualifications, intent, and intended audience and market analysis (comprehensive list of similar titles and detailed explanation of how your book stands out from the field), along with your promotional plan, outline, 2 sample chapters (note: for early childhood submissions, the entire text is required for evaluation), resume, SASE. Do not send original copies of work. Responds to proposals within 6 months.

ILLUSTRATION Works with 5 illustrators/year. Submit samples to creative director for consideration. If appropriate, samples will be kept on file and artist will be contacted if a suitable project comes up. Enclose SASE if you'd like materials returned.

PHOTOGRAPHY Uses stock photos. Does not accept photography submissions.

TERMS Book catalog and guidelines online.

TIPS "Our books are issue-oriented, jargon-free, and solution-focused. Our audience is children, teens, teachers, parents and youth counselors. We are especially concerned with kids' social and emotional well-being and look for books with ready-to-use strategies for coping with today's issues at home or in school—written in everyday language. We are not looking for academic or religious materials, or books that analyze problems with the nation's school systems. Instead, we want books that offer practical, positive advice so kids can help themselves, and parents and teachers can help kids succeed."

FULCRUM PUBLISHING

4690 Table Mountain Dr., Suite 100, Golden CO 80403. **E-mail:** acquisitions@fulcrumbooks.com. **Website:** www.fulcrum-books.com. **Contact:** T. Baker, acquisitions editor. In physics, the word fulcrum denotes the point at which motion begins. We strive to create books that will inspire you to move forward in your life or to take action. Whether it's exploring the world around you or discussing the ideas and issues that shape that world, our books provide the tools to create forward motion in your life. Our mission is simple, yet profound: Publish books that inspire readers to live life to the fullest and to learn something new every day. More than thirty years ago, when Bob Baron started Fulcrum Publishing, his goal was to publish high-quality books from extraordinary authors. Fulcrum recognizes that good books can't exist without the best authors. To that end, we have published books from prominent politicians (Governors Richard Lamm and Bill Ritter, Jr., Senators Gary Hart and Eugene McCarthy), influential Native Americans (Wilma Mankiller, Vine Deloria Jr., and Joseph Bruchac), master gardeners (Lauren Springer, Tom Peace, and Richard Hartlage), and important organizations in the environmental community (Campaign for America's Wilderness, World Wilderness Congress, Defenders of Wildlife). Our books have received accolades from the likes of Tom Brokaw, Elizabeth Dole, Nelson Mandela, Paul Newman, William Sears, MD, Gloria Steinem, Dr. Henry Louis Gates, Jr., and Kurt Vonnegut. In addition, Fulcrum authors have received awards from prestigious organizations such as the American Booksellers Association, American Library Association, Colorado Center for the Book, ForeWord magazine, National Book Foundation, National Parenting Publications, New York Public Library, PEN USA Literary Awards, Smithsonian National Museum of the American Indian, Teacher's Choice, Harvey Awards, and

more. **40% of books from first-time authors. 90% from unagented writers.**

NONFICTION Looking for nonfiction-based graphic novels and comics, U.S. history and culture, Native American history or culture studies, conservation-oriented materials. "We do not accept memoir or fiction manuscripts."

HOW TO CONTACT "Your submission must include: a proposal of your work, including a brief synopsis, 2-3 sample chapters, brief biography of yourself, description of your audience, your assessment of the market for the book, list of competing titles, and what you can do to help market your book. We are a green company and therefore only accept e-mailed submissions. Paper queries submitted via US Mail or any other means (including fax, FedEx/UPS, and even door-to-door delivery) will not be reviewed or returned. Please help us support the preservation of the environment by e-mailing your query to acquisitions@fulcrumbooks.com." 200 Because of the volume of submissions we receive, we can only reply to submissions we are interested in pursuing, and it may take up to three months for a reply. No editorial remarks will be supplied. We do not provide consulting services for authors on the suitability of their mss. Ms published 18-24 months after acceptance.

PHOTOGRAPHY Works on assignment only.

TERMS Pays authors royalty based on wholesale price. Offers advances. Catalog for SASE. Your submission must include: A proposal of your work, including a brief synopsis; 2-3 sample chapters; a brief biography of yourself; a description of your audience; your assessment of the market for the book; a list of competing titles; what you can do to help market your book.

TIPS "Research our line first. We look for books that appeal to the school market and trade."

GIBBS SMITH

P.O. Box 667, Layton UT 84041. (801)544-9800. **Fax:** (801)544-8853. **E-mail:** debbie.uribe@gibbs-smith.com. **Website:** www.gibbs-smith.com. **Publishes 3 titles/year. 50% of books from first-time authors. 50% from unagented writers.**

NONFICTION Middle readers: activity, arts/crafts, cooking, how-to, nature/environment, science. Average word length: picture books—under 1,000 words; activity books—under 15,000 words.

HOW TO CONTACT Submit an outline and writing samples for activity books; query for other types of books. Responds in 2 months. Publishes ms 1-2 years after acceptance.

ILLUSTRATION Works with 2 illustrators/year. Reviews ms/illustration packages from artists. Query. Submit ms with 3-5 pieces of final art. Illustrations only: Query with samples; provide résumé, promo sheet, slides (duplicate slides, not originals). Responds only if interested. Samples returned with SASE; samples filed.

TERMS Pays illustrators by the project or royalty of 2% based on retail price. Sends galleys to authors; color proofs to illustrators. Original artwork returned at job's completion. Pays authors royalty of 2% based on retail price or work purchased outright ($500 minimum). Offers advances (average amount: $2,000). Book catalog available for 9×12 SAE and $2.30 postage. Ms guidelines available by e-mail.

TIPS "We target ages 5-11. We do not publish young adult novels or chapter books."

THE GLENCANNON PRESS

P.O. Box 1428, El Cerrito CA 94530. (510)455-9027. **E-mail:** merships@yahoo.com. **Website:** www.glencannon.com. **Contact:** Bill Harris (maritime, maritime children's). "We publish quality books about ships and the sea." Average print order: 300. Member PMA, BAIPA. Promotes titles through direct mail, magazine advertising and word of mouth. Accepts unsolicited mss. Often comments on rejected mss. Publishes hardcover and paperback originals and hardcover reprints. **Publishes 3-4 titles/year. 25% of books from first-time authors. 100% from unagented writers.**

NONFICTION "We specialize on books about ships and the sea, with an emphasis on the U.S. merchant marine and navy."

HOW TO CONTACT Submit complete ms. Include brief bio, list of publishing credits. Send SASE for return of ms or send a disposable ms and SASE for reply only. 20 Responds in 1 month to queries; 2 months to mss. Publishes ms 6-24 months after acceptance.

TERMS Pays 10-20% royalty. Does not pay advance. Available on request. Submit complete paper ms with SASE. "We do not look at electronic submissions due to the danger of computer viruses."

TIPS "Write a good story in a compelling style."

Ⓐ DAVID R. GODINE, PUBLISHER

15 Court Square, Suite 320, Boston MA 02108. (617)451-9600. **Fax:** (617)350-0250. **E-mail:** info@godine.com. **Website:** www.godine.com. "We publish books that matter for people who care." This publisher is no longer considering unsolicited mss of any type. Only interested in agented material.

HOW TO CONTACT Only interested in agented material.

ILLUSTRATION Only interested in agented material. Works with 1-3 illustrators/year. "Please do not send original artwork unless solicited. Almost all of the children's books we accept for publication come to us with the author and illustrator already paired up. Therefore, we rarely use freelance illustrators."

ⒶⒸ GOLDEN BOOKS FOR YOUNG READERS GROUP

An imprint of Penguin Random House LLC, 1745 Broadway, New York NY 10019. **Website:** www.penguinrandomhouse.com. "Random House Books aims to create books that nurture the hearts and minds of children, providing and promoting quality books and a rich variety of media that entertain and educate readers from 6 months to 12 years." *Random House-Golden Books does not accept unsolicited mss, only agented material.* They reserve the right not to return unsolicited material. **2% of books from first-time authors.**

TERMS Pays authors in royalties; sometimes buys mss outright. Book catalog free on request.

GOOSEBOTTOM BOOKS

E-mail: submissions@goosebottombooks.com. **Website:** goosebottombooks.com. **Contact:** Pamela Livingston. Goosebottom Books is a small press dedicated to "fun non-fiction"representing the histories of under-represented voices. Founded by Shirin Yim Bridges, author of *Ruby's Wish*. *The Thinking Girl's Treasury of Dastardly Dames* was named by *Booklist* as one of the Top 10 Nonfiction Series for Youth. *Horrible Hauntings* made the IRA Children's Choices list with a mention that it "motivated even the most reluctant reader." And *Call Me Ixchel, Goddess of the Moon* was named one of the Top 10 Middle Grade Novels 2013 by Foreword Reviews. The Last Celt, by A.E. Conran, has been awarded First Place for Middle Grade Fiction and Charity/Making a Difference Categories in the Purple Dragonfly Awards 2018; Finalist in three categories, Children's Fiction, First Novel and War/Military (Fiction and Non-Fiction) of the Independent Author Network Book of the Year Awards, 2018; 2016 Gold Medal Winner for Children's Chapter Books from The Military Writers Society of America; and listed as a Top 100 Notable Book: Shelf Unbound Magazine Best in Independent Publishing Competition, 2018. Middle grade nonfiction and fiction. **Publishes less than 6 titles/year. 50%% of books from first-time authors. 75%% from unagented writers.**

FICTION Gosling Press is a new partnership publishing imprint for children's middle grade fiction. Any fiction for adults.

HOW TO CONTACT 1,000 submissions received/year. We are not currently accepting submissions. Publishes ms 18-36 months after acceptance.

ILLUSTRATION Considers samples.

TERMS Goosebottom Books: Pays work-for-hire only at this time; Gosling Press: Pays royalties only. Catalog online. Goosebottom Books is not accepting submissions at this time. Goosebottom Books never accepts hard copy submissions. "We like trees."

GREENHAVEN PRESS

27500 Drake Rd., Farmington Hills MI 48331. (800)877-4523. **Website:** www.gale.com/greenhaven. Publishes 220 young adult academic reference titles/year. 50% of books by first-time authors. Greenhaven continues to print quality nonfiction anthologies for libraries and classrooms. "Our well-known Opposing Viewpoints series is highly respected by students and librarians in need of material on controversial social issues." Greenhaven accepts no unsolicited mss. Send query, resume, and list of published works by e-mail. Work purchased outright from authors; write-for-hire, flat fee.

NONFICTION Young adults (high school): controversial issues, social issues, history, literature, science, environment, health.

Ⓐ GREENWILLOW BOOKS

HarperCollins Publishers, 10 E. 53rd St., New York NY 10022. (212)207-7000. **Website:** www.greenwillowblog.com. *Does not accept unsolicited mss.* "Unsolicited mail will not be opened and will not be returned." Publishes hardcover originals, paperbacks, e-books, and reprints. **Publishes 40-50 titles/year.**

HOW TO CONTACT *Agented submissions only.* Publishes ms 2 years after acceptance.

TERMS Pays 10% royalty on wholesale price for first-time authors. Offers variable advance.

Ⓐ GROSSET & DUNLAP PUBLISHERS

Penguin Random House, 1745 Broadway, New York NY 10019. **Website:** www.penguinrandomhouse.com. Grosset & Dunlap publishes children's books that show children that reading is fun, with books that speak to their interests, and that are affordable so that children can build a home library of their own. Focus on licensed properties, series and readers. "Grosset & Dunlap publishes high-interest, affordable books for children ages 0-10 years. We focus on original series, licensed properties, readers and novelty books." Publishes hardcover (few) and mass market paperback originals. **Publishes 140 titles/year.**

HOW TO CONTACT *Agented submissions only. Agented submissions only.*

TERMS Pays royalty. Pays advance.

GRYPHON HOUSE, INC.

P.O. Box 10, 6848 Leon's Way, Lewisville NC 27023. (800)638-0928. **E-mail:** info@ghbooks.com. **Website:** www.gryphonhouse.com. "At Gryphon House, our goal is to publish books that help teachers and parents enrich the lives of children from birth through age 8. We strive to make our books useful for teachers at all levels of experience, as well as for parents, caregivers, and anyone interested in working with children." Query. Submit outline/synopsis and 2 sample chapters. Responds to queries/mss in 6 months. Publishes a book 18 months after acceptance. Will consider simultaneous submissions, e-mail submissions. Book catalog and ms guidelines available via website or with SASE. Publishes trade paperback originals. **Publishes 12-15 titles/year.**

NONFICTION Currently emphasizing social-emotional intelligence and classroom management; de-emphasizing literacy after-school activities.

HOW TO CONTACT "We prefer to receive a letter of inquiry and/or a proposal, rather than the entire manuscript. Please include: the proposed title, the purpose of the book, table of contents, introductory material, 20-40 sample pages of the actual book. In addition, please describe the book, including the intended audience, why teachers will want to buy it, how it is different from other similar books already published, and what qualifications you possess that make you the appropriate person to write the book. If you have a writing sample that demonstrates that you write clear, compelling prose, please include it with your letter." Responds in 3-6 months to queries.

ILLUSTRATION Works with 4-5 illustrators/year. Uses b&w realistic artwork only. Query with samples, promo sheet. Responds in 2 months. Samples returned with SASE; samples filed. Pays illustrators by the project.

PHOTOGRAPHY Pays photographers by the project or per photo. Sends edited ms copy to authors. Original artwork returned at job's completion.

TERMS Pays royalty on wholesale price. Guidelines available online.

TIPS "We are looking for books of creative, participatory learning experiences that have a common conceptual theme to tie them together. The books should be on subjects that parents or teachers want to do on a daily basis."

HACHAI PUBLISHING

527 Empire Blvd., Brooklyn NY 11225. (718)633-0100. **Fax:** (718)633-0103. **E-mail:** info@hachai.com; dlr@hachai.com. **Website:** www.hachai.com. **Contact:** Devorah Leah Rosenfeld, editor. Hachai is dedicated to producing high quality Jewish children's literature, ages 2-10. Story should promote universal values such as sharing, kindness, etc. Publishes hardcover originals. **Publishes 5 titles/year. 75% of books from first-time authors.**

○ "All books have spiritual/religious themes, specifically traditional Jewish content. We're seeking books about morals and values; the Jewish experience in current and Biblical times; and Jewish observance, Sabbath and holidays."

FICTION Picture books and young readers: contemporary, historical fiction, religion. Middle readers: adventure, contemporary, problem novels, religion. Does not want to see fantasy, animal stories, romance, problem novels depicting drug use or violence.

HOW TO CONTACT Submit complete ms. Submit complete ms. Responds in 2 months to mss.

ILLUSTRATION Works with 4 illustrators/year. Uses primary color artwork, some b&w illustration. Reviews ms/illustration packages from authors. Submit ms with 1 piece of final art. Illustrations only: Query with samples; arrange personal portfolio

review. Responds in 6 weeks. Samples returned with SASE; samples filed.

TERMS Work purchased outright from authors for $800-1,000. Guidelines online.

TIPS "We are looking for books that convey the traditional Jewish experience in modern times or long ago; traditional Jewish observance such as Sabbath and holidays and mitzvos such as mezuzah, blessings etc.; positive character traits (middos) such as honesty, charity, respect, sharing, etc. We are also interested in historical fiction for young readers (7-10) written with a traditional Jewish perspective and highlighting the relevance of Torah in making important choices. Please, no animal stories, romance, violence, preachy sermonizing. Write a story that incorporates a moral, not a preachy morality tale. Originality is the key. We feel Hachai publications will appeal to a wider readership as parents become more interested in positive values for their children."

HARMONY INK PRESS

Dreamspinner Press, 5032 Capital Circle SW, Suite 2 PMB 279, Tallahassee FL 32305. (850)632-4648. **Fax:** (888)308-3739. **E-mail:** submissions@harmonyinkpress.com. **Website:** harmonyinkpress.com. **Contact:** Anne Regan. Teen and new adult fiction featuring at least 1 strong LGBTQ+ main character who shows significant personal growth through the course of the story. **Publishes 26 titles/year.**

FICTION "We are looking for stories in all subgenres, featuring primary characters across the whole LGBTQ+ spectrum between the ages of 14 and 21 that explore all the facets of young adult, teen, and new adult life. Sexual content should be appropriate for the characters and the story."

HOW TO CONTACT Submit complete ms.

TERMS Pays royalty. Pays $500-1,000 advance.

Ⓐ HARPERCOLLINS CHILDREN'S BOOKS/ HARPERCOLLINS PUBLISHERS

195 Broadway, New York NY 10007. (212)207-7000. **Website:** www.harpercollins.com. HarperCollins, one of the largest English language publishers in the world, is a broad-based publisher with strengths in academic, business and professional, children's, educational, general interest, and religious and spiritual books, as well as multimedia titles. Publishes hardcover and paperback originals and paperback reprints. **Publishes 500 titles/year.**

FICTION "We look for a strong story line and exceptional literary talent."

NONFICTION *No unsolicited mss or queries.*

HOW TO CONTACT Agented submissions only. *All unsolicited mss returned.* Agented submissions only. Unsolicited mss returned unopened. Responds in 1 month, will contact only if interested. Does not accept any unsolicited texts.

TERMS Negotiates payment upon acceptance. Catalog online.

TIPS "We do not accept any unsolicited material."

HEYDAY

c/o Acquisitions Editor, Box 9145, Berkeley CA 94709. **E-mail:** editor@heydaybooks.com. **Website:** www.heydaybooks.com. **Contact:** Marthine Satris, acquisitions editor. Heyday is an independent, nonprofit publisher with a focus on California and the American West. We publish nonfiction books that explore history, celebrate Native cultural renewal, fight injustice, and honor nature. Publishes hardcover originals, trade paperback originals and reprints. **Publishes 15-20 titles/year. 50% of books from first-time authors. 90% from unagented writers.**

NONFICTION Books about California only.

HOW TO CONTACT Responds in 3 months. Publishes book ~18 months after acceptance.

TERMS Book catalog online. If you think that Heyday would be an appropriate publisher for your manuscript, send us a query or proposal by email to editor (at) heydaybooks (dot) com (please include "Heyday" in your subject line, or your proposal may be discarded), or by post to Heyday, P.O. Box 9145, Berkeley, CA 94709 (please include a self-addressed stamped envelope if you would like your submission materials returned). Please include the following: A cover letter introducing yourself and your qualifications. A brief description of your project. An annotated table of contents and list of illustrations (if any). Notes on the audiences you are trying to reach and why your book will appeal to them. A list of comparable titles and a brief description of the ways your book adds to the existing literature. Estimates of your book's expected length and your timeline for completing the writing. A sample chapter. We will do our best to respond to your query within twelve weeks of receiving it. No follow-up calls, please.

HOLIDAY HOUSE, INC.

425 Madison Ave., New York NY 10017. (212)688-0085. **Fax:** (212)421-6134. **E-mail:** info@holidayhouse.com. **Website:** holidayhouse.com. "Holiday House publishes children's and young adult books for the school and library markets. We have a commitment to publishing first-time authors and illustrators. We specialize in quality hardcovers from picture books to young adult, both fiction and nonfiction, primarily for the school and library market." Publishes hardcover originals and paperback reprints. **Publishes 50 titles/year. 5% of books from first-time authors. 50% from unagented writers.**

FICTION Children's books only.

HOW TO CONTACT Query with SASE. No phone calls, please. Please send the entire ms, whether submitting a picture book or novel. "All submissions should be directed to the Editorial Department, Holiday House. We do not accept certified or registered mail. There is no need to include a SASE. We do not consider submissions by e-mail or fax. Please note that you do not have to supply illustrations. However, if you have illustrations you would like to include with your submission, you may send detailed sketches or photocopies of the original art. Do not send original art." Responds in 4 months. Publishes 1-2 years after acceptance.

ILLUSTRATION Accepting art samples, not returned.

TERMS Pays royalty on list price, range varies. Guidelines for #10 SASE.

TIPS "We need manuscripts with strong stories and writing."

HOUGHTON MIFFLIN HARCOURT BOOKS FOR CHILDREN

Imprint of Houghton Mifflin Trade & Reference Division, 222 Berkeley St., Boston MA 02116. (617)351-5000. **Fax:** (617)351-1111. **Website:** www.houghtonmifflinbooks.com. Houghton Mifflin Harcourt gives shape to ideas that educate, inform, and above all, delight. *Does not respond to or return mss unless interested.* Publishes hardcover originals and trade paperback originals and reprints. **Publishes 100 titles/year. 10% of books from first-time authors. 60% from unagented writers.**

NONFICTION Interested in innovative books and subjects about which the author is passionate.

HOW TO CONTACT Submit complete ms. Query with SASE. Submit sample chapters, synopsis. 5,000 queries received/year. 14,000 mss received/year.

Responds in 4-6 months to queries. Publishes ms 2 years after acceptance.

TERMS Pays 5-10% royalty on retail price. Pays variable advance. Guidelines online.

IMPACT PUBLISHERS, INC.

5674 Shattuck Ave., Oakland CA 94609. **E-mail:** proposals@newharbinger.com. **Website:** www.newharbinger.com/imprint/impact-publishers. **Contact:** Acquisitions Department. "Our purpose is to make the best human services expertise available to the widest possible audience. We publish only popular psychology and self-help materials written in everyday language by professionals with advanced degrees and significant experience in the human services." **Publishes 3-5 titles/year. 20% of books from first-time authors.**

NONFICTION Young readers, middle readers, young adults: self-help.

HOW TO CONTACT Query or submit complete ms, cover letter, résumé. Responds in 3 months.

ILLUSTRATION Works with 1 illustrator/year. Not accepting freelance illustrator queries.

TERMS Pays authors royalty of 10-12%. Offers advances. Book catalog for #10 SASE with 2 first-class stamps. Guidelines for SASE.

TIPS "Please do not submit fiction, poetry or narratives."

INVERTED-A

P.O. Box 267, Licking MO 65542. **E-mail:** katzaya@gmail.com. **Website:** inverteda.com. **Contact:** Aya Katz, chief editor (poetry, novels, political); Nets Katz, science editor (scientific, academic). Books: POD. Distributes through Amazon, Bowker, Barnes Noble. Publishes paperback originals.

HOW TO CONTACT Does not accept unsolicited mss. Query with SASE. Reading period open from January 2 to March 15. Accepts queries by e-mail. Include estimated word count. Responds in 1 month to queries; 3 months to mss. Publishes ms 1 year after acceptance.

TERMS Pays 10 author's copies. Guidelines for SASE.

TIPS "Read our books. Read the *Inverted-A Horn*. We are different. We do not follow industry trends."

JEWISH LIGHTS PUBLISHING

LongHill Partners, Inc., Sunset Farm Offices, Rt. 4, P.O. Box 237, Woodstock VT 05091. (802)457-4000. **Fax:** (802)457-4004. **E-mail:** submissions@turner-publishing.com. **Website:** www.jewishlights.com. "Jewish Lights publishes books for people of all faiths and all backgrounds who yearn for books that attract, engage, educate and spiritually inspire. Our authors are at the forefront of spiritual thought and deal with the quest for the self and for meaning in life by drawing on the Jewish wisdom tradition. Our books cover topics including history, spirituality, life cycle, children, self-help, recovery, theology and philosophy. We do not publish autobiography, biography, fiction, haggadot, poetry or cookbooks. At this point we plan to do only two books for children annually, and one will be for younger children (ages 4-10)." Publishes hardcover and trade paperback originals, trade paperback reprints. **Publishes 30 titles/year. 50% of books from first-time authors. 75% from unagented writers.**

FICTION Picture books, young readers, middle readers: spirituality. "We are not interested in anything other than spirituality."

NONFICTION Picture book, young readers, middle readers: activity books, spirituality. "We do *not* publish haggadot, biography, poetry, memoirs, or cookbooks."

HOW TO CONTACT Query with outline/synopsis and 2 sample chapters; submit complete ms for picture books. Query. Responds in 6 months to queries. Publishes ms 1 year after acceptance.

TERMS Pays authors royalty of 10% of revenue received; 15% royalty for subsequent printings. Book catalog and guidelines online.

TIPS "We publish books for all faiths and backgrounds that also reflect the Jewish wisdom tradition. Explain in your cover letter why you're submitting your project to us in particular. Make sure you know what we publish."

JOURNEYFORTH

Imprint of BJU Press, 1430 Wade Hampton Blvd., Greenville SC 29609. **E-mail:** journeyforth@bjupress.com. **Website:** www.journeyforth.com. **Contact:** Nancy Lohr. JourneyForth Books publishes fiction and nonfiction that reflects a worldview based solidly on the Bible and that encourages Christians to live out their faith. JourneyForth is an imprint of BJU Press. Publishes paperback originals. **Publishes 6-8 titles/year. 30% of books from first-time authors. 80% from unagented writers.**

FICTION "Our fiction is for the youth market only and is based on a Christian worldview. Our catalog ranges from first chapter books to YA titles." Does not want picture books, short stories, romance, speculative fiction, poetry, or fiction for the adult market.

NONFICTION Christian living, Bible studies, church and ministry, church history. "We produce books for the adult Christian market that are from a conservative Christian worldview."

HOW TO CONTACT Submit proposal with synopsis, market analysis of competing works, and first 5 chapters. Will look at simultaneous submissions, but not multiple submissions. 300+ Responds in 1 month to queries; 3 months to mss. Publishes book 12-18 months after acceptance.

TERMS Pays authors royalty based on wholesale price. Pays royalty. Pays advance. Book catalog available free in SASE or online. Guidelines online—https://www.bjupress.com/books/freelance.php

TIPS "Study the publisher's guidelines. We are looking for engaging text and a biblical worldview. Will read hard copy submissions, but prefer e-mail queries/proposals/submissions."

JUST US BOOKS, INC.

P.O. Box 5306, East Orange NJ 07019. (973)672-7701. **Fax:** (973)677-7570. **Website:** justusbooks.com. "Just Us Books is the nation's premier independent publisher of Black-interest books for young people. Our books focus primarily on the culture, history, and contemporary experiences of African Americans."

FICTION Just Us Books is currently accepting queries for chapter books and middle reader titles only. "We are not considering any other works at this time."

HOW TO CONTACT Query with synopsis and 3-5 sample pages.

TERMS Guidelines online.

TIPS "We are looking for realistic, contemporary characters; stories and interesting plots that introduce both conflict and resolution. We will consider various themes and story-lines, but before an author submits a query we urge them to become familiar with our books."

Ⓐ KANE/MILLER BOOK PUBLISHERS

4901 Morena Blvd., Suite 213, San Diego CA 92117. (858)456-0540. **Fax:** (858)456-9641. **Website:** www.kanemiller.com. **Contact:** Editorial Department. "Kane/Miller Book Publishers is a division of EDC Publishing, specializing in award-winning children's books from around the world. Our books bring the children of the world closer to each other, sharing stories and ideas, while exploring cultural differences and similarities. Although we continue to look for books from other countries, we are now actively seeking works that convey cultures and communities within the US. We are committed to expanding our picture book list and are interested in great stories with engaging characters, especially those with particularly American subjects. When writing about the experiences of a particular community, we will express a preference for stories written from a first-hand experience." Submission guidelines on site.

FICTION Picture Books: concept, contemporary, health, humor, multicultural. Young Readers: contemporary, multicultural, suspense. Middle Readers: contemporary, humor, multicultural, suspense. "At this time, we are not considering holiday stories (in any age range) or self-published works."

HOW TO CONTACT If interested, responds in 90 days to queries.

TIPS "We like to think that a child reading a Kane/Miller book will see parallels between his own life and what might be the unfamiliar setting and characters of the story. And that by seeing how a character who is somehow or in some way dissimilar—an outsider—finds a way to fit comfortably into a culture or community or situation while maintaining a healthy sense of self and self-dignity, she might be empowered to do the same."

KAR-BEN PUBLISHING

Lerner Publishing Group, 241 North First St., Minneapolis MN 55401. **E-mail:** editorial@karben.com. **Website:** www.karben.com. **Contact:** Joni Sussman. Kar-Ben publishes exclusively Jewish-themed children's books. Publishes hardcover, trade paperback, board books and e-books. **Publishes 25 titles/year. 20% of books from first-time authors. 70% from unagented writers.**

FICTION "We seek picture book mss 800-1,000 words on Jewish-themed topics for children." Picture books: Adventure, concept, folktales, history, humor, multicultural, religion, special needs; must be on a Jewish theme. Average word length: picture books–1,000. Recently published titles: *The Count's Hanukkah Countdown*, *Sammy Spider's First Book of Jewish Holidays*, *The Cats of Ben Yehuda Street*.

NONFICTION "In addition to traditional Jewish-themed stories about Jewish holidays, history, folktales and other subjects, we especially seek stories that reflect the rich diversity of the contemporary Jewish community." Picture books, young readers; Jewish history, Israel, Holocaust, folktales, religion, social issues, special needs; must be of Jewish interest. No textbooks, games, or educational materials.

HOW TO CONTACT Submit full ms. Picture books only. Submit completed ms. 800 mss received/year. Only responds if interested. Most mss published within 2 years.

TERMS Pays 5% royalty on NET sale. Pays $500-2,500 advance. Book catalog online; free upon request. Guidelines online.

TIPS "Authors: Do a literature search to make sure similar title doesn't already exist. Illustrators: Look at our online catalog for a sense of what we like—bright colors and lively composition."

KREGEL PUBLICATIONS

2450 Oak Industrial Dr. NE, Grand Rapids MI 49505. (616)451-4775. **Fax:** (616)451-9330. **E-mail:** kregelbooks@kregel.com. **Website:** www.kregelpublications.com. "Our mission as an evangelical Christian publisher is to provide—with integrity and excellence—trusted, Biblically based resources that challenge and encourage individuals in their Christian lives. Works in theology and Biblical studies should reflect the historic, orthodox Protestant tradition." Publishes hardcover and trade paperback originals and reprints. **Publishes 90 titles/year. 20% of books from first-time authors. 10% from unagented writers.**

FICTION Fiction should be geared toward the evangelical Christian market. Wants books with fast-paced, contemporary storylines presenting a strong Christian message in an engaging, entertaining style.

NONFICTION "We serve evangelical Christian readers and those in career Christian service."

HOW TO CONTACT Finds works through The Writer's Edge and Christian Manuscript Submissions ms screening services. Finds works through The Writer's Edge and Christian Manuscript Submissions

ms screening services. Responds in 2-3 months. Publishes ms 12-16 months after acceptance.

TERMS Pays royalty on wholesale price. Pays negotiable advance. Guidelines online.

TIPS "Our audience consists of conservative, evangelical Christians, including pastors and ministry students."

LANTANA PUBLISHING

London , United Kingdom. **E-mail:** info@lantana-publishing.com. **Website:** www.lantanapublishing.com. Lantana Publishing is a young, independent publishing house producing inclusive picture books for children. "Our mission is to publish outstanding writing for young readers by giving new and aspiring BAME authors and illustrators a platform to publish in the UK and by working with much-loved authors and illustrators from around the world. Lantana's award-winning titles have so far received high praise, described as 'dazzling', 'delectable', 'enchanting' and 'exquisite' by bloggers and reviewers. They have been nominated for a Kate Greenaway Medal (three times), received starred Kirkus reviews (three times), been shortlisted for the Teach Early Years Awards, the North Somerset Teachers' Book Awards, and the Sheffield Children's Books Awards, and won the Children's Africana Best Book Award. Lantana's founder, Alice Curry, is the recipient of the 2017 Kim Scott Walwyn Prize for women in publishing."

FICTION "We primarily publish picture books for 4-8 year-olds with text no longer than 500 words (and we prefer 200-400 words). We love writing that is contemporary and fun. We particularly like stories with modern-day settings in the UK or around the world, especially if they feature BAME families, and stories that lend themselves to great illustration."

NONFICTION "We accept some nonfiction content for the 7-11 range if it is international in scope."

HOW TO CONTACT Responds in 6 weeks.

TERMS Pays royalty. Pays advance. Guidelines online.

LEE & LOW BOOKS

95 Madison Ave., #1205, New York NY 10016. (212)779-4400. **E-mail:** general@leeandlow.com. **Website:** www.leeandlow.com. "Our goals are to meet a growing need for books that address children of color, and to present literature that all children can identify with. We only consider multicultural children's books. Sponsors a yearly New Voices Award for first-time

picture book authors of color. Contest rules online at website or for SASE." Publishes hardcover originals and trade paperback reprints. **Publishes 12-14 titles/year. 20% of books from first-time authors. 50% from unagented writers.**

FICTION Picture books, young readers: anthology, contemporary, history, multicultural, poetry. Picture book, middle reader: contemporary, history, multicultural, nature/environment, poetry, sports. Average word length: picture books—1,000-1,500 words. "We do not publish folklore or animal stories."

NONFICTION Picture books: concept. Picture books, middle readers: biography, history, multicultural, science and sports. Average word length: picture books-1,500-3,000.

HOW TO CONTACT Submit complete ms. Submit complete ms. Receives 100 queries/year; 1,200 mss/year. Responds in 6 months to mss if interested. Publishes book 2 years after acceptance.

ILLUSTRATION Works with 12-14 illustrators/year. Uses color artwork only. Reviews ms/illustration packages from artists. Contact: Louise May. Illustrations only: Query with samples, résumé, promo sheet and tearsheets. Responds only if interested. Samples returned with SASE; samples filed. Original artwork returned at job's completion.

PHOTOGRAPHY Buys photos from freelancers. Works on assignment only. Model/property releases required. Submit cover letter, résumé, promo piece and book dummy.

TERMS Pays net royalty. Pays authors advances against royalty. Pays illustrators advance against royalty. Photographers paid advance against royalty. Book catalog available online. Guidelines available online or by written request with SASE.

TIPS "Check our website to see the kinds of books we publish. Do not send mss that don't fit our mission."

ARTHUR A. LEVINE BOOKS

Scholastic, Inc., 557 Broadway, New York NY 10012. (212)343-4436. **Fax:** (212)343-6143. **Website:** www.arthuralevinebooks.com. Publishes hardcover, paperback, and e-book editions.

FICTION "Arthur A. Levine is looking for distinctive literature, for children and young adults, for whatever's extraordinary." Averages 18-20 total titles/year.

HOW TO CONTACT Query. Please follow submission guidelines. Responds in 1 month to queries; 5 months to mss. Publishes a book 18 months after acceptance.

TERMS Picture Books: Query letter and full text of pb. Novels: Send Query letter, first 2 chapters and synopsis. Other: Query letter, 10-page sample and synopsis/proposal.

Ⓐ LITTLE, BROWN BOOKS FOR YOUNG READERS

Hachette Book Group USA, 1290 Avenue of the Americas, New York NY 10104. (212)364-1100. **Fax:** (212)364-0925. **Website:** littlebrown.com. "Little, Brown and Co. Children's Publishing publishes all formats including board books, picture books, middle grade fiction, and nonfiction YA titles. We are looking for strong writing and presentation, but no predetermined topics." *Only interested in solicited agented material.* **Publishes 100-150 titles/year.**

FICTION Average word length: picture books—1,000; young readers—6,000; middle readers—15,000- 50,000; young adults—50,000 and up.

NONFICTION "Writers should avoid looking for the 'issue' they think publishers want to see, choosing instead topics they know best and are most enthusiastic about/inspired by."

HOW TO CONTACT *Agented submissions only. Agented submissions only.* Responds in 1-2 months. Publishes ms 2 years after acceptance.

ILLUSTRATION Works with 40 illustrators/year. Illustrations only: Query art director with b&w and color samples; provide résumé, promo sheet or tearsheets to be kept on file. Does not respond to art samples. Do not send originals; copies only. Accepts illustration samples by postal mail or e-mail.

PHOTOGRAPHY Works on assignment only. Model/property releases required; captions required. Publishes photo essays and photo concept books. Uses 35mm transparencies. Photographers should provide résumé, promo sheets or tearsheets to be kept on file.

TERMS Pays authors royalties based on retail price. Pays illustrators and photographers by the project or royalty based on retail price. Sends galleys to authors; dummies to illustrators. Pays negotiable advance.

TIPS "In order to break into the field, authors and illustrators should research their competition and try to come up with something outstandingly different."

LITTLE PICKLE PRESS

3701 Sacramento St., #494, San Francisco CA 94118. (415)340-3344. **Fax:** (415)366-1520. **E-mail:** info@ march4thinc.com. **Website:** www.littlepicklepress. com. Little Pickle Press is a 21st Century publisher dedicated to helping parents and educators cultivate conscious, responsible little people by stimulating explorations of the meaningful topics of their generation through a variety of media, technologies, and techniques. Submit through submission link on site. Includes YA imprint Relish Media.

TERMS Uses Author.me for submissions for Little Pickle and YA imprint Relish Media. Guidelines available on site.

TIPS "We have lots of manuscripts to consider, so it will take up to 8 weeks before we get back to you."

Ⓐ LITTLE SIMON

Imprint of Simon & Schuster, 1230 Avenue of the Americas, New York NY 10020. (212)698-1295. **Fax:** (212)698-2794. **Website:** www.simonandschuster. com/kids. "Our goal is to provide fresh material in an innovative format for preschool to age 8. Our books are often, if not exclusively, format driven." Publishes novelty and branded books only.

FICTION Novelty books include many things that do not fit in the traditional hardcover or paperback format, such as pop-up, board book, scratch and sniff, glow in the dark, lift the flap, etc. Children's/juvenile. No picture books. Large part of the list is holiday-themed.

NONFICTION "We publish very few nonfiction titles." No picture books.

HOW TO CONTACT *Currently not accepting unsolicited mss. Currently not accepting unsolicited mss.*

TERMS Offers advance and royalties.

MAGINATION PRESS

750 First St. NE, Washington DC 20002. (202)336-5618. **Fax:** (202)336-5624. **E-mail:** magination@apa. org. **Website:** www.apa.org. Magination Press is an imprint of the American Psychological Association. "We publish books dealing with the psycho/therapeutic resolution of children's problems and psychological issues with a strong self-help component." Submit complete ms. Full guidelines available on site. Materials returned only with SASE. **Publishes 12 titles/year. 75% of books from first-time authors.**

FICTION All levels: psychological and social issues, self-help, health, parenting concerns and, special needs. Picture books, middle school readers.

NONFICTION All levels: psychological and social issues, self-help, health, multicultural, special needs.

HOW TO CONTACT Responds to queries in 1-2 months; mss in 2-6 months. Publishes a book 18-24 months after acceptance.

ILLUSTRATION Works with 10-15 illustrators/year. Reviews ms/illustration packages. Will review artwork for future assignments. Responds only if interested, or immediately if SASE or response card is included. "We keep samples on file."

Ⓞ MASTER BOOKS

P.O. Box 726, Green Forest AR 72638. **E-mail:** submissions@newleafpress.net. **Website:** www.masterbooks. com. **Contact:** Craig Froman, acquisitions editor. Publishes 3 middle readers/year; 2 young adult nonfiction titles/year; 10 homeschool curriculum titles; 20 adult trade books/year. **5% of books from first-time authors. 99% from unagented writers.**

NONFICTION Picture books: activity books, animal, nature/environment, creation. Young readers, middle readers, young adults: activity books, animal, biography Christian, nature/environment, science, creation.

HOW TO CONTACT Submission guidelines on website. http://www.nlpg.com/submissions 500 We are no longer able to respond to every query. If you have not heard from us within 90 days, it means we are unable to partner with you on that particular project. Publishes book 1 year after acceptance.

TERMS Pays authors royalty of 3-15% based on wholesale price. Book catalog available upon request. Guidelines online.

TIPS "All of our children's books are creation-based, including topics from the Book of Genesis. We look also for home school educational material as we are expanding our home school curriculum resources."

MARGARET K. MCELDERRY BOOKS

Imprint of Simon & Schuster Children's Publishing Division, 1230 Sixth Ave., New York NY 10020. (212)698-7200. **Website:** imprints.simonandschuster.biz/margaret-k-mcelderry-books. "Margaret K. McElderry Books publishes hardcover and paperback trade books for children from pre-school age through young adult. This list includes picture books, middle grade and teen fiction, poetry, and fantasy. The style and subject matter of the books we publish is almost unlimited. We do not publish textbooks, coloring and activity books, greeting cards, magazines, pamphlets, or religious publications." **Publishes 30 titles/year. 15% of books from first-time authors. 50% from unagented writers.**

FICTION *No unsolicited mss.*

NONFICTION *No unsolicited mss. Agented submissions only.*

HOW TO CONTACT *Agented submissions only.*

TERMS Pays authors royalty based on retail price. Pays illustrator royalty of by the project. Pays photographers by the project. Original artwork returned at job's completion. Offers $5,000-8,000 advance for new authors. Guidelines for #10 SASE.

TIPS "Read! The children's book field is competitive. See what's been done and what's out there before submitting. We look for high quality: an originality of ideas, clarity and felicity of expression, a well organized plot, and strong character-driven stories. We're looking for strong, original fiction, especially mysteries and middle grade humor. We are always interested in picture books for the youngest age reader. Study our titles."

MEDIA LAB BOOKS

Topix Media Lab, 14 Wall St., Suite 4B, New York NY 10005. **Website:** onnewsstandsnow.com. **Contact:** Phil Sexton, vice president and publisher. Media Lab Books is a premier imprint that partners with industry leaders to publish branded titles designed to inform, educate and entertain readers around the world. "With brand partners that run the gamut, our books are widely variable in category and topic. From John Wayne to Disney and every brand in between, our partners have loyal followings, strong media presences and amazing stories to tell. While leveraging the platforms of our brand partners, we publish highly visual, illustrated books that surprise and delight readers of all ages. From *Jack Hanna's Big Book of Why* to *The John Wayne Code*, we truly have something for everyone. In the end, our aim is to match great ideas with amazing brands. We're looking for creative nonfiction ideas from authors with a voice (and a platform). Though we specialize in creating visually dynamic books built around big brands, we're also interested in original works focusing on popular or trending topics in most nonfiction categories, but given a unique, one-of-a-kind spin that demands

publication. For example, *I'm Just Here for the Drinks*, by Sother Teague." Publishes cooking, children's books, games, puzzles, reference, humor, biography, history. **Publishes 20 titles/year. 20% of books from first-time authors. 20% from unagented writers.**

HOW TO CONTACT Responds in 30 days. Publishes ms 12-18 months after acceptance.

TERMS Catalog available. Electronic submissions only. On the first page of the document, please include author's name and contact information. Please send full submission packet, including overview, USP (unique selling proposition), comparable titles, proposed TOC, and 1-3 sample chapters (no more than 50 pages).

TIPS "Be sure to check out the kind of books we've already published. You'll see that most of them are brand-driven. The ones that are author-driven address popular topics with a unique approach. More general books are of no interest unless the topic in question is trending and there's minimal competition in the market."

MILKWEED EDITIONS

1011 Washington Ave. S., Suite 300, Minneapolis MN 55415. (612)332-3192. **Fax:** (612)215-2550. **Website:** www.milkweed.org. Publishes 3-4 middle readers/ year. 25% of books by first-time authors. "Milkweed Editions publishes with the intention of making a humane impact on society, in the belief that literature is a transformative art uniquely able to convey the essential experiences of the human heart and spirit. To that end, Milkweed Editions publishes distinctive voices of literary merit in handsomely designed, visually dynamic books, exploring the ethical, cultural, and esthetic issues that free societies need continually to address." Publishes hardcover, trade paperback, and electronic originals; trade paperback and electronic reprints. **Publishes 15-20 titles/year. 25% of books from first-time authors. 75% from unagented writers.**

FICTION Novels for adults and for readers 8-13. High literary quality. For adult readers: literary fiction, nonfiction, poetry, essays. Middle readers: adventure, contemporary, fantasy, multicultural, nature/environment, suspense/mystery. Average length: middle readers—90-200 pages. No romance, mysteries, science fiction.

HOW TO CONTACT "Please submit a query letter with three opening chapters (of a novel) or three representative stories (of a collection). Publishes YR." Responds in 6 months. Publishes book in 18 months.

TERMS Pays authors variable royalty based on retail price. Offers advance against royalties. Pays varied advance from $500-10,000. Book catalog online. Only accepts submissions during open submission periods. See website for guidelines.

TIPS "We are looking for excellent writing with the intent of making a humane impact on society. Please read submission guidelines before submitting and acquaint yourself with our books in terms of style and quality before submitting. Many factors influence our selection process, so don't get discouraged. Nonfiction is focused on literary writing about the natural world, including living well in urban environments."

⚪ THE MILLBROOK PRESS

Lerner Publishing Group, 1251 Washington Ave N, Minneapolis MN 55401. **E-mail:** info@lernerbooks.com. **Website:** www.lernerbooks.com. **Contact:** Carol Hinz, editorial director. "Millbrook Press publishes informative picture books, illustrated nonfiction titles, and inspiring photo-driven titles for grades K–5. Our authors approach curricular topics with a fresh point of view. Our fact-filled books engage readers with fun yet accessible writing, high-quality photographs, and a wide variety of illustration styles. We cover subjects ranging from the parts of speech and other language arts skills; to history, science, and math; to art, sports, crafts, and other interests. Millbrook Press is the home of the best-selling Words Are CATegorical® series and Bob Raczka's Art Adventures. We do not accept unsolicited manuscripts from authors. Occasionally, we may put out a call for submissions, which will be announced on our website."

MITCHELL LANE PUBLISHERS

2001 S.W. 31st Ave., Hallandale FL 33009. (954)985-9400. **Fax:** (800)223-3251. **E-mail:** phil@mitchelllane.com; customerservice@mitchelllane.com. **Website:** www.mitchelllane.com. **Contact:** Phil Comer. Publishes hardcover and library bound originals and has it's own eBook platform and delivery system. **Publishes 80 titles/year. 90% from unagented writers.**

NONFICTION Young readers, middle readers, young adults: biography, nonfiction, and curriculum-related subjects. Average word length: 4,000-50,000 words. Recently published: *My Guide to US Citizenship*, *Rivers of the World* and *Vote America*.

HOW TO CONTACT Query with SASE. *All unsolicited mss discarded.* 100 queries/year; 5 mss received/year. Responds only if interested to queries. Publishes ms 1 year after acceptance.

ILLUSTRATION Works with 2-3 illustrators/year. Reviews ms/illustration packages from artists. Query. Illustration only: Query with samples; send résumé, portfolio, slides, tearsheets. Responds only if interested. Samples not returned; samples filed.

PHOTOGRAPHY Buys stock images. Needs photos of famous and prominent minority figures. Captions required. Uses color prints or digital images. Submit cover letter, résumé, published samples, stock photo list.

TERMS Work purchased outright from authors (range: $350-2,000). Pays illustrators by the project (range: $40-400). Book catalog available free.

TIPS "We hire writers on a 'work-for-hire' basis to complete book projects we assign. Send résumé and writing samples that do not need to be returned."

ⒶMOODY PUBLISHERS

Moody Bible Institute, 820 N. LaSalle Blvd., Chicago IL 60610. (800)678-8812. **Fax:** (312)329-4157. **Website:** www.moodypublishers.org. **Contact:** Acquisitions Coordinator. "The mission of Moody Publishers is to educate and edify the Christian and to evangelize the non-Christian by ethically publishing conservative, evangelical Christian literature and other media for all ages around the world, and to help provide resources for Moody Bible Institute in its training of future Christian leaders." Publishes hardcover, trade, and mass market paperback originals. **Publishes 60 titles/year. 1% of books from first-time authors. 80% from unagented writers.**

NONFICTION "We are no longer reviewing queries or unsolicited manuscripts unless they come to us through an agent, are from an author who has published with us, an associate from a Moody Bible Institute ministry or a personal contact at a writer's conference. Unsolicited proposals will be returned only if proper postage is included. We are not able to acknowledge the receipt of your unsolicited proposal."

HOW TO CONTACT *Agented submissions only.* Does not accept unsolicited nonfiction submissions. 1,500 queries received/year. 2,000 mss received/year. Responds in 2-3 months to queries. Publishes book 1 year after acceptance.

TERMS Royalty varies. Book catalog for 9×12 envelope and 4 first-class stamps. Guidelines online.

TIPS "In our fiction list, we're looking for Christian storytellers rather than teachers trying to present a message. Your motivation should be to delight the reader. Using your skills to create beautiful works is glorifying to God."

MSI PRESS LLC

1760-F Airline Hwy, #203, Hollister CA 95023. **Fax:** (831)886-2486. **E-mail:** editor@msipress.com. **Website:** www.msipress.com. **Contact:** Betty Lou Leaver, managing editor (self-help, spirituality, religion, memoir, mind/body/spirit, some humor, popular psychology, foreign language & culture, parenting). "We are a small press that specializes in award-winning quality publications, refined through strong personal interactions and productive working relationships between our editors and our authors. A small advance may be offered to previously published authors with a strong book, strong platform, and solid sales numbers. We will accept first-time authors with credibility in their fields and a strong platform, but we do not offer advances to first-time authors. We may refer authors with a good book but little experience or lacking a strong platform to San Juan Books, our hybrid publishing venture." Publishes trade paperback originals and corresponding e-books. **Publishes 10-15 titles/year. 50%% of books from first-time authors. 100% from unagented writers.**

NONFICTION "We continue to expand our spirituality, psychology, and self-help lines and are interested in adding to our collection of books in Spanish. We do not do or publish translations." Does not want erotica.

HOW TO CONTACT Submit proposal package, including: annotated outline, 1 sample chapter, professional resume, platform information. Electronic submissions preferred. We are open to foreign writers (non-native speakers of English), but please have an English editor proofread the submission prior to sending; if the query letter or proposal is written in poor English, we will not take a chance on a manuscript. 100-200 Responds in 2 weeks to queries sent by e-mail and to proposals submitted via the template on our website. If response not received in 2 weeks, okay to query. Publishes ms 6-10 months after acceptance.

TERMS Pays 10% royalty on retail price for paperbacks and hard cover books; pays 50% royalty on net for e-books. By exception, pays small advance to previously published authors with good sales history. Catalog online. Guidelines online.

TIPS "Learn the mechanics of writing. Too many submissions are full of grammar and punctuation errors and poorly worded with trite expressions. Read to write; observe and analyze how the great authors of all time use language to good avail. Capture our attention with active verbs, not bland description. Before writing your book, determine its audience, write to that audience, and go about developing your credibility with that audience—and then tell us what you have done and are doing in your proposal."

Ⓐ NATIONAL GEOGRAPHIC CHILDREN'S BOOKS

1145 17th St. NW, Washington DC 20090-8199. (800)647-5463. **Website:** kids.nationalgeographic.com. National Geographic CHildren's Books provides quality nonfiction for children and young adults by award-winning authors. *This market does not currently accept unsolicited mss.*

NATUREGRAPH PUBLISHERS, INC.

P.O. Box 1047, 3543 Indian Creek Rd., Happy Camp CA 96039. (530)493-5353. **Fax:** (530)493-5240. **E-mail:** nature@sisqtel.net. **Website:** www.naturegraph.com. **Contact:** Barbara Brown, owner. Publishes trade paperback originals. **Publishes 2 titles/year. 80% of books from first-time authors. 90% from unagented writers.**

HOW TO CONTACT 100 queries; 6 mss received/year. Responds in 1 month to queries; 2 months to mss. Publishes ms 2 years after acceptance.

TERMS Pays royalties. Does not pay advance. Book catalog for #10 SASE.

TIPS "Please-always send a stamped reply envelope. Publishers get hundreds of manuscripts yearly."

TOMMY NELSON

Imprint of Thomas Nelson, Inc., P.O. Box 141000, Nashville TN 37214-1000. (615)889-9000. **Fax:** (615)902-2219. **Website:** www.tommynelson.com. "Tommy Nelson publishes children's Christian nonfiction and fiction for boys and girls up to age 14. We honor God and serve people through books, videos, software and Bibles for children that improve the lives of our customers." Publishes hardcover and trade paperback originals. **Publishes 50-75 titles/year.**

FICTION No stereotypical characters.

HOW TO CONTACT *Does not accept unsolicited mss. Does not accept unsolicited mss.*

TERMS Guidelines online.

TIPS "Know the Christian Booksellers Association market. Check out the Christian bookstores to see what sells and what is needed."

NIGHTSCAPE PRESS

P.O. Box 1948, Smyrna TN 37167. **E-mail:** info@night-scapepress.com. **Website:** www.nightscapepress.com. Nightscape Press is seeking quality book-length words of at least 50,000 words (40,000 for young adult).

FICTION "We are not interested in erotica or graphic novels."

HOW TO CONTACT Query.

TERMS Pays monthly royalties. Offers advance. Guidelines online. Currently closed to submissions. Will announce on site when they re-open to submissions.

NOMAD PRESS

2456 Christain St., White River Junction VT 05001. (802)649-1995. **E-mail:** info@nomadpress.net. **Website:** www.nomadpress.net. **Contact:** Acquisitions Editor. "We produce nonfiction children's activity books that bring a particular science or cultural topic into sharp focus. Nomad Press does not accept unsolicited manuscripts. If authors are interested in contributing to our children's series, please send a writing resume that includes relevant experience/expertise and publishing credits."

◯ Nomad Press does not accept picture books, fiction, or cookbooks.

NONFICTION Middle readers: activity books, history, science. Average word length: middle readers—30,000.

HOW TO CONTACT Responds to queries in 3-4 weeks. Publishes book 1 year after acceptance.

TERMS Pays authors royalty based on retail price or work purchased outright. Offers advance against royalties. Catalog online.

TIPS "We publish a very specific kind of nonfiction children's activity book. Please keep this in mind when querying or submitting."

NORTHSOUTH BOOKS

600 Third Ave., 2nd Floor, New York NY 10016. **E-mail:** submissionsb@gmail.com. **Website:** www.northsouth.com. **Contact:** Beth Terrill.

FICTION Looking for fresh, original fiction with universal themes that could appeal to children ages 3-8. "We typically do not acquire rhyming texts, since our books must also be translated into German."

HOW TO CONTACT Submit picture book mss (1,000 words or less) via e-mail.

TERMS Guidelines online.

⬤ NOSY CROW PUBLISHING

The Crow's Nest, 10a Lant St., London SE1 1QR, United Kingdom. (44)(0)207-089-7575. **Fax:** (44)(0)207-089-7576. **E-mail:** hello@nosycrow.com. **Website:** nosycrow.com. "We publish books for children 0-14. We're looking for 'parent-friendly' books, and we don't publish books with explicit sex, drug use or serious violence, so no edgy YA or edgy crossover. And whatever New Adult is, we don't do it. We also publish apps for children from 2-7, and may publish apps for older children if the idea feels right."

FICTION "As a rule, we don't like books with 'issues' that are in any way overly didactic."

HOW TO CONTACT Prefers submissions by e-mail, but post works if absolutely necessary. Prefers submissions by e-mail, but post works if absolutely necessary.

TERMS Guidelines online.

TIPS "Please don't be too disappointed if we reject your work! We're a small company and can only publish a few new books and apps each year, so do try other publishers and agents: publishing is necessarily a hugely subjective business. We wish you luck!"

ONSTAGE PUBLISHING

(256)542-3213. **E-mail:** submissions@onstagepublishing.com. **Website:** www.onstagepublishing.com. **Contact:** Dianne Hamilton, senior editor. "At this time, we only produce fiction books for ages 8-18. We have added an e-book only side of the house for mysteries for grades 6-12. See our website for more information. We will not do anthologies of any kind. Query first for nonfiction projects as nonfiction projects must spark our interest. We no longer are accepting written submissions. We want e-mail queries and submissions. For submissions: Put the first 3 chapters in the body of the e-mail. Do not use attachments! We will delete any submission with an attachment without acknowledgment." Suggested ms lengths: Chapter books: 3,000-9,000 words, Middle Grade novels: 10,000-40,000 words, Young adult novels: 40,000-60,000 words. **Publishes 1-5 titles/year. 80% of books from first-time authors. 95% from unagented writers.**

FICTION Middle readers: adventure, contemporary, fantasy, history, nature/environment, science fiction, suspense/mystery. Young adults: adventure, contemporary, fantasy, history, humor, science fiction, suspense/mystery. Average word length: chapter books—4,000-6,000 words; middle readers—5,000 words and up; young adults—25,000 and up. Recently published *Mission: Shanghai* by Jamie Dodson (an adventure for boys ages 12+); *Birmingham, 1933: Alice* (a chapter book for grades 3-5). "We do not produce picture books."

HOW TO CONTACT 500 + Responds in 1-6 months.

TERMS Pays authors/illustrators/photographers advance plus royalties. Pays advance. Guidelines online.

TIPS "Study our titles and get a sense of the kind of books we publish, so that you know whether your project is likely to be right for us."

ON THE MARK PRESS

15 Dairy Ave., Napanee ON K7R 1M4, Canada. (800)463-6367. **Fax:** (800)290-3631. **Website:** www. onthemarkpress.com. Publishes books for the Canadian curriculum. **15% of books from first-time authors.**

PHOTOGRAPHY Buys stock images.

OOLIGAN PRESS

369 Neuberger Hall, 724 SW Harrison St., Portland OR 97201. (503)725-9410. **Website:** ooligan.pdx.edu. **Contact:** Acquisitions Co-Managers. "We seek to publish regionally significant works of literary, historical, and social value.
We define the Pacific Northwest as Northern California, Oregon, Idaho, Washington, British Columbia, and Alaska. We recognize the importance of diversity, particularly within the publishing industry, and are committed to building a literary community that includes traditionally underrepresented voices; therefore, we are interested in works originating from, or focusing on, marginalized communities of the Pacific Northwest." Publishes trade paperbacks, electronic originals, and reprints. **Publishes 3-4 titles/year. 90% of books from first-time authors. 90% from unagented writers.**

FICTION "We seek to publish regionally significant works of literary, historical, and social value.
We define the Pacific Northwest as Northern California, Oregon, Idaho, Washington, British Columbia, and Alaska."
We recognize the importance of diversity, particularly within the publishing industry, and are committed to building a literary community that includes traditionally underrepresented voices; therefore, we are interested in works originating from, or focusing on, marginalized communities of the Pacific Northwest. Does not want romance, horror, westerns, incomplete mss.

NONFICTION Cookbooks, self-help books, how-to manuals.

HOW TO CONTACT Query with SASE. *"At this time we cannot accept science fiction or fantasy submissions."* Submit a query through Submittable. If accepted, then submit proposal package, outline, 4 sample chapters, projected page count, audience, marketing ideas, and a list of similar titles. 250-500 queries; 50-75 mss received/year. Responds in 3 weeks for queries; 3 months for proposals. Publishes ms 12-18 months after acceptance.

TERMS Pays negotiable royalty on retail price. Catalog online. Guidelines online.

TIPS "Search the blog for tips."

ORCHARD BOOKS (US)

557 Broadway, New York NY 10012. **Website:** www. scholastic.com. *Orchard is not accepting unsolicited mss.* **Publishes 20 titles/year. 10% of books from first-time authors.**

FICTION Picture books, early readers, and novelty: animal, contemporary, history, humor, multicultural, poetry.

TERMS Most commonly offers an advance against list royalties.

HALF RICHARD C. OWEN PUBLISHERS, INC.

P.O. Box 585, Katonah NY 10536. (914)232-3903; (800)262-0787. **E-mail:** richardowen@ rcowen.com. **Website:** www.rcowen.com. **Contact:** Richard Owen, publisher. "We publish child-focused books, with inherent instructional value, about characters and situations with which 5, 6, and 7-year-old children can identify—books that can be read for meaning, entertainment, enjoyment and information. We include multicultural stories that present minorities in a positive and natural way. Our stories show the diversity in America." Not interested in lesson plans, or books of activities for literature studies or other content areas. Submit complete ms and cover letter.

"Due to high volume and long production time, we are currently limiting to nonfiction submissions only."

NONFICTION "Our books are for kindergarten, first- and second-grade children to read on their own. The stories are very brief—up to 2,000 words—yet well structured and crafted with memorable characters, language, and plots. Picture books, young readers: animals, careers, history, how-to, music/dance, geography, multicultural, nature/environment, science, sports. Multicultural needs include: Good stories respectful of all heritages, races, cultural—African-American, Hispanic, American Indian, Asian, European, Middle Eastern." Wants lively stories. No "encyclopedic" type of information stories. Average word length: under 500 words.

HOW TO CONTACT Responds to mss in 1 year. Publishes book 2-3 years after acceptance.

ILLUSTRATION Works with 20 illustrators/year. Uses color artwork only. Illustration only: Send color copies/reproductions or photos of art or provide tearsheets; do not send slides or originals. Include SASE and cover letter. Responds only if interested; samples filed.

TERMS Pays authors royalty of 5% based on net price or outright purchase (range: $25-500). Offers no advances. Pays illustrators by the project (range: $100-2,000) or per photo (range: $50-150). Book catalog available with SASE. Ms guidelines with SASE or online.

PAGESPRING PUBLISHING

P.O. Box 2113, Columbus OH 43221. **E-mail:** sales@pagespringpublishing.com. **Website:** www.pagespringpublishing.com. **Contact:** Lucky Marble Books Editor or Cup of Tea Books Editor. PageSpring Publishing publishes women's fiction under the Cup of Tea Books imprint and YA/middle grade titles under the Lucky Marble Books imprint. Visit the PageSpring Publishing website for submission details. Publishes trade paperback and electronic originals. **Publishes 4-7 titles/year. 50% of books from first-time authors. 90% from unagented writers.**

FICTION Cup of Tea Books publishes women's fiction. Lucky Marble Books specializes in middle grade and young adult fiction.

HOW TO CONTACT submissions@pagespringpublishing.com Send submissions for both Cup of Tea Books and Lucky Marble Books to submissions@pagespringpublishing.com. Send a query, synopsis, and the first 30 pages of the manuscript in the body of the email. please. NO attachments. Endeavors to respond to queries within 3 months. Publishes ms 9-12 months after acceptance.

TERMS Pays royalty on wholesale price. Catalog online. Guidelines online.

TIPS Cup of Tea Books would love to see more cozy mysteries and humor. Lucky Marble Books is looking for humor and engaging contemporary stories for middle grade and young adult readers.

PAGESPRING PUBLISHING

PageSpring Publishing, P.O. Box 21133, Columbus OH 43221. **Website:** www.pagespringpublishing.com. PageSpring Publishing is a small independent publisher with two imprints: Cup of Tea Books and Lucky Marble Books. Cup of Tea Books publishes women's fiction, with particular emphasis on mystery and humor. Lucky Marble Books publishes young adult and middle grade fiction. "We are looking for engaging characters and well-crafted plots that keep our readers turning the page. We accept e-mail queries only; see our website for details." Publishes trade paperback and electronic originals. **Publishes 4-5 titles/year. 75%% of books from first-time authors. 100%% from unagented writers.**

FICTION Lucky Marble Books publishes middle grade and young adult novels. Cup of Tea Books publishes women's fiction. Lucky Marble Books publishes middle grade and young adult novels. No children's picture books.

HOW TO CONTACT Submit proposal package via e-mail only. Include synopsis and 30 sample pages. Responds in 3 months. Publishes ms 12 months after acceptance.

TERMS Pays royalty. Guidelines online.

TIPS "Cup of Tea Books is particularly interested in cozy mystery novels. Lucky Marble Books is looking for funny, age-appropriate tales for middle grade and young adult readers."

PANTS ON FIRE PRESS

2062 Harbor Cove Way, Winter Garden FL 34787. (863)546-0760. **E-mail:** submission@pantsonfirepress.com. **Website:** www.pantsonfirepress.com. **Contact:** Becca Goldman, senior editor; Emily Gerety, editor. Pants On Fire Press is an award-winning book publisher of picture, middle-grade, young adult, and adult books. Publishes hardcover originals and reprints, trade paperback originals and reprints, and electronic originals and reprints. **Publishes 10**

titles/year. 50% of books from first-time authors. 80% from unagented writers.

Pants On Fire Press is an award-winning boutique book publisher of middle-grade, young adult and fictional books for adults. We publish in both print and e-book format. We love big story ideas and meaty characters. We are always on the lookout for the following subjects: Action, Adventure, Christian, Detective, Drama, Dystopian, Fantasy, Historical Fiction, Horror, Humor, Jewish, Love, Mystery, Paranormal, Romance, Science Fiction, Supernatural, Suspense and Thriller stories.

FICTION Publishes big story ideas with high concepts, new worlds, and meaty characters for children, teens, and discerning adults.

HOW TO CONTACT Submit a proposal package including a synopsis, 3 sample chapters, and a query letter via e-mail. Receives 36,300 queries and mss per year. Responds in 3 months. Publishes ms approximately 7 months after acceptance.

TERMS Pays 10-50% royalties on wholesale price. Catalog online. Guidelines online.

PAUL DRY BOOKS

1700 Sansom St., Suite 700, Philadelphia PA 19103. (215)231-9939. **Fax:** (215)231-9942. **E-mail:** editor@pauldrybooks.com. **Website:** pauldrybooks.com. "We publish fiction, both novels and short stories, and nonfiction, biography, memoirs, history, and essays, covering subjects from Homer to Chekhov, bird watching to jazz music, New York City to shogunate Japan." Hardcover and trade paperback originals, trade paperback reprints.

HOW TO CONTACT "We do not accept unsolicited manuscripts." "We do not accept unsolicited manuscripts."

TERMS Book catalog online.

TIPS "Our aim is to publish lively books 'to awaken, delight, and educate'—to spark conversation. We publish fiction and nonfiction, and essays covering subjects from Homer to Chekhov, bird watching to jazz music, New York City to shogunate Japan."

PAULINE BOOKS & MEDIA

50 St. Paul's Ave., Boston MA 02130. (617)522-8911. **Fax:** (617)541-9805. **E-mail:** design@paulinemedia.com; editorial@paulinemedia.com. **Website:** www.pauline.org. "Submissions are evaluated on adherence to Gospel values, harmony with the Catholic faith tradition, relevance of topic, and quality of writing." For board books and picture books, the entire manuscript should be submitted. For easy-to-read, young readers, and middle reader books and teen books, please send a cover letter accompanied by a synopsis and two sample chapters. "Electronic submissions are encouraged. We make every effort to respond to unsolicited submissions within 2 months." Publishes trade paperback originals and reprints. **Publishes 40 titles/year. 5% from unagented writers.**

FICTION Children's and teen fiction only. "We are now accepting submissions for easy-to-read and middle reader chapter, and teen well documented historical fiction. We would also consider well-written fantasy, fairy tales, myths, science fiction, mysteries, or romance if approached from a Catholic perspective and consistent with church teaching. Please see our writer's guidelines."

NONFICTION Picture books, young readers, middle readers, teen: religion and fiction. Average word length: picture books—500-1,000; young readers—8,000-10,000; middle readers—15,000-25,000; teen—30,000-50,000. Recently published children's titles: *Bible Stores for Little Ones* by Genny Monchapm; *I Forgive You: Love We Can Hear, Ask For and Give* by Nicole Lataif; *Shepherds To the Rescue* (first place Catholic Book Award Winner) by Maria Grace Dateno; *FSP; Jorge from Argentina; Prayers for Young Catholics.* Teen Titles: *Teens Share the Mission* by Teens; *Martyred: The Story of Saint Lorenzo Ruiz; Ten Commandmenst for Kissing Gloria Jean* by Britt Leigh; *A.K.A. Genius* (2nd Place Catholic Book Award Winner) by Marilee Haynes; *Tackling Tough Topics* with Faith and Fiction by Diana Jenkins. No memoir/autobiography, poetry, or strictly nonreligious works currently considered.

HOW TO CONTACT "Submit proposal package, including synopsis, 2 sample chapters, and cover letter; complete ms." Submit proposal package, including outline, 1-2 sample chapters, cover letter, synopsis, intended audience and proposed length. Responds in 2 months. Publishes a book approximately 11-18 months after acceptance.

ILLUSTRATION Works with 10-15 illustrators/year. Uses color and black-and-white- artwork. Samples and résumés will be kept on file unless return is requested and SASE provided.

TERMS Varies by project, but generally are royalties with advance. Flat fees sometimes considered for smaller works. Book catalog online. Guidelines online.

TIPS "Manuscripts may or may not be explicitly catechetical, but we seek those that reflect a positive worldview, good moral values, awareness and appreciation of diversity, and respect for all people. All material must be relevant to the lives of readers and must conform to Catholic teaching and practice."

PAULIST PRESS

997 Macarthur Blvd., Mahwah NJ 07430. (201)825-7300. **Fax:** (201)825-8345. **E-mail:** submissions@paulistpress.com. **Website:** www.paulistpress.com. **Contact:** Trace Murphy, Editorial Director. Paulist Press publishes ecumenical theology, Roman Catholic studies, and books on scripture, liturgy, spirituality, church history, and philosophy, as well as works on faith and culture. Also publishes 2-3 children's titles a year. **10% of books from first-time authors. 95% from unagented writers.**

HOW TO CONTACT Accepts submissions via e-mail. Receives 400 submissions/year. Responds in 3 months to queries and proposals; 3-4 months on mss. Publishes a book 12-18 months after receipt of final, edited ms.

TERMS Royalties and advances are negotiable. Pays negotiable advance. Book catalog online. Guidelines online.

PEACHTREE PUBLISHING COMPANY INC.

Peachtree Publishing Company Inc., 1700 Chattahoochee Ave., Atlanta GA 30318. (404)876-8761. **Fax:** (404)875-2578. **E-mail:** hello@peachtree-online.com. **Website:** www.peachtree-online.com. **Contact:** Helen Harriss, submissions editor. "We publish a broad range of subjects and perspectives, with emphasis on innovative plots and strong writing." Publishes hardcover and trade paperback originals. **Publishes 30 titles/year. 25% of books from first-time authors. 25% from unagented writers.**

FICTION Looking for very well-written middle grade and young adult novels. No adult fiction. No collections of poetry or short stories; no romance or science fiction.

NONFICTION No e-mail or fax queries of mss.

HOW TO CONTACT Submit complete ms with SASE. Submit complete ms with SASE, or summary and 3 sample chapters with SASE. Responds in 6 months and mss. Publishes ms 1 year after acceptance.

TERMS Pays royalty on retail price. Book catalog for 6 first-class stamps. Guidelines online.

PEACHTREE PUBLISHING COMPANY INC.

1700 Chattahoochee Ave., Atlanta GA 30318. (404)876-8761. **Fax:** (404)875-2578. **E-mail:** hello@peachtree-online.com. **Website:** www.peachtree-online.com. **Publishes 30-35 titles/year.**

FICTION Picture books, young readers: adventure, animal, concept, history, nature/environment. Middle readers: adventure, animal, history, nature/environment, sports. Young adults: fiction, mystery, adventure. Does not want to see science fiction, romance.

NONFICTION Picture books: animal, history, nature/environment. Young readers, middle readers, young adults: animal, biography, nature/environment. Does not want to see religion.

HOW TO CONTACT Submit complete manuscript by postal mail only. Submit complete ms by postal mail only. Responds in 6-9 months. Publishes book 1-2 years after acceptance.

ILLUSTRATION Works with 8-10 illustrators/year. Illustrations only: Query production manager or art director with samples, résumé, slides, color copies to keep on file. Responds only if interested. Samples returned with SASE; samples filed.

PELICAN PUBLISHING COMPANY

1000 Burmaster St., Gretna LA 70053. (504)368-1175. **Fax:** (504)368-1195. **E-mail:** editorial@pelicanpub.com. **Website:** www.pelicanpub.com. "We believe ideas have consequences. One of the consequences is that they lead to a best-selling book. We publish books to improve and uplift the reader. Currently emphasizing business and history titles." Publishes 20 young readers/year; 1 middle reader/year. "Our children's books (illustrated and otherwise) include history, biography, holiday, and regional. Pelican's mission is to publish books of quality and permanence that enrich the lives of those who read them." Publishes hardcover, trade paperback and mass market paperback originals and reprints.

FICTION We publish no adult fiction. Young readers: history, holiday, science, multicultural and regional. Middle readers: Louisiana History. Multicultural needs include stories about African-Americans, Irish-Americans, Jews, Asian-Americans, and Hispanics. Does not want animal stories, general Christmas stories, "day at school" or "accept yourself" stories. Maximum word length: young readers—1,100; middle readers—40,000. No young adult, romance, science fiction, fantasy, gothic, mystery, erotica, confession, horror, sex, or violence. Also no psychological novels.

NONFICTION "We look for authors who can promote successfully. We require that a query be made first. This greatly expedites the review process and can save the writer additional postage expenses." Young readers: biography, history, holiday, multicultural. Middle readers: Louisiana history, holiday, regional. No multiple queries or submissions.

HOW TO CONTACT Submit outline, clips, 2 sample chapters, SASE. Full guidelines on website. Responds in 1 month to queries; 3 months to mss. Requires exclusive submission. Publishes a book 9-18 months after acceptance.

ILLUSTRATION Works with 20 illustrators/year. Reviews ms/illustration packages from artists. Query first. Illustrations only: Query with samples (no originals). Responds only if interested. Samples returned with SASE; samples kept on file.

TERMS Pays authors in royalties; buys ms outright "rarely." Illustrators paid by "various arrangements." Advance considered. Book catalog and ms guidelines online.

TIPS "We do extremely well with cookbooks, popular histories, and business. We will continue to build in these areas. The writer must have a clear sense of the market and knowledge of the competition. A query letter should describe the project briefly, give the author's writing and professional credentials, and promotional ideas."

Ⓐ PENGUIN RANDOM HOUSE, LLC

Division of Bertelsmann Book Group, 1745 Broadway, New York NY 10019. (212)782-9000. **Website:** www.penguinrandomhouse.com. Penguin Random House LLC is the world's largest English-language general trade book publisher. *Agented submissions only. No unsolicited mss.*

PERSEA BOOKS

277 Broadway, Suite 708, New York NY 10007. (212)260-9256. **Fax:** (212)267-3165. **E-mail:** info@perseabooks.com. **Website:** www.perseabooks.com. The aim of Persea is to publish works that endure by meeting high standards of literary merit and relevance. "We have often taken on important books other publishers have overlooked, or have made significant discoveries and rediscoveries, whether of a single work or writer's entire oeuvre. Our books cover a wide range of themes, styles, and genres. We have published poetry, fiction, essays, memoir, biography, titles of Jewish and Middle Eastern interest, women's studies, American Indian folklore, and revived classics, as well as a notable selection of works in translation."

HOW TO CONTACT Queries should include a cover letter, author background and publication history, a detailed synopsis of the proposed work, and a sample chapter. Please indicate if the work is simultaneously submitted. Responds in 8 weeks to proposals; 10 weeks to mss.

TERMS Guidelines online.

Ⓐ PHILOMEL BOOKS

Imprint of Penguin Group (USA), Inc., 375 Hudson St., New York NY 10014. (212)414-3610. **Website:** www.penguin.com. **Contact:** Michael Green, president/publisher. "We look for beautifully written, engaging manuscripts for children and young adults." Publishes hardcover originals. **Publishes 8-10 titles/year. 5% of books from first-time authors. 20% from unagented writers.**

NONFICTION Picture books.

HOW TO CONTACT *No unsolicited mss. Agented submissions only.*

ILLUSTRATION Works with 8-10 illustrators/year. Reviews ms/illustration packages from artists. Query with art sample first. Illustrations only: Query with samples. Send résumé and tearsheets. Responds to art samples in 1 month. Original artwork returned at job's completion. Samples returned with SASE or kept on file.

TERMS Pays authors in royalties. Average advance payment "varies." Illustrators paid by advance and in royalties. Pays negotiable advance.

PIANO PRESS

P.O. Box 85, Del Mar CA 92014. (619)884-1401. **Fax:** (858)755-1104. **E-mail:** pianopress@pianopress.com. **Website:** www.pianopress.com. **Contact:** Elizabeth C. Axford, editor. "We publish music-related books, either fiction or nonfiction, music-related coloring books, songbooks, sheet music, CDs, and music-related poetry."

FICTION Picture books, young readers, middle readers, young adults: folktales, multicultural, poetry, music. Average word length: picture books—1,500-2,000.

NONFICTION Picture books, young readers, middle readers, young adults: multicultural, music/dance. Average word length: picture books—1,500-2,000.

HOW TO CONTACT Responds if interested. Publishes book 1 year after acceptance.

ILLUSTRATION Works with 1 or 2 illustrators/year. Reviews ms/illustration packages from artists. Query. Illustrations only: Query with samples. Responds in 3 months. Samples returned with SASE; samples filed.

PHOTOGRAPHY Buys stock and assigns work. Looking for music-related, multicultural. Model/property releases required. Uses glossy or flat, color or b&w prints. Submit cover letter, résumé, client list, published samples, stock photo list.

TERMS Pays authors, illustrators, and photographers royalties based on the retail price. Book catalog online.

TIPS "We are looking for music-related material only for the juvenile market. Please do not send non-music-related materials. Query by e-mail first before submitting anything."

PIÑATA BOOKS

Imprint of Arte Publico Press, University of Houston, 4902 Gulf Fwy., Bldg. 19, Room 100, Houston TX 77204-2004. (713)743-2845. **Fax:** (713)743-3080. **E-mail:** submapp@uh.edu. **Website:** www.artepublicopress.com. "Piñata Books is dedicated to the publication of children's and young adult literature focusing on U.S. Hispanic culture by U.S. Hispanic authors. Arte Publico's mission is the publication, promotion and dissemination of Latino literature for a variety of national and regional audiences, from early childhood to adult, through the complete gamut of delivery systems, including personal performance as well as print and electronic media." Publishes hardcover and trade paperback originals. **Publishes 10-15 titles/year. 80% of books from first-time authors.**

NONFICTION Piñata Books specializes in publication of children's and young adult literature that authentically portrays themes, characters and customs unique to U.S. Hispanic culture.

HOW TO CONTACT Submissions made through online submission form. Submissions made through online submission form. Responds in 2-3 months to queries; 4-6 months to mss. Publishes book 2 years after acceptance.

ILLUSTRATION Works with 6 illustrators/year. Uses color artwork only. Reviews ms/illustration packages from artists. Query or send portfolio (slides, color copies). Illustrations only: Query with samples or send résumé, promo sheet, portfolio, slides, client list and tearsheets. Responds only if interested. Samples not returned; samples filed.

TERMS Pays 10% royalty on wholesale price. Pays $1,000-3,000 advance. Book catalog and guidelines online.

TIPS "Include cover letter with submission explaining why your manuscript is unique and important, why we should publish it, who will buy it, etc."

PINEAPPLE PRESS, INC.

P.O. Box 3889, Sarasota FL 34230. (941)706-2507. **Fax:** (800)746-3275. **Website:** www.pineapplepress.com. **Contact:** June Cussen, executive editor. "We are seeking quality nonfiction on diverse topics for the library and book trade markets. Our mission is to publish good books about Florida." Publishes hardcover and trade paperback originals. **Publishes 21 titles/year. 50% of books from first-time authors. 95% from unagented writers.**

FICTION Picture books, young readers, middle readers, young adults: animal, folktales, history, nature/environment.

NONFICTION Picture books: animal, history, nature/environmental, science. Young readers, middle readers, young adults: animal, biography, geography, history, nature/environment, science.

HOW TO CONTACT Query or submit outline/synopsis and 3 sample chapters. Query or submit outline/synopsis and intro and 3 sample chapters. 1,000 queries; 500 mss received/year. Responds in 2 months. Publishes a book 1 year after acceptance.

ILLUSTRATION Works with 2 illustrators/year. Reviews ms/illustration packages from artists. Query with nonreturnable samples. Contact: June Cussen, executive editor. Illustrations only: Query with brochure, nonreturnable samples, photocopies, résumé. Responds only if interested. Samples returned with SASE, but prefers nonreturnable; samples filed.

TERMS Pays authors royalty of 10-15%. Book catalog for 9×12 SAE with $1.32 postage. Guidelines online.

TIPS "Quality first novels will be published, though we usually only do one or two novels per year and they must be set in Florida. We regard the author/editor relationship as a trusting relationship with communication open both ways. Learn all you can about the publishing process and about how to promote your book once it is published. A query on a novel without a brief sample seems useless."

POLIS BOOKS

E-mail: info@polisbooks.com. **Website:** www.polisbooks.com. "Polis Books is an independent publishing company actively seeking new and established authors for our growing list. We are actively acquiring titles in mystery, thriller, suspense, procedural, traditional crime, science fiction, fantasy, horror, supernatural, urban fantasy, romance, erotica, commercial women's fiction, commercial literary fiction, young adult and middle grade books." **Publishes 40 titles/ year. 33% of books from first-time authors. 10% from unagented writers.**

HOW TO CONTACT Query with 3 sample chapters and bio via e-mail. 500+ Only responds to submissions if interested For e-book originals, ms published 6-9 months after acceptance. For front list print titles, 9-15 months.

TERMS Offers advance against royalties. Guidelines online.

Ⓐ PRICE STERN SLOAN, INC.

An imprint of Penguin Random House LLC, 1745 Broadway, New York NY 10019. (212)782-9000. **Website:** www.penguinrandomhouse.com. "Price Stern Sloan publishes quirky mass market novelty series for childrens as well as licensed movie tie-in books." Price Stern Sloan only responds to submissions it's interested in publishing.

FICTION Publishes picture books and novelty/board books.

HOW TO CONTACT *Agented submissions only.*

TERMS Book catalog online.

TIPS "Price Stern Sloan publishes unique, fun titles."

Ⓐ PUFFIN BOOKS

Imprint of Penguin Random House LLC, 1745 Broadway, New York NY 10019. (212)782-2000. **Website:** www.penguinrandomhouse.com. "Puffin Books publishes high-end trade paperbacks and paperback reprints for preschool children, beginning and middle readers, and young adults." Publishes trade paperback originals and reprints. **Publishes 175-200 titles/year.**

NONFICTION "Women in history books interest us."

HOW TO CONTACT *No unsolicited mss. Agented submissions only. No unsolicited mss. Agented submissions only.* Publishes book 1 year after acceptance.

ILLUSTRATION Reviews artwork. Send color copies.

PHOTOGRAPHY Reviews photos. Send color copies.

TIPS "Our audience ranges from little children 'first books' to young adult (ages 14-16). An original idea has the best luck."

Ⓐ G.P. PUTNAM'S SONS HARDCOVER

Imprint of Penguin Random House LLC, 1745 Broadway, New York NY 10019. (212)782-9000. **Fax:** (212)366-2664. **Website:** www.penguinrandomhouse. com. Publishes hardcover originals.

HOW TO CONTACT *Agented submissions only. Agented submissions only. No unsolicited mss.*

TERMS Pays variable royalties on retail price. Pays varies advance. Request book catalog through mail order department.

Ⓐ RANDOM HOUSE CHILDREN'S BOOKS

1745 Broadway, New York NY 10019. (212)782-9000. **Website:** www.penguinrandomhouse.com. "Producing books for preschool children through young adult readers, in all formats from board to activity books to picture books and novels, Random House Children's Books brings together world-famous franchise characters, multimillion-copy series and top-flight, award-winning authors, and illustrators." Submit mss through a literary agent.

FICTION "Random House publishes a select list of first chapter books and novels, with an emphasis on fantasy and historical fiction." Chapter books, middle-grade readers, young adult.

HOW TO CONTACT *Does not accept unsolicited mss.*

ILLUSTRATION The Random House publishing divisions hire their freelancers directly. To contact the appropriate person, send a cover letter and résumé to the department head at the publisher as follows: "Department Head" (e.g., Art Director, Production Director), "Publisher/Imprint" (e.g., Knopf, Doubleday, etc.), 1745 Broadway New York, NY 10019. Works with 100-150 freelancers/year. Works on assignment only. Send query letter with résumé, tearsheets and printed samples; no originals. Samples are filed. Negotiates rights purchased. Assigns 5 freelance design jobs/year. Pays by the project.

TIPS "We look for original, unique stories. Do something that hasn't been done before."

⚫💲 RANDOM HOUSE CHILDREN'S PUBLISHERS UK

20 Vauxhall Bridge Rd., London SW1V 2SA, United Kingdom. **Website:** www.randomhousechildrens. co.uk. *Only interested in agented material.* **Publishes 250 titles/year.**

FICTION Picture books: adventure, animal, anthology, contemporary, fantasy, folktales, humor, multicultural, nature/environment, poetry, suspense/mystery. Young readers: adventure, animal, anthology, contemporary, fantasy, folktales, humor, multicultural, nature/environment, poetry, sports, suspense/mystery. Middle readers: adventure, animal, anthology, contemporary, fantasy, folktales, humor, multicultural, nature/environment, problem novels, romance, sports, suspense/mystery. Young adults: adventure, contemporary, fantasy, humor, multicultural, nature/environment, problem novels, romance, science fiction, suspense/mystery. Average word length: picture books—800; young readers—1,500-6,000; middle readers—10,000-15,000; young adults—20,000-45,000.

ILLUSTRATION Works with 50 illustrators/year. Reviews ms/illustration packages from artists. Query with samples. Contact: Margaret Hope. Samples are returned with SASE (IRC).

PHOTOGRAPHY Buys photos from freelancers. Contact: Margaret Hope. Photo captions required. Uses color or b&w prints. Submit cover letter, published samples.

TERMS Pays authors royalty. Offers advances.

TIPS "Although Random House is a big publisher, each imprint only publishes a small number of books each year. Our lists for the next few years are already full. Any book we take on from a previously unpublished author has to be truly exceptional. Manuscripts should be sent to us via literary agents."

RAZORBILL

Penguin Young Readers Group, 345 Hudson St., New York NY 10014. (212)414-3427. **E-mail:** asanchez@ penguinrandomhouse.com; bschrank@penguinrandomhouse.com; jharriton@penguinrandomhouse.com. **Website:** www.razorbillbooks.com. **Contact:** Jessica Almon, executive editor; Casey McIntyre, associate publisher; Deborah Kaplan, vice president and executive art director, Marissa Grossman; assistant editor, Tiffany Liao; associate editor. "This division of Penguin Young Readers is looking for the best and the most original of commercial contemporary fiction titles for middle grade and YA readers. A select quantity of nonfiction titles will also be considered." **Publishes 30 titles/year.**

FICTION Middle Readers: adventure, contemporary, graphic novels, fantasy, humor, problem novels. Young adults/teens: adventure, contemporary, fantasy, graphic novels, humor, multicultural, suspense, paranormal, science fiction, dystopian, literary, romance. Average word length: middle readers—40,000; young adult—60,000.

NONFICTION Middle readers and young adults/teens: concept.

HOW TO CONTACT Submit cover letter with up to 30 sample pages. Submit cover letter with up to 30 sample pages. Responds in 1-3 months. Publishes book 1-2 after acceptance.

TERMS Offers advance against royalties.

TIPS "New writers will have the best chance of acceptance and publication with original, contemporary material that boasts a distinctive voice and well-articulated world. Check out website to get a better idea of what we're looking for."

⚫ REBELIGHT PUBLISHING, INC.

23-845 Dakota St., Suite 314, Winnipeg Manitoba R2M 5M3, Canada. **Website:** www.rebelight.com. **Contact:** Editor. Rebelight Publishing is interested in "crack the spine, blow your mind" manuscripts for middle grade, young adult and new adult novels. *Only considers submissions from Canadian writers.* Publishes paperback and electronic originals. **Publishes 6-10 titles/year. 25-50% of books from first-time authors. 100% from unagented writers.**

FICTION All genres are considered, provided they are for a middle grade, young adult, or new adult audience. "Become familiar with our books. Study our website. Stick within the guidelines. Our tag line is 'crack the spine, blow your mind'—we are looking for well-written, powerful, fresh, fast-paced fiction. Keep us turning the pages. Give us something we just have to spread the word about."

HOW TO CONTACT Submit proposal package, including a synopsis and 3 sample chapters. Read guidelines carefully. Receive about 500 submissions/year. Responds in 3 months to queries and mss. Submissions accepted via email only. Publishes ms 12-18 months after acceptance.

TERMS Pays 12-22% royalties on retail price. Does not offer an advance. Catalog online or PDF available via e-mail request. Guidelines online.

TIPS "Review your manuscript for passive voice prior to submitting! (And that means get rid of it.)"

☯ RED DEER PRESS

195 Allstate Pkwy., Markham ON L3R 4TB, Canada. (905)477-9700. **Fax:** (905)477-9179. **E-mail:** rdp@ reddeerpress.com. **Website:** www.reddeerpress.com. **Contact:** Richard Dionne, publisher.

○ Red Deer Press is an award-winning publisher of children's and young adult literary titles.

FICTION Publishes young adult, adult science fiction, fantasy, and paperback originals "focusing on books by, about, or of interest to Canadians." Books: offset paper; offset printing; hardcover/perfect-bound. Average print order: 5,000. First novel print order: 2,500. Distributes titles in Canada and the US, the UK, Australia and New Zealand. Young adult (juvenile and early reader), contemporary. No romance or horror.

HOW TO CONTACT Publishes ms 18 months after acceptance.

ILLUSTRATION Works with 4-6 illustrators/year. Illustrations only: Query with samples. Responds only if interested. Samples not returned; samples filed for six months. Canadian illustrators only.

PHOTOGRAPHY Buys stock and assigns work. Model/property releases required. Submit cover letter, résumé and color promo piece.

TERMS Pays illustrators and photographers by the project or royalty (depends on the project). Originals returned to artist at job's completion. Pays 8-10% royalty. Book catalog for 9 x 12 SASE.

TIPS "We're very interested in young adult and children's fiction from Canadian writers with a proven track record (either published books or widely published in established magazines or journals) and for manuscripts with regional themes and/or a distinctive voice. We publish Canadian authors exclusively."

REDLEAF LANE

Redleaf Press, 10 Yorkton Ct., St. Paul MN 55117. (800)423-8309. **E-mail:** info@redleafpress.org. **Website:** www.redleafpress.org. **Contact:** David Heath, director. Redleaf Lane publishes engaging, high-quality picture books for children. "Our books are unique because they take place in group-care settings and reflect developmentally appropriate practices and research-based standards."

TERMS Guidelines online.

RIPPLE GROVE PRESS

P.O. Box 910, Shelburne VT 05482. **Website:** www.ripplegrovepress.com. **Contact:** Robert Broder. Ripple Grove Press is an independent, family-run children's book publisher. "We started Ripple Grove Press because we have a passion for well-told and beautifully illustrated stories for children. Our mission is to bring together great writers and talented illustrators to make the most wonderful books possible. We hope our books find their way to the cozy spot in your home." Publishes hardcover originals. **Publishes 3-6 titles/year.**

FICTION We are looking for something unique, that has not been done before; an interesting story that captures a moment with a timeless feel. We are looking for picture driven stories for children ages 2-6. Please do not send early readers, middle grade, or YA mss. No religious stories. Please do not submit your story with page breaks or illustration notes. Do not submit a story with doodles or personal photographs. Do not send your "idea" for a story, send your story in manuscript form.

HOW TO CONTACT Submit completed mss. Accepts submissions by mail and e-mail. E-mail preferred. Please submit a cover letter including a summary of your story, the age range of the story, a brief biography of yourself, and contact information. 3,000 submissions/year. "Given the volume of submissions we receive we are no longer able to individually respond to each. Please allow 5 months for us to review your submission. If we are interested in your story, you can expect to hear from us within that time. If you do not hear from us after that time, we are not interested in publishing your story. It's not you, it's us! We receive thousands of submissions and only publish a few books each year. Don't give up!" Average length of time between acceptance of a book-length ms and publication is 12-18 months.

TERMS Authors and illustrators receive royalties on net receipts. Pays negotiable advance. Catalog online. Guidelines online.

TIPS "Please read children's picture books. Please read our books to see what we look for in a story and in art. We create books that capture a moment, so that a child can create their own."

A ROARING BROOK PRESS

Macmillan Children's Publishing Group, 175 Fifth Ave., New York NY 10010. (646)307-5151. **Website:** us.macmillan.com. Roaring Brook Press is an imprint of MacMillan, a group of companies that includes Henry Holt and Farrar, Straus & Giroux. *Roaring Brook is not accepting unsolicited mss.*

FICTION Picture books, young readers, middle readers, young adults: adventure, animal, contemporary, fantasy, history, humor, multicultural, nature/environment, poetry, religion, science fiction, sports, suspense/mystery.

NONFICTION Picture books, young readers, middle readers, young adults: adventure, animal, contemporary, fantasy, history, humor, multicultural, nature/environment, poetry, religion, science fiction, sports, suspense/mystery.

HOW TO CONTACT *Not accepting unsolicited mss or queries. Not accepting unsolicited mss or queries.*

ILLUSTRATION Works with 25 illustrators/year. Illustrations only: Query with samples. Do not send original art; copies only through the mail. Samples returned with SASE.

TERMS Pays authors royalty based on retail price.

TIPS "You should find a reputable agent and have him/her submit your work."

ROSEN PUBLISHING

29 E. 21st St., New York NY 10010. (800)237-9932. **Fax:** (888)436-4643. **Website:** www.rosenpublishing. com. Artists and writers should contact customer service team through online form for information about contributing to Rosen Publishing. Rosen Publishing is an independent educational publishing house, established to serve the needs of students in grades Pre-K-12 with high interest, curriculum-correlated materials. Rosen publishes more than 700 new books each year and has a backlist of more than 7,000.

SADDLEBACK EDUCATIONAL PUBLISHING

3120-A Pullman St., Costa Mesa CA 92626. (888)735-2225. **E-mail:** contact@sdlback.com. **Website:** www. sdlback.com. Saddleback is always looking for fresh, new talent. "Please note that we primarily publish books for kids ages 12-18."

FICTION "We look for diversity for our characters and content."

HOW TO CONTACT Mail typed submission along with a query letter describing the work simply and where it fits in with other titles.

SASQUATCH BOOKS

1904 Third Ave., Suite 710, Seattle WA 98101. (206)467-4300. **Fax:** (206)467-4301. **E-mail:** custserv@sasquatchbooks.com. **Website:** www.sasquatch-books.com. "Sasquatch Books publishes books for and from the Pacific Northwest, Alaska, and California is the nation's premier regional press. Sasquatch Books' publishing program is a veritable celebration of regionally written words. Undeterred by political or geographical borders, Sasquatch defines its region as the magnificent area that stretches from the Brooks Range to the Gulf of California and from the Rocky Mountains to the Pacific Ocean. Our top-selling Best Places® travel guides serve the most popular destinations and locations of the West. We also publish widely in the areas of food and wine, gardening, nature, photography, children's books, and regional history, all facets of the literature of place. With more than 200 books brimming with insider information on the West, we offer an energetic eye on the lifestyle, landscape, and worldview of our region. Considers queries and proposals from authors and agents for new projects that fit into our West Coast regional publishing program. We can evaluate query letters, proposals, and complete mss." Publishes regional hardcover and trade paperback originals. **Publishes 30 titles/year. 20% of books from first-time authors. 75% from unagented writers.**

FICTION Young readers: adventure, animal, concept, contemporary, humor, nature/environment.

NONFICTION "We are seeking quality nonfiction works about the Pacific Northwest and West Coast regions (including Alaska to California). The literature of place includes how-to and where-to as well as history and narrative nonfiction." Picture books: activity books, animal, concept, nature/environment. "We publish a variety of nonfiction books, as well as children's books under our Little Bigfoot imprint."

HOW TO CONTACT Query first, then submit outline and sample chapters with SASE. Send submissions to The Editors. E-mailed submissions and queries are not recommended. Please include return postage if you want your materials back. Responds to queries in 3 months. Publishes book 6-9 months after acceptance.

ILLUSTRATION Accepts material from international illustrators. Works with 5 illustrators/year. Uses both color and b&w. Reviews ms/illustration packages. For ms/illustration packages: Query. Submit ms/illustration packages to The Editors. Reviews work for future assignments. If interested in illustrating future titles, query with samples. Samples returned with SASE. Samples filed.

TERMS Pays royalty on cover price. Pays wide range advance. Guidelines online.

TIPS "We sell books through a range of channels in addition to the book trade. Our primary audience consists of active, literate residents of the West Coast."

SCHOLASTIC, INC.

557 Broadway, New York NY 10012. (212)343-6100. **Website:** www.scholastic.com.

Scholastic Trade Books is an award-winning publisher of original children's books. Scholastic publishes approximately 600 new hardcover, paperback and novelty books each year. The list includes the phenomenally successful publishing properties Harry Potter, Goosebumps, Captain Underpants, Dog Man, and The Hunger Games; best-selling and award-winning authors and illustrators, including Suzanne Collins, Christopher Paul Curtis, Ann M. Martin, Dav Pilkey, J.K. Rowling, Pam Muñoz Ryan, Lauren Tarshis, Brian Selznick, David Shannon, Mark Teague, and Walter Wick, among others; as well as licensed properties such as Star Wars and Rainbow Magic.

SCHOLASTIC CHILDREN'S BOOKS UK

Euston House, 24 Eversholt St., London VI NW1 1DB, United Kingdom. **E-mail:** contactus@scholastic.co.uk. **Website:** www.scholastic.co.uk.

Scholastic UK does not accept unsolicited submissions. Unsolicited illustrations are accepted, but please do not send any original artwork as it will not be returned.

TIPS "Getting work published can be a frustrating process, and it's often best to be prepared for disappointment, but don't give up."

SCHOLASTIC LIBRARY PUBLISHING

90 Old Sherman Turnpike, Danbury CT 6816. (203)797-3500. **Fax:** (203)797-3197. **E-mail:** slpservice@scholastic.com. **Website:** www.scholastic.com/librarypublishing. **Contact:** Phil Friedman, vice president/publisher; Kate Nunn, editor-in-chief; Marie O'Neil, art director. "Scholastic Library is a leading publisher of reference, educational, and children's books. We provide parents, teachers, and librarians with the tools they need to enlighten children to the pleasure of learning and prepare them for the road ahead. Publishes informational (nonfiction) for K-12; picture books for young readers, grades 1-3." Publishes hardcover and trade paperback originals.

Accepts agented submissions only.

FICTION Publishes 1 picture book series, Rookie Readers, for grades 1-2. Does not accept unsolicited mss.

NONFICTION Photo-illustrated books for all levels: animal, arts/crafts, biography, careers, concept, geography, health, history, hobbies, how-to, multicultural, nature/environment, science, social issues, special needs, sports. Average word length: young readers—2,000; middle readers—8,000; young adult—15,000.

HOW TO CONTACT *Does not accept fiction proposals.* Query; submit outline/synopsis, resume, and/or list of publications, and writing sample. SASE required for response.

ILLUSTRATION Works with 15-20 illustrators/year. Uses color artwork and line drawings. Illustrations only: Query with samples or arrange personal portfolio review. Responds only if interested. Samples returned with SASE. Samples filed. Do not send originals. No phone or e-mail inquiries; contact only by mail.

TERMS Pays authors royalty based on net or work purchased outright. Pays illustrators at competitive rates.

SCHOLASTIC PRESS

Imprint of Scholastic, Inc., 557 Broadway, New York NY 10012. (212)343-6100. **Fax:** (212)343-4713. **Website:** www.scholastic.com. Scholastic Press publishes fresh, literary picture book fiction and nonfiction; fresh, literary nonseries or nongenre-oriented middle grade and young adult fiction. Currently emphasizing subtly handled treatments of key relationships in children's lives; unusual approaches to commonly dry subjects, such as biography, math, history, or science. De-emphasizing fairy tales (or retellings), board books, genre, or series fiction (mystery, fantasy, etc.). Publishes hardcover originals. **Publishes 60 titles/year. 1% of books from first-time authors.**

FICTION Looking for strong picture books, young chapter books, appealing middle grade novels (ages

8-11) and interesting and well-written young adult novels. Wants fresh, exciting picture books and novels—inspiring, new talent.

HOW TO CONTACT *Agented submissions only.* Agented submissions and previously published authors only. 2,500 queries received/year. Responds in 3 months to queries; 6-8 months to mss. Publishes book 2 years after acceptance.

ILLUSTRATION Works with 30 illustrators/year. Uses both b&w and color artwork. Illustrations only: Query with samples; send tearsheets. Responds only if interested. Samples returned with SASE. Original artwork returned at job's completion.

TERMS Pays royalty on retail price. Pays variable advance.

TIPS "Read *currently* published children's books. Revise, rewrite, rework and find your own voice, style and subject. We are looking for authors with a strong and unique voice who can tell a great story and have the ability to evoke genuine emotion. Children's publishers are becoming more selective, looking for irresistible talent and fairly broad appeal, yet still very willing to take risks, just to keep the game interesting."

SEEDLING CONTINENTAL PRESS

520 E. Bainbridge St., Elizabethtown PA 17022. (800)233-0759. **Website:** www.continentalpress. com. "Continental publishes educational materials for grades K-12, specializing in reading, mathematics, and test preparation materials. We are not currently accepting submissions for Seedling leveled readers or instructional materials."

FICTION Young readers: adventure, animal, folktales, humor, multicultural, nature/environment. Does not accept texts longer than 12 pages or over 300 words. Average word length: young readers—100.

NONFICTION Young readers: animal, arts/crafts, biography, careers, concept, multicultural, nature/environment, science. Does not accept texts longer than 12 pages or over 300 words. Average word length: young readers—100.

HOW TO CONTACT Submit complete ms. Responds to mss in 6 months. Publishes book 1-2 years after acceptance.

ILLUSTRATION Works with 8-10 illustrators/year. Uses color artwork only. Reviews ms/illustration packages from artists. Submit ms with dummy. Illustrations only: Color copies or line art. Responds only if interested. Samples returned with SASE only; samples filed if interested.

PHOTOGRAPHY Buys photos from freelancers. Works on assignment only. Model/property releases required. Uses color prints and 35mm transparencies. Submit cover letter and color promo piece.

TERMS Work purchased outright from authors.

TIPS "See our website. Follow writers' guidelines carefully and test your story with children and educators."

SILVER DOLPHIN BOOKS

(858)457-2500. **E-mail:** infosilverdolphin@readerlink.com. **Website:** www.silverdolphinbooks.com. Silver Dolphin Books publishes activity, novelty, and educational nonfiction books for preschoolers to 12-year-olds. Highly interactive formats such as the Field Guides and Uncover series both educate and entertain older children. "We will consider submissions only from authors with previously published works."

HOW TO CONTACT Submit cover letter with full proposal and SASE.

Ⓐ SIMON & SCHUSTER BOOKS FOR YOUNG READERS

Imprint of Simon & Schuster Children's Publishing, 1230 Avenue of the Americas, New York NY 10020. (212)698-7000. **Fax:** (212)698-2796. **Website:** www. simonsayskids.com. "Simon and Schuster Books For Young Readers is the Flagship imprint of the S&S Children's Division. We are committed to publishing a wide range of contemporary, commercial, award-winning fiction and nonfiction that spans every age of children's publishing. BFYR is constantly looking to the future, supporting our foundation authors and franchises, but always with an eye for breaking new ground with every publication. We publish high-quality fiction and nonfiction for a variety of age groups and a variety of markets. Above all, we strive to publish books that we are passionate about." *No unsolicited mss.* All unsolicited mss returned unopened. Publishes hardcover originals. **Publishes 75 titles/year.**

NONFICTION Picture books: concept. All levels: narrative, current events, biography, history. "We're looking for picture books or middle grade nonfiction that have a retail potential. No photo essays."

HOW TO CONTACT *Agented submissions only. Agented submissions only.* Publishes ms 2-4 years after acceptance.

ILLUSTRATION Works with 70 illustrators/year. Do not submit original artwork. Does not accept unsolicited or unagented illustration submissions.

TERMS Pays variable royalty on retail price. Guidelines online.

TIPS "We're looking for picture books centered on a strong, fully-developed protagonist who grows or changes during the course of the story; YA novels that are challenging and psychologically complex; also imaginative and humorous middle-grade fiction. And we want nonfiction that is as engaging as fiction. Our imprint's slogan is 'Reading You'll Remember.' We aim to publish books that are fresh, accessible and family-oriented; we want them to have an impact on the reader."

SKINNER HOUSE BOOKS

The Unitarian Universalist Association, 24 Farnsworth St., Boston MA 02210. (617)742-2100, ext. 603. **Fax:** (617)948-6466. **E-mail:** bookproposals@uua.org. **Website:** www.uua.org/publications/skinnerhouse. **Contact:** Betsy Martin. "We publish titles in Unitarian Universalist faith, liberal religion, history, biography, worship, and issues of social justice. Most of our children's titles are intended for religious education or worship use. They reflect Unitarian Universalist values. We also publish inspirational titles of poetic prose and meditations. Writers should know that Unitarian Universalism is a liberal religious denomination committed to progressive ideals. Currently emphasizing social justice concerns." Publishes trade paperback originals and reprints. **Publishes 10-20 titles/year. 30% of books from first-time authors. 100% from unagented writers.**

FICTION Only publishes fiction for children's titles for religious instruction.

NONFICTION All levels: activity books, multicultural, music/dance, nature/environment, religion.

HOW TO CONTACT Query. Query or submit proposal with cover letter, TOC, 2 sample chapters. Responds to queries in 1 month. Publishes book 1 year after acceptance.

ILLUSTRATION Works with 2 illustrators/year. Uses both color and b&w. Reviews ms/illustration packages from artists. Query. Contact: Suzanne Morgan, design director. Responds only if interested. Samples returned with SASE.

PHOTOGRAPHY Buys stock images and assigns work. Contact: Suzanne Morgan, design director. Uses inspirational types of photo's. Model/property releases required; captions required. Uses color, b&w. Submit cover letter, resume.

TERMS Book catalog for 6×9 SAE with 3 first-class stamps. Guidelines online.

TIPS "From outside our denomination, we are interested in manuscripts that will be of help or interest to liberal churches, Sunday School classes, parents, ministers, and volunteers. Inspirational/spiritual and children's titles must reflect liberal Unitarian Universalist values."

Ⓐ LIZZIE SKURNICK BOOKS

(718)797-0676. **Website:** lizzieskurnickbooks.com. Lizzie Skurnick Books, an imprint of Ig Publishing, is devoted to reissuing the very best in young adult literature, from the classics of the 1930s and 1940s to the social novels of the 1970s and 1980s. Ig does not accept unsolicited mss, either by e-mail or regular mail. If you have a ms that you would like Ig to take a look at, send a query through online contact form. If interested, they will contact. All unsolicited mss will be discarded.

SKY PONY PRESS

307 W. 36th St., 11th Floor, New York NY 10018. (212)643-6816. **Fax:** (212)643-6819. **Website:** skyponypress.com. Sky Pony Press is the children's book imprint of Skyhorse Publishing. "Following in the footsteps of our parent company, our goal is to provide books for readers with a wide variety of interests."

FICTION "We will consider picture books, early readers, midgrade novels, novelties, and informational books for all ages."

NONFICTION "Our parent company publishes many excellent books in the fields of ecology, independent living, farm living, wilderness living, recycling, and other green topics, and this will be a theme in our children's books. We are also searching for books that have strong educational themes and that help inform children of the world in which they live."

HOW TO CONTACT Submit ms or proposal. Submit proposal via e-mail.

TERMS Guidelines online.

SLEEPING BEAR PRESS

2395 South Huron Parkway #200, Ann Arbor MI 48104. (800)487-2323. **Fax:** (734)794-0004. **E-mail:** submissions@sleepingbearpress.com. **Website:** www.sleepingbearpress.com. **Contact:** Manuscript Submissions.

FICTION Picture books: adventure, animal, concept, folktales, history, multicultural, nature/environment, religion, sports. Young readers: adventure, animal, concept, folktales, history, humor, multicultural, nature/environment, religion, sports. Average word length: picture books—1,800.

HOW TO CONTACT Accepts unsolicited queries 3 times per year. See website for details. Query with sample of work (up to 15 pages) and SASE. Please address packages to Manuscript Submissions.

TERMS Book catalog available via e-mail.

SOURCEBOOKS FIRE

1935 Brookdale Rd., Suite 139, Naperville IL 60563. (630)961-3900. **Fax:** (630)961-2168. **E-mail:** submissions@sourcebooks.com. **Website:** www.sourcebooks.com. "We're actively acquiring knockout books for our YA imprint. We are particularly looking for strong writers who are excited about promoting and building their community of readers, and whose books have something fresh to offer the ever-growing young adult audience. We are not accepting any unsolicited or unagented manuscripts at this time. Unfortunately, our staff can no longer handle the large volume of manuscripts that we receive on a daily basis. We will continue to consider agented manuscripts." See website for details.

HOW TO CONTACT Query with the full ms attached in Word doc.

SPENCER HILL PRESS

27 W. 20th St., Suite 1102, New York NY 10011. **Website:** www.spencerhillpress.com. Spencer Hill Press is an independent publishing house specializing in sci-fi, urban fantasy, and paranormal romance for young adult readers. "Our books have that 'I couldn't put it down!' quality."

FICTION "We are interested in young adult, new adult, and middle grade sci-fi, psych-fi, paranormal, or urban fantasy, particularly those with a strong and interesting voice."

HOW TO CONTACT Check website for open submission periods.

TERMS Guidelines online.

SPINNER BOOKS

University Games, 2030 Harrison St., San Francisco CA 94110. (415)503-1600. **Fax:** (415)503-0085. **E-mail:** info@ugames.com. **Website:** www.ugames.com. "Spinners Books publishes books of puzzles, games and trivia."

NONFICTION Picture books: games and puzzles.

HOW TO CONTACT Query. Responds to queries in 3 months; mss in 2 months only if interested. Publishes book 6 months after acceptance.

ILLUSTRATION Only interested in agented material. Uses both color and b&w. Illustrations only: Query with samples. Responds in 3 months only if interested. Samples not returned.

SPLASHING COW BOOKS

P.O. Box 867, Manchester VT 05254. **Website:** www.splashingcowbooks.com. **Contact:** Gordon McClellan, publisher. Splashing Cow Books publishes books under three imprints: Splashing Cow (children), Blue Boot (women) and Yellow Dot (family). Publishes mass market paperback and hardcover books. We do not publish digital books. **Publishes 10 titles/year. 100% of books from first-time authors. 100% from unagented writers.**

FICTION Interested in a wide range of subject matter for children, women and families.

NONFICTION Open to any topic that would be of interest to children, women or families.

HOW TO CONTACT Please check our website for submission guidelines. We try to reply as soon as possible, but may take up to 3 months.

TERMS Pays royalties on retail price. Does not offer an advance. Catalog online. Guidelines online.

STANDARD PUBLISHING

Standex International Corp., 4050 Lee Vance View, Colorado Springs CO 80918. (800)323-7543. **Fax:** (800)323-0726. **Website:** www.standardpub.com. Publishes resources that meet church and family needs in the area of children's ministry.

TERMS Guidelines online.

STAR BRIGHT BOOKS

13 Landsdowne St., Cambridge MA 02139. (617)354-1300. **Fax:** (617)354-1399. **E-mail:** lolabush@starbrightbooks.com. **Website:** www.starbrightbooks.com. **Contact:** Lola Bush. Star Bright Books accepts unsolicited mss and art submissions. "We welcome submissions for picture books and longer works, both fiction and particularly nonfiction." Also beginner readers and chapter books. Currently seeking bios, math infused books. **Publishes 12 titles/year. 75% of books from first-time authors. 99% from unagented writers.**

NONFICTION Almost anything of interest to children. Very keen on Biographies and any thing of interest to children.

HOW TO CONTACT How things work, how things are made, nature.. history, multi-ethnic. Responds in several months. Publishes ms 1-3 years after acceptance.

TERMS Pays advance. as well as flat fee Catalog online.

STERLING PUBLISHING CO., INC.

1166 Avenue of the Americas, 17th Floor, New York NY 10036. (212)532-7160. **Website:** www.sterling-publishing.com. "Sterling publishes highly illustrated, accessible, hands-on, practical books for adults and children. Our mission is to publish high-quality books that educate, entertain, and enrich the lives of our readers." Publishes hardcover and paperback originals and reprints. **15% of books from first-time authors.**

FICTION Publishes fiction for children.

NONFICTION Proposals on subjects such as crafting, decorating, outdoor living, and photography should be sent directly to Lark Books at their Asheville, North Carolina offices. Complete guidelines can be found on the Lark site: www.larkbooks.com/submissions. Publishes nonfiction only.

HOW TO CONTACT Submit to attention of "Children's Book Editor." Submit outline, publishing history, 1 sample chapter (typed and double-spaced), SASE. "Explain your idea. Send sample illustrations where applicable. For children's books, please submit full mss. We do not accept electronic (e-mail) submissions. Be sure to include information about yourself with particular regard to your skills and qualifications in the subject area of your submission. It is helpful for us to know your publishing history—whether or not you've written other books and, if so, the name of the publisher and whether those books are currently in print."

ILLUSTRATION Works with 50 illustrators/year. Reviews ms/illustration packages from artists. Illustrations only: Send promo sheet. Contact: Karen Nelson, creative director. Responds in 6 weeks. Samples returned with SASE; samples filed.

PHOTOGRAPHY Buys stock and assigns work. Contact: Karen Nelson.

TERMS Pays royalty or work purchased outright. Offers advances (average amount: $2,000). Catalog online. Guidelines online.

TIPS "We are primarily a nonfiction activities-based publisher. We have a picture book list, but we do not publish chapter books or novels. Our list is not trend-driven. We focus on titles that will backlist well. "

STONE ARCH BOOKS

1710 Roe Crest Rd., North Mankato MN 56003. **Website:** www.stonearchbooks.com.

FICTION Imprint of Capstone Publishers.Young readers, middle readers, young adults: adventure, contemporary, fantasy, humor, light humor, mystery, science fiction, sports, suspense. Average word length: young readers—1,000-3,000; middle readers and early young adults—5,000-10,000.

HOW TO CONTACT Submit outline/synopsis and 3 sample chapters. Electronic submissions preferred. Full guidelines available on website.

ILLUSTRATION Works with 35 illustrators/year. Uses both color and b&w.

TERMS Work purchased outright from authors. Catalog online.

TIPS "A high-interest topic or activity is one that a young person would spend their free time on without adult direction or suggestion."

SUNSTONE PRESS

Box 2321, Santa Fe NM 87504. (800)243-5644. **Website:** www.sunstonepress.com. **Contact:** Submissions Editor. Sunstone's original focus was on nonfiction subjects that preserved and highlighted the richness of the American Southwest but it has expanded its view over the years to include mainstream themes and categories—both nonfiction and fiction—that have a more general appeal.

HOW TO CONTACT Query with 1 sample chapter. Query with 1 sample chapter.

TERMS Guidelines online.

Ⓐ KATHERINE TEGEN BOOKS

HarperCollins, 10 E. 53rd St., New York NY 10022. **Website:** www.harpercollins.com. Katherine Tegen Books publishes high-quality, commercial literature for children of all ages, including teens. Talented authors and illustrators who offer powerful narratives that are thought-provoking, well-written, and entertaining are the core of the Katherine Tegen Books imprint. *Katherine Tegen Books accepts agented work only.*

THUNDERSTONE BOOKS

6575 Horse Dr., Las Vegas NV 89131. **E-mail:** info@thunderstonebooks.com. **Website:** www.thunderstonebooks.com. **Contact:** Rachel Noorda, editorial director. "At ThunderStone Books, we aim to publish children's books that have an educational aspect. We are not looking for curriculum for learning certain subjects, but rather stories that encourage learning for children, whether that be learning about a new language/culture or learning more about science and math in a fun, fictional format. We want to help children to gain a love for other languages and subjects so that they are curious about the world around them. We are currently accepting fiction and nonfiction submissions. Picture books without accompanying illustration will not be accepted." Publishes hardcover, trade paperback, mass market paperback, and electronic originals. **Publishes 2-5 titles/year. 100% of books from first-time authors. 100% from unagented writers.**

FICTION Interested in multicultural stories with an emphasis on authentic culture and language (these may include mythology).

NONFICTION Looking for engaging educational materials, not a set curriculum, but books that teach as well as have some fun. Open to a variety of educational subjects, but specialty and main interest lies in language exposure/learning, science, math, and history.

HOW TO CONTACT "If you think your book is right for us, send a query letter with a word attachment of the first 50 pages to info@thunderstonebooks.com. If it is a picture book or chapter book for young readers that is shorter than 50 pages send the entire manuscript." Receives 30 queries and mss/year. Responds in 3 months. Publishes ms 6 months after acceptance.

TERMS Pays 5-15% royalties on retail price. Pays $300-1,000 advance. Catalog available for SASE. Guidelines available.

TILBURY HOUSE PUBLISHERS

WordSplice Studio, Inc., 12 Starr St., Thomaston ME 04861. (207)582-1899. **Fax:** (207)582-8772. **E-mail:** info@tilburyhouse.com. **Website:** www.tilburyhouse.com. **Publishes 24 titles/year.**

FICTION Picture books: multicultural, nature/environment. Special needs include books that teach children about and honoring diversity.

NONFICTION Regional history/maritime/nature, and children's picture books that deal with issues, such as bullying, multiculturalism, etc. science/nature.

HOW TO CONTACT Send art/photography samples and/or complete ms to info@tilburyhouse.com. Submit complete ms for picture books or outline/synopsis for longer works. Now uses online submission form. Responds to mss in 6 months. Publishes ms 1.5 years after acceptance.

PHOTOGRAPHY Buys photos from freelancers. Works on assignment only.

TERMS Pays royalty based on wholesale price. Guidelines and catalog online.

TIPS "We are always interested in stories that will encourage children to understand the natural world and the environment, as well as stories with social justice themes. We really like stories that engage children to become problem solvers as well as those that promote respect, tolerance and compassion."

TOR BOOKS

Tom Doherty Associates, 175 Fifth Ave., New York NY 10010. **Website:** www.tor-forge.com. Tor Books is the "world's largest publisher of science fiction and fantasy, with strong category publishing in historical fiction, mystery, western/Americana, thriller, YA." **Publishes 10-20 titles/year.**

HOW TO CONTACT Submit first 3 chapters, 3-10 page synopsis, dated cover letter, SASE.

TERMS Pays author royalty. Pays illustrators by the project. Book catalog available. Guidelines online.

TRIANGLE SQUARE

Seven Stories Press, 140 Watts St., New York NY 10013. (212)226-8760. **Fax:** (212)226-1411. **E-mail:** info@sevenstories.com. **Website:** https://www.sevenstories.com/imprints/triangle-square. Triangle Square is a children's and young adult imprint of Seven Story Press.

HOW TO CONTACT Send a cover letter with 2 sample chapters and SASE. Send c/o Acquisitions.

TU BOOKS

Lee & Low Books, 95 Madison Ave., Suite #1205, New York NY 10016. **Website:** www.leeandlow.com/imprints/3. **Contact:** Stacy Whitman, publisher. The Tu Books imprint spans many genres: science fiction, fantasy, mystery, contemporary, and more. We don't believe in labels or limits, just great stories. Join us at the crossroads where fantasy and real life collide. You'll be glad you did. Publishes young adult and middle grade novels and graphic novels: science fiction, fantasy, contemporary realism, mystery, historical fiction, and more, with particular interest in books with strong literary hooks. Also seeking middle grade and young adult nonfiction. **Publishes 6-8 titles/year. 40%% of books from first-time authors.**

For new writers of color, please be aware of the New Visions Award writing contest, which runs every year from May-August. Previously unpublished writers of color and Native American writers may submit their middle grade and young adult novels and graphic novels. See submission guidelines for the contest online.

FICTION At Tu Books, an imprint of Lee & Low Books, our focus is on well-told, exciting, adventurous fantasy, science fiction, and mystery novels and graphic novels starring people of color. We also selectively publish realism and nonfiction that explores the contemporary and historical experiences of people of color. We look for fantasy set in worlds inspired by non-Western folklore or culture, contemporary mysteries and fantasy set all over the world starring POC, and science fiction that centers the possibilities for people of color in the future. We welcome intersectional narratives that feature LGBTQIA and disabled POC as heroes in their own stories. We are looking specifically for stories for both middle grade (ages 8-12) and young adult (ages 12-18) readers. Occasionally a manuscript might fall between those two categories; if your manuscript does, let us know. (We are not looking for picture books, chapter books, or short stories at this time. Please do not send submissions in these categories.) Manuscript Submissions: * Please include a synopsis and first three chapters of the novel. Do not send the complete manuscript. * Manuscripts should be doubled-spaced. * Manuscripts should be accompanied by a cover letter that includes a brief biography of the author, including publishing history. The letter should also state if the manuscript is a simultaneous or an exclusive submission. * We're looking for middle grade (ages 8-12) and young adult (ages 12 and up) books. We are not looking for chapter books (ages 6 to 9) at this time. * Be sure to include full contact information on the first page of the manuscript. Page numbers and your last name/title of the book should appear on subsequent pages. Unsolicited

manuscripts should be submitted online at https://tubooks.submittable.com/submit. "Our focus is on fiction and narrative nonfiction centering people of color or Native people. We are interested in both middle grade stories for ages 8 to 12 and young adult stories for ages 12 to 18. Occasionally a manuscript might fall between these two categories; if your manuscript does, let us know. We look for fantasy set in worlds inspired by non-Western folklore or culture, contemporary mystery and fantasy set all over the world, and science fiction that centers the possibilities for people of color or Native people in the future. We also selectively publish realism and narrative nonfiction that explores the contemporary and historical experiences of people of color or Native people. We welcome intersectional narratives that feature LGBTQIA and disabled people as heroes in their own stories. Stacy Whitman and Cheryl Klein both acquire titles for Tu Books, and we ask that you identify which of them you wish to consider your submission. As loose rules of thumb, Cheryl has a more literary bent and does not acquire graphic novels, while Stacy has a more commercial focus and does not acquire narrative nonfiction." Not seeking picture books or chapter books.

NONFICTION "We selectively publish narrative nonfiction that explores the contemporary and historical experiences of people of color or Native people. We welcome intersectional narratives that feature LGBTQIA and disabled people as heroes in their own stories."

HOW TO CONTACT Submit via Submittable page. Please include a synopsis and first three chapters of the novel. Do not send the complete ms. Mss should be typed doubled-spaced. Mss should be accompanied by a cover letter that includes a brief biography of the author, including publishing history. The letter should be addressed to either Stacy Whitman or Cheryl Klein, and should also state if the ms is a simultaneous or an exclusive submission. "We're looking for middle grade (ages 8-12) and young adult (ages 12 and up) books. We are not looking for chapter books (ages 6 to 9) at this time. Be sure to include full contact information on the cover letter and first page of the manuscript. Page numbers and your last name/title of the book should appear on subsequent pages." Responds only if interested.

ILLUSTRATION Tu Books, an imprint of Lee & Low Books, is not interested in illustrations for picture books, but will consider artwork for graphic novels and for book covers and spot illustrations for novels aimed at older readers (ages 8-18). Artists are welcome to submit a sample with the address of their website portfolio following the guidelines below. Our books feature children and teens of color and include a variety of fantasy, science fiction, and mystery. We are particularly interested in hearing from illustrators whose cultural, ethnic, or racial backgrounds and experiences support their knowledge of diverse cultures. We are open to seeing work from professional illustrators and artists at all levels of experience. Illustrators who have worked in other fields and are interested in creating cover and spot art for novels are also welcome.

TERMS Advance against royalties. Pays advance. Catalog available online. Please see our full submissions guidelines online.

TUMBLEHOME LEARNING

P.O. Box 71386, Boston MA 02117. **E-mail:** info@tumblehomelearning.com. **Website:** www.tumblehomelearning.com. **Contact:** Pendred Noyce, editor. Tumblehome Learning helps kids imagine themselves as young scientists or engineers and encourages them to experience science through adventure and discovery. "We do this with exciting mystery and adventure tales as well as experiments carefully designed to engage students from ages 8 and up." Publishes hardcover, trade paperback, and electronic originals. **Publishes 8-10 titles/year. 50% of books from first-time authors. 100% from unagented writers.**

FICTION "All our fiction has science at its heart. This can include using science to solve a mystery (see *The Walking Fish* by Rachelle Burk or *Something Stinks!* by Gail Hedrick), realistic science fiction, books in our Galactic Academy of Science series, science-based adventure tales, and the occasional picture book with a science theme, such as appreciation of the stars and constellations in *Elizabeth's Constellation Quilt* by Olivia Fu. A graphic novel about science would also be welcome."

NONFICTION Rarely publishes nonfiction. Book would need to be sold to trade, not just the school market.

HOW TO CONTACT Submit completed ms electronically. Receives 20 queries and 20 mss/year. Responds in 1 month to queries and proposals, and 2 months to mss. Publishes ms 8 months after acceptance.

TERMS Pays authors 8-12% royalties on retail price. Pays $500 advance. Catalog available online. Guidelines available on request for SASE.

TIPS "Please don't submit to us if your book is not about science. We don't accept generic books about animals or books with glaring scientific errors in the first chapter. That said, the book should be fun to read and the science content can be subtle. We work closely with authors, including first-time authors, to edit and improve their books. As a small publisher, the greatest benefit we can offer is this friendly and respectful partnership with authors."

Ⓐ TYNDALE HOUSE PUBLISHERS, INC.

351 Executive Dr., Carol Stream IL 60188. (800)323-9400. **Fax:** (800)684-0247. **Website:** www.tyndale.com. "Tyndale House publishes practical, user-friendly Christian books for the home and family." Publishes hardcover and trade paperback originals and mass paperback reprints. **Publishes 15 titles/year.**

FICTION "Christian truths must be woven into the story organically. No short story collections. Youth books: character building stories with Christian perspective. Especially interested in ages 10-14. We primarily publish Christian historical romances, with occasional contemporary, suspense, or standalones."

HOW TO CONTACT *Agented submissions only. No unsolicited mss. Agented submissions only. No unsolicited mss.*

ILLUSTRATION Uses full-color for book covers, b&w or color spot illustrations for some nonfiction. Illustrations only: Query with photocopies (color or b&w) of samples, résumé.

PHOTOGRAPHY Buys photos from freelancers. Works on assignment only.

TERMS Pays negotiable royalty. Pays negotiable advance. Guidelines online.

TIPS "All accepted manuscripts will appeal to Evangelical Christian children and parents."

Ⓐ VIKING CHILDREN'S BOOKS

An imprint of Penguin Random House LLC, 1745 Broadway, New York NY 10019. **Website:** www.penguinrandomhouse.com. "Viking Children's Books is known for humorous, quirky picture books, in addition to more traditional fiction. We publish the highest quality fiction, nonfiction, and picture books for pre-schoolers through young adults." *Does not accept unsolicited submissions.* Publishes hardcover originals. **Publishes 70 titles/year.**

FICTION All levels: adventure, animal, contemporary, fantasy, history, humor, multicultural, nature/environment, poetry, problem novels, romance, science fiction, sports, suspense/mystery.

NONFICTION All levels: biography, concept, history, multicultural, music/dance, nature/environment, science, and sports.

HOW TO CONTACT *Accepts agented mss only. Agented submissions only.* Responds in 6 months. Publishes book 1-2 years after acceptance.

ILLUSTRATION Works with 30 illustrators/year. Responds to artist's queries/submissions only if interested. Samples returned with SASE only or samples filed. Originals returned at job's completion.

TERMS Pays 2-10% royalty on retail price or flat fee. Pays negotiable advance.

TIPS "No 'cartoony' or mass-market submissions for picture books."

WESTMINSTER JOHN KNOX PRESS

Flyaway Books, Division of Presbyterian Publishing Corp., 100 Witherspoon St., Louisville KY 40202. **Fax:** (502)569-5113. **E-mail:** submissions@wjkbooks.com. **Website:** www.wjkbooks.com. Flyaway Books is a new imprint for children's picture books that intentionally publishes diverse content, authors, and illustrators. See our website www.flyawaybooks.com for more details and submission instructions. "All WJK books have a religious/spiritual angle, but are written for various markets-scholarly, professional, and the general reader. Flyaway Books is a new children's picture book imprint that is intentionally diverse in content and authorship.

Email submissions only. No submissions by mail. No phone queries. We do not publish fiction, poetry, or dissertations. We do not return or respond to submissions received by mail and do not respond to unsolicited phone messages. Westminster John Knox is affiliated with the Presbyterian Church (U.S.A.). " Publishes hardcover and paperback originals. **Publishes 60 titles/year. 10% of books from first-time authors. 75% from unagented writers.**

 Looking for fresh and challenging voices writing about social justice issues (race, LGBTQI,

immigration, women's rights, economic justice, etc.) from a religious, spiritual, or humanitarian perspective. Looking for biblical studies and theology texts for graduate and seminary students and core textbooks in Bible for undergraduates. See more at www.wjkbooks.com. Flyaway Books is looking for picture books for a trade, school, and progressive church audience. See more at www.flyawaybooks.com.

NONFICTION No dissertations.

HOW TO CONTACT submissions@flyawaybooks.com Submit proposal package according to the WJK book proposal guidelines found online. 1,000 submissions received/year. Responds in 2-3 months.

ILLUSTRATION Contact submissions@flyawaybooks.com.

TERMS net royalty with advance Pays royalty on net price. Pays advance. Catalog online. Proposal guidelines online.

WHITE MANE KIDS

73 W. Burd St., Shippensburg PA 17257. (717)532-2237. **Fax:** (717)532-6110. **E-mail:** marketing@whitemane.com. **Website:** www.whitemane.com. **Contact:** Harold Collier, acquisitions editor.

FICTION Middle readers, young adults: history (primarily American Civil War). Average word length: middle readers—30,000. Does not publish picture books.

NONFICTION Middle readers, young adults: history. Average word length: middle readers—30,000. Does not publish picture books.

HOW TO CONTACT Query. Submit outline/synopsis and 2-3 sample chapters. Book proposal form on website. Responds to queries in 1 month, mss in 6-9 months. Publishes book 18 months after acceptance.

ILLUSTRATION Works with 4 illustrators/year. Illustrations used for cover art only. Responds only if interested. Samples returned with SASE.

PHOTOGRAPHY Buys stock and assigns work. Submit cover letter and portfolio.

TERMS Pays authors royalty of 7-10%. Pays illustrators and photographers by the project. Book catalog and writer's guidelines available for SASE.

TIPS "Make your work historically accurate. We are interested in historically accurate fiction for middle and young adult readers. We do *not* publish picture books. Our primary focus is the American Civil War and some America Revolution topics."

ALBERT WHITMAN & COMPANY

250 S. Northwest Hwy., Suite 320, Park Ridge IL 60068. (800)255-7675. **Fax:** (847)581-0039. **E-mail:** submissions@albertwhitman.com. **Website:** www.albertwhitman.com. Albert Whitman & Company publishes books for the trade, library, and school library market. Interested in reviewing the following types of projects: Picture book manuscripts for ages 2-8; novels and chapter books for ages 8-12; young adult novels; nonfiction for ages 3-12 and YA; art samples showing pictures of children. Best known for the classic series The Boxcar Children® Mysteries. "We are no longer reading unsolicited queries and manuscripts sent through the US mail. We now require these submissions to be sent by e-mail. You must visit our website for our guidelines, which include instructions for formatting your e-mail. E-mails that do not follow this format may not be read. We read every submission within 4 months of receipt, but we can no longer respond to every one. If you do not receive a response from us after four months, we have declined to publish your submission." Publishes in original hardcover, paperback, boardbooks. **Publishes 60 titles/year. 10% of books from first-time authors. 50% from unagented writers.**

FICTION Picture books (up to 1,000 words); middle grade (up to 35,000 words); young adult (up to 70,000 words).

NONFICTION Picture books up to 1,000 words.

HOW TO CONTACT For picture books, submit cover letter and brief description. For middle grade and young adult, send query, synopsis, and first 3 chapters. Submit cover letter, brief description.

TERMS Guidelines online.

Ⓐ PAULA WISEMAN BOOKS

1230 Sixth Ave., New York NY 10020. (212)698-7000. **Fax:** (212)698-2796. **Website:** kids.simonandschuster.com. Paula Wiseman Books is an imprint of Simon & Schuster Children's Publishing that launched in 2003. It has since gone on to publish over 70 award-winning and bestselling books, including picture books, novelty books, and novels. The imprint focuses on stories and art that are childlike, timeless, innovative, and centered in emotion. "We strive to publish books that entertain while expanding the experience of the children who read them, as well as stories that will endure, including those based in other cultures. We are committed to publishing new talent in both picture books and novels. We are actively seeking submissions from new and published authors and artists through agents and from SCBWI conferences." **Publishes 30 titles/year. 15% of books from first-time authors.**

FICTION Considers all categories. Average word length: picture books—500; others standard length.

NONFICTION Picture books: animal, biography, concept, history, nature/environment. Young readers: animal, biography, history, multicultural, nature/environment, sports. Average word length: picture books—500; others standard length.

HOW TO CONTACT Does not accept unsolicited or unagented mss.

ILLUSTRATION Works with 15 illustrators/year. Does not accept unsolicited or unagented illustrations or submissions.

Ⓐ WORDSONG

815 Church St., Honesdale PA 18431. **Fax:** (570)253-0179. **Website:** www.wordsongpoetry.com. "We publish fresh voices in contemporary poetry."

HOW TO CONTACT Responds to mss in 3 months.

ILLUSTRATION Works with 7 illustrators/year. Reviews ms/illustration packages from artists. Submit complete ms with 1 or 2 pieces of art. Illustrations only: Query with samples best suited to the art (postcard, 8½ × 11, etc.). Label package "Art Sample Submission." Responds only if interested. Samples returned with SASE.

PHOTOGRAPHY Assigns work.

TERMS Pays authors royalty or work purchased outright.

TIPS "Collections of original poetry, not anthologies, are our biggest need at this time. Keep in mind that the strongest collections demonstrate a facility with multiple poetic forms and offer fresh images and insights. Check to see what's already on the market and on our website before submitting."

WORLD BOOK, INC.

180 N. LaSalle St., Suite 900, Chicago IL 60601. (312)729-5800. **Fax:** (312)729-5600. **E-mail:** service@worldbook.com. **Website:** www.worldbook.com. World Book, Inc. (publisher of The World Book Encyclopedia), publishes reference sources and nonfiction series for children and young adults in the areas of science, mathematics, English-language skills, basic

academic and social skills, social studies, history, and health and fitness. "We publish print and non-print material appropriate for children ages 3-14. WB does not publish fiction, poetry, or wordless picture books."

NONFICTION Young readers: animal, arts/crafts, careers, concept, geography, health, reference. Middle readers: animal, arts/crafts, careers, geography, health, history, hobbies, how-to, nature/environment, reference, science. Young adult: arts/crafts, careers, geography, health, history, hobbies, how-to, nature/environment, reference, science.

HOW TO CONTACT Query. Responds to queries in 2 months. Publishes book 18 months after acceptance.

ILLUSTRATION Works with 10-30 illustrators/year. Illustrations only: Query with samples. Responds only if interested. Samples returned with SASE; samples filed "if extra copies and if interested."

PHOTOGRAPHY Buys stock and assigns work. Needs broad spectrum; editorial concept, specific natural, physical and social science spectrum. Model/property releases required; captions required. Submit cover letter, résumé, promo piece (color and b&w).

TERMS Payment negotiated on project-by-project basis.

WORLD WEAVER PRESS

Website: www.worldweaverpress.com. **Contact:** WWP Editors. World Weaver Press publishes digital and print editions of speculative fiction at various lengths for adult, young adult, and new adult audiences. "We believe in great storytelling." **Publishes 6-9 titles/year. 95% from unagented writers.**

FICTION "We believe that publishing speculative fiction isn't just printing words on the page — it's the act of weaving brand new worlds. Seeking speculative fiction in many varieties: protagonists who have strength, not fainting spells; intriguing worlds with well-developed settings; characters that are to die for (we'd rather find ourselves in love than just in lust)." Full list of interests on website. Not currently open to full-length fiction. Check anthology submission guidelines for short fiction calls.

HOW TO CONTACT Not currently open for queries. Full guidelines will be updated approximately one month before queries re-open. Frequently open for submissions for themed short story anthologies. Check website for details. Responds to query letters within 3 weeks. Responses to mss requests take longer. Publishes ms 6-24 months after acceptance.

TERMS Average royalty rate of 39% net on all editions. No advance. Catalog online. Guidelines on website.

WORTHYKIDS

Hachette Book Group, 6100 Tower Circle, Suite 210, Franklin TN 37067. (615)932-7600. **E-mail:** idealsinfo@worthypublishing.com. **Website:** www.worthypublishing.com. "WorthyKids is an imprint of Hachette Book Group and publishes 20-30 new children's titles a year, primarily for 2-8 year-olds. Our backlist includes more than 400 titles, including The Berenstain Bears, VeggieTales, and Frosty the Snowman. We publish picture books, activity books, board books, and novelty/sound books covering a wide array of topics, such as Bible stories, holidays, early learning, history, family relationships, and values. Our bestselling titles include *The Story of Christmas*, *The Story of Easter*, *The Sparkle Box*, *Seaman's Journal*, *How Do I Love You?*, *God Made You Special*, *The Berenstain Bears' Please and Thank You Book*, and *My Daddy and I*. Through our dedication to publishing high-quality and engaging books, we never forget our obligation to our littlest readers to help create those special moments with books."

FICTION WorthyKids/Ideals publishes fiction and nonfiction picture books for children ages 2 to 8. Subjects include holiday, faith/inspirational, family values, and patriotic themes; relationships and values; and general fiction. Picture book mss should be no longer than 800 words. Board book mss should be no longer than 250 words.

HOW TO CONTACT Editors will review complete mss only; please do not send query letters or proposals. Previous publications, relevant qualifications or background, and a brief synopsis of your manuscript may be included in a cover letter. Please send copies only—we cannot be responsible for an original ms. Include your name, address, and phone number or e-mail address on every page. Do not include original art or photographs. We do not accept digital submissions via e-mail or other electronic means. Send complete mss to: WorthyKids, Attn: SUBMISSIONS, 6100 Tower Circle, Suite 210, Franklin TN 37067. Due to the high volume of submissions, we are only able to respond to unsolicited manuscripts of interest to our publishing program. We cannot discuss submissions by telephone or in person and we cannot provide detailed editorial feedback.

WORTHY KIDS/IDEALS BOOKS

6100 Tower Circle, Suite 210, Franklin TN 37067. **Website:** www.idealsbooks.com.

FICTION Picture books: animal, concept, history, religion. Board books: animal, history, nature/environment, religion. Worthy Kids/Ideals publishes for ages birth to 8, no longer than 800 words.

NONFICTION Worthy Kids/Ideals publishes for ages birth to 8, no longer than 800 words.

HOW TO CONTACT Submit complete ms. Submit complete ms.

ZEST BOOKS

2443 Fillmore St., Suite 340, San Francisco CA 94115. (415)777-8654. **Fax:** (415)777-8653. **Website:** zestbooks.net. **Contact:** Dan Harmon, publishing director. Zest Books is a leader in young adult nonfiction, publishing books on entertainment, history, science, health, fashion, and lifestyle advice since 2006. Zest Books is distributed by Houghton Mifflin Harcourt.

HOW TO CONTACT Submit proposal.

ILLUSTRATION "If you are interested in becoming part of our team of illustrators, please send examples of printed work to adam@zestbooks.net."

TERMS Guidelines online.

TIPS "If you're interested in becoming a member of our author pool, send a cover letter stating why you are interested in young adult nonfiction, plus your specific areas of interest and specialties, your resume, 3-5 writing samples."

ZUMAYA PUBLICATIONS, LLC

3209 S. Interstate 35, Austin TX 78741. (512)333-4055. **Fax:** (512)276-6745. **E-mail:** business@zumayapublishing.com. **Website:** www.zumayapublications.com. **Contact:** Elizabeth K. Burton. Zumaya Publications is a digitally-based micro-press publishing mainly in on-demand trade paperback and e-book formats in an effort to reduce environmental impact. "We currently offer approximately 190 fiction titles in the mystery, SF/F, historical, romance, LGBTQ, horror, and occult genres in adult, young adult, and middle reader categories. In 2016, we plan to officially launch our graphic and illustrated novel imprint, Zumaya Fabled Ink. We publish approximately 10-15 new titles annually, at least five of which are from new authors. We do *not* publish erotica or graphic erotic romance at this time. We accept only electronic queries; all others will be discarded unread. A working knowledge of computers and relevant software is a necessity, as our production process is completely digital." Publishes trade paperback and electronic originals. **Publishes 10-15 titles/year. 5% of books from first-time authors. 100% from unagented writers.**

Zumaya was publishing diversity before it became a thing, and is always looking for fiction that presents the wonderful multiplicity of cultures in the world in ways that can lower the divisions that are too often keeping us from understanding one another. We also love books about people who are often either overlooked altogether or presented in clichéd ways. A romance between two 80-year-olds? Bring it on. A police procedural where the officers have happy home lives? Yes, please. We like the idea of having fiction that reflects the manifold realities of people everywhere, even if the world they inhabit resides only in the author's imagination.

FICTION "We are open to all genres, particularly GLBT and YA/middle grade, historical and western, New Age/inspirational (no overtly Christian materials, please), non-category romance, thrillers. We encourage people to review what we've already published so as to avoid sending us more of the same, at least, insofar as the plot is concerned. While we're always looking for good mysteries, especially cozies, mysteries with historical settings, and police procedurals, we want original concepts rather than slightly altered versions of what we've already published. We do not publish erotica or graphically erotic romance at this time." Does not want erotica, graphically erotic romance, experimental, literary (unless it fits into one of our established imprints).

NONFICTION "The easiest way to figure out what we're looking for is to look at what we've already done. Our main nonfiction interests are in collections of true ghost stories, ones that have been investigated or thoroughly documented, memoirs that address specific regions and eras from a 'normal person' viewpoint and books on the craft of writing. That doesn't mean we won't consider something else."

HOW TO CONTACT A copy of our rules of submission is posted on our website and can be downloaded. They are rules rather than guidelines and should be read carefully before submitting. It will save everyone time and frustration. Electronic query only. 1,000 queries; 50 mss requested/year. Responds in 3 months to queries and proposals; 6 months to mss. Publishes book 2 years after acceptance.

TERMS Pay 20% of net on paperbacks, net defined as cover price less printing and other associated costs; 50% of net on all e-books. Does not pay advance. Catalog online. Guidelines online. "We do not accept hard-copy queries or submissions."

TIPS "We're catering to readers who may have loved last year's best seller but not enough to want to read 10 more just like it. Have something different. If it does not fit standard pigeonholes, that's a plus. On the other hand, it has to have an audience. And if you're not prepared to work with us on promotion and marketing, particularly via social media, it would be better to look elsewhere."

MAGAZINES

//

Children's magazines are a great place for unpublished writers and illustrators to break into the market. Writers, illustrators, and photographers alike may find it easier to get book assignments if they have tearsheets from magazines. Having magazine work under your belt shows you're professional and have experience working with editors and art directors and meeting deadlines.

But magazines aren't merely a breaking-in point. Writing, illustration and photo assignments for magazines let you see your work in print quickly, and the magazine market can offer steady work and regular paychecks (a number of them pay on acceptance). Book authors and illustrators may have to wait a year or two before receiving royalties from a project. The magazine market is also a good place to use research material that didn't make it into a book project you're working on. You may even work on a magazine idea that blossoms into a book project.

TARGETING YOUR SUBMISSIONS

It's important to know the topics typically covered by different children's magazines. To help you match your work with the right publications, we've included several indexes in the back of this book. The **Subject Index** lists both book and magazine publishers by the fiction and nonfiction subjects they're seeking.

If you're a writer, use the Subject Index in conjunction with the **Age-Level Index** to narrow your list of markets. Targeting the correct age group with your submission is an important consideration. Many rejection slips are sent because a writer has not targeted a manuscript to the correct age. Few magazines are aimed at children of all ages, so you must be certain your manuscript is written for the audience level of the particular magazine you're submitting to. Magazines for children (just as magazines for adults) may also target a specific gender.

Each magazine has a different editorial philosophy. Language usage also varies between periodicals, as does the length of feature articles and the use of artwork and photographs. Reading magazines *before* submitting is the best way to determine if your material is appropriate. Also, because magazines targeted to specific age groups have a natural turnover in readership every few years, old topics (with a new slant) can be recycled.

If you're a photographer, look for listings with the **Photos** subhead. Use this strategy in combination with the subject index to narrow your search. For instance, if you photograph sports, look under Sports in the Subject Index to see which accept photos.

Because many kids' magazines sell subscriptions through direct mail or schools, you may not be able to find a particular publication at bookstores or newsstands. Check your local library, or send for copies of the magazines you're interested in. Most magazines in this section have sample copies available and will send them for a SASE or small fee.

Also, many magazines have submission guidelines and theme lists available for a SASE. Check magazines' websites, too. Many offer excerpts of articles, submission guidelines, and theme lists and will give you a feel for the editorial focus of the publication.

Watch for the Canadian ☼ and International ☻ symbols. These publications' needs and requirements may differ from their United States counterparts.

AQUILA

Studio 2 Willowfield Studios, 67a Willowfield Rd., Eastbourne BN22 8AP, England. (44)(132)343-1313. **E-mail:** editor@aquila.co.uk. **Website:** www.aquila.co.uk. *"Aquila* is an educational magazine for readers ages 8-13 including factual articles (no pop/celebrity material), arts/crafts, and puzzles." Entire publication aimed at juvenile market. Estab. 1993. Circ. 40,000.

FICTION , Young Readers: animal, contemporary, fantasy, folktales, health, history, humorous, multicultural, nature/environment, problem solving, religious, science fiction, sports, suspense/mystery. Middle Readers: animal, contemporary, fantasy, folktales, health, history, humorous, multicultural, nature/environment, problem solving, religious, romance, science fiction, sports, suspense/mystery. Length: 1,000-1,150 words. Pays £90.

NONFICTION , Young Readers: animal, arts/crafts, concept, cooking, games/puzzles, health, history, how-to, interview/profile, math, nature/environment, science, sports. Middle Readers: animal, arts/crafts, concept, cooking, games/puzzles, health, history, interview/profile, math, nature/environment, science, sports. Query. Length: 600-800 words. Pays £90.

HOW TO CONTACT Accepts queries by mail, e-mail.

TERMS Pays on publication. Sample copy: £5. Guidelines online.

TIPS "We only accept a high level of educational material for children ages 8-13 with a good standard of literacy and ability."

ASK

E-mail: ask@cricketmedia.com. **Website:** www.cricketmedia.com. *"Ask* is a magazine of arts and sciences for curious kids ages 7-10 who like to find out how the world works." Estab. 2002.

NONFICTION Needs humor, photo feature, profile. *"ASK* commissions most articles but welcomes queries from authors on all nonfiction subjects. Particularly looking for odd, unusual, and interesting stories likely to interest science-oriented kids. Writers interested in working for *ASK* should send a résumé and writing sample (including at least 1 page unedited) for consideration." Length: 200-1,600.

HOW TO CONTACT Send submissions to: Art Submissions Coordinator, Cricket Media, 70 E. Lake St., Suite 800, Chicago IL 60601. Accepts queries by e-mail, online submission form.

ILLUSTRATION Illustrations are by assignment only. PLEASE DO NOT send original artwork. Send postcards, promotional brochures, or color photocopies. Be sure that each sample is marked with your name, address, phone number, and website or blog. Art submissions will not be returned.

TERMS Rights vary. Byline given. Guidelines online.

BABYBUG

Cricket Media, Inc., 7926 Jones Branch Dr., Suite 870, McLean VA 22102. (703)885-3400. **Website:** www.cricketmedia.com. *"Babybug,* a look-and-listen magazine, presents simple poems, stories, nonfiction, and activities that reflect the natural playfulness and curiosity of babies and toddlers." Estab. 1994. Circ. 45,000.

FICTION Wants very short, clear fiction. , rhythmic, rhyming. Submit complete ms via online submissions manager. Length: up to 6 sentences. Pays up to 25¢/word.

NONFICTION , "First Concepts," a playful take on a simple idea, expressed through very short nonfiction. See recent issues for examples. Submit through online submissions manager: cricketmag.submittable.com/submit. Length: up to 6 sentences. Pays up to 25¢/word.

POETRY "We are especially interested in rhythmic and rhyming poetry. Poems may explore a baby's day, or they may be more whimsical." Submit via online submissions manager. Pays up to $3/line; $25 minimum.

HOW TO CONTACT Send submissions to: Art Submissions Coordinator, Cricket Media, 70 E. Lake St., Suite 800, Chicago IL 60601. Responds in 3-6 months to mss. Accepts queries by online submission form.

ILLUSTRATION "Please **do not** send original artwork. Send postcards, promotional brochures, or color photocopies. Be sure that each sample is marked with your name, address, phone number and website or blog. Art submissions will not be returned."

TERMS Rights vary. Byline given. Pays on publication. 50% freelance written. Guidelines online.

TIPS "We are particularly interested in mss that explore simple concepts, encourage very young children's imaginative play, and provide opportunities for adult readers and babies to interact. We welcome work that reflects diverse family cultures and traditions."

BREAD FOR GOD'S CHILDREN

Bread Ministries, INC., P.O. Box 1017, Arcadia FL 34265. (863)494-6214. **E-mail:** bread@breadminis-tries.org. **Website:** www.breadministries.org. **Contact:** Judith M. Gibbs, editor. An interdenominational Christian teaching publication published 4-6 times/year written to aid children and youth in leading a Christian life. Estab. 1972. Circ. 10,000 (U.S. and Canada).

FICTION "We are looking for writers who have a solid knowledge of Biblical principles and are concerned for the youth of today living by those principles. Stories must be well written, with the story itself getting the message across—no preaching, moralizing, or tag endings." Needs historical, religious. , Young readers, middle readers, young adult/teen: adventure, religious, problem-solving, sports. Looks for "teaching stories that portray Christian lifestyles without preaching.". Send complete ms. Length: 600-800 words for young children; 900-1,500 words for older children. Pays $40-50.

NONFICTION Needs inspirational. All levels: how-to. "We do not want anything detrimental to solid family values. Most topics will fit if they are slanted to our basic needs.". Send complete ms. Length: 500-800 words On publication

HOW TO CONTACT Responds in 6 months to mss. Publishes ms an average of 6 months after acceptance. Accepts queries by mail.

ILLUSTRATION "The only illustrations we purchase are those occasional good ones accompanying an accepted story."

TERMS Pays on publication. Pays $30-50 for stories; $30 for articles. Sample copies free for 9x12 SAE and 5 first-class stamps (for 2 copies). Buys first rights. Byline given. Publication No kill fee. 10% freelance written. Sample copy for 9x12 SAE and 5 first-class stamps. Guidelines for #10 SASE.

TIPS "We want stories or articles that illustrate overcoming obstacles by faith and living solid, Christian lives. Know our publication and what we have used in the past. Know the readership and publisher's guidelines. Stories should teach the value of morality and honesty without preaching. Edit carefully for content and grammar."

BRILLIANT STAR

1233 Central St., Evanston IL 60201. (847)853-2354. **E-mail:** brilliant@usbnc.org; hparsons@usbnc.org.

Website: www.brilliantstarmagazine.org. **Contact:** Heidi Parsons, associate editor. "*Brilliant Star* empowers kids to explore their roles as world citizens. Inspired by the principles of peace and unity in the Baha'i Faith, the magazine and website encourage readers to use their virtues to make the world a better place. Universal values of good character, such as kindness, courage, creativity, and helpfulness, are presented through fiction, nonfiction, activities, interviews, puzzles, cartoons, games, music, and art. " Estab. 1969.

FICTION "We print fiction with kids ages 10-12 as the protagonists who resolve their problems themselves." Submit complete ms. Length: 700-1,400 words. Pays 3 contributor's copies.

NONFICTION , Middle readers: arts/crafts, games/puzzles, geography, how-to, humorous, multicultural, nature/environment, religion, social issues. Query. Length: 300-700 words. Pays 3 contributor's copies.

POETRY "We only publish poetry written by children at the moment."

HOW TO CONTACT Accepts queries by e-mail.

ILLUSTRATION Reviews ms/illustration packages from artists. Illustrations only; query with samples. Contact: Aaron Kreader, graphic designer, at brilliant@usbnc.org. Responds only if interested. Samples kept on file. Credit line given.

PHOTOS Buys photos with accompanying ms only. Model/property release required; captions required. Responds only if interested.

TERMS Buys first rights and reprint rights for mss, artwork, and photos. Byline given. Guidelines available for SASE or via e-mail.

TIPS "*Brilliant Star*'s content is developed with a focus on children in their 'tween' years, ages 8-12. This is a period of intense emotional, physical, and psychological development. Familiarize yourself with the interests and challenges of children in this age range. Protagonists in our fiction are usually in the upper part of our age range: 10-12 years old. They solve their problems without adult intervention. We appreciate seeing a sense of humor but not related to bodily functions or put-downs. Keep your language and concepts age-appropriate. Use short words, sentences, and paragraphs. Activities and games may be submitted in rough or final form. Send us a description of your activity along with short, simple instructions. We avoid long, complicated activities that require adult supervision. If you think they will be helpful, please provide step-by-step rough sketches of the instructions. You may also submit photographs to illustrate the activity."

CADET QUEST MAGAZINE

Calvinist Cadet Corps, 1333 Alger St. SE, Grand Rapids MI 49507. (616)241-5616. **Fax:** (616)241-5558. **E-mail:** submissions@calvinistcadets.org. **Website:** www.calvinistcadets.org. **Contact:** Steve Bootsma, editor. Magazine published 7 times/year. *Cadet Quest Magazine* shows boys 9-14 how God is at work in their lives and in the world around them. Estab. 1958. Circ. 6,000.

FICTION "Fast-moving, entertaining stories that appeal to a boy's sense of adventure or to his sense of humor are welcomed. Stories must present Christian life realistically and help boys relate Christian values to their own lives. Stories must have action without long dialogues. Favorite topics for boys include sports and athletes, humor, adventure, mystery, friends, etc. They must also fit the theme of that issue of *Cadet Quest*. Stories with preachiness and/or clichés are not of interest to us." No fantasy, science fiction, fashion, horror, or erotica. Send complete ms by mail or e-mail (in body of e-mail; no attachments). Length: 1,000-1,300 words. Pays 5¢/word and 1 contributor's copy.

NONFICTION , informational. Send complete ms via postal mail or e-mail (in body of e-mail; no attachments). Length: up to 1,500 words. Pays 5¢/word and 1 contributor's copy.

HOW TO CONTACT Responds in 2 months to mss. Publishes ms 4-11 months after acceptance. Accepts queries by mail, e-mail.

ILLUSTRATION Works on assignment only. Reviews ms/illustration packages from artists.

PHOTOS Pays $5 each for photos purchased with ms.

TERMS Buys all rights, first rights, and second rights. Rights purchased vary with author and material. Byline given. Pays on acceptance. No kill fee. Sample copy for 9x12 SASE and $1.45 postage. Guidelines online.

TIPS "The best time to submit stories/articles is early in the year (January-April). Also remember readers are boys ages 9-14. Stories must reflect or add to the theme of the issue and be from a Christian perspective."

COLLEGEXPRESS MAGAZINE

Carnegie Communications, LLC, 2 LAN Dr., Suite 100, Westford MA 01886. **E-mail:** info@carnegiecomm.com. **Website:** www.collegexpress.com. *CollegeXpress Magazine*, formerly *Careers and Colleges*, provides juniors and seniors in high school with editorial, tips, trends, and websites to assist them in the transition to college, career, young adulthood, and independence.

○ Distributed to 10,000 high schools and reaches 1.5 million students.

TIPS "Articles with great quotes, good reporting, good writing. Rich with examples and anecdotes. Must tie in with the objective to help teenaged readers plan for their futures. Current trends, policy changes and information regarding college admissions, financial aid, and career opportunities."

CRICKET

Cricket Media, Inc., 7926 Jones Branch Dr., Suite 870, McLean VA 22102. (703)885-3400. **Website:** www.cricketmag.com. *Cricket* is a monthly literary magazine for ages 9-14. Publishes 9 issues/year. Estab. 1973. Circ. 73,000.

FICTION , realistic, contemporary, historic, humor, mysteries, fantasy, science fiction, folk/fairy tales, legend, myth. No didactic, sex, religious, or horror stories. Submit via online submissions manager (cricketmag.submittable.com). Length: 1,200-1,800 words. Pays up to 25¢/word.

NONFICTION , *Cricket* publishes thought-provoking nonfiction articles on a wide range of subjects: history, biography, true adventure, science and technology, sports, inventors and explorers, architecture and engineering, archaeology, dance, music, theater, and art. Articles should be carefully researched and include a solid bibliography that shows that research has gone beyond reviewing websites. Submit via online submissions manager (cricketmag.submittable.com). Length: 1,200-1,800 words. Pays up to 25¢/word.

POETRY *Cricket* publishes both serious and humorous poetry. Poems should be well-crafted, with precise and vivid language and images. Poems can explore a variety of themes, from nature, to family and friendships, to whatever you can imagine that will delight our readers and invite their wonder and emotional response. Length: up to 35 lines/poem. Most poems run 8-15 lines. Pays up to $3/line.

HOW TO CONTACT Send submissions to: Art Submissions Coordinator, Cricket Media, 70 E. Lake St., Suite 800, Chicago IL 60601. Responds in 3-6 months to mss. Accepts queries by online submission form.

ILLUSTRATION "Please do not send original artwork. Send postcards, promotional brochures, or color photocopies. Be sure that each sample is marked with your name, address, phone number and website or blog. Art submissions will not be returned."

TERMS Byline given. Pays on publication. Sample copy available online. Guidelines available online.

TIPS Writers: "Read copies of back issues and current issues. Adhere to specified word limits. *Please* do not query." Would currently like to see more fantasy and science fiction. Illustrators: "Send only your best work and be able to reproduce that quality in assignments. Put name and address on *all* samples. Know a publication before you submit."

CRICKET MEDIA, INC.

f/k/a Carus Publishing, Cricket Media Services, 70 East Lake St., Suite 800, Chicago IL 60601. **Website:** www.cricketmedia.com. Cricket Media® is a global education company creating high-quality print and multi-media products for children, families, mentors, teachers, and partners that improve learning opportunities for everyone. Led by our 10 award-winning children's magazines and our customizable research-tested collaborative learning platform, we are committed to creating and supporting innovative learning experiences that help children safely explore and engage with their expanding world.

HOW TO CONTACT Accepts queries by e-mail.

DEVOZINE

1908 Grand Ave., P.O. Box 340004, Nashville TN 37203-0004. **E-mail:** devozine@upperroom.org. **Website:** www.devozine.org. **Contact:** Sandy Miller, editor. *devozine,* published bimonthly, is a 64-page devotional magazine for youth (ages 14-19) and adults who care about youth. Offers meditations, scripture, prayers, poems, stories, songs, and feature articles to "aid youth in their prayer life, introduce them to spiritual disciplines, help them shape their concept of God, and encourage them in the life of discipleship."

NONFICTION Submit devotionals by mail or e-mail listed above. Submit feature article **queries** by e-mail to smiller@upperroom.org. Length: 150-250 words

for devotionals; 500-600 words for feature articles. Pays $25-100.

POETRY Considers poetry by teens. Submit by postal mail with SASE, or by e-mail. Include name, age/birth date (if younger than 25), mailing address, e-mail address, phone number, and fax number (if available). Always publishes theme issues (available for SASE or online). Indicate theme you are writing for. Length: 10-20 lines/poem. Pays $25.

HOW TO CONTACT Accepts queries by mail, e-mail, online submission form.

DRAMATICS MAGAZINE

Educational Theatre Association, 2343 Auburn Ave., Cincinnati OH 45219. (513)421-3900. **E-mail:** gbossler@schooltheatre.org. **Website:** schooltheatre.org. **Contact:** Gregory Bossler, editor-in-chief. *Dramatics* is for students (mainly high school age) and teachers of theater. The magazine wants student readers to grow as theater artists and become a more discerning and appreciative audience. Material is directed to both theater students and their teachers, with strong student slant. Tries to portray the theater community in all its diversity. Estab. 1929. Circ. 45,000.

FICTION Young adults: drama (one-act and full-length plays). "We prefer unpublished scripts that have been produced at least once." Does not want to see plays that show no understanding of the conventions of the theater. No plays for children, no Christmas or didactic "message" plays. Submit complete ms. Buys 5-9 plays/year. Emerging playwrights have better chances with résumé of credits. Length: 10 minutes to full length. Pays $100-500 for plays.

NONFICTION Needs how-to, profile. , practical articles on acting, directing, design, production, and other facets of theater; career-oriented profiles of working theater professionals. Submit complete ms. Length: 750-3,000 words. Pays $50-500 for articles.

HOW TO CONTACT Publishes ms 3 months after acceptance. Accepts queries by mail, e-mail.

ILLUSTRATION Buys 3-8 illustrations/year. Works on assignment only. Arrange portfolio review; send résumé, promo sheets, and tearsheets. Responds only if interested. Samples returned with SASE; sample not filed. Credit line given. Pays up to $300 for illustrations.

PHOTOS Buys photos with accompanying ms only. Looking for "good-quality production or candid photography to accompany article. We very occasionally publish photo essays." Model/property release and captions required. Prefers hi-res JPG files. Will consider prints or transparencies. Query with résumé of credits. Responds only if interested.

TERMS Byline given. Pays on acceptance. Sample copy available for 9x12 SAE with 4-ounce first-class postage. Guidelines available for SASE.

TIPS "Obtain our writer's guidelines and look at recent back issues. The best way to break in is to know our audience—drama students, teachers, and others interested in theater—and write for them. Writers who have some practical experience in theater, especially in technical areas, have an advantage, but we'll work with anybody who has a good idea. Some freelancers have become regular contributors."

FCA MAGAZINE

Fellowship of Christian Athletes, 8701 Leeds Rd., Kansas City MO 64129. (816)921-0909; (800)289-0909. **Fax:** (816)921-8755. **E-mail:** mag@fca.org. **Website:** www.fca.org/mag. **Contact:** Clay Meyer, editor; Matheau Casner, creative director. Published 6 times/year. *FCA Magazine*'s mission is to serve as a ministry tool of the Fellowship of Christian Athletes by informing, inspiring and involving coaches, athletes and all whom they influence, that they may make an impact for Jesus Christ. Estab. 1959. Circ. 75,000.

NONFICTION Needs inspirational, personal experience, photo feature. Articles should be accompanied by at least 3 quality photos. Query and submit via e-mail. Length: 1,000-2,000 words. Pays $150-400 for assigned and unsolicited articles.

HOW TO CONTACT Responds to queries/mss in 3 months. Publishes ms an average of 4 months after acceptance.

PHOTOS Purchases photos separately. Looking for photos of sports action. Uses color prints and high resolution electronic files of 300 dpi or higher. State availability. Reviews contact sheets. Payment based on size of photo.

TERMS Buys first rights and second serial (reprint) rights. Byline given. Pays on publication. No kill fee. 50% freelance written. Prefers to work with published/established writers, but works with a growing number of new/unpublished writers each year. Sample copy for $2 and 9x12 SASE with 3 first-class stamps. Guidelines available at www.fca.org/mag/media-kit.

TIPS "Profiles and interviews of particular interest to coed athlete, primarily high school and college age.

Our graphics and editorial content appeal to youth. The area most open to freelancers is profiles on or interviews with well-known athletes or coaches (male, female, minorities) who have been or are involved in some capacity with FCA."

THE FRIEND MAGAZINE

The Church of Jesus Christ of Latter-day Saints, 50 E. North Temple St., Salt Lake City UT 84150. (801)240-2210. **Fax:** (801)240-2270. **E-mail:** friend@ldschurch.org. **Website:** www.lds.org/friend. **Contact:** Paul B. Pieper, editor; Mark W. Robison, art director. Monthly magazine for 3-12 year olds. "The *Friend* is published by The Church of Jesus Christ of Latter-day Saints for boys and girls up to 3-12 years of age." Estab. 1971.

FICTION Wants illustrated stories and "For Little Friends" stories. See guidelines online.

NONFICTION Needs historical, humor, inspirational.

POETRY Pays $30 for poems.

ILLUSTRATION Illustrations only: Query with samples; arrange personal interview to show portfolio; provide résumé and tearsheets for files.

TERMS Available online.

FUN FOR KIDZ

P.O. Box 227, Bluffton OH 45817. 419-358-4610. **Website:** funforkidz.com. **Contact:** Marilyn Edwards, articles editor. "*Fun For Kidz* is an activity magazine that maintains the same wholesome values as the other publications. Each issue is also created around a theme. There is nothing in the magazine to make it out dated. *Fun For Kidz* offers creative activities for children with extra time on their hands." Estab. 2002.

NONFICTION , picture-oriented material, young readers, middle readers: animal, arts/crafts, cooking, games/puzzles, history, hobbies, how-to, humorous, problem-solving, sports, carpentry projects. Submit complete ms with SASE, contact info, and notation of which upcoming theme your content should be considered for. Length: 300-750 words. Pays minimum 5¢/word for articles; variable rate for games and projects, etc.

HOW TO CONTACT Accepts queries by mail.

ILLUSTRATION Works on assignment mostly. "We are anxious to find artists capable of illustrating stories and features. Our inside art is pen and ink." Query with samples. Samples kept on file. Pays $35 for full page and $25 for partial page.

PHOTOS "We use a number of b&w photos inside the magazine; most support the articles used." Photos should be in color. Pays $5 per photo.

TERMS Buys first North American serial rights. Byline given. Pays on acceptance. Sample copy: $6 in U.S., $9 in Canada, and $12.25 internationally. Guidelines online.

TIPS "Our point of view is that every child deserves the right to be a child for a number of years before he or she becomes a young adult. As a result, *Fun for Kidz* looks for activities that deal with timeless topics, such as pets, nature, hobbies, science, games, sports, careers, simple cooking, and anything else likely to interest a child."

GIRLS' LIFE

3 S. Frederick St., Suite 806, Baltimore MD 21202. (410)426-9600. **Fax:** (866)793-1531. **Website:** www.girlslife.com. **Contact:** Karen Bokram, founding editor and publisher; Kelsey Haywood, senior editor; Chun Kim, art director. Bimonthly magazine covering girls ages 9-15. Estab. 1994. Circ. 2.16 million.

FICTION "We accept short fiction. They should be stand-alone stories and are generally 2,500-3,500 words." Needs short stories.

NONFICTION Needs book excerpts, essays, general interest, how-to, humor, inspirational, interview, new product, travel. Query by mail with published clips. Submit complete ms on spec only. "Features and articles should speak to young women ages 10-15 looking for new ideas about relationships, family, friends, school, etc. with fresh, savvy advice. Front-of-the-book columns and quizzes are a good place to start." Length: 700-2,000 words. Pays $350/regular column; $500/feature.

HOW TO CONTACT Editorial lead time 4 months. Responds in 1 month to queries. Publishes an average of 3 months after acceptance. Accepts queries by mail, e-mail.

PHOTOS State availability with submission if applicable. Reviews contact sheets, negatives, transparencies. Negotiates payment individually. Captions, identification of subjects, model releases required. State availability. Captions, identification of subjects, model releases required. Reviews contact sheets, negatives, transparencies. Negotiates payment individually.

TERMS Buys all rights. Byline given. Pays on publication. Sample copy for $5 or online. Guidelines online.

TIPS "Send thought-out queries with published writing samples and detailed résumé. Have fresh ideas and a voice that speaks to our audience—not down to them. And check out a copy of the magazine or visit girlslife.com before submitting."

GREEN TEACHER

Green Teacher, 95 Robert St., Toronto ON M5S 2K5, Canada. (416)960-1244. **Fax:** (416)925-3474. **E-mail:** tim@greenteacher.com; info@greenteacher.com. **Website:** www.greenteacher.com. **Contact:** Tim Grant, co-editor; Amy Stubbs, editorial assistant. "We're a nonprofit organization dedicated to helping educators, both inside and outside of schools, promote environmental awareness among young people aged 6-19." Estab. 1991. Circ. 15,000.

NONFICTION , multicultural, nature, environment. Query. Submit one-page summary or outline. Length: 1,500-3,500 words.

HOW TO CONTACT Responds to queries in 1 week. Publishes ms 8 months after acceptance. Accepts queries by mail, e-mail.

ILLUSTRATION Buys 3 illustrations/issue from freelancers; 10 illustrations/year from freelancers. B&w artwork only. Works on assignment only. Reviews ms/illustration packages from artists. Query with samples; tearsheets. Responds only if interested. Samples not returned. Samples filed. Credit line given.

PHOTOS Purchases photos both separately and with accompanying mss. "Activity photos, environmental photos." Query with samples. Responds only of interested.

HIGHLIGHTS FOR CHILDREN

803 Church St., Honesdale PA 18431. (570)253-1080. **Fax:** (570)251-7847. **E-mail:** eds@highlights.com (Do not send submissions to this address.). **Website:** www.highlights.com. **Contact:** Christine French Cully, editor-in-chief. Monthly magazine for children ages 6-12. "This book of wholesome fun is dedicated to helping children grow in basic skills and knowledge, in creativeness, in ability to think and reason, in sensitivity to others, in high ideals, and worthy ways of living—for children are the world's most important people." We publish stories and articles for beginning and advanced readers. Up to 400 words for beginning readers, up to 750 words for advanced readers. Guidelines updated regularly at Highlights.submittable.com. Estab. 1946. Circ. Approximately 1 million.

FICTION Stories appealing to girls and boys ages 6-12. Vivid, full of action. Engaging plot, strong characterization, lively language. Prefers stories in which a child protagonist solves a dilemma through his or her own resources. No stories glorifying war, crime or violence. See Highlights.submittable.com. Up to 475 words for beginning readers. Up to 750 words for advanced readers. Pays $175 and up.

NONFICTION See guidelines online. Up to 400 words for beginning readers. Up to 750 words for advanced readers. Pays $175 and up for articles; pays $40 and up for crafts, activities, and puzzles.

POETRY See Highlights.submittable.com. No previously published poetry. Buys all rights. 16 lines maximum. Pays $50 and up.

HOW TO CONTACT Responds in 2 months. Accepts queries by online submission form.

TERMS Buys all rights. Byline given. Pays on acceptance. 70% freelance written. Guidelines online.

TIPS "We update our guidelines and current needs regularly at Highlights.submittable.com. Read several recent issues of the magazine before submitting. In addition to fiction, nonfiction, and poetry, we purchase crafts, puzzles, and activities that will stimulate children mentally and creatively. We judge each submission on its own merits. Expert reviews and complete bibliography are required for nonfiction. Include special qualifications, if any, of author. Speak to today's kids. Avoid didactic, overt messages. Even though our general principles haven't changed over the years, we are contemporary in our approach to issues."

HUNGER MOUNTAIN

Vermont College of Fine Arts, 36 College St., Montpelier VT 05602. (802)828-8517. **E-mail:** hungermtn@vcfa.edu. **Website:** www.hungermtn.org. "We accept picture book, middle grade, YA, and YA crossover work (text only—for now). We're looking for polished pieces that entertain, that show the range of adolescent experience, and that are compelling, creative, and will appeal to the devoted followers of the kid-lit craft, as well as the child inside us all." Editor: Erin Stalcup. **Contact:** Cameron Finch, managing editor. Annual perfect-bound journal covering high-quality fiction, poetry, creative nonfiction, craft essays, writing for children, and artwork. Four contests held annually, one in each genre. Accepts high-quality work from unknown, emerging, or successful writers. Publishing fiction, creative nonfiction, poetry, and young adult & children's writing. Four writing contests annually. *Hunger Mountain* is a print and online journal of the arts. The print journal is about 200 pages, 7x9, professionally printed, perfect-bound, with full-bleed color artwork on cover. Press run is 1,000. Over 10,000 visits online monthly. Uses online submissions manager (Submittable). Member: CLMP. Estab. 2002. Circ. 1,000.

FICTION "We look for work that is beautifully crafted and tells a good story, with characters that are alive and kicking, storylines that stay with us long after we've finished reading, and sentences that slay us with their precision." Needs experimental, humorous, novel excerpts, short stories, slice-of-life vignettes. No genre fiction, meaning science fiction, fantasy, horror, detective, erotic, etc. Submit ms using online submissions manager: https://hungermtn.submittable.com/submit. Length: up to 10,000 words. Pays $50 for general fiction.

NONFICTION , "We welcome an array of traditional and experimental work, including, but not limited to, personal, lyrical, and meditative essays, memoirs, collages, rants, and humor. The only requirements are recognition of truth, a unique voice with a firm command of language, and an engaging story with multiple pressure points.". Submit complete ms using online submissions manager at Submittable. Length: up to 10,000 words. Pays $50 for general fiction or creative nonfiction, for both children's lit and general adult lit.

POETRY Submit 1-5 poems at a time. "We are looking for truly original poems that run the aesthetic gamut: lively engagement with language in the act of pursuit. Some poems remind us in a fresh way of our own best thoughts; some poems bring us to a place beyond language for which there aren't quite words; some poems take us on a complicated language ride that is, itself, its own aim. Complex poem-architectures thrill us and still-points in the turning world do, too. Send us the best of what you have." Submit using online submissions manager. No light verse, humor/quirky/catchy verse, greeting card verse. Pays $25 for poetry up to 2 poems (plus $5/poem for additional poems).

HOW TO CONTACT Responds in 4-6 months to mss. Publishes ms an average of 1 year after acceptance. Accepts queries by online submission form.

PHOTOS Send photos.

TERMS Buys first worldwide serial rights. Byline given. Pays on publication. No kill fee. Single issue: $12; subscription: $18 for 2 issues/2 years; back issue: $8. Checks payable to Vermont College of Fine Arts, or purchase online. Guidelines online.

TIPS "Mss must be typed, prose double-spaced. Poets submit poems as one document. No multiple genre submissions. Fresh viewpoints and human interest are very important, as is originality and diversity. We are committed to publishing an outstanding journal of the arts. Do not send entire novels, mss, or short story collections. Do not send previously published work."

IMAGINATION CAFÉ

Imagination Café, P.O. Box 1536, Valparaiso IN 46384. (219)510-4467. **E-mail:** editor@imagination-cafe.com. **Website:** www.imagination-cafe.com. **Contact:** Rosanne Tolin, contact. "*Imagination Café* is dedicated to empowering kids and tweens by encouraging curiosity in the world around them, as well as exploration of their talents and aspirations. *Imagination Café*'s mission is to offer children tools to discover their passions by providing them with reliable information, resources and safe opportunities for self-expression." Estab. 2006.

NONFICTION Manuscripts are preferred over queries. Varies. Under 1,000 words.

HOW TO CONTACT Accepts queries by e-mail.

JACK AND JILL

U.S. Kids, P.O. Box 88928, Indianapolis IN 46208. (317)634-1100. **E-mail:** jackandjill@uskidsmags.com. **Website:** www.uskidsmags.com. Bimonthly magazine published for children ages 6-12. *Jack and Jill* is an award-winning magazine for children ages 6-12. It promotes the healthy educational and creative growth of children through interactive activities and articles. The pages are designed to spark a child's curiosity in a wide range of topics through articles, games, and activities. Inside you will find: current real-world topics in articles in stories; challenging puzzles and games; and interactive entertainment through experimental crafts and recipes. Please do not send artwork. "We prefer to work with professional illustrators of our own choosing. Write entertaining and imaginative stories for kids, not just about them. Writers should understand what is funny to kids, what's important to them, what excites them. Don't write from an adult 'kids are so cute' perspective. We're also looking for

health and healthful lifestyle stories and articles, but don't be preachy." Estab. 1938. Circ. 40,000.

FICTION Submit complete ms via postal mail; no e-mail submissions. The tone of the stories should be fun and engaging. Stories should hook readers right from the get-go and pull them through the story. Humor is very important! Dialogue should be witty instead of just furthering the plot. The story should convey some kind of positive message. Possible themes could include self-reliance, being kind to others, appreciating other cultures, and so on. There are a million positive messages, so get creative! Kids can see preachy coming from a mile away, though, so please focus on telling a good story over teaching a lesson. The message—if there is one—should come organically from the story and not feel tacked on. Length: 600-800 words. Pays $25 minimum.

NONFICTION Submit complete ms via postal mail; no e-mail submissions. Queries not accepted. We are especially interested in features or Q&As with regular kids (or groups of kids) in the *Jack and Jill* age group who are engaged in unusual, challenging, or interesting activities. No celebrity pieces, please. Length: up to 700 words. Pays $25 minimum.

POETRY Submit via postal mail; no e-mail submissions. Wants light-hearted poetry appropriate for the age group. Mss must be typewritten with poet's contact information in upper-right corner of each poem's page. SASE required. Length: up to 30 lines/poem. Pays $25-50.

HOW TO CONTACT Responds to mss in 3 months. Publishes ms an average of 8 months after acceptance. Accepts queries by mail.

TERMS Buys all rights. Byline given. Pays on publication. 50% freelance written. Guidelines online.

TIPS "We are constantly looking for new writers who can tell good stories with interesting slants—stories that are not full of outdated and time-worn expressions. We like to see stories about kids who are smart and capable but not sarcastic or smug. Problem-solving skills, personal responsibility, and integrity are good topics for us. Obtain current issues of the magazine and study them to determine our present needs and editorial style."

KEYS FOR KIDS DEVOTIONAL

Keys for Kids Ministries, PO Box 1001, Grand Rapids MI 49501. **E-mail:** editorial@keysforkids.org. **Website:** www.keysforkids.org. **Contact:** Courtney Lasater, editor. Quarterly devotional featuring stories and Scripture verses for children ages 6-12 that help kids dig into God's Word and apply it to their lives. Please put your name and contact information on the first page of your submission. "We prefer to receive submissions via our website." Story length is typically 340-375 words. To see full guidelines or submit a story, please go to www.keysforkids.org/writersguidelines. Estab. 1982. Circ. 60,000 print (not including digital circulation).

FICTION Need short contemporary stories with spiritual applications for kids. Please suggest a key verse and an appropriate Scripture passage, generally 3-10 verses, to reinforce the theme of your story. (See guidelines for more details on our devotional format.) Length: Up to 375 words. Pays $30.

HOW TO CONTACT Editorial lead time 6-8 months. Responds in 2-4 months. Typically publishes stories 6-9 months after acceptance. Accepts queries by e-mail, online submission form.

TERMS Buys all rights. Byline given. Pays on acceptance. 95% freelance. Sample copy online. Guidelines online.

TIPS "We love devotional stories that use an everyday object/situation to illustrate a spiritual truth (especially in a fresh, unique way) with characters that pull the reader into the story."

LEADING EDGE MAGAZINE

Brigham Young University, 4087 JKB, Provo UT 84602. **E-mail:** editor@leadingedgemagazine.com; fiction@leadingedgemagazine.com; art@leadingedgemagazine.com; poetry@leadingedgemagazine.com; nonfiction@leadingedgemagazine.com. **Website:** www.leadingedgemagazine.com. **Contact:** Abigail Miner, editor-in-chief. Semiannual magazine covering science fiction and fantasy. "*Leading Edge* is a magazine dedicated to new and upcoming talent in the fields of science fiction, fantasy, and horror. We strive to encourage developing and established talent and provide high-quality speculative fiction to our readers." Does not accept mss with sex, excessive violence, or profanity. Accepts unsolicited submissions. Estab. 1981. Circ. 200.

FICTION Needs fantasy, horror, science fiction. Send complete ms with cover letter and SASE. Include estimated word count. Length: up to 15,000 words. Pays 1¢/word; $50 maximum.

NONFICTION Needs essays, expose, interview, personal experience, reviews. Send complete ms with cover letter and SASE. Include estimated word count. Send to nonfiction@leadingedgemagazine.com. Length: up to 15,000 words. Pays 1¢/word; $50 maximum.

POETRY Publishes 2-4 poems per issue. Poetry should reflect both literary value and popular appeal and should deal with science fiction- or fantasy-related themes. Cover letter is preferred. Include name, address, phone number, length of poem, title, and type of poem at the top of each page. Please include SASE with every submission. Pays $10 for first 4 pages; $1.50/each subsequent page.

HOW TO CONTACT Responds within 12 months to mss. Publishes ms an average of 2-4 months after acceptance. Accepts queries by mail, e-mail.

ILLUSTRATION Buys 24 illustrations/issue; 48 illustrations/year. Uses b&w artwork only. Works on assignment only. Contact: Art Director. Illustrations only: Send postcard sample with portfolio, samples, URL. Responds only if interested. Samples filed. Credit line given.

TERMS Buys first North American serial rights. Byline given. Pays on publication. No kill fee. 90% freelance written. Single copy: $6.99. "We no longer provide subscriptions, but *Leading Edge* is now available on Amazon Kindle, as well as print-on-demand." Guidelines online.

TIPS "Buy a sample issue to know what is currently selling in our magazine. Also, make sure to follow the writer's guidelines when submitting."

THE LOUISVILLE REVIEW

Spalding University, 851 S. Fourth St., Louisville KY 40203. (502)873-4398. **E-mail:** louisvillereview@spalding.edu. **Website:** www.louisvillereview.org. **Contact:** Ellyn Lichvar, managing editor. *The Louisville Review*, published twice/year, prints poetry, fiction, nonfiction, and drama. Has a section devoted to poetry by writers under age 18 (grades K-12) called "The Children's Corner." *The Louisville Review* is 150 pages, digest-sized, flat-spined. Receives about 700 submissions/year, accepts about 10%. Estab. 1976.

FICTION Needs novel excerpts, short stories. Submit complete ms by mail or online submissions manager. Also publishes plays. No word limit, but prefers shorter pieces. Pays contributor's copies.

NONFICTION Needs essays. Submit via online submissions manager. No word limit, but prefers shorter pieces. Pays contributor's copies.

MAGAZINES

POETRY Accepts submissions via online manager; please see website for more information. "Poetry by children must include permission of parent to publish if accepted. Address those submissions to 'The Children's Corner.'" Reads submissions year round. Has published poetry by Wendy Bishop, Gary Fincke, Michael Burkard, and Sandra Kohler. Pays contributor's copies.

HOW TO CONTACT Responds in 3-6 months to mss. Accepts queries by e-mail.

TERMS Sample copy: $5. Single copy: $8. Subscription: $14/year, $27/2 years, $40/3 years (foreign subscribers add $6/year for s&h). Guidelines online.

MAGIC DRAGON

Association for Encouragement of Children's Creativity, P.O. Box 687, Webster NY 14580. **Website:** www.magicdragonmagazine.com. **Contact:** Patricia A. Roesch. Quarterly magazine publishes children's writing and art (no photography). "All work is created by children age 12 and younger (elementary school grades). We consider stories, poems, and artwork. Queries, writing, and art accepted by USPS mail and by e-mail.". Non-profit, educational magazine. Estab. 2005. Circ. 3,500.

○ Magic Dragon exists solely to encourage creative expression in young children and to support the arts in education.

FICTION Needs adventure, fantasy, historical, humorous. Submit complete ms. Pays 1 contributor's copy.

NONFICTION Needs essays, humor, inspirational, personal experience. Send complete ms. Length: up to 250 words. Pays 1 contributor's copy.

POETRY Length: up to 30 lines/poem. Pays 1 contributor's copy.

HOW TO CONTACT Editorial lead time 3-6 months. Time between acceptance and publication varies. Accepts queries by mail, e-mail.

TERMS No rights purchased. Byline given. Pays contributor's copy on publication. No kill fee. No freelance. Sample: $4. Guidelines online.

TIPS "Artists: Include an SASE with adequate postage with all original artwork. If it's a copy, make sure the colors and copy are the same and the lines are clear. Include an explanation of how you created the art (crayon, watercolor, paper sculpture, etc.)."

NATIONAL GEOGRAPHIC KIDS

National Geographic Society, 1145 17th St. NW, Washington DC 20036. **E-mail:** ashaw@ngs.org. **Website:** www.kids.nationalgeographic.com. **Contact:** Michelle Tyler, editorial assistant. Magazine published 10 times/year. "It's our mission to find fresh ways to entertain children while educating and exciting them about their world." Estab. 1975. Circ. 1.3 million.

○ "We do not want poetry, sports, fiction, or story ideas that are too young—our audience is between ages 6-14."

NONFICTION Needs general interest, humor, interview, technical. Query with published clips and résumé. Length: 100-1,000 words. Pays $1/word for assigned articles.

HOW TO CONTACT Editorial lead time 6+ months. Publishes ms an average of 6 months after acceptance. Accepts queries by mail.

PHOTOS State availability. Captions, identification of subjects, model releases required. Reviews contact sheets, negatives, transparencies, prints. Negotiates payment individually.

TERMS Buys all rights. Makes work-for-hire assignments. Byline given. Pays on acceptance. Offers 10% kill fee. 70% freelance written. Sample copy for #10 SASE. Guidelines online.

TIPS "Submit relevant clips. Writers must have demonstrated experience writing for kids. Read the magazine before submitting."

POCKETS

The Upper Room, P.O. Box 340004, Nashville TN 37203. (615)340-7333. **E-mail:** pockets@upperroom. org. **Website:** pockets.upperroom.org. **Contact:** Lynn W. Gilliam, editor. Magazine published 11 times/year. "*Pockets* is a Christian devotional magazine for children ages 6-12. All submissions should address the broad theme of the magazine. Each issue is built around a theme with material which can be used by children in a variety of ways. Scripture stories, fiction, poetry, prayers, art, graphics, puzzles and activities are included. Submissions do not need to be overtly religious. They should help children experience a Christian lifestyle that is not always a neatly wrapped moral package but is open to the continuing revelation of God's will. Seasonal material, both secular and liturgical, is desired." Estab. 1981.

○ Does not accept e-mail or fax submissions.

FICTION "Stories should contain lots of action, use believable dialogue, be simply written, and be relevant to the problems faced by this age group in everyday life." Submit complete ms by mail. No e-mail submissions. Length: 600-1,000 words.

NONFICTION , Picture-oriented, young readers, middle readers: cooking, games/puzzles. Submit complete ms by mail. No e-mail submissions. Length: 400-1,000 words. Pays 14¢/word.

POETRY Both seasonal and theme poems needed. Considers poetry by children. Length: up to 20 lines. Pays $25 minimum.

HOW TO CONTACT Responds in 8 weeks to mss. Publishes ms an average of 1 year after acceptance.

PHOTOS Send 4-6 close-up photos of children actively involved in peacemakers at work activities. Send photos, contact sheets, prints, or digital images. Must be 300 dpi. Pays $25/photo.

TERMS Buys first North American serial rights. Byline given. Pays on acceptance. No kill fee. 60% freelance written. Each issue reflects a specific theme. Guidelines online.

TIPS "Theme stories, role models, and retold scripture stories are most open to freelancers. Poetry is also open. It is very helpful if writers read our writers' guidelines and themes on our website."

SHINE BRIGHTLY

GEMS Girls' Clubs, 1333 Alger St., SE, Grand Rapids MI 49507. (616)241-5616. **Fax:** (616)241-5558. **E-mail:** shinebrightly@gemsgc.org. **Website:** www.gemsgc. org. **Contact:** Kelli Gilmore, managing editor. Monthly magazine from September to May with a double issue for September/October. "Our purpose is to lead girls into a living relationship with Jesus Christ and to help them see how God is at work in their lives and the world around them. Puzzles, crafts, stories, and articles for girls ages 9-14." Estab. 1970. Circ. 13,000.

FICTION Does not want "unrealistic stories and those with trite, easy endings. We are interested in manuscripts that show how real girls can change the world." Needs ethnic, historical, humorous, mystery, religious, slice-of-life vignettes. Believable only. Nothing too preachy. Submit complete ms in body of e-mail. No attachments. Length: 700-900 words. Pays up to $35, plus 2 copies.

NONFICTION Needs humor, inspirational, interview, personal experience, photo feature, religious, travel. Submit complete ms in body of e-mail. No attachments. Length: 100-800 words. Pays up to $35, plus 2 copies.

POETRY Limited need for poetry. Pays $5-15.

HOW TO CONTACT Responds in 2 months to mss. Publishes ms an average of 4 months after acceptance.

ILLUSTRATION Samples returned with SASE. Credit line given.

PHOTOS Purchased with or without ms. Appreciate multicultural subjects. Reviews 5x7 or 8x10 clear color glossy prints. Pays $25-50 on publication.

TERMS Buys first North American serial rights, buys second serial (reprint) rights, buys simultaneous rights. Byline given. Pays on publication. No kill fee. 60% freelance written. Works with new and published/established writers. Sample copy with 9x12 SASE with 3 first class stamps and $1. Guidelines online.

TIPS Writers: "Please check our website before submitting. We have a specific style and theme that deals with how girls can impact the world. The stories should be current, deal with pre-adolescent problems and joys, and help girls see God at work in their lives through humor as well as problem-solving." Prefers not to see anything on the adult level, secular material, or violence. Writers frequently oversimplify the articles and often write with a Pollyanna attitude. An author should be able to see his/her writing style as exciting and appealing to girls ages 9-14. The style can be fun, but also teach a truth. Subjects should be current and important to *SHINE brightly* readers. Use our theme update as a guide. We would like to receive material with a multicultural slant."

SKIPPING STONES

A Multicultural Literary Magazine, Skipping Stones. Inc., P.O. Box 3939, Eugene OR 97403-0939. (541)342-4956. **E-mail:** editor@skippingstones.org. **Website:** www.skippingstones.org. **Contact:** Arun Toké, editor. "*Skipping Stones* is an award-winning multicultural, nonprofit magazine designed to promote cooperation, creativity and celebration of cultural and ecological richness. We encourage submissions by children of color, minorities and under-represented populations. We want material meant for children and young adults/teenagers with multicultural or ecological awareness themes. Think, live and write as if you were a child, tween or teen. We want material that gives insight to cultural celebrations, lifestyle, customs and traditions, glimpse of daily life in other countries and cultures. Photos, songs, artwork are most welcome if they illustrate/highlight the points. Translations are invited if your submission is in a language other than English." Themes may include cultural celebrations, living abroad, challenging disability, hospitality customs of various cultures, cross-cultural understanding, African, Asian and Latin American cultures, humor, international understanding, turning points and magical moments in life, caring for the earth, spirituality, and multicultural awareness. *Skipping Stones* is magazine-sized, saddle-stapled, printed on recycled paper. Published quarterly during the school year (4 issues). Estab. 1988. Circ. 1,200 print, plus online and Web.

FICTION Middle readers, young adult/teens: contemporary, meaningful, humorous. All levels: folktales, multicultural, nature/environment. Multicultural needs include: bilingual or multilingual pieces; use of words from other languages; settings in other countries, cultures or multi-ethnic communities. Needs adventure, ethnic, historical, humorous. , multicultural, international, social issues. No suspense or romance stories. Send complete ms. Length: 1,000 words maximum. Pays 6 contributor's copies.

NONFICTION Needs essays, general interest, humor, inspirational, interview, opinion, personal experience, photo feature, travel. , All levels: animal, biography, cooking, games/puzzles, history, humorous, interview/profile, multicultural, nature/environment, creative problem-solving, religion and cultural celebrations, sports, travel, social and international awareness. Does not want to see preaching, violence or abusive language. Send complete ms. Length: 1,000 words maximum. Pays 6 contributor's copies.

POETRY Submit up to 5 poems at a time. Considers simultaneous submissions; no previously published poems. Accepts e-mail submissions. Cover letter is preferred. "Include your cultural background, experiences, and the inspiration behind your creation." Time between acceptance and publication is 6-9 months. "A piece is chosen for publication when most of the editorial staff feel good about it." Seldom comments on rejected poems. Publishes multi-theme issues. Responds in up to 4 months. Poems by youth under the age of 19 only. Length: 30 lines maximum. Pays 2 contributor's copies, offers 40% discount for more copies and subscription, if desired.

HOW TO CONTACT Editorial lead time 3-4 months. Responds only if interested. Send nonreturnable samples. Publishes ms an average of 4-8 months after acceptance. Accepts queries by mail, e-mail.

ILLUSTRATION Prefers illustrations by teenagers and young adults. Will consider all illustration packages. Manuscript/illustration packages: Query; submit complete ms with final art; submit tearsheets. Responds in 4 months. Credit line given.

PHOTOS Black & white photos preferred, but color photos with good contrast are welcome. Needs: youth 7-17, international, nature, celebrations. Send photos. Captions required. Reviews 4X6 prints, low-res JPEG files. Offers no additional payment for photos.

TERMS Buys first North American serial rights, nonexclusive reprint, and electronic rights. Byline given. No kill fee. 80% freelance written. Sample: $7. Subscription: $25. Guidelines available online or for SASE.

TIPS "Be original and innovative. Use multicultural, nature, or cross-cultural themes. Multilingual submissions are welcome."

SOUL FOUNTAIN

E-mail: soulfountain@antarcticajournal.com. **Website:** www.antarcticajournal.com/soul-fountain/. **Contact:** Tone Bellizzi, editor. *Soul Fountain* is produced by The Antarctica Journal, a not-for-profit arts project of the Hope for the Children Foundation, committed to empowering young and emerging artists of all disciplines at all levels to develop and share their talents through performance, collaboration, and networking. Digitally publishes poetry, art, photography, short fiction, and essays on the antarcticajournal.com website. Open to all. Publishes quality submitted work, and specializes in emerging voices. Favors visionary, challenging, and consciousness-expanding material. Estab. 1997.

FICTION Submit by e-mail only. No cover letters, please.

POETRY Submit 2-3 poems by e-mail. No cover letters, please. Does not want poems about pets, nature, romantic love, or the occult. Sex and violence themes not welcome. Welcomes poetry by teens.

HOW TO CONTACT Accepts queries by e-mail.
TERMS Guidelines online.

STONE SOUP

E-mail: editor@stonesoup.com. **Website:** https://stonesoup.com. **Contact:** Emma Wood, editor.

Monthly magazine of writing and art by children age 13 and under, including fiction, poetry, book reviews, and art. We also publish blogposts by children and educators on our site. *Stone Soup,* a digital magazine with a print annual, is the national magazine of writing and art by kids, founded in 1973. Receives 5,000 poetry submissions/year, accepts about 20. Subscription: $24.99/year (U.S.). "We have a preference for writing and art based on real-life experiences; no formula stories or poems. We only publish writing by children up to (and including) age 13. We do not publish writing by adults." Subscription includes downloadable PDFs of each issue as well as more than 15 years of back issues online. Estab. 1973.

FICTION Needs adventure, ethnic, experimental, fantasy, historical, humorous, mystery, science fiction, slice-of-life vignettes, suspense. "We do not like assignments or formula stories of any kind." We only accept submissions through Submittable. Length: 150-5,000 words. Pays in a contributor copy of the print annual (a collection of the years' issues along with bonus content from the blogs), discounted subscription rates.

NONFICTION Needs historical, humor, memoir, personal experience, reviews. Submit complete ms; no SASE. Pays in a contributor copy of the print annual (a collection of the years' issues along with bonus content from the blogs), discounted subscription rates.

POETRY Prefers free verse but considers all kinds. Pays in a contributor copy of the print annual (a collection of the years' issues along with bonus content from the blogs), discounted subscription rates.

HOW TO CONTACT Publishes ms an average of 4 months after acceptance. Accepts queries by e-mail.

TERMS Buys all rights. Pays on publication. 100% freelance written. View a PDF sample copy online. Guidelines online.

TIPS "All writing we publish is by young people ages 13 and under. We do not publish any writing by adults. We can't emphasize enough how important it is to read a couple of issues of the magazine. You can read stories and poems from past issues online. We have a strong preference for writing on subjects that mean a lot to the author. If you feel strongly about something that happened to you or something you observed, use that feeling as the basis for your story or poem. Stories should have good descriptions, realistic dialogue, and a point to make. In a poem, each word must be chosen carefully. Your poem should present a view of your subject, and a way of using words that are special and all your own."

YOUNG RIDER

2030 Main Street, Irvine CA 92614. (949) 855-8822. **Fax:** (949) 855-3045. **E-mail:** yreditor@i5publishing.com. **Website:** www.youngrider.com. "*Young Rider* magazine teaches young people, in an easy-to-read and entertaining way, how to look after their horses properly, and how to improve their riding skills safely."

FICTION, young adults: adventure, animal, horses. "We would prefer funny stories, with a bit of conflict, which will appeal to the 13-year-old age group. They should be written in the third person, and about kids.". Query. Length: 800-1,000 words. Pays $150.

NONFICTION, young adults: animal, careers, famous equestrians, health (horse), horse celebrities, riding. Query with published clips. Length: 800-1,000 words. Pays $200/story.

PHOTOS Buys photos with accompanying ms only. Uses high-res digital images only—in focus, good light. Model/property release required; captions required.

TERMS Byline given. Guidelines available online.

TIPS "Fiction must be in third person. Read magazine before sending in a query. No 'true story from when I was a youngster.' No moralistic stories. Fiction must be up-to-date and humorous, teen-oriented. No practical or how-to articles—all done in-house."

AGENTS & ART REPS

///

This section features listings of literary agents and art reps who either specialize in, or represent a good percentage of, children's writers and/or illustrators. While there are a number of children's publishers who are open to nonagented material, using the services of an agent or rep can be beneficial to a writer or artist. Agents and reps can get your work seen by editors and art directors more quickly. They are familiar with the market and have insights into which editors and art directors would be most interested in your work. Also, they negotiate contracts and will likely be able to get you a better deal than you could get on your own.

Agents and reps make their income by taking a percentage of what writers and illustrators receive from publishers. The standard percentage for agents is 10 to 15 percent; art reps generally take 25 to 30 percent. We have not included any agencies in this section that charge reading fees.

WHAT TO SEND

When putting together a package for an agent or rep, follow the guidelines given in their listings. Most agents open to submissions prefer initially to receive a query letter describing your work. For novels and longer works, some agents ask for an outline and a number of sample chapters, but you should send these only if you're asked to do so. Never fax or e-mail query letters or sample chapters to agents without their permission. Just as with publishers, agents receive a large volume of submissions. It may take them a long time to reply, so you may want to query several agents at one time. It's best, however, to have a complete manuscript considered by only one agent at a time. Always include a self-addressed, stamped envelope (SASE).

For initial contact with art reps, send a brief query letter and self-promo pieces, following the guidelines given in the listings. If you don't have a flier or brochure, send photocopies. Always include a SASE.

For those who both write and illustrate, some agents listed will consider the work of author/illustrators. Read through the listings for details.

As you consider approaching agents and reps with your work, keep in mind that they are very choosy about whom represent. Your work must be high quality and presented professionally to make an impression on them. For more information on approaching agents and additional listings, see *Guide to Literary Agents* (Writer's Digest Books).

AN ORGANIZATION FOR AGENTS

In some listings of agents you'll see references to AAR (The Association of Authors' Representatives). This organization requires its members to meet an established list of professional standards and code of ethics.

The objectives of AAR include keeping agents informed about conditions in publishing and related fields; encouraging cooperation among literary organizations; and assisting agents in representing their author-clients' interests. Officially, members are prohibited from directly or indirectly charging reading fees. They offer writers a list of member agents on their website. They also offer a list of recommended questions an author should ask an agent and other FAQs, all found on their website. They can be contacted at AAR, 676A 9th Ave. #312, New York NY 10036. (212)840-5777. E-mail: aarinc@mindspring.com. Website: www.aar-online.org.

A+B WORKS

Website: http://aplusbworks.com. **Contact:** Amy Jameson, Brandon Jameson.

HANDLES Does not want women's fiction, or any other books for adults.

HOW TO CONTACT Query via online submission form. "Due to the high volume of queries we receive, we can't guarantee a response." Accepts simultaneous submissions.

ADAMS LITERARY

7845 Colony Rd., C4 #215, Charlotte NC 28226. (704)542-1440. **Fax:** (704)542-1450. **E-mail:** info@ adamsliterary.com. **Website:** www.adamsliterary. com. **Contact:** Tracey Adams, Josh Adams. Adams Literary is a full-service literary agency exclusively representing children's and young adult authors and artists.

○ Temporarily closed to submissions.

HANDLES Represents "the finest children's book and young adult authors and artists."

RECENT SALES *The Cruelty*, by Scott Bergstrom (Feiwel & Friends); *The Little Fire Truck*, by Margery Cuyler (Christy Ottaviano); *Unearthed*, by Amie Kaufman and Meagan Spooner (Disney-Hyperion); *A Handful of Stars*, by Cynthia Lord (Scholastic); *Under Their Skin*, by Margaret Peterson Haddix (Simon & Schuster); *The Secret Horses of Briar Hill*, by Megan Shepherd (Delacorte); *The Secret Subway*, by Shana Corey (Schwartz & Wade); *Impyrium*, by Henry Neff (HarperCollins).

TERMS Agent receives 15% commission on domestic sales; 20% on foreign sales. Offers written contract.

HOW TO CONTACT Submit through online form on website only. Send e-mail if that is not operating correctly. All submissions and queries should first be made through the online form on website. Will not review—and will promptly recycle—any unsolicited submissions or queries received by mail. Before submitting work for consideration, review complete guidelines online, as the agency sometimes shuts off to new submissions. Accepts simultaneous submissions. "While we have an established client list, we do seek new talent—and we accept submissions from both published and aspiring authors and artists."

TIPS "Guidelines are posted (and frequently updated) on our website."

AEVITAS CREATIVE MANAGEMENT

19 W. 21st St., Suite 501, New York NY 10010. (212)765-6900. **Website:** aevitascreative.com.

HOW TO CONTACT Find specific agents on the Aevitas website to see their specific interests and guidelines. Accepts simultaneous submissions.

ALIVE LITERARY AGENCY

7680 Goddard St., Suite 200, Colorado Springs CO 80920. (719)260-7080. **Fax:** (719)260-8223. **E-mail:** info@aliveliterary.com. **Website:** www.aliveliterary.com. **Contact:** Rick Christian. Alive is the largest, most influential literary agency for inspirational content and authors.

HANDLES This agency specializes in inspirational fiction, Christian living, how-to, and commercial nonfiction. Actively seeking inspirational, literary and mainstream fiction, inspirational nonfiction, and work from authors with established track records and platforms. Does not want to receive poetry, scripts, or dark themes.

TERMS Agent receives 15% commission on domestic sales. Offers written contract; two-month notice must be given to terminate contract.

HOW TO CONTACT "Because all our agents have full client loads, they are only considering queries from authors referred by clients and close contacts. Please refer to our guidelines at http://aliveliterary. com/submissions. Authors referred by an Alive client or close contact are invited to send proposals to submissions@aliveliterary.com." Your submission should include a referral (name of referring Alive client or close contact in the e-mail subject line. In the e-mail, please describe your personal or professional connection to the referring individual), a brief author biography (including recent speaking engagements, media appearances, social media platform statistics, and sales histories of your books), a synopsis of the work for which you are seeking agency representation (including the target audience, sales and marketing hooks, and comparable titles on the market), and the first 3 chapters of your manuscript. Alive will respond to queries meeting the above guidelines within 8-10 weeks.

TIPS Rewrite and polish until the words on the page shine. Endorsements, a solid platform, and great connections may help, provided you can write with power and passion. Hone your craft by networking with publishing professionals, joining critique groups, and attending writers' conferences.

AZANTIAN LITERARY AGENCY

Website: www.azantianlitagency.com. **Contact:** Jennifer Azantian.

HANDLES Stories that explore meaningful human interactions against fantastic backdrops, underrepresented voices, obscure retold fairy tales, quirky middle grade, modernized mythologies, psychological horror, literary science fiction, historical fantasy, magical realism, internally consistent epic fantasy, and spooky stories for younger readers.

HOW TO CONTACT During open submission windows only: send your query letter, 1-2 page synopsis, and first 10 pages through the form on ALA's website. Accepts simultaneous submissions.

THE BENT AGENCY

19 W. 21st St., #201, New York NY 10010. **E-mail:** info@thebentagency.com. **Website:** www.thebentagency.com. **Contact:** Jenny Bent.

RECENT SALES *Caraval*, by Stephanie Garber (Flatiron); *Rebel of the Sands*, by Alwyn Hamilton (Viking Children's/Penguin BFYR); *The Square Root of Summer*, by Harriet Reuter Hapgood (Roaring Brook/Macmillan); *Dirty Money*, by Lisa Renee Jones (Simon & Schuster); *True North*, by Liora Blake (Pocket Star).

HOW TO CONTACT "Tell us briefly who you are, what your book is, and why you're the one to write it. Then include the first 10 pages of your material in the body of your e-mail. We respond to all queries; please resend your query if you haven't had a response within 4 weeks." Accepts simultaneous submissions.

DAVID BLACK LITERARY AGENCY

335 Adams St., Suite 2707, Brooklyn NY 11201. (718)-852-5500. **Fax:** (718)852-5539. **Website:** www.davidblackagency.com. **Contact:** David Black, owner.

RECENT SALES Some of the agency's best-selling authors include: Erik Larson, Stuart Scott, Jeff Hobbs, Mitch Albom, Gregg Olsen, Jim Abbott, and John Bacon.

HOW TO CONTACT "To query an individual agent, please follow the specific query guidelines outlined in the agent's profile on our website. Not all agents are currently accepting unsolicited queries. To query the agency, please send a 1-2 page query letter describing your book, and include information about any pre-

viously published works, your audience, and your platform." Do not e-mail your query unless an agent specifically asks for an e-mail. Accepts simultaneous submissions.

BOND LITERARY AGENCY

4340 E. Kentucky Ave., Suite 471, Denver CO , 80246. (303)781-9305. **Website:** www.bondliteraryagency.com. **Contact:** Sandra Bond. The agency is small, with a select list of writers. Represents adult and young adult fiction, both literary and commercial, including mysteries and women's fiction. Nonfiction interests include narrative, history, science and business.

HANDLES Agency does not represent romance, poetry, young reader chapter books, children's picture books, or screenplays.

RECENT SALES *The Past is Never*, by Tiffany Quay Tyson; *Cold Case: Billy the Kid*, by W.C. Jameson; *Women in Film: The Truth and the Timeline*, by Jill S. Tietjen and Barbara Bridges; Books 7 & 8 in the Hiro Hattori Mystery Series, by Susan Spann.

TERMS No Fees

HOW TO CONTACT Please submit query by e-mail (absolutely no attachments unless requested). No unsolicited mss. "They will let you know if they are interested in seeing more material. No phone calls, please." Accepts simultaneous submissions.

THE BOOK GROUP

20 W. 20th St., Suite 601, New York NY 10011. (212)803-3360. **Website:** www.thebookgroup.com. The Book Group is a full service literary agency located in the heart of Manhattan. Launched in 2015 by publishing industry veterans. The Book Group shares a singular passion: to seek out and cultivate writers, and to serve as their champions throughout their careers. "We represent a wide range of distinguished authors, including critically acclaimed and bestselling novelists, celebrated writers of children's literature, and award-winning historians, food writers, memoirists and journalists."

HANDLES Please do not send poetry or screenplays.

RECENT SALES *This Is Not Over*, by Holly Brown; *Perfect Little World*, by Kevin Wilson; *City of Saints & Thieves*, by Natalie C. Anderson; *The Runaway Midwife*, by Patricia Harman; *Always*, by Sarah Jio; *The Young Widower's Handbook*, by Tom McAllister.

HOW TO CONTACT Send a query letter and 10 sample pages to submissions@thebookgroup.com, with the first and last name of the agent you are querying in the subject line. All material must be in the body of the e-mail, as the agents do not open attachments. "If we are interested in reading more, we will get in touch with you as soon as possible." Accepts simultaneous submissions.

BOOKSTOP LITERARY AGENCY

(925)254-2664. **E-mail:** info@bookstopliterary.com. **Website:** www.bookstopliterary.com. BookStop Literary represents authors and illustrators of books for children and young adults. "We do not accept submissions for the general adult audience. Please visit our website and look at agent bios for more information."

HANDLES Please see agent bios on our website for more information. Special interest in Hispanic, Asian-American, African-American, and multicultural writers. Also seeking quirky picture books; clever adventure/mystery novels; eye-opening nonfiction; heartfelt middle-grade; unusual teen romance; and illustrators. Please see agent bios on our website for more information.

TERMS Agent receives 15% commission on domestic sales. Offers written contract, binding for 1 year.

HOW TO CONTACT Please look at agent bios on our website and address your submission to the appropriate agent. E-mail all submissions to: info@bookstopliterary.com with the following information in subject line: "submission," writer's last name, and title of project. Fiction: paste a cover letter and the first 10 pages of ms into body of e-mail. For picture books, paste the entire text into the body of the e-mail. Nonfiction: paste a cover letter, proposal, and two sample chapters into the body of your e-mail. Illustrators: send a cover letter and a link to your online portfolio. Do not send original artwork. Accepts simultaneous submissions.

BRADFORD LITERARY AGENCY

5694 Mission Center Rd., #347, San Diego CA 92108. (619)521-1201. **E-mail:** queries@bradfordlit.com. **Website:** www.bradfordlit.com. **Contact:** Laura Bradford, Natalie Lakosil, Sarah LaPolla, Kari Sutherland, Jennifer Chen Tran. "The Bradford Literary Agency is a boutique agency which offers a full range of representation services to authors who are both published and pre-published. Our mission at the Bradford Literary Agency is to form true partnerships with our clients and build long-term relationships that extend from writing the first draft through the length of the author's career."

○ Picture book writers should contact Natalie only at this agency.

HANDLES Laura Bradford does not want to receive poetry, screenplays, short stories, westerns, horror, new age, religion, crafts, cookbooks, gift books. Natalie Lakosil does not want to receive inspirational novels, memoir, romantic suspense, adult thrillers, poetry, screenplays. Sarah LaPolla does not want to receive nonfiction, picture books, inspirational/spiritual novels, romance, or erotica. Kari Sutherland does not want to receive horror, romance, erotica, memoir, adult sci-fi/fantasy, thrillers, cookbooks, business, spiritual/religious, poetry, or screenplays. Jennifer Chen Tran does not want to receive picture books, sci-fi/fantasy, urban fantasy, westerns, erotica, poetry, or screenplays.

RECENT SALES Sold 80 titles in the last year, including Vox by Christina Dalcher (Berkley); *The Last 8*, by Laura Pohl (Sourcebooks Fire); *You'll Miss Me When I'm Gone*, by Rachel Solomon (Simon Pulse); *Monday's Not Coming*, by Tiffany Jackson (Harper Collins); *Where She Fell*, by Kaitlin Ward (Adaptive); *Into the Nightfell Wood*, by Kristin Bailey (Katherine Tegen Books); *Yasmin the Explorer*, by Saadia Faruqi (Capstone); *Fix Her Up*, by Tessa Bailey (Entangled); *The Protector*, by HelenKay Dimon (Avon); *The Spitfire Girls*, by Soraya Lane (St. Martins); *Highland Wrath*, by Madeline Martin (Diversion); *Everybody's Favorite Book*, by Mike Allegra (Macmillan); *The Hook Up*, by Erin McCarthy (PRH); *Next Girl to Die*, by Dea Poirier (Thomas & Mercer); *The Fearless King*, by Katee Robert (Entangled); *Noble Hops*, by Layla Reyne (Carina Press); *The Rogue on Fifth Avenue*, by Joanna Shupe (Kensington).

TERMS Agent receives 15% commission on domestic sales; 25% commission on foreign sales. Offers written contract. Charges for extra copies of books for foreign submissions.

HOW TO CONTACT Accepts e-mail queries only; For submissions to Laura Bradford, send to queries@bradfordlit.com. For submissions to Natalie Lakosil, use the form listed on the website under the "How to Submit" page. For submissions to Sarah LaPolla, send to sarah@bradfordlit.com. For submissions to Kari Sutherland, send to kari@bradfordlit.com. For submissions to Jennifer Chen Tran, send to jen@bradfordlit.com. The entire submission must appear in the body of the e-mail and not as an attachment. The subject line should begin as follows: "QUERY: (the title of the ms or any short message that is important should follow)." For fiction: e-mail a query letter along with the first chapter of ms and a synopsis. Include the genre and word count in your query letter. Nonfiction: e-mail full nonfiction proposal including a query letter and a sample chapter. Accepts simultaneous submissions. Obtains most new clients through queries.

BRANDT & HOCHMAN LITERARY AGENTS, INC.

1501 Broadway, Suite 2310, New York NY 10036. (212)840-5760. **Fax:** (212)840-5776. **Website:** brandthochman.com. **Contact:** Gail Hochman or individual agent best suited for the submission.

HANDLES No screenplays or textbooks.

RECENT SALES This agency sells 40-60 new titles each year. A full list of their hundreds of clients is on the agency website.

TERMS Agent receives 15% commission on domestic sales; 20% commission on foreign sales.

HOW TO CONTACT "We accept queries by e-mail and regular mail; however, we cannot guarantee a response to e-mailed queries. For queries via regular mail, be sure to include a SASE for our reply. Query letters should be no more than 2 pages and should include a convincing overview of the book project and information about the author and his or her writing credits. Address queries to the specific Brandt & Hochman agent whom you would like to consider your work. Agent e-mail addresses and query preferences may be found at the end of each agent profile on the 'Agents' page of our website." Accepts simultaneous submissions. Obtains most new clients through recommendations from others.

TIPS "Write a letter which will give the agent a sense of you as a professional writer—your long-term interests as well as a short description of the work at hand."

M. COURTNEY BRIGGS

Derrick & Briggs, LLP, 100 N. Broadway Ave., 28th Floor, Oklahoma City OK 73102. (405)235-1900. **Fax:** (405)235-1995. **Website:** www.derrickandbriggs.com. "M. Courtney Briggs combines her primary work as a literary agent with expertise in intellectual property, entertainment law, and estates and probate. Her clients are published authors (exclusively), theatres, and a variety of small businesses and individuals."

CURTIS BROWN, LTD.

10 Astor Place, New York NY 10003. (212)473-5400. **Fax:** (212)598-0917. **Website:** www.curtisbrown.com. Represents authors and illustrators of fiction, nonfiction, picture books, middle grade, young adult.

RECENT SALES This agency prefers not to share information on specific sales.

TERMS Agent receives 15% commission on domestic sales; 20% on foreign sales. Offers written contract. 75-day notice must be given to terminate contract. Charges for some postage (overseas, etc.).

HOW TO CONTACT Please refer to the "Agents" page on the website for each agent's submission guidelines. Accepts simultaneous submissions. Obtains most new clients through recommendations from others, solicitations, conferences.

BROWNE & MILLER LITERARY ASSOCIATES

(312)922-3063. **Website:** www.browneandmiller.com. **Contact:** Danielle Egan-Miller, president. Founded in 1971 by Jane Jordan Browne, Browne & Miller Literary Associates is the Chicago area's leading literary agency. Danielle Egan-Miller became president of the agency in 2003 and has since sold hundreds of books with a heavy emphasis on commercial adult fiction. Her roster includes several New York Times best-selling authors and numerous prize- and award-winning writers. She loves a great story well told.

"We are very hands-on and do much editorial work with our clients. We are passionate about the books we represent and work hard to help clients reach their publishing goals."

HANDLES Browne & Miller is most interested in literary and commercial fiction, women's fiction, women's historical fiction, literary-leaning crime fiction, dark suspense/domestic suspense,romance, and Christian/inspirational fiction by established authors, and a wide range of platform-driven nonfiction by nationally-recognized author-experts. "We do not represent children's books of any kind or Young Adult; no adult Memoirs; we do not represent horror, science fiction or fantasy, short stories, poetry, original screenplays,or articles."

HOW TO CONTACT Query via e-mail only; no attachments. Do not send unsolicited mss. Accepts simultaneous submissions.

ANDREA BROWN LITERARY AGENCY, INC.

E-mail: andrea@andreabrownlit.com; caryn@andreabrownlit.com; lauraqueries@gmail.com; jennifer@

andreabrownlit.com; kelly@andreabrownlit.com; jennL@andreabrownlit.com; jamie@andreabrownlit.com; jmatt@andreabrownlit.com; kathleen@andreabrownlit.com; lara@andreabrownlit.com; soloway@andreabrownlit.com. **Website:** www.andreabrownlit.com. The Andrea Brown Literary Agency was founded in August 1981 and has offices in the San Francisco Bay area, San Diego, Los Angeles, New York, and Chicago. "Our agency specializes in children's literature. We work to bring to light the voices and perspectives of new writers as well as to nurture and develop the careers of experienced authors. Our goal, whether seeking to secure a publishing contract for a first book or a fiftieth book, is to make sure that clients are not only published, but published well. Our philosophy is to remain a 'small' agency at heart. We invest a great deal of personal care and attention in each project, and we are hands-on in all aspects of our interactions with clients. We work closely with clients in an editorial capacity and we devise a strategy at every stage of the writing process that will enable us to find the best publisher for each book. In doing so, we think about both short term and long term goals for our clients, always keeping the trajectory of a successful career in mind. Our agents have backgrounds in New York publishing, editing, academia, business, teaching, writing and film, and one of our strengths as an agency is that we work collaboratively. Our clients have the benefit not only of their individual agent's expertise but of the combined experience and vision of the group. As a West Coast based agency, we follow a tradition of West Coast innovation in our passion for discovering new voices, in our efforts to make New York publishing more inclusive of voices from other parts of the country, and in our attempt to see publishing trends that result from this broader perspective. We combine this approach with access, standing, and visibility in the publishing community at large. Our agents make regular trips to New York, attend industry conventions, and participate as faculty at writers' conferences all over the country. We ensure a high profile for our clients and actively keep our fingers on the pulse of publishing."

🗨 Writers should review the large agent bios on the agency website to determine which agent to contact. Please choose only one agent to query. The agents share queries, so a no from one agent at Andrea Brown Literary Agency is a no from all. *E-queries only.*

HANDLES Specializes in all kinds of children's books—illustrators and authors. 98% juvenile books. Considers: nonfiction, fiction, picture books, young adult.

RECENT SALES Supriya Kelkar's middle grade novel *American As Paneer Pie* to Jennifer Ung at Aladdin, at auction, for publication in summer 2020, by Kathleen Rushall. Mitali Perkins's *You Bring the Distant Near* , sold at auction, in a two-book deal, to Grace Kendall at Farrar, Straus Children's, by Laura Rennert. Cynthia Salaysay's YA novel *Private Lessons* to Kate Fletcher at Candlewick, for publication in the spring of 2020, by Jennifer March Soloway. Dev Petty's picture book text, *The Bear Must Go On* to Talia Benamy at Philomel, for publication in spring 2021, by Jennifer Rofe. Carrie Pearson's nonfiction picture book text *A Girl Who Leaped, A Woman Who Soared* to Simon Boughton at Norton Children's by Kelly Sonnack. K. C. Johnson's YA novel, *This is My America* to Chelsea Eberly at Random House Children's in a two-book deal by Jennifer March Soloway. Nancy Castaldo's nonfiction YA, *Water* to Elise Howard at Algonquin Young Readers, by Jennifer Laughran. Kate Messner's picture book text, *The Next President* to Melissa Manlove at Chronicle Children's, in a two book deal, by Jennifer Laughran. Amber Lough's YA novel, *Summer of War* to Amy Fitzgerald at Carolrhoda Lab by Laura Rennert and Jennifer March Soloway. Andrea Zimmerman and David Clemesha's picture book *All Buckled Up!* to Jeffrey Salane at Little Simon, in a two-book deal by Jamie Weiss Chilton. Jennifer Berne's picture book *Dinosaur Doomsday* to Melissa Manlove at Chronicle Children's by Caryn Wiseman. Tami Charles's *Serena Williams—G.O.A.T.: Making the Case for the Greatest of All Time*, a sports biography of Serena Williams to Ada Zhang at Sterling Children's by Lara Perkins. Katy Loutzenhiser's YA *If You're Out There* to Donna Bray at Balzer & Bray in a two-book deal by Jennifer Mattson. Barry Eisler's *The Killer Collective,* as well as a John Rain prequel, and two more in the Livia Lone series, to Gracie Doyle at Thomas & Mercer, in a major deal by Laura Rennert. Maggie Stiefvater's The Raven Cycle series to Universal Cable Productions by Laura Rennert.

TERMS Agent receives 15% commission on domestic sales; 25% commission on foreign sales. Offers written contract. No fees.

HOW TO CONTACT Writers should review the large agent bios on the agency website to determine which agent to contact. Please choose only one agent to query. The agents share queries, so a no from one agent at Andrea Brown Literary Agency is a no from all. (Note that Jennifer Laughran and Kelly Sonnack only receive queries by querymanager - please visit the agency's website for information.) For picture books, submit a query letter and complete ms in the body of the e-mail. For fiction, submit a query letter and the first 10 pages in the body of the e-mail. For nonfiction, submit proposal, first 10 pages in the body of the e-mail. Illustrators: submit a query letter and 2-3 illustration samples (in jpeg format), link to online portfolio, and text of picture book, if applicable. "We only accept queries via e-mail. No attachments, with the exception of jpeg illustrations from illustrators." Visit the agents' bios on our website and choose only one agent to whom you will submit your e-query. Send a short e-mail query letter to that agent with "QUERY" in the subject field. Accepts simultaneous submissions. Obtains most new clients through queries and referrals from editors, clients and agents. Check website for guidelines and information.

KIMBERLEY CAMERON & ASSOCIATES

1550 Tiburon Blvd., #704, Tiburon CA 94920. (415)789-9191. **Website:** www.kimberleycameron. com. **Contact:** Kimberley Cameron.

HANDLES "We are looking for a unique and heartfelt voice that conveys a universal truth."

HOW TO CONTACT Prefers queries via site. Only query one agent at a time. For fiction, fill out the correct submissions form for the individual agent and attach the first 50 pages and a synopsis (if requested) as a Word doc or PDF. For nonfiction, fill out the correct submission form of the individual agent and attach a full book proposal and sample chapters (includes the first chapter and no more than 50 pages) as a Word doc or PDF. Accepts simultaneous submissions. Obtains new clients through recommendations from others, solicitations.

CHALBERG & SUSSMAN

115 W. 29th St., Third Floor, New York NY 10001. (917)261-7550. **Website:** www.chalbergsussman.com.
RECENT SALES The agents' sales and clients are listed on their website.
HOW TO CONTACT To query by e-mail, please contact one of the following: terra@chalbergsuss-

man.com, rachel@chalbergsussman.com, nicole@ chalbergsussman.com, lana@chalbergsussman.com. To query by regular mail, please address your letter to one agent and include SASE. Accepts simultaneous submissions.

THE CHUDNEY AGENCY

72 N. State Rd., Suite 501, Briarcliff Manor NY 10510. (914)465-5560. **E-mail:** steven@thechudneyagency. com. **Website:** www.thechudneyagency.com. **Contact:** Steven Chudney.

○ Please always check our website before you contact us for the latest information about our agnecy and what we're looking for.

HANDLES "At this time, the agency is only looking for author/illustrators (one individual), who can both write and illustrate wonderful picture books. The author/illustrator must really know and understand the prime audience's needs and wants of the child reader! Storylines should be engaging, fun, with a hint of a life lessons and cannot be longer than 800 words. With chapter books, middle grade and teen novels, I'm primarily looking for quality, contemporary literary fiction: novels that are exceedingly well-written, with wonderful settings and developed, unforgettable characters. I'm looking for historical fiction that will excite me, young readers, editors, and reviewers, and will introduce us to unique characters in settings and situations, countries, and eras we haven't encountered too often yet in children's and teen literature." Does not want most fantasy and no science fiction.

HOW TO CONTACT No snail mail submissions for fiction/novels. Queries only. Submission package info from us to follow should we be interested in your project. For children's picture books, we only want author/illustrator projects. Submit a pdf with full text and at least 5-7 full-color illustrations. Accepts simultaneous submissions.

DON CONGDON ASSOCIATES INC.

110 William St., Suite 2202, New York NY 10038. (212)645-1229. **Fax:** (212)727-2688. **E-mail:** dca@doncongdon.com. **Website:** doncongdon.com.
HANDLES Susan Ramer: "Not looking for romance, science fiction, fantasy, espionage, mysteries, politics, health/diet/fitness, self-help, or sports." Katie Kotchman: "Please do not send her screenplays or poetry."
RECENT SALES This agency represents many best-selling clients such as David Sedaris and Kathryn Stockett.

HOW TO CONTACT "For queries via e-mail, you must include the word 'query' and the agent's full name in your subject heading. Please also include your query and sample chapter in the body of the e-mail, as we do not open attachments for security reasons. Please query only one agent within the agency at a time. If you are sending your query via regular mail, please enclose a SASE for our reply. If you would like us to return your materials, please make sure your postage will cover their return." Accepts simultaneous submissions.

CORVISIERO LITERARY AGENCY

275 Madison Ave., at 40th, 14th Floor, New York NY 10016. (646)856-4032. **Fax:** (646)217-3758. **E-mail:** consult@corvisieroagency.com. **Website:** www.corvisieroagency.com. **Contact:** Marisa A. Corvisiero, Founder, Senior Agent, Attorney. "We are a boutique literary agency founded by Marisa A Corvisiero, Esq. This agency is a place where authors can find professional and experienced representation." *Does not accept unsolicited mss.*

HOW TO CONTACT Accepts submissions via QueryManager. Include query letter, 5 pages of complete and polished ms, and a 1-2 page synopsis. For nonfiction, include a proposal instead of the synopsis. Each agent profile on website has a button for direct submissions. Accepts simultaneous submissions.

D4EO LITERARY AGENCY

7 Indian Valley Rd., Weston CT 06883. (203)544-7180. **Fax:** (203)544-7160. **Website:** www.d4eoliteraryagency.com. **Contact:** Bob Diforio.

TERMS Offers written contract, binding for 2 years; automatic renewal unless 60 days notice given prior to renewal date. Charges for photocopying and submission postage.

HOW TO CONTACT Each of these agents has a different submission e-mail and different tastes regarding how they review material. See all on their individual agent pages on the agency website. Obtains most new clients through recommendations from others.

LAURA DAIL LITERARY AGENCY, INC.

121 W. 27th St., Suite 1201, New York NY 10001. (212)239-7477. **E-mail:** literary@ldlainc.com. **Website:** www.ldlainc.com.

HANDLES Specializes in women's fiction, literary fiction, young adult fiction, as well as both practical and idea-driven nonfiction. "Due to the volume of queries and mss received, we apologize for not answering every e-mail and letter. None of us handles children's picture books or chapter books. No New Age. We do not handle screenplays or poetry."

HOW TO CONTACT "If you would like, you may include a synopsis and no more than 10 pages. If you are mailing your query, please be sure to include a self-addressed, stamped envelope; without it, you may not hear back from us. To save money, time and trees, we prefer queries by e-mail to queries@ldlainc.com. We get a lot of spam and are wary of computer viruses, so please use the word 'Query' in the subject line and include your detailed materials in the body of your message, not as an attachment." Accepts simultaneous submissions.

DARHANSOFF & VERRILL LITERARY AGENTS

133 W. 72nd St., Room 304, New York NY 10023. (917)305-1300. **Website:** www.dvagency.com. "We are most interested in literary fiction, narrative nonfiction, memoir, sophisticated suspense, and both fiction and nonfiction for younger readers. Please note we do not represent theatrical plays or film scripts."

RECENT SALES A full list of clients is available on their website.

HOW TO CONTACT Send queries via e-mail. Accepts simultaneous submissions.

LIZA DAWSON ASSOCIATES

(212)465-9071. **Website:** www.lizadawsonassociates.com. **Contact:** Caitie Flum.

HANDLES Multiple agents at this agency represent young adult mss. This agency specializes in readable literary fiction, thrillers, mainstream historicals, women's fiction, young adult, middle-grade, academics, historians, journalists, and psychology.

TERMS Agent receives 15% commission on domestic sales; 20% commission on foreign sales. Offers written contract.

HOW TO CONTACT Query by e-mail only. No phone calls. Each of these agents has their own specific submission requirements, which you can find online at the agency's website. Obtains most new clients through recommendations from others, conferences, and queries.

THE JENNIFER DE CHIARA LITERARY AGENCY

299 Park Ave., 6th Floor, New York NY 10171. (212)739-0803. **E-mail:** jenndec@aol.com. **Website:** www.jdlit.com. **Contact:** Jennifer De Chiara.

TERMS Agent receives 15% commission on domestic sales. Offers written contract.

HOW TO CONTACT Each agent has their own e-mail submission address and submission instructions; check the website for the current updates, as policies do change. Accepts simultaneous submissions. Obtains most new clients through recommendations from others, conferences, query letters.

DEFIORE & COMPANY

47 E. 19th St., 3rd Floor, New York NY 10003. (212)925-7744. **Fax:** (212)925-9803. **Website:** www. defliterary.com.

HANDLES "Please be advised that we are not considering dramatic projects at this time."

TERMS Agent receives 15% commission on domestic sales; 20% commission on foreign sales. Offers written contract; 10-day notice must be given to terminate contract. Charges clients for photocopying and overnight delivery (deducted only after a sale is made).

HOW TO CONTACT Query with SASE or e-mail to submissions@defliterary.com. "Please include the word 'query' in the subject line. All attachments will be deleted; please insert all text in the body of the e-mail. For more information about our agents, their individual interests, and their query guidelines, please visit our 'About Us' page on our website." Accepts simultaneous submissions. Obtains most new clients through recommendations from others.

JOELLE DELBOURGO ASSOCIATES, INC.

101 Park St., Montclair NJ 07042. (973)773-0836. **E-mail:** joelle@delbourgo.com. **Website:** www.delbourgo.com. **Contact:** Joelle Delbourgo. "We are a boutique agency representing a wide range of nonfiction and fiction. Nonfiction: narrative, research-based and prescriptive nonfiction, including history, current affairs, education, psychology and personal development, parenting, science, business and economics, diet and nutrition, and cookbooks. Adult and young adult commercial and literary fiction, some middle grade. We do not represent plays, screenplays, poetry and picture books."

HANDLES "We are former publishers and editors with deep knowledge and an insider perspective. We have a reputation for individualized attention to clients, strategic management of authors' careers, and creating strong partnerships with publishers for our clients." We are looking for strong narrative and prescriptive nonfiction including science, history, health and medicine, business and finance, sociology, parenting, women's issues. We prefer books by credentialed experts and seasoned journalists, especially ones that are research-based. We are taking on very few memoir projects. In fiction, you can send mystery and thriller, commercial women's fiction, book club fiction and literary fiction. Do not send scripts, picture books, poetry.

RECENT SALES *The Rule of St. Benedict*, translated by Philip Freeman (St. Martins Essentials); *Holly Banks Full of Angst* & Untitled Novel 2, Julie Valerie (Lake Union); *Flat, Fluid & Fast*, Brynne S. Kennedy (McGraw-Hill); *The Dog Went Over the Mountain*, Peter Zheutlin (Pegasus), *The Remarriage Manual*, Terry Gaspard (Sounds True); *The Narcissistic Family*, Julie Hall (Da Capo Lifelong/Hachette); *Queen of the West*, Theresa Kaminski (Rowman & Littlefield); *The Wealth Creator's Playbook*, John C. Christianson (Praeger).

TERMS Agent receives 15% commission on domestic sales and 20% commission on foreign sales as well as television/film adaptation when a co-agent is involved. Offers written contract. Standard industry commissions. Charges clients for postage and photocopying.

HOW TO CONTACT E-mail queries only are accepted. Query one agent directly, not multiple agents at our agency. No attachments. Put the word "Query" in the subject line. If you have not received a response in 60 days you may consider that a pass. Do not send us copies of self-published books. Let us know if you are sending your query to us exclusively or if this is a multiple submission. For nonfiction, wait to send your query when you have a completed proposal. For fiction and memoir, embed the first 10 pages of ms into the e-mail after your query letter. Please no attachments. If we like your first pages, we may ask to see your synopsis and more manuscript. Please do not cold call us or make a follow-up call unless we call you. Accepts simultaneous submissions. Our clients come via referral, and occasionally over the transom.

TIPS "Do your homework. Do not cold call. Read and follow submission guidelines before contacting us. Do not call to find out if we received your material. No e-mail queries. Treat agents with respect, as you would any other professional, such as a doctor, lawyer or financial advisor."

SANDRA DIJKSTRA LITERARY AGENCY

1155 Camino del Mar, PMB 515, Del Mar CA 92014. **E-mail:** queries@dijkstraagency.com. **Website:** www.dijkstraagency.com. The Dijkstra Agency was established over 35 years ago and is known for guiding the careers of many best-selling fiction and non-fiction authors, including Amy Tan, Lisa See, Maxine Hong Kingston, Chitra Divakaruni, Eric Foner, Marcus Rediker, and many more. "We handle nearly all genres, except for poetry." Please see www.dijkstraagency.com for each agent's interests.

TERMS Works in conjunction with foreign and film agents. Agent receives 15% commission on domestic sales and 20% commission on foreign sales. Offers written contract. No reading fee.

HOW TO CONTACT "Please see guidelines on our website, www.dijkstraagency.com. Please note that we only accept e-mail submissions. Due to the large number of unsolicited submissions we receive, we are only able to respond those submissions in which we are interested." Accepts simultaneous submissions.

TIPS "Remember that publishing is a business. Do your research and present your project in as professional a way as possible. Only submit your work when you are confident that it is polished and ready for prime-time. Make yourself a part of the active writing community by getting stories and articles published, networking with other writers, and getting a good sense of where your work fits in the market."

DONAGHY LITERARY GROUP

(647)527-4353. **E-mail:** stacey@donaghyliterary.com. **Website:** www.donaghyliterary.com. **Contact:** Stacey Donaghy. "Donaghy Literary Group provides full-service literary representation to our clients at every stage of their writing career. Specializing in commercial fiction, we seek middle grade, young adult, new adult and adult novels."

TERMS Agent receives 15% commission on domestic sales; 20% commission on foreign sales. Offers written contract, 30-day notice must be given to terminate contract.

HOW TO CONTACT Visit agency website for "new submission guidelines" Do not e-mail agents directly. This agency only accepts submissions through the QueryManager database system. Accepts simultaneous submissions.

TIPS "Only submit to one DLG agent at a time, we work collaboratively and often share projects that may be better suited to another agent at the agency."

DUNHAM LITERARY, INC.

110 William St., Suite 2202, New York NY 10038. (212)929-0994. **Website:** www.dunhamlit.com. **Contact:** Jennie Dunham.

HANDLES "We are not looking for Westerns, genre romance, poetry, or individual short stories."

RECENT SALES *The Bad Kitty Series*, by Nick Bruel (Macmillan); *Believe*, by Robert Sabuda (Candlewick); *The Gollywhopper Games* and Sequels, by Jody Feldman (HarperCollins); *Foolish Hearts*, by Emma Mills (Macmillan); *Gangster Nation*, by Tod Goldberg (Counterpoint); *A Shadow All of Light*, by Fred Chappell (Tor).

TERMS Agent receives 15% commission on domestic sales; 20% commission on foreign sales.

HOW TO CONTACT E-mail queries preferred, with all materials pasted in the body of the e-mail. Attachments will not be opened. Paper queries are also accepted. Please include a SASE for response and return of materials. Please include the first 5 pages with the query. Accepts simultaneous submissions. Obtains most new clients through recommendations from others.

DUNOW, CARLSON, & LERNER AGENCY

27 W. 20th St., Suite 1107, New York NY 10011. (212)645-7606. **E-mail:** mail@dclagency.com. **Website:** www.dclagency.com.

RECENT SALES A full list of agency clients is on the website.

HOW TO CONTACT Query via snail mail with SASE, or by e-mail. E-mail preferred, paste 10 sample pages below query letter. No attachments. Will respond only if interested. Accepts simultaneous submissions.

DYSTEL, GODERICH & BOURRET LLC

1 Union Square W., Suite 904, New York NY 10003. (212)627-9100. **Fax:** (212)627-9313. **Website:** www.dystel.com.

○ "We have discovered many of our most talented authors in the slush pile. We read everything that is sent to us, whether we decide to represent it or not." Dystel & Goderich Literary Management recently acquired the client list of Bedford Book Works.

HANDLES "We are actively seeking fiction for all ages, in all genres." No plays, screenplays, or poetry.

TERMS Agent receives 15% commission on domestic sales; 19% commission on foreign sales. Offers written contract.

HOW TO CONTACT Query via e-mail and put "Query" in the subject line. "Synopses, outlines or sample chapters (say, one chapter or the first 25 pages of your manuscript) should either be included below the cover letter or attached as a separate document. We won't open attachments if they come with a blank e-mail." Accepts simultaneous submissions. Obtains most new clients through recommendations from others, solicitations, conferences.

TIPS "DGLM prides itself on being a full-service agency. We're involved in every stage of the publishing process, from offering substantial editing on mss and proposals, to coming up with book ideas for authors looking for their next project, negotiating contracts and collecting monies for our clients. We follow a book from its inception through its sale to a publisher, its publication, and beyond. Our commitment to our writers does not, by any means, end when we have collected our commission. This is one of the many things that makes us unique in a very competitive business."

EDEN STREET LITERARY

P.O. Box 30, Billings NY 12510. **E-mail:** info@edenstreetlit.com. **Website:** www.edenstreetlit.com. **Contact:** Liza Voges. Eden Street represents over 40 authors and author-illustrators of books for young readers from pre-school through young adult. Their books have won numerous awards over the past 30 years. Eden Street prides themselves on tailoring services to each client's goals, working in tandem with them to achieve literary, critical, and commercial success. Welcomes the opportunity to work with additional authors and illustrators. This agency gives priority to members of SCBWI.

○ At the moment we are not open to submisssions except to those attending SCBWI conferences where we are attending, if that should change, we will update the information.

RECENT SALES *Dream Dog*, by Lou Berger; *Biscuit Loves the Library*, by Alyssa Capucilli; *The Scraps Book*, by Lois Ehlert; *Two Bunny Buddies*, by Kathryn O. Galbraith; *Between Two Worlds*, by Katherine Kirkpatrick.

HOW TO CONTACT E-mail a picture book ms or dummy; a synopsis and 3 chapters of a MG or YA novel; a proposal and 3 sample chapters for nonfiction. Accepts simultaneous submissions.

JUDITH EHRLICH LITERARY MANAGEMENT, LLC

146 Central Park W., 20E, New York NY 10023. (646)505-1570. **Fax:** (646)505-1570. **E-mail:** jehrlich@judithehrlichliterary.com. **Website:** www.judithehrlichliterary.com. Judith Ehrlich Literary Management LLC, established in 2002 and based in New York City, is a full service agency. "We represent nonfiction and fiction, both literary and commercial for the mainstream trade market. Our approach is very hands on, editorial, and constructive with the primary goal of helping authors build successful writing careers." Special areas of interest include compelling narrative nonfiction, outstanding biographies and memoirs, lifestyle books, works that reflect our changing culture, women's issues, psychology, science, social issues, current events, parenting, health, history, business, and prescriptive books offering fresh information and advice. "We also seek and represent stellar commercial and literary fiction, including romance and other women's fiction, historical fiction, literary mysteries, and select thrillers. Our agency deals closely with all major and independent publishers. When appropriate, we place our properties with foreign agents and co-agents at leading film agencies in New York and Los Angeles."

HANDLES Does not want to receive novellas, poetry, textbooks, plays, or screenplays.

RECENT SALES Fiction: *The Bicycle Spy*, by Yona Zeldis McDonough (Scholastic); *The House on Primrose Pond*, by Yona McDonough (NAL/Penguin); *You Were Meant for Me*, by Yona McDonough (NAL/Penguin); *Echoes of Us: The Hybrid Chronicles*, Book 3 by Kat Zhang (HarperCollins); *Once We Were: The Hybrid Chronicles* Book 2, by Kat Zhang (HarperCollins). Nonfiction: *Listen to the Echoes: The Ray Bradbury Interviews (Deluxe Edition)*, by Sam Weller (Hat & Beard Press); *What are The Ten Commandments?*, by Yona McDonough (Grosset & Dunlap); *Little Author in the Big Woods: A Biography of Laura Ingalls Wilder*, by

Yona McDonough (Christy Ottaviano Books/Henry Holt); *Ray Bradbury: The Last Interview: And Other Conversations*, by Sam Weller (Melville House); *Who Was Sojourner Truth?*, by Yona McDonough (Grosset & Dunlap); *Power Branding: Leveraging the Success of the World's Best Brands*, by Steve McKee (Palgrave Macmillan); *Confessions of a Sociopath: A Life Spent Hiding in Plain Sight*, by M.E. Thomas (Crown); *Luck and Circumstance: A Coming of Age in New York* and *Hollywood* and *Points Beyond*, by Michael Lindsay-Hogg (Knopf).

HOW TO CONTACT E-query, with a synopsis and some sample pages. The agency will respond only if interested. Accepts simultaneous submissions.

EINSTEIN LITERARY MANAGEMENT

27 W. 20th St., No. 1003, New York NY 10011. (212)221-8797. **E-mail:** info@einsteinliterary.com. **Website:** http://einsteinliterary.com. **Contact:** Susanna Einstein.

HANDLES "As an agency we represent a broad range of literary and commercial fiction, including upmarket women's fiction, crime fiction, historical fiction, romance, and books for middle-grade children and young adults, including picture books and graphic novels. We also handle non-fiction including cookbooks, memoir and narrative, and blog-to-book projects. Please see agent bios on the website for specific information about what each of ELM's agents represents." Does not want poetry, textbooks, or screenplays.

HOW TO CONTACT Please submit a query letter and the first 10 double-spaced pages of your manuscript in the body of the e-mail (no attachments). Does not respond to mail queries or telephone queries or queries that are not specifically addressed to this agency. Accepts simultaneous submissions.

EMPIRE LITERARY

115 W. 29th St., 3rd Floor, New York NY 10001. (917)213-7082. **E-mail:** abarzvi@empireliterary.com. **Website:** www.empireliterary.com.

HOW TO CONTACT Please only query one agent at a time. "If we are interested in reading more we will get in touch with you as soon as possible." Accepts simultaneous submissions.

DIANA FINCH LITERARY AGENCY

116 W. 23rd St., Suite 500, New York NY 10011. (917)544-4470. **E-mail:** diana.finch@verizon.net. **Website:** dianafinchliteraryagency.blogspot.com. **Con-**tact: Diana Finch. A boutique agency in Manhattan's Chelsea neighborhood. "Many of the agency's clients are journalists, and I handle book-related magazine assignments as well as book deals. I am the Chair of the AAR's International Committee, attend overseas book fairs, and actively handle foreign rights to my clients' work."

HANDLES For news about the agency and agency clients, see the agency Facebook page at https://www.facebook.com/DianaFinchLitAg/. "Does not want romance or children's picture books."

RECENT SALES *The Journeys of the Trees*, by Zach St George (W. W. Norton); *Owls of the Eastern Ice*, by Jonathan SIaght (FSG/Scientific American); *Uncolor: on toxins in personal products*, by Ronnie Citron-Fink (Island Press); *Cutting School* , by Professor Noliwe Rooks (The New Press); *Merchants of Men*, by Loretta Napoleoni (Seven Stories Press); *Beyond $15*, by Jonathan Rosenblum (Beacon Press); *The Age of Inequality*, by the Editors of In These Times (Verso Books); *Seeds of Resistance*, by Mark Schapiro (Hot Books/Skyhorse).

TERMS Agent receives 15% commission on domestic sales; 20% commission on foreign sales. Offers written contract. "I charge for overseas postage, galleys, and books purchased, and try to recoup these costs from earnings received for a client, rather than charging outright."

HOW TO CONTACT This agency prefers submissions via its online form. Accepts simultaneous submissions. Obtains most new clients through recommendations from others.

TIPS "Do as much research as you can on agents before you query. Have someone critique your query letter before you send it. It should be only 1 page and describe your book clearly—and why you are writing it—but also demonstrate creativity and a sense of your writing style."

FINEPRINT LITERARY MANAGEMENT

207 W. 106th St., Suite 1D, New York NY 10025. (212)279-1412. **Website:** www.fineprintlit.com. **Contact:** Peter Rubie.

TERMS Agent receives 15% commission on domestic sales; 20% commission on foreign sales.

HOW TO CONTACT E-query. For fiction, send a query, synopsis, bio, and 30 pages pasted into the e-mail. No attachments. For nonfiction, send a query only; proposal requested later if the agent is interested. Accepts simultaneous submissions. Obtains most new clients through recommendations from others, solicitations.

JAMES FITZGERALD AGENCY

118 Waverly Place, #1B, New York NY 10011. **E-mail:** submissions@jfitzagency.com. **Website:** www.jfitzagency.com. **Contact:** Anna Tatelman. "As an agency, we primarily represent books that reflect the popular culture of today being in the forms of fiction, nonfiction, graphic and packaged books. In order to have your work considered for possible representation, the following information must be submitted. Please submit all information in English even if your manuscript is in another language."

RECENT SALES A full and diverse list of titles are on this agency's website.

HOW TO CONTACT Query via e-mail or snail mail. This agency's online submission guidelines page explains all the elements they want to see. Accepts simultaneous submissions.

FLANNERY LITERARY

1140 Wickfield Ct., Naperville IL 60563. **E-mail:** jennifer@flanneryliterary.com. **Website:** flanneryliterary.com. **Contact:** Jennifer Flannery. "Flannery Literary is a Chicago-area literary agency representing writers of books for children and young adults because the most interesting, well-written, and time-honored books are written with young people in mind."

HANDLES This agency specializes in children's and young adult fiction and nonfiction. It also accepts picture books. 100% juvenile books. Actively seeking middle grade and young adult novels. No rhyming picture books nor bodily function topics, please. Also I do not open attachments unless instructed.

TERMS Agent receives 15% commission on domestic sales; 20% commission on foreign sales. Offers written contract, binding for life of book in print.

HOW TO CONTACT Query by e-mail only. "Multiple queries are fine, but please inform us. Please no attachments. If you're sending a query about a novel, please embed in the e-mail the first 5-10 pages; if it's a picture book, please embed the entire text in the e-mail. We do not open attachments unless they have been requested." Accepts simultaneous submissions. Obtains new clients through referrals and queries.

TIPS "Write an engrossing, succinct query describing your work. We are always looking for a fresh new voice."

FLETCHER & COMPANY

78 Fifth Ave., 3rd Floor, New York NY 10011. **Website:** www.fletcherandco.com. **Contact:** Christy Fletcher. Today, Fletcher & Co. is a full-service literary management and production company dedicated to writers of upmarket nonfiction as well as commercial and literary fiction.

RECENT SALES *The Profiteers*, by Sally Denton; *The Longest Night*, by Andrea Williams; *Disrupted: My Misadventure in the Start-Up Bubble*, by Dan Lyons; *Free Re-Fills: A Doctor Confronts His Addiction*, by Peter Grinspoon, M.D.; *Black Man in a White Coat: A Doctor's Reflections on Race and Medicine*, by Damon Tweedy, M.D.

HOW TO CONTACT Send queries to info@fletcherandco.com. Please do not include e-mail attachments with your initial query, as they will be deleted. Address your query to a specific agent. No snail mail queries. Accepts simultaneous submissions.

FOLIO LITERARY MANAGEMENT, LLC

The Film Center Building, 630 Ninth Ave., Suite 1101, New York NY 10036. (212)400-1494. **Fax:** (212)967-0977. **Website:** www.foliolit.com.

This agency has many agents, and their specialties are listed on the website.

HANDLES No poetry, stage plays, or screenplays.

HOW TO CONTACT Query via e-mail only (no attachments). Read agent bios online for specific submission guidelines and e-mail addresses, and to check if someone is closed to queries. "All agents respond to queries as soon as possible, whether interested or not. If you haven't heard back from the individual agent within the time period that they specify on their bio page, it's possible that something has gone wrong, and your query has been lost–in that case, please e-mail a follow-up."

TIPS "Please do not submit simultaneously to more than one agent at Folio. If you're not sure which of us is exactly right for your book, don't worry. We work closely as a team, and if one of our agents gets a query that might be more appropriate for someone else, we'll always pass it along. It's important that you check each agent's bio page for clear directions as to how to submit, as well as when to expect feedback."

FOUNDRY LITERARY + MEDIA

33 W. 17th St., PH, New York NY 10011. (212)929-5064. **Fax:** (212)929-5471. **Website:** www.foundrymedia.com.

HOW TO CONTACT Target one agent only. Send queries to the specific submission e-mail of the agent. For fiction: send query, synopsis, author bio, first 3 chapters—all pasted in the e-mail. For nonfiction, send query, sample chapters, TOC, author bio (all pasted). "We regret that we cannot guarantee a response to every submission we receive. If you do not receive a response within 8 weeks, your submission is not right for our lists at this time." Accepts simultaneous submissions.

TIPS "Consult website for each agent's submission instructions."

FOX LITERARY

110 W. 40th St., Suite 2305, New York NY 10018. **Website:** foxliterary.com. Fox Literary is a boutique agency which represents commercial fiction, along with select works of literary fiction and nonfiction that have broad commercial appeal.

HOW TO CONTACT E-mail query and first 5 pages in body of e-mail. E-mail queries preferred. For snail mail queries, must include an e-mail address for response and no response means no. Do not send SASE. No e-mail attachments. Accepts simultaneous submissions.

REBECCA FRIEDMAN LITERARY AGENCY

E-mail: queries@rfliterary.com. **Website:** www.rfliterary.com.

RECENT SALES A complete list of agency authors is available online.

HOW TO CONTACT Please submit your brief query letter and first chapter (no more than 15 pages, double-spaced). No attachments. Accepts simultaneous submissions.

FULL CIRCLE LITERARY, LLC

Website: www.fullcircleliterary.com. **Contact:** Stefanie Von Borstel. "Full Circle Literary is a full-service literary agency, offering a full circle approach to literary representation. Our team has diverse experience in book publishing including editorial, marketing, publicity, legal and rights, which we use collectively to build careers book by book. We work with both award-winning veteran and debut writers and artists and our team has a knack for finding and developing new and diverse talent. Learn more about our agency and submission guidelines by visiting our website." This agency goes deeply into depth about what they are seeking and submission guidelines on their agency website.

HANDLES Actively seeking nonfiction and fiction projects that offer new and diverse viewpoints, and literature with a global or multicultural perspective. "We are particularly interested in books with a Latino or Middle Eastern angle."

TERMS Agent receives 15% commission on domestic sales; 25% commission on foreign sales. Offers written contract which outlines responsibilities of the author and the agent.

HOW TO CONTACT Online submissions only via submissions form online. Please complete the form and submit cover letter, author information and sample writing. For sample writing: fiction please include the first 10 ms pages. For nonfiction, include a proposal with 1 sample chapter. Accepts simultaneous submissions. Obtains most new clients through recommendations from others and conferences.

FUSE LITERARY

Foreword Literary, Inc. dba FUSE LITERARY, P.O. Box 258, La Honda CA 94020. **E-mail:** info@fuseliterary.com. **Website:** www.fuseliterary.com. **Contact:** Contact each agent directly via e-mail. Fuse Literary is a full-service, hybrid literary agency based in San Francisco with offices in New York, Chicago, Dallas, North Dakota and Vancouver. "We blend the tried-and-true methods of traditional publishing with the brash new opportunities engendered by digital publishing, emerging technologies, and an evolving author-agent relationship. Fuse manages a wide variety of clients, from bestsellers to debut authors, working with fiction and nonfiction for children and adults worldwide. We combine technical efficiency with outside-the-covers creative thinking so that each individual client's career is specifically fine-tuned for them. We are not an agency that sells a book and then washes our hands of the project. We realize that our ongoing success directly results from that of our clients, so we remain at their side to cultivate and strategize throughout the many lives of each book, both before and after the initial sale. Innovations, such as our Short Fuse client publishing program, help bridge the gaps between books, growing and maintaining the author's fan base without lag. The partners launched Fuse following tenures at established agencies, bringing with them experience in writing, teaching, professional editing, book marketing, blogging and social media, running high-tech companies, and marketing new technologies. A boutique, collaborative agency, Fuse provides each client with the expertise and forward vision of the group. We pride ourselves on our flexibility and passion for progression in an ever-changing publishing environment. We believe that the agency of the future will not just react to change but will actively create change, pushing markets and advancing formats to provide authors with the best possible outlets for their art."

RECENT SALES Seven-figure and six-figure deals for NYT bestseller Julie Kagawa (YA); six-figure deal for debut Melissa D. Savage (MG); seven-figure and six-figure deals for Kerry Lonsdale (suspense); two six-figure audio deals for fantasy author Brian D. Anderson; *First Watch*, by Dale Lucas (fantasy); *This Is What a Librarian Looks Like*, by Kyle Cassidy (photo essay); *A Big Ship at the Edge of the Universe*, by Alex White (sci-fi); Runebinder Chronicles, by Alex Kahler (YA); *Perceptual Intelligence*, by Dr. Brian Boxler Wachler (science); *The Night Child*, by Anna Quinn (literary); *Hollywood Homicide*, by Kellye Garrett (mystery); Breakup Bash Series, by Nina Crespo (romance); *America's Next Reality Star*, by Laura Heffernan (women's fiction); *Losing the Girl*, by MariNaomi (graphic novel); *Maggie and Abby's Neverending Pillow Fort*, by Will Taylor (MG); *Idea Machine*, by Jorjeana Marie (how-to).

TERMS "We earn 15% on negotiated deals for books and with our co-agents earn between 20-30% on foreign translation deals depending on the territory; 20% on TV/Movies/Plays; other multimedia deals are so new there is no established commission rate. The author has the last say, approving or not approving all deals." After the initial 90-day period, there is a 30-day termination of the agency agreement clause. No fees.

HOW TO CONTACT E-query an individual agent. Check the website to see if any individual agent has closed themselves to submissions, as well as for a description of each agent's individual submission preferences. (You can find these details by clicking on each agent's photo.) Accepts simultaneous submissions. Only accepts e-mailed queries that follow our online guidelines.

GALLT AND ZACKER LITERARY AGENCY

273 Charlton Ave., South Orange NJ 07079. **Website:** www.galltzacker.com. **Contact:** Nancy Gallt, Marietta Zacker. "At the Gallt and Zacker Literary Agency

we represent people, not projects. We aim to bring to life stories and artwork that help readers throughout the world become life-long book enthusiasts and to inspire and entertain readers of all ages."

HANDLES Books for children and young adults. Actively seeking author, illustrators, author/illustrators who create books for young adults and younger readers.

RECENT SALES Rick Riordan's Books (Hyperion); *Trace*, by Pat Cummings (Harper); *I Got Next*, by Daria Peoples-Riley (Bloomsbury); *Gondra's Treasure*, illustrated by Jennifer Black Reinhardt (Clarion/HMH); *Caterpillar Summer*, by Gillian McDunn (Bloomsbury); *It Wasn't Me*, by Dana Alison Levy (Delacorte/Random House); *Five Midnights*, by Ann Dávila Cardinal (Tor/Macmillan); *Patron Saints of Nothing*, by Randy Ribay (Kokila/Penguin); *Rot*, by Ben Clanton (Simon & Schuster). *The Year They Fell*, by David Kreizman (Imprint/Macmillan); *Manhattan Maps*, by Jennifer Thermes (Abrams); *The Moon Within*, by Aida Salazar (Scholastic); *Artist in Space*, by Dean Robbins (Scholastic); *Where Are You From?*, by Mary Amato (Holiday House); *Where Are You From?*, by Yamile Saied Méndez (Harper); *The Girl King*, by Mimi Yu (Bloomsbury); *Narwhal and Jelly*, by Ben Clanton (Tundra/Penguin Random House Canada).

TERMS Agent receives 15% commission on domestic sales; 20% commission on foreign sales. Offers written contract; 30-day notice must be given to terminate contract.

HOW TO CONTACT Submission guidelines on our website: http://galltzacker.com/submissions.html. No e-mail queries, please. Accepts simultaneous submissions. Obtains new clients through submissions, conferences and recommendations from others.

TIPS "Writing and illustrations stand on their own, so submissions should tell the most compelling stories possible—whether visually, in narrative, or both."

GELFMAN SCHNEIDER/ICM PARTNERS

850 7th Ave., Suite 903, New York NY 10019. **Website:** www.gelfmanschneider.com. **Contact:** Jane Gelfman, Deborah Schneider.

HANDLES "Among our diverse list of clients are novelists, journalists, playwrights, scientists, activists & humorists writing narrative nonfiction, memoir, political & current affairs, popular science and popular culture nonfiction, as well as literary & commercial fiction, women's fiction, and historical fiction." Does not currently accept screenplays or scripts, poetry, or picture book queries.

TERMS Agent receives 15% commission on domestic sales; 20% commission on foreign sales; 15% commission on film sales. Offers written contract. Charges clients for photocopying and messengers/couriers.

HOW TO CONTACT Query. Check Submissions page of website to see which agents are open to queries and further instructions. Accepts simultaneous submissions.

THE GERNERT COMPANY

136 E. 57th St., New York NY 10022. (212)838-7777. **E-mail:** info@thegernertco.com. **Website:** www.thegernertco.com. "Our client list is as broad as the market; we represent equal parts fiction and nonfiction."

RECENT SALES *Partners*, by John Grisham; *The River Why*, by David James Duncan; *The Thin Green Line*, by Paul Sullivan; *A Fireproof Home for the Bride*, by Amy Scheibe; *The Only Girl in School*, by Natalie Standiford.

HOW TO CONTACT Please send us a query letter by e-mail to info@thegernertco.com describing the work you'd like to submit, along with some information about yourself and a sample chapter if appropriate. Please indicate in your letter which agent you are querying. Please do not send e-mails directly to individual agents. It's our policy to respond to your query only if we are interested in seeing more material, usually within 4-6 weeks. See company website for more instructions. Accepts simultaneous submissions. Obtains most new clients through recommendations from others, solicitations.

BARRY GOLDBLATT LITERARY LLC

320 7th Ave. #266, Brooklyn NY 11215. **Website:** www.bgliterary.com. **Contact:** Barry Goldblatt; Jennifer Udden.

HANDLES "Please see our website for specific submission guidelines and information on our particular tastes."

RECENT SALES *Trolled*, by Bruce Coville; *Grim Tidings*, by Caitlin Kittridge; *Max at Night*, by Ed Vere.

TERMS Agent receives 15% commission on domestic sales; 20% on foreign and dramatic sales. Offers written contract. 60 days notice must be given to terminate contract.

HOW TO CONTACT "E-mail queries can be sent to query@bgliterary.com and should include the word 'query' in the subject line. To query Jen Udden specifically, e-mail queries can be sent to query.judden@gmail.com. Please know that we will read and respond to every e-query that we receive, provided it is properly addressed and follows the submission guidelines below. We will not respond to e-queries that are addressed to no one, or to multiple recipients. Your e-mail query should include the following within the body of the e-mail: your query letter, a synopsis of the book, and the first 5 pages of your manuscript. We will not open or respond to any e-mails that have attachments. If we like the sound of your work, we will request more from you. Our response time is 4 weeks on queries, 6-8 weeks on full manuscripts. If you haven't heard from us within that time, feel free to check in via e-mail." Accepts simultaneous submissions. Obtains clients through referrals, queries, and conferences.

TIPS "We're a hands-on agency, focused on building an author's career, not just making an initial sale. We don't care about trends or what's hot; we just want to sign great writers."

IRENE GOODMAN LITERARY AGENCY

27 W. 24th St., Suite 700B, New York NY 10010. **E-mail:** miriam.queries@irenegoodman.com, barbara.queries@irenegoodman.com, rachel.queries@irenegoodman.com, kim.queries@irenegoodman.com, victoria.queries@irenegoodman.com, irene.queries@irenegoodman.com, brita.queries@irenegoodman.com. **Website:** www.irenegoodman.com. **Contact:** Brita Lundberg.

HANDLES Commercial and literary fiction and nonfiction. No screenplays, poetry, or inspirational fiction.

TERMS 15% commission.

HOW TO CONTACT Query. Submit synopsis, first 10 pages pasted into the body of the email. E-mail queries only! See the website submission page. No e-mail attachments. Query 1 agent only. Accepts simultaneous submissions.

TIPS "We are receiving an unprecedented amount of e-mail queries. If you find that the mailbox is full, please try again in two weeks. E-mail queries to our personal addresses will not be answered. E-mails to our personal inboxes will be deleted."

DOUG GRAD LITERARY AGENCY, INC.

156 Prospect Park West, #3L, Brooklyn NY 11215. **Website:** www.dgliterary.com. **Contact:** Doug Grad. Throughout Doug's editorial career, he was always an author's advocate—the kind of editor authors wanted to work with because of his keen eye, integrity, and talent for developing projects. He was also a skillful negotiator, sometimes to the chagrin of literary agents. For the last 10 years, he has been bringing those experiences to the other side of the table in offering publishers the kind of high-quality commercial fiction and nonfiction that he himself was proud to publish. He has sold award-winning and bestselling authors.

HANDLES Does not want fantasy, young adult, or children's picture books.

RECENT SALES *Net Force* series created by Tom Clancy and Steve Pieczenik, written by Jerome Preisler (Hanover Square); *A Serial Killer's Daughter* by Kerri Rawson (Thomas Nelson); *The Next Greatest Generation*, by Joseph L. Galloway and Marvin J. Wolf (Thomas Nelson); *All Available Boats* by L. Douglas Keeney (Lyons Press); *Here Comes the Body*, Book 1 in the Catering Hall mystery series, by Agatha Award-winner Ellen Byron writing as Maria DiRico (Kensington); *Please Don't Feed the Mayor* and *Alaskan Catch,* by Sue Pethick (Kensington).

TERMS None

HOW TO CONTACT Query by e-mail first. No sample material unless requested; no printed submissions by mail. Accepts simultaneous submissions.

SANFORD J. GREENBURGER ASSOCIATES, INC.

55 Fifth Ave., New York NY 10003. (212)206-5600. **Fax:** (212)463-8718. **Website:** www.greenburger.com. "Large enough to be a full service agency, including international rights, but small enough to manage and service clients personally, SJGA works closely with authors to edit and fine-tune proposals, refine concepts and ensure that the best work reaches editors. The agents freely share information and expertise, creating a collaborative partnership unique to the industry. The combined result is reflected in the numerous successes of the agency's authors (including Dan Brown, Patrick Rothfuss, and Robin Preiss Glasser)."

HANDLES No screenplays.

RECENT SALES *Origin*, by Dan Brown; *Sweet Pea and Friends: A Sheepover,* by

JOHN CHURCHMAN and Jennifer Churchman; *Code of Conduct*, by Brad Thor.

TERMS Agent receives 15% commission on domestic sales; 20% commission on foreign sales. Charges for photocopying and books for foreign and subsidiary rights submissions.

HOW TO CONTACT E-query. "Please look at each agent's profile page for current information about what each agent is looking for and for the correct email address to use for queries to that agent. Please be sure to use the correct query e-mail address for each agent." Obtains most new clients through recommendations from others.

THE GREENHOUSE LITERARY AGENCY

E-mail: submissions@greenhouseliterary.com. **Website:** www.greenhouseliterary.com. **Contact:** Sarah Davies.

"At Greenhouse we aim to establish strong, long-term relationships with clients and work hard to find our authors the very best publisher and deal for their writing. We often get very involved editorially, working creatively with authors where necessary. Our goal is to submit high-quality manuscripts to publishers while respecting the role of the editor who will have their own publishing vision."

HANDLES "We represent authors writing fiction and nonfiction for children and teens. The agency has offices in both the US and UK, and the agency's commission structure reflects this—taking 15% for sales to both US and UK, thus treating both as 'domestic' market." All genres of children's and YA fiction. Occasionally, a nonfiction proposal will be considered. Does not want to receive picture books texts (ie, written by writers who aren't also illustrators) or short stories, educational or religious/inspirational work, pre-school/novelty material, screenplays. Represents novels and some nonfiction.Considers these fiction areas: juvenile, chapter book series, middle grade, young adult. Does not want to receive poetry, picture book texts (unless by author/illustrators) or work aimed at adults; short stories, educational or religious/inspirational work, pre-school/novelty material, or screenplays.

RECENT SALES *Agents of the Wild*, by Jennifer Bell & Alice Lickens (Walker UK); *Bookshop Girl in Paris*, by Chloe Coles (Hot Key); *Votes for Women*, by Winifred Conkling (Algonquin); *The Monster Catchers*, by George Brewington (Holt); *City of the Plague God*, by Sarwat Chadda (Disney-Hyperion); *Whiteout*, by Gabriel Dylan (Stripes); *The Lying Woods*, by Ashley Elston (Disney-Hyperion); *When You Trap a Tiger*, by Tae Keller (Random House); *We Speak in Storms*, by Natalie Lund (Philomel); *When We Wake*, by Elle Cosimano (HarperCollins); *Carpa Fortuna*, by Lindsay Eagar (Candlewick); *Instructions Not Included*, by Tami Lewis Brown & Debbie Loren Dunn (Disney-Hyperion); *Fake*, by Donna Cooner (Scholastic); *Unicorn Academy*, by Julie Sykes (Nosy Crow); *The Girl Who Sailed the Stars*, by Matilda Woods (Scholastic UK/Philomel US).

TERMS Agent receives 15% commission on domestic sales; 25% commission on foreign sales. Offers written contract. This agency occasionally charges for submission copies to film agents or foreign publishers.

HOW TO CONTACT Query 1 agent only. Put the target agent's name in the subject line. Paste the first 5 pages of your story after the query. Please see our website for up-to-date information as occasionally we close to queries for short periods of time. Accepts simultaneous submissions.

TIPS "Before submitting material, authors should visit the Greenhouse Literary Agency website and carefully read all submission guidelines."

KATHRYN GREEN LITERARY AGENCY, LLC
157 Columbus Ave., Suite 510, New York NY 10023. (212)245-4225. **E-mail:** query@kgreenagency.com. **Website:** www.kathryngreenliteraryagency.com. **Contact:** Kathy Green.

HANDLES "Considers all types of fiction but particularly like historical fiction, cozy mysteries, young adult and middle grade. For nonfiction, I am interested in memoir, parenting, humor with a pop culture bent, and history. Quirky nonfiction is also a particular favorite." Does not want to receive science fiction, fantasy, children's picture books, screenplays, or poetry.

RECENT SALES *Jigsaw Jungle*, by Kristin Levine; *Jane, Anonymous*, by Laurie Faria Stolarz; *To Woo a Wicked Widow, Wedding the Widow*, and *What a Widow Wants*, by Jenna Jaxon; *The Pennypackers Take a Vacation*, by Lisa Doan; *Comfort in Hard Times*, by Earl Johnson.

TERMS Agent receives 15% commission on domestic sales; 20% commission on foreign sales.

HOW TO CONTACT Query by e-mail. Send no attachments unless requested. Do not send queries via regular mail. Responds in 4 weeks. "Queries do not have to be exclusive; however if further material is requested, please be in touch before accepting other representation." Accepts simultaneous submissions. Obtains most new clients through recommendations from others, solicitations, conferences.

JILL GRINBERG LITERARY MANAGEMENT, LLC
392 Vanderbilt Ave., Brooklyn NY 11238. (212)620-5883. **Website:** www.jillgrinbergliterary.com. "Our authors are novelists, historians, and scientists; memoirists and journalists; illustrators and musicians, cultural critics and humanitarians. They are passionate about what they write. They have strong, authentic voices, whether they are writing fiction or writing nonfiction. They are brilliant storytellers. Our authors have won the American Book Award, the National Book Award and the Pulitzer Prize, as well as the Printz Award and Newbery Honor award. They appear on The New York Times and international bestseller lists. We don't make a habit of dividing our list by category—our authors transcend category. Our authors write for every audience, picture book to adult. They are not easily boxed or contained within any neat, singular label. They often cross categories, are 'genre busting.' We love books, but we take on authors. Our authors are career authors. We are deeply invested in their careers and in making every book count. We are committed to developing ongoing relationships with writers and have represented a good number of our authors for 10 years plus. We understand the importance of the author–publisher connection and put great focus on matching our authors to the right editors and publishers. We fiercely advocate for our authors while maintaining a strong network of top editors and publishers. We have many years of publicity and marketing experience between us, and we give tremendous thought to positioning. Every project requires a tailored, personalized plan. Every author is a unique. Every author has a different path."

HANDLES "We do not accept unsolicited queries for screenplays."

HOW TO CONTACT "Please send queries via e-mail to info@jillgrinbergliterary.com–include your query letter, addressed to the agent of your choice, along with the first 50 pages of your ms pasted into the body of the e-mail or attached as a doc. or docx. file. We also accept queries via mail, though e-mail is much preferred. Please send your query letter and the first 50 pages of your ms by mail, along with a SASE, to the attention of your agent of choice. Please note that unless a SASE with sufficient postage is provided, your materials will not be returned. As submissions are shared within the office, please only query one agent with your project." Accepts simultaneous submissions.

TIPS "We prefer submissions by electronic mail."

HARTLINE LITERARY AGENCY

123 Queenston Dr., Pittsburgh PA 15235-5429. (412)829-2483. **E-mail:** jim@hartlineliterary.com. **Website:** www.hartlineliterary.com. **Contact:** James D. Hart. Many of the agents at this agency are generalists. This agency also handles inspirational and Christian works.

HANDLES "This agency specializes in the Christian bookseller market." We also represent general market, but no graphic sex or language. Actively seeking adult fiction, all genres, self-help, social issues, Christian living, parenting, marriage, business, biographies, narrative non-fiction, creative nonfiction. Does not want to receive erotica, horror, graphic violence or graphic language.

RECENT SALES *Coral*, by Sara Ella (Thomas Nelson); *The Dating Charade*, by Melisa Ferguson (Thomas Nelson); *The Beautiful Ashes of Gomez Gomez*, by Buck Storm (Kregel); *The Mr. Rogers Effect*, by Dr. Anita Knight (Baker Books); *People Can Change*, by Dr. Mark W. Baker (Fortress); *Obedience Over Hustle*, by Malinda Fuller (Barbour); *Keller's Heart*, by John Gray, Illustrations Shanna Oblenus (Paraclete); *Create Your Yes*, by Angela Marie Hutchinson (Source Books); *Simply Spirit Filled*, by Dr. Andrew K. Gabriel (Thomas Nelson).

TERMS Agent receives 15% commission on domestic sales. Offers written contract.

HOW TO CONTACT E-mail submissions are preferred. Target one agent only. Each agent has specific interests, please refer to our web page for that information. All e-mail submissions sent to Hartline Agents should be sent as a MS Word doc attached to an e-mail with 'submission: title, authors name and word count' in the subject line. A proposal is a single document, not a collection of files. Place the query letter in the email itself. Do not send the entire proposal in the body of the e-mail. Further guidelines online. Accepts simultaneous submissions. Obtains most new clients through recommendations from others, and at conferences.

TIPS Please follow the guidelines on our web site www.hartlineliterary for the fastest response to your proposal. E-mail proposals only.

ANTONY HARWOOD LIMITED

103 Walton St., Oxford OX2 6EB, United Kingdom. (44)(018)6555-9615. **Website:** www.antonyharwood. com. **Contact:** Antony Harwood; James Macdonald Lockhart; Jo Williamson.

TERMS Agent receives 15% commission on domestic sales; 20% commission on foreign sales.

HOW TO CONTACT "We are happy to consider submissions of fiction and nonfiction in every genre and category except for screenwriting and poetry. If you wish to submit your work to us for consideration, please send a covering letter, brief outline and the opening 50 pages by e-mail. If you want to post your material to us, please be sure to enclose an SAE or the cost of return postage." Replies if interested. Accepts simultaneous submissions.

HERMAN AGENCY

350 Central Park W., Apt. 41, New York NY 10025. (212)749-4907. **E-mail:** ronnie@hermanagencyinc. com. **Website:** www.hermanagencyinc.com. Literary and artistic agency. Member of SCBWI, Graphic Artists' Guild and Authors' Guild. Some of the illustrators represented: Michael Rex, Troy Cummings, Mike Lester, Geoffrey Hayes. Currently not accepting new clients unless they have been successfully published by major trade publishing houses. **Contact:** Ronnie Ann Herman. "We are a small boutique literary agency that represents authors and artists for the children's book market. We are not accepting any submission except picture books or graphic middle grade by author/artists/

We are accepting very few new clients. If you do to hear from us within 8 weeks, please understand that that means we are not able to represent your work.

HANDLES Specializes in childrens' books of all genres. We only want author/artist projects

TERMS Agent receives 15% commission. Exclusive contract.

HOW TO CONTACT e-mail only. Responds in 8-16 weeks. For first contact, artists or author/artists should e-mail a link to their website with bio and list of published books as well as new picture book manuscript or dummy to Ronnie. We will contact you only if your samples are right for us. For first contact, authors of middle-grade should e-mail bio, list of published books and first ten pages. Finds illustrators and authors through recommendations from others, conferences, queries/solicitations. Submit via e-mail only. Accepts simultaneous submissions. Obtains extremely few new clients.

TIPS "Check our website to see if you belong with our agency." Remember only author/artist works.

HILL NADELL LITERARY AGENCY

6442 Santa Monica Blvd., Suite 201, Los Angeles CA 90038. (310)860-9605. **E-mail:** queries@hillnadell.com. **Website:** www.hillnadell.com.

TERMS Agent receives 15% commission on domestic and film sales; 20% commission on foreign sales. Charges clients for photocopying and foreign mailings.

HOW TO CONTACT Send a query and SASE. If you would like your materials returned, please include adequate postage. To submit electronically: Send your query letter and the first 5-10 pages to queries@hillnadell.com. No attachments. Due to the high volume of submissions the agency receives, it cannot guarantee a response to all e-mailed queries. Accepts simultaneous submissions.

HOLLOWAY LITERARY

P.O. Box 771, Cary NC 27512. **E-mail:** submissions@hollowayliteraryagency.com. **Website:** hollowayliteraryagency.com. **Contact:** Nikki Terpilowski. A full-service boutique literary agency located in Raleigh, NC.

HANDLES "Note to self-published authors: While we are happy to receive submissions from authors who have previously self-published novels, we do not represent self-published works. Send us your unpublished manuscripts only." Nikki is open to submissions and is selectively reviewing queries for cozy mysteries with culinary, historical or book/publishing industry themes written in the vein of Jaclyn Brady, Laura Childs, Julie Hyzy and Lucy Arlington; women's fiction with strong magical realism similar to Meena van Praag's *The Dress Shop of Dreams*, Sarah Addison Allen's *Garden Spells, Season of the Dragonflies* by Sarah Creech and Mary Robinette Kowal's *Glamourist Series*. She would love to find a wine-themed mystery series similar to Nadia Gordon's Sunny McCoskey series or Ellen Crosby's Wine County Mysteries that combine culinary themes with lots of great Southern history. Nikki is also interested in seeing contemporary romance set in the southern US or any wine county or featuring a culinary theme, dark, edgy historical romance, gritty military romance or romantic suspense with sexy Alpha heroes and lots of technical detail. She is also interested in acquiring historical fiction written in the vein of Alice Hoffman, Lalita Tademy and Isabel Allende. Nikki is also interested in espionage, military, political and AI thrillers similar to Tom Clancy, Robert Ludlum, Steve Berry, Vince Flynn, Brad Thor and Daniel Silva. Nikki has a special interest in non-fiction subjects related to governance, politics, military strategy and foreign relations; food and beverage, mindfulness, southern living and lifestyle. Does not want horror, true crime or novellas.

RECENT SALES A list of recent sales are listed on the agency website's "news" page.

HOW TO CONTACT Send query and first 15 pages of ms pasted into the body of e-mail to submissions@hollowayliteraryagency.com. In the subject header write: (Insert Agent's Name)/Title/Genre. Holloway Literary does accept submissions via mail (query letter and first 50 pages). Expect a response time of at least 3 months. Include e-mail address, phone number, social media accounts, and mailing address on your query letter. Accepts simultaneous submissions.

HSG AGENCY

37 W. 28th St., 8th Floor, New York NY 10001. **E-mail:** channigan@hsgagency.com; jsalky@hsgagency.com; jgetzler@hsgagency.com; sroberts@hsgagency.com; leigh@hsgagency.com. **Website:** hsgagency.com. **Contact:** Carrie Hannigan; Jesseca Salky; Josh Getzler; Soumeya Roberts; Julia Kardon; Rhea Lyons. Hannigan Salky Getzler (HSG) Agency is a boutique literary agency, formed by Carrie Hannigan, Jesseca Salky and Josh Getzler in 2011. "Our agents have over 40 years combined experience in the publishing industry and represent a diverse list of best-selling and award-winning clients. HSG is a full-service literary agency that through collaborative and client-focused representation manages all aspects of an author's career, from manuscript shaping, to sale and publication, subsidiary rights management, marketing and publicity strategy, and beyond. Our diverse and skilled team represents all

types of fiction and non-fiction, for both adults and children, and has strong relationships with every major publisher as well as familiarity with independent and start-up publishers offering a different approach to publishing. Our clients have access to the resources and expertise of every member of our agency team, which includes in-house lawyers and contracts professionals, foreign rights managers, and royalty and accounting specialists. Most importantly, our worth is measured by the success of our clients, and so you will find in each HSG agent not only a staunch advocate but a career-long ally."

HANDLES Carrie Hannigan: In the kidlit world, right now Carrie is looking for humorous books and books with warmth, heart and a great voice in both contemporary and fantasy. She is also open to graphic novels and nonfiction. Jesseca Salky: Jesseca is looking for literary fiction submissions that are family stories (she loves a good mother/daughter tale), have a strong sense of place (where the setting feels like its own character), or a daring or unique voice (think Jamie Quatro), as well as upmarket fiction that can appeal to men and women and has that Tropper/Hornby/Matt Norman quality to it. Josh Getzler: Josh is particularly into foreign and historical fiction; both women's fiction (your Downton Abbey/ Philippa Gregory Mashups), straight ahead historical fiction (think Wolf Hall or The Road to Wellville); and thrillers and mysteries (The Alienist, say; or Donna Leon or Arianna Franklin). He'd love a strong French Revolution novel. In nonfiction, he's very interested in increasing his list in history (including micro-histories), business, and political thought–but not screeds. Soumeya Roberts: In fiction, Soumeya is seeking literary and upmarket novels and collections, and also represents realistic young-adult and middle-grade. She likes books with vivid voices and compelling, well-developed story-telling, and is particularly interested in fiction that reflects on the post-colonial world and narratives by people of color. In nonfiction, she is primarily looking for idea-driven or voice-forward memoirs, personal essay collections, and approachable narrative nonfiction of all stripes. Leigh Eisenman: Leigh seeks submissions in the areas of literary and upmarket commercial fiction for adults, and is particularly drawn to: flawed protagonists she can't help but fall in love with (Holden Caulfield was her first crush); stories that take place in contemporary New York, but also any well-defined, vivid setting;

explorations of relationships (including journeys of self-discovery); and of course, excellent writing. On the nonfiction side, Leigh is interested in cookbooks, food/travel-related works, health and fitness, lifestyle, humor/gift, and select narrative nonfiction. Please note that we do not represent screenplays, romance fiction, or religious fiction.

RECENT SALES *A Spool of Blue Thread*, by Anne Tyler (Knopf); *Blue Sea Burning*, by Geoff Rodkey (Putnam); *The Partner Track*, by Helen Wan (St. Martin's Press); *The Thrill of the Haunt*, by E.J. Copperman (Berkley); *Aces Wild*, by Erica Perl (Knopf Books for Young Readers); *Steve & Wessley: The Sea Monster*, by Jennifer Morris (Scholastic); *Infinite Worlds*, by Michael Soluri (Simon & Schuster).

HOW TO CONTACT Please send a query letter and the first 5 pages of your ms (within the e-mail–no attachments please) to the appropriate agent for your book. If it is a picture book, please include the entire ms. If you were referred to us, please mention it in the first line of your query. Please note that we do not represent screenplays, romance fiction, or religious fiction. All agents are open to new clients.

ICM PARTNERS

65 E. 55th St., New York NY 10022. (212)556-5600. **E-mail:** careersny@icmpartners.com. **Website:** www. icmtalent.com. **Contact:** Literary Department. With the most prestigious literary publications department in the world, ICM Partners represents a wide range of writers, including the authors of best-selling fiction, self-help and nonfiction books, as well as journalists who write for prominent newspapers and magazines. In addition to handling the sale of publication rights, ICM Partners' literary agents in New York work closely with a team of agents in Los Angeles dedicated exclusively to seeking out opportunities for film and television adaptations. Its foreign rights department works in partnership with the Curtis Brown agency in England, which sells book and magazine projects in the UK and other English-speaking countries as well foreign language translations throughout the world. **HOW TO CONTACT** Accepts simultaneous submissions.

INKLINGS LITERARY AGENCY

3419 Virginia Beach Blvd. #183, Virginia Beach VA 23452. **E-mail:** michelle@inklingsliterary.com. **Website:** www.inklingsliterary.com. Inklings Literary Agency is a full service, hands-on literary agency seeking submissions from established authors as well as talented new authors. "We represent a broad range of commercial and literary fiction as well as memoirs and true crime. We are not seeking short stories, poetry, screenplays, or children's picture books."

TERMS Agent takes 15% domestic, 20% subsidiary commission. Charges no fees.

HOW TO CONTACT E-queries only. To query, type "Query (Agent Name)" plus the title of your novel in the subject line, then please send your query letter, short synopsis, and first 10 pages pasted into the body of the e-mail to query@inklingsliterary.com. Check the agency website to make sure that your targeted agent is currently open to submissions. Accepts simultaneous submissions.

INKWELL MANAGEMENT, LLC

521 Fifth Ave., Suite 2600, New York NY 10175. (212)922-3500. **Fax:** (212)922-0535. **E-mail:** info@ inkwellmanagement.com. **Website:** www.inkwell-management.com.

TERMS Agent receives 15% commission on domestic sales; 20% commission on foreign sales. Offers written contract.

HOW TO CONTACT "In the body of your e-mail, please include a query letter and a short writing sample (1-2 chapters). We currently accept submissions in all genres except screenplays. Due to the volume of queries we receive, our response time may take up to 2 months. Feel free to put 'Query for [Agent Name]: [Your Book Title]' in the e-mail subject line." Accepts simultaneous submissions. Obtains most new clients through recommendations from others.

TIPS "We will not read mss before receiving a letter of inquiry."

INTERNATIONAL TRANSACTIONS, INC.

P.O. Box 97, Gila NM 88038-0097. (845)373-9696. **Website:** www.intltrans.com. **Contact:** Peter Riva. Since 1975, the company has specialized in international idea and intellectual property brokerage catering to multi-national, multi-lingual, licensing and rights' representation of authors and publishers as well as producing award-winning TV and other media. They have been responsible for over 40 years of production, in both media and product, resulting in excess of $1.6 billion in retail sales and several international historic events (the memorabilia of which are on permanent display in national institutions in America, Germany, and France as well as touring

internationally). In 2000 by JoAnn Collins BA, RN joined the company and acts as an Associate Editor specializing in women's voices and issues. In 2013 they created an imprint, published by Skyhorse Publishing, called Yucca Publishing which featured over 40 new and independent voices–exciting additions to the book world. In 2015 they created an imprint, Horseshoe Books, to facilitate out-of-print backlist titles to re-enter the marketplace.

HANDLES "We specialize in large and small projects, helping qualified authors perfect material for publication." Actively seeking intelligent, well-written innovative material that breaks new ground. Authors of non-fiction must have an active and wide-reaching platform to help promote their work (since publishers rarely work at that any more). Does not want to receive material influenced by TV (too much dialogue); a rehash of previous successful novels' themes, or poorly prepared material. Does not want to be sent any material being reviewed by others.

RECENT SALES Averaging 20+ book placements per year.

TERMS Agent receives 15% (25%+ on illustrated books) commission on domestic sales; 20% commission on foreign sales and media rights. Offers written contract; 100-day notice must be given to terminate contract. No additional fees, ever.

HOW TO CONTACT In 2018, we will be extremely selective of new projects. First, e-query with an outline or synopsis. E-queries only. Put "Query: [Title]" in the e-mail subject line. Submissions or emails received without these conditions met are automatically discarded. Obtains most new clients through recommendations from others.

TIPS "'Book'—a published work of literature. That last word is the key. Not a string of words, not a book of (TV or film) 'scenes,' and never a stream of consciousness unfathomable by anyone outside of the writer's coterie. A writer should only begin to get 'interested in getting an agent' if the work is polished, literate and ready to be presented to a publishing house. Anything less is either asking for a quick rejection or is a thinly disguised plea for creative assistance—which is often given but never fiscally sound for the agents involved. Writers, even published authors, have difficulty in being objective about their own work. Friends and family are of no assistance in that process either. Writers should attempt to get their work read by the most unlikely and stern critic as part of the editing process, months before any agent is approached. In another matter: the economics of our job have changed as well. As the publishing world goes through the transition to e-books (much as the music industry went through the change to downloadable music)—a transition we expect to see at 95% within 10 years—everyone is nervous and wants 'assured bestsellers' from which to eke out a living until they know what the new e-world will continue to bring. This makes the sales rate and, especially, the advance royalty rates, plummet. Hence, our ability to take risks and take on new clients' work is increasingly perilous financially for us and all agents."

JABBERWOCKY LITERARY AGENCY

49 W. 45th St., 12th Floor, New York NY 10036. **Website:** www.awfulagent.com. **Contact:** Joshua Bilmes. Each agent at this agency is different in terms of openness to submissions. As of the agency updating this listing, Joshua Bilmes, Eddie Schneider, and Lisa Rodgers are open to queries. Check the agency website for more info.

HANDLES This agency represents quite a lot of genre fiction (science fiction & fantasy), romance, and mystery; and is actively seeking to increase the amount of nonfiction projects. It does not handle children's or picture books. Book-length material and novellas only—no poetry, articles, or short fiction.

RECENT SALES *Alcatraz #5* by Brandon Sanderson; *Aurora Teagarden*, by Charlaine Harris; *The Unnoticeables*, by Robert Brockway; *Messenger's Legacy*, by Peter V. Brett; *Slotter Key*, by Elizabeth Moon. Other clients include Tanya Huff, Simon Green, Jack Campbell, Myke Cole, Marie Brennan, Daniel Jose Older, Jim Hines, Mark Hodder, Toni Kelner, Ari Marmell, Ellery Queen, Erin Tettensor, and Walter Jon Williams.

TERMS Agent receives 15% commission on domestic sales; 20% commission on foreign sales. Offers written contract, binding for 1 year. Charges clients for book purchases, photocopying, international book/ms mailing.

HOW TO CONTACT "We are currently open to unsolicited queries. No e-mail, phone, or fax queries, please. Query with SASE. Please check our website, as there may be times during the year when we are not accepting queries. Query letter only; no manuscript material unless requested." Accepts simultaneous submissions. Obtains most new clients through solicitations, recommendation by current clients.

TIPS "In approaching with a query, the most important things to us are your credits and your biographical background to the extent it's relevant to your work. I (and most agents) will ignore the adjectives you may choose to describe your own work."

JANKLOW & NESBIT ASSOCIATES

285 Madison Ave., 21st Floor, New York NY 10017. (212)421-1700. **Fax:** (212)355-1403. **E-mail:** info@janklow.com. **Website:** www.janklowandnesbit.com.

HOW TO CONTACT Be sure to address your submission to a particular agent. For fiction submissions, send an informative cover letter, a brief synopsis and the first 10 pages. "If you are sending an e-mail submission, please include the sample pages in the body of the e-mail below your query. For nonfiction submissions, send an informative cover letter, a full outline, and the first 10 pages of the ms. If you are sending an e-mail submission, please include the sample pages in the body of the e-mail below your query. For picture book submissions, send an informative cover letter, full outline, and include a picture book dummy and at least one full-color sample. If you are sending an e-mail submission, please attach a picture book dummy as a PDF and the full-color samples as JPEGs or PDFs." Accepts simultaneous submissions. Obtains most new clients through recommendations from others.

TIPS "Please send a short query with first 10 pages or artwork."

HARVEY KLINGER, INC.

300 W. 55th St., Suite 11V, New York NY 10019. (212)581-7068. **Website:** www.harveyklinger.com. **Contact:** Harvey Klinger. Always interested in considering new clients, both published and unpublished.

HANDLES This agency specializes in big, mainstream, contemporary fiction and nonfiction. Great debut or established novelists and in nonfiction, authors with great ideas and a national platform already in place to help promote one's book. No screenplays, poetry, textbooks or anything too technical.

RECENT SALES *The Far River*, by Barbara Wood; *I Am Not a Serial Killer*, by Dan Wells; *Me, Myself and Us*, by Brian Little; *The Secret of Magic*, by Deborah Johnson; *Children of the Mist*, by Paula Quinn. Other clients include George Taber, Terry Kay, Scott Mebus, Jacqueline Kolosov, Jonathan Maberry, Tara Altebrando, Alex McAuley, Eva Nagorski, Greg Kot, Justine Musk, Michael Northrup, Nina LaCour, Ashley

Kahn, Barbara De Angelis, Robert Patton, Augusta Trobaugh, Deborah Blum, Jonathan Skariton.

TERMS Agent receives 15% commission on domestic sales; 25% commission on foreign sales. Offers written contract. Charges for photocopying mss and overseas postage for mss.

HOW TO CONTACT Use online e-mail submission form on the website, or query with SASE via snail mail. No phone or fax queries. Don't send unsolicited mss or e-mail attachments. Make submission letter to the point and as brief as possible. A bit of biographical information is always welcome, particularly with non-fiction submissions where one's national platform is vitally important. Accepts simultaneous submissions. Obtains most new clients through recommendations from others.

THE KNIGHT AGENCY

232 W. Washington St., Madison GA 30650. **E-mail:** deidre.knight@knightagency.net. **Website:** http://knightagency.net/. **Contact:** Deidre Knight. The Knight Agency is a full-service literary agency with a focus on genre-based adult fiction, YA, MG and select nonfiction projects. With 9 agents and a full-time support staff, our agency strives to give our clients individualized attention. "Our philosophy emphasizes building the author's entire career, from editorial, to marketing, to subrights and social media. TKA has earned a reputation for discovering vivid, original works, and our authors routinely land bestsellers on the New York Times, USA Today, Publishers Weekly, Los Angeles Times, Barnes & Noble Bestseller and Amazon.com Hot 100 lists. Awards received by clients include the RITA, the Hugo, the Newberry Medal, Goodreads Choice Award, the Lambda, the Christy, and Romantic Times' Reviewer Choice Awards, to name only a few."

HANDLES Actively seeking Romance in all sub-genres, including romantic suspense, paranormal romance, historical romance (a particular love of mine), LGBT, contemporary, and also category romance. Occasionally I represent new adult. I'm also seeking women's fiction with vivid voices, and strong concepts (think me before you). Further seeking YA and MG, and select nonfiction in the categories of personal development, self-help, finance/business, memoir, parenting and health. Does not want to receive screenplays, short stories, poetry, essays, or children's picture books.

TERMS 15% Simple agency agreement with open-ended commitment. 15% commission on all domestic sales, 20% on foreign and film.

HOW TO CONTACT E-queries only. "Your submission should include a one page query letter and the first five pages of your manuscript. All text must be contained in the body of your e-mail. Attachments will not be opened nor included in the consideration of your work. Queries must be addressed to a specific agent. Please do not query multiple agents." Accepts simultaneous submissions.

KT LITERARY, LLC

9249 S. Broadway, #200-543, Highlands Ranch CO 80129. **E-mail:** contact@ktliterary.com. **Website:** www.ktliterary.com. **Contact:** Kate Schafer Testerman, Sara Megibow, Renee Nyen, Hannah Fergesen, Hilary Harwell. KT Literary is a full-service literary agency operating out of Highlands Ranch, in the suburbs of Denver, Colorado, where every major publishing house is merely an e-mail or phone call away. We believe in the power of new technology to connect writers to readers, and authors to editors. We bring over a decade of experience in the New York publishing scene, an extensive list of contacts, and a lifetime love of reading to the foothills of the Rocky Mountains.

HANDLES Kate is looking only at young adult and middle grade fiction, especially #OwnVoices, and selective nonfiction for teens and tweens. Sara seeks authors in middle grade, young adult, romance, science fiction, and fantasy. Renee is looking for young adult and middle grade fiction only. Hannah is interested in speculative fiction in young adult, middle grade, and adult. Hilary is looking for young adult and middle grade fiction only. "We're thrilled to be actively seeking new clients with great writing, unique stories, and complex characters, for middle grade, young adult, and adult fiction. We are especially interested in diverse voices." Does not want adult mystery, thrillers, or adult literary fiction.

RECENT SALES *Most Likely*, by Sarah Watson, *All of Us With Wings*, by Michelle Ruiz Keil, *Postcards for a Songbird*, by Rebekah Crane, *The Tourist Trap*, by Sarah Morgenthaler, *The Last Year of James and Kat*, by Amy Spalding, and many more. A full list of clients and most recent sales are available on the agency website and some recent sales are available on Publishers Marketplace.

TERMS Agent receives 15% commission on domestic sales; 20% commission on foreign sales. Offers written contract; 30-day notice must be given to terminate contract.

HOW TO CONTACT "To query us, please select one of the agents at kt literary at a time. If we pass, you can feel free to submit to another. Please e-mail your query letter and the first 3 pages of your manuscript in the body of the e-mail to either Kate at katequery@ktliterary.com, Sara at saraquery@ktliterary.com, Renee at reneequery@ktliterary.com, Hannah at hannahquery@ktliterary.com, or Hilary at hilaryquery@ktliterary.com. The subject line of your e-mail should include the word 'Query' along with the title of your manuscript. Queries should not contain attachments. Attachments will not be read, and queries containing attachments will be deleted unread. We aim to reply to all queries within 4 weeks of receipt. For examples of query letters, please feel free to browse the About My Query archives on the KT Literary website. In addition, if you're an author who is sending a new query, but who previously submitted a novel to us for which we requested chapters but ultimately declined, please do say so in your query letter. If we like your query, we'll ask for the first 5 chapters and a complete synopsis. For our purposes, the synopsis should include the full plot of the book including the conclusion. Don't tease us. Thanks! We are not accepting snail mail queries or queries by phone at this time. We also do not accept pitches on social media." Accepts simultaneous submissions. Obtains most new clients through query slush pile.

LEVINE GREENBERG ROSTAN LITERARY AGENCY, INC.

307 Seventh Ave., Suite 2407, New York NY 10001. (212)337-0934. **Fax:** (212)337-0948. **E-mail:** submit@lgrliterary.com. **Website:** www.lgrliterary.com.

RECENT SALES Notorious **RBG**, by Irin Carmon and Shana Knizhnik; **Pogue's Basics: Life**, by David Pogue; **Invisible City**, by Julia Dahl; **Gumption**, by Nick Offerman; **All the Bright Places**, by Jennifer Niven.

TERMS Agent receives 15% commission on domestic sales; 20% commission on foreign sales. Offers written contract. Charges clients for out-of-pocket expenses—telephone, fax, postage, photocopying—directly connected to the project.

HOW TO CONTACT E-query to submit@lgrliterary.com, or online submission form. "If you would like to direct your query to one of our agents specifically, please feel free to name them in the online form or in the email you send." Cannot respond to submissions by mail. Do not attach more than 50 pages. "Due to the volume of submissions we receive, we are unable to respond to each individually. If we would like more information about your project, we'll contact you within 3 weeks (though we do get backed up on occasion!)." Accepts simultaneous submissions. Obtains most new clients through recommendations from others.

TIPS "We focus on editorial development, business representation, and publicity and marketing strategy."

LKG AGENCY

60 Riverside Blvd., #1101, New York NY 10069. **E-mail:** query@lkgagency.com. **Website:** lkgagency.com. **Contact:** Lauren Galit; Caitlen Rubino-Bradway. The LKG Agency was founded in 2005 and is based on the Upper West Side of Manhattan. "We are a boutique literary agency that specializes in middle grade and young adult fiction, as well as nonfiction, both practical and narrative, with a particular interest in women-focused how-to. We invest a great deal of care and personal attention in each of our authors with the aim of developing long-term relationships that last well beyond the sale of a single book."

HANDLES "The LKG Agency specializes in nonfiction, both practical and narrative, as well as middle grade and young adult fiction." Actively seeking parenting, beauty, celebrity, dating & relationships, entertainment, fashion, health, diet & fitness, home & design, lifestyle, memoir, narrative, pets, psychology, women's focused, middle grade & young adult fiction. Does not want history, biography, true crime, religion, picture books, spirituality, screenplays, poetry any fiction other than middle grade or young adult.

HOW TO CONTACT For nonfiction submissions, please send a query letter to nonfiction@lkgagency.com, along with a TOC and 2 sample chapters. The TOC should be fairly detailed, with a paragraph or 2 overview of the content of each chapter. Please also make sure to mention any publicity you have at your disposal. For middle grade and young adult submissions, please send a query, synopsis, and the three (3) chapters, and address all submissions to mgya@lkgagency.com. On a side note, while both Lauren and Caitlen consider young adult and middle grade, Lauren tends to look more for middle grade, while

Caitlen deals more with young adult fiction. Please note: due to the high volume of submissions, we are unable to reply to every one. If you do not receive a reply, please consider that a rejection. Accepts simultaneous submissions.

STERLING LORD LITERISTIC, INC.

115 Broadway, New York NY 10006. (212)780-6050. **Fax:** (212)780-6095. **E-mail:** info@sll.com. **Website:** www.sll.com.

TERMS Agent receives 15% commission on domestic sales; 20% commission on foreign sales. Offers written contract.

HOW TO CONTACT Query via snail mail. "Please submit a query letter, a synopsis of the work, a brief proposal or the first 3 chapters of the manuscript, a brief bio or resume, and SASE for reply. Original artwork is not accepted. Enclose sufficient postage if you wish to have your materials returned to you. We do not respond to unsolicited e-mail inquiries." Accepts simultaneous submissions.

LOWENSTEIN ASSOCIATES INC.

115 E. 23rd St., Floor 4, New York NY 10010. (212)206-1630. **Website:** www.lowensteinassociates.com. **Contact:** Barbara Lowenstein.

HANDLES Barbara Lowenstein is currently looking for writers who have a platform and are leading experts in their field, including business, women's issues, psychology, health, science and social issues, and is particularly interested in strong new voices in fiction and narrative nonfiction. Does not want westerns, textbooks, children's picture books and books in need of translation.

TERMS Agent receives 15% commission on domestic sales; 20% commission on foreign sales. Offers written contract. Charges for large photocopy batches, messenger service, international postage.

HOW TO CONTACT "For fiction, please send us a 1-page query letter, along with the first 10 pages pasted in the body of the message by e-mail to assistant@bookhaven.com. If nonfiction, please send a 1-page query letter, a table of contents, and, if available, a proposal pasted into the body of the e-mail. Please put the word 'QUERY' and the title of your project in the subject field of your e-mail and address it to the agent of your choice. Please do not send an attachment as the message will be deleted without being read and no reply will be sent." Accepts simultaneous submissions.

Obtains most new clients through recommendations from others, solicitations, conferences.

TIPS "Know the genre you are working in and read!"

ANDREW LOWNIE LITERARY AGENCY, LTD.

36 Great Smith St., London SW1P 3BU, United Kingdom. (44)(207)222-7574. **Fax:** (44)(207)222-7576. **E-mail:** lownie@globalnet.co.uk. **Website:** www.andrewlownie.co.uk. **Contact:** Andrew Lownie, nonfiction. The Andrew Lownie Literary Agency Ltd is one of the UK's leading boutique literary agencies with some 200 nonfiction authors. Its authors regularly win awards and appear in the bestseller lists. It prides itself on its personal attention to its clients and specializes both in launching new writers and taking established writers to a new level of recognition. According to Publishers Marketplace, Andrew Lownie has been the top selling nonfiction agent in the world for the last few years. He has also been shortlisted for 'Agent of the Year' at the British Bookseller Awards many times.

HANDLES This agent has wide publishing experience, extensive journalistic contacts, and a specialty in showbiz/celebrity memoir. Actively seeking showbiz memoirs, narrative histories, and biographies. No fiction, poetry, short stories, children's, academic, or scripts.

RECENT SALES Sells about fifty books a year, with over a dozen top 10 bestsellers including many number ones, as well as the memoirs of Queen Elizabeth II's press officer Dickie Arbiter, Lance Armstrong's masseuse Emma O'Reilly, actor Warwick Davis, Multiple Personality Disorder sufferer Alice Jamieson, round-the-world yachtsman Mike Perham, poker player Dave 'Devilfish' Ulliott, David Hasselhoff, Sam Faiers and Kirk Norcross from TOWIE, Spencer Matthews from Made in Chelsea, singer Kerry Katona. Other clients: Juliet Barker, Guy Bellamy, Joyce Cary estate, Roger Crowley, Patrick Dillon, Duncan Falconer, Cathy Glass, Timothy Good, Robert Hutchinson, Lawrence James, Christopher Lloyd, Sian Rees, Desmond Seward, Daniel Tammet, Casey Watson and Matt Wilven.

TERMS Agent receives 15% commission on domestic sales; 20% commission on foreign sales. Offers written contract; 30-day notice must be given to terminate contract.

HOW TO CONTACT Query by e-mail only. For nonfiction, submit outline and one sample chapter. Accepts simultaneous submissions. Obtains most new clients through recommendations from others and unsolicited through website.

GINA MACCOBY LITERARY AGENCY

P.O. Box 60, Chappaqua NY 10514. (914)238-5630. **Website:** www.publishersmarketplace.com/members/ginamaccoby/. **Contact:** Gina Maccoby. Gina Maccoby is a New York literary agent representing authors of literary and upmarket fiction and narrative nonfiction for adults and children, including New York Times bestselling and award-winning titles. First and foremost she is captured by an engaging, compelling voice; across all forms she is looking for strong storytelling and fresh perspectives. Areas of interest in nonfiction include history, biography, current events, long-form journalism, and popular science. In fiction she is looking for upmarket novels, mysteries and thrillers, middle grade, and young adult. Gina served four terms on the Board of Directors of the Association of Authors' Representatives and is a member of both the Royalties and Contracts Committees. She belongs to SCBWI and is a longtime member of the Authors Guild. Prior to establishing her own agency in 1986, she was a literary agent at Russell & Volkening for 6 years where she handled her own clients as well as first serial, foreign and movie rights for the agency. Gina grew up mostly in Northern California and graduated with Honors from Harvard College.

TERMS Agent receives 15% commission on domestic sales; 20-25% commission on foreign sales, which includes subagents commissions. May recover certain costs, such as purchasing books, shipping books overseas by airmail, legal fees for vetting motion picture contracts, bank fees for electronic funds transfers, overnight delivery services.

HOW TO CONTACT Query by e-mail only. Accepts simultaneous submissions. Obtains most new clients through recommendations.

MANSION STREET LITERARY MANAGEMENT

E-mail: querymansionstreet@gmail.com. **Website:** mansionstreet.com. **Contact:** Jean Sagendorph; Michelle Witte.

HANDLES Jean is not interested in memoirs or medical/reference. Typically sports and self-help are not a good fit; also does not represent travel books. Michelle is not interested in fiction or nonfiction for adults.

RECENT SALES *Shake and Fetch*, by Carli Davidson; *Bleed, Blister, Puke and Purge*, by J. Marin Younker; *Spectrum*, by Ginger Johnson; *I Left You a Present* and *Movie Night Trivia*, by Robb Pearlman; *Open Sesame!*, by Ashley Evanson; *Fox Hunt*, by Nilah Magruder; *ABC Now You See Me*, by Kim Siebold.

HOW TO CONTACT Mansion Street Literary Management has changed how we accept queries, so we now use a submission form. To query Jean, go to http://QueryMe.Online/mansionstreet. To query Michelle, go to http://QueryMe.Online/michellewitte. Accepts simultaneous submissions.

MARJACQ SCRIPTS LTD

Box 412, 19/12 Crawford St., London W1H 1PJ, United Kingdom. (44)(207)935-9499. **Fax:** (44)(207)935-9115. **E-mail:** enquiries@marjacq.com. **Website:** www.marjacq.com. **Contact:** Submissions: individual agent. Business matters: Guy Herbert.. Founded in 1974 by Jacqui Lyons and the late screenwriter and novelist George Markstein, Marjacq is a full-service literary agency with a diverse range of authors across both fiction and non-fiction for adults, young adults and children. We work closely with our authors at every stage of the process, from editorial guidance and negotiating deals, to long-term career management - including selling their work into as many languages as possible and seeking the best opportunities for adaptation to Film, TV and other media. We are a member of the Association of Authors' Agents (AAA).

HANDLES Actively seeking quality fiction, nonfiction, children's books, and young adult books. Does not want to receive stage plays or poetry.

RECENT SALES 3-book deal for Stuart McBride (HarperCollins UK) (repeated *Sunday Times* #1 bestseller); 3-book deal for Howard Linskey.

TERMS Agent receives 15% commission on direct book sales; 20% on foreign rights, film etc. Offers written contract. Services include in-house business affairs consultant. No service fees other than commission. Recharges bank fees for money transfers.

HOW TO CONTACT Email submissions direct to the individual agent who you feel is the best fit. Submit outline, synopsis, 3 sample chapters, bio, covering letter, SASE. "Do not bother with fancy bindings and folders. Keep synopses, bio, and covering letter short." Accepts simultaneous submissions. Obtains most new clients through recommendations from others, solicitations, conferences.

TIPS "Keep trying! If one agent rejects you, you can try someone else. Perseverance and self-belief are important, but do listen to constructive criticism, and 'no' does mean no. Be warned, few agents will give you advice as a non-client. We just don't have the time. Be aware of what is being published. If you show awareness of what other writers are doing in your field/genre, you might be able to see how your book fits in and why an editor/agent might be interested in taking it on. Take care with your submissions. Research the agency and pay attention to presentation: Always follow the specific agency submission guidelines. Doing so helps the agent assess your work. Join writers groups. Sharing your work is a good way to get constructive criticism. If you know anyone in the industry, use your contacts. A personal recommendation will get more notice than cold calling."

MARSAL LYON LITERARY AGENCY, LLC

PMB 121, 665 San Rodolfo Dr. 124, Solana Beach CA 92075. **E-mail:** jill@marsallyonliteraryagency.com; kevan@marsallyonliteraryagency.com; patricia@marsallyonliteraryagency.com; deborah@marsallyonliteraryagency.com; shannon@marsallyonliteraryagency.com. **Website:** www.marsallyonliteraryagency.com.

Please see our web site and visit the pages for each agent to best match your submission to our agents' interests.

RECENT SALES All sales are posted on Publishers' Marketplace.

HOW TO CONTACT Query by e-mail. Query only one agent at this agency at a time. "Please visit our website to determine who is best suited for your work. Write 'query' in the subject line of your e-mail. Please allow up to several weeks to hear back on your query." Accepts simultaneous submissions.

TIPS "Our agency's mission is to help writers achieve their publishing dreams. We want to work with authors not just for a book but for a career; we are dedicated to building long-term relationships with our authors and publishing partners. Our goal is to help find homes for books that engage, entertain, and make a difference."

MARTIN LITERARY AND MEDIA MANAGEMENT

E-mail: sharlene@martinlit.com. **Website:** www.martinlit.com. **Contact:** Sharlene Martin. "Please see our website at www.martinlit.com for company overview, testimonials, bios of literary managers."

HANDLES This agency has strong ties to film/TV. Sharlene Martin has an overall deal with ITV for unscripted television. Actively seeking nonfiction that is highly commercial and that can be adapted to film. "We are being inundated with queries and submissions that are wrongfully being submitted to us, which only results in more frustration for the writers. Please review our Submission Page on our website and direct your query accordingly."

RECENT SALES *Chasing Cosby*, by Nicole Weisensee Egan; *Taking My Life Back*, by Rebekah Gregory with Anthony Flacco; *Breakthrough*, by Jack Andraka; *In the Matter of Nikola Tesla: A Romance of the Mind*, by Anthony Flacco; *Honor Bound: My Journey to Hell and Back with Amanda Knox*, by Raffaele Sollecito; *Impossible Odds: The Kidnapping of Jessica Buchanan and Dramatic Rescue by SEAL Team Six*, by Jessica Buchanan, Erik Landemalm and Anthony Flacco; *Walking on Eggshells*, by Lisa Chapman; *Newtown: An American Tragedy*, by Matthew Lysiak; *Publish Your Nonfiction Book*, by Sharlene Martin and Anthony Flacco.

TERMS Agent receives 15% commission on domestic sales. We are exclusive for foreign sales to Taryn Fagerness Agency. Offers written contract, binding for 1 year; 1-month notice must be given to terminate contract. 99% of materials are sent electronically to minimize charges to author for postage and copying.

HOW TO CONTACT Query via e-mail with MS Word only. No attachments on queries; place letter in body of e-mail. Accepts simultaneous submissions. Obtains most new clients through recommendations from others.

TIPS "Have a strong platform for nonfiction. Please don't call. (I can't tell how well you write by the sound of your voice.) I welcome e-mail. I'm very responsive when I'm interested in a query and work hard to get my clients' materials in the best possible shape before submissions. Do your homework prior to submission and only submit your best efforts. Please review our website carefully to make sure we're a good match for your work. If you read my book, *Publish Your Nonfiction Book: Strategies For Learning the Industry, Selling Your Book and Building a Successful Career* (Writer's Digest Books) you'll know exactly how to charm me."

MASSIE & MCQUILKIN

27 W. 20th St., Suite 305, New York NY 10011. **E-mail:** info@lmqlit.com. **Website:** www.lmqlit.com.

HANDLES "Massie & McQuilkin is a full-service literary agency that focuses on bringing fiction and nonfiction of quality to the largest possible audience."

RECENT SALES Clients include Roxane Gay, Peter Ho Davies, Kim Addonizio, Natasha Trethewey, David Sirota, Katie Crouch, Uwen Akpan, Lydia Millet, Tom Perrotta, Jonathan Lopez, Chris Hayes, Caroline Weber.

TERMS Agent receives 15% commission on domestic sales; 20% commission on foreign sales. Offers written contract; 30-day notice must be given to terminate contract. Only charges for reasonable business expenses upon successful sale.

HOW TO CONTACT E-query preferred. Include the word "Query" in the subject line of your e-mail. Review the agency's online page of agent bios (lmqlit. com/contact.html), as some agents want sample pages with their submissions and some do not. If you have not heard back from the agency in 4 weeks, assume they are not interested in seeing more. Accepts simultaneous submissions. Obtains most new clients through recommendations from others, solicitations, conferences.

MB ARTISTS

775 Sixth Ave., #6, New York NY 10001. (212)689-7830. **E-mail:** mela@mbartists.com. **Website:** www. mbartists.com. **Contact:** Mela Bolinao. MB Artists represents illustrators whose work is primarily intended for the juvenile market in books, editorial publications, licensing merhandise, advertising, games, puzzles, and toys.

HANDLES Specializes in illustration for juvenile markets. Markets include: advertising agencies; editorial/magazines; publishing/books, board games, stationary, etc.

TERMS Rep receives 25% commission. No geographic restrictions. Advertising costs are split: 75% paid by talent; 25% paid by representative.

HOW TO CONTACT For first contact, send query letter, direct mail flier/brochure, website address, tearsheets, slides, photographs or color copies and SASE or send website link to mela@mbartists.com. Portfolio should include at least 12 images appropriate for the juvenile market. Accepts simultaneous submissions.

MARGRET MCBRIDE LITERARY AGENCY

P.O. Box 9128, La Jolla CA 92038. (858)454-1550. **Website:** www.mcbrideliterary.com. The Margret McBride Literary Agency has been in business for almost 40 years and has successfully placed over 300 books with mainstream publishers such as Hachette, Hyperion, HarperCollins, Penguin Random House, Simon & Schuster, Rodale, Macmillan, John Wiley & Sons, Houghton Mifflin Harcourt, Workman and Thomas Nelson. We are always looking for new and interesting projects to get excited about. For information about submitting your work for our consideration, please see our website: www.mcbrideliterary. com."

🔾 Only accepts e-mail queries. No snail mail please.

HANDLES This agency specializes in mainstream nonfiction and some commercial fiction. Actively seeking commercial nonfiction, business, health, self-help. Does not want screenplays, romance, poetry, or children's.

RECENT SALES *Millennial Money*, by Grant Sabatier (Atria/Penguin Random House); *Nimble*, by Baba Prasad (Perigee/Penguin Random House—US and World rights excluding India); *Carefrontation*, by Dr. Arlene Drake (Regan Arts/Phaidon); *There Are No Overachievers*, by Brian Biro (Crown Business/Penguin Random House); *Cheech Is Not My Real Name*, by Richard Marin (Grand Central Books/Hachette); *Killing It!*, by Sheryl O'Loughlin (Harper Business/HarperCollins); *Scrappy*, by Terri Sjodin (Portfolio/Penguin Random House).

TERMS Agent receives 15% commission on domestic sales; 25% commission on translation rights sales (15% to agency, 10% to sub-agent). Charges for overnight delivery and photocopying.

HOW TO CONTACT Please check our website, as instructions are subject to change. Only e-mail queries are accepted: staff@mcbridelit.com. In your query letter, provide a brief synopsis of your work, as well as any pertinent information about yourself. We recommend that authors look at book jacket copy of professionally published books to get an idea of the style and content that should be included in a query letter. Essentially, you are marketing yourself and your work to us, so that we can determine whether we feel we can market you and your work to publishers. There are detailed nonfiction proposal guidelines on our website, but we recommend author's get a copy of How to Write a Book Proposal by Michael Larsen for further instruction. **Please note: The McBride Agency will not respond to queries sent by mail, and will not be responsible for the return of any material submitted by mail.** Accepts simultaneous submissions.

TIPS "E-mail queries only. Please don't call to pitch your work by phone."

SEAN MCCARTHY LITERARY AGENCY

E-mail: submissions@mccarthylit.com. **Website:** www.mccarthylit.com. **Contact:** Sean McCarthy.

HANDLES Sean is drawn to flawed, multifaceted characters with devastatingly concise writing in YA, and character-driven work or smartly paced mysteries/adventures in MG. In picture books, he looks more for unforgettable characters, off-beat humor, and especially clever endings. He is not currently interested in issue-driven stories or query letters that pose too many questions.

HOW TO CONTACT E-query. "Please include a brief description of your book, your biography, and any literary or relevant professional credits in your query letter. If you are a novelist: Please submit the first 3 chapters of your manuscript (or roughly 25 pages) and a 1-page synopsis in the body of the e-mail or as a Word or PDF attachment. If you are a picture book author: Please submit the complete text of your manuscript. We are not currently accepting picture book manuscripts over 1,000 words. If you are an illustrator: Please attach up to 3 JPEGs or PDFs of your work, along with a link to your website." Accepts simultaneous submissions.

ANNE MCDERMID & ASSOCIATES, LTD

320 Front St. W., Suite 1105, Toronto ON M5V 3B6, Canada. (647)788-4016. **Fax:** (416)324-8870. **E-mail:** admin@mcdermidagency.com. **Website:** www.mcdermidagency.com. **Contact:** Anne McDermid.

HANDLES The agency represents literary novelists and commercial novelists of high quality, and also writers of nonfiction in the areas of memoir, biography, history, literary travel, narrative science, and investigative journalism. "We also represent a certain number of children's and YA writers and writers in the fields of science fiction and fantasy."

HOW TO CONTACT Query via e-mail or mail with a brief bio, description, and first 5 pages of project only. Accepts simultaneous submissions. *No unsolicited manuscripts.* Obtains most new clients through recommendations from others.

MCINTOSH & OTIS, INC.

353 Lexington Ave., New York NY 10016. (212)687-7400. **Fax:** (212)687-6894. **E-mail:** info@mcintoshandotis.com. **Website:** www.mcintoshandotis.com. **Contact:** Elizabeth Winick Rubinstein. McIntosh & Otis has a long history of representing authors of adult and children's books. The children's department is a separate division.

HANDLES Actively seeking "books with memorable characters, distinctive voices, and great plots."

TERMS Agent receives 15% commission on domestic sales; 20% on foreign sales.

HOW TO CONTACT E-mail submissions only. Each agent has their own e-mail address for subs. For fiction: Please send a query letter, synopsis, author bio, and the first 3 consecutive chapters (no more than 30 pages) of your novel. For nonfiction: Please send a query letter, proposal, outline, author bio, and 3 sample chapters (no more than 30 pages) of the ms. For children's & young adult: Please send a query letter, synopsis and the first 3 consecutive chapters (not to exceed 25 pages) of the ms. Accepts simultaneous submissions. Obtains clients through recommendations from others, editors, conferences and queries.

HOWARD MORHAIM LITERARY AGENCY

30 Pierrepont St., Brooklyn NY 11201. (718)222-8400. **Fax:** (718)222-5056. **E-mail:** info@morhaimliterary.com. **Website:** www.morhaimliterary.com.

HANDLES Agent Kate McKean represents young adult and middle grade when she is open to submissions. Concerning books for children and teens, she seeks "middle grade and young adult full-length novels only in the areas of: mystery, thriller, horror, romance, LGBTQ issues, contemporary fiction, sports, magical realism, fantasy, and science fiction." Concerning what not to send her, avoid sending the following: "books that feature dragons, angels/demons/Grim Reaper, werewolves/vampires/zombies etc., zany middle grade stories about a character's wacky adventures, stories about bullying, stories t hat center around orphans or parents who die in car crashes, ghost-teens back to right wrongs. No novels in verse. No picture books or chapter books." Kate McKean is open to many subgenres and categories of YA and MG fiction. Check the website for the most details. Actively seeking fiction, nonfiction, and young adult novels.

HOW TO CONTACT Query via e-mail with cover letter and 3 sample chapters. See each agent's listing for specifics. Accepts simultaneous submissions.

MOVEABLE TYPE MANAGEMENT

244 Madison Ave., Suite 334, New York NY 10016. **E-mail:** achromy@movabletm.com. **Website:** www.movabletm.com. **Contact:** Adam Chromy.

HANDLES Mr. Chromy is a generalist, meaning that he accepts fiction submissions of virtually any kind (except juvenile books aimed for middle grade and younger) as well as nonfiction. He has sold books in the following categories: new adult, women's, romance, memoir, pop culture, young adult, lifestyle, horror, how-to, general fiction, and more.

RECENT SALES *The Wedding Sisters*, by Jamie Brenner (St. Martin's Press); *Rage*, by (AmazonCrossing); *Sons Of Zeus*, by Noble Smith (Thomas Dunne Books); *World Made By Hand And Too Much Magic*, by James Howard Kunstler (Grove/Atlantic Press); *Dirty Rocker Boys*, by Bobbie Brown (Gallery/S&S).

HOW TO CONTACT E-queries only. Responds if interested. For nonfiction: Send a query letter in the body of an e-mail that precisely introduces your topic and approach, and includes a descriptive bio. For journalists and academics, please also feel free to include a CV. Fiction: Send your query letter and the first 10 pages of your novel in the body of an e-mail. Your subject line needs to contain the word "Query" or your message will not reach the agency. No attachments and no snail mail. Accepts simultaneous submissions.

ERIN MURPHY LITERARY AGENCY

824 Roosevelt Trail, #290, Windham ME 04062. **Website:** emliterary.com. **Contact:** Erin Murphy, president; Ammi-Joan Paquette, senior agent; Tricia Lawrence, agent; Kevin Lewis, agent; Tara Gonzalez, associate agent.

This agency only represents children's books. "We do not accept unsolicited manuscripts or queries. We consider new clients by referral or personal contact only (such as meeting at writers conferences)."

HANDLES Specializes in children's books only.

TERMS Agent receives 15% commission on domestic sales; 20-30% on foreign sales. Offers written contract. 30 days notice must be given to terminate contract.

HOW TO CONTACT Accepts simultaneous submissions.

TIPS "Please do not submit to more than one agent at EMLA at a time."

JEAN V. NAGGAR LITERARY AGENCY, INC.

JVNLA, Inc., 216 E. 75th St., Suite 1E, New York NY 10021. (212)794-1082. **Website:** www.jvnla.com. **Contact:** Jennifer Weltz.

HANDLES This agency specializes in mainstream fiction and nonfiction and literary fiction with commercial potential as well as young adult, middle grade, and picture books. Does not want to receive screenplays.

RECENT SALES *Mort(e)*, by Robert Repino; *The Paying Guests*, by Sarah Waters; *The Third Victim*, by Phillip Margolin; *Every Kind of Wanting*, by Gina Frangello; *The Lies They Tell*, by Gillian French; *Dietland*, by Sarai Walker; *Mr. Rochester*, by Sarah Shoemaker; *Not If I See You First*, by Eric Lindstrom.

TERMS Agent receives 15% commission on domestic sales; 20% commission on foreign and film sales. Offers written contract. Charges for overseas mailing, messenger services, book purchases, photocopying—all deductible from royalties received.

HOW TO CONTACT "Visit our website to send submissions and see what our individual agents are looking for. No snail mail submissions please!" Accepts simultaneous submissions.

TIPS "We recommend courage, fortitude, and patience: the courage to be true to your own vision, the fortitude to finish a novel and polish it again and again before sending it out, and the patience to accept rejection gracefully and wait for the stars to align themselves appropriately for success."

NELSON LITERARY AGENCY

1732 Wazee St., Suite 207, Denver CO 80202. (303)292-2805. **E-mail:** query@nelsonagency.com. **Website:** www.nelsonagency.com. **Contact:** Kristin Nelson, President. Kristin Nelson established Nelson Literary Agency, LLC, in 2002 and over the last decade of her career, she has represented over thirty-five *New York Times* bestselling titles and many *USA Today* bestsellers. Editors call her "a hard-working bulldog agent that will fight for you." When not busy selling books, she is quite sporty. She attempts to play tennis and golf. She also loves playing Bridge (where she is the youngest person in the club). On weekends, she and her husband can be found in the mountains hiking with their 12-year old rat terrier, Chutney. "I'm looking for a good story well told. How you tell that story doesn't need to fit in a neat little category. For specifics, check out the examples on the Submission Guidelines page, follow the clear directions posted there, then submit a query directly to."

○ Kristin is looking for a good story well told. How you tell that story doesn't need to fit in a neat little category. For those looking for more specifics, the below might be helpful: Young adult and upper-level middle-grade novels in all subgeneres; big crossover novels with one foot squarely in genre (*Wool, The Night Circus, Gone Girl*); literary commercial novels (*Hotel on the Corner of Bitter and Sweet, Major Pettigrew's Last Stand, The Art of Racing in the Rain*); upmarket women's fiction (*Keepsake, My Sister's Keeper, Still Alice*); single-title romance, historicals especially (*Ravishing The Heiress, The Ugly Duchess, The Heir*); lead title or hardcover science fiction and fantasy (*Soulless, Game of Thrones, Old Man's War*).

HANDLES NLA specializes in representing commercial fiction and high-caliber literary fiction. "We represent many popular genre categories, including historical romance, steampunk, and all subgenres of YA." Regardless of genre, "we are actively seeking good stories well told." Does not want nonfiction, memoir, stage plays, screenplays, short story collections, poetry, children's picture books, early reader chapter books, or material for the Christian/inspirational market.

TERMS Agent charges industry standard commission.

HOW TO CONTACT "Please visit our website and carefully read our submission guidelines. We do not accept any queries on Facebook or Twitter." Accepts simultaneous submissions.

TIPS "If you would like to learn how to write an awesome pitch paragraph for your query letter or would like any info on how publishing contracts work, please visit Kristin's popular industry blog Pub Rants: http://nelsonagency.com/pub-rants/."

NEW LEAF LITERARY & MEDIA, INC.

110 W. 40th St., Suite 2201, New York NY 10018. (646)248-7989. **Fax:** (646)861-4654. **Website:** www. newleafliterary.com. "We are a passionate agency with a relentless focus on building our clients' careers. Our approach is big picture, offering a one-stop shop built without silos and access to a variety of services including international sales, film and television, and branding resources for all clients. Our aim is to challenge conformity and re-imagine the marketplace while equipping our clients with the tools necessary to navigate an evolving landscape and succeed."

RECENT SALES *Carve the Mark*, by Veronica Roth (HarperCollins); *Red Queen*, by Victoria Aveyard (HarperCollins); *Lobster is the Best Medicine*, by Liz Climo (Running Press); *Ninth House*, by Leigh Bardugo (Henry Holt); *A Snicker of Magic*, by Natalie Lloyd (Scholastic).

HOW TO CONTACT Send query via e-mail. Please do not query via phone. The word "Query" must be in the subject line, plus the agent's name, i.e.–Subject: Query, Suzie Townsend. You may include up to 5 double-spaced sample pages within the body of the e-mail. No attachments, unless specifically requested. Include all necessary contact information. You will receive an auto-response confirming receipt of your query. "We only respond if we are interested in seeing your work."

PARK LITERARY GROUP, LLC

50 Broadway, Suite 1601, New York NY 10006. (212)691-3500. **Fax:** (212)691-3540. **E-mail:** info@ parkliterary.com. **Website:** www.parkliterary.com.

HANDLES The Park Literary Group represents fiction and nonfiction with a boutique approach: an emphasis on servicing a relatively small number of clients, with the highest professional standards and focused personal attention. Does not want to receive poetry or screenplays.

RECENT SALES This agency's client list is on their website. It includes bestsellers Nicholas Sparks, Soman Chainani, Emily Giffin, and Debbie Macomber.

HOW TO CONTACT Please specify the first and last name of the agent to whom you are submitting in the subject line of the e-mail. All materials must be in the body of the e-mail. Responds if interested. For fiction submissions, please include a query letter with short synopsis and the first 3 chapters of your work. Accepts simultaneous submissions.

RUBIN PFEFFER CONTENT

648 Hammond St., Chestnut Hill MA 02467. **E-mail:** info@rpcontent.com. **Website:** www.rpcontent.com. **Contact:** Rubin Pfeffer. Rubin Pfeffer Content is a literary agency exclusively representing children's and

young adult literature, as well as content that will serve educational publishers and digital developers. Working closely with authors and illustrators, RPC is devoted to producing long-lasting children's literature: work that exemplifies outstanding writing, innovative creativity, and artistic excellence.

HANDLES High-quality children's fiction and non-fiction, including picture books, middle-grade, and young adult. No manuscripts intended for an adult audience.

HOW TO CONTACT Note: Rubin Pfeffer accepts submissions by referral only. Melissa Nasson is open to queries for picture books, middle-grade, and young adult fiction and nonfiction. To query Melissa, email her at melissa@rpcontent.com, include the query letter in the body of the email, and attach the first 50 pages as a Word doc or PDF. If you wish to query Rubin Pfeffer by referral only, specify the contact information of your reference when submitting. Authors/illustrators should send a query and a 1-3 chapter ms via e-mail (no postal submissions). The query, placed in the body of the e-mail, should include a synopsis of the piece, as well as any relevant information regarding previous publications, referrals, websites, and biographies. The ms may be attached as a .doc or a .pdf file. Specifically for illustrators, attach a PDF of the dummy or artwork to the e-mail. Accepts simultaneous submissions.

PIPPIN PROPERTIES, INC.

(212)338-9310. **E-mail:** info@pippinproperties.com. **Website:** www.pippinproperties.com. **Contact:** Holly McGhee. Pippin Properties, Inc. opened its doors in 1998, and for the past 17 years we have been privileged to help build careers for authors and artists whose work stands the test of time, many of whom have become household names in their own right such as Peter H. Reynolds, Kate DiCamillo, Sujean Rim, Doreen Cronin, Renata Liwska, Sarah Weeks, Harry Bliss, Kate & Jim McMullan, Katherine Applegate, David Small, and Kathi Appelt. We also love to launch new careers for amazing authors and artists such as Jason Reynolds, Anna Kang and Chris Weyant, and Jandy Nelson.

HANDLES "We are strictly a children's literary agency devoted to the management of authors and artists in all media. We are small and discerning in choosing our clientele."

TERMS Agent receives 15% commission on domestic sales; 25% commission on foreign sales. Offers written contract; 30-day notice must be given to terminate contract.

HOW TO CONTACT If you are a writer who is interested in submitting a ms, please query us via e-mail, and within the body of that e-mail please include: the first chapter of your novel with a short synopsis of the work or the entire picture book ms. For illustrators interested in submitting their work, please send a query letter detailing your background in illustration and include links to website with a dummy or other examples of your work. Direct all queries to the agent whom you wish to query and please do not query more than one. No attachments, please. Accepts simultaneous submissions. Obtains most new clients through recommendations from others.

TIPS "Please do not call after sending a submission."

PRENTIS LITERARY

PMB 496 6830 NE Bothell Way, Kenmore WA 98028. **Website:** prentisliterary.com. **Contact:** Autumn Frisse, acquisitions; Terry Johnson, business manager. A boutique author focused agency with a devotion to words and the innovative voices that put those words to good use. The agency has always centered on finding books we are passionate about homes. When Linn Prentis was alive, this was her mission and long before she passed, it indeed has been ours as well. Many a time passion has lead us to love, champion and sell books that defy pat definition. While we obviously are seeking the commercially successful, we also demand good writing which we admire that sparks our passion.

HANDLES Special interest in sci-fi and fantasy, but fiction is what truly interests us. Nonfiction projects have to be something we just can't resist. Actively seeking science fiction/fantasy, POC/intersectional, women's fiction, LBGTQ+, literary fiction, children's fiction, YA, MG, mystery, horror, romance, nonfiction/memoir. Please visit website for comprehensive list. Does not want to "receive books for little kids."

RECENT SALES Sales include The Relic Hunter: A Gina Miyoko Mystery NYT best selling author, Maya Bohnhoff, Substrate Phantoms for Jessica Reisman, Vienna for William Kirby; Hunting Ground, Frost Burned and Night Broken titles in two series for NY Times bestselling author Patricia Briggs (as well as a graphic novel *Homecoming*) and a story collection; with more coming; a duology of novels for A.M. Dellamonica whose first book, *Indigo Springs*, won Canada's annual award for best fantasy, as well as several books abroad for client Tachyon Publications. **TERMS** Agent receives 15% commission on domestic sales; 20% commission on foreign sales. Offers written contract; 60-day notice must be given to terminate contract.

HOW TO CONTACT No phone or fax queries. No surface mail. For submission use our submission form posted on our submission page or e-mail acquisitions afrisse@prentisliterary.com. For other business business questions e-mail: tjohnson@prentisliterary.com. Accepts simultaneous submissions. Obtains most new clients through recommendations from others, solicitations.

PROSPECT AGENCY

551 Valley Rd., PMB 377, Upper Montclair NJ 07043. (718)788-3217. **Fax:** (718)360-9582. **Website:** www.prospectagency.com. "Prospect Agency was founded in 2005 with the goal of offering clients top notch representation, creating a community-centered haven for authors and illustrators, and taking a leadership role in creating bold, innovative literature. The agency focuses on both the adult and children's markets, and is currently looking for the next generation of writers and illustrators to shape the literary landscape. We are a small, personal agency that helps each client reach success through hands-on editorial assistance and professional contract negotiations. We also strive to be on the cutting edge of technologically. The agents here spend a lot of time forming personal relationships with authors and their work. Every agent here has incredibly strong editorial skills, and works directly with clients to balance the goals of selling individual books and managing a career."

HANDLES Handles nonfiction, fiction, picture books, middle grade, young adult. "We're looking for strong, unique voices and unforgettable stories and characters."

TERMS Agent receives 15% on domestic sales, 20% on foreign sales sold directly and 25% on sales using a subagent. Offers written contract.

HOW TO CONTACT All submissions are electronic and must be submitted through the portal at prospectagency.com/submit.html. We do not accept any submissions through snail mail. Accepts simultaneous submissions. Obtains new clients through

conferences, recommendations, queries, and some scouting.

P.S. LITERARY AGENCY

2010 Winston Park Dr., 2nd Floor, Oakville ON L6H 5R7, Canada. **E-mail:** info@psliterary.com. **Website:** www.psliterary.com. **Contact:** Curtis Russell, principal agent; Carly Watters, senior agent; Maria Vicente, literary agent; Eric Smith; literary agent; Kurestin Armada, associate agent.. The P.S. Literary Agency (PSLA) represents both fiction and nonfiction works to leading publishers in North America, Europe and throughout the World. We maintain a small but select client list that receives our undivided attention and focused efforts. PSLA seeks to work with clients who are professional and committed to their goals. It is our desire to work with clients for the duration of their careers.

"The P.S. Literary Agency represents both fiction and nonfiction in a variety of categories. Seeking both new and established writers."

HANDLES Actively seeking both fiction and nonfiction. Seeking both new and established writers. Does not want to receive poetry or screenplays.

TERMS Agent receives 15% commission on domestic sales; 25% commission on foreign sales. "We offer a written contract, with 30-days notice to terminate."

HOW TO CONTACT Query letters should be directed to query@psliterary.com. PSLA does not accept or respond to phone, paper, or social media queries. Obtains most new clients through solicitations.

TIPS "Please review our website for the most up-to-date submission guidelines. We do not charge reading fees. We do not offer a critique service."

THE PURCELL AGENCY

E-mail: tpaqueries@gmail.com. **Website:** www.thepurcellagency.com. **Contact:** Tina P. Schwartz. This is an agency for authors of children's and teen literature.

HANDLES This agency also takes juvenile nonfiction for MG and YA markets. At this point, the agency is not considering fantasy, science fiction or picture book submissions.

RECENT SALES *Seven Suspects*, by Renee James; *A Kind of Justice*, by Renee James; *Adventures at Hound Hotel*, by Shelley Swanson Sateren; *Adventures at Tabby Towers*, by Shelley Swanson Sateren; *Keys to Freedom*, by Karen Meade.

HOW TO CONTACT Check the website to see if agency is open to submissions and for submission guidelines. Accepts simultaneous submissions.

RED SOFA LITERARY

(651)224-6670. **E-mail:** dawn@redsofaliterary.com laura@redsofaliterary.com; amanda@redsofaliterary.com; stacey@redsofaliterary.com; erik@redsofaliterary.com; liz@redsofaliterary.com. **Website:** www.redsofaliterary.com. **Contact:** Dawn Frederick, owner/literary agent; Laura Zats, literary agent; Amanda Rutter, associate literary agent; Stacey Graham, associate literary agent; Erik Hane, associate literary agent; Liz Rahn, subrights agent.

HANDLES Dawn Frederick: "I am always in search of a good work of nonfiction that falls within my categories (see my specific list at our website). I especially love pop culture, interesting histories, social sciences/advocacy, humor and books that are great conversation starters. As for fiction, I am always in search of good YA and MG titles. For YA I will go a little darker on the tone, as I enjoy a good gothic, contemporary or historical YA novel. For MG, I will always want something fun and lighthearted, but would love more contemporary themes too." **Laura Zats:** " Diverse YA of all kinds, I'm looking for all genres here, and am especially interested in settings or characters I haven't seen before and queer romantic relationships if there's a romance. Adult science fiction and fantasy.Please note I have an anthropology degree, I'm interested in well-drawn cultures and subverting traditional Chosen One, quest, and colonial narratives. I will fall on the floor and salivate if your writing reminds me of N.K. Jemisin or Nnedi Okorafor. No white dudes on quests, dreams, or Western ideas of Hell, please. Romance/erotica - I am looking for all settings and subgenres here. Must have verbal consent throughout and a twist to traditional romance tropes. If you send me the next The Hating Game, I will be the happiest agent in all the land. Please no rape, querying anything shorter than 60K, or shifters" **Amanda Rutter:** "Science fiction/fantasy, the non-YA ideas, young adult and middle grade–science fiction/fantasy." **Stacey Graham:** "Middle-grade with a great voice — especially funny and/or spooky, Nonfiction (MG/YA/Adult), Romance, and Mystery with a humorous bent." **Erik Hane:** "Literary fiction, Nonfiction [no memoirs]." These are the things we are not actively seeking: **Dawn:** "Memoirs, it seems everyone ignores this request. I also prefer to represent books that aren't overly sappy, overly romantic, or any type of didactic/moralistic."**Laura:** "Nonfiction, including memoir. Adult mystery/thriller/literary fiction. Fiction without quirky or distinctive hooks. Books that follow or fit in trends." **Amanda:** "I am definitely not a non-fiction person. I rarely read it myself, so wouldn't know where to start where to represent! Also, although I enjoy middle grade fiction and would be happy to represent, I won't take on picture books." **Stacey:** "At this time, I do not want to represent YA, fantasy, sci-fi, or romance." **Erik:** "I definitely don't want to represent fiction that sets out at the start to be 'genre.' I like reading it, but I don't think it's for me as an agent. Bring me genre elements, but I think I'd rather let the classification happen naturally. I also don't want memoir unless you've really, really got something unique and accessible. I also don't want to represent children's lit; that's another thing I really do love and appreciate but don't quite connect with professionally."

TERMS Agent receives 15% commission on domestic sales; 20% commission on foreign sales. Offers written contract.

HOW TO CONTACT Query by e-mail or mail with SASE. No attachments, please. Submit full proposal (for nonfiction especially, for fiction it would be nice) plus 3 sample chapters (or first 50 pages) and any other pertinent writing samples upon request by the specific agent. Do not sent within or attached to the query letter. Pdf/doc/docx is preferred, no rtf documents please. Accepts simultaneous submissions. Obtains new clients through queries, also through recommendations from others, solicitations.

TIPS "Always remember the benefits of building an author platform, and the accessibility of accomplishing this task in today's industry. Most importantly, research the agents queried. Avoid contacting every literary agent about a book idea. Due to the large volume of queries received, the process of reading queries for unrepresented categories (by the agency) becomes quite the arduous task. Investigate online directories, printed guides (like *Writer's Market*), individual agent websites, and more, before beginning the query process. It's good to remember that each agent has a vision of what s/he wants to represent and will communicate this information accordingly. We're simply waiting for those specific book ideas to come in our direction."

REES LITERARY AGENCY

14 Beacon St., Suite 710, Boston MA 02108. (617)227-9014. **E-mail:** lorin@reesagency.com. **Website:** reesagency.com.

TERMS Agent receives 15% commission on domestic sales; 20% commission on foreign sales.

HOW TO CONTACT Consult website for each agent's submission guidelines and e-mail addresses, as they differ. Accepts simultaneous submissions. Obtains most new clients through recommendations from others, conferences, submissions.

REGAL HOFFMANN & ASSOCIATES LLC

143 West 29th St., Suite 901, New York NY 10001. (212)684-7900. **Website:** www.rhaliterary.com. Regal Hoffmann & Associates LLC, a full-service agency based in New York, was founded in 2002. We represent works in a wide range of categories, with an emphasis on literary fiction, outstanding thriller and crime fiction, and serious narrative nonfiction.

HANDLES We represent works in a wide range of categories, with an emphasis on literary fiction, outstanding thriller and crime fiction, and serious narrative nonfiction. Actively seeking literary fiction and narrative nonfiction. Does not want romance, science fiction, poetry, or screenplays.

RECENT SALES *Wily Snare*, by Adam Jay Epstein; *Perfectly Undone*, by Jamie Raintree; *A Sister in My House*, by Linda Olsson; *This Is How It Really Sounds*, by Stuart Archer Cohen; *Autofocus*, by Lauren Gibaldi; *We've Already Gone This Far*, by Patrick Dacey; *A Fierce and Subtle Poison*, by Samantha Mabry; *The Life of the World to Come*, by Dan Cluchey; *Willful Disregard*, by Lena Andersson; *The Sweetheart*, by Angelina Mirabella.

TERMS Agent receives 15% commission on domestic sales; 20% commission on foreign sales. We charge no reading fees.

HOW TO CONTACT Query with SASE or via Submittable (https://rhaliterary.submittable.com/submit). No phone calls. Submissions should consist of a 1-page query letter detailing the book in question, as well as the qualifications of the author. For fiction, submissions may also include the first 10 pages of the novel or one short story from a collection. Accepts simultaneous submissions.

TIPS "We are deeply committed to every aspect of our clients' careers, and are engaged in everything from the editorial work of developing a great book proposal or line editing a fiction manuscript to negotiating state-of-the-art book deals and working to promote and publicize the book when it's published. We are at the forefront of the effort to increase authors' rights in publishing contracts in a rapidly changing commercial environment. We deal directly with co-agents and publishers in every foreign territory and also work directly and with co-agents for feature film and television rights, with extraordinary success in both arenas. Many of our clients' works have sold in dozens of translation markets, and a high proportion of our books have been sold in Hollywood. We have strong relationships with speaking agents, who can assist in arranging author tours and other corporate and college speaking opportunities when appropriate."

✪ THE RIGHTS FACTORY

P.O. Box 499, Station C, Toronto ON M6J 3P6, Canada. (416)966-5367. **Website:** www.therightsfactory.com. "The Rights Factory is an international literary agency."

HANDLES Plays, screenplays, textbooks.

HOW TO CONTACT There is a submission form on this agency's website. Accepts simultaneous submissions.

RODEEN LITERARY MANAGEMENT

3501 N. Southport #497, Chicago IL 60657. **E-mail:** info@rodeenliterary.com. **Website:** www.rodeenliterary.com. **Contact:** Paul Rodeen.

HANDLES Actively seeking "writers and illustrators of all genres of children's literature including picture books, early readers, middle-grade fiction and nonfiction, graphic novels and comic books, as well as young adult fiction and nonfiction." This is primarily an agency devoted to children's books.

HOW TO CONTACT Unsolicited submissions are accepted by e-mail only. Cover letters with synopsis and contact information should be included in the body of your e-mail. An initial submission of 50 pages from a novel or a longer work of nonfiction will suffice and should be pasted into the body of your e-mail. Accepts simultaneous submissions.

ANDY ROSS LITERARY AGENCY

767 Santa Ray Ave., Oakland CA 94610. (510)238-8965. **E-mail:** andyrossagency@hotmail.com. **Website:** www.andyrossagency.com. **Contact:** Andy Ross. "I opened my literary agency in 2008. Prior to that, I was the owner of the legendary Cody's Books in Berkeley for 30 years. My agency represents books in a wide range

of nonfiction genres including: narrative nonfiction, science, journalism, history, popular culture, memoir, and current events. I also represent literary, commercial, historical, crime, upmarket women's fiction, and YA fiction. For nonfiction, I look for writing with a strong voice, robust story arc, and books that tell a big story about culture and society by authors with the authority to write about their subject. In fiction, I like stories about real people in the real world. No vampires and trolls, thank you very much. I don't represent poetry, science fiction, paranormal, and romance. Authors I represent include: Daniel Ellsberg, Jeffrey Moussaieff Masson, Anjanette Delgado, Elisa Kleven, Tawni Waters, Randall Platt, Mary Jo McConahay, Gerald Nachman, Michael Parenti, Paul Krassner, Milton Viorst, and Michele Anna Jordan. I am a member of the Association of Author Representatives (AAR). Check out my website and blog."

HANDLES "This agency specializes in general nonfiction, politics and current events, history, biography, journalism and contemporary culture as well as literary, commercial, and YA fiction." Does not want to receive poetry.

RECENT SALES See my website.

TERMS Agent receives 15% commission on domestic sales; 20% commission on foreign sales or other deals made through a sub-agent. Offers written contract.

HOW TO CONTACT Queries should be less than half page. Please put the word "query" in the title header of the e-mail. In the first sentence, state the category of the project. Give a short description of the book and your qualifications for writing. Accepts simultaneous submissions.

VICTORIA SANDERS & ASSOCIATES

(212)633-8811. **E-mail:** queriesvsa@gmail.com. **Website:** www.victoriasanders.com. **Contact:** Victoria Sanders.

HANDLES Various agents at this agency handle juvenile books, such as young adult and picture books.

TERMS Agent receives 15% commission on domestic sales; 20% commission on foreign/film sales. Offers written contract.

HOW TO CONTACT Authors who wish to contact us regarding potential representation should send a query letter with the first 3 chapters (or about 25 pages) pasted into the body of the message to queriesvsa@gmail.com. We will only accept queries via e-mail. Query letters should describe the project and

the author in the body of a single, 1-page e mail that does not contain any attached files. Important note: Please paste the first 3 chapters of your manuscript (or about 25 pages, and feel free to round up to a chapter break) into the body of your e-mail. Accepts simultaneous submissions.

TIPS "Limit query to letter (no calls) and give it your best shot. A good query is going to get a good response."

WENDY SCHMALZ AGENCY

402 Union St., #831, Hudson NY 12534. (518)672-7697. **E-mail:** wendy@schmalzagency.com. **Website:** www.schmalzagency.com. **Contact:** Wendy Schmalz.

HANDLES Not looking for picture books, science fiction or fantasy.

TERMS Agent receives 15% commission on domestic sales; 20% on foreign sales; 25% for Asia.

HOW TO CONTACT Accepts only e-mail queries. Paste synopsis into the e-mail. Do not attach the ms or sample chapters or synopsis. Replies to queries only if they want to read the ms. If you do not hear from this agency within 2 weeks, consider that a no. Accepts simultaneous submissions. Obtains clients through recommendations from others.

SUSAN SCHULMAN LITERARY AGENCY LLC

454 W. 44th St., New York NY 10036. (212)713-1633. **E-mail:** susan@schulmanagency.com. **Website:** www.publishersmarketplace.com/members/schulman/. **Contact:** Susan Schulman. "A literary agency specializes in representing foreign rights, motion picture, television and allied rights, live stage including commercial theater, opera and dance adaptations, new media rights including e-book and digital applications, and other subsidiary rights on behalf of North American publishers and independent literary agents. The agency also represents its own clients domestically and internationally in all markets. The agency has a particular interest in fiction and nonfiction books for, by and about women and women's issues and interests. The agency's areas of focus include: commercial and literary fiction and nonfiction, specifically narrative memoir, politics, economics, social issues, history, urban planning, finance, law, health, psychology, body/mind/spirit, and creativity and writing."

HANDLES "We specialize in books for, by and about women and women's issues including nonfiction self-help books, fiction, and theater projects. We also handle the film, television. and allied rights for several agencies as well as foreign rights for several publishing houses." Actively seeking new nonfiction. Considers plays. Does not want to receive poetry, television scripts or concepts for television.

RECENT SALES Sold 70 titles in the last year; hundreds of subsidiary rights deals.

TERMS Agent receives 15% commission on domestic sales; 20% commission on foreign sales. Offers written contract; 30-day notice must be given to terminate contract.

HOW TO CONTACT "For fiction: query letter with outline and three sample chapters, resume and SASE. For nonfiction: query letter with complete description of subject, at least one chapter, resume and SASE. Queries may be sent via regular mail or e-mail. Please do not submit queries via UPS or Federal Express. Please do not send attachments with e-mail queries Please incorporate the chapters into the body of the e-mail." Accepts simultaneous submissions. Obtains most new clients through recommendations from others, solicitations, conferences.

TIPS "Keep writing!" Schulman describes her agency as "professional boutique, long-standing, eclectic."

SELECTIC ARTISTS

9 Union Square, #123, Southbury CT 06488. **E-mail:** christopher@selectricartists.com. **Website:** www. selectricartists.com. **Contact:** Christopher Schelling. "Selectric Artists is an agency for literary and creative management founded and run by Christopher Schelling. Selectric's client list includes best-selling and critically-acclaimed authors in many genres, as well as a few New York pop-rock musicians. Schelling has been an agent for over twenty years and previously held executive editor positions at Dutton and HarperCollins."

HOW TO CONTACT E-mail only. Consult agency website for status on open submissions. Accepts simultaneous submissions.

SERENDIPITY LITERARY AGENCY, LLC

305 Gates Ave., Brooklyn NY 11216. **E-mail:** rbrooks@ serendipitylit.com; info@serendipitylit.com. **Website:** www.serendipitylit.com; facebook.com/serendipitylit. **Contact:** Regina Brooks.

"Authors who have a hook, platform, and incredible writing are ideal. Must be willing to put efforts into promotion."

TERMS Agent receives 15% commission on domestic sales; 20% commission on foreign sales. Offers written contract; 2-month notice must be given to terminate contract. Charges clients for office fees, which are taken from any advance.

HOW TO CONTACT Check the website, as there are online submission forms for fiction, nonfiction and juvenile. Website will also state if we're temporarily closed to submissions to any areas. Accepts simultaneous submissions. Obtains most new clients through conferences, referrals and social media.

TIPS "See the books *Writing Great Books For Young Adults* and *You Should Really Write A Book: How To Write Sell And Market Your Memoir.* We are looking for high concept ideas with big hooks. If you get writer's block try possibiliteas.co, it's a muse in a cup."

THE SEYMOUR AGENCY

475 Miner St., Canton NY 13617. (239)398-8209. **E-mail:** nicole@theseymouragency.com; julie@theseymouragency.com. **Website:** www.theseymouragency. com. We work with both fiction and nonfiction authors across the spectrum of topics and genres.

TERMS Agent receives 12-15% commission on domestic sales.

HOW TO CONTACT Accepts e-mail queries. Check online for guidelines. Accepts simultaneous submissions.

SPENCERHILL ASSOCIATES

8131 Lakewood Main St., Building M, Suite 205, Lakewood Ranch FL 34202. (941)907-3700. **E-mail:** submission@spencerhillassociates.com. **Website:** www.spencerhillassociates.com. **Contact:** Karen Solem, Nalini Akolekar, Amanda Leuck, Sandy Harding, and Ali Herring. Karen Solem founded Spencerhill in 2001 to represent authors of commercial, general-interest fiction. Specializing in romance and women's fiction, we work with talented writers in every genre at any stage of their career-from the well-known, successfully published and established author to the debut writer with an exciting new voice. Based in Florida, our agents travel to industry conferences nationally and internationally. Our goal is to maximize the careers of our authors by placing them with the right editors and publishers so their readerships can expand. In a complex and dynamic industry our personal approach provides experienced guidance through every phase of the publishing process.

HANDLES "We handle mostly commercial women's fiction, historical novels, romance (historical, contemporary, paranormal, urban fantasy), thrillers, and mysteries. We also represent Christian fiction only—no nonfiction." No nonfiction, poetry, children's picture books, or scripts.

RECENT SALES A full list of sales and clients is available on the agency website.

TERMS Agent receives 15% commission on domestic sales; 20% commission on foreign sales. Offers written contract; 3-month notice must be given to terminate contract.

HOW TO CONTACT "We accept electronic submissions only. Please send us a query letter in the body of an e-mail, pitch us your project and tell us about yourself: Do you have prior publishing credits? Attach the first three chapters and synopsis preferably in .doc, rtf or txt format to your email. Send all queries to submission@spencerhillassociates.com. Or submit through the QueryManager link on our website. We do not have a preference for exclusive submissions, but do appreciate knowing if the submission is simultaneous. We receive thousands of submissions a year and each query receives our attention. Unfortunately, we are unable to respond to each query individually. If we are interested in your work, we will contact you within 12 weeks." Accepts simultaneous submissions.

THE SPIELER AGENCY

27 W. 20 St., Suite 302, New York NY 10011. (212)757-4439, ext. 1. **Fax:** (212)333-2019. **Website:** thespieleragency.com. **Contact:** Joe Spieler.

TERMS Agent receives 15% commission on domestic sales. Charges clients for messenger bills, photocopying, postage.

HOW TO CONTACT "Before submitting projects to the Spieler Agency, check the listings of our individual agents and see if any particular agent shows a general interest in your subject (e.g. history, memoir, YA, etc.). Please send all queries either by e-mail or regular mail. If you query us by regular mail, we can only reply to you if you include a SASE." Accepts simultaneous submissions. Obtains most new clients through recommendations, listing in *Guide to Literary Agents*.

STIMOLA LITERARY STUDIO

308 Livingston Ct., Edgewater NJ 07020. **E-mail:** info@stimolaliterarystudio.com. **Website:** www.stimolaliterarystudio.com. **Contact:** Rosemary B. Stimola. "A full service literary agency devoted to representing authors and author/illustrators of fiction and nonfiction, pre-school through young adult, who bring unique and substantive contributions to the industry."

HANDLES Actively seeking remarkable middle grade, young adult fiction, and debut picture book author/illustrators. Also seeking fresh graphic novels for juvenile and adult readers. No institutional books.

RECENT SALES *King Alice*, by Matthew Cordell; *Snakes on a Train*, by Kathryn Dennis; *Mapping Sam*, by Joyce Hesselberth; *Butterfly Yellow*, by Thanhha Lai; *Killing November*, by Adriana Mather; *Two Can Keep a Secret*, by Karen M. McManus; *Monster Street*, by J.H. Reynolds; *Death Prefers Blondes*, by Caleb Roehrig; *Through the Window*, by Barb Rosenstock and Mary GrandPre; *I Am Human*, by Susan Verde.

TERMS Agent receives 15% commission on domestic sales; 20% (if subagents are employed) commission on foreign sales. Offers written contract, binding for all children's projects. 60 days notice must be given to terminate contract.

HOW TO CONTACT Query via e-mail as per submission guidelines on website. Author/illustrators of picture books may attach text and sample art. with query. A PDF dummy is preferred. Accepts simultaneous submissions. While unsolicited queries are welcome, most clients come through editor, agent, client referrals.

TIPS Agent is hands-on, no-nonsense. May request revisions. Does not line edit but may offer suggestions for improvement before submission. Well-respected by clients and editors. "A firm but reasonable deal negotiator."

STONESONG

270 W. 39th St. #201, New York NY 10018. (212)929-4600. **E-mail:** editors@stonesong.com. **Website:** stonesong.com.

HANDLES Does not represent plays, screenplays, picture books, or poetry.

RECENT SALES *Sweet Laurel*, by Laurel Gallucci and Claire Thomas; *Terrain: A Seasonal Guide to Nature at Home*, by Terrain; *The Prince's Bane*, by Alexandra Christo; *Deep Listening*, by Jillian Pransky; *Change Resilience*, by Lior Arussy; *A Thousand Words*, by Brigit Young.

HOW TO CONTACT Accepts electronic queries for fiction and nonfiction. Submit query addressed to a specific agent. Include first chapter or first 10 pages of ms. Accepts simultaneous submissions.

THE STRINGER LITERARY AGENCY LLC

P.O. Box 111255, Naples FL 34108. **E-mail:** mstringer@stringerlit.com. **Website:** www.stringerlit.com. **Contact:** Marlene Stringer. This agency focuses on commercial fiction for adults and teens.

HANDLES This agency specializes in fiction. "We are an editorial agency, and work with clients to make their manuscripts the best they can be in preparation for submission. We focus on career planning, and help our clients reach their publishing goals. We advise clients on marketing and promotional strategies to help them reach their target readership. Because we are so hands-on, we limit the size of our list; however, we are always looking for exceptional voices and stories that demand we read to the end. You never know where the next great story is coming from." This agency is seeking thrillers, crime fiction (not true crime), mystery, women's fiction, single title and category romance, fantasy (all subgenera), grounded science fiction (no space opera, aliens, etc.), and YA/teen. Does not want to receive picture books, MG, plays, short stories, or poetry. This is not the agency for inspirational romance or erotica. No space opera. The agency is not seeking nonfiction as of this time.

RECENT SALES *Don't Believe It by Charlie Donlea; The Waiting Room*, by Emily Bleeker; *The Numina Trilogy*, by Charlie N. Holmberg; *Belle Chasse*, by Suzanne Johnson; *The Evermore Chronicles by Emily R. King; Wilds of the Bayou*, by Susannah Sandlin; Death In The Family by Tessa Wegert; *The Vine Witch by Luanne Smith; The Scottish Trilogy*, by Anna Bradley; *Fly By Night*, by Andrea Thalasinos; The Dragonsworn Series, by Caitlyn McFarland; *The Devious Dr. Jekyll*, by Viola Carr; *The Dragon's Price*, by Bethany Wiggins; The Hundredth Queen Series by Emily R. King; Film Rights to *The Paper Magician*, by Charlie N. Holmberg.

TERMS Standard commission. "We do not charge fees."

HOW TO CONTACT Electronic submissions through website only. Please make sure your ms is as good as it can be before you submit. Agents are not first readers. For specific information on what we like to see in query letters, refer to the information at www.stringerlit.com. Accepts simultaneous submissions. Obtains new clients through referrals, submissions, conferences.

TIPS "If your ms falls between categories, or you are not sure of the category, query and we'll let you know if we'd like to take a look. We strive to respond as quickly as possible. If you have not received a response in the time period indicated on website, please requery."

THE STROTHMAN AGENCY, LLC

63 E. 9th St., 10X, New York NY 10003. **E-mail:** info@strothmanagency.com. **Website:** www.strothmanagency.com. **Contact:** Wendy Strothman, Lauren MacLeod. The Strothman Agency, LLC is a highly selective literary agency operating out of New York and Nashville, TN dedicated to advocating for authors of significant books through the entire publishing cycle. Recent Strothman Agency authors have won the Pulitzer Prize for Biography, the National Book Critics Circle Award for Non-Fiction, the Lincoln Prize, and many other awards. Clients have appeared on New York Times bestsellers lists, on National Book Award Long Lists, and two were Finalists for the Pulitzer Prize in History.

HANDLES Specializes in history, science, biography, politics, narrative journalism, nature and the environment, current affairs, narrative nonfiction, business and economics, young adult fiction and nonfiction, and middle grade fiction and nonfiction. "The Strothman Agency seeks out scholars, journalists, and other acknowledged and emerging experts in their fields. We specialize in history, science, narrative journalism, nature and the environment, current affairs, narrative nonfiction, business and economics, young adult fiction and nonfiction, middle grade fiction and nonfiction. We are not signing up projects in romance, science fiction, picture books, or poetry."

TERMS Agent receives 15% commission on domestic sales; 20% commission on foreign sales. Offers written contract; 30-day notice must be given to terminate contract.

HOW TO CONTACT Accepts queries only via e-mail. See submission guidelines online. Accepts simultaneous submissions. "All e-mails received will be responded to with an auto-reply. If we have not replied to your query within 6 weeks, we do not feel that it is right for us." Accepts simultaneous submissions. Obtains most new clients through recommendations from others.

EMMA SWEENEY AGENCY, LLC

245 E 80th St., Suite 7E, New York NY 10075. **E-mail:** info@emmasweeneyagency.com. **Website:** www. emmasweeneyagency.com.

HANDLES Does not want erotica.

HOW TO CONTACT "We accept only electronic queries, and ask that all queries be sent to queries@ emmasweeneyagency.com rather than to any agent directly. Please begin your query with a succinct (and hopefully catchy) description of your plot or proposal. Always include a brief cover letter telling us how you heard about ESA, your previous writing credits, and a few lines about yourself. We cannot open any attachments unless specifically requested, and ask that you paste the first 10 pages of your proposal or novel into the text of your e-mail." Accepts simultaneous submissions.

TALCOTT NOTCH LITERARY SERVICES, LLC

31 Cherry St., Suite 100, Milford CT 06460. (203) 876-4959. **Fax:** (203)876-9517. **E-mail:** editorial@talcottnotch.net. **Website:** www.talcottnotch.net. **Contact:** Gina Panettieri, founder. Talcott Notch Literary is a four-member full-service literary and sub-rights agency with offices covering the East Coast, representing award-winning and bestselling adult and juvenile fiction and nonfiction from the freshest upcoming writers from the U.S. and the abroad.

HANDLES "We are most actively seeking projects featuring diverse characters and stories which expand the reader's understanding of our society and the wider world we live in."

RECENT SALES Agency sold 65 titles in the last year, including *Lies She Told* , by Cate Holahan (Crooked Lane Books); *American Operator*, by Brian Andrews and Jeffrey Wilson (Thomas & Mercer); *Reset*, by Brian Andrews (Thomas & Mercer); *A Lover's Pinch*, by Peter Tupper (Rowman & Littlefield); *Everlasting Nora*, by Marie Cruz (Tor); *A Borrowing of Bones*, by Paula Munier (St. Martin's); *Muslim Girls Rise*, by Saira Mir (Salaam Reads), *Belabored*, by Lyz Lenz (Nation Books); *Tarnished Are The Stars*, by Rosiee Thor (Scholastic): *The Complicated Math of Two Plus One*, by Cathleen Barnhart (Harper Children's); and many others.

TERMS Agent receives 15% commission on domestic sales; 20% commission on foreign sales. Offers written contract, binding for 1 year.

HOW TO CONTACT Query via e-mail (preferred) with first 10 pages of the ms pasted within the body of the e-mail, not as an attachment. Accepts simultaneous submissions. We find many of our new clients through conferences and online events that allow us to interact one-on-one with the authors, as well as through referrals by our clients.

TIPS "Know your market and how to reach them. A strong platform is essential in your book proposal. Can you effectively use social media/Are you a strong networker: Are you familiar with the book bloggers in your genre? Are you involved with the interest-specific groups that can help you? What can you do to break through the 'noise' and help present your book to your readers? Check our website for more tips and information on this topic."

THOMPSON LITERARY AGENCY

115 W. 29th St., Third Floor, New York NY 10001. (716)257-8149. **Website:** thompsonliterary.com. **Contact:** Meg Thompson, founder.

HANDLES The agency is always on the lookout for both commercial and literary fiction, as well as young adult and children's books. "Nonfiction, however, is our specialty, and our interests include biography, memoir, music, popular science, politics, blog-to-book projects, cookbooks, sports, health and wellness, fashion, art, and popular culture." "Please note that we do not accept submissions for poetry collections or screenplays, and we only consider picture books by established illustrators."

HOW TO CONTACT "For fiction: Please send a query letter, including any salient biographical information or previous publications, and attach the first 25 pages of your manuscript. For nonfiction: Please send a query letter and a full proposal, including biographical information, previous publications, credentials that qualify you to write your book, marketing information, and sample material. You should address your query to whichever agent you think is best suited for your project." Accepts simultaneous submissions.

THREE SEAS LITERARY AGENCY

P.O. Box 444, Sun Prairie WI 53590. (608)834-9317. **E-mail:** threeseaslit@aol.com. **Website:** threeseasagency.com. **Contact:** Michelle Grajkowski, Cori Deyoe.

HANDLES "We represent more than 50 authors who write romance, women's fiction, science fiction/fantasy, thrillers, young adult and middle grade fiction, as well as select nonfiction titles. Currently, we are looking for fantastic authors with a voice of their own." 3 Seas does not represent poetry or screenplays.

RECENT SALES REPRESENTS Bestselling authors, including Jennifer Brown, Katie MacAlister, Kerrelyn Sparks, and C.L. Wilson.

TERMS Agent receives 15% commission on domestic sales; 20% commission on foreign sales. Offers written contract.

HOW TO CONTACT E-mail queries only; no attachments, unless requested by agents. For fiction, please e-mail the first chapter and synopsis along with a cover letter. Also, be sure to include the genre and the number of words in your manuscript, as well as pertinent writing experience in your query letter. For nonfiction, e-mail a complete proposal, including a query letter and your first chapter. For picture books, query with complete text. Accepts simultaneous submissions. Obtains most new clients through recommendations from others, conferences.

✪ TRANSATLANTIC LITERARY AGENCY

2 Bloor St. E., Suite 3500, Toronto ON M4W 1A8, Canada. (416)488-9214. **E-mail:** info@transatlanticagency.com. **Website:** transatlanticagency.com. The Transatlantic Agency represents adult and children's authors of all genres, including illustrators. We do not handle stage plays, musicals or screenplays. Please review the agency website and guidelines carefully before making any inquiries, as each agent has their own particular submission guidelines.

HANDLES "In both children's and adult literature, we market directly into the US, the United Kingdom and Canada." Represents adult and children's authors of all genres, including illustrators. Does not want to receive picture books, musicals, screenplays or stage plays.

RECENT SALES Sold 250 titles in the last year.

TERMS Agent receives 15% commission on domestic sales; 20% commission on foreign sales. Offers written contract; 45-day notice must be given to terminate contract. This agency charges for photocopying and postage when it exceeds $100.

HOW TO CONTACT Always refer to the website, as guidelines will change, and only various agents are open to new clients at any given time. Obtains most new clients through recommendations from others.

SCOTT TREIMEL NY

434 Lafayette St., New York NY 10003. (212)505-8353. **E-mail:** general@scotttreimelny.com. **Website:** scotttreimelny.blogspot.com; www.scotttreimelny.com. **Contact:** Chris Hoyt.

HANDLES This agency specializes in tightly focused segments of the trade and institutional markets, representing both authors and illustrators of books for children and teens.

RECENT SALES *Misunderstood Shark*, by Ame Dyckman (Scholastic); *Crimson*, by Arthur Slade (HarperCanada); *Willa and the Bear*, by Philomena O'Neill (Sterling); *Wee Beastie Series*, by Ame Dyckman (Simon & Schuster); *A Bike Like Sergio's*, by Maribeth Boelts (Candlewick); *Lucky Jonah*, by Richard Scrimger (HarperCanada); *Other Word-ly*, by Yee-Lum Mak (Chronicle); *The Passover Cowboy*, by Barbara Diamond Golden (Apples & Honey Press); *Dandy*, by Ame Dyckman (Little Brown); *You Don't Want a Unicorn*, by Ame Dyckman (Little Brown); *Par-Tay*, by Eloise Greenfield (Alazar Press); *The Women Who Caught the Babies*, by Eloise Greenfield (Alazar Books); *Pupunzel*, by Maribeth Boelts (Random House); *The Fairy Dog Mother*, by Maribeth Boelts (Random House); *Flickers*, by Arthur Slade (HarperCanada).

TERMS Agent receives 15% commission on domestic sales; 20% commission on foreign sales. Offers verbal or written contract, standard terms. Only charges fees for books needed to sell subsidiary rights—foreign, film, etc.

HOW TO CONTACT No longer accepts unsolicited submissions. Wants—via e-mail only—queries from writers recommended by his clients and/or editor pals or that he has met at conferences. Accepts simultaneous submissions.

TIPS "We look for dedicated authors and illustrators able to sustain longtime careers in our increasingly competitive field. I want fresh, not derivative story concepts with overly familiar characters. We look for gripping stories, characters, pacing, and themes. We read for an authentic (to the age) point-of-view, and look for original voices. We spend significant time hunting for the best new work, and do launch debut talent each year. It is best not to send warm-up manuscripts or those already seen all over town."

TRIADA US

P.O. Box 561, Sewickley PA 15143. (412)401-3376. **E-mail:** uwe@triadaus.com; brent@triadaus.com; laura@triadaus.com; lauren@triadaus.com; amelia@triadaus.com. **Website:** www.triadaus.com. **Contact:** Dr. Uwe Stender, President. Triada US was founded by Dr. Uwe Stender over twelve years ago. Since then, the agency has built a high-quality list of fiction and nonfiction for kids, teens, and adults. Triada US titles are consistently critically acclaimed and translated into multiple languages.

HANDLES Actively seeking fiction and non-fiction across a broad range of categories of all age levels.

RECENT SALES *Playing Back the 80s* by Jim Beviglia (Rowman & Littlefield), *Game of Stars* by Sayantani DasGupta (Scholastic), *The Voice in My Head* by Dana Davis (Inkyard), *The Sound of Stars* by Alechia Dow (Inkyard), *Fake Blood* by Whitney Gardner (Simon & Schuster), *Maiden & Princess* by Daniel Haack and Isabel Galupo (Little Bee), *Bear No Malice* by Clarissa Harwood (Pegasus), *The Last Chance Dance* by Kate Hattemer (Knopf), *Hunting Annabelle* by Wendy Heard (Mira), *Beside Herself* by Elizabeth LaBan (Lake Union), *Don't Date Rosa Santos* by Nina Moreno (Disney-Hyperion), *Don't Call the Wolf* by Aleksandra Ross (HarperTeen), *Empire of Sand* by Tasha Suri (Orbit), *Ghost Wood Song* by Erica Waters (HarperTeen), *The Light Between Worlds* by Laura Weymouth (HarperTeen), *Going Off-Script* by Jen Wilde (Swoon Reads).

TERMS Triada US retains 15% commission on domestic sales and 20% commission on foreign and translation sales. Offers written contract; 30-day notice must be given prior to termination.

HOW TO CONTACT E-mail queries preferred. Please paste your query letter and the first 10 pages of your ms into the body of a message e-mailed to the agent of your choice. Do not simultaneously query multiple Triada agents. Please query one and wait for their response before moving onto another agent within our agency. Obtains most new clients through submission inbox (query letters and requested mss), client referrals, and conferences.

TRIDENT MEDIA GROUP

41 Madison Ave., 36th Floor, New York NY 10010. (212)333-1511. **E-mail:** info@tridentmediagroup.com. **Website:** www.tridentmediagroup.com. **Contact:** Ellen Levine.

HANDLES Actively seeking new or established authors in a variety of fiction and nonfiction genres.

HOW TO CONTACT Submit through the agency's online submission form on the agency website. Query only one agent at a time. If you e-query, include no attachments. Accepts simultaneous submissions.

TIPS "If you have any questions, please check FAQ page before e-mailing us."

THE UNTER AGENCY

23 W. 73rd St., Suite 100, New York NY 10023. (212)401-4068. **E-mail:** jennifer@theunteragency.com. **Website:** www.theunteragency.com. **Contact:** Jennifer Unter.

HANDLES This agency specializes in children's, nonfiction, and quality fiction.

RECENT SALES A full list of recent sales/titles is available on the agency website.

HOW TO CONTACT Send an e-query. There is also an online submission form. If you do not hear back from this agency within 3 months, consider that a no. Accepts simultaneous submissions.

UPSTART CROW LITERARY

244 Fifth Avenue, 11th Floor, New York NY 10001. **Website:** www.upstartcrowliterary.com. **Contact:** Danielle Chiotti, Alexandra Penfold.

HOW TO CONTACT Submit a query and 20 pages pasted into an e-mail. Accepts simultaneous submissions.

WELLS ARMS LITERARY

Website: www.wellsarms.com. Wells Arms Literary represents children's book authors and illustrators to the trade children's book market.

HANDLES "We focus on books for young readers of all ages: board books, picture books, readers, chapter books, middle grade, and young adult fiction." Actively seeking middle grade, young adult, magical realism, contemporary, romance, fantasy. "We do not represent to the textbook, magazine, adult romance or fine art markets."

HOW TO CONTACT Wells Arms Literary is currently closed to queries or submissions "unless you've met me at a conference." Accepts simultaneous submissions.

WERNICK & PRATT AGENCY

Website: www.wernickpratt.com. **Contact:** Marcia Wernick; Linda Pratt; Emily Mitchell. "Wernick & Pratt Agency provides each client with personal attention and the highest quality of advice and service that has been the hallmark of our reputations in the industry. We have the resources and accumulated knowledge to assist clients in all aspects of their creative lives including editorial input, contract negotiations, and subsidiary rights management. Our goal is to represent and manage the careers of our clients so they may achieve industry wide and international recognition, as well as the highest level of financial potential."

Dedicated to children's books.

HANDLES "Wernick & Pratt Agency specializes in children's books of all genres, from picture books through young adult literature and everything in between. We represent both authors and illustrators. We do not represent authors of adult books." Wants people who both write and illustrate in the picture book genre; humorous young chapter books with strong voice, and which are unique and compelling; middle grade/YA novels, both literary and commercial. No picture book mss of more than 750 words, or mood pieces; work specifically targeted to the educational market; fiction about the American Revolution, Civil War, or World War II unless it is told from a very unique perspective.

HOW TO CONTACT Submit via e-mail only to submissions@wernickpratt.com. "Please indicate to which agent you are submitting." Detailed submission guidelines available on website. "Submissions will only be responded to further if we are interested in them. If you do not hear from us within 6 weeks of your submission, it should be considered declined." Accepts simultaneous submissions.

WESTWOOD CREATIVE ARTISTS, LTD.

386 Huron St., Toronto ON M5S 2G6, Canada. (416)964-3302. **E-mail:** wca_office@wcaltd.com. **Website:** www.wcaltd.com. Westwood Creative Artists is Canada's largest literary agency. It's also one of the oldest and most respected. "Situated in Toronto's Annex neighbourhood, our staff of 11 includes 6 full-time book agents who are supported by an in-house international rights agent and an outstanding network of twenty-four international co-agents. We take great pride in the enthusiastic response to our list from publishers around the world and in the wide praise our writers receive from Canadian and international critics. We are honored that many of the writers we represent have won and been shortlisted for such esteemed prizes as the Man Booker Prize, the Nobel Prize, and the Scotiabank Giller Prize."

HANDLES "We take on children's and young adult writers very selectively. The agents bring their diverse interests to their client lists, but are generally looking for authors with a mastery of language, a passionate, expert or original perspective on their subject, and a gift for storytelling." "Please note that WCA does not represent screenwriters, and our agents are not currently seeking poetry or children's picture book submissions."

HOW TO CONTACT E-query only. Include credentials, synopsis, and no more than 10 pages. No attachments. Accepts simultaneous submissions.

TIPS "We will reject outright complete, unsolicited manuscripts, or projects that are presented poorly in the query letter. We prefer to receive exclusive submissions and request that you do not query more than one agent at the agency simultaneously. It's often best if you approach WCA after you have accumulated some publishing credits."

WHIMSY LITERARY AGENCY, LLC

49 N. 8th St., 6G, Brooklyn NY 11249. (212)674-7162. **E-mail:** whimsynyc@aol.com. **Contact:** Jackie Meyer. Whimsy Literary Agency LLC, specializes in nonfiction books and authors that educate, entertain, and inspire people.

HANDLES "Whimsy looks for nonfiction projects that are concept- and platform-driven. We seek books that educate, inspire, and entertain." Actively seeking experts in their field with integrated and established platforms.

TERMS Agent receives 15% commission on domestic sales; 20% commission on foreign sales. Offers written contract.

HOW TO CONTACT Send your proposal via e-mail to whimsynyc@aol.com (include your media platform, table of contents with full description of each chapter). First-time authors: "We appreciate proposals that are professional and complete. Please consult the many fine books available on writing book proposals. We are not considering poetry, or screenplays. Please Note: Due to the volume of queries and submissions, we are unable to respond unless they are of interest to us." Accepts simultaneous submissions. Obtains most new clients through recommendations from others, solicitations.

WRITERS HOUSE

21 W. 26th St., New York NY 10010. (212)685-2400. **Fax:** (212)685-1781. **Website:** www.writershouse.com.

HANDLES This agency specializes in all types of popular fiction and nonfiction, for both adult and juvenile books as well as illustrators. Does not want to receive scholarly, professional, poetry, plays, or screenplays.

TERMS Agent receives 15% commission on domestic sales. Agent receives 20% commission on foreign sales. Offers written contract, binding for 1 year. Agency charges fees for copying mss/proposals and overseas airmail of books.

HOW TO CONTACT Individual agent email addresses are available on the website. "Please e-mail us a query letter, which includes your credentials, an explanation of what makes your book unique and special, and a synopsis. Some agents within our agency have different requirements. Please consult their individual Publisher's Marketplace (PM) profile for details. We respond to all queries, generally within six to eight weeks." If you prefer to submit my mail, address it to an individual agent, and please include SASE for our reply. (If submitting to Steven Malk: Writers House, 7660 Fay Ave., #338H, La Jolla, CA 92037.) Accepts simultaneous submissions. Obtains most new clients through recommendations from authors and editors.

TIPS "Do not send mss. Write a compelling letter. If you do, we'll ask to see your work. Follow submission guidelines and please do not simultaneously submit your work to more than one Writers House agent."

WRITERS HOUSE

7660 Fay Ave., #338H, La Jolla CA 92037. **E-mail:** smalk@writershouse.com. **Website:** writershouse.com.

HOW TO CONTACT Accepts simultaneous submissions.

JASON YARN LITERARY AGENCY

3544 Broadway, No. 68, New York NY 10031. **Website:** www.jasonyarnliteraryagency.com.

HOW TO CONTACT Please e-mail your query to jason@jasonyarnliteraryagency.com with the word "Query" in the subject line, and please paste the first 10 pages of your manuscript or proposal into the text of your e-mail. Do not send any attachments. "Visit the About page for information on what we are interested in, and please note that JYLA does not accept queries for film, TV, or stage scripts." Accepts simultaneous submissions.

CLUBS & ORGANIZATIONS

Contacts made through organizations such as the ones listed in this section can be quite beneficial for children's writers and illustrators. Professional organizations provide numerous educational, business, and legal services in the form of newsletters, workshops, or seminars. Organizations can provide tips about how to be a more successful writer or artist, as well as what types of business cards to keep, health and life insurance coverage to carry, and competitions to consider.

An added benefit of belonging to an organization is the opportunity to network with those who have similar interests, creating a support system. As in any business, knowing the right people can often help your career, and important contacts can be made through your peers. Membership in a writer's or artist's organization also shows publishers you're serious about your craft. This provides no guarantee your work will be published, but it gives you an added dimension of credibility and professionalism.

Some of the organizations listed here welcome anyone with an interest, while others are only open to published writers and professional artists. Organizations such as the Society of Children's Book Writers and Illustrators (SCBWI, www.scbwi.org) have varying levels of membership. SCBWI offers associate membership to those with no publishing credits, and full membership to those who have had work for children published. International organizations such as SCBWI also have regional chapters throughout the US and the world. Write or call for more information regarding any group that interests you, or check the websites of the many organizations that list them. Be sure to get information about local chapters, membership qualifications, and services offered.

AMERICAN ALLIANCE FOR THEATRE & EDUCATION

718 7th St. NW, Washington DC 20001. (202)909-1194. **E-mail:** info@aate.com. **Website:** www.aate.com. Purpose of organization: to promote standards of excellence in theatre and drama education. "We achieve this by assimilating quality practices in theatre and theatre education, connecting artists, educators, researchers and scholars with each other, and by providing opportunities for our members to learn, exchange and diversify their work, their audiences and their perspectives." Membership cost: $115 annually for individual in U.S. and Canada, $220 annually for organization, $60 annually for students, and $70 annually for retired people, $310 annually for University Departmental memberships; add $30 outside Canada and U.S. Holds annual conference (July or August). Contests held for unpublished play reading project and annual awards in various categories. Awards plaque and stickers for published playbooks. Publishes list of unpublished plays deemed worthy of performance and stages readings at conference. Contact national office at number above or see website for contact information for Playwriting Network Chairpersons.

AMERICAN SOCIETY OF JOURNALISTS AND AUTHORS

355 Lexington Ave., 15th Floor, New York NY 10017. (212)997-0947. **Website:** www.asja.org. Qualifications for membership: "Need to be a professional freelance nonfiction writer. Refer to website for further qualifications." Membership cost: Application fee—$50; annual dues—$210. Group sponsors national conferences. Professional seminars online and in person around the country. Workshops/conferences open to nonmembers. Publishes a newsletter for members that provides confidential information for nonfiction writers. **Contact:** Holly Koenig, interim executive director.

ARIZONA AUTHORS' ASSOCIATION

6939 East Chaparral Rd., Paradise Valley AZ 85253. (602)510-8076. **E-mail:** azauthors@gmail.com. **Website:** www.azauthors.com. Since 1978, Arizona Authors' Association has served to offer professional, educational and social opportunities to writers and authors and serves as an informational and referral network for the literary community. Members must be authors, writers working toward publication, agents, publishers, publicists, printers, illustrators, etc. Az Authors' publishes a bimonthly newsletter and the renown annual *Arizona Literary Magazine*. The Association sponsors the international Arizona Literary Contest including poetry, essays, short stories, new drama writing, novels, and published books with cash prizes and awards bestowed at a Fall ceremony. Winning entries are published or advertised in the *Arizona Literary Magazine*. First and second place winners in poetry, essay and short story categories are entered in the annual Pushcart Prize. Learn more online. **Contact:** Lisa Aquilina, President.

THE AUTHORS GUILD, INC.

31 E. 32nd St., 7th Floor, New York NY 10016. (212)563-5904. **Fax:** (212)564-5363. **E-mail:** staff@authorsguild.org. **Website:** www.authorsguild.org. Purpose of organization: to offer services and materials intended to help authors with the business and legal aspects of their work, including contract problems, copyright matters, freedom of expression and taxation. Guild has 8,000 members. Qualifications for membership: Must be book author published by an established American publisher within 7 years or any author who has had 3 works (fiction or nonfiction) published by a magazine or magazines of general circulation in the last 18 months. Associate membership also available. Different levels of membership include: associate membership with all rights except voting available to an author who has a firm contract offer or is currently negotiating a royalty contract from an established American publisher. "The Guild offers free contract reviews to its members. The Guild conducts several symposia each year at which experts provide information, offer advice and answer questions on subjects of interest and concern to authors. Typical subjects have been the rights of privacy and publicity, libel, wills and estates, taxation, copyright, editors and editing, the art of interviewing, standards of criticism and book reviewing. Transcripts of these symposia are published and circulated to members. The *Authors Guild Bulletin*, a quarterly journal, contains articles on matters of interest to writers, reports of Guild activities, contract surveys, advice on problem clauses in contracts, transcripts of Guild and League symposia and information on a variety of professional topics. Subscription included in the cost of the annual dues. **Contact:** Mary Rasenberger, executive director.

⟳ CANADIAN SOCIETY OF CHILDREN'S AUTHORS, ILLUSTRATORS AND PERFORMERS

720 Bathurst St., Suite 503, Toronto ON M5S 2R4, Canada. (416)515-1559. **E-mail:** office@canscaip.org. **Website:** www.canscaip.org. Purpose of organization: development of Canadian children's culture and support for authors, illustrators and performers working in this field. Qualifications for membership: Members—professionals who have been published (not self-published) or have paid public performances/records/tapes to their credit. Friends—share interest in field of children's culture. Sponsors workshops/conferences. Manuscript evaluation services; publishes newsletter: includes profiles of members; news round-up of members' activities countrywide; market news; news on awards, grants, etc; columns related to professional concerns. **Contact:** Helena Aalto, administrative director.

LEWIS CARROLL SOCIETY OF NORTH AMERICA

11935 Beltsville Dr., Beltsville MD 20705. **E-mail:** secretary@lewiscarroll.org. **Website:** www.lewiscarroll.org. "We are an organization of Carroll admirers of all ages and interests and a center for Carroll studies." Qualifications for membership: "An interest in Lewis Carroll and a simple love for Alice (or the Snark for that matter)." Membership cost: $35 (regular membership), $50 (foreign membership), $100 (sustaining membership). The Society meets twice a year—in spring and in fall; locations vary. Publishes a semi-annual journal, *Knight Letter*, and maintains an active publishing program. **Contact:** Sandra Lee Parker, secretary.

HORROR WRITERS ASSOCIATION

P.O. Box 56687, Sherman Oaks CA 91413. (818)220-3965. **E-mail:** hwa@horror.org; membership@horror.org; admin@horror.org. **Website:** www.horror.org. Purpose of organization: To encourage public interest in horror and dark fantasy and to provide networking and career tools for members. Qualifications for membership: Complete membership rules online at www.horror.org/memrule.htm. At least one low-level sale is required to join as an affiliate. Non-writing professionals who can show income from a horror-related field may join as an associate (booksellers, editors, agents, librarians, etc.). To qualify for full active membership, you must be a published, professional writer of horror. Membership cost: $69 annually. Holds annual Stoker Awards Weekend and HWA Business Meeting. Publishes monthly newsletter focusing on market news, industry news, HWA business for members. Sponsors awards. We give the Bram Stoker Awards for superior achievement in horror annually. Awards include a handmade Stoker trophy designed by sculptor Stephen Kirk. Awards open to nonmembers. **Contact:** Brad Hodson, Administrator.

INTERNATIONAL READING ASSOCIATION

P.O. Box 8139, Newark DE 19714. (302)731-1600. **E-mail:** councils@reading.org. **Website:** www.reading.org. The International Reading Association seeks to promote high levels of literacy for all by improving the quality of reading instruction through studying the reading process and teaching techniques; serving as a clearinghouse for the dissemination of reading research through conferences, journals, and other publications; and actively encouraging the lifetime reading habit. Its goals include professional development, advocacy, partnerships, research, and global literacy development. Sponsors annual convention. Publishes a newsletter called "Reading Today." Sponsors a number of awards and fellowships. More information online.

INTERNATIONAL WOMEN'S WRITING GUILD

International Women's Writing Guild, 5 Penn Plaza, 19th Floor, PMB# 19059, New York NY 10001. (917)720-6959. **E-mail:** iwwgquestions@gmail.com. **Website:** www.iwwg.wildapricot.org. IWWG is a network for the personal and professional empowerment of women through writing. Open to any woman connected to the written word regardless of professional portfolio. IWWG sponsors several annual conferences in all areas of the U.S. The major event, held in the summer, is a week-long conference attracting hundreds of women writers from around the globe. **Contact:** Marj Hahne, Interim Director of Operations.

LITERARY MANAGERS AND DRAMATURGS OF THE AMERICAS

P.O. Box 604074, Bayside NY 11360. (800)680-2148. **E-mail:** info@lmda.org. **Website:** www.lmda.org. LMDA is a not-for-profit service organization for the professions of literary management and dramaturgy. Student Membership: $30/year. Open to students in dramaturgy, performing arts and literature programs, or related disciplines. Proof of student status required. Includes national conference, New Dramaturg activities, local symposia, job phone and select membership meetings. Individual Membership: $75/year. Open to full-time and part-time professionals working in the fields of literary management and dramaturgy. All privileges and services including voting rights and eligibility for office. Institutional Membership: $200/year. Open to theaters, universities, and other organizations. Includes all privileges and services except voting rights and eligibility for office. Publishes a newsletter featuring articles on literary management, dramaturgy, LMDA program updates and other articles of interest. Spotlight sponsor membership $500/year; Open to theatres, universities, and other organizations; includes all priviledges for up to six individual members, plus additional promotional benefits.

THE NATIONAL LEAGUE OF AMERICAN PEN WOMEN

Pen Arts Building, 1300 17th St. N.W., Washington D.C. 20036-1973. (202)785-1997. **Fax:** (202)452-6868. **E-mail:** contact@nlapw.org. **Website:** www.americanpenwomen.org. Purpose of organization: to promote professional female work in art, letters, and music since 1897. Qualifications for membership: An applicant must show "proof of sale" in each chosen category—art, letters, and music. Levels of membership include: Active, Associate, International Affiliate, Members-at-Large, Honorary Members (in one or more of the following classifications: Art, Letters, and Music). Holds workshops/conferences. Publishes magazine 4 times/year titled *The Pen Woman*. Sponsors various contests in areas of Art, Letters, and Music. Awards made at Biennial Convention. Biannual scholarships awarded to non-Pen Women for mature women. Awards include cash prizes—up to $1,000. Specialized contests open to nonmembers. **Contact:** Nina Brooks, corresponding secretary.

NATIONAL WRITERS ASSOCIATION

10940 S. Parker Rd., #508, Parker CO 80138. **E-mail:** natlwritersassn@hotmail.com. **Website:** www.nationalwriters.com. Association for freelance writers. Qualifications for membership: associate membership—must be serious about writing; professional membership—must be published and paid writer (cite credentials). Sponsors workshops/conferences: TV/screenwriting workshops, NWAF Annual Conferences, Literary Clearinghouse, editing and

critiquing services, local chapters, National Writer's School. Open to non-members. Publishes industry news of interest to freelance writers; how-to articles; market information; member news and networking opportunities. Sponsors poetry contest; short story contest; article contest; novel contest. Awards cash for top 3 winners; books and/or certificates for other winners; honorable mention certificate places 5-10. Contests open to nonmembers.

NATIONAL WRITERS UNION

256 W. 38th St., Suite 703, New York NY 10018. (212)254-0279. **Fax:** (212)254-0673. **E-mail:** nwu@nwu.org. **Website:** www.nwu.org. Advocacy for freelance writers. Qualifications for membership: "Membership in the NWU is open to all qualified writers, and no one shall be barred or in any manner prejudiced within the Union on account of race, age, sex, sexual orientation, disability, national origin, religion or ideology. You are eligible for membership if you have published a book, a play, three articles, five poems, one short story or an equivalent amount of newsletter, publicity, technical, commercial, government or institutional copy. You are also eligible for membership if you have written an equal amount of unpublished material and you are actively writing and attempting to publish your work." Holds workshops throughout the country. Members only section on website offers rich resources for freelance writers. Skilled contract advice and grievance help for members.

PEN AMERICAN CENTER

588 Broadway, Suite 303, New York NY 10012. (212)334-1660. **E-mail:** info@pen.org. **Website:** www.pen.org. An association of writers working to advance literature, to defend free expression, and to foster international literary fellowship. PEN welcomes to its membership all writers and those belonging to the larger literary community. We ask that writers have at least one book published or be writers with proven records as professional writers; playwrights and screenwriters should have at least one work produced in a professional setting. Others should have achieved recognition in the literary field. Editors, literary agents, literary scouts, publicists, journalists, bloggers, and other literary professionals are all invited to join as Professional Members. If you feel you do not meet these guidelines, please consider joining as an Advocate Member. Candidates for membership may be nominated by a PEN member

or they may nominate themselves with the support of two references from the literary community or from a current PEN member. PEN members receive a subscription to the PEN journal, the PEN Annual Report, and have access to medical insurance at group rates. Members living in the New York metropolitan and tri-state area, or near the Branches, are invited to PEN events throughout the year. Membership in PEN American Center includes reciprocal privileges in PEN American Center branches and in foreign PEN Centers for those traveling abroad. Application forms are available online. PEN American Center is the largest of the 141 centers of PEN International, the world's oldest human rights organization and the oldest international literary organization. PEN International was founded in 1921 to dispel national, ethnic, and racial hatreds and to promote understanding among all countries. PEN American Center, founded a year later, works to advance literature, to defend free expression, and to foster international literary fellowship. The Center has a membership of 3,400 distinguished writers, editors, and translators. In addition to defending writers in prison or in danger of imprisonment for their work, PEN American Center sponsors public literary programs and forums on current issues, sends prominent authors to inner-city schools to encourage reading and writing, administers literary prizes, promotes international literature that might otherwise go unread in the United States, and offers grants and loans to writers facing financial or medical emergencies.

SCIENCE-FICTION AND FANTASY WRITERS OF AMERICA, INC.

P.O. Box 3238, Enfield CT 06083. **Website:** www. sfwa.org. Purpose of organization: to encourage public interest in science fiction literature and provide organization format for writers/editors/artists within the genre. Qualifications for membership: at least 1 professional sale or other professional involvement within the field. Different levels of membership include: active—requires 3 professional short stories or 1 novel published; associate—requires 1 professional sale; or affiliate—which requires some other professional involvement such as artist, editor, librarian, bookseller, teacher, etc. Workshops/conferences: annual awards banquet, usually in April or May. Open to nonmembers. Publishes quarterly journal, the *SFWA Bulletin*. Sponsors Nebula Awards for best published science fiction or fantasy in the categories

of novel, novella, novelette and short story. Awards trophy. Also presents the Damon Knight Memorial Grand Master Award for Lifetime Achievement, and, beginning in 2006, the Andre Norton Award for Outstanding Young Adult Science Fiction or Fantasy Book of the Year.

SOCIETY OF CHILDREN'S BOOK WRITERS AND ILLUSTRATORS

4727 Wilshire Blvd #301, Los Angeles CA 90010. (323)782-1010. **Fax:** (323)782-1892. **E-mail:** scbwi@ scbwi.org; membership@scbwi.org. **Website:** www. scbwi.org. Purpose of organization: to assist writers and illustrators working or interested in the field. Qualifications for membership: an interest in children's literature and illustration. Membership cost: $80/year. Plus one time $95 initiation fee. Different levels of membership include: P.A.L. membership—published by publisher listed in SCBWI Market Surveys; full membership—published authors/illustrators (includes self-published); associate membership—unpublished writers/illustrators. Holds 100 events (workshops/conferences) worldwide each year. National Conference open to nonmembers. Publishes bi-monthly magazine on writing and illustrating children's books. Sponsors annual awards and grants for writers and illustrators who are members. **Contact:** Stephen Mooser, president; Lin Oliver, executive director.

SOCIETY OF ILLUSTRATORS

128 E. 63rd St., New York NY 10065. (212)838-2560. **Fax:** (212)838-2561. **E-mail:** info@societyillustrators.org. **Website:** www.societyillustrators.org. "Our mission is to promote the art and appreciation of illustration, its history and evolving nature through exhibitions, lectures and education. Annual dues for nonresident illustrator members (those living more than 125 air miles from SI's headquarters): $300. Dues for resident illustrator members: $500 per year; resident associate members: $500. Artist members shall include those who make illustration their profession and earn at least 60% of their income from their illustration. Associate members are those who earn their living in the arts or who have made a substantial contribution to the art of illustration. This includes art directors, art buyers, creative supervisors, instructors, publishers and like categories. The candidate must complete and sign the application form, which requires a brief biography, a listing of schools attended, other training and a résumé of his

or her professional career. Candidates for illustrators membership, in addition to the above requirements, must submit examples of their work." **Contact:** Anelle Miller, executive director.

SOCIETY OF MIDLAND AUTHORS

P.O. Box 10419, Chicago IL 60610. **Website:** www.midlandauthors.com. Purpose of organization: create closer association among writers of the Middle West; stimulate creative literary effort; maintain collection of members' works; encourage interest in reading and literature by cooperating with other educational and cultural agencies. Qualifications for membership: membership by invitation only. Must be author or co-author of a book demonstrating literary style and published by a recognized publisher and be identified through residence with Illinois, Indiana, Iowa, Kansas, Michigan, Minnesota, Missouri, Nebraska, North Dakota, Ohio, South Dakota or Wisconsin. **Open to students** (if authors). Membership cost: $40/year dues. Different levels of membership include: regular—published book authors; associate, nonvoting—not published as above but having some connection with literature, such as librarians, teachers, publishers and editors. Program meetings held 5 times a year, featuring authors, publishers, editors or the like individually or on panels. Usually second Tuesday of October, November, February, March and April. Also holds annual awards dinner in May. Publishes a newsletter focusing on news of members and general items of interest to writers. Sponsors contests. "Annual awards in six categories, given at annual dinner in May. Monetary awards for books published that premiered professionally in previous calendar year. Send SASE to contact person for details." Categories include adult fiction, adult nonfiction, juvenile fiction, juvenile nonfiction, poetry, biography. No picture books. Contest open to nonmembers. **Contact:** Meg Tebo, president.

SOCIETY OF SOUTHWESTERN AUTHORS

Fax: (520)751-7877. **E-mail:** wporter202@aol.com. **Website:** www.ssa-az.org. Purpose of organization: to promote fellowship among professional and associate members of the writing profession, to recognize members' achievements, to stimulate further achievement, and to assist persons seeking to become professional writers. Qualifications for membership: Professional Membership: proof of publication of a book, articles, TV screenplay, etc. Associate Membership: proof of

desire to write, and/or become a professional. Self-published authors may receive status of Professional Membership at the discretion of the board of directors. Membership cost: see website. Sometimes this organization hosts writing events, such as its cosponsorship of the Arizona Writing Workshops in Phoenix and Tucson in November 2014.

○ TEXT & ACADEMIC AUTHORS ASSOCIATION (TAA)

TAA, P.O. Box 367, Fountain City WI 54629. (727)563-0020. **E-mail:** info@taaonline.net. **Website:** www.taaonline.net. TAA's overall mission is "To support textbook and academic authors in the creation of top-quality educational and scholarly works that stimulate the love of learning and foster the pursuit of knowledge." Qualifications for membership: all authors and prospective authors are welcome. Membership cost: $20-$200. Workshops/conferences: June each year. Newsletter focuses on all areas of interest to textbook and academic authors.

THEATRE FOR YOUNG AUDIENCES/USA

c/o The Theatre School, 2350 N. Racine Ave., Chicago IL 60614. (773)325-7981. **Fax:** (773)325-7920. **E-mail:** info@tyausa.org. **Website:** tyausa.org. Purpose of organization: to promote theater for children and young people by linking professional theaters and artists together; sponsoring national, international and regional conferences and providing publications and information. Also serves as U.S. Center for International Association of the Theatre for Children and Young People. Different levels of memberships include: organizations, individuals, students, retirees, libraries. TYA Today includes original articles, reviews and works of criticism and theory, all of interest to theater practitioners (included with membership). Publishes *Marquee*, a directory that focuses on information on members in U.S.

VOLUNTEER LAWYERS FOR THE ARTS

1 E. 53rd St., 6th Floor, New York NY 10022. (212)319-2787, ext. 1. **Fax:** (212)752-6575. **E-mail:** vlany@vlany.org. **Website:** www.vlany.org. Purpose of organization: Volunteer Lawyers for the Arts is dedicated to providing free arts-related legal assistance to low-income artists and not-for-profit arts organizations in all creative fields. Over 1,000 attorneys in the New York area donate their time through VLA to artists and arts organizations unable to afford legal counsel. Everyone is welcome to use

VLA's Art Law Line, a legal hotline for any artist or arts organization needing quick answers to arts-related questions. VLA also provides clinics, seminars, and publications designed to educate artists on legal issues that affect their careers. Members receive discounts on publications and seminars as well as other benefits.

✪ WRITERS' FEDERATION OF NEW BRUNSWICK

P.O. Box 4528, Rothesay NB E2E 5X2, Canada. (506)224-0364. **E-mail:** info@wfnb.ca. **Website:** www.wfnb.ca. Purpose of organization: "to promote New Brunswick writing and to help writers at all stages of their development." Qualifications for membership: interest in writing. Membership cost: $50 basic annual membership; $5, high school students; $50, institutional membership. Holds workshops/conferences. Publishes a newsletter with articles concerning the craft of writing, member news, contests, markets, workshops and conference listings. Sponsors annual literary competition, $20-$35 entry fee for members, $25-$40 for nonmembers. Categories: fiction, nonfiction, poetry, children's literature. **Contact:** Cathy Fynn, executive director.

✪ WRITERS' FEDERATION OF NOVA SCOTIA

1113 Marginal Rd., Halifax NS B3H 4P7, Canada. (902)423-8116. **Fax:** (902)422-0881. **E-mail:** director@writers.ns.ca. **Website:** www.writers.ns.ca. Purpose of organization: "to foster creative writing and the profession of writing in Nova Scotia; to provide advice and assistance to writers at all stages of their careers; and to encourage greater public recognition of Nova Scotian writers and their achievements." Regional organization open to anybody who writes. Currently has 800+ members. Offerings include resource library with over 2,500 titles, promotional services, workshop series, annual festivals, mentorship program. Publishes *Eastword*, a bimonthly newsletter containing "a plethora of information on who's doing what; markets and contests; and current writing events and issues." Members and nationally known writers give readings that are open to the public. Additional information online. **Contact:** Marilyn Smulders, executive director.

✪ WRITERS' GUILD OF ALBERTA

11759 Groat Rd. NW, Edmonton AB T5M 3K6, Canada. (780)422-8174. **E-mail:** mail@writersguild.ca. **Website:** writersguild.ca. Purpose of organization: to support, encourage and promote writers and writing, to safeguard the freedom to write and to read, and to advocate for the well-being of writers in Alberta. Currently has over 1,000 members. Offerings include retreats/conferences; monthly events; bimonthly magazine that includes articles on writing and a market section; weekly electronic bulletin with markets and event listings; and the Stephan G. Stephansson Award for Poetry (Alberta residents only). Holds workshops/conferences. Publishes a newsletter focusing on markets, competitions, contemporary issues related to the literary arts (writing, publishing, censorship, royalties etc.). Sponsors annual literary awards in 5 categories (novel, nonfiction, children's literature, poetry, drama). Awards include $1,500. Open to nonmembers. **Contact:** Carol Holmes.

CONFERENCES & WORKSHOPS

Writers and illustrators eager to expand their knowledge of the children's publishing industry should consider attending one of the many conferences and workshops held each year. Whether you're a novice or seasoned professional, conferences and workshops are great places to pick up information on a variety of topics and network with experts in the publishing industry, as well as with your peers.

Listings in this section provide details about what conference and workshop courses are offered, where and when they are held, and the costs. Some of the national writing and art organizations also offer regional workshops throughout the year. Write, call, or visit websites for information.

Members of the Society of Children's Book Writers and Illustrators (SCBWI) can find information on conferences in national and local SCBWI newsletters. Nonmembers may attend SCBWI events as well. (Some SCBWI regional events are listed in this section.) For information on SCBWI's annual national conferences and all of their regional events, check their website (scbwi.org) for a complete calendar of conferences and happenings.

AGENTS & EDITORS CONFERENCE

Writers' League of Texas, 611 S. Congress Ave., Suite 200 A-3, Austin TX 78704. (512)499-8914. **Website:** www.writersleague.org/38/conference. **Contact:** Michael Noll, program director. Annual conference held in summer. 2019 dates: June 28-June 30. This standout conference gives each attendee the opportunity to become a publishing insider. Meet more than 25 top agents, editors, and industry professionals through one-on-one consultations and receptions. Get tips and strategies for revising and improving your manuscript from keynote speakers and presenters (including award-winning and bestselling writers). Discounted rates are available at the conference hotel.

COSTS Registration for the 2019 conference opens in November for WLT members and n December for everyone.

ALASKA CONFERENCE FOR WRITERS & ILLUSTRATORS

Alaska Writers Guild, SCBWI Alaska, & RWA Alaska, P.O. Box 670014, Chugiak AK 99567. **E-mail:** alaskawritersguild.awg@gmail.com. **Website:** alaskawritersguild.com. Join the Alaska Writers Guild, SCBWI Alaska, and Alaska RWA for this annual 2-day conference event! Optional Friday workshops and round tables, 1:1 Manuscript Reviews and pitches, and an all-day event of keynotes, panels, and breakout sessions. Topics range from writing 101 to advanced revisions, traditional to self published, and Kidlit to steamy romance. Plus everything in between! Our 2019 dates are already set for September 20 & 21 at the BP Energy Center in Anchorage, Alaska, so mark your calendars!

AMERICAN CHRISTIAN WRITERS CONFERENCES

P.O. Box 110390, Nashville TN 37222. (800)219-7483 or (615)331-8668. **E-mail:** acwriters@aol.com. **Website:** www.acwriters.com. **Contact:** Reg Forder, director. ACW hosts a dozen annual two-day writers conferences and mentoring retreats across America taught by editors and professional freelance writers. These events provide excellent instruction, networking opportunities, and valuable one-on-one time with editors. Open to all forms of Christian writing (fiction, nonfiction, and scriptwriting). Conferences are held between March and November during each year.

Special rates are available at the host hotel (usually a major chain like Holiday Inn).

COSTS Costs vary and may depend on type of event (conference or mentoring retreat).

ADDITIONAL INFORMATION E-mail or call for conference brochures.

ANNUAL SPRING POETRY FESTIVAL

City College, 160 Convent Ave., New York NY 10031. (212)650-6356. **Website:** www.ccny.cuny.edu/poetry/festival. **Contact:** Pamela Laskin. Friday, May 3, 2019, (9 a.m.-5 p.m.) Workshops geared to all levels. Open to students. Write for more information. Site: Theater B of Aaron Davis Hall.

ATLANTA WRITERS CONFERENCE

Atlanta Writers Club, Westin Atlanta Airport Hotel, 4736 Best Rd., Atlanta GA 30337. **E-mail:** awconference@gmail.com. **Website:** www.atlantawritersconference.com. **Contact:** George Weinstein. Annual conference held in spring and fall. 2019 dates: October 25-26. Literary agents and editors are in attendance to take pitches and critique ms samples and query letters. Conference offers a writing craft workshop, instructional sessions with local authors, and separate question-and-answer panels with the agents and editors. Site: Westin Airport Atlanta Hotel. A block of rooms is reserved at the conference hotel. Booking instructions will be sent in the registration confirmation e-mail.

COSTS Manuscript critiques are $170 each (2 spots/waitlists maximum). Pitches are $70 each (2 spots/waitlists maximum). There's no charge for waitlists unless a spot opens. Query letter critiques are $70 (1 spot maximum). Other workshops and panels may also cost extra; see website. The "all activities" option is $620 and includes 2 manuscript critiques, 2 pitches, and 1 of each remaining activity.

ADDITIONAL INFORMATION A free shuttle runs between the airport and the hotel.

BIG SUR WRITING WORKSHOP

Henry Miller Library, Hwy. 1, Big Sur CA 93920. (831)667-2574. **E-mail:** lisa@bigsurchildrenswriters.com. **Website:** https://www.bigsurchildrenswriters.com/. Annual workshop focusing on children's writing (picture books, middle-grade, and young adult). Held every spring in Big Sur Lodge in Pfeiffer State Park. Cost of workshop includes meals, lodging, workshop, and Saturday evening reception. This event is helmed by the literary agents of the Andrea Brown Literary Agency. All attendees meet with at least 2 faculty members to have their work critiqued. Conference dates: December 6 8, 2019.

🕮 Full editorial schedule and much more available online. The Lodge is located 25 miles south of Carmel in Big Sur's Pfeiffer State Park, 47225 Hwy. 1, Big Sur CA 93920.

BOOKS-IN-PROGRESS CONFERENCE

Carnegie Center for Literacy and Learning, 251 W. Second St., Lexington KY 40507. (859)254-4175. **E-mail:** ccll1@carnegiecenterlex.org. **Website:** carnegiecenterlex.org. **Contact:** Laura Whitaker, program director. This is an annual writing conference at the Carnegie Center for Literacy and Learning in Lexington, Kentucky. It typically happens in June. 2019 event held May 30-June1. "Each conference will offer writing and publishing workshops and includes a keynote presentation." Literary agents are flown in to meet with writers and hear pitches. Website is updated several months prior to each annual event. See website for list of area hotels.

🕮 "Personal meetings with faculty (agents and editors) are only available to full conference participants. Limited slots available. Please choose only one agent; only one pitching session per participant."

CAPE COD WRITERS CENTER ANNUAL CONFERENCE

P.O. Box 408, Osterville MA 02655. (508)420-0200. **E-mail:** writers@capecodwriterscenter.org. **Website:** www.capecodwriterscenter.org. **Contact:** Nancy Rubin Stuart, executive director. Announcing the 57th broad-based literary conference August 1-4, 2019 at the Resort and Conference Center at Hyannis, MA. Workshops in fiction, nonfiction, poetry, memoir, mystery, thrillers, writing for children, social media, screenwriting, promotion, pitches and queries, agent meetings and ms mentorship with agents, editors, and faculty. Resort and Conference Center of Hyannis, Massachusetts.

COSTS Costs vary, depending on the number of courses selected, beginning at $125. Several scholarships are available.

CELEBRATION OF SOUTHERN LITERATURE

Southern Lit Alliance, 301 E. 11th St., Suite 301, Chattanooga TN 37403. (423)267-1218. **Fax:** (866)483-6831. **Website:** www.southernlitalliance.

org. Biennial conference held in odd-numbered years. "The Celebration of Southern Literature stands out because of its unique collaboration with the Fellowship of Southern Writers, an organization founded by towering literary figures like Eudora Welty, Cleanth Brooks, Walker Percy, and Robert Penn Warren to recognize and encourage literature in the South. The Fellowship awards 11 literary prizes and inducts new members, making this event the place to discover up-and-coming voices in Southern literature. The Southern Lit Alliance's Celebration of Southern Literature attracts more than 1,000 readers and writers from all over the United States. It strives to maintain an informal atmosphere where conversations will thrive, inspired by a common passion for the written word. The Southern Lit Alliance (formerly the Arts & Education Council) started as one of 12 pilot agencies founded by a Ford Foundation grant in 1952. The Alliance is the only organization of the 12 still in existence. The Southern Lit Alliance celebrates Southern writers and readers through community education and innovative literary arts experiences."

CLARKSVILLE WRITERS CONFERENCE

1123 Madison St., Clarksville TN 37040. (931)551-8870. **E-mail:** artsandheritage@cdelightband.net. **Website:** www.artsandheritage.us/writers. **Contact:** Ellen Kanervo. Annual conference held in the summer at Austin Peay State University. 2019 dates: June 6-7. Features a variety of presentations on fiction, nonfiction, and more. Past presenting authors include Tom Franklin, Frye Gaillard, William Gay, Susan Gregg Gilmore, Will Campbell, John Seigenthaler Sr., Alice Randall, George Singleton, Alanna Nash, and Robert Hicks. "Our presentations and workshops are valuable to writers and interesting to readers."

COSTS Costs available online; prices vary depending on how long attendees stay and if they attend the banquet dinner.

ADDITIONAL INFORMATION Multiple literary agents are flown in to the event every year to meet with writers and take pitches.

CONFERENCE FOR WRITERS & ILLUSTRATORS OF CHILDREN'S BOOKS

Book Passage, 51 Tamal Vista Blvd., Corte Madera CA 94925. (415)927-0960, ext. 401. **E-mail:** plivingston@bookpassage.com. **Website:** www.bookpassage.com. Conference for writers and illustrators geared toward beginner and intermediate levels. Sessions cover such topics as the nuts and bolts of writing and illustrating, publisher's spotlight, market trends, developing characters, finding a voice, and the author–agent relationship. 2019 dates: August 8-11 for travel writers and photographers. August 22-25 for mystery writers.

COSTS Travel Writers and Photographers: New Attendee Price: $650; Alumni Price: $575

Mystery Writers: New Attendee Price: $575; Alumni Price: $500

GOTHAM WRITERS WORKSHOP

writingclasses.com, 555 Eighth Ave., Suite 1402, New York NY 10018. (212)974-8377. **E-mail:** contact@gothamwriters.com. **Website:** www.writingclasses.com. Offers craft-oriented creative writing courses in general creative writing, fiction writing, screenwriting, nonfiction writing, article writing, stand-up comedy writing, humor writing, memoir writing, novel writing, children's book writing, playwriting, poetry, songwriting, mystery writing, science fiction writing, romance writing, television writing, article writing, travel writing, and business writing, as well as classes on freelancing, selling your screenplay, blogging, writing a nonfiction book proposal, and getting published. Also, the workshop offers a teen program, private instruction, and a mentoring program. Classes are held at various schools in New York as well as online. Online classes are held throughout the year. Agents and editors participate in some workshops.

ADDITIONAL INFORMATION See the website for courses, pricing, and instructors.

HAMPTON ROADS WRITERS CONFERENCE

Hampton Roads Writers, P.O. Box 56228, Virginia Beach VA 23456. (757)639-6146. **E-mail:** hrwriters@cox.net. **Website:** hamptonroadswriters.org. Annual conference held in September. 2019 dates: September 19-21 at Holiday Inn

Virginia Beach-Norfolk Hotel & Conference Center. Workshops cover fiction, nonfiction, memoir, poetry, lyric writing, screenwriting, and the business of getting published. A bookshop, 3 free contests with cash prizes, free evening networking social, and many networking opportunities will be available. Multiple literary agents are in attendance each year to meet with writers and hear ten-minute pitches. Much more information available on the website.

COSTS Costs vary. There are discounts for members, for early bird registration, for students, and more.

HIGHLAND SUMMER CONFERENCE

P.O. Box 7014, Radford University, Radford VA 24142. **E-mail:** tburriss@radford.edu. **Website:** tinyurl.com/q8z8ej9. **Contact:** Dr. Theresa Burriss. The Highland Summer Writers' Conference is a 4-day lecture-seminar workshop combination conducted by well known guest writers. 2019 details: "The 42nd annual HSC will be held at Radford University's beautiful Selu Conservancy the entire week of July 8-12. Multi-genre Affrilachian author Crystal Wilkinson will serve as guest writer/facilitator. Interested individuals can enroll in the conference to obtain traditional three-hour course credit at the graduate or undergraduate level, or register through the Appalachian Regional & Rural Studies Center at a reduced rate for continuing education credits or to simply participate. For more information, please contact Theresa Burriss." It offers the opportunity to study and practice creative and expository writing within the context of regional culture. The evening readings are free and open to the public. Services at a reduced rate for continuing education credits or to simply participate.

HIGHLIGHTS FOUNDATION FOUNDERS WORKSHOPS

814 Court St., Honesdale PA 18431. (877)288-3410. **Fax:** (570)253-0179. **E-mail:** klbrown@highlightsfoundation.org. **Website:** highlightsfoundation.org. 814 Court St.Honesdale PA 18431. (570)253-1192. **Fax:** (570)253-0179. **E-mail:** contact@highlightsfoundation.org. **Website:** www.highlightsfoundation.org. **Contact:** Kent Brown, director. Workshops geared toward those interested in writing and illustrating for children, intermediate and advanced levels. Classes offered include: Writing Novels for Young Adults, Biography, Nonfiction Writing, Writing Historical Fiction, Wordplay: Writing Poetry for Children, Heart of the Novel, Nature Writing for Kids, Visual Art of the Picture Book, The Whole Novel Workshop, and more (see website for updated list). Workshops held near Honesdale, PA. Workshops limited to between 8 and 14 people. Cost of workshops range from $695 and up. Cost of workshop includes tuition, meals, conference supplies and private housing. Call for application and more information. **Contact:** Kent L. Brown, Jr.. Offers more than 40 workshops per year. Duration: 3-7 days. Attendance: limited to 10-14. Genre-specific workshops and retreats on children's writing, including fiction, nonfiction, poetry, and

promotions. "Our goal is to improve, over time, the quality of literature for children by educating future generations of children's authors." Retreat center location: Highlights Founders' home in Boyds Mills, Pennsylvania. Coordinates pickup at local airport. Offers overnight accommodations. Participants stay in guest cabins on the wooded grounds surrounding Highlights Founders' home adjacent to the house/conference center.

○ "Applications will be reviewed and accepted on a first-come, first-served basis. Applicants must demonstrate specific experience in the writing area of the workshop they are applying for—writing samples are required for many of the workshops."

COSTS Prices vary based on workshop. Check website for details.

ADDITIONAL INFORMATION Some workshops require pre-workshop assignment. Brochure available for SASE, by e mail, on website, by phone, by fax. Accepts inquiries by phone, fax, e-mail, SASE. Editors attend conference.

IOWA SUMMER WRITING FESTIVAL

The University of Iowa, 250 Continuing Education Facility, University of Iowa, Iowa City IA 52242. (319)335-4160. **Fax:** (319)335-4039. **E-mail:** iswfestival@uiowa.edu. **Website:** https://iowasummerwritingfestival.org/. Annual festival held in June and July. More than 100 workshops and more than 50 instructors. Workshops are 1 week or a weekend. Attendance is limited to 12 people per class, with more than 1,500 participants throughout the summer. Offers courses across the genres: novel, short story, poetry, essay, memoir, humor, travel, playwriting, screenwriting, writing for children, and women's writing. Held at the University of Iowa campus. Speakers have included Marvin Bell, Lan Samantha Chang, John Dalton, Hope Edelman, Katie Ford, Patricia Foster, Bret Anthony Johnston, and Barbara Robinette Moss. Accommodations available at area hotels. Information on overnight accommodations available by phone or on website.

COSTS See website for registration and conference fees.

ADDITIONAL INFORMATION Brochures are available in February. Inquire via e-mail or on website. "Register early. Classes fill quickly."

IWWG SPRING BIG APPLE CONFERENCE

(917)720-6959. **E-mail:** iwwgquestions@iwwg.org. **Website:** www.iwwg.org. One or 2-day annual conference held from in New days York in spring and includes writing workshops, new-authors panel discussing publishing trends, fairs agents panel, and open one-on-one pitch sessions.

JAMES RIVER WRITERS CONFERENCE

2319 E. Broad St., Richmond VA 23223. (804)433-3790. **E-mail:** info@jamesriverwriters.org. **Website:** www.jamesriverwriters.org. **Contact:** Katharine Herndon. Nonprofit supporting writers in the Richmond, VA, area and beyond. Annual conference held in October. The event has master classes, agent pitching, critiques, panels, and more. Previous attending speakers include Ellen Oh, Margot Lee Shetterly, David Baldacci, Jeannette Walls, Adriana Trigiani, Jacqueline Woodson, and more. 2019 dates: October 12-13 with pre-conference master classes on October 11.

○ The James River Writers conference is frequently recognized for its friendly atmosphere and southern hospitality.

COSTS Check website for updated pricing.

KENTUCKY WRITERS CONFERENCE

Southern Kentucky Book Fest, WKU South Campus, 2355 Nashville Rd., Bowling Green KY 42101. (270)745-4502. **E-mail:** sara.volpi@wku.edu. **Website:** www.sokybookfest.org. **Contact:** Sara Volpi. This event is entirely free to the public. 2019 date: April 26-27. Duration: 2 days. Part of the 2-day Southern Kentucky Book Fest. Authors who will be participating in the Book Fest on Saturday will give attendees at the conference the benefit of their wisdom on Friday (16 sessions available). For the first time, additional workshops will be offered on Saturday! Free workshops on a variety of writing topics will be presented. Sessions run for 75 minutes, and the day begins at 9 a.m. and ends at 3:30 p.m. The conference is open to anyone who would like to attend, including high school students, college students, teachers, and the general public. Registration will open online in February.

○ Since the event is free, interested attendees are asked to register in advance. Information on how to do so is on the website.

KINDLING WORDS EAST

Website: www.kindlingwords.org. Annual retreat held early in the year near Burlington, Vermont. 2020 dates: January 30-February 2. A retreat with 3 strands: writer, illustrator, and editor; professional level. Intensive workshops for each strand and an open schedule for conversations and networking. Registration limited to approximately 70. Hosted by the 4-star Inn at Essex (room and board extra). Participants must be published by a CCBC listed publisher, or if in publishing, occupy a professional position. Registration opens August 1 or as posted on the website and fills quickly. Check website to see if spaces are available, to sign up to be notified when registration opens each year, or for more information. Inquire via contact form on the website.

KINDLING WORDS WEST

Website: www.kindlingwords.org. Annual retreat specifically for children's book writers held in spring out west. 2020 dates: April 4-11. 2020 location: Whidbey Institute, a retreat off the coast of Seattle. Kindling Words West is an artist's colony–style week with workshops by gifted teachers followed by a working retreat. Participants gather just before dinner to have white-space discussions; evenings include fireside readings, star gazing, and songs. Participants must be published by CBC-recognized publisher.

LA JOLLA WRITERS CONFERENCE

P.O. Box 178122, San Diego CA 92177. **E-mail:** akuritz@san.rr.com. **Website:** www.lajollawritersconference.com. **Contact:** Jared Kuritz, director. Annual conference held in fall. 2019 dates: October 25-27. Conference duration: 3 days. Attendance: 200 maximum. The LaJolla Writers Conference covers all genres in both fiction and nonfiction as well as the business of writing. "We take particular pride in educating our attendees on the business aspect of the book industry and have agents, editors, publishers, publicists, and distributors teach classes. There is unprecedented access to faculty. Our conference offers lecture sessions that run for 50 minutes and workshops that run for 110 minutes. Each block period is dedicated to either workshop or lecture-style classes with 6-8 classes on various topics available each block. For most workshop classes, you are encouraged to bring written work for review. Literary agents from prestigious agencies such as the Andrea Brown Literary Agency, the Dijkstra Agency, the McBride Agency, Full Circle Literary Group, the Zimmerman Literary Agency, the Van Haitsma Literary Agency, the Farris Literary Agency, and more

have participated in the past, teaching workshops in which they are familiarized with attendee work. Late night and early bird sessions are also available. The conference creates a strong sense of community, and it has seen many of its attendees successfully published."
COSTS $395 for full 2019 conference registration (doesn't include lodging or breakfast).

LEAGUE OF UTAH WRITERS' ANNUAL WRITER'S CONFERENCES

Spring Conference and Quills Conference, 1042 East Fort Union Blvd. #443, Midvale UT 84047. (385)434-0355. **E-mail:** president@leagueofutahwriters.org. **Website:** https://www.leagueofutahwriters.com. **Contact:** Johnny Worthen. The annual Spring Conference presented by League of Utah Writers includes a full day of workshops and presentations focused on improving your skills as a writer. Please join us! The Quills Conference is an Intermountain West professional writer's weekend. Come learn from industry professionals what you need to be successful in writing and publishing. This 2-day event is packed with presentations on poetry, prose, and screenwriting and includes dining with an award-winning catering staff at the beautiful University Marriott adjacent to the University of Utah campus. Conference meals include Friday dinner and Saturday lunch. Awards banquet is optional. Register for the appropriate ticket if you wish to attend the Saturday night banquet where the 2019 Quill Awards will be announced. 2019 dates: Spring Conference is June 15. The Quills Conference is August 22-24.

⊙ The Spring Conference is held at Utah State University in the Eccles Conference Center. The Quills Conference is held at Salt Lake City Marriott University Park.

COSTS Spring Conference is $25 early bird pricing. Quills Conference starts at $230. See website for details.

MIDWEST WRITERS WORKSHOP

(765)282-1055. **E-mail:** midwestwriters@yahoo.com. **Website:** www.midwestwriters.org. **Contact:** Jama Kehoe Bigger, director. Writing conferences in east central Indiana, geared toward writers of all levels, including craft and business sessions. Topics include most genres. Faculty/speakers have included Angie Thomas, Becky Albertalli, Julie Murphy, Joyce Carol Oates, Marcus Sakey, William Kent Krueger, William Zinsser, John Gilstrap, Jane Friedman, and numerous best-selling mystery, literary fiction, young adult, and children's authors. Conferences with agent pitch sessions, ms evaluation, query letter critiques.

COSTS $155-425. Some meals included.

ADDITIONAL INFORMATION See website for more information. Keep in touch with the MWW at facebook.com/midwestwriters and twitter.com/midwestwriters.

MONTROSE CHRISTIAN WRITERS' CONFERENCE

Montrose Bible Conference, 218 Locust St., Montrose PA 18801. (570)278-1001 or (800)598-5030. **Fax:** (570)278-3061. **E-mail:** mbc@montrosebible.org. **Website:** www.montrosebible.org. "Annual conference held in July. Offers workshops, editorial appointments, and professional critiques. We try to meet writing needs, for beginners and advanced, covering fiction, poetry, and writing for children. It is small enough to allow personal interaction between attendees and faculty. Speakers have included William Petersen, Mona Hodgson, Jim Watkins, and Bob Hostetler." Held in Montrose. Will meet planes in Binghamton, New York, and Scranton, Pennsylvania. On-site accommodations: room and board $360-490/conference, including food (2018 rates). RV court available.

COSTS Tuition is around $200.

ADDITIONAL INFORMATION "Writers can send work ahead of time and have it critiqued for a small fee." The attendees are usually church related. The writing has a Christian emphasis. Conference information available in April. For brochure, visit website, e-mail, or call. Accepts inquiries by phone or e-mail.

MOUNT HERMON CHRISTIAN WRITERS CONFERENCE

P.O. Box 413, Mount Hermon CA 95041. **E-mail:** info@mounthermon.org. **Website:** writers.mounthermon.org. **Contact:** Kathy Ide, director. Annual professional conference held over Palm Sunday weekend. Friday lunch through Tuesday breakfast. Pre-conference mentoring clinics run from Wednesday dinner till Friday lunch. Average attendance: 350-400. Sponsored by and held at the 440-acre Mount Hermon Christian Conference Center near San Jose, California, in the heart of the coastal redwoods. We are a broad-ranging conference for all areas of Christian writing, including fiction, nonfiction, sci-fi/fantasy, children's, teen, young adult, poetry, magazines, and devotional writing. This is a working, how-to conference, with Major Morning Tracks in several genres (including tracks for teen writers and professional authors), Morning Mentoring Clinics, and 40 or more afternoon workshops. Faculty-to-student ratio is about 1 to 6. Many of our more than 70 faculty members are literary agents, acquisitions editors, and representatives from major Christian publishing houses nationwide. Attendees can submit up to two manuscript samples to faculty members for review or critique for no additional charge. Ample opportunities for one-on-one appointments. Options include modern cabins (with full kitchens) or lodges (similar to hotel rooms), available in economy, standard, and deluxe. See website for pricing.

MUSE AND THE MARKETPLACE

Grub Street, 162 Boylston St., 5th Floor, Boston MA 02116. (617)695-0075. **E-mail:** info@grubstreet.org. **Website:** museandthemarketplace.com. GrubStreet's national conference for writers. Held in the spring, such as in early April. 2020 dates: April 3-5. Conference duration: 3 days. Average attendance: 550. Dozens of agents are in attendance to meet writers and give direct one-on-one feedback on manuscript samples. The conference has sessions on all aspects of writing. Boston Park Plaza Hotel.

The Muse and the Marketplace is designed to give aspiring writers a better understanding of the craft of writing fiction and nonfiction, to prepare them for the changing world of publishing and promotion, and to create opportunities for meaningful networking. On all 3 days, prominent and nationally recognized, established and emerging authors lead sessions on the craft of writing—the "muse" side of things—while editors, literary agents, publicists, and other industry professionals lead sessions on the business side—the "marketplace."

NORTH CAROLINA WRITERS' NETWORK FALL CONFERENCE

P.O. Box 21591, Winston-Salem NC 27120. (336)293-8844. **E-mail:** mail@ncwriters.org. **Website:** www.ncwriters.org. Annual Fall Conference the first weekend of November rotates throughout the state each year. Average attendance: 225. This organization hosts 2 conferences: 1 in the spring and 1 in the fall. Each conference is a weekend full of workshops, panels, book signings, and readings (including open mic).

There will be a keynote speaker, a variety of sessions on the craft and business of writing, and an opportunity to meet with agents and editors.

COSTS Approximately $260 (all days, with meals).

NORTHERN COLORADO WRITERS CONFERENCE

407 Cormorant Ct., Fort Collins CO 80525. (970)227-5746. **E-mail:** april@northerncoloradowriters.com. **Website:** www.northerncoloradowriters.com. Annual conference held in Fort Collins. 2019 dates: May 3-4. Duration: 2-3 days. The conference features a variety of speakers, agents, and editors. There are workshops and presentations on fiction, nonfiction, screenwriting, children's books, marketing, magazine writing, staying inspired, and more. Previous agents who have attended and taken pitches from writers include Jessica Regel, Kristen Nelson, Jennifer March Soloway, Andrea Brown, Ken Sherman, Jessica Faust, Gordon Warnock, and Taylor Martindale. Each conference features more than 30 workshops from which to choose from. Previous keynotes include Chuck Wendig, Andrew McCarthy, and Stephen J. Cannell. Conference hotel offers rooms at a discounted rate.

COSTS Prices vary depending on a number of factors. See website for details.

ODYSSEY FANTASY WRITING WORKSHOP

P.O. Box 75, Mont Vernon NH 03057. (603)673-6234. **E-mail:** jcavelos@odysseyworkshop.org. **Website:** www.odysseyworkshop.org. **Contact:** Jeanne Cavelos. Saint Anselm College, 100 Saint Anselm Dr., Manchester NH 03102. Annual workshop held in June (through July). Conference duration: 6 weeks. Average attendance: 15. A workshop for fantasy, science fiction, and horror writers that combines an intensive learning and writing experience with in-depth feedback on students' mss. Held on the campus of Saint Anselm College in Manchester, New Hampshire. Speakers have included George R.R. Martin, Elizabeth Hand, Jane Yolen, Catherynne M. Valente, Holly Black, and Dan Simmons. Most students stay in Saint Anselm College apartments to get the full Odyssey experience. Each apartment has 2 bedrooms and can house a total of 2 to 3 people (with each bedroom holding 1 or 2 students). The apartments are equipped with kitchens, so you may buy and prepare your own food, which is a money-saving option, or you may eat at the college's Coffee Shop or Dining Hall. Wireless internet access and use of laundry facilities are provided at no cost. Students with cars will receive a campus parking permit.

Since its founding in 1996, the Odyssey Writing Workshop has become one of the most highly respected workshops for writers of fantasy, science fiction, and horror in the world. Top authors, editors and agents have served as guests at Odyssey. Fifty-nine percent of graduates have gone on to be professionally published. Among Odyssey's graduates are *New York Times* bestsellers, Amazon bestsellers, and award winners.

COSTS $2,060 tuition, $195 textbook, $892 housing (double room), $1,784 housing (single room), $40 application fee, $600 food (approximate), $1,000 optional processing fee to receive college credit.

ADDITIONAL INFORMATION Students must apply and include a writing sample. Application deadline: April 1. Students' works are critiqued throughout the 6 weeks. Workshop information available in October. For brochure/guidelines, send SASE, e-mail, visit website, or call.

OHIO KENTUCKY INDIANA CHILDREN'S LITERATURE CONFERENCE

Northern Kentucky University, 405 Steely Library, Highland Heights KY 41099. (859)572-6620. **Fax:** (859)572-5390. **E-mail:** smithjen@nku.edu. **Website:** https://swonlibraries.org/mpage/oki. **Contact:** Jennifer Smith. Annual conference held in November for writers and illustrators, geared toward all levels. Open to all. Emphasizes multicultural literature for children and young adults. Contact Jennifer Smith for more information.

COSTS $85; includes registration/attendance at all workshop sessions, continental breakfast, lunch, and author/illustrator signings. Manuscript critiques are available for an additional cost. E-mail or call for more information.

OKLAHOMA WRITERS' FEDERATION, INC. ANNUAL CONFERENCE

9800 South Hwy. 137, Miami OK 74354. **Website:** www.owfi.org. Annual conference held first weekend in May, just outside Oklahoma City. Writer workshops geared toward all levels. "The goal of the conference is to create good stories with strong bones. We will be exploring cultural writing and cultural sensitivity in writing." Several literary agents are in attendance each year to meet with writers and hear pitches.

COSTS Costs vary depending on when registrants sign up. Cost includes awards banquet and famous author banquet. 3 extra sessions are available for an extra fee. Visit the event website for more information and a complete faculty list.

OUTDOOR WRITERS ASSOCIATION OF AMERICA ANNUAL CONFERENCE

2814 Brooks St., Box 442, Missoula MT 59801. (406)728-7434. **E-mail:** info@owaa.org. **Website:** owaa.org. **Contact:** Jessica Seitz, conference and membership coordinator. Outdoor communicator workshops geared toward all levels. Annual 3-day conference includes craft improvement seminars and newsmaker sessions. 2019 dates: June 22-24. Site: Little Rock, Arkansas. Cost includes attendance at all workshops and meals.

COSTS Full 3 Days - $249; 2 Days - $200; One Day - $100.

OZARK CREATIVE WRITERS, INC. CONFERENCE

P.O. Box 9076, Fayetteville AR 72703. **E-mail:** ozarkcreativewriters@ozarkcreativewriters.com. **Website:** www.ozarkcreativewriters.com. The annual event is held in October at the Inn of the Ozarks, in the resort town of Eureka Springs, Arkansas. Approximately 200 writers attend each year; many also enter the creative writing competitions. Open to professional and amateur writers, workshops are geared toward all levels and all forms of the creative process and literary arts; sessions sometimes also include songwriting. Includes presentations by best-selling authors, editors, and agents. Offering writing competitions in all genres.

○ A full list of sessions and speakers is online. The conference usually has agents and/or editors in attendance to meet with writers.

COSTS Full Conference Early Bird Registration: $185.00; after August 25:$ 248.00. Conference Only Registration: $140.00; after August 25: $150.00.

PACIFIC COAST CHILDREN'S WRITERS WHOLE-NOVEL WORKSHOP: FOR ADULTS AND TEENS

P.O. Box 244, Aptos CA 95001. **Website:** www.childrenswritersworkshop.com. Annual conference held in fall. 2019 dates: September 20-22. Offers semi-advanced through published writers an editor and/or agent critique on their full novel or 15-page partial. (The latter may include mid-book and synopsis critiques.) Focus is on craft as a marketing tool. Team-taught master classes (open clinic ms critiques) explore topics such as "Story Architecture and Arcs."

Offers continuous close contact with faculty, who have included Andrea Brown (agent, president of Andrea Brown Literary) and Simon Boughton (vice president/executive editor of 3 Macmillan imprints). Attendance: 16 maximum. For the most critique options and early bird discount, submit e-application in May (dates on website); registration is open until all places are filled. Content: character-driven upper middle-grade and young adult novels. Collegial; highly hands-on. Reading peer mss before master class observations and discussions maximizes learning. Usually at least 1 enrollee lands a book deal with faculty. A concurrent workshop is open to teens who give adults smart target-reader feedback.

COSTS Visit website for tiered fees (includes lodging, meals), schedule, and more; e-mail Director Nancy Sondel via the contact form.

PENNWRITERS CONFERENCE

P.O. Box 685, Dalton PA 18414. **E-mail:** conferenceco@pennwriters.org; info@pennwriters.org. **Website:** pennwriters.org/conference. The mission of Pennwriters, Inc. is to help writers of all levels, from the novice to the award-winning and multi-published, improve and succeed in their craft. The annual Pennwriters conference is held every year in May in Pennsylvania, switching between locations—Lancaster in even numbered years and Pittsburgh in odd numbered years. 2019 dates: May 17-19 at the Pittsburgh Airport Marriott. Literary agents are in attendance to meet with writers. Costs vary. Pennwriters members in good standing get a slightly reduced rate.

○ As the official writing organization of Pennsylvania, Pennwriters has 8 different areas with smaller writing groups that meet. Each of these areas sometimes has their own, smaller event during the year in addition to the annual writing conference.

ADDITIONAL INFORMATION Sponsors contest. Published authors judge fiction in various categories. Agent/editor appointments are available on a first-come, first-served basis.

PHILADELPHIA WRITERS' CONFERENCE

P.O. Box 7171, Elkins Park PA 19027. (215)619-7422. **E-mail:** info@pwcwriters.org. **Website:** pwcwriters.org. Annual conference held in June. Duration: 3 days. Average attendance: 160-200. Conference covers many forms of writing: novel, short story, genre fiction, nonfiction book, magazine writing, blogging, juvenile, poetry. 2019 dates: June 7-9. See website for details. Hotel may offer discount for early registration.

Offers 14 workshops, usually 4 seminars, several "manuscript rap" sessions, a Friday Round-table Forum Buffet with speaker, and the Saturday Annual Awards Banquet with speaker. Attendees may submit mss in advance for criticism by the workshop leaders and are eligible to submit entries in more than 10 contest categories. Cash prizes and certificates are given to first and second place winners, plus full tuition for the following year's conference to first place winners.

ADDITIONAL INFORMATION Accepts inquiries by e-mail. Agents and editors attend the conference. Many questions are answered online.

PIKES PEAK WRITERS CONFERENCE

Pikes Peak Writers, P.O. Box 64273, Colorado Springs CO 80962. (719)244-6220. **E-mail:** registrar@pikespeakwriters.com. **Website:** www.pikespeakwriters.com/ppwc. Annual conference held in April. 2019 dates: May 3-5. Conference duration: 3 days. Average attendance: 300. Workshops, presentations, and panels focus on writing and publishing mainstream and genre fiction (romance, science fiction/fantasy, suspense/thrillers, action/adventure, mysteries, children's, young adult). Agents and editors are available for meetings with attendees on Saturday. Speakers have included Jeff Lindsay, Rachel Caine, and Kevin J. Anderson. Marriott Colorado Springs holds a block of rooms at a special rate for attendees until late March.

COSTS $405-465 (includes all 7 meals).

ADDITIONAL INFORMATION Readings with critiques are available on Friday afternoon. Registration forms are online; brochures are available in January. Send inquiries via e-mail.

PNWA SUMMER WRITERS CONFERENCE

Writers' Cottage, 317 NW Gilman Blvd. Suite 8, Issaquah WA 98027. (425)673-2665. **E-mail:** pnwa@pnwa.org. **Website:** www.pnwa.org. Annual conference. 2019 dates: September 12-15. Duration: 4 days. Average attendance: 400. Attendees have the chance to meet agents and editors, learn craft from authors, and uncover marketing secrets. Speakers have included J.A. Jance, Sheree Bykofsky, Kimberley Cameron, Jennie Dunham, Donald Maass, Jandy Nelson, Robert Dugoni, and Terry Brooks.

COSTS See website for costs and early bird registration.

ROCKY MOUNTAIN FICTION WRITERS COLORADO GOLD CONFERENCE

Rocky Mountain Fiction Writers, Denver Renaissance Hotel, Denver CO **E-mail:** conference@rmfw.org. **Website:** www.rmfw.org. **Contact:** Pamela Nowak and Susan Brooks. Annual conference held in September. Duration: 3 days. Average attendance: 400+. Themes include general fiction, genre fiction, contemporary romance, mystery, science fiction/fantasy, mainstream, young adult, screenwriting, short stories, and historical fiction, as well as marketing and career management. 2019 keynote speakers are Anne Hillerman, John Gilstrap and Marie Force. Past speakers have included Kate Moretti, James Scott Bell, Christopher Paolini, Diana Gabaldon, Sherry Thomas, Lori Rader-Day, Ann Hood, Robert J. Sawyer, Jeffery Deaver, William Kent Krueger, Margaret George, Jodi Thomas, Bernard Cornwell, Terry Brooks, Dorothy Cannell, Patricia Gardner Evans, Diane Mott Davidson, Constance O'Day, and Connie Willis. Approximately 16 acquiring editors and agents attend annually. Special rates will be available at conference hotel.

COSTS Available on website.

ADDITIONAL INFORMATION Pitch appointments available at no charge. Add-on options include agent and editor critiques, master classes, pitch coaching, query letter coaching, special critiques, and more.

SAN DIEGO STATE UNIVERSITY WRITERS' CONFERENCE

SDSU College of Extended Studies, 5250 Campanile Dr., San Diego State University, San Diego CA 92182. (619)594-2099. **Fax:** (619)594-8566. **E-mail:** sdsuwritersconference@mail.sdsu.edu. **Website:** ces.sdsu.edu/writers. Just as all good literary works must come to an end, so must we. The San Diego State Writers' Conference bids you farewell, and wishes you every success in your writing endeavors. Use your conference memories, epiphanies, and connections as fuel to maintain your momentum in pursuing your goals.

SAN FRANCISCO WRITERS CONFERENCE

Hyatt Regency Embarcadero, San Francisco (925) 420-6223. **E-mail:** barbara@sfwriters.org. **Website:** sfwriters.org. **Contact:** Barbara Santos, marketing director. SFWC Main Office, P.O. Box 326, Oakley CA 94561 2019 dates: February 14-17. Annual conference held

President's Day weekend in February. Average attendance: 700. "More than 100 top authors, respected literary agents, and major publishing houses are at the event so attendees can make face-to-face contact with all the right people. Writers of nonfiction, fiction, poetry, and specialty writing (children's books, lifestyle books, etc.) will all benefit from the event. There are important sessions on marketing, self-publishing, technology, and trends in the publishing industry. Plus, there's an optional session called Speed Dating with Agents where attendees can meet with literary agents. Past speakers have included Jane Smiley, Debbie Macomber, Clive Cussler, Guy Kawasaki, Jennifer Crusie, R.L. Stine, Lisa See, Steve Berry, and Jacquelyn Mitchard. Bestselling authors, agents and several editors from traditional publishing houses participate each year, and many will be available for meetings with attendees." The Hyatt Regency Embarcadero offers a discounted SFWC rate (based on availability. Use Code WR19). Call directly: (415) 788-1234. Across from the Ferry Building in San Francisco, the hotel is located so that everyone arriving at the Oakland or San Francisco airport can take the BART to the Embarcadero exit, directly in front of the hotel.

Keynoters for 2019 include Catherine Coulther, Jose Antonio Vargas, and Jane Friedman. Attendees can take educational sessions and network with the 100+ presenters from the publishing world. Free editorial and PR consults, exhibitor hall, pitching and networking opportunities available throughout the four-day event. Also several free sessions offered to the public. See website for details or sign up for the SFWC Newsletter for updates.

COSTS Full registration is $895 with a $795 early bird registration rate until December 31, 2018

ADDITIONAL INFORMATION "Present yourself in a professional manner, and the contacts you will make will be invaluable to your writing career. Fliers, details, and registration information are online."

SANTA BARBARA WRITERS CONFERENCE
27 W. Anapamu St., Suite 305, Santa Barbara CA 93101. (805)568-1516. **E-mail:** info@sbwriters.com. **Website:** www.sbwriters.com. Annual conference held in June. 2019 dates: June 16-21 at Santa Barbara Hyatt for 47th anniversary. Average attendance: 200. 30+ writing workshops, panels, speakers, agents, and fellow word crafters. Covers fiction,

nonfiction, journalism, memoir, poetry, playwriting, screenwriting, travel writing, young adult, children's literature, humor, and marketing. Speakers have included Ray Bradbury, William Styron, Eudora Welty, James Michener, Sue Grafton, Charles M. Schulz, Clive Cussler, Fannie Flagg, Elmore Leonard, and T.C. Boyle. Agents will appear on a panel; in addition, there will be an agents and editors day that allows writers to pitch their projects in one-on-one meetings. Hyatt Santa Barbara.

COSTS $150 for single-day; $699 for full conference.

ADDITIONAL INFORMATION Register online or contact for brochure and registration forms.

✚ SCBWI—AUSTIN CONFERENCE
E-mail: austin@scbwi.org; scbwi@scbwi.org. **Website:** austin.scbwi.org. **Contact:** Samantha Clark, regional advisor. 2019 dates: May 18-19. Annual conference features a faculty of published authors and illustrators. Our conference has expanded this year. The schedule includes two keynotes; a publishing panel; 16 breakout sessions on writing, illustrating and professional development; intensives on picture books, novels and illustration; along with critiques, pitches, portfolio showcase, cookies and more. Editors and agents are in attendance to meet with writers. The schedule consists of keynotes and breakout sessions with tracks for writing (picture book and novel), illustrating, and professional development.

COSTS Costs vary for members, students and non-members, and discounted early-bird pricing is available. Visit website for full pricing options.

☯ SCBWI—CANADA EAST
E-mail: canadaeast@scbwi.org; almafullerton@alma-fullerton.com. **Website:** www.canadaeast.scbwi.org. **Contact:** Alma Fullerton, regional advisor. Writer and illustrator events geared toward all levels. Usually offers one event in spring and another in the fall. Check website for updated information.

SCBWI—CENTRAL-COASTAL CALIFORNIA; FALL CONFERENCE
E-mail: cencal@scbwi.org. **Website:** cencal.scbwi.org. **Contact:** Rebecca Langston-George, Regional Advisor. Annual children's writing conference held in October. Geared to all levels. Speakers include editors, authors, illustrators, and agents. Fiction and nonfiction picture books, middle-grade, and young adult novels, and magazine submissions addressed.

There is an annual writing contest in all genres plus illustration display. For fees and other information, e-mail or visit website.

SCBWI—COLORADO/WYOMING (ROCKY MOUNTAIN); EVENTS

E-mail: rmc@scbwi.org. **Website:** www.rmc.scbwi.org. **Contact:** Todd Tuell and Lindsay Eland, regional advisors. SCBWI Rocky Mountain chapter (Colorado/Wyoming) offers special events, schmoozes, meetings, and conferences throughout the year. Major events: Fall Conference (annual, September); Summer Retreat, "Big Sur in the Rockies" (bi- and tri-annual). More info on website.

SCBWI—EASTERN NEW YORK; FALLING LEAVES MASTER CLASS RETREAT

Silver Bay NY **E-mail:** easternny@scbwi.org. **Website:** easternny.scbwi.org. **Contact:** Nancy Castaldo, regional advisor. P.O. Box 159, Valatie NY 12184 We'll return next year for a weekend focused on picture books! The dates will be announced soon. Watch for the call for applications in June 2019. Annual master class retreat hosted by SCBWI Eastern New York and held in November in Silver Bay on Lake George. Holds ms and portfolio critiques, question-and-answer and speaker sessions, intensives, and more, with respected authors and editors. Theme varies each year between picture books, novels, and nonfiction. See website for more information.

SCBWI—MID-ATLANTIC; ANNUAL FALL CONFERENCE

P.O. Box 3215, Reston VA 20195-1215. **E-mail:** midatlantic@scbwi.org. **Website:** midatlantic.scbwi.org/. **Contact:** Ellen R. Braaf, Regional Advisor. For updates and details, visit website. Registration limited to 250. Conference fills quickly. Includes continental breakfast and boxed lunch. Optional craft-focused workshops and individual consultations with conference faculty are available for additional fees.

🖰 This conference takes place in October. Previous conferences have been held in Sterling, Virginia.

SCBWI—NEW ENGLAND; WHISPERING PINES WRITER'S RETREAT

West Greenwich RI **E-mail:** whisperingpinesretreat@yahoo.com. **Website:** newengland.scbwi.org; www.whisperingpinesretreat.org. **Contact:** Pam Vaughan, Director; Julia Boyce, Assistant Director. Three-day retreat (with stays overnight). 2019 dates: October 25-27. A working retreat. No frills. No faculty. Just focus.

Come alone or bring your critique group. Write. Illustrate. Outline. Draft. Revise. Outstanding accommodations and delicious food. Let's get down to work! Registration details coming soon. Save the Dates for 2020:

Back to our regular programming with mentor meetings, presentations, etc.: WPWR-1-October 2-4, 2020 and WPWR-2-October 22-24, 2020. Offers the opportunity to work intimately with professionals in an idyllic setting. Attendees will work with others who are committed to quality children's literature in small groups and will benefit from a 30-minute one-on-one critique with a mentor. Also includes mentors' presentations and an intimate question-and-answer session, Team Kid Lit Jeopardy with prizes, and more. Retreat limited to 32 full-time participants.

COSTS $175-615 depending on day/overnight attendee, participation level, member/non-member, etc. Please see website for details.

SCBWI—NEW JERSEY; ANNUAL SUMMER CONFERENCE

New Jersey NJ **Website:** newjersey.scbwi.org. **Contact:** Regional Advisor Tisha Hamiliton,; Co-Assistant Regional Advisor Rosanne Kurstedt; Co-Assistant Regional Advisor

Kelly Calabrese. 2019 dates: June 1-2 at Hyatt Regency New Brunswick, NJ. This weekend conference is held in the summer. Highlights include multiple one-on-one critiques; "how to" workshops for every level; first page sessions; agent pitches; and interaction with the faculty of editors, agents, art director, and authors. On Friday, attendees can sign up for writing intensives or register for illustrators' day with the art directors. Published authors attending the conference can sign up to participate in the bookfair to sell and autograph their books; illustrators have the opportunity to display their artwork. Attendees have the option to participate in group critiques after dinner on Saturday evening and attend a mix-and-mingle with the faculty on Friday night. Meals are included with the cost of admission. Conference is known for its high ratio of faculty to attendees and interaction opportunities.

COSTS Registration for 2019 is now closed.

SCBWI WINTER CONFERENCE ON WRITING AND ILLUSTRATING FOR CHILDREN

4727 Wilshire Blvd #301, Los Angeles CA 90010. (323)782-1010. **Fax:** (323)782-1892. **E-mail:** scbwi@scbwi.org. **Website:** www.scbwi.org. **Contact:** Stephen Mooser. 2019 conference: February 8-10 in New York City. Average attendance: 1,000. Conference is to promote writing and illustrating for children (picture books, middle-grade, and young adult) and to give participants an opportunity to network with professionals. Covers financial planning for writers, marketing your book, art exhibitions, and more. The winter conference is held in Manhattan; the summer conference in Los Angeles.

COSTS See website for current cost and conference information; $525-675.

ADDITIONAL INFORMATION SCBWI also holds an annual summer conference in August in Los Angeles.

SOUTH CAROLINA WRITERS WORKSHOP

4711 Forest Dr., Suite 3, P.M.B. 189, Columbia SC 29206. **E-mail:** scwwliaison@gmail.com. **Website:** www.myscwa.org. Conference held in October at the Metropolitan Conference Center in Columbia. Held almost every year. Conference duration: 3 days. Features critique sessions, open mic readings, and presentations from agents and editors. More than 50 different workshops for writers to choose from, dealing with all subjects of writing craft, writing business, getting an agent, and more. Agents will be in attendance.

SOUTHEASTERN WRITERS ASSOCIATION— ANNUAL WRITERS WORKSHOP

E-mail: southeasternwriters@gmail.com. **Website:** www.southeasternwriters.org. Annual 4-day workshop, held in Epworth By The Sea, St. Simons Island, Georgia. Open to all writers. 2019 dates: June 7-11. Tuition includes 3 free evaluation conferences with instructors (minimum 2-day registration). Offers contests with cash prizes. Manuscript deadlines: May 15 for both contests and evaluations. Lodging at Epworth and throughout St. Simons Island. Visit website for more information.

Instruction offered for novel writing, short fiction, young adult, humor, columns, poetry, memoir, and self-publishing. Includes agent in residence, publisher in residence, and photographer for author head shots.

COSTS Cost of workshop: $445 for 4 days or lower prices for daily tuition or early bird special. (See website for tuition pricing.)

STEAMBOAT SPRINGS WRITERS CONFERENCE

A Day For Writers, Steamboat Springs Arts Council, Eleanor Bliss Center for the Arts at the Depot, P.O. Box 774284, Steamboat Springs CO 80477. (970)879-9008. **E-mail:** info@steamboatwriters.com. **Website:** www.steamboatwriters.com. **Contact:** Barbara Sparks. 1001 13th St., Steamboat Springs CO 80487. Annual event will be Saturday July 27, 2019. Instructors Juan Morales, poet, and Emily Sinclair, essayist. Workshops geared toward intermediate levels. Open to professionals and amateurs alike. Average attendance: 35-40 (registration limited, conference fills quickly). Optional pre-conference gathering Friday night. Meet-and-greet buffet social followed by Five Minutes of Fame session for conference participants to share their work.

"A Day for Writers" emphasizes instruction within the seminar format. Novices and polished professionals benefit from a unique feature that offers one workshop at a time. All participants engage together, adding to the informal and intimate community feeling. It's perfect for nonfiction writers seeking a combination of inspiration, craft techniques and camaraderie.

COSTS $60 early registration; $75 after May 31. Registration fee includes continental breakfast and luncheon.

SURREY INTERNATIONAL WRITERS' CONFERENCE

SiWC, 151-10090 152 St., Suite 544, Surrey BC V3R 8X8, Canada. **E-mail:** kathychung@siwc.ca. **Website:** www.siwc.ca. **Contact:** Kathy Chung, proposals contact and conference coordinator. Annual professional development writing conference outside Vancouver, Canada, held every October. Writing workshops geared toward beginner, intermediate, and advanced levels. More than 80 workshops and panels, on all topics and genres, plus pre-conference master classes. Blue Pencil and agent/editor pitch sessions included. Different conference price packages available. Check the conference website for more information. This event has many literary agents in attendance taking pitches. Annual fiction writing contest open to all with $1,000 prize for first place. Conference registration opens in early June every year. Register very early to avoid disappointment as the conference is likely to sell out quickly.

TEXAS WRITING RETREAT

Navasota TX **E-mail:** paultcuclis@gmail.com. **Website:** www.texaswritingretreat.com. **Contact:** Paul Cuclis, coordinator. The Texas Writing Retreat is an intimate event with a limited number of attendees. 2017 dates: January 11-16. Held on a private residence ranch an hour outside of Houston, the retreat has an agent and editor in attendance teaching. All attendees get to pitch the attending agent. Meals, excursions, and amenities are included. This is a unique event that combines craft sessions, business sessions, time for writing, relaxation, and more. The retreat is not held every year; it's best to check the website.

COSTS Costs vary per event. There are different pricing options for those staying on-site versus commuters.

THE UNIVERSITY OF WINCHESTER WRITERS' FESTIVAL

University of Winchester, Winchester Hampshire S022 4NR, United Kingdom. (44)(0)1962-827238. **E-mail:** sara.gangai@winchester.ac.uk. **Website:** www.writersfestival.co.uk. **Contact:** Sara Okaya Gangai, festival director. The 38th Winchester Writers' Festival (2019) takes place on June 14-16 at the University of Winchester, offering inspiration, learning, and networking for new and emerging writers working in all forms and genres. Choose from 18 day-long workshops and 28 talks, plus book up to 4 one-to-one appointments per attendee with leading literary agents, commissioning editors, and award-winning authors to help you harness your creative ideas, turn them into marketable work, and pitch to publishing professionals. If you cannot attend, you may still enter one of our 9 writing competitions. Enjoy a creative writing weekend in Winchester, the oldest city in England. Only 1 hour from London. To view festival details, including all the competition details, please go to the official event website. Booking opens in February. On-site student single ensuite accommodation available. Also, a range of hotels and bed and breakfasts nearby in the city.

COSTS See festival program.

ADDITIONAL INFORMATION Lunch, and tea/coffee/cake included in the booking cost. Dinner can be booked separately. All dietary needs catered for.

TMCC WRITERS' CONFERENCE

Truckee Meadows Community College, 7000 Dandini Blvd., Reno NV 89512. (775)673-7111. **E-mail:** wdce@tmcc.edu. **Website:** wdce.tmcc.edu. Annual conference held in April. 2019 date: April 13. Average attendance: 150. Conference focuses on strengthening mainstream/literary fiction and nonfiction works and how to market them to agents and publishers. Site: Truckee Meadows Community College in Reno. "There is always an array of speakers and presenters with impressive literary credentials, including agents and editors." Speakers have included Chuck Sambuchino, Sheree Bykofsky, Andrea Brown, Dorothy Allison, Karen Joy Fowler, James D. Houston, James N. Frey, Gary Short, Jane Hirschfield, Dorrianne Laux, and Kim Addonizio. Literary agents are on site to take pitches from writers. Contact the conference manager to learn about accommodation discounts.

ADDITIONAL INFORMATION "The conference is open to all writers, regardless of their level of experience. Brochures are available online and mailed in January. Send inquiries via e-mail."

UNICORN WRITERS CONFERENCE

17 Church Hill Rd., Redding CT 06896, USA. (203)938-7405. **E-mail:** unicornwritersconference@gmail.com. **Website:** www.unicornwritersconference.com. **Contact:** Jan L. Kardys, chair. 2019 website: The next conference will be held from 7:30 AM to 8:00 PM on (Date Coming Soon) at Reid Castle at Manhattanville College. For all the information about our guest agents, editors, and speakers, manuscript review sessions, and workshops please take a look through our site.

This writers conference draws upon its close proximity to New York and pulls in over 40 literary agents and 15 major New York editors to pitch each year. There are manuscript review sessions (40 pages equals 30 minutes with an agent/editor), query/manuscript review sessions, and 6 different workshops every hour. Cost: $325, includes all workshops and 3 meals. Held at Reid Castle, Purchase, New York. Directions available on event website.

"The forty pages for manuscript reviews are read in advance by your selected agents/editors, but follow the submission guidelines on the website. Check the genre chart for each agent and editor before you make your selection."

ADDITIONAL INFORMATION The first self-published authors will be featured on the website, and the bookstore will sell their books at the event.

UNIVERSITY OF WISCONSIN AT MADISON WRITERS INSTITUTE

21 N. Park St., Madison WI 53715. (608)265-3972. **E-mail:** laurie.scheer@wisc.edu. **Website:** uwwritersinstitute.wisc.edu. Annual conference. 2019 dates: April 4-7. Conference on fiction, nonfiction, marketing, and publishing held at the University of Wisconsin at Madison. Guest speakers are published authors and publishing executives. Agents and publishing companies take pitches. Theme: Pathway to Publication.

COSTS $265-345, depending on discounts and if you attend one day or multiple days.

WESLEYAN WRITERS CONFERENCE

Wesleyan University, 294 High St., Room 207, Middletown CT 06459. (860)685-3604. **Fax:** (860)685-2441. **E-mail:** agreene@wesleyan.edu. **Website:** www.wesleyan.edu/writing/conference. **Contact:** Anne Greene, director. Annual conference held in June. 2018 dates: June 12-16. Average attendance: 100. Focuses on the novel, fiction techniques, short stories, poetry, screenwriting, nonfiction, literary journalism, memoir, mixed media work, and publishing. The conference is held on the campus of Wesleyan University, in the hills overlooking the Connecticut River. Features a faculty of award-winning writers, seminars, and readings of new fiction, poetry, nonfiction, and mixed media forms—as well as guest lectures on a range of topics including publishing. Both new and experienced writers are welcome. Participants may attend seminars in all genres. Speakers have included Esmond Harmsworth (Zachary Shuster Harmsworth), Daniel Mandel (Sanford J. Greenburger Associates), Amy Williams (ICM and Collins McCormick), and many others. Agents will be speaking and available for meetings with attendees. Participants are often successful in finding agents and publishers for their mss. Wesleyan participants are also frequently featured in the anthology *Best New American Voices*. Meals are provided on campus. Lodging is available on campus or in town.

ADDITIONAL INFORMATION Ms critiques are available but not required.

WHIDBEY ISLAND WRITERS' CONFERENCE

(360)331-0307. **E-mail:** http://writeonwhidbey.org. **Website:** http://writeonwhidbey.org. P.O. Box 1289, Langley, WA 98260. (360)331-6714. **E-mail:** writers@whidbey.com. **Website:** www.writeonwhidbey.org. **Writers Contact:** Conference Director. Three days focused on the tools you need to become a great writer. Learn from a variety of award-winning children's book authors and very experienced literary agents. Variety of preconference workshops and conference topics. Conference held in early spring. Registration limited to 290. Cost: $395; early bird and member discounts available. Registration includes workshops, fireside chats, book-signing reception, various activities, and daily luncheons. The conference offers consultation appointments with editors and agents. Registrants may reduce the cost of their conference by volunteering. See the website for more information. "The uniquely personal and friendly weekend is designed to be highly interactive." 2019: No current info found.

Annual conference held in early spring. Registration limited to 290. Registration includes workshops, fireside chats, book-signing reception, various activities, and daily luncheons. The conference offers consultation appointments with editors and agents. Registrants may reduce the cost of their conference by volunteering. See the website for more information. "The uniquely personal and friendly weekend is designed to be highly interactive." There are a variety of sessions on topics such as fiction, craft, poetry, platform, agents, screenwriting, and much more. Topics are varied, and there is something for all writers. Multiple agents and editors are in attendance. The schedule and faculty change every year, and those changes are reflected online

WILLAMETTE WRITERS CONFERENCE

5331 SW Macadam Ave.
Suite 258, PMB 215, Portland OR 97239. (971) 200-5382. **E-mail:** conf.chair@willamettewriters.org. **Website:** willamettewriters.com/wwcon/; willamettewriters.org; wilwrite@Willamettewriters.org. 2019 dates: August 2-4 at Sheraton Portland Airport Hotel. Over 700 attendees will gather for a weekend that's all about writers and writing. Meet industry professionals, learn from world-class faculty, and keynotes, and connect with a community of writers. 50th consecutive year Willamette Writers has hosted

one of the largest and most-beloved writing conferences in North America. We have worked tirelessly to reach our golden anniversary, providing a wide array of opportunities for writers to build their craft, meet successful professionals, and become part of a dynamic group of writers from all walks of life.

COSTS Pricing schedule available online. Conference price includes breakfast, lunch, and an appetizer reception on Friday and Saturday. Workshops on Friday, Saturday, and Sunday are included — first come, first serve. No additional registration is required for workshops. You must sign up at an additional cost to participate in Master Classes and Sunday Intensives.

WINTER POETRY & PROSE GETAWAY

Murphy Writing of Stockton University, 30 Front Street, Hammonton NJ 08037, USA. (609)626-3594. E-mail: info@wintergetaway.com. **Website:** www.stockton.edu/wintergetaway; stockton.edu/murphywriting. **Contact:** Amanda Murphy, Director. 2020 dates: January 17-20. Annual January conference at the Jersey Shore. Join us at the historic Seaview Hotel near Atlantic City. Enjoy challenging and supportive workshops, insightful feedback and an encouraging community. Choose from workshops in poetry, fiction, nonfiction, memoir, and more. Room packages at the historic Stockton Seaview Hotel are available.

○ "At most conferences, writers listen to talks and panels and sit in sessions where previously written work is discussed. At the Getaway, they write. Most workshops are limited to 10 or fewer participants. By spending the entire weekend in one workshop, participants will venture deeper into their writing, making more progress than they thought possible."

COSTS See website or call for past fee information. Scholarships available.

ADDITIONAL INFORMATION Previous faculty has included Julianna Baggott, Christian Bauman, Laure-Anne Bosselaar, Kurt Brown, Mark Doty (National Book Award winner), Stephen Dunn (Pulitzer Prize winner), Dorianne Laux, Carol Plum-Ucci, James Richardson, Mimi Schwartz, Terese Svoboda, and more.

WOMEN WRITING THE WEST

8547 E. Araphoe Rd., Box J-541, Greenwood Village CO 80112-1436. **E-mail:** conference@womenwritingthewest.org; cmassey2@satx.rr.com. **Website:** www.womenwritingthewest.org. 2019: 25th Annual Conference October 10-13 Writing to Remember - Remembering Why We Write. Held at: Omni La Mansion del Rio Hotel San Antonio, Texas. "Women Writing the West is a nonprofit association of writers, editors, publishers, agents, booksellers, and other professionals writing and promoting the women's West. As such, women writing their stories in the American West in a way that illuminates them authentically. In addition, the organization provides support, encouragement, and inspiration to all women writing about any facet of the American West. Membership is open to all interested persons worldwide, including students. WWW membership also allows the choice of participation in our marketing marvel, the annual WWW Catalog of Author's Books. An annual conference is held every fall. The event covers research, writing techniques, multiple genres, marketing/promotion, and more. Agents and editors share ideas in a panel format as well as meeting one-on-one for pitch sessions with attendees. Conference location changes each year. The blog and social media outlets publish current WWW activities, features market research, and share articles of interest pertaining to American West literature and member news. WWW annually sponsors the WILLA Literary Award, which is given in several categories for outstanding literature featuring women's stories, set in the West. The winner of a WILLA literary Award receives a cash award and a trophy at the annual conference. Contest is open to non-members. See website for location and accommodation details.

COSTS See website. Discounts available for members.

WRITEAWAYS

E-mail: writeawaysinfo@gmail.com. **Website:** https://www.writeaways.com. **Contact:** Mimi Herman. "We created Writeaways—writing getaways—to help you find the time you need to write. We provide writing instruction, fabulous food and company in beautiful places, and an inspiring place for you to take a writing vacation with your muse. We pamper you while providing rigorous, supportive assistance to help you become the best writer possible. We have week-long workshops in France and Italy, and weekend-plus-optional-retreat programs in North Carolina." North Carolina: The Whitehall, Camden, North Carolina. France: Chateau du Pin, near Champtocé-sur Loire (18 miles west of Angers). Italy: Villas Cini and Casanova, near Bucine, between Siena and Arezzo.

For 2019, consider these dates: Workshop by the River (NC): May 17-19; Retreat by the River (NC): May 19-21; France (Chateau du Pin): September 26-October 3; Italy (Villas Cini and Casanova): October 5-12; The Grand Tour (France and Italy back to back): September 26 -October 12.

COSTS North Carolina workshop: Price TBA (check web site for the latest information). France and Italy: $2,350 single room, $2,100 shared rooms. The Grand Tour (France and Italy): $4,200 each single room, $4,000 each shared room.

WRITE-BY-THE-LAKE WRITER'S WORKSHOP & RETREAT

21 N. Park St., 7th Floor, Madison WI 53715. (608)262-3447. **E-mail:** christine.desmet@wisc.edu. **Website:** www.dcs.wisc.edu/lsa/writing. **Contact:** Christine DeSmet, director. Open to all writers and students; 12 or more workshops for all levels. Includes classes for full novel critique and one master class for 50 pages. Usually held the third week of June on the University of Wisconsin-Madison campus. Registration limited to 15 each section; fewer in master classes. Writing facilities available; computer labs, wifi in all buildings and on the outdoor lakeside terrace. E-mail for more information. "Registration opens every January for following June."

COSTS $425 before May 20, 2019; $475 after that. Additional cost for master classes and college credits. Cost includes instruction, welcome luncheon, pastry/coffee each day, open mic, guest speaker presentations, one-on-one meetings with the Writing Doctor.

WRITE CANADA

The Word Guild, Box 77001, Markham Ontario L3P 0C8, Canada. **E-mail:** info@thewordguild.com. **Website:** https://thewordguild.com/. Annual conference in Ontario for Christian writers of all types and at all stages. 2019 dates: June 13-15. Conference duration: 3 days. Offers solid instruction, stimulating interaction, exciting challenges, and worshipful community.

"Write Canada is the nation's largest Christian writers' conference held annually. Each year hundreds of writers and editors—authors, journalists, columnists, bloggers, poets and playwrights—gather to hone their craft. Over the past 3 decades, Write Canada has successfully equipped writers and editors, beginner to professional, from all across North America."

COSTS See website for details and registration.

WRITE IN THE HARBOR

Website: continuingedtacoma.com/writeintheharbor. 3993 Hunt St., Gig Harbor WA 98335. (253)460-2424. **Website:** continuingedtacoma.com/writeintheharbor. Annual conference held in fall. 2019 dates: November 1-2. Offers workshops geared toward beginner, intermediate, advanced, and professional levels. Includes welcome reception, keynote speaker, and several presenters. Registration limited to 150. Early bird enrollment opens July 1. See website for more information. Annual conference held in fall. 2019 dates: November 1-2. Offers workshops geared toward beginner, intermediate, advanced, and professional levels. Includes welcome reception, keynote speaker, and several presenters. Registration limited to 80.

COSTS See website.

WRITE ON THE SOUND

WOTS, City of Edmonds Arts Commission, Frances Anderson Center, 700 Main St., Edmonds WA 98020. (425)771-0228. **E-mail:** wots@edmondswa.gov. **Website:** www.writeonthesound.com. **Contact:** Laurie Rose, Conference Organizer or Frances Chapin, Edmonds Arts Commission Mgr. Small, affordable annual conference focused on the craft of writing. Held the first weekend in October. 2019 dates: October 4-6. Conference duration: 3 days. Average attendance: 275. Features over 30 presenters, keynote, writing contest, ms critique appts, round table discussions, book signing reception, onsite bookstore, and opportunity to network with faculty and attendees. Edmonds is located just north of Seattle on the Puget Sound. Best Western Plus/Edmonds Harbor Inn is a conference partner.

Past attendee says, "I came away from every session with ideas to incorporate into my own writer's toolbox. The energy was wonderful because everyone was there for a single purpose: to make the most of a weekend for writers, whatever the level of expertise. I can't thank all the organizers, presenters, and volunteers enough for a wonderful experience."

COSTS $90-300 (not including optional fees).

ADDITIONAL INFORMATION Schedule posted on website late spring/early summer. Registration opens mid-July. Attendees are required to select the sessions when they register. Wait lists for conference and manuscript appointments are available.

WRITE-TO-PUBLISH CONFERENCE

WordPro Communication Services, 9118 W. Elmwood Dr., Suite 1G, Niles IL 60714. (847)296-3964. **E-mail:** lin@writetopublish.com. **Website:** www.writetopublish.com. **Contact:** Lin Johnson, director. Annual conference. 2019 dates: June 19-22. Average attendance: 175. Conference is focused on the Christian market and includes classes for writers at all levels and appointments with editors and agents. Open to high school students. Site: Wheaton College, Wheaton, Illinois (Chicago area). [This is not a function of Wheaton College.] Campus residence hall rooms available. See the website for current information and costs.

COSTS See the website for current costs.

ADDITIONAL INFORMATION Conference information available in late January or early February. For details, visit website, or email brochure@writetopublish.com. Accepts inquiries by e-mail, phone.

WRITING AND ILLUSTRATING FOR YOUNG READERS CONFERENCE

1480 E. 9400 S., Sandy UT 84093. **E-mail:** staff@wifyr.com. **Website:** www.wifyr.com. Brigham Young University, 348 Harman Continuing Education Bldg. Provo, UT 84602-1532. (801)442-2568. **Fax:** (801)422-0745. **E-mail:** cw348@byu.edu. **Website:** http://wifyr.byu.edu. Annual workshop held in June. 5-day workshop designed for people who want to write for children or teenagers. Participants focus on a single market during daily 4-hour morning writing workshops: picture books, book-length fiction (novels), fantasy/science fiction, nonfiction, mystery, beginning writing or illustration. Afternoon workshop sessions feature a variety of topics of interest to writers for all youth ages. See website for workshop cost. Afternoon-only registration available; participants may attend these sessions all 5 days. See website for cost. Attendance at the Thursday evening banquet is included in addition to the afternoon mingle, plenary, and breakout sessions. Annual workshop held in June. 2019 dates: June 10-14. Duration: 5 days. Average attendance: more than 100. Learn how to write, illustrate, and publish in the children's and young adult markets. Beginning and advanced writers and illustrators are tutored in a small-group workshop setting by published authors and artists and receive instruction from and network with editors, major publishing house representatives, and literary agents. Afternoon attendees get to hear practical writing and publishing tips from published authors, literary agents, and editors. Site: Waterford School in Sandy, UT. Speakers have included John Cusick, Stephen Fraser, Alyson Heller, and Ruth Katcher. A block of rooms is available at the Best Western Cotton Tree Inn in Sandy, UT, at a discounted rate. This rate is good as long as there are available rooms.

Guidelines and registration are on the website.

ADDITIONAL INFORMATION There is an online form to contact this event.

WRITING FOR THE SOUL

Jerry B. Jenkins Christian Writers Guild, P.O. Box 88288, Black Forest CO 80908. (866)495-7551. **Fax:** (719)494-1299. **E-mail:** jerry@jerryjenkins.com. **Website:** www.jerryjenkins.com. Conferences as announced, covering fiction, nonfiction, and online writing. Nationally known, best-selling authors as keynote speakers, hosted by Jerry B. Jenkins. See website for pricing, locations, dates, and accommodations.

WYOMING WRITERS ANNUAL CONFERENCE

P. O. Box 454, Riverton WY 82501. **E-mail:** wyowriters@gmail.com. **Website:** wyowriters.org. **Contact:** J.G. Matheny, president. This is a three-day conference for writers of all genres, with attendees generally coming from Wyoming and neighboring states. Each year multiple published authors, editors, and literary agents come to meet with attendees, hold educational sessions, and take pitches. Open reading sessions, peer critique, and keynote speakers highlight the event. Each year the conference location moves to different Wyoming locales, so that attendees can experience the true flavor of this smaller western conference.

CONTESTS, AWARDS & GRANTS

Publication is not the only way to get your work recognized. Contests and awards can also be great ways to gain recognition in the industry. Grants, offered by organizations like the Society of Children's Book Writers and Illustrators (SCBWI), offer monetary recognition to writers, giving them more financial freedom as they work on projects.

When considering contests or applying for grants, be sure to study guidelines and requirements. Regard entry deadlines as gospel and follow the rules to the letter.

Note that some contests require nominations. For published authors and illustrators, competitions provide an excellent way to promote your work. Your publisher may not be aware of local competitions such as state-sponsored awards—if your book is eligible, have the appropriate person at your publishing company nominate or enter your work for consideration.

To select potential contests and grants, read through the listings that interest you, then send for more information about the types of written or illustrated material considered and other important details. A number of contests offer information through websites given in their listings.

If you are interested in knowing who has received certain awards in the past, check your local library or bookstores or consult *Children's Books: Awards & Honors*, compiled and edited by the Children's Book Council (www.cbcbooks.org). Many bookstores have special sections for books that are Caldecott and Newbery Medal winners. Visit the American Library Association website, www.ala.org, for information on the Caldecott, Newbery, Coretta Scott King, and Printz Awards. Visit www.hbook.com for information on The Boston Globe-Horn Book Award. Visit www.scbwi.org/awards.htm for information on The Golden Kite Award.

JANE ADDAMS CHILDREN'S BOOK AWARD

Jane Addams Peace Association, 777 United Nations Plaza, 6th Floor, New York NY 10017. (212)682-8830. **E-mail:** info@janeaddamspeace.org. **Website:** www.janeaddamspeace.org. **Contact:** Heather Palmer, Co-Chair.. The Jane Addams Children's Book Award annually recognizes children's books, published the preceding year, that effectively promote the cause of peace, social justice, world community, and the equality of the sexes and all races, as well as meeting conventional standards for excellence. Books eligible for this award may be fiction, poetry, or nonfiction. Books may be any length. Entries should be suitable for ages 2-12. See website for specific details on guidelines and required book themes. Deadline: December 31. Judged by a national committee of WILPF members concerned with children's books and their social values is responsible for making the choices each year.

☺ ALCUIN SOCIETY AWARDS FOR EXCELLENCE IN BOOK DESIGN IN CANADA

The Alcuin Society, P.O. Box 3216, Stn. Terminal, Vancouver BC V6B 3X8, Canada. **E-mail:** awards@alcuinsociety.com; info@alcuinsociety.com. **Website:** www.alcuinsociety.com. **Contact:** Leah Gordon. The Alcuin Society Awards for Excellence in Book Design in Canada is the only national competition for book design in Canada. Winners are selected from books designed and published in Canada. Awards are presented annually at appropriate ceremonies held each year. Winning books are exhibited nationally and internationally at the Tokyo, Frankfurt, and Leipzig Book Fairs, and are Canada's entries in the international competition in Leipzig, "Book Design from all over the World", in the following spring. Submit previously published material from the year before the award's call for entries. Submissions made by the publisher (Canadian), author (any), or designer (Canadian). Deadline: varies annually. Prizes: 1st, 2nd, 3rd, and Honourable Mention in each category (at the discretion of the judges). Judged by professionals and those experienced in the field of book design.

AMERICA & ME ESSAY CONTEST

Farm Bureau Insurance, P.O. Box 30400, Lansing MI 48909. **E-mail:** lfedewa@fbinsmi.com. **Website:** FarmBureauInsurance.com. **Contact:** Lisa Fedewa.. Focuses on encouraging students to write about their personal Michigan heroes: someone who lives in the state and who has encouraged them, taught them important lessons, and helped them pursue their dreams. Open to Michigan eighth graders. Contest rules and entry form available on website. Encourages Michigan youth to recognize the heroes in their communities and their state. Deadline: November 18. Prize: $1,000, plaque, and medallion for top 10 winners. Home office volunteers.

AMERICAN ASSOCIATION OF UNIVERSITY WOMEN YOUNG PEOPLE'S LITERATURE AWARD

4610 Mail Service Center, Raleigh NC 27699-4610. (919)807-7290. **E-mail:** michael.hill@ncdcr.gov. **Website:** www.ncdcr.gov. **Contact:** Michael Hill, Awards Coordinator.. Annual award. Book must be published during the year ending June 30. Submissions made by author, author's agent. or publisher. SASE for contest rules. Author must have maintained either legal residence or actual physical residence, or a combination of both, in the state of North Carolina for 3 years immediately preceding the close of the contest period. Only published work (books) eligible. Recognizes the year's best work of juvenile literature by a North Carolina resident. Deadline: July 15. Prize: Awards a cup to the winner and winner's name inscribed on a plaque displayed within the North Carolina Office of Archives and History. Judged by 3-judge panel.

○ Competition receives 10-15 submissions per category.

☻ HANS CHRISTIAN ANDERSEN AWARD

Nonnenweg 12, Postfach Basel CH-4009, Switzerland. **E-mail:** liz.page@ibby.org. **E-mail:** ibby@ibby.org. **Website:** www.ibby.org. **Contact:** Liz Page, Director. The Hans Christian Andersen Award, awarded every two years by the International Board on Books for Young People (IBBY), is the highest international recognition given to an author and an illustrator of children's books. The Author's Award has been given since 1956, the Illustrator's Award since 1966. Her Majesty Queen Margrethe II of Denmark is the Patron of the Hans Christian Andersen Awards. The awards are presented at the biennial congresses of IBBY. Awarded to an author and to an illustrator, living at the time of the nomination, who by the outstanding value of their work are judged to have made a lasting contribution to literature for children and young people. The complete works of the author and of the illustrator will be taken into consideration in awarding the medal, which will be accompanied by a diploma. Candidates are nominated by National Sections of IBBY in good standing. Prize: Awards medals according to literary and artistic criteria. Judged by the Hans Christian Andersen International Jury.

☯ MARILYN BAILLIE PICTURE BOOK AWARD

The Canadian Children's Book Centre, 40 Orchard View Blvd., Suite 217, Toronto ON M4R 1B9, Canada. (416)975-0010, ext. 222. **Fax:** (416)975-8970. **E-mail:** meghan@bookcentre.ca. **Website:** www.bookcentre. ca. **Contact:** Meghan Howe. The Marilyn Baillie Picture Book Award honors excellence in the illustrated picture book format. To be eligible, the book must be an original work in English, aimed at children ages 3-8, written and illustrated by Canadians. Books published in Canada or abroad are eligible. Eligible genres include fiction, non-fiction and poetry. Books must be published between Jan. 1 and Dec. 31 of the previous calendar year. New editions or re-issues of previously published books are not eligible for submission. Send 5 copies of title along with a completed submission form. Deadline: mid-December annually. Prize: $20,000.

MILDRED L. BATCHELDER AWARD

Association for Library Service to Children, Division of the American Library Association, 50 E. Huron St., Chicago IL 60611-2795. (800)545-2433. **Fax:** (312)280-5271. **Website:** www.ala.org/alsc/awards-grants/bookmedia/batchelderaward. The Batchelder Award is given to the most outstanding children's book originally published in a language other than English in a country other than the United States, and subsequently translated into English for publication in the US. Visit website for terms and criteria of award. The purpose of the award, a citation to an American publisher, is to encourage international exchange of quality children's books by recognizing US publishers of such books in translation. Deadline: December 31.

☯ THE GEOFFREY BILSON AWARD FOR HISTORICAL FICTION FOR YOUNG PEOPLE

The Canadian Children's Book Centre, 40 Orchard View Blvd., Suite 217, Toronto ON M4R 1B9, Canada. (416)975-0010, ext. 222. **Fax:** (416)975-8970. **Website:** www.bookcentre.ca. **Contact:** Meghan Howe. Awarded annually to reward excellence in the writing of an outstanding work of historical fiction for young readers, by a Canadian author, published between Jan

1 and Dec 31 of the previous calendar year. Open to Canadian citizens and/or permanent residents of Canada. Books must be published between January 1 and December 31 of the previous year. Books must be first foreign or first Canadian editions. Autobiographies are not eligible. Jury members will consider the following: historical setting and accuracy; strong character and plot development; well-told, original story; and stability of book for its intended age group. Send 5 copies of the title along with a completed submission form. Deadline: January 15th, annually. Prize: $5,000.

THE IRMA S. AND JAMES H. BLACK AWARD

Bank Street College of Education, 610 W. 112th St., New York NY 10025-1898. (212)875-4458. **Fax:** (212)875-4558. **E-mail:** kfreda@bankstreet.edu. **Website:** http://bankstreet.edu/center-childrens-literature/irma-black-award/. **Contact:** Kristin Freda. Award give to an outstanding book for young children—a book in which text and illustrations are inseparable, each enhancing and enlarging on the other to produce a singular whole. Entries must have been published during the previous calendar year. Publishers submit books. Submit only 1 copy of each book. Does not accept unpublished mss. Deadline: December 6. A scroll with the recipient's name, and a gold seal designed by Maurice Sendak. Judged by a committee of older children and children's literature professionals. Final judges are first-, second-, and third-grade classes at a number of cooperating schools.

☜ BOROONDARA LITERARY AWARDS

City of Boroondara, 340 Camberwell Rd., Camberwell VIC 3124, Australia. **E-mail:** bla@boroondara. vic.gov.au. **Website:** www.boroondara.vic.gov.au/ literary-awards. Contest for unpublished work in 2 categories: Open Short Story from residents of Australia (1,500-3,000 words); and Young Writers who live, go to school or work in the City of Boroondara: 5th-6th grade (Junior), 7th-9th grade (Middle), and 10th-12th grade (Senior), prose and poetry on any theme. Deadline: 5pm on the last Friday of August. Prizes: Young Writers, Junior: 1st Place: $300; 2nd Place: $200; 3rd Place: $100. Young Writers, Middle: 1st Place: $450; 2nd Place: $300; 3rd Place: $150 and Senior: 1st Place: $600; 2nd Place: $400; 3rd Place: $200. Open Short Story: 1st Place: $1,500; 2nd Place: $1000; 3rd Place $500.

BOSTON GLOBE-HORN BOOK AWARDS

The Boston Globe, Horn Book, Inc., 300 The Fenway, Palace Road Building, Suite P-311, Boston MA 02115. (617)278-0225. **Fax:** (617)278-6062. **E-mail:** bghb@hbook.com; info@hbook.com. **Website:** www.hbook.com/bghb/. Offered annually for excellence in literature for children and young adults (published June 1-May 31). Categories: picture book, fiction and poetry, nonfiction. Judges may also name up to 2 honor books in each category. Books must be published in the US, but may be written or illustrated by citizens of any country. The Horn Book Magazine publishes speeches given at awards ceremonies. Guidelines for submitting books online. Submit a book directly to each of the judges. See www.hbook.com/bghb-submissions for details on submitting, as well as contest guidelines. Deadline: May 15. Prize: $500 and an engraved silver bowl; honor-book recipients receive an engraved silver plate. Judged by a panel of 3 judges selected each year.

◑ ANN CONNOR BRIMER BOOK AWARD

(902)490-2742. **Website:** www.atlanticbookawards.ca/. **Contact:** Laura Carter, Atlantic Book Awards Festival Coordinator. In 1990, the Nova Scotia Library Association established the Ann Connor Brimer Award for writers residing in Atlantic Canada who have made an outstanding contribution to writing for Atlantic Candian young people. Author must be alive and residing in Atlantic Canada at time of nomination. Book intended for youth up to the age of 15. Book in print and readily available. Fiction or nonfiction (except textbooks). Book must have been published within the previous year. November 1. Prize: $2,000. Two shortlisted titles: $250 each.

CALIFORNIA YOUNG PLAYWRIGHTS CONTEST

Playwrights Project, 3675 Ruffin Rd., Suite 330, San Diego CA 92123-1870. (858)384-2970. **Fax:** (858)384-2974. **E-mail:** write@playwrightsproject.org. **Website:** www.playwrightsproject.org/programs/contest/. **Contact:** Cecelia Kouma, Executive Director. The California Young Playwrights Contest is open to Californians under age 19. Every year, young playwrights submit original scripts to the contest. Every writer who requests feedback receives an individualized script critique. Selected writers win script readings or full professional productions in Plays by Young Writers festival. Distinguished artists from major theatres select festival scripts and write comments to the play-

wrights. Submissions are required to be unpublished and not produced professionally. Submissions made by the author. SASE for contest rules and entry form. Scripts must be a minimum of 10 standard typewritten pages. Scripts will *not* be returned. If requested, entrants receive detailed evaluation letter. Guidelines available online. Deadline: June 1. Prize: Scripts will be produced in spring at a professional theatre in San Diego. Writers submitting scripts of 10 or more pages receive a detailed script evaluation letter upon request. Judged by professionals in the theater community, a committee of 5-7; changes somewhat each year.

CHILDREN'S AFRICANA BOOK AWARD

Outreach Council of the African Studies Association, c/o Rutgers University-Livingston campus, 54 Joyce Kilmer Ave., Piscataway NJ 08854, USA. (703)549-8208; (301)585-9136. **E-mail:** africaaccess@aol.com. **E-mail:** Harriet@AfricaAccessReview.org. **Website:** www.africaaccessreview.org. **Contact:** Brenda Randolph, Chairperson. The Children's Africana Book Awards are presented annually to the authors and illustrators of the best books on Africa for children and young people published or distributed in the U.S. The awards were created by the Outreach Council of the African Studies Association (ASA) to dispel stereotypes and encourage the publication and use of accurate, balanced children's materials about Africa. The awards are presented in 2 categories: Young Children and Older Readers. Entries must have been published in the calendar year previous to the award. Work submitted for awards must be suitable for children ages 4-18; a significant portion of book's content must be about Africa; must by copyrighted in the calendar year prior to award year; and must be published or distributed in the US. Books should be suitable for children and young adults, ages 4-18. A significant portion of the book's content should be about Africa. Deadline: December 31 of the year book is published. Judged by African Studies and Children's Literature scholars. Nominated titles are read by committee members and reviewed by external African Studies scholars with specialized academic training.

CHILDREN'S BOOK GUILD AWARD FOR NONFICTION

E-mail: theguild@childrensbookguild.org. **Website:** www.childrensbookguild.org. Annual award. "One doesn't enter. One is selected. Our jury annually selects one author for the award." Honors an author or illustrator whose total work has contributed significantly to the quality of nonfiction for children. Prize: Cash and an engraved crystal paperweight. Judged by a jury of Children's Book Guild specialists, authors, and illustrators.

CHILDREN'S LITERATURE LEGACY AWARD

50 E. Huron, Chicago IL 60611. (800)545-2433. **Fax:** (312)280-5271. **E-mail:** alscawards@ala.org. **Website:** http://www.ala.org/alsc/awardsgrants/bookmedia/clla. The Children's Literature Legacy Award honors an author or illustrator whose books, published in the United States, have made, over a period of years, a significant and lasting contribution to children's literature through books that demonstrate integrity and respect for all children's lives and experiences. The candidates must be nominated by ALSC members. Medal presented at Newbery/Caldecott/Legacy banquet during annual conference. Judging by Legacy Award Selection Committee.

CHRISTIAN BOOK AWARD® PROGRAM

ECPA/Christian Book Award®, 5801 S. McClintock Dr, Suite 104, Tempe AZ 85283. (480)966-3998. **Fax:** (480)966-1944. **E-mail:** info@ecpa.org. **Website:** www.ecpa.org. **Contact:** Stan Jantz, ED. The Evangelical Christian Publishers Association (ECPA) recognizes quality and encourages excellence by presenting the ECPA Christian Book Awards® (formerly known as Gold Medallion) each year. Categories include Christian Living, Biography & Memoir, Faith & Culture, Children, Young People's Literature, Devotion & Gift, Bibles, Bible Reference Works, Bible Study, Ministry Resources and New Author. All entries must be evangelical in nature and submitted through an ECPA member publisher. Books must have been published in the calendar year prior to the award. Publishing companies submitting entries must be ECPA members in good standing. See website for details. The Christian Book Award® recognizes the highest quality in Christian books and is among the oldest and most prestigious awards program in Christian publishing. Submission period runs September 1-30. Judged by experts, authors, and retailers with years of experience in their field.

○ Book entries are submitted by ECPA member publishers according to criteria including date of publication and category.

THE CITY OF VANCOUVER BOOK AWARD

Cultural Services Dept., Woodward's Heritage Building, 111 W. Hastings St., Suite 501, Vancouver BC V6B 1H4, Canada. (604)871-6634. **Fax:** (604)871-6005. **E-mail:** marnie.rice@vancouver.ca; culture@vancouver.ca. **Website:** https://vancouver.ca/people-programs/city-of-vancouver-book-award.aspx. The annual City of Vancouver Book Award recognizes authors of excellence of any genre that reflect Vancouver's unique character, rich diversity and culture, history and residents. The book must exhibit excellence in one or more of the following areas: content, illustration, design, format. The book must not be copyrighted prior to the previous year. Submit four copies of book. See website for details and guidelines. Deadline: May 22. Prize: $3,000. Judged by an independent jury.

MARGARET A. EDWARDS AWARD

50 East Huron St., Chicago IL 60611-2795. (312)280-4390 or (800)545-2433. **Fax:** (312)280-5276. **E-mail:** yalsa@ala.org. **Website:** www.ala.org/yalsa/edwards. **Contact:** Nichole O'Connor. Annual award administered by the Young Adult Library Services Association (YALSA) of the American Library Association (ALA) and sponsored by *School Library Journal* magazine. Awarded to an author whose book or books, over a period of time, have been accepted by young adults as an authentic voice that continues to illuminate their experiences and emotions, giving insight into their lives. The book or books should enable them to understand themselves, the world in which they live, and their relationship with others and with society. The book or books must be in print at the time of the nomination. Submissions must be previously published no less than 5 years prior to the first meeting of the current Margaret A. Edwards Award Committee at Midwinter Meeting. Nomination form is available on the YALSA website. Deadline: December 1. Prize: $2,000. Judged by members of the Young Adult Library Services Association.

SHUBERT FENDRICH MEMORIAL PLAYWRITING CONTEST

Pioneer Drama Service, Inc., Pioneer Drama Service, Inc. - Att'n: Submissions Editor, P.O. Box 4267, Englewood CO 80155-4267. (303)779-4035. **Fax:** (303)779-4315. **E-mail:** editors@pioneerdrama.com. **E-mail:** submissions@pioneerdrama.com. **Web-**

site: www.pioneerdrama.com. **Contact:** Brian Taylor, Acquisitions Editor. Annual competition that encourages the development of quality theatrical material for educational, community, and children's theatre markets. Previously unpublished submissions only. Only considers mss with a running time between 20-120 minutes. Open to all writers not currently published by Pioneer Drama Service. Guidelines available online. No entry fee. Cover letter, SASE for return of ms, and proof of production or staged reading must accompany all submissions. Deadline: Ongoing contest; a winner is selected by June 1 each year from all submissions received the previous year. Prize: $1,000 royalty advance in addition to publication. Judged by editors.

DOROTHY CANFIELD FISHER CHILDREN'S BOOK AWARD

Midstate Library Service Center, Dorothy Canfield Fisher Book Award Committee

Vermont Department of Libraries, c/o Vermont Department of Libraries, 60 Washington Street St., Suite 2, Barre VT 05641. (802)828-6954. **E-mail:** grace.greene@state.vt.us. **Website:** https://libraries.vermont.gov/services/children_and_teens/book_awards/dcf. **Contact:** Grace W. Greene. Annual award to encourage Vermont children to become enthusiastic and discriminating readers by providing them with books of good quality by living American or Canadian authors published in the current year. E-mail for entry rules. Titles must be original work, published in the U.S., and be appropriate to children in grades 4-8. The book must be copyrighted in the current year. It must be written by an American author living in the U.S. or Canada, or a Canadian author living in Canada or the U.S. Deadline: December of year book was published. Prize: Awards a scroll presented to the winning author at an award ceremony. Judged by children, grades 4-8, who vote for their favorite book.

✪ THE NORMA FLECK AWARD FOR CANADIAN CHILDREN'S NON-FICTION

The Canadian Children's Book Centre, Norma Fleck Award for Canadian Children's Non-Fiction, c/o The Canadian Children's Book Centre, Suite 217, 40 Orchard View Blvd., Toronto ON M4R 1B9, Canada. (416)975-0010 ext. 222. **Fax:** (416)975-8970. **E-mail:** meghan@bookcentre.ca. **Website:** www.bookcentre.ca. **Contact:** Meghan Howe. The Norma Fleck Award was established by the Fleck Family Foundation to recognize and raise the profile of exceptional nonfiction books for children. Offered annually for books published between January 1 and December 31 of the previous calendar year. Open to Canadian citizens and/or permanent residents. Books must be first foreign or first Canadian editions. Nonfiction books in the following categories are eligible: culture and the arts, science, biography, history, geography, reference, sports, activities, and pastimes. Deadline: January 15. Prize: $10,000. The award will go to the author unless 40% or more of the text area is composed of original illustrations, in which case the award will be divided equally between author and illustrator.

FLICKER TALE CHILDREN'S BOOK AWARD

Fargo Public Library, 102 3rd Street North, Fargo ND 58102. **E-mail:** aemery@fargolibrary.org. **Website:** www.ndla.info/flickertale. **Contact:** Amber Emery. Award gives children across the state of North Dakota a chance to vote for their book of choice from a nominated list of 20: 4 in the picture book category, 4 in the intermediate category, 4 in the juvenile category (for more advanced readers), and 4 in the upper-grade-level nonfiction category. Also promotes awareness of quality literature for children. Previously published submissions only. Submissions nominated by librarians and teachers across the state of North Dakota. Deadline: April 1. Prize: A plaque from North Dakota Library Association and banquet dinner. Judged by children in North Dakota.

DON FREEMAN ILLUSTRATOR GRANTS

4727 Wilshire Blvd Suite 301, Los Angeles CA 90010. (323)782-1010. **Fax:** (323)782-1010. **E-mail:** grants@scbwi.org; sarahbaker@scbwi.org. **Website:** www.scbwi.org. **Contact:** Sarah Baker. The grant-in-aid is available to both full and associate members of the SCBWI who, as artists, seriously intend to make picture books their chief contribution to the field of children's literature. Applications and prepared materials are available in October. Grant awarded and announced in August. SASE for award rules and entry forms. SASE for return of entries. Enables picture-book artists to further their understanding, training, and work in the picture-book genre. Deadline: March 31. Submission period begins March 1. Prize: Two grants of $1,000 each awarded annually. One grant to a published illustrator and one to a pre-published illustrator.

THEODOR SEUSS GEISEL AWARD

Association for Library Service to Children, Division of the American Library Association, 50 E. Huron, Chicago IL 60611. (800)545-2433. **Fax:** (312)280-5271. **E-mail:** alscawards@ala.org. **Website:** http://www.ala.org/alsc/awardsgrants/bookmedia/geiselaward. The Theodor Seuss Geisel Award is given annually to the author(s) and illustrator(s) of the most distinguished American book for beginning readers published in English in the United States during the preceding year. The award is to recognize the author(s) and illustrator(s) who demonstrate great creativity and imagination in his/her/their literary and artistic achievements to engage children in reading. Terms and criteria for the award are listed on the website. Entry will not be returned. Deadline: December 31. Prize: Medal, given at awards ceremony during the ALA Annual Conference.

☾ JOHN GLASSCO TRANSLATION PRIZE

Literary Translators' Association of Canada, ATTLC | LTAC; Concordia University, LB-601, 1455 de Maisonneuve Boulevard West, Montréal QC H3G 1M8, Canada. (514)848-2424, ext. 8702. **E-mail:** info@attlc-ltac.org. **Website:** attlc-ltac.org/john-glassco-translation-prize. **Contact:** Glassco Prize Committee. Offered annually for a translator's first book-length literary translation into French or English, published in Canada during the previous calendar year. The translator must be a Canadian citizen or permanent resident. Eligible genres include fiction, creative nonfiction, poetry, and children's books. Deadline: July 9. Prize: $1,000 and a 1-year membership to LTAC.

GOLDEN KITE AWARDS

Society of Children's Book Writers and Illustrators (SCBWI), SCBWI Golden Kite Awards, 8271 Beverly Blvd., Los Angeles CA 90048-4515. (323)782-1010. **Fax:** (323)782-1892. **E-mail:** bonniebader@sbcwi.org. **Website:** www.scbwi.org. **Contact:** Bonnie Bader, Golden Kite Coordinator. Given annually to recognize excellence in children's literature in 4 categories: fiction, nonfiction, picture-book text, and picture-book illustration. Books submitted must be published in the previous calendar year. Both individuals and publishers may submit. Submit 4 copies of book. Submit to one category only, except in the case of picture books. Must be a current member of the SCBWI. SUBMISSIONS FOR THE 2020 AWARDS WILL OPEN IN TWO WAVES: May 1 – June 30, 2019 (for books published between January-June 2019); July 1 – November 15, 2019 (for books published between July-December 2019). Prize: One Golden Kite Award Winner and at least one Honor Book will be chosen per category. Winners and Honorees will receive a commemorative poster, also sent to publishers, bookstores, libraries, and schools; a press release; and an announcement on the SCBWI website and on SCBWI Social Networks.

☾ GOVERNOR GENERAL'S LITERARY AWARDS

Canada Council for the Arts, 150 Elgin St., P.O. Box 1047, Ottawa ON K1P 5V8, Canada. (800)263-5588, ext. 5573 or (613)566-4414, ext. 5573. **Website:** ggbooks.ca. The Canada Council for the Arts provides a wide range of grants and services to professional Canadian artists and art organizations in dance, media arts, music, theatre, writing, publishing, and the visual arts. Books must be first-edition literary trade books written, translated, or illustrated by Canadian citizens or permanent residents of Canada and published in Canada or abroad in the previous year. In the case of translation, the original work must also be a Canadian-authored title. For complete eligibility criteria, deadlines, and submission procedures, please visit the website at www.canadacouncil.ca. The Governor General's Literary Awards are given annually for the best English-language and French-language work in each of 7 categories, including fiction, non-fiction, poetry, drama, young people's literature (text), young people's literature (illustrated books), and translation. Deadline: Depends on the book's publication date. See website for details. Prize: Each GG winner receives $25,000. Non-winning finalists receive $1,000. Publishers of the winning titles receive a $3,000 grant for promotional purposes. Evaluated by fellow authors, translators, and illustrators. For each category, a jury makes the final selection.

GREEN PIECES PRESS ARIZONA LITERARY CONTEST BOOK AWARDS

Green Pieces Press, 6939 East Chaparral Rd., Paradise Valley AZ 85253-7000. (480)219-4559. **E-mail:** Director@AzLiteraryContest.com. **Website:** www.AzLiteraryContest.com. **Contact:** Lisa Aquilina, publisher. Green Pieces Press is honored to receive the baton from its contest predecessor and sponsor a refreshed, retooled 2019 annual literary competition for published books, unpublished novels, and Arizona Book of the Year. Cash prizes awarded ($1,000 Book of the Year) from Green Pieces Press. First Place in each of the nine categories ($200), Second Place $100, Third Place $50. All category finalists in 2019 have their literary works published in the *Arizona Literary Magazine 2020*. NEW PRIZE in 2019 for Unpublished Novel category. All Finalists have their completed manuscript submitted to Ingram Elliot Book Publishers for consideration and potential award of a standard, traditional publishing contract. All published work must have 2018 or 2019 copyright date at time of submission. Poetry, short story, essay, and new drama writing submissions must be unpublished. Work must have been published in the current or immediate past calendar year. Considers simultaneous submissions. Entry form and guidelines available on website or upon request. Deadline: September 1, 2019. Begins accepting submissions January 1, 2019. Finalists notified by Labor Day weekend. Prizes: Grand Prize, Arizona Book of the Year Award: $1,000. All categories: 1st Prize: $200; 2nd Prize: $100; 3rd Prize: $50. Unpublished Novel finallists also have their manuscripts submitted to IngramElliott Book Publishers for consideration to be awarded traditional publishing contract. Features in *Arizona Literary Magazine 2020*. Judged by nationwide published authors, editors, literary agents, and reviewers. Winners announced prior to Thanksgiving 2019. International entries encouraged; only caveat, all entries must be written in English.

○ Competition receives approximately 1,000+ entries per year. Submissions welcome from authors worldwide. All entries must be published or written in English. The Contest Directors reserve the right not to award a prize in any or all categories if the entries received are insufficient for viable competition and/or entries received do not meet international literary standards.

GUGGENHEIM FELLOWSHIPS

John Simon Guggenheim Memorial Foundation, John Simon Guggenheim Memorial Foundation, 90 Park Ave., New York NY 10016. (212)687-4470. **E-mail:** fellowships@gf.org. **Website:** www.gf.org. Often characterized as "midcareer" awards, Guggenheim Fellowships are intended for men and women who have already demonstrated exceptional capacity for productive scholarship or exceptional creative ability in the arts. Fellowships are awarded through two annual competitions: one open to citizens and permanent residents of the United States and Canada, and the other open to citizens and permanent residents of Latin America and the Caribbean. Candidates must apply to the Guggenheim Foundation in order to be considered in either of these competitions. The Foundation receives between 3,500 and 4,000 applications each year. Although no one who applies is guaranteed success in the competition, there is no prescreening: all applications are reviewed. Approximately 200 Fellowships are awarded each year. Deadline: September 17.

HACKNEY LITERARY AWARDS

Hackney Literary Awards, 4650 Old Looney Mill Rd., Birmingham AL 35243. **E-mail:** info@hackneyliteraryawards.org. **Website:** www.hackneyliteraryawards.org. **Contact:** Myra Crawford, PhD, Executive Director. Offered annually for unpublished novels, short stories (maximum 5,000 words), and poetry (50 line limit). Guidelines on website. Deadline: September 30 (novels), November 30 (short stories and poetry). Prize: $5,000 in annual prizes for poetry and short fiction ($2,500 national and $2,500 state level). 1st Place: $600; 2nd Place: $400; 3rd Place: $250; plus $5,000 for an unpublished novel. Competition winners will be announced on the website each March.

ERIC HOFFER AWARD

Ztasy; Historical Fiction; Short Story/Anthology; Mystery/Crime; Children (titles for young children); Middle Reader; Young Adult (titles aimed at the juvenile and teen markets); Culture (titles demonstrating the human or world experience); Memoir (titles relating to personal experience); Business (titles with application to today's business environment and emerging trends); Reference (titles from traditional and emerging reference areas); Home (titles with practical applications to home or home-related issues, including family); Health (titles promoting physical, mental, and emotional well-being); Self-help (titles involving new and emerging topics in self-help); Spiritual (titles involving the mind and spirit, including relgion); Legacy Fiction and Nonfiction (titles over 2 years of age that hold particular relevance to any subject matter or form); E-book Fiction; E-book Nonfiction. Open to any writer of published work within the last 2 years, including categories for older books. This contest recognizes excellence in independent publishing in many unique categories. Also awards the Montaigne Medal for most though-provoking book, the Da Vinci Eye for best cover, and the First Horizon Award for best new authors. Results published in the US Review of Books. Deadline: January 21. Grand Prize: $2,500; honors (winner, runner-up, honorable mentions) in each category, including the Montaigne Medal (most thought-provoking), da Vinci Art (cover art), First Horizon (first book), and Best in Press (small, academic, micro, self-published).

MARILYN HOLLINSHEAD VISITING SCHOLARS FELLOWSHIP

University of Minnesota, Marilyn Hollinshead Visiting Scholars Fellowship, 113 Anderson Library, 222 21st Ave. South, Minneapolis MN 55455. **Website:** http://www.lib.umn.edu/clrc/awards-grants-and-fellowships. Marilyn Hollinshead Visiting Scholars Fund for Travel to the Kerlan Collection is available for research study. Applicants may request up to $1,500. Send a letter with the proposed purpose, plan to use specific research materials (manuscripts and art), dates, and budget (including airfare and per diem). Travel and a written report on the project must be completed and submitted in the previous year. Deadline: January 30.

THE JULIA WARD HOWE/BOSTON AUTHORS AWARD

The Boston Authors Club, The Boston Authors Club, Boston Authors Club, Attn. Mary Cronin, 2400 Beacon Street, Unit 208, Chestnut Hill MA 02467. **E-mail:** bostonauthors@aol.com. **Website:** www.bostonauthorsclub.org. **Contact:** Alan Lawson. This annual award honors Julia Ward Howe and her literary friends who founded the Boston Authors Club in 1900. It also honors the membership over 110 years; consisting of novelists, biographers, historians, governors, senators, philosophers, poets, playwrights, and other luminaries. Boston Authors Club has been awarding the Julia Ward Howe Prizes (named after the Club's first President) to outstanding adult and young-reader books for over 20 years. These awards recognize exceptional books by Boston-area authors in four separate categories: Fiction, Nonfiction, Poetry, and the Young Reader category. Authors must live or have lived (college counts) within a hundred 100-mile radius of Boston within the last 5 years. Sub-

sidized books, cook books and picture books are not eligible. Deadline: January 31. Prize: $1,000. Judged by the members.

CAROL OTIS HURST CHILDREN'S BOOK PRIZE

Westfield Athenaeum, 6 Elm St., Westfield MA 01085. (413)562-6158, Ext. 5. **Website:** www.westath.org. **Contact:** Sarah Scott, Youth Services Librarian. The Carol Otis Hurst Children's Book Prize honors outstanding works of fiction and nonfiction, including biography and memoir, written for children and young adults through the age of 18, which exemplify the highest standards of research, analysis, and authorship in their portrayal of the New England Experience. The prize will be presented annually to an author whose book treats the region's history as broadly conceived to encompass one or more of the following elements: political experience, social development, fine and performing artistic expression, domestic life and arts, transportation and communication, changing technology, military experience at home and abroad, schooling, business and manufacturing, workers and the labor movement, agriculture and its transformation, racial and ethnic diversity, religious life and institutions, immigration and adjustment, sports at all levels, and the evolution of popular entertainment. The public presentation of the prize will be accompanied by a reading and/or talk by the recipient at a mutually agreed upon time during the spring immediately following the publication year. Books must have been copyrighted in their original format during the calendar year, January 1 to December 31, of the year preceding the year in which the prize is awarded. Any individual, publisher, or organization may nominate a book. See website for details and guidelines. Deadline: December 31. Prize: $500.

INSIGHT WRITING CONTEST

Insight Magazine, Insight Writing Contest, 55 W. Oak Ridge Dr., Hagerstown MD 21740-7390. **Fax:** (301)393-4055. **E-mail:** insight@rhpa.org. **Website:** www.insightmagazine.org. **Contact:** Omar Miranda, Editor. Annual contest for writers in the categories of student short story, general short story, and student poetry. Unpublished submissions only. General category is open to all writers; student categories must be age 22 and younger. Deadline: July 31. Prizes: Student Short and General Short Story: 1st Prize: $250; 2nd

Prize: $200; 3rd Prize: $150. Student Poetry: 1st Prize: $100; 2nd Prize: $75; 3rd Prize: $50.

INTERNATIONAL LITERACY ASSOCIATION CHILDREN'S AND YOUNG ADULT'S BOOK AWARDS

P.O. Box 8139, 800 Barksdale Rd., Newark DE 19714-8139. (302)731-1600, ext. 221. **E-mail:** kbaughman@reading.org. **E-mail:** committees@reading.org. **Website:** www.literacyworldwide.org. **Contact:** Kathy Baughman. The ILA Children's and Young Adults Book Awards are intended for newly published authors who show unusual promise in the children's and young adult's book field. Awards are given for fiction and nonfiction in each of 3 categories: primary, intermediate, and young adult. Books from all countries and published in English for the first time during the previous calendar year will be considered. See website for eligibility and criteria information. Entry should be the author's first or second book. Deadline: March 15. Prize: $1,000.

✪ THE IODE ONTARIO JEAN THROOP BOOK AWARD

IODE Ontario, c/o Linda Dennis, 45 Frid Street, Suite 9, Hamilton ON L8P 4M3, Canada. (905)522-9537. **E-mail:** iodeontario@gmail.com. **Website:** www.iode-ontario.ca. **Contact:** Linda Dennis. Each year, IODE Ontario presents an award intended to encourage the publication of books for children between the ages of 6-12 years. The award winner must be a Canadian citizen, resident in Toronto or the surrounding area, and the book must be published in Canada. Deadline: December 31. Prize: Award and cash prize of $2,000. The Selection Committee for the Award is comprised of members from the Toronto IODE Primary Chapters and members from the IODE Ontario Executive.

JEFFERSON CUP AWARD

P.O. Box 56312, Virginia Beach VA 23456. (757)689-0594. **Website:** www.vla.org. **Contact:** Salena Sullivan, Jefferson Cup Award Chairperson. The Jefferson Cup honors a distinguished biography, historical fiction, or American history book for young people. The Jefferson Cup Committee's goal is to promote reading about America's past; to encourage the quality writing of United States history, biography, and historical fiction for young people; and to recognize authors in these disciplines. Deadline: January 31.

THE EZRA JACK KEATS BOOK AWARD FOR NEW WRITER AND NEW ILLUSTRATOR

University of Southern Mississippi, de Grummond Children's Literature Collection, 118 College Dr., #5148, Hattiesburg MS 39406-0001. **E-mail:** ellen.ruffin@usm.edu or claire.thompson@usm.edu. **Website:** https://www.degrummond.org/. **Contact:** Ellen Ruffin, Curator of the de Grummond Children's Literature Collection and Claire Thompson, Ezra Jack Keats Book Award Coordinator.. Annual award to an outstanding new author and new illustrator of children's books that portray universal qualities of childhood in our multicultural world. Many past winners have gone on to distinguished careers, creating books beloved by parents, children, librarians, and teachers around the world. Writers and illustrators must have had no more than 3 books previously published. Prize: The winning author and illustrator will each receive a cash award of $3,000. Judged by a distinguished selection committee of early childhood education specialists, librarians, illustrators, and experts in children's literature.

EZRA JACK KEATS/KERLAN MEMORIAL FELLOWSHIP

University of Minnesota Libraries, 113 Elmer L. Andersen Library, 222 21st Ave. S, Minneapolis MN 55455. **E-mail:** asc-clrc@umn.edu. **Website:** https://www.lib.umn.edu/clrc/awards-grants-and-fellowships. This fellowship from the Ezra Jack Keats Foundation will provide $3,000 to a talented writer and/or illustrator of children's books who wishes to use the Kerlan Collection for the furtherance of his or her artistic development. Special consideration will be given to someone who would find it difficult to finance a visit to the Kerlan Collection. The Ezra Jack Keats Fellowship recipient will receive transportation costs and a per diem allotment. See website for application deadline and for digital application materials. Winner will be notified in February. Study and written report must be completed within the calendar year. Deadline: January 30. $3,000 to fund a trip to visit the Kerlan Collection.

KENTUCKY BLUEGRASS AWARD

Website: www.kasl.us. The Kentucky Bluegrass Award is a student-choice program. The KBA promotes and encourages Pre-K through 12th-grade students to read a variety of quality literature. Each year, a KBA committee for each grade category chooses the books for the 4 Master Lists (K-2, 3-5, 6-8, and 9-12). All Kentucky public and private schools, as well as public libraries, are welcome to participate in the program. To nominate a book, see the website for form and details. Deadline: March 1. Judged by students who read books and choose their favorite.

CORETTA SCOTT KING BOOK AWARDS

ALA American Library Association, 50 E. Huron St., Chicago IL 60611-2795. (800)545-2433. **E-mail:** olos@ala.org. **Website:** www.ala.org/csk. **Contact:** Office for Diversity, Literacy and Outreach Services. The Coretta Scott King Book Awards are given annually to outstanding African American authors and illustrators of books for children and young adults that demonstrate an appreciation of African American culture and universal human values. The award commemorates the life and work of Dr. Martin Luther King, Jr., and honors his wife, Mrs. Coretta Scott King, for her courage and determination to continue the work for peace and world brotherhood. Must be written for a youth audience in 1 of 3 categories: preschool-4th grade; 5th-8th grade; or 9th-12th grade. Book must be published in the year preceding the year the award is given, evidenced by the copyright date in the book. See website for full details, criteria, and eligibility concerns. Purpose is to encourage the artistic expression of the African American experience via literature and the graphic arts; including biographical, historical, and social history treatments by African American authors and illustrators. Deadline: December 2nd at 4pm CST. Judged by the Coretta Scott King Book Awards Committee.

☻ THE STEPHEN LEACOCK MEMORIAL MEDAL FOR HUMOUR

Bette Walker, 149 Peter St. N., Orillia ON L3V 4Z4, Canada. (705)326-9286. **E-mail:** awardschair@leacock.ca. **Website:** www.leacock.ca. **Contact:** Bette Walker, Award Committee, Stephen Leacock Associates. The Leacock Associates awards the prestigious Leacock Medal for the best book of literary humor written by a Canadian and published in the current year. The winning author also receives a cash prize of $15,000, thanks to the generous support of the TD Financial Group. 2 runners-up are each awarded a cash prize of $3,000. Deadline: Postmarked before December 31. Prize: $15,000.

LEAGUE OF UTAH WRITERS WRITING CONTEST

The League of Utah Writers, The League of Utah Writers, P.O. Box 64, Lewiston UT 84320. (435)755-7609. **E-mail:** luwcontest@gmail.com; luwriters@gmail.com. **Website:** www.luwriters.org. Open to any writer, the LUW Contest provides authors an opportunity to get their work read and critiqued. Multiple categories are offered; see website for details. Entries must be the original and unpublished work of the author. Winners are announced at the Annual Writers Round-Up in September. Those not present will be notified by e-mail. Deadline: May 31. Submissions period begins March 1. Prize: Cash prizes are awarded. Judged by professional authors and editors from outside the League.

MCKNIGHT ARTIST FELLOWSHIPS FOR WRITERS, LOFT AWARD(S) IN CHILDREN'S LITERATURE/CREATIVE PROSE/POETRY

The Loft Literary Center, 1011 Washington Ave. S., Suite 200, Open Book, Minneapolis MN 55415. (612)215-2575. **Fax:** (612)215-2576. **E-mail:** loft@loft.org. **Website:** www.loft.org. **Contact:** Bao Phi. The Loft administers the McKnight Artists Fellowships for Writers. Five $25,000 awards are presented annually to accomplished Minnesota writers and spoken word artists. Four awards alternate annually between creative prose (fiction and creative nonfiction) and poetry/spoken word. The fifth award is presented in children's literature and alternates annually for writing for ages 8 and under and writing for children older than 8. The awards provide the writers the opportunity to focus on their craft for the course of the fellowship year. Prize: $25,000, plus up to $3,000 in reimbursement for a writer's retreat or conference. The judge is announced after selections are made.

☻ THE VICKY METCALF AWARD FOR LITERATURE FOR YOUNG PEOPLE

The Writers' Trust of Canada, 460 Richmond St. W., Suite 600, Toronto ON M5V 1Y1, Canada. (416)504-8222. **E-mail:** djackson@writerstrust.com. **Website:** www.writerstrust.com. **Contact:** Devon Jackson. The Vicky Metcalf Award is presented to a Canadian writer for a body of work in children's literature at The Writers' Trust Awards event held in Toronto each fall. Open to Canadian citizens and permanent residents only. Prize: $25,000.

MILKWEED PRIZE FOR CHILDREN'S LITERATURE

Milkweed Editions, 1011 Washington Ave. S., Suite 300, Minneapolis MN 55415. (612)332-3192. **Fax:** (612)215-2550. **E-mail:** editor@milkweed.org. **Website:** www.milkweed.org. Milkweed Editions will award the Milkweed Prize for Children's Literature to the best mss for young readers that Milkweed accepts for publication during the calendar year by a writer not previously published by Milkweed. All mss for young readers submitted for publication by Milkweed are automatically entered into the competition. Seeking full-length fiction between 90-200 pages. Does not consider picture books or poetry collections for young readers. Recognizes an outstanding literary novel for readers ages 8-13, and encourage writers to turn their attention to readers in this age group. Prize: $10,000 cash, in addition to a publishing contract negotiated at the time of acceptance. Judged by the editors of Milkweed Editions.

MINNESOTA BOOK AWARDS

The Friends of the Saint Paul Public Library, 1080 Montreal Ave., Suite 2, St. Paul MN 55116. (651)222-3242. **Fax:** (651)222-1988. **E-mail:** mnbookawards@thefriends.org. **Website:** www.mnbookawards.org. **Contact:** Bailey Veesenmeyer: bailey@thefriends.org. A year-round program celebrating and honoring Minnesota's best books, culminating in an annual awards ceremony. Recognizes and honors achievement by members of Minnesota's book and book arts community. All books must be the work of a Minnesota author or primary artistic creator (current Minnesota resident who maintains a year-round residence in Minnesota). All books must be published within the calendar year prior to the Awards presentation. Deadline: Books should be entered by 5 p.m. on the third Friday in November.

NATIONAL BOOK AWARDS

The National Book Foundation, 90 Broad St., Suite 604, New York NY 10004. (212)685-0261. **E-mail:** nationalbook@nationalbook.org. **Website:** www.nationalbook.org. The National Book Foundation and the National Book Awards celebrate the best of American literature, expand its audience, and enhance the cultural value of great writing in America. The contest offers prizes in 4 categories: fiction, nonfiction, poetry, and young people's literature. Books should be published between December 1 and November 30 of the previous year. Submissions must be previously published and must be entered by the publisher. General guidelines available on website. Interested publishes should phone or e-mail the Foundation. Deadline: Submit entry form, payment, and a copy of the book by May 15. Prize: $10,000 in each category. Finalists will each receive a prize of $1,000. Judged by a category specific panel of 5 judges for each category.

NATIONAL OUTDOOR BOOK AWARDS

921 S. 8th Ave., Stop 8128, Pocatello ID 83209. (208)282-3912. **E-mail:** wattron@isu.edu. **Website:** www.noba-web.org. **Contact:** Ron Watters. Nine categories: History/biography, outdoor literature, instructional texts, outdoor adventure guides, nature guides, children's books, design/artistic merit, natural history literature, and nature and the environment. Additionally, a special award, the Outdoor Classic Award, is given annually to books which, over a period of time, have proven to be exceptionally valuable works in the outdoor field. Application forms and eligibility requirements are available online. Applications for the Awards program become available in early June. Deadline: August 22. Prize: Winning books are promoted nationally and are entitled to display the National Outdoor Book Award (NOBA) medallion.

NATIONAL WRITERS ASSOCIATION SHORT STORY CONTEST

NWA Short Story Contest, 10940 S. Parker Rd., #508, Parker CO 80134. **E-mail:** natlwritersassn@hotmail.com. **Website:** www.nationalwriters.com. Any genre of short story manuscript may be entered. All entries must be postmarked by July 1. Contest opens April 1. Only unpublished works may be submitted. All manuscripts must be typed, double-spaced, in the English language. Maximum length is 5,000 words. Those unsure of proper manuscript format should request Research Report #35. The entry must be accompanied by an entry form (photocopies are acceptable) and return SASE if you wish the material and rating sheets returned. Submissions will be destroyed, otherwise. Receipt of entry will not be acknowledged without a return postcard. Author's name and address must appear on the first page. Entries remain the property of the author and may be submitted during the contest as long as they are not published before the final notification of winners.

Final prizes will be awarded in June. The purpose of the National Writers Assn. Short Story Contest is to encourage the development of creative skills, recognize and reward outstanding ability in the area of short story writing. July 1 (postmarked). Prize: 1st Prize: $250; 2nd Prize: $100; 3rd Prize: $50; 4th-10th places will receive a book. 1st-3rd place winners may be asked to grant one-time rights for publication in *Authorship* magazine. Honorable Mentions receive a certificate. Judging will be based on originality, marketability, research, and reader interest. Copies of the judges' evaluation sheets will be sent to entrants furnishing an SASE with their entry.

NATIONAL YOUNGARTS FOUNDATION

National YoungArts Foundation, 2100 Biscayne Blvd., Miami FL 33137. (305)377-1140. **Fax:** (305)377-1149. **E-mail:** info@youngarts.org; apply@youngarts.org. **Website:** www.youngarts.org. The National YoungArts Foundation (formerly known as the National Foundation for Advancement in the Arts) was established in 1981 by Lin and Ted Arison to identify and support the next generation of artists and to contribute to the cultural vitality of the nation by investing in the artistic development of talented young artists in the visual, literary, design, and performing arts. Each year, there are approximately 11,000 applications submitted to YoungArts from 15-18 year old (grades 10-12) artists. From these, approximately 700 winners are selected who are eligible to participate in programs in Miami, New York, Los Angeles, and Washington D.C. (with Chicago and other regions in the works). YoungArts provides these emerging artists with life-changing experiences and validation by renowned mentors, access to significant scholarships, national recognition, and other opportunities throughout their careers to help ensure that the nation's most outstanding emerging artists are encouraged to pursue careers in the arts. See website for details about applying. Prize: Cash awards up to $10,000.

JOHN NEWBERY MEDAL

Association for Library Service to Children, Division of the American Library Association, 50 E. Huron, Chicago IL 60611. (800)545-2433. **Fax:** (312)280-5271. **E-mail:** alscawards@ala.org. **Website:** http://www.ala.org/alsc/awardsgrants/bookmedia/newberymedal/newberymedal. The Newbery Medal is awarded annually by the American Library Association for the most distinguished contribution to American literature for children. Previously published submissions only; must be published prior to year award is given. SASE for award rules. Entries not returned. Medal awarded at Caldecott/Newbery/Legacy banquet during ALA annual conference. Deadline: December 31. Judged by Newbery Award Selection Committee.

NEW ENGLAND BOOK AWARDS

NEIBA, 1955 Massachusetts Ave., #2, Cambridge MA 02140. (617)547-3642. **Fax:** (617)547-3759. **E-mail:** ali@neba.org. **Website:** www.newenglandbooks.org. **Contact:** Nan Sorensen, Administrative Coordinator. All books must be either written by a New-England-based author or be set in New England. Eligible books must be published between September 1, 2017 and August 31, 2018 in either hardcover or paperback. Submissions made by New England booksellers and publishers. Submit written nominations only; actual books should not be sent. Award is given to a specific title: fiction, nonfiction, children's, or young adult. The titles must be either about New England, set in New England. or by an author residing in the New England. The titles must be hardcover, paperback original, or reissue that was published between September 1 and August 31. Entries must be still in print and available. Deadline: June 14. Prize: Winners will receive $250 for literacy to a charity of their choice. Judged by NEIBA membership.

NEW VOICES AWARD

Website: www.leeandlow.com. Open to students. Annual award. Lee & Low Books is one of the few minority-owned publishing companies in the country, and has published more than 100 first-time writers and illustrators. Winning titles include *The Blue Roses*, winner of a Patterson Prize for Books for Young People; *Janna and the Kings*, an IRA Children's Book Award Notable; and *Sixteen Years in Sixteen Seconds*, selected for the Texas Bluebonnet Award Masterlist. Submissions made by author. SASE for contest rules or visit website. Restrictions of media for illustrators: The author must be a writer of color who is a resident of the U.S. and who has not previously published a children's picture book. For additional information, send SASE or visit Lee & Low's website. Encourages writers of color to enter the world of children's books. Deadline: August 31. Prize: $2,000, standard publi-

CONTESTS, AWARDS, & GRANTS

cation contract (regardless of whether or not writer has an agent), and an advance against royalties; New Voices Honor Award: $1000 prize. Judged by Lee & Low editors.

NORTH AMERICAN INTERNATIONAL AUTO SHOW HIGH SCHOOL POSTER CONTEST

Detroit Auto Dealers Association, 1900 W. Big Beaver Rd., Troy MI 48084-3531, USA. (248)643-0250. **Fax:** (248)283-5148. **E-mail:** sherp@dada.org. **Website:** www.naias.com. **Contact:** Sandy Herp. Open to students. Annual contest. Submissions made by the author and illustrator. Entrants must be Michigan high school students enrolled in grades 10-12. Winning posters may be displayed at the NAIAS and reproduced in the official NAIAS program, which is available to the public, international media, corporate executives and automotive suppliers. Winning posters may also be displayed on the official NAIAS website at the sole discretion of the NAIAS. Contact Detroit Auto Dealers Association (DADA) for contest rules and entry forms or retrieve rules from website. Deadline: November. Prize: Chairman's Award: $1,000; State Farm Insurance Award: $1,000; Designer's Best of Show (Digital and Traditional): $500; Best Theme: $250; Best Use of Color: $250; Most Creative: $250. A winner will be chosen in each category from grades 10, 11 and 12. Prizes: 1st place in 10, 11, 12: $500; 2nd place: $250; 3rd place: $100. Judged by an independent panel of recognized representatives of the art community.

NORTHERN CALIFORNIA BOOK AWARDS

Northern California Book Reviewers Association, Northern California Book Awards, c/o Poetry Flash, 1450 Fourth St. #4, Att'n: NCBR, Berkeley CA 94710. (510)525-5476. **E-mail:** ncbr@poetryflash.org; editor@poetryflash.org. **Website:** www.poetryflash.org. **Contact:** Joyce Jenkins, Executive Director. Annual Northern California Book Award for outstanding book in literature; open to books published in the current calendar year by Northern California authors. NCBR presents annual awards to Bay Area (northern California) authors annually in fiction, nonfiction, poetry, and children's literature. Previously published books only. Must be published the calendar year prior to spring awards ceremony. Submissions nominated by publishers; author or agent could also nominate published work. Send 3 copies of the book to attention: NCBR. Encourages writers and stimulates interest in books and reading. Deadline: January 18. Prize: $100 honorarium and award certificate. Judging by voting members of the Northern California Book Reviewers.

⚙ NOVA WRITES COMPETITION FOR UNPUBLISHED MANUSCRIPTS

Writers' Federation of Nova Scotia, 1113 Marginal Rd., Halifax NS B3H 4P7. (902)423-8116. **Fax:** (902)422-0881. **E-mail:** programs@writers.ns.ca. **Website:** www.writers.ns.ca. **Contact:** Robin Spittal, Communications and Development Officer. Annual program designed to honor work by unpublished writers in all 4 Atlantic Provinces. Entry is open to writers unpublished in the category of writing they wish to enter. Prizes are presented in the fall of each year. Categories include: short form creative nonfiction, long form creative nonfiction, novel, poetry, short story, and writing for children/young adult novel. Judges return written comments when competition is concluded. Page lengths and rules vary based on categories. See website for details. Anyone resident in the Atlantic Provinces since September 1st immediately prior to the deadline date is eligible to enter. Only 1 entry per category is allowed. Each entry requires its own entry form and registration fee. Deadline: January 3. Prizes vary based on categories. See website for details.

OHIOANA BOOK AWARDS

Ohioana Library Association, 274 E. First Ave., Suite 300, Columbus OH 43201-3673. (614)466-3831. **Fax:** (614)728-6974. **E-mail:** ohioana@ohioana.org. **Website:** www.ohioana.org. **Contact:** David Weaver, executive director. Writers must have been born in Ohio or lived in Ohio for at least 5 years, but books about Ohio or an Ohioan need not be written by an Ohioan. Finalists announced in May and winners in July. Winners notified by mail in early summer. Offered annually to bring national attention to Ohio authors and their books, published in the last year. (Books can only be considered once.) Categories: Fiction, nonfiction, juvenile, poetry, and books about Ohio or an Ohioan. Deadline: December 31. Prize: $1,000 cash prize, certificate, and glass sculpture. Judged by a jury selected by librarians, book reviewers, writers and other knowledgeable people.

OKLAHOMA BOOK AWARDS

200 NE 18th St., Oklahoma City OK 73105. (405)521-2502. **Fax:** (405)525-7804. **E-mail:** connie.arm-

strong@libraries.ok.gov. **Website:** www.odl.state.ok.us/ocb. **Contact:** Connie Armstrong, executive director. This award honors Oklahoma writers and books about Oklahoma. Awards are presented to best books in fiction, nonfiction, children's, design and illustration, and poetry books about Oklahoma or books written by an author who was born, is living or has lived in Oklahoma. SASE for award rules and entry forms. Winner will be announced at banquet in Oklahoma City. The Arrell Gibson Lifetime Achievement Award is also presented each year for a body of work. Previously published submissions only. Submissions made by the author, author's agent, or entered by a person or group of people, including the publisher. Must be published during the calendar year preceding the award. Deadline: January 10. Prize: Awards a medal. Judging by a panel of 5 people for each category, generally a librarian, a working writer in the genre, booksellers, editors, etc.

OREGON BOOK AWARDS

925 SW Washington St., Portland OR 97205. (503)227-2583. **Fax:** (503)241-4256. **E-mail:** la@literary-arts.org. **Website:** www.literary-arts.org. **Contact:** Susan Denning, director of programs and events. The annual Oregon Book Awards celebrate Oregon authors in the areas of poetry, fiction, nonfiction, drama and young readers' literature published between August 1 and July 31 of the previous calendar year. Awards are available for every category. See website for details. Entry fee determined by initial print run; see website for details. Entries must be previously published. Oregon residents only. Accepts inquiries by phone and e-mail. Finalists announced in January. Winners announced at an awards ceremony in November. List of winners available in April. Deadline: August 26. Prize: Grant of $2,500. (Grant money could vary.) Judged by writers who are selected from outside Oregon for their expertise in a genre. Past judges include Mark Doty, Colson Whitehead and Kim Barnes.

OREGON LITERARY FELLOWSHIPS

925 S.W. Washington, Portland OR 97205. (503)227-2583. **E-mail:** susan@literary-arts.org. **Website:** www.literary-arts.org. **Contact:** Susan Moore, Director of programs and events. Oregon Literary Fellowships are intended to help Oregon writers initiate, develop, or complete literary projects in poetry, fiction, literary nonfiction, drama, and young readers literature. Writers in the early stages of their career are encouraged to apply. The awards are merit-based. Guidelines available in February for SASE. Accepts inquiries by e-mail, phone. Oregon residents only. Recipients announced in January. Deadline: Last Friday in June. Prize: $3,000 minimum award, for approximately 8 writers and 2 publishers. Judged by out-of-state writers

THE ORIGINAL ART

128 E. 63rd St., New York NY 10065. (212)838-2560. **Fax:** (212)838-2561. **E-mail:** kim@societyillustrators.org; info@societyillustrators.org. **Website:** www.societyillustrators.org. **Contact:** Kate Feirtag, exhibition director. The Original Art is an annual exhibit created to showcase illustrations from the year's best children's books published in the US. For editors and art directors, it's an inspiration and a treasure trove of talent to draw upon. Previously published submissions only. Request "call for entries" to receive contest rules and entry forms. Works will be displayed at the Society of Illustrators Museum of American Illustration in New York City October-November annually. Deadline: July 18. Judged by 7 professional artists and editors.

HELEN KEATING OTT AWARD FOR OUTSTANDING CONTRIBUTION TO CHILDREN'S LITERATURE

CSLA, 10157 SW Barbur Blvd. #102C, Portland OR 97219. (503)244-6919. **Fax:** (503)977-3734. **E-mail:** sharper1@kent.edu. **Website:** www.cslainfo.org. **Contact:** S. Meghan Harper, awards chair. Annual award given to a person or organization that has made a significant contribution to promoting high moral and ethical values through children's literature. Recipient is honored in July during the conference. Awards certificate of recognition, the awards banquet, and one-night's stay in the hotel. A nomination for an award may be made by anyone. An application form is available online. Elements of creativity and innovation will be given high priority by the judges.

PATERSON PRIZE FOR BOOKS FOR YOUNG PEOPLE

The Poetry Center at Passaic County Community College, One College Blvd., Paterson NJ 07505. (973)684-6555. **Fax:** (973)523-6085. **E-mail:** mgillan@pccc.edu. **Website:** www.pccc.edu/poetry. **Contact:** Maria Mazziotti Gillan, executive director. Award for a book published in the previous year in each age category (Pre-K-Grade 3, Grades 4-6, Grades 7-12). Deadline: February 1. Prize: $500.

THE KATHERINE PATERSON PRIZE FOR YOUNG ADULT AND CHILDREN'S WRITING

Hunger Mountain, Vermont College of Fine Arts, 36 College St., Montpelier VT 05602. (802)828-8517. **E-mail:** hungermtn@vcfa.edu. **Website:** www.hungermtn.org. **Contact:** Cameron Finch, managing editor. The annual Katherine Paterson Prize for Young Adult and Children's Writing honors the best in young adult and children's literature. Submit young adult or middle grade mss, and writing for younger children, short stories, picture books, poetry, or novel excerpts, under 10,000 words. Guidelines available on website. Deadline: March 1. Prize: $1,000 and publication for the first place winner; $100 each and publication for the three category winners. Judged by a guest judge every year.

PENNSYLVANIA YOUNG READERS' CHOICE AWARDS PROGRAM

Pennsylvania School Librarians Association, 134 Bisbing Road, Henryville PA 18332. **E-mail:** pyrca.psla@gmail.com. **Website:** www.psla.org. **Contact:** Alice L. Cyphers, co-coordinator. Submissions nominated by a person or group. Must be published within 5 years of the award—for example, books published in 2013 to present are eligible for the 2018-2019 award. Check the Program wiki at pyrca.wikispaces.com for submission information. View information at the Pennsylvania School Librarians' website or the Program wiki. Must be currently living in North America. The purpose of the Pennsylvania Young Reader's Choice Awards Program is to promote the reading of quality books by young people in the Commonwealth of Pennsylvania, to encourage teacher and librarian collaboration and involvement in children's literature, and to honor authors whose works have been recognized by the students of Pennsylvania. Deadline: September 15. Prize: Framed certificate to winning authors. Four awards are given, one for each of the following grade level divisions: K-3, 3-6, 6-8, YA. Judged by children of Pennsylvania (they vote).

PEN/PHYLLIS NAYLOR WORKING WRITER FELLOWSHIP

E-mail: awards@pen.org. **Website:** www.pen.org/awards. **Contact:** Arielle Anema, Literary Awards Coordinator. Offered annually to an author of children's or young-adult fiction. The Fellowship has been developed to help writers whose work is of high literary caliber but who have not yet attracted a broad readership. The Fellowship is designed to assist a writer at a crucial moment in his or her career to complete a book-length work-in-progress. Candidates have published at least one novel for children or young adults which have been received warmly by literary critics, but have not generated sufficient income to support the author. Writers must be nominated by an editor or fellow author. See website for eligibility and nomination guidelines. Deadline: Submissions open during the summer of each year. Visit PEN.org/awards for up-to-date information on deadlines. Prize: $5,000.

PLEASE TOUCH MUSEUM BOOK AWARD

Memorial Hall in Fairmount Park, 4231 Avenue of the Republic, Philadelphia PA 19131. (215)578-5153. **Fax:** (215)578-5171. **E-mail:** hboyd@pleasetouchmuseum.org. **Website:** www.pleasetouchmuseum.org. **Contact:** Heather Boyd. This prestigious award has recognized and encouraged the publication of high quality books. The award was exclusively created to recognize and encourage the writing of publications that help young children enjoy the process of learning through books, while reflecting PTM's philosophy of learning through play. The awards to to books that are imaginative, exceptionally illustrated, and help foster a child's life-long love of reading. To be eligible for consideration, a book must be distinguished in text, illustration, and ability to explore and clarify an idea for young children (ages 7 and under). Deadline: October 1. Books for each cycle must be published within previous calendar year (September-August). Judged by a panel of volunteer educators, artists, booksellers, children's authors, and librarians in conjunction with museum staff.

PNWA LITERARY CONTEST

Pacifc Northwest Writers Association, PMB 2717, 1420 NW Gilman Blvd., Suite 2, Issaquah WA 98027. (452)673-2665. **Fax:** (452)961-0768. **E-mail:** pnwa@pnwa.org. **Website:** www.pnwa.org. Annual literary contest with 12 different categories. See website for details and specific guidelines. Each entry receives 2 critiques. Winners announced at the PNWA Summer Conference, held annually in mid-July. Deadline: February 20. Prize: 1st Place: $600; 2nd Place:

$300; 3rd Place: $100. Judged by an agent or editor attending the conference.

POCKETS FICTION-WRITING CONTEST

P.O. Box 340004, Nashville TN 37203-0004. (615)340-7333. **Fax:** (615)340-7267. **E-mail:** pockets@upper-room.org. **Website:** www.pockets.upperroom.org. **Contact:** Lynn W. Gilliam, senior editor. Designed for 6- to 12-year-olds, *Pockets* magazine offers wholesome devotional readings that teach about God's love and presence in life. The content includes fiction, scripture stories, puzzles and games, poems, recipes, colorful pictures, activities, and scripture readings. Freelance submissions of stories, poems, recipes, puzzles and games, and activities are welcome. Stories should be 750-1,000 words. Multiple submissions are permitted. Past winners are ineligible. The primary purpose of *Pockets* is to help children grow in their relationship with God and to claim the good news of the gospel of Jesus Christ by applying it to their daily lives. *Pockets* espouses respect for all human beings and for God's creation. It regards a child's faith journey as an integral part of all of life and sees prayer as undergirding that journey. Deadline: August 15. Submission period begins March 15. Prize: $500 and publication in magazine.

EDGAR ALLAN POE AWARD

1140 Broadway, Suite 1507, New York NY 10001. (212)888-8171. **E-mail:** mwa@mysterywriters.org. **Website:** www.mysterywriters.org. Mystery Writers of America is the leading association for professional crime writers in the United States. Members of MWA include most major writers of crime fiction and nonfiction, as well as screenwriters, dramatists, editors, publishers, and other professionals in the field. Categories include: Best Novel, Best First Novel by an American Author, Best Paperback/E-Book Original, Best Fact Crime, Best Critical/Biographical, Best Short Story, Best Juvenile Mystery, Best Young Adult Mystery, Best Television Series Episode Teleplay, and Mary Higgins Clark Award. Purpose of the award: Honor authors of distinguished works in the mystery field. Previously published submissions only. Submissions should be made by the publisher. Work must be published/produced the year of the contest. Deadline: November 30. Prize: Awards ceramic bust of "Edgar" for winner; certificates for all nominees. Judged by active status members of Mystery Writers of America (writers).

MICHAEL L. PRINTZ AWARD

Young Adult Library Services Association, Division of the American Library Association, 50 E. Huron, Chicago IL 60611. (800)545-2433. **Fax:** (312)280-5276. **E-mail:** yalsa@ala.org. **Website:** www.ala.org/yalsa/printz. **Contact:** Nichole O'Connor, program officer for events and conferences. The Michael L. Printz Award annually honors the best book written for teens, based entirely on its literary merit, each year. In addition, the Printz Committee names up to 4 honor books, which also represent the best writing in young adult literature. The award-winning book can be fiction, nonfiction, poetry or an anthology, and can be a work of joint authorship or editorship. The books must be published between January 1 and December 31 of the preceding year and be designated by its publisher as being either a young adult book or one published for the age range that YALSA defines as young adult, e.g. ages 12 through 18. Deadline: December 1. Judged by an award committee.

PURPLE DRAGONFLY BOOK AWARDS

Story Monsters LLC, 4696 W Tyson St, Chandler AZ 85226-2903. (480)940-8182. **Fax:** (480)940-8787. **E-mail:** linda@storymonsters.com. **Website:** www.dragonflybookawards.com. **Contact:** Cristy Bertini, contest coordinator. The Purple Dragonfly Book Awards were conceived with children in mind. Not only do we want to recognize and honor accomplished authors in the field of children's literature, but we also want to highlight up-and-coming, newly published authors, and younger published writers. Divided into 55 distinct subject categories ranging from books on the environment and cooking to sports and family issues, and even marketing collateral that complements a book, the Purple Dragonfly Book Awards are geared toward stories that appeal to children of all ages. We are looking for books that are original, innovative and creative in both content and design. A Purple Dragonfly Book Awards seal on your book's cover, marketing materials, or website tells parents, grandparents, educators, and caregivers that they are giving children the very best in reading excellence. Our judges are industry experts with specific knowledge about the categories over which they preside. Being honored with a Purple Dragonfly Book Award confers credibility upon the winner and gives published authors the recognition they deserve and provide a helping hand to further their careers. The awards are open to books published in any calendar year and in any country that are available for purchase. Books entered must be printed in English. Traditionally published, partnership published and self-published books are permitted, as long as they fit the above criteria. Submit materials to: Cristy Bertini, Attn: Dragonfly Book Awards, 1271 Turkey St., Ware, MA 01082. Deadline: May 1. The grand prize winner will receive a $500 cash prize, a certificate commemorating their accomplishment, 100 Grand Prize seals, a one-hour marketing consulting session with Linda F. Radke, a news release announcing the winners sent to a comprehensive list of media outlets, and a listing on the Dragonfly Book Awards website. All first-place winners of categories will be put into a drawing for a $100 prize. In addition, each first-place winner in each category receives a certificate commemorating their accomplishment, 25 foil award seals, and mention on Dragonfly Book Awards website. All winners receive certificates and are listed in Story Monsters Ink magazine. Judged by industry experts with specific knowledge about the categories over which they preside.

QUILL AND SCROLL WRITING, PHOTO AND MULTIMEDIA CONTEST AND BLOGGING COMPETITION

School of Journalism, Univ. of Iowa, 100 Adler Journalism Bldg., Iowa City IA 52242-2004. (319)335-3457. **E-mail:** quill-scroll@uiowa.edu. **E-mail:** quill-scroll@uiowa.edu. **Website:** quillandscroll.org. **Contact:** Jeffrey Browne, Contest Director.. Entries must have been published in a high school or professional newspaper or website during the previous year, and be the work of a currently enrolled high school student when published. Open to students. Annual contest. Previously published submissions only. Submissions made by the author or school media adviser. Deadline: February 5. Prize: Winners will receive *Quill and Scroll*'s National Award Gold Key and, if seniors, are eligible to apply for one of the scholarships offered by *Quill and Scroll*. All winning entries are automatically eligible for the International Writing and Photo Sweepstakes Awards. Engraved plaque awarded to sweepstakes winners.

THE RED HOUSE CHILDREN'S BOOK AWARD

Red House Children's Book Award, 123 Frederick Road, Cheam, Sutton, Surrey SM1 2HT, United Kingdom. **E-mail:** info@rhcba.co.uk. **Website:** www.redhousechildrensbookaward.co.uk. **Con-**

tact: Sinead Kromer, national coordinator. The Red House Children's Book Award is the only national book award that is entirely voted for by children. A shortlist is drawn up from children's nominations and any child can then vote for the winner of the three categories: Books for Younger Children, Books for Younger Readers and Books for Older Readers. The book with the most votes is then crowned the winner of the Red House Children's Book Award. Deadline: December 31.

TOMÁS RIVERA MEXICAN AMERICAN CHILDREN'S BOOK AWARD

Dr. Jesse Gainer, Texas State University, 601 University Drive, San Marcos TX 78666-4613. (512)245-2357. **E-mail:** riverabookaward@txstate.edu. **Website:** www.riverabookaward.org. **Contact:** Dr. Jesse Gainer, award director. Texas State University College of Education developed the Tomas Rivera Mexican American Children's Book Award to honor authors and illustrators who create literature that depicts the Mexican American experience. The award was established in 1995 and was named in honor of Dr. Tomas Rivera, a distinguished alumnus of Texas State University. The book will be written for younger children, ages pre-K to 5th grade (awarded in even years), or older children, ages 6th grade to 12 grade (awarded in odd years). The text and illustrations will be of highest quality. The portrayal/representations of Mexican Americans will be accurate and engaging, avoid stereotypes, and reflect rich characterization. The book may be fiction or nonfiction. See website for more details and directions. Deadline: November 1.

ROCKY MOUNTAIN BOOK AWARD: ALBERTA CHILDREN'S CHOICE BOOK AWARD

Box 42, Lethbridge AB T1J 3Y3, Canada. **E-mail:** rockymountainbookaward@shaw.ca. **Website:** www.rmba.info. **Contact:** Michelle Dimnik, contest director. Annual contest. No entry fee. Awards: Gold medal and author tour of selected Alberta schools. Judging by students. Canadian authors and/or illustrators only. Submit entries to Richard Chase. Previously unpublished submissions only. Submissions made by author's agent or nominated by a person or group. Must be published within the 3 years prior to that year's award. Register before January 20th to take part in the Rocky Mountain Book Award. SASE for contest rules and entry forms. Purpose of contest: "Reading motivation for students, promotion of Canadian authors, illustrators and publishers." Gold Medal and sponsored visit to several Alberta Schools or Public Libraries. Judged by students.

☼ SASKATCHEWAN BOOK AWARDS

315-1102 8th Ave., Regina SK S4R 1C9, Canada. (306)569-1585. **E-mail:** director@bookawards.sk.ca. **Website:** www.bookawards.sk.ca. **Contact:** Courtney Bates-Hardy, executive director. Saskatchewan Book Awards celebrates, promotes, and rewards Saskatchewan authors and publishers worthy of recognition through 14 awards, granted on an annual or semiannual basis. Awards: Fiction, Nonfiction, Poetry, Scholarly, First Book, Prix du Livre Français, Regina, Saskatoon, Indigenous Peoples' Writing, Indigenous Peoples' Publishing, Publishing in Education, Publishing, Children's Literature/Young Adult Literature, Book of the Year. November 1. Prize: $2,000 (CAD) for all awards except Book of the Year, which is $3,000 (CAD). Juries are made up of writing and publishing professionals from outside of Saskatchewan.

○   Saskatchewan Book Awards is the only provincially focused book award program in Saskatchewan and a principal ambassador for Saskatchewan's literary community. Its solid reputation for celebrating artistic excellence in style is recognized nationally.

SCBWI MAGAZINE MERIT AWARDS

4727 Wilshire Blvd., Suite 301, Los Angeles CA 90010. (323)782-1010. **Fax:** (323)782-1892. **E-mail:** grants@scbwi.org. **Website:** www.scbwi.org. **Contact:** Stephanie Gordon, award coordinator. The SCBWI is a professional organization of writers and illustrators and others interested in children's literature. Membership is open to the general public at large. All magazine work for young people by an SCBWI member—writer, artist or photographer—is eligible during the year of original publication. In the case of co-authored work, both authors must be SCBWI members. Members must submit their own work. Requirements for entrants: 4 copies each of the published work and proof of publication (may be contents page) showing the name of the magazine and the date of issue. Previously published submissions only. For rules and procedures see website. Must be a SCBWI member. Recognizes outstanding original magazine work for young people published during that year, and having been written or illustrated by members of SCBWI. Deadline: December 15 of the year of publication. Submission period begins January 1. Prize: Awards plaques and honor certificates for each of 4 categories (fiction, nonfiction, illustration and poetry). Judged by a magazine editor and two "full" SCBWI members.

SHEEHAN YA BOOK PRIZE

Elephant Rock Books, P.O. Box 119, Ashford CT 06278. **E-mail:** elephantrockbooksya@gmail.com. **Website:** elephantrockbooks.com/ya.html. **Contact:** Jotham Burrello and Amanda Hurley. Elephant Rock is a small independent publisher. Their first YA book, *The Carnival at Bray* by Jessie Ann Foley was a Morris Award Finalist, and Printz Honor Book. Runs contest every other year. Check website for details. Guidelines are available on the website: http://www.elephantrockbooks.com./about.html#submissions. "Elephant Rock Books' teen imprint is looking for a great story to follow our critically acclaimed novel, *The Carnival at Bray*. We're after quality stories with heart, guts, and a clear voice. We're especially interested in the quirky, the hopeful, and the real. We are not particularly interested in genre fiction and prefer standalone novels, unless you've got the next *Hunger Games*. We seek writers who believe in the transformative power of a great story, so show us what you've got." Deadline: July 1. Prize: $1,000 as an advance. Judges vary year-to-year.

SKIPPING STONES BOOK AWARDS

Skipping Stones, P.O. Box 3939, Eugene OR 97403-0939. **E-mail:** editor@skippingstones.org. **Website:** www.skippingstones.org/wp. **Contact:** Arun N. Toke', Exec. Editor. Open to published books, publications/magazines, educational videos, and DVDs. Annual awards. Submissions made by the author or publishers and/or producers. Send request for contest rules and entry forms or visit website. Many educational publications announce the winners of our book awards. The winning books and educational videos/DVDs are announced in the July-September issue of *Skipping Stones* and also on the website. In addition to announcements on social media pages, the reviews of winning titles are posted on website. For several years now, Multicultural Education, a quarterly journal has been republishing all the book award winners' reviews. *Skipping Stones* multicultural magazine has been published for over 28 years. Recognizes exceptional, literary and artistic contributions to juvenile/children's literature, as well as teaching resources and educational audio/video resources in the areas of multicultural awareness, nature and ecology, social issues, peace, and nonviolence. Deadline: February 28. Prize: Winners receive gold honor award seals, attractive honor certificates, and publicity via multiple outlets. Judged by a multicultural selection committee of editors, students, parents, teachers, and librarians.

AWARD WINNING PUB SKIPPING STONES YOUTH AWARDS

P.O. Box 3939, Eugene OR 97403-0939. (541)342-4956. **Fax:** (541)342-4956. **E-mail:** editor@skippingstones. org. **Website:** www.skippingstones.org. **Contact:** Arun N. Toké. Annual awards to promote creativity as well as multicultural and nature awareness in youth. Cover letter should include name, address, phone, and e-mail. Entries must be unpublished. Length: 1,000 words maximum; 30 lines maximum for poems. Open to any writer between 7 and 17 years old. Guidelines available by SASE, e-mail, or on website. Accepts inquiries by e-mail or phone. Results announced in the October-December issue of *Skipping Stones*. Winners notified by mail. For contest results, visit website. Everyone who enters receives the issue which features the award winners. Deadline: June 25. Prize: Publication in the autumn issue of *Skipping Stones*, honor certificate, subscription to magazine, plus 5 multicultural and/or nature books. Judged by editors and reviewers at *Skipping Stones* magazine.

SKIPPING STONES YOUTH HONOR AWARDS

P. O. Box 3939, Eugene OR 97403-0939. (541)342-4956. **E-mail:** editor@skippingstones.org. **Website:** www.SkippingStones.org/wp. **Contact:** Arun N. Toké, editor. Now celebrating its 30th year, *Skipping Stones* is a winner of N.A.M.E., EDPRESS, Newsstand Resources, Writer and Parent's Choice Awards. Open to students ages 7 to 17. Annual awards. Submissions made by the author. The winners are published in the October-December issue of *Skipping Stones*. Everyone who enters the contest receives the Autumn issue featuring Youth Awards. SASE for contest rules or download from website. Entries must include certificate of originality by a parent and/or teacher and a cover letter that included cultural background information on the author. Submissions can either be mailed or e-mailed. Up to ten awards are given in three categories: (1) Compositions (essays, poems, short stories, songs, travelogues, etc.): Entries should be typed (double-spaced) or neatly handwritten. Fiction or nonfiction should be limited to 1,000 words; poems to 30 lines. Non-English writings are also welcome. (2) Artwork (drawings, cartoons, paintings or photo essays with captions): Entries should have the artist's name, age and address on the back of each page. Send the originals with SASE. Black & white photos are especially welcome. Limit: 8 pieces. (3) Youth Organizations: Describe how your club or group works to: (a) preserve the nature and ecology in your area, (b) enhance the quality of life for low-income, minority or disabled or (c) improve racial or cultural harmony in your school or community. Use the same format as for compositions. Recognizes youth, 7 to 17, for their contributions to multicultural awareness, nature and ecology, social issues, peace and nonviolence. Also promotes creativity, self-esteem and writing skills and to recognize important work being done by youth organizations. Deadline: June 25. Judged by *Skipping Stones* staff.

KAY SNOW WRITING CONTEST

Willamette Writers, Willamette Writers, 2108 Buck St., West Linn OR 97068. (503)305-6729. **Fax:** (503)344-6174. **E-mail:** reg@willamettewriters.com. **Website:** www.willamettewriters.org. Willamette Writers is the largest writers' organization in Oregon and one of the largest writers' organizations in the United States. It is a non-profit, tax-exempt Oregon corporation led by volunteers. Elected officials and directors administer an active program of monthly meetings, special seminars, workshops, and an annual writing conference. Continuing with established programs and starting new ones is only made possible by strong volunteer support. See website for specific details and rules. There are six different categories writers can enter: Adult Fiction, Adult Nonfiction, Poetry, Juvenile Short Story, Screenwriting, and Student Writer. The purpose of this annual writing contest, named in honor of Willamette Writer's founder, Kay Snow, is to help writers reach professional goals in writing in a broad array of categories and to encourage student writers. Deadline: April 23. Submission deadline begins January 15. Prize: One first prize of $300, one second place prize of $150, and a third place prize of $50 per winning entry in each of the six categories. Student first prize is $50, $20 for second place, $10 for third.

SOCIETY OF MIDLAND AUTHORS AWARD

Society of Midland Authors, P.O. Box 10419, Chicago IL 60610-0419. **E-mail:** marlenetbrill@comcast.net. **Website:** www.midlandauthors.com. **Contact:** Marlene Targ Brill, awards chair. Since 1957, the Society has presented annual awards for the best books written by Midwestern authors. The Society began in 1915. The contest is open to any title published within the year prior to the contest year. Open to adult and children's authors/poets who reside in, were born in, or have strong ties to a Midland state, which includes Illinois, Indiana, Iowa, Kansas, Michigan, Minnesota, Missouri, Nebraska, North Dakota, South Dakota, Ohio, and Wisconsin. The Society of Midland Authors (SMA) Award is presented to one title in each of 6 categories: adult nonfiction, adult fiction, adult biography and memoir, children's nonfiction, children's fiction, and poetry. There may be honor book winners as well. Books and entry forms must be mailed to the 3 judges in each category; for a list of judges and the entry and payment forms, visit the SMA website. Do not mail books to the society's P.O. box. The fee can be sent to the SMA P.O. box or paid via Paypal. Deadline: The first Saturday in January for books from the previous year. Prize: $500 and a plaque that is awarded at the SMA banquet in May in Chicago. Honorary winners receive a plaque. Check the SMA website for each year's judges at the end of October.

STORY MONSTER APPROVED BOOK AWARDS

Story Monsters LLC, 4696 W. Tyson St., Chandler AZ 85226. (480)940-8182. **Fax:** (480)940-8787. **E-mail:** linda@storymonsters.com. **E-mail:** cristy@story-monsters.com. **Website:** www.dragonflybookawards.com. **Contact:** Cristy Bertini. The Story Monsters Approved! book designation program was developed to recognize and honor accomplished authors in the field of children's literature that inspire, inform, teach, or entertain. A Story Monsters seal of approval on your book tells teachers, librarians, and parents they are giving children the very best. Kids know when they see the Story Monsters Approved! seal, it means children their own age enjoyed the book and are recommending they read it, too. How do they know that? Because after books pass a first round of rigorous judging by industry experts, the books are

then judged by a panel of youth judges who must also endorse the books before they can receive the official seal of approval. Guidelines available online. Send submissions to Cristy Bertini, Attn.: Dragonfly Book Awards, 1271 Turkey St., Ware, MA 01082. There is no deadline to enter. Books are sent for judging as they are received. The Book of the Year winner will receive a feature interview and a full-page ad in Story Monsters Ink® magazine, a certificate commemorating their accomplishment, and 50 Story Monsters Approved! seals. All authors earning a Story Monsters Approved! designation receive a certificate commemorating their accomplishment; 50 award seals, a news release sent to a comprehensive list of media outlets, and listings on our website and in Story Monsters Ink® magazine. Our judging panel includes industry experts in the fields of education and publishing, and student judges.

SYDNEY TAYLOR BOOK AWARD

E-mail: chair@sydneytaylorbookaward.org. **Website:** www.sydneytaylorbookaward.org. **Contact:** Ellen Tilman, chair. The Sydney Taylor Book Award is presented annually to outstanding books for children and teens that authentically portray the Jewish experience. Deadline: November 30. Cannot guarantee that books received after November 30 will be considered. Prize: Gold medals are presented in 3 categories: younger readers, older readers, and teen readers. Honor books are awarded in silver medals, and notable books are named in each category. Winners are selected by a committee of the Association of Jewish Libraries. Each committee member must receive an individual copy of each book that is to be considered. ○ Please contact the chair for submission details.

SYDNEY TAYLOR MANUSCRIPT COMPETITION

Association of Jewish Libraries, Sydney Taylor Manuscript Award Competition, 204 Park St., Montclair NJ 07042-2903. **E-mail:** stmacajl@aol.com. **Website:** www.jewishlibraries.org/main/Awards/SydneyTaylorManuscriptAward.aspx. **Contact:** Aileen Grossberg. This competition is for unpublished writers of juvenile fiction. Material should be for readers ages 8-13. The manuscript should have universal appeal and reveal positive aspects of Jewish life that will serve to deepen the understanding of Judaism for all children. Download rules and forms from website. Must be an unpublished fiction writer or a student; also, books must range from 64-200 pages in length.

"AJL assumes no responsibility for publication, but hopes this cash incentive will serve to encourage new writers of children's stories with Jewish themes for all children." To encourage new fiction of Jewish interest for readers ages 8-13. Deadline: September 30. Prize: $1,000. Judging by qualified judges from within the Association of Jewish Libraries.

TD CANADIAN CHILDREN'S LITERATURE AWARD

The Canadian Children's Book Centre, 40 Orchard View Blvd., Suite 217, Toronto ON M4R 1B9, Canada. (416)975-0010, ext. 222. **Fax:** (416)975-8970. **E-mail:** meghan@bookcentre.ca. **Website:** www.bookcentre.ca. **Contact:** Meghan Howe. The TD Canadian Children's Literature Award is for the most distinguished book of the year. All books, in any genre, written and illustrated by Canadians and for children ages 1-12 are eligible. Only books published in Canada are eligible for submission. Books must be published between January 1 and December 31 of the previous calendar year. Open to Canadian citizens and/or permanent residents of Canada. Deadline: mid-December. Prizes: Two prizes of $50,000, 1 for English, 1 for French. $20,000 will be divided among the Honour Book English titles and Honour Book French titles, to a maximum of 4; $2,500 shall go to each of the publishers of the English and French grand-prize winning books for promotion and publicity.

TORONTO BOOK AWARDS

City of Toronto c/o Toronto Arts & Culture, Cultural Partnerships, City Hall, 9E, 100 Queen St. W., Toronto ON M5H 2N2, Canada. **E-mail:** shan@toronto.ca. **Website:** www.toronto.ca/book_awards. The Toronto Book Awards honor authors of books of literary or artistic merit that are evocative of Toronto. There are no separate categories; all books are judged together. Any fiction or nonfiction book published in English for adults and/or children that are evocative of Toronto are eligible. To be eligible, books must be published between January 1 and December 31 of previous year. Deadline: April 30. Prize: Each finalist receives $1,000 and the winning author receives $10,000 ($15,000 total in prize money available).

VEGETARIAN ESSAY CONTEST

The Vegetarian Resource Group, P.O. Box 1463, Baltimore MD 21203. (410)366-VEGE. **Fax:** (410)366-8804. **E-mail:** vrg@vrg.org. **Website:** www.vrg.org. Write a 2-3 page essay on any aspect of veganism/vegetarianism. Entrants should base their paper on interviewing, research, and/or personal opinion. You need not be a vegetarian to enter. Three different entry categories: age 14-18; age 9-13; and age 8 and under. Prize: $50.

VFW VOICE OF DEMOCRACY

Veterans of Foreign Wars of the U.S., National Headquarters, 406 W. 34th St., Kansas City MO 64111. (816)968-1117. **E-mail:** kharmer@vfw.org. **Website:** https://www.vfw.org/VOD/. The Voice of Democracy Program is open to students in grades 9-12 (on the Nov. 1 deadline), who are enrolled in a public, private or parochial high school or home study program in the United States and its territories. Contact your local VFW Post to enter (entry must not be mailed to the VFW National Headquarters, only to a local, participating VFW Post). Purpose is to give high school students the opportunity to voice their opinions about their responsibility to our country and to convey those opinions via the broadcast media to all of America. Deadline: November 1. Prize: Winners receive awards ranging from $1,000-30,000.

WESTERN AUSTRALIAN PREMIER'S BOOK AWARDS

State Library of Western Australia, Perth Cultural Centre, 25 Francis St., Perth WA 6000, Australia. (61)(8)9427-3151. **E-mail:** premiersbookawards@slwa.wa.gov.au. **Website:** pba.slwa.wa.gov.au. **Contact:** Karen de San Miguel. Annual competition for Australian citizens or permanent residents of Australia, or writers whose work has Australia as its primary focus. Categories: children's books, digital narrative, fiction, nonfiction, poetry, scripts, writing for young adults, West Australian history, and Western Australian emerging writers. Submit 5 original copies of the work to be considered for the awards. All works must have been published between January 1 and December 31 of the prior year. See website for details and rules of entry. Deadline: January 31. Prize: Awards $25,000 for Premier's Prize; awards $15,000 each for the Children's Books, Digital Narrative, Fiction, and Nonfiction categories; awards $10,000 each for the Poetry, Scripts, Western Australian History, Western Australian Emerging Writers, and Writing for Young Adults; awards $5,000 for People's Choice Award.

WESTERN HERITAGE AWARDS

National Cowboy & Western Heritage Museum, 1700 NE 63rd St., Oklahoma City OK 73111-7997. (405)478-2250. **Fax:** (405)478-4714. **Website:** www.national-cowboymuseum.org. **Contact:** Jessica Limestall. The National Cowboy & Western Heritage Museum Western Heritage Awards were established to honor and encourage the legacy of those whose works in literature, music, film, and television reflect the significant stories of the American West. Accepted categories for literary entries: western novel, nonfiction book, art book, photography book, juvenile book, magazine article, or poetry book. Previously published submissions only; must be published the calendar year before the awards are presented. Requirements for entrants: The material must pertain to the development or preservation of the West, either from a historical or contemporary viewpoint. Literary entries must have been published between December 1 and November 30 of calendar year. Five copies of each published work must be furnished for judging with each entry, along with the completed entry form. Works recognized during special awards ceremonies held annually at the museum. There is an autograph party preceding the awards. Awards ceremonies are sometimes broadcast. The WHA are presented annually to encourage the accurate and artistic telling of great stories of the West through 16 categories of western literature, television, film and music; including fiction, nonfiction, children's books and poetry. See website for details and category definitions. Deadline: November 30. Prize: Awards a Wrangler bronze sculpture designed by famed western artist, John Free. Judged by a panel of judges selected each year with distinction in various fields of western art and heritage.

WESTERN WRITERS OF AMERICA

271 CR 219, Encampment WY 82325. (307)329-8942. **E-mail:** wwa.moulton@gmail.com. **Website:** www.westernwriters.org. **Contact:** Candy Moulton, executive director. Eighteen Spur Award categories in various aspects of the American West. Send entry form with your published work. Accepts multiple submissions, each with its own entry form, available on our website. The nonprofit Western Writers of America has promoted and honored the best in Western literature with the annual Spur Awards, selected by panels of judges. Awards, for material published last year, are given for works whose inspirations, image and literary excellence best represent the reality and spirit of the American West. Deadline: January 4. Judged by independent Judges.

JACKIE WHITE MEMORIAL NATIONAL CHILDREN'S PLAY WRITING CONTEST

1800 Nelwood Dr., Columbia MO 65202-1447. (573)874-5628. **E-mail:** jwmcontest@cectheatre.org. **Website:** www.cectheatre.org. **Contact:** Tom Phillips. Annual contest that encourages playwrights to write quality plays for family audiences. Previously unpublished submissions only. Submissions made by author. Play may be performed during the following season. All submissions will be read by at least 3 readers. Author will receive a written evaluation of the script. Guidelines available online. Deadline: June 1. Prize: $500 with production possible. Judging by current and past board members of CEC and by non-board members who direct plays at CEC.

WILLA LITERARY AWARD

E-mail: 2019willachair@gmail.com. **Website:** www.womenwritingthewest.org. **Contact:** Carmen Peone. The WILLA Literary Award honors the year's best in published literature featuring women's or girls' stories set in the West. Women Writing the West (WWW), a nonprofit association of writers and other professionals writing and promoting the Women's West, underwrites and presents the nationally recognized award annually (for work published between January 1 and December 31). The award is named in honor of Pulitzer Prize winner Willa Cather, one of the country's foremost novelists. The award is given in 8 categories: historical fiction, contemporary fiction, original softcover fiction, creative nonfiction, scholarly nonfiction, poetry, children's fiction and nonfiction and young adult fiction/nonfiction. Entry forms available on the website. Deadline: November 1–February 1. Prize: $150 and a trophy. Finalist receives a plaque. Both receive digital and sticker award emblems for book covers. Notice of Winning and Finalist titles mailed to more than 4,000 booksellers, libraries, and others. Award announcement is in early August, and awards are presented to the winners and finalists at the annual WWW Fall Conference. Also, the eight winners will participate in a drawing for 2 two week all expenses paid residencies donated by Playa at Summer Lake in Oregon. Judged by professional librarians not affiliated with WWW.

RITA WILLIAMS YOUNG ADULT PROSE PRIZE CATEGORY

Soul-Making Keats Literary Competition, The Webhallow House, 1544 Sweetwood Dr., Broadmoor Vlg. CA 94015-2029. (650)756-5279. **Fax:** (650)756-5279. **E-mail:** soulkeats@mail.com. **Website:** www.soulmakingcontest.us. **Contact:** Eileen Malone. For writers in grades 9-12 or equivalent age. Up to 3,000 words in prose form of choice. Complete rules and guidelines available online. Deadline: November 30 (postmarked). Prize: $100 for first place; $50 for second place; $25 for third place. Judged (and sponsored) by Rita Wiliams, an Emmy-award winning investigative reporter with KTVU-TV in Oakland, California.

PAUL A. WITTY OUTSTANDING LITERATURE AWARD

P.O. Box 8139, Newark DE 19714-8139. (800)336-7323. **Fax:** (302)731-1057. **Website:** www.reading. org. **Contact:** Marcie Craig Post, executive director. This award recognizes excellence in original poetry or prose written by students. Elementary and secondary students whose work is selected will receive an award. Deadline: February 2. Prize: Not less than $25 and a citation of merit.

WORK-IN-PROGRESS GRANT

Society of Children's Book Writers and Illustrators (SCBWI), 8271 Beverly Blvd., Los Angeles CA 90048. (323)782-1010. **E-mail:** grants@scbwi.org; wipgrant@scbwi.org. **Website:** www.scbwi.org. Six grants—one designated specifically for picture book text, chapter book/early readers, middle grade, young adult fiction, nonfiction, and multicultural fiction or nonfiction—to assist SCBWI members in the completion of a specific project. Open to SCBWI members only. Deadline: March 31. Open to submissions on March 1.

WRITE NOW

Indiana Repertory Theatre, 140 W. Washington St., Indianapolis IN 46204. 480-921-5770. **E-mail:** info@writenow.co. **Website:** www.writenow.co. The purpose of this biennial workshop is to encourage writers to create strikingly original scripts for young audiences. It provides a forum through which each playwright receives constructive criticism and the support of a development team consisting of a professional director and dramaturg. Finalists will spend approximately one week in workshop with their development team. At the end of the week, each play will be read as a part of the Write Now convening. Guidelines available online. Deadline: August 15.

WRITER'S DIGEST SELF-PUBLISHED BOOK AWARDS

Writer's Digest, 5720 Flatiron Pkwy, Boulder CO 80301. **E-mail:** writersdigestselfpublishingcompetition@aimmedia.com. **Website:** www.writersdigest. com. **Contact:** Nicole Howard. Contest open to all English-language, self-published books for which the authors have paid the full cost of publication, or the cost of printing has been paid for by a grant or as part of a prize. Categories include: Mainstream/Literary Fiction, Genre Fiction, Nonfiction, Inspirational (spiritual/new age), Life Stories (biographies/autobiographies/family histories/memoirs), Children's Books, Reference Books (directories/encyclopedias/guide books), Poetry, and Middle-Grade/Young Adult Books. Judges reserve the right to recategorize entries. Judges reserve the right to withhold prizes in any category. All winners will be notified in October. Entrants must send a printed and bound book. Entries will be evaluated on content, writing quality, and overall quality of production and appearance. No handwritten books are accepted. Books must have been published within the past 5 years from the competition deadline. Books which have previously won awards from *Writer's Digest* are not eligible. Early bird deadline: April 2. Prizes: Grand Prize: $8,000, a trip to the Writer's Digest Conference, promotion in *Writer's Digest*, 10 copies of the book will be sent to major review houses, and a guaranteed review in *Midwest Book Review*; 1st Place (9 winners): $1,000 and promotion in *Writer's Digest*; Honorable Mentions: promotion on writersdigest. com. All entrants will receive a brief commentary from one of the judges.

WRITER'S DIGEST SELF-PUBLISHED E-BOOK AWARDS

Writer's Digest, 5720 Flatiron Pkwy, Boulder CO 80301. **E-mail:** writersdigestselfpublishingcompetition@aimmedia.com. **Website:** www.writersdigest. com. **Contact:** Nicole Howard. Contest open to all English-language, self-published e-books for which the authors have paid the full cost of publication, or the cost of publication has been paid for by a grant or as part of a prize. Categories include: Mainstream/Literary Fiction, Genre Fiction, Nonfiction (includes reference books), Inspirational (spiritual/new age),

Life Stories (biographies/autobiographies/family histories/memoirs), Children's Books, Poetry, and Middle-Grade/Young Adult Books. Judges reserve the right to re-categorize entries. Judges reserve the right to withhold prizes in any category. All winners will be notified by December 31. Entrants must enter online. Entrants may provide a file of the book or submit entry by the Amazon gifting process. Acceptable file types include: .epub, .mobi, .ipa. Word processing documents will not be accepted. Entries will be evaluated on content, writing quality, and overall quality of production and appearance. Books must have been published within the past 5 years from the competition deadline. Books which have previously won awards from *Writer's Digest* are not eligible. Early bird deadline: August 1; Deadline: September 4. Prizes: Grand Prize: $5,000, promotion in *Writer's Digest*, and more; 1st Place (9 winners): $1,000 and promotion in *Writer's Digest*; Honorable Mentions: promotion on writersdigest.com. All entrants will receive a brief commentary from one of the judges.

WRITERS-EDITORS NETWORK INTERNATIONAL WRITING COMPETITION

CNW Publishing, P.O. Box A, North Stratford NH 03590-0167. **E-mail:** contestentry@writers-editors.com. **E-mail:** info@writers-editors.com. **Website:** www.writers-editors.com. **Contact:** Dana K. Cassell, executive director. Annual award to recognize publishable talent. New categories and awards for 2018: Nonfiction (unpublished or self-published; may be an article, blog post, essay/opinion piece, column, nonfiction book chapter, children's article or book chapter); fiction (unpublished or self-published; may be a short story, novel chapter, Young Adult [YA] or children's story or book chapter); poetry (unpublished or self-published; may be traditional or free verse poetry or children's verse). Guidelines available online. Open to any writer. Maximum length: 4,000 words. Accepts inquiries by e-mail, phone and mail. Entry form online. Results announced May 31. Winners notified by mail and posted on website. Results available for SASE or visit website. Deadline: March 15. Prize: 1st Place: $150 plus one year Writers-Editors membership; 2nd Place: $100; 3rd Place: $75. All winners and Honorable Mentions will receive certificates as warranted. Most Promising entry in each category will receive a free critique by a contest judge. Judged by editors, librarians, and writers.

✪ WRITERS' GUILD OF ALBERTA AWARDS

Writers' Guild of Alberta, Percy Page Centre, 11759 Groat Rd., Edmonton AB T5M 3K6, Canada. (780)422-8174. **Fax:** (780)422-2663. **E-mail:** mail@writersguild.ca. **Website:** writersguild.ca. **Contact:** Executive Director. Offers the following awards: Wilfrid Eggleston Award for Nonfiction; Georges Bugnet Award for Fiction; Howard O'Hagan Award for Short Story; Stephan G. Stephansson Award for Poetry; R. Ross Annett Award for Children's Literature; Gwen Pharis Ringwood Award for Drama; Jon Whyte Memorial Essay Award; James H. Gray Award for Short Nonfiction. Eligible entries will have been published anywhere in the world between January 1 and December 31 of the current year. The authors must have been residents of Alberta for at least 12 of the 18 months prior to December 31. Unpublished mss, except in the drama and essay categories, are not eligible. Anthologies are not eligible. Works may be submitted by authors, publishers, or any interested parties. Deadline: December 31. Prize: Winning authors receive $1,500; short piece prize winners receive $700.

WRITERS' LEAGUE OF TEXAS BOOK AWARDS

Writers' League of Texas, 611 S. Congress Ave., Suite 200A-3, Austin TX 78704. (512)499-8914. **Fax:** (512)499-0441. **E-mail:** sara@writersleague.org. **Website:** www.writersleague.org. **Contact:** Sara Kocek. Open to Texas authors of books published the previous year. To enter this contest, you must be a Texas author. "Texas author" is defined as anyone who (whether currently a resident or not) has lived in Texas for a period of 3 or more years. This contest is open to indie or self-published authors as well as traditionally-published authors. Deadline: February 28. Open to submissions October 7. Prize: $1,000 and a commemorative award.

WRITING CONFERENCE WRITING CONTESTS

P.O. Box 664, Ottawa KS 66067-0664. (785)242-2947. **Fax:** (785)242-2473. **E-mail:** jbushman@writingconference.com. **E-mail:** support@studentq.com. **Website:** www.writingconference.com. **Contact:** John H. Bushman, contest director. Unpublished submissions only. Submissions made by the author or teacher. Purpose of contest: To further writing by students with awards for narration, exposition and poetry at the elementary, middle school, and high school levels. Deadline: January 8. Prize: Awards plaque and publication of winning entry in The Writers' Slate online, April issue. Judged by a panel of teachers.

YEARBOOK EXCELLENCE CONTEST

100 Adler Journalism Building, Iowa City IA 52242-2004. (319)335-3457. **Fax:** (319)335-3989. **E-mail:** quill-scroll@uiowa.edu. **Website:** www.quilland-scroll.org. **Contact:** Jeff Browne, executive director. High school students who are contributors to or staff members of a student yearbook at any public or private high school are invited to enter the competition. Awards will be made in each of the 18 divisions. There are two enrollment categories: Class A: more than 750 students; Class B: 749 or less. Winners will receive Quill and Scroll's National Award Gold Key and, if seniors, are eligible to apply for one of the Edward J. Nell Memorial or George and Ophelia Gallup scholarships. Open to students whose schools have Quill and Scroll charters. Previously published submissions only. Submissions made by the author or school yearbook adviser. Must be published in the 12-month span prior to contest deadline. Visit website for list of current and previous winners. Purpose is to recognize and reward student journalists for their work in yearbooks and to provide student winners an opportunity to apply for a scholarship to be used freshman year in college for students planning to major in journalism. Deadline: October 10.

✪ THE YOUNG ADULT FICTION PRIZE

Victorian Premier's Literary Awards, State Government of Victoria, The Wheeler Centre, 176 Little Lonsdale Street, Melbourne VIC 3000, Australia. (61)(3)90947800. **E-mail:** vpla@wheelercentre.com. **Website:** http://www.wheelercentre.com/projects/victorian-premier-s-literary-awards-2016/about-the-awards. **Contact:** Project Officer. Visit website for guidelines and nomination forms. Prize: $25,000.

YOUNG READER'S CHOICE AWARD

E-mail: hbray@missoula.lib.mt.us. **Website:** www.pnla.org. **Contact:** Honore Bray, president. The Pacific Northwest Library Association's Young Reader's Choice Award is the oldest children's choice award in the U.S. and Canada. Nominations are taken only from children, teachers, parents and librarians in the Pacific Northwest: Alaska, Alberta, British Columbia, Idaho, Montana and Washington. Nominations will not be accepted from publishers. Nominations may include fiction, nonfiction, graphic novels, anime, and manga. Nominated titles are those published 3 years prior to the award year. Deadline: February 1. Books will be judged on popularity with readers. Age appropriateness will be considered when choosing which of the three divisions a book is placed. Other considerations may include reading enjoyment; reading level; interest level; genre representation; gender representation; racial diversity; diversity of social, political, economic, or religions viewpoints; regional consideration; effectiveness of expression; and imagination. The Pacific Northwest Library Association is committed to intellectual freedom and diversity of ideas. No title will be excluded because of race, nationality, religion, gender, sexual orientation, political or social view of either the author or the material.

THE YOUTH HONOR AWARDS

Skipping Stones Youth Honor Awards, Skipping Stones Magazine, Skipping Stones Magazine, P.O. Box 3939, Eugene OR 97403. (541)342-4956. **E-mail:** info@skippingstones.org. **E-mail:** editor@skippingstones.org. **Website:** www.skippingstones.org/wp. **Contact:** Arun N. Toke, Editor and Publisher. *Skipping Stones* is an international, literary, and multicultural, children's magazine that encourages cooperation, creativity, and celebration of cultural and linguistic diversity. It explores stewardship of the ecological and social webs that nurture us. It offers a forum for communication among children from different lands and backgrounds. *Skipping Stones* expands horizons in a playful, creative way. This is a non-commercial, non-profit magazine with no advertisements. In its 31st year. Original writing and art from youth, ages 7 to 17, should be typed or neatly handwritten. The entries should be appropriate for ages 7 to 17. Prose under 1,000 words; poems under 30 lines. Word limit: 1,000. Poetry: 30 lines. Non-English and bilingual writings are welcome. To promote multicultural, international and nature awareness. Deadline: June 25. Prize: An Honor Award Certificate, issues of Skipping Stones magazine and five nature and/or multicultural books. They are also invited to join the Student Review Board. Everyone who enters the contest receives the autumn issue featuring the ten winners and other noteworthy entries. Editors and interns at the *Skipping Stones* magazine

○ Youth awards are for children only; you must be under 18 years of age to qualify.

ANNA ZORNIO MEMORIAL CHILDREN'S THEATRE PLAYWRITING COMPETITION

University of New Hampshire, Department of Theatre and Dance, PCAC, 30 Academic Way, Durham NH 03824. **E-mail:** mike.wood@unh.edu. **Website:** cola. unh.edu/theatre-dance/program/anna-zornio-chil-drens-theatre-playwriting-award. **Contact:** Michael Wood. Offered every 4 years for unpublished well-written plays or musicals appropriate for young audiences with a maximum length of 60 minutes. May submit more than 1 play, but not more than 3. Honors the late Anna Zornio, an alumna of The University of New Hampshire, for dedication to and inspiration of playwriting for young people, K-12th grade. Deadline: March 1, 2021. Prize: $500.

PUBLISHERS & THEIR IMPRINTS

///

The publishing world is in constant transition. With all the buying, selling, reorganizing, consolidating, and dissolving, it's hard to keep publishers and their imprints straight. To help make sense of these changes, here's a breakdown of major publishers (and their divisions)—who owns whom and which imprints are under each company umbrella. Keep in mind that this information changes frequently. The website of each publisher is provided to help you keep an eye on this ever-evolving business.

HACHETTE BOOK GROUP

www.hachettebookgroup.com

GRAND CENTRAL PUBLISHING

Forever

Forever Yours

Goop Press

Grand Central Life & Style

Twelve

HACHETTE AUDIO

Wattpad

HACHETTE NASHVILLE

Center Street

Faith Words

Worthy Books

LITTLE, BROWN AND COMPANY

Back Bay Books

JIMMY Patterson

Little, Brown Spark

Mulholland Books

Voracious

LITTLE, BROWN BOOKS FOR YOUNG READERS

LB Kids

Poppy

ORBIT

Orbit Publishing

Redhook

PERSEUS

Avalon Travel

Basic Books

Black Dog & Leventhal

Bold Type Books

Da Capo

Economist Books

Hachette Books

Moon Travel

PublicAffairs

Rick Steves

Running Press

Seal Press

HARPERCOLLINS

www.harpercollins.com

ADULT

Amistad

Anthony Bourdain Books

Avon

Avon Inspire

Avon Red

Broadside Books

Custom House

Dey Street

Ecco Books

Harper Books

Harper Business

Harper Design

Harper Luxe

Harper Perennial

Harper Voyager

Harper Wave

HarperAudio

HarperCollins 360

HarperLegend

HarperOne

Morrow Gift

William Morrow

Witness

CHILDREN'S

Amistad

Balzer + Bray

Greenwillow Books

HarperChildren's Audio

HarperCollins Children's Books

HarperFestival

HarperTeen

HarperTeen Impulse

Katherine Tegen Books

Walden Pond Press

CHRISTIAN PUBLISHING

Bible Gateway

Editorial Vida

FaithGateway

Grupo Nelson

Nelson Books

Olive Tree

Thomas Nelson

Tommy Nelson

W Publishing Group

WestBow Press

Zonderkidz

Zondervan

Zondervan Academic

HARLEQUIN

Carina Press

Harlequin Books

Harlequin TEEN

HQN Books

Kimani Press

Love Inspired

MIRA Books

Worldwide Mystery

HARPERCOLLINS AUSTRALIA

HARPERCOLLINS BRAZIL

Thomas Nelson Brazil

HARPERCOLLINS CANADA

Collins

Harper Avenue

Harper Perennial

Harper Weekend

HarperCollins Canada

Patrick Crean Editions

HARPERCOLLINS FRANCE

HARPERCOLLINS GERMANY

HARPERCOLLINS HOLLAND

HARPERCOLLINS INDIA

HARPERCOLLINS ITALY

HARPERCOLLINS JAPAN

HARPERCOLLINS MEXICO

HARPERCOLLINS NEW ZEALAND

HARPERCOLLINS POLAND

HARPERCOLLINS SPAIN

HARPERCOLLINS SWEDEN

HARPERCOLLINS SWITZERLAND

HARPERCOLLINS UK

4th Estate

Avon

Collins

Harper Audio

Harper Inspire

Harper Voyager

Harper360

HarperCollins Children's Books

HarperCollins in Ireland

HarperFiction

HarperImpulse

HarperNonFiction

HQ

HQ Digital

Mills & Boon

Mudlark

The Borough Press

Times Books

William Collins

MACMILLAN PUBLISHERS

us.macmillan.com

CELADON BOOKS

DISTRIBUTED PUBLISHERS

Bloomsbury USA and Walker & Company

The College Board

Drawn and Quarterly

Entangled Publishing

Graywolf Press

Guinness World Records

Media Lab Books

Page Street Publishing Co.

Papercutz

FARRAR, STRAUS AND GIROUX

Faber and Faber Inc.

Farrar, Straus and Giroux Books for Young Readers

FSG Originals

Hill and Wang

North Point Press

Sarah Crichton Books

Scientific American

FIRST SECOND

FLATIRON BOOKS

HENRY HOLT & CO.

Henry Holt

Henry Holt Books for Young Readers

Holt Paperbacks

Metropolitan Books

Times Books

MACMILLAN AUDIO

MACMILLAN CHILDREN'S

Farrar, Straus & Giroux for Young Readers

Feiwel & Friends

Henry Holt Books for Young Readers

Imprint

Kingfisher

Macmillan Children's Publishing Group

Odd Dot

Priddy Books

Roaring Brook Press

Square Fish

Tor Children's

PICADOR

QUICK AND DIRTY TIPS

ST. MARTIN'S PRESS

All Points Books

Castle Books

Griffin

Minotaur Books

St. Martin's Press Paperbacks

Thomas Dunne Books

Truman Talley Books

Wednesday Books

TOR/FORGE
Starscape

Tor Teen Books

PENGUIN RANDOM HOUSE

www.penguinrandomhouse.com

DK
DK

Prima Games

KNOPF DOUBLEDAY PUBLISHING GROUP
Alfred A. Knopf

Anchor Books

Doubleday

Everyman's Library

Nan A. Talese

Pantheon Books

Schocken Books

Vintage Books

Vintage Espanol

PENGUIN PUBLISHING GROUP

Avery

Berkley

Blue Rider Press

DAW

Dutton

F+W

G.P. Putnam's Sons

Grosset & Dunlap

Penguin

Peguin Classics

Penguin Press

Plume

Portfolio

Riverhead

Speak

Sentinel

TarcherPerigee

Viking Books

RANDOM HOUSE PUBLISHING GROUP

Ballantine Books

Bantam

B\D\W\Y

Clarkson Potter

Convergent Books

Crown

Crown Archetype

Crown Forum

Currency

Delacorte Press

Dell

Del Rey

The Dial Press

Harmon

Hogarth

Image

Lorena Jones Books

Loveswept

Lucas Books

The Modern Library

One World

Random House

Rodale

SJP for Hogarth

Spiegel & Grau

Ten Speed Press

Three Rivers Press

Tim Duggan Books

Waterbrook Multnomah

Watson-Guptill

PENGUIN YOUNG READERS GROUP

Dial Books for Young Readers

Dutton Children's Books

Firebird

Frederick Warne & Co.

G.P. Putnam's Sons Books for Young Readers

Kathy Dawson Books

Kokila

Nancy Paulson Books

Penguin Workshop

Philomel

Puffin

Razorbill

Speak

Viking Children's Books

PENGUIN RANDOM HOUSE CHILDREN'S BOOKS

Alfred A. Knopf

Crown

Delacorte Press

Doubleday

Dragonfly Books

Ember

Golden Books

Laurel-Leaf Books

Now I'm Reading!

The Princeton Review

Random House Books for Young Readers

Schwartz & Wade Books

Sylvan Learning

Wendy Lamb Books

Yearling Books

PENGUIN RANDOM HOUSE AUDIO PUBLISHING GROUP

Books on Tape

Listening Library

Living Language

Penguin Random House Audio Publishing

RH Large Print

Random House Puzzles and Games

Random House Reference

RH INTERNATIONAL

Penguin Random House Australia

The Penguin Random House Group (UK)

Penguin Random House Grupo Editorial (Argentina)

Penguin Random House Grupo Editorial (Chile)

Penguin Random House Grupo Editorial (Colombia)

Penguin Random House Grupo Editorial (Mexico)

Penguin Random House Grupo Editorial (Peru)

Penguin Random House Grupo Editorial (Spain)

Penguin Random House Grupo Editorial (Uruguay)

Penguin Random House India

Penguin Random House New Zealand

Penguin Random House of Canada

Penguin Random House Struik (South Africa)

Verlagsgruppe Penguin Random House

SIMON & SCHUSTER

www.simonandschuster.com

SIMON & SCHUSTER ADULT PUBLISHING

Adams Media

Atria

Emily Bestler Books

Enliven

Folger Shakespeare Library

Free Press

Gallery

Howard

Jeter Publishing

Pocket

Pocket Star

Scout Press

Scribner

Simon & Schuster

Threshold

Touchstone

SIMON & SCHUSTER CHILDREN'S PUBLISHING

Aladdin

Atheneum

Simon & Schuster Books for Young Readers

Beach Lane Books

Little Simon

Margaret K. McElderry

Paula Wiseman Books

Saga Press

Salaam Reads

Simon Pulse

Simon Spotlight

SIMON & SCHUSTER AUDIO PUBLISHING

Pimsleur

Simon & Schuster Audio

SIMON & SCHUSTER INTERNATIONAL

Simon & Schuster Australia

Simon & Schuster Canada

Simon & Schuster UK

GLOSSARY OF INDUSTRY TERMS

Common terminology and lingo.

//

AAR. Association of Authors' Representatives.

ABA. American Booksellers Association.

ABC. Association of Booksellers for Children.

ADVANCE. A sum of money a publisher pays a writer or illustrator prior to the publication of a book. It is usually paid in installments, such as one half on signing the contract, one half on delivery of a complete and satisfactory manuscript. The advance is paid against the royalty money that will be earned by the book.

ALA. American Library Association.

ALL RIGHTS. The rights contracted to a publisher permitting the use of material anywhere and in any form, including movie and book club sales, without additional payment to the creator.

ANTHOLOGY. A collection of selected writings by various authors or gatherings of works by one author.

ANTHROPOMORPHIZATION. The act of attributing human form and personality to things not human (such as animals).

ASAP. As soon as possible.

ASSIGNMENT. An editor or art director asks a writer, illustrator, or photographer to produce a specific piece for an agreed-upon fee.

B&W. Black and white.

BACKLIST. A publisher's list of books not published during the current season but still in print.

BEA. BookExpo America.

BIENNIALLY. Occurring once every two years.

BIMONTHLY. Occurring once every two months.

BIWEEKLY. Occurring once every two weeks.

BOOK PACKAGER. A company that draws all elements of a book together, from the initial concept to writing and marketing strategies, then sells the book package to a book publisher and/or movie producer. Also known as book producer or book developer.

BOOK PROPOSAL. Package submitted to a publisher for consideration, usually consisting of a synopsis and outline as well as sample chapters.

BUSINESS-SIZE ENVELOPE. Also known as a #10 envelope. The standard size used in sending business correspondence.

CAMERA-READY. Refers to art that is completely prepared for copy camera platemaking.

CAPTION. A description of the subject matter of an illustration or photograph; photo captions include persons' names where appropriate. Also called cutline.

CBC. Children's Book Council.

CLEAN-COPY. A manuscript free of errors that needs no editing; it is ready for typesetting.

CLIPS. Samples, usually from newspapers or magazines, of a writer's published work.

CONCEPT BOOKS. Books that deal with ideas, concepts and large-scale problems, promoting an understanding of what's happening in a child's world. Most prevalent are alphabet and counting books, but also includes books dealing with specific concerns facing young people (such as divorce, birth of a sibling, friendship, or moving).

CONTRACT. A written agreement stating the rights to be purchased by an editor, art director, or producer and the amount of payment the writer, illustrator, or photographer will receive for that sale.

CONTRIBUTOR'S COPIES. The magazine issues sent to an author, illustrator, or photographer in which her work appears.

CO-OP PUBLISHER. A publisher that shares production costs with an author but, unlike subsidy publishers, handles all marketing and distribution. An author receives a high percentage of royalties until her initial investment is recouped, then standard royalties. (Children's Writer's & Illustrator's Market does not include co-op publishers.)

COPY. The actual written material of a manuscript.

COPYEDITING. Editing a manuscript for grammar usage, spelling, punctuation, and other general style.

COPYRIGHT. A means to legally protect an author's/illustrator's/photographer's work. This can be shown by writing the creator's name and the year of the work's creation.

COVER LETTER. A brief letter, accompanying a complete manuscript, especially useful if responding to an editor's request for a manuscript. May also accompany a book proposal.

CUTLINE. See caption.

DIVISION. An unincorporated branch of a company.

DUMMY. A loose mock-up of a book showing placement of text and artwork.

ELECTRONIC SUBMISSION. A submission of material by e-mail or Web form.

FINAL DRAFT. The last version of a polished manuscript ready for submission to an editor.

FIRST NORTH AMERICAN SERIAL RIGHTS. The right to publish material in a periodical for the first time, in the U.S. or Canada.

F&GS. Folded and gathered sheets. An early, not-yet-bound copy of a picture book.

FLAT FEE. A one-time payment.

GALLEYS. The first typeset version of a manuscript that has not yet been divided into pages.

GENRE. A formulaic type of fiction, such as horror, mystery, romance, fantasy, suspense, thriller, science fiction, or western.

GLOSSY. A photograph with a shiny surface, as opposed to one with a matte finish.

GOUACHE. Opaque watercolor with an appreciable film thickness and an actual paint layer.

HALFTONE. Reproduction of a continuous tone illustration with the image formed by dots produced by a camera lens screen.

HARD COPY. The printed copy of a computer's output.

HARDWARE. Refers to all the mechanically integrated components of a computer that are not software—circuit boards, transistors and the machines that are the actual computer.

HI-LO. High interest, low reading level.

HOME PAGE. The first page of a website.

IBBY. International Board on Books for Young People.

IMPRINT. Name applied to a publisher's specific line of books.

IRA. International Reading Association.

IRC. International Reply Coupon. Sold at the post office to enclose with text or artwork sent to a recipient outside your own country to cover postage costs when replying or returning work.

KEYLINE. Identification of the positions of illustrations and copy for the printer.

LAYOUT. Arrangement of illustrations, photographs, text and headlines for printed material.

LGBTQ. Lesbian/gay/bisexual/trans/queer.

LINE DRAWING. Illustration done with pencil or ink using no wash or other shading.

MASS MARKET BOOKS. Paperback books directed toward an extremely large audience sold in supermarkets, drugstores, airports, newsstands, online retailers, and bookstores.

MECHANICALS. Paste-up or preparation of work for printing.

MIDDLE-GRADE OR MID-GRADE. See middle reader.

MIDDLE READER. The general classification of books written for readers approximately ages nine to twelve. Often called middle-grade or mid-grade.

MS (MSS). Manuscript(s).

MULTIPLE SUBMISSIONS. See simultaneous submissions.

NCTE. National Council of Teachers of English.

NEW ADULT (NA). Novels with characters in their late teens or early twenties who are exploring what it means to be an adult.

ONE-TIME RIGHTS. Permission to publish a story in periodical or book form one time only.

PACKAGE SALE. The sale of a manuscript and illustrations/photos as a "package" paid for with one check.

PAYMENT ON ACCEPTANCE. The writer, artist, or photographer is paid for her work at the time the editor or art director decides to buy it.

PAYMENT ON PUBLICATION. The writer, artist, or photographer is paid for her work when it is published.

PICTURE BOOK. A type of book aimed at preschoolers to eight-year-olds that tells a story using a combination of text and artwork, or artwork only.

PRINT. An impression pulled from an original plate, stone, block, screen, or negative; also a positive made from a photographic negative.

PROOFREADING. Reading text to correct typographical errors.

QUERY. A letter to an editor or agent designed to capture interest in an article or book you have written or propose to write. (See the article "Before Your First Sale.")

READING FEE. Money charged by some agents and publishers to read a submitted manuscript. (Children's Writer's & Illustrator's Market does not include agencies that charge reading fees.)

REPRINT RIGHTS. Permission to print an already published work whose first rights have been sold to another magazine or book publisher.

RESPONSE TIME. The average length of time it takes an editor or art director to accept or reject a query or submission, and inform the creator of the decision.

RIGHTS. The bundle of permissions offered to an editor or art director in exchange for printing a manuscript, artwork, or photographs.

ROUGH DRAFT. A manuscript that has not been checked for errors in grammar, punctuation, spelling, or content.

ROUGHS. Preliminary sketches or drawings.

ROYALTY. An agreed percentage paid by a publisher to a writer, illustrator, or photographer for each copy of her work sold.

SAE. Self-addressed envelope.

SASE. Self-addressed, stamped envelope.

SCBWI. The Society of Children's Book Writers and Illustrators.

SECOND SERIAL RIGHTS. Permission for the reprinting of a work in another periodical after its first publication in book or magazine form.

SEMIANNUAL. Occurring every six months or twice a year.

SEMIMONTHLY. Occurring twice a month.

SEMIWEEKLY. Occurring twice a week.

SERIAL RIGHTS. The rights given by an author to a publisher to print a piece in one or more periodicals.

SIMULTANEOUS SUBMISSIONS. Queries or proposals sent to several publishers at the same time. Also called multiple submissions. (See the article "Before Your First Sale.")

SLANT. The approach to a story or piece of artwork that will appeal to readers of a particular publication.

SLUSH PILE. Editors' term for their collections of unsolicited manuscripts.

SOFTWARE. Programs and related documentation for use with a computer.

SOLICITED MANUSCRIPT. Material that an editor has asked for or agreed to consider before being sent by a writer.

SPAR. Society of Photographers and Artists Representatives.

SPECULATION (SPEC). Creating a piece with no assurance from an editor or art director that it will be purchased or any reimbursements for material or labor paid.

SUBSIDIARY RIGHTS. All rights other than book publishing rights included in a book contract, such as paperback, book club, and movie rights.

SUBSIDY PUBLISHER. A book publisher that charges the author for the cost of typesetting, printing and promoting a book. Also called a vanity publisher. (Note: Children's Writer's & Illustrator's Market does not include subsidy publishers.)

SYNOPSIS. A summary of a story or novel. Usually a page to a page and a half, single-spaced, if part of a book submission.

TABLOID. Publication printed on an ordinary newspaper page turned sideways and folded in half.

TEARSHEET. Page from a magazine or newspaper containing your printed art, story, article, poem or photo.

THUMBNAIL. A rough layout in miniature.

TRADE BOOKS. Books sold in bookstores and through online retailers, aimed at a smaller audience than mass market books, and printed in smaller quantities by publishers.

TRANSPARENCIES. Positive color slides; not color prints.

UNSOLICITED MANUSCRIPT. Material sent without an editor's, art director's, or agent's request.

VANITY PUBLISHER. See subsidy publisher.

WORK-FOR-HIRE. An arrangement between a writer, illustrator, or photographer and a company under which the company retains complete control of the work's copyright.

YA. See young adult.

YOUNG ADULT. The general classification of books written for readers approximately ages twelve to sixteen. Often referred to as YA.

YOUNG READER. The general classification of books written for readers approximately ages five to eight.

GENERAL INDEX

SUBJECT INDEX

Animal

Multicultural NF

Poetry

Poetry NF

Problem Novels

AGE-LEVEL INDEX